新航道 NEW CHANNEL

北京新航道学校 [illegible] 教材

剑桥雅思

真题全解

3·4·5

IELTS

胡敏 主编

中国广播电视出版社
CHINA RADIO & TELEVISION PUBLISHING HOUSE

图书在版编目（CIP）数据

剑桥雅思真题全解 / 胡敏主编. 一北京：中国广播电视出版社，2006.10
ISBN 7-5043-5150-4

Ⅰ.剑... Ⅱ.胡... Ⅲ.英语－高等学校－入学考试，国外－解题 Ⅳ.H319.6

中国版本图书馆CIP数据核字（2006）第124835号

剑桥雅思真题全解

主　　编	胡　敏
特约编辑	周　壮
责任编辑	刘　君
监　　印	赵　宁
监　　制	张曲波
出版发行	中国广播电视出版社
电　　话	86093580　86093583
社　　址	北京市西城区真武庙二条9号(邮政编码 100045)
经　　销	各地新华书店和外文书店
印　　刷	保定华泰印刷有限公司
开　　本	787毫米×1092毫米　1/16
字　　数	826(千)字
印　　张	30.5
版　　次	2006年10月第1版　2006年10月第1次印刷
书　　号	ISBN 7-5043-5150-4 / H·299
定　　价	39.00元

做中国最好的雅思培训

由于多方利好消息，2006 年雅思考试高歌猛进，全线飘红，已呈现与托福势均力敌之态，这应验了七年前我在伦敦面对当时的英国文化委员会雅思总裁肖恩·海德时所说的一句话："雅思考试具备巨大的市场潜力，肯定会异军突起。"说这句话之前，我刚刚开完第一个雅思班，带着教学心得以及对雅思进一步了解的愿望，来到了伦敦，来到了肖恩·海德面前。在聊到竞争对手托福考试时，肖恩·海德说了一句话："TOEFL is an empire.（托福是一个帝国。）"言下之意雅思无法与之抗衡，我则充满信心地回应了开始的那一句话。而今，风云际会，天时具矣。

当年我从英国回到国内立刻着手研发了一套系统的雅思教材，这套教材是国内第一套正式出版的真正意义上的雅思考试培训教材。两年后，经过不断总结教学经验，我又率领研发团队开发了拥有完全自主知识产权的第二代雅思教材。由于教材的独创性、可操作性和高效度，很快在学员当中赢得了巨大的知名度和认可度，许多已经在国外读预科班的学员，纷纷向国内求购这套教材，因此学员和同行给了我"胡雅思"这个称呼。对我来说，这个称呼更多地意味着一种期待和激励。为了不辜负大家的期望，我不断对这一教材进行升级，新航道成立之后研发出的已经是第四代雅思教材了，而七年来使用过这套教材的学员也接近五十万人。在新航道，我再次组织了一批优秀的中外语言培训专家，投入巨资，利用一年多的时间研发了中国第一套基础版雅思培训教材，填补了又一项国内雅思培训领域的空白。同时，北京新航道学校所采用的教学模式，也是我和新航道同事们在多年教学经验的基础上，经过科学研发设计而成，许多培训机构纷纷模仿。这些附带大量学术和技术含量、拥有自主知识产权、凝结了我和大批中外语言培训专家心血的研发成果，使得北京新航道学校在北京乃至全国建立了为广大学员和同行所承认的学术形象。多年生聚，地利得矣。

新航道的理念和理想聚集了一大批在雅思培训界从业多年的精英，其中不乏巨擘大腕，也屡见年轻新锐，既有外籍专家和留学人士的加盟，也有多年纵横于讲台的国内培训精英支持。千金难求的人才，给了新航道千载难逢的机会，更造就了我为之自豪的新航道顶级雅思培训团队——雅思梦之队。这个团队的弟子桃李满英伦，学员遍布英联邦各国大学，当我在英国、澳大利亚等国的街头、校园漫步时，经常会有年轻朋友迎面走来："胡老师，我是新航道的学员……"他们亲切自信的问候常常使我欣慰怡然，人心所向，人和备矣。

天时、地利、人和，三者俱全，终于让新航道有机会实现自己的梦想——做中国最好的雅思培训！

这个梦想让我在雅思培训领域坚持七年、不断进取！

这个梦想让我和新航道的全体同事卧薪尝胆、厚积薄发！

这个梦想让大批优秀人才在新航道构筑的崭新平台上齐心协力、共同创业！

这个梦想会让新航道不断为学员贡献最好的教材、最好的课程、最好的教师，最终将梦想变为现实。

北京新航道学校校长 ——胡敏

2006 年 10 月于北京

Contents

剑桥雅思真题全解 3

剑桥雅思真题全解 4

剑桥雅思真题全解 5

剑 桥 雅 思

真题全解 3

Test 1

LISTENING

SECTION 1

谈话场景:租房场景,电话交谈。

人物关系:房客和房产公司工作人员。

谈话话题:寻租合适的住房,讨论付款以及看房条件。

词汇注释

(此处词汇释义指在本段文章中的特定含义,后文同)

property *n.* 财产,房地产

enquiry (= **inquiry**) *n.* 咨询 make enquiries of sb. about sth. 向某人询问某事

suburb *n.* 郊区

range *v.* (在一定范围内)变动,变化

depend on 取决于,视…而定

factor *n.* 因素,要素

garage *n.* 车库,汽车修理厂

necessarily *adv.* 必然地,必定地,必需地

file *n.* 档案,文件夹

suit *v.* 适合,中…的意

bill *n.* 账单;water bill 自来水账单

rental *n.* 租费,租金

available *adj.* 可以使用的,可以找到的,(某人)有空的

availability *n.* 可用性,可得性,可得到的东西(或人员)

reference *n.* (关于品行,能力的)证明书(人); reference letter 推荐信,证明信

employer *n.* 雇主,工作单位

deposit *n.* 押金,定金,预付金

amount *n.* 总数,数量,数额

contract *n.* 合同,契约

交际与语言表达

1. 接听电话时,接听一方一般要自报家门,打进一方进行确认,由此可以了解电话接听者的身份和本段对话的主题。对话开始时女声首先提到 Flagstone,男声问 Is that Flagstone Properties? (Flagstone 房产公司),已基本表明双方的人物关系。
2. 男声提及自己打电话的原委,这个句型可以适用于任何电话交谈场景。**I'm ringing just to** make enquiries about renting a house. 此后房产公司的工作人员(女声)开始询问他的租房条件和要求,所以交谈为**"一问一答"**式。由此可以推测下文肯定涉及到房屋的地理位置、租金、配套的设施以及安排看房的时间等。这些均是租房场景中经常讨论的话题。雅思考生在备考听力时,应该背诵一些常用句型,以不变应万变。
3. Well... 在口语中位于句首,本身并没有什么特定含义,一般用来作为短暂思考时的口头禅。类似于我们平常说话中的"嗯……"、"这个……"。
4. We were most interested in the Northern areas actually. 我们实际上对北部地区很感兴趣。most 此处当 very 理解。
5. Could you give me some idea? 你能让我了解一下(有关情况吗)?
   这样的问题后面经常会跟出一些重要的信息点,考试时应当特别小心。

6. And a garage pushes up the price. 再增加一个车库会使价格更高。
此处 push up 比 increase 或 add 更为形象。
7. Would you like to have a look at a couple of properties, sir? 先生,您想不想去看看一些房子呢? would you like to do sth. 的问法与 do you want to 相比,更加委婉和客气。
8. Hang on. 稍等。这是电话中常用的术语,本意是"拿着话机,别挂电话",也可以说 just a moment, just a minute, just a second 等。
9. Yep. 口语中相当于 yes,相应的 no 也可以经常说成 nope。
10. Got that. (我)知道了,记住了,明白了。口语中经常省略主语,接近于 I see.
11. No, I'm afraid not. 不,恐怕没有。I'm afraid... 使说话的语气更加缓和。
12. It **does** include the telephone rental. (房租)的确包括了电话费。这句话的正常表达为 It includes the telephone rental. 用 does 来强调所表达内容的重要性。
13. When would you be available to see them? 您什么时候有空能来看房? available 一词用法极其活泛,可指人指物,在不同的语境中可以产生不同的含义。
14. ... say... 是 let's say 的缩略用法,表示"比如说,即使说,大约……"。如 Shall we go camping sometime later next week, say, Friday?
15. How about Wednesday afternoon? 星期三下午如何? how about... 经常用来引出说话者提出的一个建议,供对方参考。
16. What sort of things do I need to get done? 什么样的事情需要我找人搞定? get sth. done 指某个事情并不是自己做的,比如:I am going to get my hair cut tomorrow.
17. Is that it? 就这些(事情)吗? 完了吗? 相对应的陈述句的表达为 That's it. 就这样了,这事到此结束了。

考题解析

Question 1

此处填空首先看清前面的 **Areas dealt with**,这个词组是一个名词词组,dealt with 是过去分词做后置定语,还原成定语从句就是:areas that are dealt with, 与磁带原文中 the main areas we deal with are the city centre itself 中的表达非常接近。在女声说完此句后,男声又重复 city centre。注意 centre 一词亦可写成 center。

Question 2

在女声问 what sort of price were you looking for 之后,考生应注意随后的说话内容。此题的关键是考生对数字的读法熟悉,且£250 在原文中重复两次。

Question 3

谈话刚开始时,女声问 what sort of price were you looking for,男声就告诉她 two-bedroomed house with **garden**,已经暗示了此处的答案。谈话进行到第三题时,女生提及房租取决于许多不同的因素,男声随即问是哪些,女声就把几个要素一一列举。提到 garden 时,男声再次说:well, as I said, we'd want a **garden**。

Questions 4–5

谈到合适的房子之后,女声提到 well, there is one on West Park Road which is £**325** a month. 男声问:Are the bills included? 女声答道:that one just includes the **water bill**. 这两道题目考查考生的基本听写能力和对所听写内容前后信息的把握。

Question 6

注意听强调句型的语气,but it **does** include the **telephone** rental.

Question 7

这道题具备初中英语水平的考生都可以听对答案,但英语专业的学生都不一定能把答案写对。不信您写写看,"星期三",怎么写?

Question 8

上文中的 letter from a/the bank 是一个很好的提示,但要注意 **employer** 的拼写。

Question 9

注意 two weeks' 的写法,最后的那一小撇是不能省略的。当然,这里写成 14 days' 也没有问题。在英式英语中,单词 fortnight 也可以指 two weeks.

Question 10

注意答案的写法。答案可以写成 1 month rent 或 one month's rent ,但不能只写 one month。因为此处讨论的对象是"钱",而非"时间"。

SECTION 2

谈话场景:家庭主妇交谈。
人物关系:新结识的邻居。
谈话话题:一方向另一方介绍当地诊所的情况。

特别提示

一般情况下,雅思听力的第二部分均为一段独白,此处出现两人交谈,在实际考试中比较少见。本部分的对话主要是一位家庭主妇向新搬来的邻居介绍附近的医疗设施,所以大部分内容都为前者所陈述,而且出题点也大多在前者所介绍的情况中,因此也可视为独白。

词汇注释

settle *v.* 安家,定居
removal *n.* 移动,搬家,迁居
van *n.* 运货车,行李车,搬运车
bother *v.* 打扰,打搅
get hold of 找到,抓到,得到
well *adj.* 健康的,良好的
practitioner *n.* 开业者(尤指医生,律师等);a general practitioner:普通医生(通看各科的开业医生)
register *v.* 登记,挂号
practice *v.* (律师,医生等)开业;practice at the bar 开业作律师 *n.* (律师,医生等的)业务,开业地点(如诊所、律师事务所)
well off 富裕的,处境不错的,条件宽松的
comparison *n.* 比较,对照;in comparison with 与…相比较
old-fashioned *adj.* 老式的,落伍的
proper *adj.* 合适的,适当的,规矩的
appointment *n.* 约会,预约
receptionist *n.* (宾馆, 诊所, 公司等)前台接待人员
fill in 填写
form *n.* 表格
brilliant *adj.* 卓越的,出色的,才华横溢的
be used to 习惯于…
elderly *adj.* 上了年纪的(对年长者尊敬的说法,比 old 正式)
tend *v.* 倾向于
patient *n.* 病人 *adj.* 有耐心的
impatient *adj.* 不耐烦的
the other day 前几天
clinic *n.* 诊所
home visit 家访,(医生)出诊
emergency *n.* 急诊

otherwise *adv.* 要不然，否则	**retired** *adj.* 退休的
surgery *n.* 外科手术，诊所	**pregnant** *adj.* 怀孕的
prescription *n.* 处方	**prescribe** *v.*（医生）开药，嘱咐，建议
medication *n.* 疗法，药物，药剂	**consultation** *n.* 咨询，询问
chemist *n.* 化学家，药剂师	**completely** *adv.* 完全地
a chemist's shop（英国）药店	**free** *adj.* 免费的
unemployed *adj.* 失业的	**resident** *n.* 居民，住户

交际与语言表达

1. 本篇文章主要介绍看病过程的细节问题，这也是雅思听力生活场景中经常涉及的内容，所以考生对于一些常用的医疗词汇和表达法要耳熟能详，还要了解一些国外看病的基本常识。
2. Are you alright? You look a bit worried. 看上去您有点着急，没事吧？Mrs. Smith 用很简单的几句话开始了与 Mrs. Sutton 的交谈，并缩短了她们之间的距离，在生活中跟不太熟悉的朋友交谈时完全可以借鉴这种说法。
3. I'm sorry to bother you so early, but I wonder if you could help me. 很抱歉这么早来打搅您，但我不知道您是否能帮我个忙。这样请求别人帮助的方式委婉且有礼貌。
4. I may have to call somebody out. 我可能得打电话请医生出诊。
5. There are two practices near here, so we're **quite well off for** doctors in this part of Manchester. 这附近有两个诊所，所以我们居住的曼彻斯特的这个地区医生并不短缺。
6. I wouldn't say he's brilliant but I suppose he's alright really. We are used to him now. 我并不是说他非常出色，但我想他还不错吧。我们现在已经习惯他了。要注意借鉴这种对一个人先部分否定又肯定的句型表达。
7. . . . but he **does** tend to get a bit impatient with children. 但他的确好像对孩子有些不耐烦。
8. If it's an emergency, you can phone at any time, night or day. It might not be your doctor that comes, **though**. . . . It doesn't really seem to make much difference. 如果是急诊，你可以白天或晚上随时打电话。不过来的不一定是你们家的医生。……（谁来）好像并没有太大的区别。注意 though 的用法。当它置于句首时表示“尽管”，但如果放在句末，则表示“但是”。
9. It is completely free as long as you are a resident here. 只要你是此地的居民，它就是完全免费的。
10. It is no trouble really, don't worry. 这一点也不麻烦，别担心。

考题解析

Question 11

此题答案比较清楚，Mrs. Sutton 担心的是她的女儿 Anna。一进门她就对 Mrs. Smith 说今天早上女儿 Anna isn't very well，后面又说她 keeps being sick and I am beginning to get a bit worried. 即使此处没有听出答案，从后文的 Mrs. Smith 主动要求照顾 Anna 也可推断出来。关键是答案的写法上。Anna 个名字是比较常见的英文名字，应该写对，当然也可拼成 Ana。如果实在不会拼写这个名字，也可以写（her）daughter 或（her）child。

Question 12

这道题要看清题目，原文是同一群这样的医生在一起的名称，而非单个的医生的称谓。这道题答不对的考生很可能是不知道 practice 一词在此处的特定含义。但该词的这一含义，在许多英语课本中出现过。

Questions 13 – 14

这两道题目答案在同一句话中出现。很多考生只注意到前面的那个数字，而忽略了后面的 four in the other。

Question 15

这道题对考生有一定的难度。首先,在看题时应该注意试卷上的关键词 appointment system 和 than,确定此处填比较级。原文并没有直接给出 Dean End 比 South Hay 怎么样,而是只单方面提到 South Hay 的预约 not proper,后面又抱怨 you have to wait for ages,意即前者的预约比后者更好,更快,更高效。所以此处答案可以直接填 more proper,或者填接近的答案,如 better, faster, more efficient。

Question 16

这道题答案比较简单,原文直接提到 elderly people,即使此处没有把握好,从后文中说该医生对孩子不耐烦也可反推答案。

Question 17

这道题答案很多考生没有填出来。问题并不在于句子本身很难理解,而是因为 back trouble 的连读很多人没有听出来。

Question 18

这道题大部分考生会错,原因在于没有抓住题目原文中的 at the health center。听力原文中先讨论医生出诊的时间,后来才提及在医疗中心的时间。听力原文的表述也故意与题目的文字有所不同,磁带中是说医疗中心每个工作日 **between 9** and 11:30,也就意味着从 9 点开始。

Question 19

原文问哪两类人可以享受免费医疗,应该注意五个选项中只有两类人可以选择。磁带中先提到 16 岁以下的孩子可以免费。后面用了一个很好的句型 **The same thing goes if you are unemployed or retired, or if you're pregnant.** 最容易混淆的一项是 E 项,people over 60 years old. 很多考生会选这一项,要注意并不是每个国家的退休年龄都是 60 岁。

Question 20

此题首先要知道原文中 charge 的意思,该词这里作"收费"理解,与听力原文中的 price 是相对应的。这道题做错的主要原因是与上题间隔太短,很多考生还在考虑上题的答案时,这道题答案已经很快读过。

SECTION 3

谈话场景:面试场景。
人物关系:面试官与应聘者。
谈话话题:讨论应聘者以前的工作经历以及应聘意向。

词汇注释

interview *n.* 面试,采访
talk through 详细地讨论,逐项讨论
application *n.* 申请
to date 迄今为止,到目前为止
degree *n.* 学历
economics *n.* 经济学
major *adj.* 主要的 *n.* 专业
strand *n.* (重要的)组成部分;(绳子的)一股,一缕
graduate *v.* 毕业
volunteer *n.* 志愿者 *v.* 主动,志愿(做某事)
in total 总共,加起来
organization *n.* 组织,机构

operate *v.* 运作,发挥作用	**look up** 好转,逐渐改善
rural *adj.* 农村的	**set up** 建立,树立,成立
co-operative *n.* 合作机构,合作社	**successful** *adj.* 成功的
variety *n.* 多样,(许多)种类;	**project** *n.* 项目,工程
a variety of = varieties of 各种各样的	**breed** *v.* 喂养,饲养
form *n.* 年级	**cattle** *n.* 牛,牛群(集合名词)
geography *n.* 地理(学)	**local** *adj.* 当地的
agriculture *n.* 农业	**fund** *n.* 资金
run *v.* 经营,管理	**see sth. through** 办好某事,把某事办到底
homesick *adj.* 想家的	**realize** *v.* 意识到,认为
miss *v.* 想念,思念	**favorite** *adj.* 最喜欢的,偏爱的 *n.* 最喜爱的事物(或人)
frustrating *adj.* 令人沮丧的	**application** *n.* 应用,用途
resource *n.* 资源	**stage** *n.* 阶段,舞台
extend *v.* 延伸,延长	
tour *n.* 旅游,旅程	

交际与语言表达

1. 面试场景中,一般由面试官首先发言,确认应聘者的身份。注意本文中面试官的提问方式十分简单明了。Jonathan Briggs, **isn't it**? 而不是 aren't you?
2. 简单的寒暄之后,面试官就告诉应聘者面试的内容和过程,基本上让应聘者清楚自己马上要经历的事情。这对考生做题也很有帮助,考生应该从面试官的介绍中了解下面题目的大概方向。
3. What organization was that with? 那是在什么机构工作? 问别人工作单位时,经常问 Which company are you working with? 而向别人介绍自己的工作时,也可以简单地说:I am with ...
4. Then in my final year I took on some Agricultural Science with the top year... that's Form 6. 最后一年我上了最高年级——6 年级的农业科学课程。
5. How interesting... 面试官在听取应聘者的介绍时,不断插入这句话。这句话本身并没有特殊的意思,也并不意味着面试官真的认为"很有趣",只不过是她承上启下的口头禅而已,与 Really? 等常用插入语作用差不多。
6. I'll be honest with you. 跟您说实话吧。类似的表达有:honestly speaking; to be frank (with you), etc.。
7. Things must have looked up then? 一切是不是慢慢好转了呢? 用 must have done (sth.) 表示对过去事情的肯定推测。
8. And you wanted to see things through? 后来你就想把事情进行到底吧? 本段对话中面试官经常用升调的陈述句来提问,实际上也是期待应聘者给她肯定的答复。

考题解析

Question 21

这道题考生只要听到 also 和 Politics,答案就完全可以做对,但很多考生此处小写成 politics,这里是用来表示学历的专有名词,必须大写,否则就得不到分数。

Question 22

这道题的关键也是大小写的问题。答案可以只写 Africa,也可以写出全部的 West Africa,但 West 要大写首字母。

Question 23

这道题很多考生会做错。因为题目中是问 Dates，所以很多考生做题时可能就准备听具体的日期，而忽略了年份。听力原文中应聘者首先提到他在那里总共工作了 three years，后面紧跟着提到 from 1990 to... umm... 1992. 这中间应聘者有 1、2 秒的思考时间，实际上也是给考生的思考时间。有些学生听到 3 年，又听到从 1990 年开始，所以后面毫不犹豫地写上 1993 年，但却犯了一个常识性错误。1990 年包括在内，往后 3 年应是 1992 年。

Question 24

这道题同样考查大小写问题。很多考生可能从未听说过 Teach South 这么一个机构，所以不敢写出答案，或者写出来后也总想猜出到底是什么意思。对于雅思听力中的专有名词，没有必要理解其含义，因为这根本就不妨碍做题和对上下文的理解。

Question 25

这道题主要考查考生词汇量。应聘者首先提出 rural co-operative 之后，面试官再次重复该词组。而这两个词并不是特别难。

Questions 26–27

这两道题的答案通过上下文的分析可以有所预测，听的时候带着对题目的分析和预测很容易得出答案。

Questions 28–30

这三道题首先要分析出都是问 reasons 的，在听的时候就要听有关原因的单词，如 because，so，why 之类。每道题都是面试官先问出 why，后面应聘者就给出答案。这三道题的关键还是考查词汇量和听写的能力。

SECTION 4

谈话场景：医疗卫生知识普及讲座。
人物关系：讲话者为医学专家。
谈话话题：介绍腰背脊椎疾病的防护和治疗。

特别提示

雅思听力的第四部分经常是讨论某一学术领域的基础知识、基本技能和简要概况，文章中会涉及一些程度较深的专业词汇。从英语听力考试的角度来讲，这些专业词汇并不会影响理解题目和得出答案，对此考生没有必要担心。但是从另一方面来讲，考生平常多看报刊杂志，扩大自己的知识面，对雅思考试也会有所裨益。

词汇注释

counsel *n.* 讨论会，忠告，商议
present *v.* 提供，做(演讲)
chief *n.* 首要的，首席的
counselor *n.* 顾问
clinic *n.* 诊所，卫生所
suffer *v.* 遭受，忍受
chronic *n.* 习惯性的，慢性的
affect *v.* 影响
all walks of life 各行各业
incapacitate *v.* 使…失去能力，使…残废

solution *n.* 解决办法
majority *n.* 大多数
vulnerable *adj.* 脆弱的,易受…攻击的
pregnancy *n.* 怀孕
osteoporosis *n.* 骨质疏松(症)
personally *adv.* 个人地,私人地
miserable *adj.* 痛苦的,难受的,可怜的
a vicious circle 恶性循环
pain killer 止痛片,止痛药剂
traditional *adj.* 传统的
response *n.* 反应,反响
unique *adj.* 独特的,唯一的
benefit *n.* 益处,好处
relaxation *n.* 松弛,放松,缓和
therapy *n.* 治疗,疗法
specialist *n.* 专家,专业人员
mishandle *v.* 错误地处理,胡乱操作
lead to 导致,引发
menace *n.* 威胁,恐吓
strain *n.* 拉伤,扭伤
blow *n.* 打击,殴打
limb *n.* 肢体
resolve *v.* 解决
injury *n.* 受伤,伤害
counter-productive *adj.* 起反作用的
strike *v.* 打击
attempt *v.* 尝试,试图
immobile *adj.* 不运动的,稳定的
muscle *n.* 肌肉
spasm *n.* 痉挛,一阵发作
twist *v.* 扭曲,曲折
spine *n.* 脊椎,脊骨
extreme *adj.* 极度的,极端的
recognize *v.* 认可,公认
overweight *adj.* 超重的
stone *n.* (重量单位,=)14 磅
diet *n.* 饮食,通常吃的食物
particularly *adv.* 尤其地,特别地
blame *v.* 指责,谴责
average *adj.* 普通的,平均的
aggravation *n.* (病情,负担)加重,恶化
slouched *adj.* 无精打采的,萎靡的,耷拉的
ligament *n.* 纽带,韧带
heal *v.* 愈合,治愈
conclusion *n.* 结论;come to a conclusion(最终)得出结论
orthopaedic *adj.* 整形外科的,矫形的
posture *n.* 身体的姿势
alignment *n.* 调整,矫正
mattress *n.* 床垫
spring *n.* 弹簧
slat *v.* 用条板制造…
hazard *n.* 危险,危害
heel *n.* 脚跟
find *n.* 发现(物或人)
insert *n.* 插入物 shoe insert 鞋垫
effective *adj.* 有效的,高效的
absolutely *adv.* 绝对地,肯定地
relief *n.* (对疼痛、困难、灾难的)减轻
battery *n.* 电池
gadget *n.* 小设备,小物品,小玩意儿
deliver *v.* 发送,递送,传送
subliminal *adj.* 微小的,难以察觉的,潜在意识的
pulse *n.* 脉搏,脉冲
indicate *v.* 表明,显示
remedy *n.* 治疗法

交际与语言表达

1. 本文是一位医学专家普及脊椎疾病的防护和医疗知识,难点在于除了使用一定的医学专业术语,她所使用的语言多为复杂的书面语言。考生在复习这篇文章时,不妨把它当作一篇阅读文章去学习。考生如果读懂了本文,可以学到很多关于脊椎疾病的生活常识,对将来的生活也会有很大的好处。
2. Today's Health Counsel is presented by..., who is ... 讲座开始时,主持人一般都要简单介绍演讲者,一句话就可以解释清楚演讲的题目和演讲者的身份。
3. Do you know what..., ... and ... have in common? 你们知道……,……和……三人的共同之处是什么吗?注意 have in common 的用法。
4. In fact, bad backs are one of the most common health problems today, affecting people in all walks of life. 实际上,背部疾病是现今最常见的健康问题,影响着各行各业的人们。注意句中分词结构的

用法,这在书面语言中比较常用,口语中可能说成 and it affects people...。本篇文章中非谓语动词结构和从句使用较多。

5. The second mistake we often make when stricken with extreme back pain is to go to bed and stay there. 我们背部十分疼痛时经常犯的第二个错误是上床休息并且在床上躺很长时间。when stricken with 可以改成 when we are stricken,但前者比较精练。
6. There are many ways in which simple day-to-day care can make all the difference. 在简单的日常生活细节中改变现状的方法有很多。
7. Also, studies have shown that just one hour sitting in a slouched position can strain ligaments in the back which can take months to heal. 研究还表明,以无精打采的姿势坐上一个小时就会拉伤背部韧带,要花上好几个月才能愈合。
8. Finally a word about the state-of-the-art relief—the TENS machine—a small battery-powered gadget which delivers subliminal electrical pulses to the skin. 最后再谈谈目前比较新潮的疼痛缓解器——TENS 机器——一种配电池的小型设计,能够把极其微弱的电脉冲传送给皮肤。这种有一定专业背景的话语其实并不影响理解和回答题目。考生在听的时候只要抓住 TENS machine 一个词就够了。

考题解析

Question 31

这道题磁带中念得比较快,很多考生可能根本不知道 incapacitated 的意思,很可能听不懂整句话的意思,但只要抓住关键的 a quarter (of a million),甚至 a million 都不用听出来,这道题也能做对。三个答案中,表达 a quarter 的只有 A 项。

Question 32

注意题干中的 **according to the speaker**,强调的是演讲者本人的观点。原文中演讲者首先提到了 pregnancy,但随后马上提到 **osteoporosis**, **which I personally believe** to be the **major** cause of problems for women. 骨质疏松这个词很多考生并不认识。对于这样的单词,在听力考试时只要注意发音即可。

Question 33

注意题干中的 **the Clinic** mainly recommends。此题与上题有相似之处,因为要强调的是演讲者所在诊所的观点。听力原文中她首先提到其他传统的治疗手段,最后提到 **at our clinic** we are beginning to realize the **unique** benefits of **relaxation therapy**。

Question 34

做选择题一定要好好分析题干和选项,把握题干中的关键词,在听的过程中定位磁带原文中相对应的词,上面两道题就是很好的例子。这道题也是这样,首先要知道本题考查的是 back 和 **other parts of the body** 的区别。磁带原文中一开始就提到 in general, the body is good at self-repair, 随后提到 **But** the body's response to back injury can be very **counter-productive.** 如果考生了解前缀 counter 一般表示"相反的",此处会有所注意。接着演讲者给大家讲解背部疾病如果只是依赖休养可能导致 **further twisting of the spine**,最后她总结性地提到 A **vicious circle** is underway. 结果是背部疼痛恶性循环的形成。这些内容有些难以理解,但如果结合好上下文,注意提示性的词语,可以确定答案为 C。

Question 35

这道题大部分考生能够做对。注意到题干中的 **bed rest** 与听力原文中的 **a short rest in bed** 的一致;在分析选项中,注意到有两项提到 **two days**,说明答案很可能与其相关。听力原文提到床上休息后,马上提到 **up to two days.** 与 **A** 项中 **a maximum of two days** 完全一致。但如果考生不知道 maximum 这一基本词汇的意义就不好办了。

Question 36

这道题讨论超重对背部疼痛的影响。提到超重者,演讲者首先提到 **back pain is not doing himself any favours.** 随后提到 the weight will... **make things worse**。与 B 项中 **worsen** 一致。

Question 37

这道题演讲者首先肯定使用 orthopaedic chairs 有时 **can be useful**,随后马上用 but 强调指出更为重要的是坐的姿势要对。先肯定,后转折,表明在部分情况下可以推荐。

Question 38

演讲者首先提到减震鞋垫是 **a real find**,真正有价值的发现,后面又进一步指出它 cheap, very effective,全力推荐该产品。

Question 39

这道题考生只要听到这么几个词:Though... for some, others... 就可以做出正确判断,没有必要完全理解原文意思。在雅思听力考试中一定要注意转折词的特殊作用。

Question 40

这道题答案有些隐晦。演讲者提到 TENS machine 之后,说 our experience indicates that your money is better spent on the more old-fashioned remedies. 我们的经验表明你的钱最好花在更传统的治疗方法上。虽然没有明确表明态度,但已经暗示不要把钱花在这种设备上了。

READING

READING PASSAGE 1

文章结构

体　　裁	说明文
主要内容	本文主要描写火箭的发展历史,主要说明反作用原理和火箭技术发展的关系,同时说明火箭技术在东方和西方作为武器应用的实际情况。
结　　构	文章按照时间顺序进行描写,首段提出主要说明内容:反作用原理对火箭技术发展具有重要意义,二、三段深入解释反作用原理和火箭技术之间的紧密联系,四、五段采用举例的方式分别说明东方和西方如何应用火箭技术,最后一段总结说明火箭技术发展意义及对未来发展预测的不确定性。
	A 段:反作用原理的发现对于火箭技术的重要意义。
	B 段:20 世纪前火箭技术未能实现转化是由于未能将反作用原理与太空旅行联系起来。
	C 段:解释火箭运作的原理(反作用原理)并说明反作用原理的实际应用在发明火箭之前。
	D 段:中国人最早发明和应用黑色炸药,并凭此技术生产各种攻击性的火箭。
	E 段:18 世纪起,欧洲人开始研究并使用火箭作为武器。
	F 段:火箭技术取得进展并使战争具有毁灭性后果,但它在未来的发展前景仍无法预测。

词汇注释

文　章

A 段

rocket *n.* 火箭；火箭发动机
concept *n.* 概念；观念；思想
mechanism *n.* 机械装置
propel *vt.* 推进；推
reaction *n.*（对刺激等的）反应；[物]反作用(力)
principle *n.* 原则；主义；原理
the reaction principle 反作用原理
represent *vt.* 代表；表示；象征
milestone *n.* 里程碑；(历史上或个人经历中的)重大事件
technology *n.* 技术；工艺
solve *vt.* 解决；阐明；解释
intrigue *vt.* 激起…的好奇心(或兴趣)；迷住
literally *adv.* 确实地，真正地，不加夸张地
exploration *n.* 探索，探究

B 段

intellectual *adj.* 知识的；智力的；理智的
breakthrough *n.* 突破性进展；突破点
automatically *adv.* 不经思索地；当然地，自然地
ensure *vt.* 保证，担保；保证获得
transition *n.* 过渡，过渡时期；转变，变迁
theory *n.* 理论；原理
practice *n.* 实践；实施，实行
despite *prep.* 不管，尽管，任凭
sporadically *adv.* 不时发生地，断断续续地，零散地
relatively *adv.* 比较而言；相对地；相当
minor *adj.*（数量、大小、程度等）较小的；较少的；较轻微的
artifact *n.* 人工制品，制造物(区别于天然物)
civilisation *n.* 文明；文明阶段；文明世界
prodigious *adj.* 巨大的；异常的；惊人的
accelerate *vt.* 使加快；促进
primitive *adj.* 原始的；早期的
rocketry *n.* 火箭学；火箭技术
sophisticated *adj.*（技术、产品等）复杂的，精密的，尖端的；高度发展的
astronaut *n.* 宇航员，航天员
generally *adv.* 一般地；通常；大体；普遍地
ignore *vt.* 不顾；不理；忽视
fiction *n.* [总称]小说
transport *vt.* 运输，运送；输送；搬运
hero *n.*（小说、戏剧、诗歌等中的）男主角，男主人公
mysterious *adj.* 神秘的；不可思议的
realm *n.* <书面语>王国；国度
fireworks *n.* 烟火
display *n.* 展示；表演
associate *vt.* 在思想上把…联系在一起
neighbouring *adj.* 邻近的，附近的

C 段

analogy *n.* 类比，类推
mount *vt.* 架置；装有(枪、炮等)
rear *n.* 后部，后边，后面；背部
discharge *n.*（枪、炮的）发射；爆炸
hence *adv.* 因此，所以；由此
motor *n.* 发动机，引擎；马达
minute *adj.* 微小的，异常小的，极小的
particle *n.* 微粒，颗粒
propellant *n.* 推进剂，发射药；火箭燃料
chamber *n.*（枪的）弹膛
ejection *n.* 喷出，射出
apply *vt.* 应用；使用，运用
practically *adv.* 实际上
invent *vt.* 发明，创造
describe *vt.* 描写，描述；形容
pigeon *n.* 鸽子
invention *n.* 发明，创造
string *n.* 细绳；线
to and fro 往复地，来回地
steam *n.* 水蒸气，蒸汽
exhaust *n.* 排气管；排气口；排气装置
port *n.* [机]汽门，风门；通道
motive *adj.*（引起）运动的；发动的，推动的
motive power（原)动力

D 段

link *v.* 联系；连接
inextricably *adv.* 分不开地；无法摆脱地
black powder（黑色）火药
credit *vt.* 认为…有(某种优点或成就等)(with)，把…归于(to)
compound *vt.* 使混合；使合成

ingredient *n.* (混合物的)组成部分,成分
saltpeter *n.* [化]硝石,钾硝,硝酸钾
charcoal *n.* 炭,木炭
sulphur *n.* 硫,硫磺,硫黄
arrow *n.* 箭,矢
rely *vi.* (relied, relied)依靠,依赖
incendiary *adj.* (物质)能(引起)燃烧的
projectile *n.* 射弹(如子弹、炮弹、枪榴弹等)
incendiary projectile 燃烧弹
explosive *adj.* 爆炸的,爆发的;会(引起)爆炸的
grenade *n.* 手榴弹;枪榴弹;(灭火、照明、催泪等用的)榴弹
cannon *n.* 大炮,火炮
leopard *n.* 豹;美洲豹,美洲虎
octagonal-shaped *adj.* 八边形的
range *n.* 射程;有效距离
saber *n.* 马刀,军刀
crossbow *n.* 弩,石弓
shaft *n.* 箭杆,矛杆
stability *n.* 稳定性,稳定度
gravity *n.* [物]重力,地心引力
apparently *adv.* 显然地,明明白白地
stabilize *vt.* 使稳定,保持…的稳定;使稳固
tail *n.* 尾,尾巴

E 段

weapon *n.* 武器,兵器
prior to 在…以前;先于;优先于
pyrotechnic *adj.* 烟火的
incentive *n.* 动机;刺激
aggressive *adj.* 侵略的;侵犯的;挑衅的
corps *n.* 队,部队
rocketeer *n.* 火箭发射(或操纵、乘坐)者
envelope *n.* 包裹物;外表;外壳
millimeter *n.* 毫米
diameter *n.* 直径
guide *vt.* 给…领路;使按特定方向移动
stick *n.* 棍,棒,杖
experiment *vi.* 进行实验
barrage *n.* 阻挡,阻塞;遮断
version *n.* (一事物的)变化形式,变体
encase *vt.* 围住,包起
stout *adj.* 结实的,坚固的
cylinder *n.* 圆柱体,圆桶
terminate *vt.* 停止,结束;终接,出现(或形成)在…的末尾
conical *adj.* 圆锥形的,圆锥的
launcher *n.* 发射装置,发射器,发射架
cylindrical *adj.* (圆)柱形的;圆筒形的
tube *n.* 管,管子
prop *vt.* 支撑(up)
thereby *adv.* 因此,由此,从而
insert *vt.* 插入;嵌入
lit *vt.* (lit or lighted)点,点燃
impressive *adj.* 给人以深刻印象的;激动人心的
predictable *adj.* 可预料的,可预测的

F 段

devastating *adj.* 毁灭性的,破坏性极大的
forum *n.* 论坛;讨论会;公开讨论的机会
nevertheless *adv.* 仍然,不过
humble *adj.* 不显要的,地位(或身份)低下的;谦逊的
previous *adj.* 以前的,先前的
foundation *n.* 基础;基本原理;根据

题目

appropriate *adj.* 适当的,恰当的
impact *n.* 影响,作用
undeveloped *adj.* 未(充分)开发的;未发展的;不发达的
military *adj.* 军事的,军用的
outcome *n.* 结果;结局;后果
major *adj.* 主要的;较重要的
indicate *vt.* 标示;指出
item *n.* 条,项;项目

考题解析

Questions 1–4

● 题型归类:List of headings

该题型考查考生抓文章结构大意,总结归纳段落中心思想的能力,是雅思阅读中较难的题型之一。做题时注意:一个 heading 只唯一对应一个自然段;将 example 中选出的 heading 首先划掉,做题时无需再看,节省时间。

● 题目解析：

题目编号	段落主题句	题解
1	Despite the fact that rockets had been used sporadically for several hundred years, they remained a relatively minor artifact of civilization until the twentieth century.	B段首句和第二句都有让步的表达，都在说火箭的理论和使用尽管很早就有，但长期都是一件并不起眼的事物。请阅读体会第二句为该段的中心句。所以对应的heading为Undeveloped for centuries。
2	A simple analogy can help us to understand how a rocket operates.	C段首句告诉我们这个自然段主要解释how a rocket operates。而通过上文我们知道reaction principle是火箭的核心。所以答案为第一个heading：How the reaction principle works。注意work和operate的对应。
3	无明显主题句。D段前面描写黑火药在中国的发明，后面谈到由黑火药做出的第一批火箭。	3题和4题较难。第3题容易错误地选择第7个heading：Rockets for military use。因为D段中描写到了大炮cannons，抗击敌人repel their enemies，有一种类似的武器one such weapon "basket of fire"，等等。但请注意E段首句，"直到18世纪时，欧洲才正式对作为战争武器的火箭本身的使用前景感兴趣，而不再局限于将它作为其他武器的助推工具。"说明D段中的描写火箭本身只是起推进器的作用，还没有自身作为武器用于军事。再加上D段首句中说到火箭的发明，所以该段应选择heading：The first rockets，第一批火箭。而第4题选择第7个heading。
4	It was not until the eighteenth century that Europe became seriously interested in the possibilities of using the rocket itself as a weapon of war and not just to propel other weapons.	

Questions 5 – 6

● 题型归类：Multiple Choice

● 题目解析：

题目编号	题目定位词	答案位置	题解
5	greatest outcome	A段第3行：reaction principle, which was the key to space travel...	题目：反作用原理的发现带来的最大成果是……当题目中有最高级形式时，应回原文中找最高级或同义表达。注意key这个单词，意思为关键，虽然不是最高级形式，但有最高级的含义。类似的单词有：crucial, essential等。
6	grestest progress	B段第2句	题目：火箭技术在何时取得了最大的进步。该题很难。正确答案D：from the late nineteenth century to the present day. 原文中表达在B段第2句："尽管火箭已被零零星星、断断续续地使用了数百年之久，但相对来说，它无非是文明社会中一件并不起眼的人造玩意儿而已。这种情况一直延续到20世纪才告结束。"通过这句话我们可以理解，在20世纪之前火箭技术都没有取得长足的发展。而只有答案D最贴近这个时间表述，其他答案错。

Questions 7–10

● 题型归类：Matching

● 题目解析：

题目编号	题目定位词	答案位置	题解
7	black powder	D 段第 1 句和第 2 句	
8	rocket-propelled arrows	第 16 页第 2 行和第 5 行	arrows like flying leopards 和 arrow as a flying sabre 这两种武器都是中国发明的，用火箭推动的箭。
9	war weapons	E 段第 5 行	“India”所在的句子。它把火箭本身作为战争的武器。
10	launcher	E 段倒数第 5 行	

Questions 11–14

● 题型归类：Matching

● 题目解析：题目本身用大写的 Chinese，Arab，Indian，British 即可在文中大致定位。

题目编号	题目定位词	答案位置	题解
11		16 页第 2 行	“basket of fire”，最突出的特点为 0.7 metre-long arrows octagonal-shaped basket，选出 B。
12		D 段倒数第 3 行	特点为 1.5m tail，two rockets attached to either side of this tail，选出 E。
13		E 段第 8 行	最突出的特点为 200 millimetres long，40 millimetres in diameter，3m-long bamboo guiding stick，选出 F。
14		E 段第 11 行	最突出的特点为 having a stick almost five metres long，选出 G。

参考译文

火箭——东始西渐的发展历程

火箭的概念，更确切地说，就是按照将物体射入空中的设想所设计的机械装置，已经存在两千年以上了。然而在反作用原理——宇宙航行的关键理论，它代表科学思想史上的伟大里程碑之一——发现之前，火箭技术一直未能得到长足的发展。它不仅解决了长期以来人类感兴趣的问题，而且更重要的是，它实际上打开了探索宇宙的大门。

一项智力上的突破，尽管很出色，也不一定会顺理成章地从理论过渡到实际应用。尽管火箭已被零零星星、断断续续地使用了数百年之久，但相对来说，它无非是文明社会中一件并不起眼的人造玩意儿而已。这种情况一直延续到 20 世纪才告结束。在上世纪两次世界大战的促进和推动下，科学家们干劲冲天，这是实现原始火箭技术的转化所必需的，于是才有可能造就掌握尖端科技的宇航员。令人感到奇怪的是：火箭之类的话题却往往被小说家们所忽略而未能将他们的主人公载运到地球以外的神秘星球上去，尽管自 13 世纪以来火箭在中国已广泛使用于烟花展演。上述情况的存在，其原因在于尚未有人将反作用原理与在太空中漫游以涉足相邻世界的想法联系起来。

一个简单的类比将有助于我们理解火箭是如何运作的。它很像安装在船尾的机关枪，作为对向后击发子弹的反作用，机枪和船只就因之前移。火箭助推器的“子弹”是精密而高速的粒子，通过点燃弹膛中的发射火药即可将这些粒子发射出去。与此同时所产生的反作用力则使火箭前移。有证据表明反作用原理的实际应用远在发明火箭之前。Aulus Gellius 在他所著的《希腊夜谭》中描写了“Archytas 的鸽子”（这是公元前360年的一个发明）：用绳子悬在空中的一个木质圆柱体，两端开有小排气孔，从中排出的蒸汽会使“鸽子”来回摆动，其动力来自对蒸汽排放时所产生的反作用力。

火箭的发明必然要与“黑色炸药”的发明联系起来。大多数技术史专家把后者的发现归功于中国人。他们的观点基于对中国典籍的研究或对早期定居或长期旅居在中国专事研究中国历史和文明的欧洲人笔记的研究。情况很可能是这样的：在十世纪的某个时期，人们首次用硝石、木炭和硫磺作为基本原料合成黑色炸药，但这并不意味着黑色炸药被立即用来推动火箭。到13世纪时，用炸药推动的火箭已司空见惯，了无新意。中国人凭借此类技术进步以生产各种烧夷弹、开花弹，可能还有大炮，来抗击敌人。有一种类似的武器就是“火筐”，或直接从汉语译过来便是“飞豹火箭”。这批箭长0.7米，近箭头处各附有一长管火药筒，它们可以从一个八边形的篮筐中同时发射，其射程可达400步之遥。另一种武器称为“飞刀利箭”，它可以用石弩发射。与其他火箭推进的各种箭型处于类似位置的火箭，其设计目的就在于延长射程。将一片微量的铁块捆绑在1.5米长的竹制箭杆的羽毛部位之下，便可将重心移至火箭下面的部位从而提高箭身的稳定性。几乎与此同时，阿拉伯人推出了“能行会烧的蛋”。此“蛋（弹）”显然满腹火药，并有一条1.5米长的“蛋”（弹）尾使其保持平衡、稳定；发射时使用弹尾两侧所附载的火箭即可。

直到18世纪时，欧洲才正式对作为战争武器的火箭本身的使用前景感兴趣，而不再局限于将它作为其他武器的助推工具。此前，火箭只是在烟花展演中使用。使火箭更具进攻性的动机并非来自欧洲大陆内部，而是来自遥远的印度。印度领导人曾组建一支火箭部队，并在18世纪后期成功地使用火箭武器抗击了英国人。用来抗击英国人的印度火箭曾被一位在印度服役的英国上尉描写成：“一个铁质外壳，长约200毫米、直径约40毫米，其顶部有尖刺若干，还配有一根3米长的竹制导杆。”19世纪初期，英国人开始做燃烧连珠弹火箭的实验。英式火箭与印度火箭的区别在于前者是完全密封在一个直径为1米的坚固的铁质圆柱体内，其终端呈为圆锥形，还配置了一根5米长的杆，这是专门用来与箭身牢牢地捆绑在一起而制作的。19世纪中叶，美国人推出一种配有专用发射装置的火箭用来对付墨西哥人。用两根棍子将一根圆柱形长管道支撑起来，并将它拴到发射装置的顶部，从而使火箭插入其中，并可从另一端予以点火发射。然而其结果有时却并不能令人如愿，因为火箭在飞行中的表现是难以预测的。

自从那个时期以来，火箭技术已取得了长足的进展，却也往往在战场上带来毁灭性的结果。尽管如此，现代太空计划在今天所取得的成功仍然要归功于头几个世纪的那些筚路蓝缕的先驱们，是他们打下并发展了反作用原理的基础。至于火箭技术在未来的发展前景如何，谁又能未卜先知呢？

READING PASSAGE 2

文章结构

体　　裁	说明文
主要内容	文章主要说明吸烟和被动吸烟的危害，列举数据证明。

结　构	第1段:introduction
	第2段:总论吸烟危害巨大。
	第3段:被动吸烟和侧烟流的危害。
	第4段:用吸烟家庭说明烟雾环境的危害。
	第5段:UCSF的研究表明二手烟雾对非烟民的危害远甚于烟民本人。
	第6段:指出被动吸烟对非烟民所产生的影响远远大于对烟民的影响。
	第7段:具体讲解吸烟致癌的多种原因。
	第8段:驳斥错误的观点。
	第9段:提出解决问题的建议。

词汇注释

文　章

第1段

risk *n.* 危险;具有危害性的事物
cigarette *n.* 香烟,卷烟
oily *adj.* 油的;含油的;多油的
essence *n.* 精油
nicotine *n.* [化]烟碱,尼古丁
active *adj.* 活性的
ingredient *n.* (混合物的)组成部分,成分
tobacco *n.* 烟草;烟叶
component *n.* (组)成(部)分
contain *vt.* 包含,容纳
chemical *adj.* 化学的;使用化学品完成(或产生、工作)的
compound *n.* 化合物
cancer *n.* 癌,恶性肿瘤
cancer-causing *adj.* 致癌的
substance *n.* 物质;材料;东西
evidence *n.* 根据;证明
vastly *adv.* 大量地;极多地;非常地
fatal *adj.* 致命的,不幸的,毁灭性的
medical *adj.* 医学的

第2段

responsible *adj.* 有责任的,可靠的,可依赖的,负责的
lung *n.* 肺,肺脏
associate with 联合,与…发生联系
amongst *prep.* 在…中间,在…之中
stomach *n.* 胃,胃部
kidney *n.* 肾,肾脏
leukemia *n.* 白血病
cervical *adj.* 子宫颈的
pneumonia *n.* [医]肺炎
bronchitis *n.* [医]支气管炎
influenza *n.* 流行性感冒
represent *vt.* 代表,扮演
preventable *adj.* 可阻止的,可预防的

第3段

passive *adj.* 被动的
puff *n.* 一阵喷烟,烟气
exhale *v.* 呼气
emphasize *vt.* 强调
particle *n.* 粒子,微粒
therefore *adv.* 因此,所以
deposit *vt.* 存放,堆积
classify *vt.* 分类,分等
category *n.* 种类,类别,范畴

第4段

illustration *n.* 说明,例证,例子
married *adj.* 已婚的,婚姻的
partner *n.* 伴侣,合伙人,股东,舞伴
latter *adj.* 后者(的)
exposure *n.* 暴露,曝露
figure *n.* 数字
spouse *n.* 配偶(指夫或妻)
pack *n.* 包、盒

calculate *v.* 计算，考虑，计划，打算
attribute to 归因于
childhood *n.* 孩童时期
adolescence *n.* 青春期(一般指成年以前由 13 岁至 15 岁的发育期)

第 5 段

leave aside（把某事）搁置一边
philosophical *adj.* 哲学的
experience *vt.* 经验，体验，经历
daily *adj.* 每日的，日常的
substantial *adj.* 真实的，很多的；大量的
adverse *adj.* 不利的，敌对的，相反的

第 6 段

journal *n.* 定期刊物，杂志
review *n.* 回顾，复习，评论
opponent *n.* 对手，反对者
suggest *vt.* 建议，提出
continually *adv.* 不断地，频繁地
cardiovascular *adj.* 心脏血管的
adapt *vt.* 使适应
compensate *v.* 偿还，补偿
inhalation *n.* 吸入
consequently *adv.* 从而，因此

第 7 段

emphasize *v.* 强调
element *n.* 要素，化学元素
monoxide *n.* 一氧化物
compete *vi.* 比赛，竞争
oxygen *n.* 氧，氧气
interfere *vi.* 干涉，干预，妨碍，打扰
deliver *vt.* 递送
life-giving *n.* 礼物，给予物
activate *vt.* 刺激，使活动
platelet *n.* [解]血小板
likelihood *n.* 可能，可能性
thereby *adv.* 因此，从而
circulation *n.* 循环，流通

第 8 段

criticize *v.* 批评，责备
consultant *n.* 顾问，商议者，咨询者
assume *vt.* 假定，设想
impact *n.* 影响，效果
underestimate *vt.* 低估，看轻
in support of 支持，支援
previous *adj.* 以前的；先的
preventable *adj.* 可阻止的，可预防的
alcohol-related *adj.* 与酒精相关的

第 9 段

illegal *adj.* 违法的，不合规定的
maintain *vt.* 维持
cost-effective *adj.* 节省成本的
establish *v.* 建立

题目

be responsible for 对…负责
intake *n.* 吸收之量，吸入
flow *n.* 流程，流动
absorption *n.* 吸收
formation *n.* 形成，构成
promote *vt.* 促进，发扬，提升
activity *n.* 活跃，活动性
take up 拿起，开始从事
teenager *n.*（13 岁到 19 岁的）少年
at risk 在危险中
finance *vt.* 为…供给资金，为…筹措资金
contract *v.* 感染，订约
oppose *vt.* 反对，使对立
subject *n.* 题目，主题，科目
solution *n.* 解决方案

考题解析

Questions 15–17

● 题型归类:Multiple Choice

● 题目解析:

题目编号	题目定位词	答案位置	题解
15	leukemia and pneumonia	第2段第3行和第5行出现这两个单词	第2段首句和第2句读完后迅速排除A、D选项。A、D选项的描述是False的表达。而C选项中lung cancer这里没有提到,这两句话的主语都是smoking,选出B。
16	carbon monoxide	第7段第2句话	原文中说一氧化碳在红血球中与氧气的对抗,干扰并妨碍血液对心脏输氧能力的发挥。抓住该句中一氧化碳的对立物质为氧。直接选出A。
17	nicotine	第7段第3句话	注意题目中问"intake of nicotine encourages..." encourage意为鼓励,促进。原文中"尼古丁"以及其他毒素激活了(activate)称作血小板的小血球,这样一来就增加了(increase)血块形成的可能性,从而对全身的血液循环产生不利的影响。正确选项C,encourage替换原文的increase。 A选项错。原文中说的是affecting,此处指不利的影响,是encourage的反意。D选项容易误选,请注意原文意思为platelets已经存在,尼古丁的作用只是激活,而不可能增加它在血液中的数量。

Questions 18–21

● 题型归类:YES/NO/NOT GIVEN

● 题目解析:

题目编号	题目定位词	答案位置	题解
18	USA 和 thirty percent	第2段最后一句话	题目:在美国30%的死亡是由吸烟相关的疾病所造成。而原文说:吸烟应对癌症死亡总数的30%负责。题目的表述明显错误理解了原文,应选NO。
19	marriage 和 partner	第4段首句	题目:如果夫妻中的一方吸烟,另一方很可能也开始吸烟。 原文没有该含义的表述,只说"就一对已婚夫妇来说,其中一位是烟民、一位是非烟民,那么后者死于心脏病的风险被认为高达30%以上,这都是被动吸烟惹的祸"。选NOT GIVEN。

20	parents, teenagers	第 4 段末句	题目:对父母吸烟的十几岁的少年来说,他们一生中患肺癌的风险很高。 原文虽然没有明显提到 parents, teenagers 等单词,但说道"有 17% 的肺癌病例可归咎于以下事实,即病人在其童年(childhood)及青少年(adolescence)时期曾深受高浓度二手烟烟雾的危害。"题目表达了同一个意思。应选 YES。
21	UCSF, opponents financed	第 5 段和第 9 段	题目:反对吸烟的人为 UCSF 的研究提供经费。 回原文先找到 UCSF,附近扫描"反对者","财务资助"等,原文都没有提到,故选 NOT GIVEN。

Questions 22–24

● 题型归类:Sentence Completion

● 题目解析:

题目编号	题目定位词	答案位置	题解
22	passive smoking	第 6 段末句	先扫描所有选项,A 到 J 选项。从语法语意上排除干扰选项。从语义上看,题干中"被动吸烟..."后能接的选项有 C, E, I, J。再回原文定位,选出 E。
23	smoker, compared	第 2 段末句和第 8 段末句	主语为 smoker,人,可能的选项有 D, F, G,再从这三个选项的意思上体会,G 选项正确。该题可以不回原文定位。
24	American Medical Association	第 4 段末句	主语为 Association 协会,可能的选项有 B, H。回原文定位,发现 B 选项是 UCSF 所做的事情,该题选 H。

Questions 25–28

● 题型归类:Matching

先划出所有题目的定位词,回原文扫描,特别留意 UCSF 和 EPA 出现的附近。

● 题目解析:

题目编号	题目定位词	答案位置	题解
25	cardiovascular	第 6 段第 6 行	"The study suggests that people who smoke cigarettes are continually damaging their cardiovascular system, which adapts in order to compensate for the effects of smoking."主语为 study,通过上文第 5 段首句知道是 UCSF 的 study,故选 A。
26	philosophical	第 5 段第 3 行	该段重点讲到 UCSF,理解"Leaving aside the philosophical question of whether anyone should have to breathe someone else's cigarette smoke..."是观点 opinion,而非 finding。

27	smoke-free public places	全文末句	UCSF的观点,而不是研究的结果发现。
28	side-stream, more harmful	第3段第4行	直接选出C。

参考译文

卷烟烟雾的危害

现在叫做尼古丁的那种油脂精原名为nicotianine,是19世纪初期发现的,它是烟草的主要活性成分。然而尼古丁只是卷烟烟雾中的一个小小组成部分。此烟雾含有4700多种化合物,包括43种致癌物。在近代,科学研究已证实:经年累月地吸烟会极度地增加患绝症的风险。

吸烟要对85%以上的肺癌患者负责,除此之外它还与口腔癌、胃癌、肾癌(其他疾病暂且不提)等有关,还有约14%的白血病和子宫颈癌也被认为是由它而起的。在1990年,由吸烟导致的死亡个案超过84000例,主要是由于患肺炎、支气管炎以及流感等病症所致。据析,吸烟应对癌症死亡总数的30%负责;吸烟在今天的美国这样的国家里,显然是最重要的可预防致癌因素。

被动吸烟——即在吸烟者每次吐纳之间,旁人吸入了香烟的燃烧端冒出的一股股侧流烟,或是吸烟者口中呼出的烟——也能引发严重的健康风险。美国环境保护局(EPA)在1992年发表的一份报告着重指出了种种危害健康的险情,特别是来自侧流烟的危害。这种类型的烟含有更多的微粒子,因而更易于沉积在肺部深处。根据这份报告,美国环境保护局将由于吸烟而使环境中产生的烟雾列入具有致癌危险的最高等级范畴之中。

现举一实例对健康方面的危害加以说明:就一对已婚夫妇来说,其中一位是烟民、一位是非烟民,那么后者死于心脏病的风险比正常情况高30%以上,这都是被动吸烟惹的祸。如果配偶一方是一位日吸四包香烟、具有烟龄20年的老烟民,那么患肺癌的风险也由于长年累月地处于被动吸烟的环境中而与日俱增,其百分比飚升至80%。据计算,有17%的肺癌病例可归咎于以下事实,即病人在其童年及青少年时期曾深受二手烟雾的侵袭。

新近由美国加州大学旧金山分校(UCSF)的研究人员所作的一次研究表明,二手烟雾对非烟民的危害远甚于烟民本人。至于人们是否应该吸入别人吐出的烟雾,这是个哲学问题,姑且搁置不论;这份研究报告提出,许多人在日常生活中所接触到的烟雾已足以对他们的心和肺产生严重的负面效果。

在美国医学协会(AMA)的学刊上发表的那份报告是以研究人员自己的早期研究成果为基础的,但是也包含了对过去几年研究工作的回顾与检论。美国医学协会代表了美国医生总数的大约一半之多,并且坚决反对吸烟。该研究报告指出,吸烟的人们正在继续损害自身的心血管系统,而该系统则进行自我调节以便抵消吸烟造成的后果。它进一步说明,不吸烟的人不具有使自己的身体适应烟雾吸入的好处。因此,被动吸烟对非烟民所产生的影响远远大于对烟民的影响。

这份报告着重指出,癌症并非由卷烟烟雾中的一个单一成分所引发;对健康的有害影响是由许多因素促成的。比如说,一氧化碳在红血球中与氧气对抗,并妨碍血液向心脏输送维持生命的氧气。卷烟烟雾中的尼古丁以及其他毒素激活了称作血小板的小血球,这样一来就增加了血块形成的可能性,从而对全身的血液循环产生不利的影响。

有些为卷烟厂服务的科学顾问作出这样的假设——卷烟烟雾对吸烟者或非吸烟者来说,其影响都是一样的;他们的这种行径受到了研究人员的批评。后者认为,那些科学家低估了被动吸烟所造成的损失;同时还引用了一些先前的研究成果以支持他们新近的调查结果。所引资料表明,美国每年都有3至6万人因为被动吸烟而死于心脏病发作。这就意味着被动吸烟是位于主动吸烟、涉酒类疾病之后的第三类最可预防的死因了。

该研究报告主张,消除被动吸烟所需要采取的行动类型应仿照针对非法吸毒及艾滋病所采取的行动。美国加州大学旧金山分校的研究人员坚称,最简单又最划算的举措便是设立禁止吸烟的工作场地、学校以及公共场所。

READING PASSAGE 3

文章结构

体　　裁	议论为主
主要内容	科学方法是假设—演绎,而非归纳。假设—演绎法的优势。
结　　构	A 段:科学方法的本质是"假设—演绎",而不是通常所认为的"归纳"。
	B 段:认识科学方法的重要。
	C 段:解释归纳。
	D 段:假设的作用。
	E 段:测试假设。
	F 段:预测结果。
	G 段:研究的方法。

词汇注释

文　　章

A 段

scientific *adj.* 科学的
hypotheses 臆测,假定
imaginative *adj.* 想象的,虚构的
inspirational *adj.* 有灵感的,给予灵感的,灵感的
adventure *n.* 冒险,冒险的经历
argue *v.* 争论,辩论
in favour of 为…而征战,参加支持…的活动
logic *n.* 逻辑;逻辑学
edition *n.* 版本,版
hypothetico-deductive 假设—推理
generally *adv.* 一般,通常,一般地
inductive *adj.* 归纳的

B 段

essential *adj.* 本质的,实质的,基本的
intending *adj.* 预计中的,未来的
interpretation *n.* 解释,阐明,口译,通译
process *n.* 过程,作用,方法,程序,步骤,进行,推移
discourage *vt.* 使气馁,阻碍
suffer *vi.* 受痛苦,受损害

C 段

myth *n.* 神话
formulation *n.* 用公式表示,明确地表达,作简洁陈述
theory *n.* 理论,学说
raw *adj.* 未加工的
unbiased *adj.* 没有偏见的
unprejudiced *adj.* 公平的,无偏见的,没有成见的
observation *n.* 观察,观测
sensory *adj.* 感觉的,感官的
data *n.* **datum** 的复数,[计] 资料,数据
commonly *adv.* 普通地,一般地
refer to 查阅,提到,谈到,打听
generalization *n.* 普遍化
disorderly *adj.* 混乱的
array *n.* 一连串(的信息)

factual *adj.* 事实的，实际的
relevant *adj.* 有关的，相应的
somehow *adv.* 不知何故
emerge *vi.* 显现，浮现，暴露，形成，（由某种状态）脱出，（事实）显现出来

D 段

function *n.* 官能，功能
otherwise *adv.* 另外，否则
experimental *adj.* 实验的，根据实验的
exploratory *adj.* 探险的，探测的
expectation *n.* 期待，预料
outcome *n.* 结果，成果
hypothesis *n.* 假设
initiative *n.* 主动
incentive *n.* 动机
inquiry *n.* 质询，调查
in the light of 按照，根据，当作
relevant *adj.*（常与 to 连用）有关的；中肯的
irrelevant *adj.* 不相关的
methodology *n.* 方法学，方法论
discard *vt.* 丢弃，抛弃
conduct *v.* 引导，管理，为人，传导
naive *adj.* 天真的
objective *adj.* 客观的

E 段

arise *vi.* 出现，发生，起因于
guesswork *n.* 臆测，猜测
inspiration *n.* 灵感
formulate *vt.* 用公式表示，明确地表达
rigorously *adv.* 严厉地，残酷地
prediction *n.* 预言，预报
deduce *vt.* 推论，演绎出
consequence *n.* 结果
modify *v.* 修改
turn out 生产
retain *vt.* 保持，保留
imagination *n.* 想象，空想
strictly *adv.* 严格地，确实地
logical *adj.* 合乎逻辑的
rigorous *adj.* 严格的，严厉的
argument *n.* 争论，辩论
hence *adv.* 因此，从此
term *n.* 学期，期限

F 段

accident *n.* 意外事件，事故
mould *n.* 模具
antidote *n.* [医]解毒剂，矫正方法
bacterial *adj.* 细菌的
infection *n.* [医] 传染，传染病，影响，感染

G 段

myth *n.* 神话
inevitable *adj.* 不可避免的，必然的
fashion *n.* 样子，方式，流行，风尚，时样
approach *n.* 方法
psychological *adj.* 心理（上）的
behaviour *n.* 行为，举止，习性
holistic *adj.* 整体的，全盘的
rework *vt.* 重做，改写，重写
blind alley *n.* 死胡同；绝路
component *n.* 成分
thesis *n.* 论题，论文
properly *adv.* 适当地，完全地
serial *adj.* 连续的
output *n.* 产量，输出，输出量
evaluate *v.* 评价
independently *adv.* 独立地，自立地
behavioural *adj.* 动作的
academic *adj.* 学院的，理论的
demonstrate *vt.* 示范，证明，论证
molecule *n.* [化]分子，些微
fascinate *vt.* 使着迷

题目

anticipate *v.* 预订，预见，可以预料
prediction *n.* 预言，预报
fulfill *vt.* 履行，实现，完成（计划等）
confirm *v.* 确认
mistaken *adj.* 犯错的，错误的
conception *n.* 观念，概念

考题解析

Questions 29–33

● 题型归类：List of Headings

● 题目解析：

题目编号	段落主题句	题解
29	The myth of the scientific method is that it is inductive: that the formulation of scientific theory starts with the basic, raw evidence of the senses—simple, unbiased, unprejudiced observation.	注意C段首句The myth of scientific method is that it is inductive：冒号后面是解释说明。
30	This expectation is a hypothesis.	注意D段中This expectation is a hypothesis. Hypotheses provide...“这种期待便是一种假设。假设为下一步的调查研究工作注入首创精神和激励因素，并对原来的工作方法产生影响。”
31	Hypotheses arise by guesswork, or by inspiration, but having been formulated they can and must be tested rigorously, using the appropriate methodology.	注意首句的表达。
32	So don't worry if you have some idea of what your results will tell you before you even begin to collect data.	理解F段首句和第二句。
33	The myth of scientific method is not only that it is inductive (which we have seen is incorrect) but also that the hypothetico-deductive method proceeds in a step-by-step, inevitable fashion.	该题比较难。段中出现的method, approach，对应done，而reported则要理解“This is much more holistic—involving guesses, reworkings, corrections, blind alleys and above all inspiration, in the deductive as well as the hypothetic component—than is immediately apparent from reading the final thesis or published papers.

Questions 34–35

● 题型归类：Short Answers

● 题目解析：

题目编号	题目定位词	答案位置	题解
34	give advice directly to the reader	B段	B段只有一句话：“It is essential that you, as an intending researcher, understand the difference between these two interpretations of the research process so that you do not become discouraged or begin to suffer from a feeling of ‘cheating’ or not going about it the right way.”

35	give advice directly to the reader	F段	F段首句:“So don’t worry if you have some idea of what your results will tell you before you even begin to collect data”.

Questions 36–39

● 题型归类:YES/NO/NOT GIVEN

● 题目解析:

题目编号	题目定位词	答案位置	题解
36	Popper	A段最后一句话	题目:Popper认为科学的方法是假设—演绎法。 原文:... arguing in favour of the position taken by Karl Popper... 支持Popper的立场, Popper的立场也就是: that the nature of the scientific method is hypothetico-deductive and not, as is generally believed, inductive.
37	prediction, fulfilled	E段第3句	题目:如果基于假设的预测实现了,那么这个假设被确定为正确。原文:如果预测应验,那就说明你的假设是获得支持的,还可能一直保留下去,直到有新的检验来否定它为止。
38	Many people, mistaken way		题目:许多人采用错误的方法做研究。 原文明显没有提到。
39	more, describing, than doing	G段最后一句	题目:与其说科学的方法是一种做研究的方法,它更是一种描述研究的方法。 原文:从这个观点来看,“科学的方法”可以被更实用地看作一种撰写调查研究文章的方法,而并非一种可以付诸实施的方法。 注意题目和原文单词的对应: Writing up—describing; carrying out—doing

Questions 40

● 题型归类:Multiple Choice

● 题目解析:

题目编号	题目定位词	答案位置	题解
40	purpose	注意文章首末两段	首段中的表达:the nature of the scientific method is hypothetico-deductive and not, inductive. 对应D选项 different conceptions。

参考译文

科学的方法

Medawar在1964年曾说过:"假设在性质上是一种想象和灵感;它们是思想上的冒险。"他是在为Karl Popper所采取的立场辩护(见《科学发现的逻辑》1972年第3版)。后者认为科学方法的本质是"假设—演绎",而不是通常所认为的"归纳"。

作为一位将要从事研究的人员,极为重要的是必须懂得对研究过程的两种诠释之间的区别,以免感到气馁,或为由此而产生一种"欺骗"的感觉而备感痛苦,或因感觉方式错误而心烦意乱。

很多人认为科学方法是归纳的:科学理论的形成始自感觉上基本的、原始的证据——简单的、不偏不倚的、不加歧视的观察。基于这些凭感觉得来的材料——通常被称为"事实"——结论便会形成。这种迷信等于在宣告,从一串杂乱无章的真实信息中总会产生出一个有条理的相关理论。但是,归纳法的出发点是毫无根据的。

世界上不存在所谓的不偏不倚的观察。我们所做的每一次观察或评论都与我们过去所见到的,或是经历过的有密切关系。所有实验性或探索性的科学工作,在开始启动的同时,人们都期待着能有所成就。这种期待便是一种假设。假设为下一步的调查研究工作注入积极性和激励因素,并对原来的工作方法会产生影响。有些观察被认为是相关而中肯的,而有些则是无关紧要的;一种方法被选用了,而其他方法被舍弃了;有些实验项目得以付诸实施,而别的项目则被取消。这一切正是根据一种期待的心理作出的抉择。你那朴素的、纯理论的、客观的研究者现在在哪里呢?

"假设"是通过推测或灵感而提出的,但在它被系统地阐述之后,能够也必须通过使用适当的方法加以严格的检验。你可以根据假设对结果进行推断,并在此基础上作出预测。如果预测未能应验的话,那么就得把你的假设予以摒弃,或者加以调整。如果预测应验,那就说明你的假设是获得支持的,还可能一直保留下去,直到有新的检验来否定它为止。你一旦得出你的假设——你头脑中想象的产物——你接着就进入以演绎的论据为基础的严格而缜密的逻辑程序,"假设—演绎"之名即由此而来。

所以,如果在你甚至尚未开始收集材料之前,你就已经意识到你的结果是什么,不要着急;世上还没有这样的科学家,他们真能坐等所有的证据都摆在面前时才开始着手搞清证据的可能含意是什么。我们会接触到的最为近似这种局面的就是某事件的偶然发生;但即便是事发当时,研究人员仍然必须制订并提出一项假设以供检验,然后才能确信,比如说,一种霉菌可能被证明为一种有效的解毒剂用以对付细菌感染。

关于"科学的方法"的这种迷信不仅认为它是归纳法(我们把它看作是错误的),而且体现在这样一个事实上:"假设—演绎法"是一个一步接一步,不可跳跃的过程。"假设—演绎法"描述了适用于大量研究工作的逻辑方法,但是它没有描述产生它的心理行为。这远比使人一读就懂的定稿论文或已发表的论文来得全面而完整,它不仅在假设成分中,而且在演绎过程中都涉及了推测、重做、修正、(陷入)困境以及最重要的灵感。这些已经被适当地整合进一个更具系列性和逻辑性的序列,以便让结果可以进行独立估算而不受行为过程的干扰,尽管这个结果是通过后者取得的。比如说吧,Crick和Watson就利用学术论文来展示DNA(脱氧核糖核酸)的分子结构,而Watson(1968)在引人入胜的《双螺旋结构》这本书中描述了他们是如何操作的——这就是前者(学术论文)与后者(科技读物《双螺旋结构》)之间的区别。从这个观点来看,"科学的方法"可能被更实用地看作一种撰写调查研究文章的方法,而并非一种展开调查的方法。

WRITING

WRITING TASK 1

范文

范文1

The graphs above reveal that as the number of Japanese tourists traveling abroad has grown, so has Australia's share of the Japanese tourist market.

The number of Japanese tourists traveling abroad increased from approximately five million in 1985 to approximately 15 million in 1995. That's a 300% increase. Australia's share of that market increased during the same period similarly from two percent in 1985 to six percent in 1994. Data is not shown for 1995. This means that more and more Japanese tourists are heading to Australia to spend their vacations.

It is interesting to note that there was a decline in the number of Japanese tourists heading to Australia in 1989 even though more Japanese tourists were traveling that year than the previous. A surge in Japanese traveling abroad in 1990 resulted in Australia regaining their share of Japanese tourists. The data also shows that fewer Japanese traveled to Australia in 1994, even though the number of Japanese traveling abroad was higher than ever. It would be interesting to examine the data for 1995 to see if this trend continued.

上表揭示出随着日本出国旅游人数的增长,澳大利亚所占日本人(出境)旅游市场的份额也得到了增长。

日本出国旅游的人数从1985年的大约500万增加到了1995年的1500万,增长了3倍。同期澳大利亚的市场份额也从1985年的2%增长到了1994年的6%。1995年的数据没有显示。这表明越来越多的日本旅游者正在前往澳大利亚度假。

一个要说明的引人注意之处在于尽管1989年的旅游人数比以往多,但是前往澳大利亚的日本旅游人数却呈现出了一个下降的趋势。1990年日本出国旅游人数增长,澳大利亚占有的份额也随之增长。同时,数据显示尽管1994年日本出国旅游人数高于以往任何一年,但是前往澳大利亚旅游的却比较少。检测1995年的数据,观察此趋势是否还在持续,将会引人关注。

范文2

Between 1985 and 1995, the number of Japanese tourists per year traveling abroad tripled, from 5 million to 15 million. There have been two significant periods of increase, the first from 1985 to 1990, when the number of tourists increased by at least one million people per year. Between 1990 and 1993, this number reached a plateau and increased only very slightly. The years 1994 and 1995 also saw great increases, which likely continued into the following years. In essence, this graph shows that the number of Japanese tourists traveling abroad increases constantly.

The second graph shows that Australia is receiving an increasingly higher percentage of Japanese tourists every year, proving that Australia is an increasingly popular destination for Japanese tourists. Between 1985 and 1995, this percentage more than tripled, from 2% to over 6%. There were two incidences of decline in this trend, but overall this graph gives evidence that Australia's share of Japan's tourist market has been on the rise and will continue to do so.

从1985到1995年间,日本每年出国旅游的人数增长了3倍,从500万增长到了1500万人。这个增长过程中有两个很显著的时期,第一个是1985年到1990年期间,每年旅游人数至少增长100

万。1990到1993年期间，这个数字稳定在一个比较高的水平，每年只有些许增长。1994年和1995年也出现了很大的增长，很可能在未来的几年里这种增长将会持续下去。基本上这个图表表明了日本出国旅游人数在迅速增长。

第二张图表显示出每年澳大利亚占有的日本人出国旅游市场的份额在持续增长，这也证明对日本人来说澳大利亚是个越来越受欢迎的旅游目的地。1985年到1995年期间这个百分比增长了3倍，从2%增长到了6%。在这个大趋势中有两次的下降，但是该图表整体上可以证明澳大利亚占有的日本人出国旅游市场份额一直处于上升阶段并且会持续增长。

谋篇布局

1. 图表作文典型的篇章结构：

一般来说，图表题的描写分为三个部分：首段交代"四要素"（图表的描述对象，数据表达形式，时间和地点），并在可能的情况下描写总体特征；中间段落进行描写；末段进行总结。但是，在实际操作过程中，我们可以进行适当的变化。

2. 题目分析：

这是一道典型的多图题，是柱状图和曲线图的组合。在常考的四种图表（曲线图、柱状图、饼状图和表格图）中，曲线图是最基本的。

3. 曲线图的描写原则：

(1)曲线图的描写要点是"趋势描写"（将曲线分段，分别描写各段上升、下降或保持不变的趋势，用关联词将这些线段连接起来）和"数据支持"（写出趋势变化关键点的数值）。

(2)单组柱状图可以先把它转换成曲线图（把每根柱子的顶端连接起来就是一根曲线），然后进行"趋势描写"和"数据支持"的工作。

(3)多条曲线组成的曲线图，除了描写各条曲线的特点以外，着重要描写两条曲线的相同点和不同点。

4. 本题的描写思路：

(1)作为多图题，最基本的思路是先写第一张图，然后写第二张图，有必要的话点出两张图的联系。上面的范文2就是按这个思路写的。

(2)其他思路：先写两张图表的总体趋势，然后写它们细节变化的联系和不同，例如范文1。

WRITING TASK 2

范文

范文1

I agree that international sporting occasions such as the Olympics and the World Cup can be very effective in easing international tensions and releasing patriotic emotions in a safe way. However, I also admit that sometimes their competitive nature makes them a forum for violence and their sheer scope has made them a target for terrorist attacks.

The Olympics is an especially good example of all nations putting aside their current agendas and coming together to participate in the Olympic legacy of fair competition. The Olympics is considered to be the highest level of competitive sport and an Olympic gold is the goal of all aspiring Olympians, no matter what their race, religion or nationality. Good sportsmanship between athletes can be an example for politicians and ordinary citizens alike; a handshake, or a pat on the back after a hard race is a gesture between two people, with no political or racial barriers. The World Cup can have a similar role, especially by giving people a forum to express patriotic emotions, by wearing representative clothing, waving flags, and cheering for their team.

On the other hand, while these two events can be a forum for easing tensions and releasing patriotic emotions, they can also be a forum for creating tensions and disaster. Case in point is the riots and fighting that often occur at the World Cup and other football competitions. Here, international tensions are actually enhanced when too much patriotic emotion is released. As for the Olympics, riots are uncommon, but the Olympic site has now become a target for terrorist action, for example the bombing at the 1996 Atlanta Olympics.

Because of these types of violence, it cannot be said that international sporting events are entirely effective in easing international tensions and releasing patriotic emotions in a safe way.

我同意诸如奥运会和世界杯足球赛之类的体育赛事对缓解国际间的紧张局势和以一种安全的方式释放爱国热情来说非常有效。然而我也承认有时候它们的竞争天性可以为暴力提供一个平台并且它们极大的范围会使它们成为恐怖分子袭击的目标。

奥运会是一个全世界各民族把近期日程放在一边来共同参与公平竞争的奥林匹克传统的极好例子。奥林匹克被认为是最高水平的竞技运动,并且奥运金牌是所有胸怀志向的奥运会选手的奋斗目标,无论他们是何种族,他们来自何地区以及他们的国籍是什么。运动员之间良好的体育精神可以成为政治家和普通老百姓之类的典范,例如一场艰苦的比赛之后,两个人之间的一次握手或者轻拍后背,没有政治和种族的界限。世界杯足球比赛也有类似的作用,尤其是通过给人们一个表达爱国热情的平台的方式,或者通过穿有代表性的衣服、挥舞旗帜和为自己的球队加油助威的方式。

另一方面,当这两种赛事能够成为缓解紧张局势和释放爱国热情的平台时,它们也可以成为创造紧张关系和灾难的平台。与此相关的情况就是经常发生在世界杯和其他足球比赛中的骚乱和斗殴。在这里当太多的爱国热情被释放出来的时候,国际间紧张的关系实际上是被加强了。对于奥运会来说爆发骚乱很不平常,不过奥运场馆现在已经成了恐怖活动的目标,例如1996年亚特兰大奥运会的爆炸案。

由于这些暴力形式的存在,就不能说国际体育赛事在缓解国际间的紧张局势和以一种安全的方式释放爱国热情完全有效。

范文2

I generally agree with this opinion, but I would not choose to use the word "essential". I would prefer to say, "play an important role." I think popular events like the World Cup and other international sporting occasions allow countries to compete in a healthy way and at the same time foster friendship and understanding across borders. One can cheer and support one's own team without needing to "hate" the opposition. One can even cheer another country's team, when it isn't directly competing with our own team.

The best example of the above would be the Olympic Games, which has grown and flourished since its beginning in 1924, despite world wars and international strife and tensions. The fact that nations can even be at war against each other but, at the same time, have their young people compete peacefully in the sports arena says something quite wonderful about the human spirit's longing for peace and goodwill. I believe all the nations which participate in the Olympics feel the Games is something very precious, to be preserved and honored, a valuable legacy to be carried on for future generations.

Another example of how an international sporting occasion led to greater understanding and the beginning of friendship is the famous "Ping Pong diplomacy" which took place in 1972 when Chinese players traveled to the US to give the well-received demonstrations. This singular event allowed the Americans to see Chinese, and China, in a new light, to gain much-needed understanding about a country long shut off from the rest of the world. At the same time, it allowed the Chinese traveling to the U. S. the chance to see, at first hand, American citizens and way of life.

In summary, international sporting occasions are very important, and some say essential, in easing international tensions and releasing patriotic emotions in a safe and healthy way.

我基本上同意这个观点,但是我不会选择使用“不可或缺”一词,我宁愿说“起了很重要的作用”。我认为诸如世界杯足球赛和其他国际体育赛事之类的大众赛事使得国家之间可以通过健康的方式来竞争,并且同时可以跨越国界,培养友谊、增强理解。一个人可以为自己的队加油喝彩,提供支持而无需“痛恨”对方。他甚至可以当其他国家队不直接与己方球队竞争时为他们呐喊助威。

以上观点最好的例证莫过于从 1924 年起就发展壮大,日益丰富的奥林匹克运动会,尽管这期间世界上还存在战争、国际冲突和紧张局势。各民族尽管在战争中互相敌对,但同时他们的年轻人却在运动场上和平竞争这样的事实,表达了人类在精神上对和平与美好心愿的渴望。我相信所有参加奥林匹克运动的民族都会觉得奥运会是一项值得珍惜,保留,骄傲并且极具价值,可为后代传承的遗产。

国际体育赛事是如何引导更大的理解与开启友谊的另一个典范就是发生在 1972 年的“乒乓外交”。中国选手到访美国做出了极受好评的示范。仅此一个单一的事件就使得美国人以一种崭新的眼光去看待中国人和中国,去赢取对一个长期与世界其他地区隔绝的国家所迫切需要的理解。同时,它可以使访美的中国人能够有机会去直接看看美国人民以及他们的生活方式。

总而言之,国际体育赛事是十分重要的,并且一部分人认为对于缓解国际间的紧张局势、以一种安全健康的方式去释放爱国热情来说是不可或缺的。

谋篇布局

1. 读题:

(1) 典型雅思议论文题目特点:

- 题目前半部分是一个事物或事件。在后半部分,在某些情况下题干可能直接会问“What is your opinion about <中心事物/事件>”。在另外一些情况下,题干中还会出现对于这个中心事物/事件或好或坏的评价,问你是否同意这种评价。
- 需要格外小心的是,有些题目还说出了或好或坏的评价的理由。这个时候你的分论点一定要围绕这个理由来写,否则就容易跑题。

(2) 本题分析:

- 中心事物是“体育比赛”。对于“体育比赛”,题干给了正评价(essential),理由是 easing international tensions and releasing patriotic emotions in a safe way。
- 如果你同意这个正评价,就意味着你需要在下面的段落中具体说明为什么体育比赛能够缓解国际紧张局势和爱国主义情绪。如果不同意,你需要说明这个正评价为什么是错误的。
- 注意,如果说体育比赛在其他方面的影响,比如说“体育比赛破坏环境”,则是跑题的。当然,如果你能从“体育比赛破坏环境”进一步说到“因为破坏环境,所以造成国际局势紧张”,这是可以的。当然,由于英语段落一般采取总分形式,所以段落的第一句话最好写成:“体育比赛造成国际紧张局势,在于它破坏了当地的环境,造成当地居民对外来人员的不满和憎恨”。

2. 写提纲:

(1) 什么叫提纲? 我们首先来看英语议论文的典型结构。

- 首段:引出要讨论的内容(中心事物/事件,或某些人对中心事物/事件的看法);表达你的观点,即总论点(你的观点可以是这个中心事物/事件是好的,也可以是不好的,或者是即好也不好)。

- 中间段落:具体说明支持你的观点的理由(一个理由就是一个分论点)。一般需要2-3个分论点。表达分论点的中心句一般放在中间段落的段首。
- 末段:重申你的观点。

(2) 如何写提纲:所谓"写提纲"就是在写作之前,构思好总论点和每一个段落的中心句,即把总论点拆分成分论点。

- 基本思路:在构思分论点的时候,可以寻找中心事物/事件的两方面内容:它的本质和它造成的后果。比如说,我们的总论点是:"在缓解紧张局势方面,体育比赛有不好的后果"。其中的一个分论点可以是:"因为体育比赛的本质,所以在缓解紧张局势方面,它容易有不好的后果"。
- 其他思路:要写更多的分论点,我们可以把不好(或者好)的后果拆分成具体的几条写出来,每一条从一个侧面写不好(或者好)。比如说,我们可以写"体育比赛导致赛场暴力","此外,体育比赛导致观众之间情绪的对立"。这些分论点都支持"体育比赛有不好的后果"。
- 范文1提供了另外一种写分论点的方法,即每一个分论点是一个例子。但是这两个例子说明的道理最好不要雷同。我们把它作为写分论点的又一条思路:当分论点要说明A(体育比赛)不能做P(疏导爱国主义情绪)时,我们可以讨论究竟怎么样才能做到P(疏导爱国主义情绪)。

3. 首段的写作:

首段写作的原则是:引出要讨论的内容+表达你的观点。下面我们来分析两篇范文。

- 范文1认为体育比赛既有好的后果,又有不好的后果。在表达作者观点的时候,它们都用了让步的方法。但是同样是让步,也表现出不同的语言手段。范文1先说体育比赛挺好,然后话锋一转,提出在缓解国际局势方面,体育比赛其实是不好的。
- 范文2认为体育比赛还是有好的后果的。在提出自己观点以后,末两句又作了进一步的解释说明。我们强调,在第一段一般不要论证。这篇文章有点特殊,因为中间段落是两个例子。

4. 中间段落的写作:

中间段落的典型结构是:首句分论点,然后是对分论点的论证。

- 最常用的论证方法是举例论证和解释论证。
- 我们还可以运用强对比论证(为了论证"某事物很好",我们可以写"某事物的对立面很不好"),正话反说论证(比如我们的分论点是"一个事物很好",我们可以这样论证:"如果没有它的话,情况将是很糟糕的")等等。
- 注意分论点和论证之间的关联词,例如在举例论证中,在论点和论据之间用:Case in point is... 还要注意同一个分论点的多条论证之间的关联词,如:This singular event allowed the Americans to see Chinese, and China, in a new light, to gain much-needed understanding about a country long shut off from the rest of the world. <u>At the same time</u>, it allowed the Chinese traveling to the U. S. the chance to see, at first hand, American citizens and way of life.

5. 末段的写作:

末段的写作相对简单一些,只要重申上面的观点即可,请参见范文1和2。

SPEAKING

I = Interviewer C = Candidate

范例 1

PART 1

I: Good morning, my name is Dinah. Could you tell me your full name, please?

C: My name is Yang Weiwei.

I: And what shall I call you?

C: You can call me Vivian, which is my English name.

I: And where are you from, Vivian?

C: I'm from Beijing.

I: Now may I see your identification, please?

C: Here you are.

I: Thanks. Let's start with some Questions about your family. Do you have a large family or a small family?

C: Well, like most Chinese families, there are three people in my family, my mother, my father and myself. My grandparents also live with us.

I: Can you tell me something about them?

C: Yes, my mother is a teacher. She teaches math in **primary school.** My father is also a teacher. He teaches computers in high school. My grandparents are retired. Before he retired, my grandfather worked as an **engineer** in a factory and my grandmother was a **government worker.**

I: How much time do you **manage** to spend with members of your family?

C: Well, since I'm quite far away at university, I only see my family during holidays. I always go home for **Spring Festival**, and usually also during the May 1st holiday and October 1st holiday. Of course I have two months off during the summer, and that gives me quite a bit of time at home. I guess I'm **luckier** than some of my classmates who live even farther away from home and are not able to get home during the May or October festivals.

I: What sorts of things do you like to do together?

C: Both my parents like **hiking**, so we often go hiking on the mountains near my home. Once a year we take a trip somewhere together. Last year we went to Hainan Island for the first time. I really enjoyed swimming at the beach. The year before that we went to Yunnan, and enjoyed traveling all around the province. The **minorities** there are very friendly and have many of their own **traditional ways.**

I: Did/do you get on well with your family? Why?

C: I feel very lucky, because I have a very close relationship with both my parents and my grandparents. When I was small, my grandmother spent a lot of time with me, and took me to many different places. My grandfather used to take me to the park on weekends. My parents are very busy with their work, but, since they are both teachers, they get the summer holiday off, and we can spend more time together then. As for why we are close, that's **hard to say**. As far back as I can remember, we have always been a close family. I have always been able to talk to my parents about my problems and **worries**. Some of my friends don't have that kind of relationship with their parents.

I: All right, now I'm going to give you a topic and I'd like you to talk about it for one to two minutes. Before you talk you'll have one minute to think about what you're going to say. You can make some notes if you wish. Do you understand?

C: Sure.

I: Ok, here is your topic, and here is some paper and a pencil for making notes. I'd like you to describe a teacher who has influenced your education.

One minute passes...

PART 2

Candidate's Notes on Paper

when met	High School
subject	English
special	creative teaching, **encouragement**
why influence	attitude towards learning, life

I: Ok? Remember, you have one to two minutes to speak. Don't worry if I stop you. I'll tell you when the time is up. Can you start speaking now?

C: Ok. I have been fortunate in having had several teachers who have had a **positive influence** on my life. If I had to choose one, I would choose my English teacher from **senior middle school**. The middle school I attended was a **joint venture** with an Australian university, and a number of teachers were from Australia. My English teacher was a lady from **Sydney.** Her name was Jennifer Brady.

I still remember the first day that I met her. She's rather tall and she has **reddish** hair. She has a very friendly smile, and makes you feel comfortable. She introduced herself to us, telling us a bit about her background, her education, and even a bit about her family in Sydney. Then she asked each of us to introduce ourselves, and tell where we were from and a bit about ourselves. Frankly, I learned more about my classmates that day than I had known before.

I think one of the special things about her was her **creative way of teaching**. Most English teachers simply have us recite passages out loud, or repeat out loud after them. Instead, Ms. Brady had us form **small groups**, gave us topics to prepare, and then had us report to the class. This way we had more of a chance to practice our English, and **took turns** reporting to the class. It also helped us in speaking out loud in front of the class.

Before taking English from Ms. Brady, I was an **average** English student, and rather shy about speaking English, especially in front of the class. After taking her class I was less shy about speaking English, and my English got much better. She always encouraged us, and **complimented** us whenever we spoke correctly. This really gave us the **courage** to keep trying to improve our English.

The most important lesson I learned from her is to always keep a positive attitude and never give up.

I: How did she teach you to keep a positive attitude?

C: She once gave us an example with a glass of water. It was half filled with water. She asked the class if the glass was half empty, and of course we said 'yes'. Then she asked if the glass was half full, and of course we also had to say 'yes'. Then she asked, what was the difference? The difference, she said, was in our attitude. The glass was both half empty and half full!

PART 3

I: Ok, we've been talking about a teacher who influenced you. Now, I'd like to ask you a few more questions on the general topic of education. How has education changed in China in the last 10 years?

C: Of course education has changed, but, unfortunately, it hasn't changed enough. We still have too much focus on exams and **memorization** in school, and students are always studying for the next exam.

I: So, do you think there should be less **emphasis** put on taking exams?

C: I understand why there have to be exams. There are too many students and not enough schools, so there needs to be a way to **eliminate** the **poorer students.** This puts a lot of **pressure** on students from the time they enter the first grade.

I: Well, then what do you **suggest**?

C: I think the schools need to put more focus on learning how to study and how to think in more original ways, and less focus on memorizing texts.

I: What changes do you **foresee** in the next 50 years?

C: I hope that by then there will be a lot more schools, and not so much pressure on students to pass exams. I hope that college students will have more freedom in choosing majors they like, and not be forced to accept majors chosen for them by the universities. I also hope that students will have more freedom to change their majors.

I: How do the **expectations** of today's **school leavers** compare with those of the **previous generation**?

C: In my parents' generation, universities usually found jobs for their graduating students. Nowadays, graduates must work hard themselves to find a good job after they graduate, and it's getting harder and harder.

I: What role do you think **extracurricular activities play** in education?

C: I personally think they play an important role, but, unfortunately, there is very little time for them. The temptation is to focus solely on schoolwork, and to not pay much attention to other activities.

I: What **method of learning** works best for you?

C: I enjoy a **balance** of studying by myself, and studying in a small group with friends. We can discuss our problems, and help each other.

I: How **beneficial** do you think it is to group students according to their level of ability?

C: I think it helps the good students become better students. But the poorer students cannot make very good **progress** this way.

I: Okay, that's the end of the interview, thank you very much.

C: I've enjoyed our talk, thank you.

范例 2

PART 1

I: Good morning, my name is Roger. Can you tell me your full name please?

C: My full name is Wang Zhiyan. You can call me Jack.

I: Okay, Jack. And where are you from?

C: I was **born and raised** in Shanghai.

I: Hmmm. I really like Shanghai. Can I see your identification please?

C: Sure, here you go.

I: Thanks. Why don't we get started? First, I'd like to ask you some questions about your family. Do you have a large family or a small family?

C: My family is a typically small family. As you know, Chinese couples are usually only allowed to have one child, so most young people these days are **only children**, like me.

I: Can you tell me something about your family?

C: My father is a doctor. Actually, I think he works too hard, but I know it's because he has a very strong **sense of responsibility** towards his family. My mother stays at home and takes care of my father and me. Even though my mother doesn't earn an **income**, I think her job is just as important as my father's. I don't know what we would do without her!

I: How much time do you **manage** to spend with members of your family?

C: You know, when I was young, I really liked spending time with my father. On the weekends, he used to take me **fishing.** We had a close relationship and I really **looked up to him**. Now, we are both so busy and rarely have a chance to get together and go fishing. It's too bad, really.

I: What sorts of things do you like to do with your family?

C: To tell you the truth, my family doesn't do a lot of things together because our schedules are so different. A couple of years ago, though, we went on a family hike up **Xiang Shan**, which is a mountain in Beijing. I remember it was a beautiful day and we had a great time together. I would really like to do it again sometime, but, like I said, we rarely have time to do things as a family.

I: Do you **get along well with** your family?

C: Yes.

I: Can you be more **specific**? Why do you think that is?

C: Of course, all families have their problems, but I think one advantage of being an only child is that there is less **arguing** within the family. I have a friend who has a sister and he says he and his sister fight all the time. With only one child, there is less **competition** and therefore less to fight about. My parents have been married for 28 years and still get along very well.

I: All right, now I'm going to give you a topic and I'd like you to talk about it for one to two minutes. Before you talk you'll have one minute to think about what you're going to say. You can make some notes if you wish. Do you understand?

C: Yes, I understand.

I: Ok, here is your topic, and here is some paper and a pencil for making notes. I'd like you to describe a teacher who influenced your education.

One minute passes...

PART 2

Candidate's Notes on Paper

where	Uni Nanjing 1998
subject	Eng.
special	interesting storytelling
influence	face difficulties fun!

I: Ok? Remember, you have one to two minutes for this, so don't worry if I stop you. I'll tell you when the time is up. Can you start speaking now, please?

C: Okay. I would like to tell you about a special teacher that had a big influence on my education. This teacher's name is Professor Wang, and I met him when I was in my second year of study at Nanjing University, which was in 1998. Professor Wang has taught English at Nanjing University for over 25 years, and he has an **excellent reputation** among students.

Unlike a lot of other English teachers, Professor Wang rarely forced us to memorize new words or **grammar patterns**; instead, he would think of interesting ways to help us remember them in the classroom. He would often make up stories or give us examples from his own life of how he learned a particular word or **verb tense**, making the lessons more like **storytelling** as opposed to **boring lectures**. He used to say that learning a language was the biggest challenge we would face in our lives, but that if we succeeded, it would be our greatest **accomplishment**. He encouraged us to **explore** the language on our own, and to speak out without **embarrassment**.

Students would often bring in articles they found on the Internet; we would photocopy them and **Professor** Wang would give the student 15 minutes at the end of class to introduce the article to the other students. We would often have discussions about these topics, during which everyone was excited to use English to **express themselves**, and over time our oral English improved because of these discussions.

I think the main thing I learned from Professor Wang is that sometimes in life we have to face difficulties, and do things that we don't want to do, and in those situations we should try to make things more fun and interesting for ourselves. Learning English is a big **headache** for Chinese students, but now I know that it can be fun as well.

I: Did you ever present an article in class?

C: Yes, once I **downloaded** an article from the New York Times and presented it to the class. Because I had to be very familiar with the article in order to answer all the students' questions, I learned a lot from that experience.

I: Do you still keep in touch with Professor Wang?

C: Sometimes I send him an **SMS** on **special occasions**, but, because I live in Beijing now, I rarely see him.

PART 3

I: Alright. We've been talking about a teacher who influenced you. Now, I'd like to ask you some more general questions about education.

C: Okay.

I: First, I would like to know how education has changed in China in the last 10 years.

C: I think the biggest change in education in China is that it has become more **available** to more people. Just recently, the government changed the rules regarding the **university entrance exam**, and now allows people of any age, married or **single**, to take the exam. In the past, only single people under 25 had the right to take the exam.

I: Really?

C: Yes, because Chinese people think that it is best to get an education when you are young. But I think this change is an excellent **step forward**. On the other hand, there is still not a lot of choice for university students regarding their **major**. The major is **assigned** to them based on their test scores, and not their **personal preferences.** Many people want to study subjects like English and **computer science** because they think they can get a high paying job. The good news is that in the past ten years hundreds of **private schools** have opened up all over China, allowing people to study what they choose just by paying the **tuition fees**. I think the education offered through private schools will help our country progress.

I: What changes do you **foresee** in the next 50 years?

C: In the next 50 years I think that the quality of education provided in China will improve greatly. The new private schools that I just **mentioned** have already started to compete with big universities for students and they often promise that the student has a better chance at a job in the future.

I: I see.

C: In my opinion, Chinese people have already started thinking of education as a **commodity**; they spend money and they want to see results. Many people now think that a university degree is useless because there are so many people graduating with **bachelor's degrees**, or even **master's** and **PhDs**, that can't find jobs. I think people will consider all their options instead of **assuming** that university is the best source of education. This **trend** has already started and it will grow in the next 50 years.

I: How do the **expectations** of today's **school leavers** compare with those of the previous generation?

C: The expectations of today's graduates are much, much lower than ever in the past. I think the main cause of this problem is that there are simply too many graduates and not enough jobs, and therefore students are often told to be **optimistic**, but not to expect too much after their graduation. In terms of both **salary** and **position** within the **hiring organization**, both are much lower than they used to be. Some young graduates even agree to do a period of **unpaid work**, in the hopes that they can prove themselves and eventually earn a salary. I think around a third of graduates don't find a job within the first two years, so some people have started to doubt the value of a university education. The luckiest graduates are the ones whose relatives or friends have **connections** within companies or **work units**, and can help them get hired. This is the easiest way to get a job, but unfortunately not everyone has this type of advantage.

I: What role do you think extracurricular activities play in education?

C: Extracurricular activities don't really **play a role** in the Chinese education system. At most, students might **engage** in some sports like ping-pong, badminton, or basketball, but students rarely have hobbies or other interests. In China, students are very competitive, and there are not enough spaces for everyone to go to university, so students don't dare to use their time on anything but their studies. If their parents forced them when they were young, some students have a special skill like playing the **piano** or **violin**, however the **majority** of students are **discouraged** from having **time-consuming hobbies**.

I've done some reading about education systems in other countries, so I know that, for example, in the United States, when students apply for university or for a job, they are **evaluated** on their grades and their other activities, like **volunteer work**, travel experience, **artistic achievements**, things like that. Unfortunately, in China, competition is **solely** based on grades, and schools and employers don't value extracurricular activities.

I: What **method of learning** works best for you?

C: I am a **visual learner**—I learn things best when I can see them. When I look at a new word or a text, I make a picture in my head that makes it easier to remember. For example, when I learn new vocabulary, I make a list with Chinese characters on one side and the English words on the other side. To test myself, I cover one set of words and write out the word in the other language. I also find that I need to review new words many times before I actually remember them, usually one or two days after I first learn them, and then a week or two later. By then I have finally memorized them! Writing new words out over and over also helps to learn them faster. I write a new word out at least 50 times before I know the spelling. Some other students I know have to say things out loud to remember them, but that method doesn't seem to help me.

I: How **beneficial** do you think it is to group students according to their level of ability?

C: I think it is very beneficial to students to group them according to their level of ability. When I was in school, there were always a few students who couldn't keep up with the teacher. The teacher would get **upset** because she didn't have time to repeat everything, and the students were upset because they didn't understand. If there had been two or more classes, students with stronger abilities could have learned faster, and the students who needed more explanation would receive it, without **disturbing** anyone else. The problem with doing this, though, is that no one likes to be grouped in a 'slow' class, even if it will help them. The other problem is that schools don't usually have the **funding** to separate classes. For example, Chinese high school classes often have 40 to 60 students, who are all of different abilities, but the school cannot afford to separate them into smaller classes of different levels. In China, the responsibility to learn is on the student, no matter what their abilities.

I: Thank you for your answers. That's the end of our interview.

词汇表

范例 1	
primary school 小学	average 水平一般的、普通的
engineer 工程师	shy 害羞的
government worker 政府职员	compliment 称赞
manage 能够	courage 勇气
Spring Festival 春节	memorization 背诵
two months off 两个月的假期	emphasis 重点
luckier 更幸运	eliminate 淘汰
hiking 远足	poorer students 水平较低的学生
minorities 少数民族	pressure 压力
traditional ways 传统习俗	suggest 建议
get on well with 与…相处融洽	foresee 预见
hard to say 很难说	expectations 期望
worries 苦恼	school leavers 即将离校的学生
encouragement 鼓励	previous generation 上届的
positive influence 正面影响	nowadays 如今
senior middle school 高中	role 作用
joint venture 合资企业	extracurricular activities 课余活动
a number of 一些	play 起(作用)
Sydney 悉尼	method of learning 学习方法
reddish 微红色的	balance 平衡
creative way of teaching 创造性的教学方法	beneficial 有益的
small groups 小组	progress 进步
take turns 依次	
范例 2	
born and raised 出生长大	manage 能够
only children 独生子	fishing 钓鱼
sense of responsibility 责任感	looked up to him 尊敬他
income 收入	Xiang Shan 香山

get along well with 与…相处融洽	master 硕士
specific 详细的、具体的	PhD 博士
argue 争论	assume 假定
competition 竞争	trend 趋势
excellent reputation 很好的声誉	expectations 期望
grammar patterns 语法结构	school leavers 即将离校的学生
verb tense 动词时态	optimistic 乐观的
storytelling 讲故事	salary 薪水
boring lectures 烦人的讲座	position 职位
accomplishment 成就	hiring organization 用人单位
explore 探索	unpaid work 不要报酬的工作
embarrassment 尴尬	connections 关系
photocopy 影印	work units 工作单位
express themselves 表达他们自己(的想法)	extracurricular activities 课余活动
headache 头疼	role 作用
download 下载	play a role 起作用
SMS 短信	engage 参加
special occasions 特殊的情况	piano 钢琴
available 可利用的	violin 小提琴
university entrance exam 大学入学考试(高考)	majority 多数
single 单身	discouraged 气馁
step forward 进一步发展	time-consuming hobbies 耗时间的习惯
major 专业	evaluate 评估
assign 分配	volunteer work 志愿者工作
personal preferences 个人志愿	artistic achievements 艺术成果
computer science 计算机科学	solely 单独地
private schools 私立学校	method of learning 学习方法
tuition fees 学费	visual learner 通过看(图、录影等)学习
foresee 预见	beneficial 受益的
mentioned 提及的	upset 烦躁
commodity 商品	disturb 打扰
bachelor's degree 学士学位	funding 资金、基金

补充词汇及句型

Part 1: Family

Family Members		
mother	siblings	uncle
father	grandmother	cousin
brother	grandfather	
sister	aunt	
Possible Activities		
going out to eat	watching movies/TV	going camping
chatting about...	going for walks	traveling

Part 2: Teacher

Stages of Schooling			
小学	elementary school	primary school	
初/高中	junior/senior high school	secondary school	junior/senior middle school
大学	university	college	
大专	vocational college	junior college	

My teacher influenced me so much because he/she...	taught me a new way to learn. led by example. showed me the importance of helping others.

Part 3: Education/Learning

Education changes	
In the last 10 years...	In the next 50 years...
testing has become more important.	technology will become more important in the classroom.
teachers have started to use more modern educational methods.	class sizes will probably decrease.
class sizes have increased.	more foreign students will come to China.

Today's school leavers...	expect to find a job in a private company, while the previous generation generally expected to work for a state-owned enterprise. are more likely to dream of going abroad to further their studies. have more pressure to find a job than the previous generation.

Extracurricular activities...	help students build character. are important in achieving balance in a student's life. supplement the education that students receive at school.

I learn best by...	listening (to lectures). reading (textbooks). doing...

Grouping students according to their ability is ...	
beneficial, because...	harmful, because...
it allows students to progress at their own pace. it makes teachers' jobs easier. students learn best when they are grouped with students of similar ability.	it creates inequality among students. it may lead to a larger gap between good and poor students.

口试要点聚焦

展开答案

关于雅思口试许多学生都有一个误解——只要把每个问题都回答正确就可以得高分。因此在回答问题时他们只用简单的“是”或“不是”,这尤其表现在口试的第一阶段。事实上,雅思口试考查的并不仅仅是你能否回答正确,更重要的是你能否有效地用英语进行交流。

还有一点很重要——回答时要努力提供更多的信息。记住,一定要把你的真才实学展示出来。这全靠你自己,与考官无关。如果你不能向考官展示你纯正的口语,证明你的实力,他们的打分自然不会高。

那么,该如何展开回答呢?展开多少呢?下面以第一、三阶段的口试为例加以说明。以下为第一阶段展开话题的两条建议:

1. 完整句子回答

如果考官问你:“What sorts of things do you like to do with your family?”

你可以回答说:“Go hiking.”

但如果这样回答会更好:“Well, I think I'd have to say that my favorite thing to do with my family is go hiking.”

两种回答从字面上看都“正确”,但第二种回答表明你具有用较复杂语言进行交流的能力。

2. 添加信息

如果考官问你:“Do you get along well with your family?”

你可以说:“Yes.”

但如果这样回答更好些:“Yes, I get along quite well with my family. I suppose we get along so well because we have similar interests, like hiking.”

跟上面一样,两种回答从字面上看都“正确”,但很明显第二种更能展示你的英语表达能力。

在口试第一阶段,通常每个问题用两到三句话回答为宜。回答时要补充说明理由、看法、特点等内容。当然,并非所有回答都长短一致,有时只用一个短句子也是可以的。

第三阶段与第一阶段不同,你遇到的话题可能不像第一阶段的那么熟悉。考官的问题经常是你从没考虑过的。在这种情况下,关键是运用你的创造力和想象力。记住,在第三阶段,清楚地表述观点是最重要的。至于你的观点是什么则无关紧要。所以发挥你的创造力和想象力就一定会答好。

然而,有时你可能需要时间思考。在口试第二阶段,你有一分钟的准备时间,但在第三阶段就没那么幸运了。那么该怎么办呢?你不能光坐在那儿沉思默想。你应该学会边想边说。一种应对办法就是先对问题加以评论。

如果考官问:“How do the expectations of today's school leavers compare with those of the previous generation?”

可你无言以对,这时你可以先这样说:“Well, you know, that's a really good question. To tell you the truth, I've never really thought about it before, and, of course, I'm not an expert on the issue. But, I suppose that the expectations of today's school leavers are quite different from those of the previous generation.”

注意,你并没有真正回答问题,但你在用英语清楚地表达自己的观点。当然,你不能每个问题都这样回答。这种应急措施的关键在于对问题进行评论的同时,思考该如何回答。因此,接下来你可以这样继续说:“For instance, graduates today are less confident about finding a job than the previous generation.”

你正在回答一个自己没有把握应对的难题,但答得不错!

Test 2

LISTENING

SECTION 1

谈话场景:新生报到会场景。
人物关系:学校接待人员和报到的新生。
谈话话题:新生入校后首日活动安排。

词汇注释

booklet *n.* 小册子,介绍手册
course *n.* 课程
activity *n.* 活动
offer *v.* 提供
outline *n.* 提纲,轮廓
program *n.* 节目单,活动安排
gather *v.* 聚集,集中
principal *n.* 校长
staff *n.* 教职员工
event *n.* (大型的)活动
last *v.* 持续,延续
director *n.* 主任,主管
requirement *n.* 要求
adviser *n.* 导师,辅导人员
various *adj.* 各种各样的
placement *n.* 放置,布置,安排
reception *n.* 前台,接待处
corridor *n.* 走廊,过道
laboratory *n.* 实验室
immediately *adv.* 直接地,立即
opposite *prep.* 在…对面
common room (主英)(师生共用的)休息室
mention *v.* 提及,提到
facility *n.* 设施

交际与语言表达

1. 新生报到的时候接待人员要面对很多人,所以有时不一定能马上接待某个学生,轮到他时很礼貌地说一声:Sorry to keep you waiting。然后再解释下一步的安排,日常生活中可以借鉴。
2. There, you see? 很简单的一句话,告诉对方自己所说明的内容所在。
3. Just let me quickly run through this morning's events first and then I'll explain how to get there. 先让我很快地过一遍今天早上的活动,然后我会给你解释怎么去那里。这一句话是整个对话的主题句,告诉了考生可能出现的两种题目:上午的活动安排和去什么地方的路线图。听到这里考生应对后文内容有大概的预测。
4. Where were we? 我们刚才说到那儿了?在口语交流中,native speaker 口中越简单的表达法,经常越难以掌握。
5. Test? I don't like the sound of that. What sort of test? 考试?我可不喜欢听见这个词!那到底是什么考试呢?学生用一种暗含幽默的说法表达了自己对考试的些许反感,但又不是完全反对。
6. You can't miss it. 你不会走丢的,不会弄错的。一般给别人指路后,加这句话可以强调自己对路线的熟悉,使对方更为放心。
7. ... immediately on your right... 就在你右边。"immediately"此处表示"直接地",相当于"directly"。
8. In a day or two, I'm sure you'll find your way around very easily. 一两天之后,我保证你会对这里非常熟悉了。

9. A：Thank you very much.

B：You are welcome.

这是最常用的表示感谢和客气的礼貌用语，考生应该应对自如，脱口而出。很多考生到考雅思的时候，仍然在考官说完 thank you 之后手足无措，其实在练听力的时候稍微用心一点，就可以学到很多有用的口语表达法。

考题解析

Questions 1–4

这几道题都非常简单，只要注意试卷中上下文的提醒，考生一般都能把答案做对。此处特别提醒考生注意的是第一题答案必须写 Main Hall，不能只写 Hall，还有要注意 Director of Studies 和 Student Adviser（Advisor 也可以）等的拼写和大小写问题。

Question 5

这道题大部分考生可能会错，最主要的原因是不知道什么是 placement test，其次不知道这道题其实也可以简单的写 English（test）即可。所谓 placement test，有些类似于我国大学入校的英语分级考试，确定学生目前的英语水平，适合上什么样的班级。

Question 6

地图题一定要注意所找地名与图中已知信息之间的关系，看图时就应该心里有数。比如这道题，看图时应该注意到所找地点在 language laboratory 的旁边，而在什么旁边用的最多的表达法是 beside 或者 next to。那么在做题时就可以等着听磁带中念到 next to language laboratory 是哪一个地方即可，因此很好确定本题答案为 library。考试时从节约时间的角度出发，不用写出完整的“library”，而只按照试卷上的提示写成“L”。

Question 7

这道题与上题息息相关。上文提到 library 时，已经带出本题答案：past the library and facing you is the **Main Hall.** 后文补充一句：**at the end of the corridor**。即使这里还没有听出来，下文中学生又补充一句：**so it's next to the Library**，可以使考生检查自己的选择是否正确。

Question 8

这道题又与上题环环相扣。原文提到行走路线前半部分与 7 题相同，但马上提到，but this time, **don't turn left, turn right, away from the Main Hall.** 后面又指出 computer lab is **immediately on your right**。这几道题磁带原文都给了考生好几种可以判断答案的方式。

Question 9

这道题磁带中给了考生 3 种可以选定答案的方式：**near the main entrance, on the left**，和 **just opposite the Reception desk.** 考生在做这样的题目时，应该先根据前文判断出答案，再根据后文进行确认检查。

Question 10

这道题给了两种可以选定答案的方式：**very close to where we are now** 和 **to the right of the Reception desk.** 对于地图题，把握好已知信息和起始点很关键。

SECTION 2

谈话场景:新生参加的非正式会议。
人物关系:演讲者为学生会工作人员,听众为新生。
谈话话题:向新生介绍如何通过热线电话寻求帮助。

词汇注释

informal *adj.* 非正式的
help line 求助热线电话
the Students Union 学生会
aim *v.* 旨在,目的在于(to)
provide *v.* 提供
service *n.* 服务
practical *adj.* 实际的,实用的
unfamiliar *adj.* 不熟悉的
financial *adj.* 财政的,金融的
grant *n.* 助学金,补助
insufficient *adj.* 不充足的,不够的
see sb. through 帮助…度过(困难等);使得以维持过(…)
query *n.* 疑问,质问,查询
regarding *prep.* 关于
overseas *adj.* 海外的,国外的
outcome *n.* 结果
domestic *adj.* 家务的,家政的
nursery *n.* 托儿所
provision *n.* 供应,提供
academic *adj.* 学术的
issue *n.* 问题,事情
arise *v.* 发生,出现
essay *n.* (作业中的)文章
deadline *n.* 截止日期
particular *adj.* 特殊的,特别的
pursue *v.* 追求,实行
participate *v.* 参加
outing *n.* 郊游
detail *n.* 细节
full-time *adj.* 专职的
employee *n.* 职员,雇员
welfare *n.* 福利
straight away 马上,立即

交际与语言表达

1. Hello, everybody and welcome to this informal meeting about the university help line. 大家好,欢迎来参加学校求助热线的非正式会议。由于本段文章是非正式会议,所以演讲者开场白也是非正式的。
2. The help line was set up ten years ago by the Students Union and it aims to provide new students to the university with a service **that** they can use **if** they need information about practical areas of student life **that** they are unfamiliar with. 求助热线是学生会 10 年前成立的。许多来到学校的新生对学生生活的实际情况不太了解,如果他们需要这方面的信息,求助热线将致力于为他们提供有帮助的服务。这句话理解起来并不难,但比较复杂,有好几重从句,黑体部分即是各从句的引导词。
3. **You may wish to** know more about essay deadlines, for example, or how to use the library. 你可能想知道更多关于交作业最后期限的事情,或者如何使用图书馆。**You may wish to** 常用于引出典型的例子。
4. . . . there are all kinds of questions you will find yourself asking and not knowing where to get quick answers from. 你会发现自己在问各种问题,又不知道从哪里能马上得到解答。find oneself (doing. . .) 发觉自己在(……)的处境中。
5. Let me give you some details so that you know where to go and who to see if you want to pay us a visit. 下面我告诉大家一些细节信息,以便在你想找我们的时候知道去哪里找谁。
6. Please note that it may not be possible for anyone to see you straight away. 请注意不太可能马上会有

人来接待您。It is (not) possible for sb. to do sth. 某人(不)可能做某事。

7. Well, enough from me. Any questions? 我就讲这么多,大家有什么问题吗?非正式演讲的结束语经常使用这句话。

考题解析

Question 11

试卷上表格里已经告诉考生要填的内容是关于"financial"的,而且上文中给出了并列的"grants",考生在做题之前应该想到要填的内容是跟钱有关的。听力原文在提到 grant 之后,马上说 you may have some queries regarding the **fees** you are paying if you are an overseas student. 答案填 fees 即可,如果知道学费还有另外一个单词 tuition 也很好。

Question 12

做题时考生应该根据后文中的 childcare 和 nurseries 推断出这类事务的大概归属范围。国外大学里很多学生是已婚或育有子女,照顾孩子和托儿所都是年轻父母所关心的家务事情。听力原文明确指出 Another area we can help with is what we generally term the "**domestic**" area. 这道题最关键的是考生是否认识这个单词,并且知道这个单词如何拼写。

Questions 13–15

这几道题考生都可以根据表格中前后左右文字的提示,去听取相关的重要信息,但要注意 13 题的核心词是 deadline,而非 essay。15 题答案写 outings 或 trips 都可以,但不能省略 s。

Question 16

此题是所有考生都不应该错的。原文一个字母接一个字母很慢地拼出这个古怪的名字,考生应该有时间全部写出。书后答案中把这个名字的每个字母都大写了,实际考试中只用大写首字母"K",后面的字母可以小写。

Question 17

这是一个简单的电话号码,注意两个数字 9 在一起可以念"nine nine"也可以读成"double nine"。

Question 18

这道题可以根据原文念的直接写出 10—4,没有必要加 a.m.,p.m.,根据上下文是上午还是下午很明了。

Question 19

注意题干中的 ring 和 visit 分别对应听力原文中的 phone 和 call ... in person 即可把握答案 appointment。

Question 20

注意题干中的 peak times 即听力原文中的 busy time,此处出题者故意设置一个思路转换的问题考查考生。试卷题干上用的句子是 there may be a ________,但听力原文中是 you may have to go on the **waiting list**,实质是一回事。

SECTION 3

谈话场景：导师指导的讨论课程。
人物关系：导师和两个学生。
谈话话题：面试中如何选择正确员工的技巧。

词汇注释

aspect *n.* 方面
applicant *n.* 申请人
tutorial *n.* (导师)个别指导，讨论课程
match *v.* 搭配，使…相配
role *n.* 角色
supervisor *n.* 管理者，监督者
imagine *v.* 想象
theoretical *adj.* 理论上的
qualification *n.* 资格，条件
certificate *n.* 证书
similar *adj.* 相似的
environment *n.* 环境
get along well with 与…相处融洽
contrast *v.* 对比，成对照
back *v.* 支持
loser *n.* 失败者
faith *n.* 信心，信任
carry out 执行
personality *n.* 性格，个性
candidate *n.* 候选人，考生，应聘者
hobby *n.* 业余爱好
involve *n.* 卷入，涉及
easy-going *adj.* 随和的
arguably *adv.* 可辩论的，可论证的
character *n.* 性格
questionnaire *n.* 调查问卷
procedure *n.* 过程
apparently *adv.* 显然地，明显地
ancient *adj.* 古代的
civil servant 文职人员，文官
military *adj.* 军队的
appropriate *adj.* 相应的
see through 看破，看穿
nature *n.* 本性，天性
compile *v.* 编写，编撰
expert *n.* 专家
indicator *n.* 指标
roughly *adv.* 基本上，大概
truthful *adj.* 真实的，诚实的
forward-looking *adj.* 有远见的，向前看的
resistant *adj.* 对…拒绝的

交际与语言表达

1. 本篇文章所涉及的场景是许多考生将来在国外学习会面临的真实情况，老师和学生讨论的是正式的问题，但在讨论过程中所使用的精练的口语对白很值得学习。
2. We've looked at various aspects of staff selection this term and I think by now you should all be beginning to see how much more there is to it than just putting applicants through a short interview or asking the 'right' questions. 我们这个学期已经研究了挑选员工的方方面面，除了让申请人参加短短的面试或问他们"正确"的问题之外，我想现在你们应该开始考虑其中有没有更多的内容。You should be doing sth. 你(们)应该马上着手做某事，表示一种比较强烈的建议。
3. So we have to put ourselves into the role of the manager or supervisor? 那我们得把自己看作是经理人或管理者吗？put oneself into the role of... 使自己扮演……的角色。
4. The point is, you can select someone—even a friend—who has all the right qualifications... degrees... certificates, whatever. 问题的关键在于，你可以挑选某个人，甚至是朋友，他具备了所有的入选资格、学历、证书什么的。当强调自己后面要表达的观点时，可以用 the point is 这个句型。

5. Well, with the best will in the world, you may be backing a loser. 那么,不管你多么努力,你可能只是在支持一个失败者。with the best will in the world 字面意思指:即使你拥有全世界最好的意愿或最强烈的愿望。

6. Wouldn't it be just a question of company training, though? 可是难道这不就是个公司培训的问题吗? 此句是反意疑问句,表达肯定的意思。

7. Even if you try, you won't find out what they are really like until they actually start work. 即使你试着这么做,你也只有到他们真正开始工作后才知道他们是什么样子的。not... until... 直到……才。

8. More and more employers around the world are making use of what are called 'personality questionnaires' to help them select new staff. 世界上越来越多的公司正在使用所谓的"性格调查问卷"来帮他们挑选新员工。make use of:利用,what are called 可以用来引出一个不太为人所知的名称。

9. They've gained a lot of ground since then. 从那以后它们不断普及发展。gain ground 普及,壮大,发展。

10. ... which makes you think that there must be something in them. 这使你觉得它们肯定有可取之处。

11. I mean, it's human nature to lie, isn't it? 我的意思是,撒谎是人类的天性,对吗? 中间的分句是用 it 作形式主语,真正的主语是 to lie。

12. Then you can go some way towards finding out whether someone's say, forward-looking... a go-ahead type of person... or resistant to change. 然后你稍稍分析就可以知道某个人是否有远见,或是会为任何事情提前做准备,或者拒绝变化。

考题解析

Question 21

考生首先要注意题干中的 At the **start** of the tutorial, 所以对于对话一开始的内容就要格外注意。导师在第一句话中就已经提到 **staff selection**,后面又提到 today's tutorial on '**matching the person to the job**'. 最后重申 we are going to talk today about **the importance of choosing that all round 'right' person**, 反复强调本次讨论的主题。

Question 22

否定词。导师首先提到 they just **don't get along with everybody else**, 与所有的人都无法融洽相处,基本可以选择答案了。后面接着举例 they've got **sharply contrasting views**,意见完全不同,听到这里可以确定答案为 C。

Question 23

注意题干中的关键词 **teamwork** 和 have **trust** in。既然是团队工作,就应该强调大家的合作,所以导师强调 people **have to have faith in each other's ability**, 基本符合 A 项的 colleagues' ability,后文继续强调 they have to **trust** that everyone will do their part of the job,是对前文的补充说明。

Question 24

这道题一些考生会选错,原因是没有分析好题干。题干中提到 **personal information**,但在听力原文中好像没有涉及。听力原文中说面试中经常会涉及应聘者的 **hobbies and what they like doing in their spare time**,实际上当然也是 personal information 的一种。后文中进一步总结说 so employers are **already involved in** the practice of doing **part of** the task,这里 task 就是指的 job interviews。

Questions 25–29

这几道题都是简单的填空题,只要把握好空格前后的单词,注意个别词汇的替换并集中注意力去听,一般不会出现错误。25 题题干中的 completed 在原文中是 filled out。26、27 题 in the past 是非常好的暗示,28 题句子由主动变被动,但题干所用均为听力原文中原词,29 题注意题干中的 written 在听力原文中是 compiled,而且答案要写 experts,不能写单数。

Question 30

这种题目在真正的雅思考试中出现得不多,其实是前面21题的翻版,而且考查的实际上是考生的阅读能力。答案根据前面的题目中的诸多提示,应该能确定选A。

SECTION 4

谈话场景:课堂讲解。

人物关系:主讲者为参加过教学实习的学生,听众为同班同学。

谈话话题:帽子的制作过程。

词汇注释

presentation *n.* 描述,介绍,课堂演示	**combination** *n.* 结合
project *n.* 项目	**phase** *n.* 时期,阶段
describe *v.* 描述,讲述	**two-dimensional** *adj.* 平面的,二维的
secondary *adj.* 中级的	**encourage** *v.* 鼓励
secondary school 中学	**small-scale** *adj.* 小规模的
subject *n.* 课程	**three-dimensional** *adj.* 立体的,三维的
pupil *n.* 学生	**experiment** *v.* 做试验
adapt *v.* 改变,改编,使适应	**impose** *v.* 把…强加于
roll *n.* (一)卷,捆	**constraint** *n.* 强制,约束
wallpaper *n.* 墙纸	**pliable** *adj.* 易弯的,柔韧的
conical *adj.* 圆锥形的	**grey (or gray)** *adj.* 灰色的
overlap *v.* 重叠,叠起来,交搭起来	**reflect** *v.* 反映
complicated *adj.* 复杂的	**enjoyable** *adj.* 令人开心的
flap *n.* (帽)沿,边;(信封的)封口	**circular** *adj.* 圆形的
bend *v.* 弯曲	**stairway** *n.* 楼梯,阶梯
stick *v.* 粘贴	**strip** *n.* 条,带
glue *n.* 胶水	**crown** *n.* 王冠
cover *n.* 桌布	**fairly** *adv.* 相当地
pillbox *n.* 药丸盒子,(平顶无边的)矮圆桶形帽子	**castle** *n.* 城堡
variation *n.* 变化,变形	**turret** *n.* 塔楼,角塔

交际与语言表达

1. 本篇文章的主干是一个monolog,但演讲者是在其导师简要介绍后才出场的。导师的几句话概括了演讲者的身份和要讲的内容,提醒考生本篇文章的主题,使考生对后文内容有大概的预测。
2. The project I chose to do was a hat-making project and I think this project could easily be adapted to suit any age. 我选定做的是制帽项目,我想这个项目可以很容易调整以适应各种年龄的人群。choose to do (sth.) 选定做某事,愿意做某事; adapt sth. to do 改动……使其适应……。
3. We went back to the classroom to make two basic hat shapes using rolls of old wallpaper. 我们回到教室,用几卷旧墙纸制作两种最基本的帽型。这句话如果让中国考生写,不少人会写成 We went back to the classroom and used... to make... 但明显不如原文的分词结构精练。
4. We each made, first of all, a conical hat by... er... if I show you now... cutting out a circle and

then making one cut up to the center and then... er... overlapping the cut like this... a conical hat that sits on your head. 我们每个人首先制作了一个圆锥形的帽子，嗯，我现在可以给大家演示一下。先剪出一个圆来，然后中间剪一刀到圆心，然后，嗯，像这样把剪开的地方叠起来，一顶圆锥帽子就可以戴在你头上了。给大家描述制帽过程时，演讲者是边想边说边做，所以在说话过程中不一定有缜密的语法思维，这在口语中比较常见。

5. I've prepared this so that I don't get glue everywhere. The pupils **do**, of course, so you need plenty of covers for the table. 我都准备好了，所以不会把胶水弄得到处都是。孩子们当然会(把胶水弄得乱七八糟)，所以你得准备大量的桌布。**do** 这里代替的是前句中 **get glue everywhere**，是一种省略的用法。

6. Then they had to translate their two-dimensional design into a form to fit their heads. 然后他们得把他们的平面设计转换成适合他们的样式。translate... into... 此处相当于 turn... into...，意为"把……变成……"。

7. I imposed certain constraints on them to keep things simple. 我给他们制订一些限制以使整个事情容易些。impose sth. on... 把某事强加于……，施加影响于……。

8. Well, it was very enjoyable and just to give you an idea of what they produced, I've brought along three hats to show you. 啊，这事的确很有趣。另外，为了让大家了解一下他们做出来的是什么样的东西，我带来三顶帽子给大家看看。and 之后的内容已经与前文没有关；to 这里相当于 in order to，引导表示目的的动词(词组)；give sb. an idea of sth. 让某人知道关于某物的些许事情。

9. There are many more that I could have brought. 我本来还可以带来更多的。I could have done sth. 是一种常用的虚拟语气表达法，表示过去本可以做某事(但没有做)。

考题解析

Questions 31–32

这两道题目大部分考生能够做对。31 题只要考生注意到题干中考查学校类型，并熟悉 **secondary school** 指中学就没有问题。

32 题注意问的是 **age**，考生在听的时候关注有关年龄的数字即可。

Questions 33–34

这两道题目最关键是要先弄清让考生做什么。试卷上有一句 Label the diagrams，这句话设置了一个陷阱，会误导考生。实际上这两道题是填空题。

33 题空白前面的 **cut into center and** 与听力原文中的 **making one cut up to the center and then** 表达的是同样的意思，后面出现的内容就是答案：**overlap(ping) the cut**。但很多考生不知道这个单词，可能会填错。

34 题做题之前应可以分析出要填的内容是 **circle** 的一部分，听的时候带着这样的目的去听即可。这道题可以填 **underside**，也可以写出比较相近的 **underneath** 或者 **bottom**。

Questions 35–37

这三道题目的难点是词汇。35 题注意听 **research**，**design**，**hat** 几个词，就可以填上 **on paper**，或者是后文中提到的 **two-dimensions**。这两个写任何一个都可以，后面这个答案很多考生可能不会写，但该词与 36 题息息相关。

36 题首先要把握好 **small-scale**，紧随其后的 **three-dimensional** 或其缩写形式 **3D** 即是答案。

37 题大部分考生没有问题，唯一要注意的是灰色的两种写法都可以：**gray** 或 **grey**。

Question 38

后三道题目大部分考生做不好，首先是因为很多考生对制作帽子的过程和所使用的词汇十分不熟悉,原因之二是很多考生总想完全听懂原文的内容,而不是听其中跟答案相关的具体细节。

38 题原文首先说帽子是按照 **a circular stairway** 设计的,但考生可以完全不理会这个说法,听好后文中的"**three**"和"**on top of the other**",可以确定是 C 项。

Question 39

此题描述的帽子制作过程虽然只有一句话,但有些不太容易理解。关键要听到原文中反复提到 **strip** 从底部到顶端,符合图中的 D 项。最后演讲者做了一个比喻,"**rather like a crown**",图中与皇冠比较接近的也是 D 项。

Question 40

听力原文提到这个帽子是 **a combination of the pillbox ... and the conical hat**,而且后者是 **on top**,听到这些关键的字词可以确定答案为 A。

READING

READING PASSAGE 1

文章结构

体　裁	说明文
主要内容	本文首先简单介绍金龟子的生活习性,然后重点说明澳大利亚农场引进金龟子并利用它们特别的生活习性使农场在多个方面获益。
结　构	第 1 段:一句话段落,直接点破题目中所说的 a remarkable beetle 就是金龟子,从而指明本文主要是介绍金龟子的情况。
	第 2 段:介绍金龟子的概况。
	第 3 段:总体说明澳大利亚引进金龟子的原因、时间、目的及大致结果。
	第 4 段:介绍把金龟子引进农场的过程及其带来改进的周期。
	第 5 段:介绍金龟子如何工作。
	第 6 段:说明需要用不同种类的金龟子相互配合以取得最大量的畜粪埋藏量。
	第 7 段:说明除了清除畜粪之外,金龟子给农场带来的其他好处。
	第 8 段:总结金龟子对澳大利亚牛奶场管理的意义。

词汇注释

文　章	
第 1 段	
remarkable *adj.* 非凡的,异常的 **beetle** *n.* 甲虫	**dung** *n.* (尤指牲畜的)粪 **dung beetle** [昆]金龟子;蜉金龟;蜣螂
第 2 段	
breed *vt.* 产(仔);孵(卵);繁殖 **species** *n.* 种;种类 **creature** *n.* 生物	**evolve** *vi.* 进化;生长;发育 **adapt** *vi.* 适应(to) **climate** *n.* 气候;气候区

native *adj.* 当地土生(或特产)的
scrub *n.* 低矮丛林,密灌丛
woodland *n.* 林地,林区
dweller *n.* 居民;居住者
specialize *vi.* 专门从事;专攻;成为专家
coarse *adj.* 粗的;粗糙的
marsupial *n.* 有袋(目)动物(如袋鼠、袋狸等)
droppings *n.* (兽、鸟等的)粪
cattle *n.* 牛
bush *n.* 灌木;灌木丛
fly *n.* 苍蝇;家蝇
buffalo *n.* (亚洲)水牛

第 3 段

premier *adj.* 首位的;首要的
introduce *vt.* 引进,传入
import *vt.* 进口
aim *vi.* (at)旨在,目的在于
match *vt.* 适应;和…相一致
climatic *adj.* 气候的
zone *n.* (地球)气候带;地带
be known to 为…所熟知
integrate(into) *vt.* 使成一体,使结合,使合并
local *adj.* 当地的;地方性的
release *vt.* 放开;释放
natural *adj.* 自然的;天然的
boundary *n.* 边界;界限

第 4 段

pasture *n.* 牧场
process *n.* 过程,进程
approximately *adv.* 接近地,近似地
handful *adj.* 少数,少量
cow pat 牛粪
beneath *prep.* 在…下方,在下面
dig *vt.* 挖掘(土等);挖…的土
tunnel *vt.* 掘,挖(隧道、地道、洞穴等)
permanent *adj.* 长期不变的;永久(性)的
self-sustaining *adj.* 能维持自己的,自给的
ecology *n.* 生态
in time 经过一段时间以后;最终,迟早
multiply *vi.* 繁殖,增殖;增加
obvious *adj.* 显然的,明显的

第 5 段

shelter *vt.* 庇护,保护;为…提供避难所
predator *n.* 食肉动物;食虫的动物(或植物)
burrow(into) *vi.* 掘地洞;钻进(或钻入)某处
tunnel *n.* 隧道,地道
hollow *vt.* 使成中空,挖空
hollow out 挖空
originate (from) *vi.* 来自;发源
excavate *vt.* 挖空;开凿,挖掘(洞、隧道等)
sausage *n.* 香肠,腊肠
sausage-shaped *adj.* 香肠形状的
brood *n.* 一次孵化的幼虫
chamber *n.* (作特殊用途的)房间;室
shallow *adj.* 浅的,不深的
pear *n.* 梨树
narrow *adj.* 窄的;狭窄的;狭小的
surface *n.* 面;表面
perfectly *adv.* 完美地;理想地
roll *vi.* 滚动;打滚
attach(to) *vt.* 使依附;使附着

第 6 段

maximum *n.* 最大量;最大值
a variety of 种种
overlap *vt.* 与…部分同时发生;与…复叠
temperate *adj.* (气候等)温带的;温和的
former *adj.* (两者中)前面的;在前的
recover (from) *vi.* 恢复;恢复正常;恢复原状
generation *n.* 代,一代
offspring *n.* 子孙;后代
latter *adj.* (通常指两者之间)后者的
annually *adv.* 年度;每年
subtropical *adj.* 副热带的,亚热带的
coastal *adj.* 近(或沿)海岸的;海岸的
commonly *adv.* 通常地,一般地;平常地

第 7 段

initially *adv.* 最初;开头;首先
with a view to doing sth. 以…为目标;指望于
evident *adj.* 明显的,明白的
larva *n.* [复]larvae 幼虫,幼体
pupation *n.* 化蛹;经历蛹期
residue *n.* 残留物;余留物

first-rate *adj.* 第一流的;最高级的;极好的	**essential** *adj.* 必不可少的;非常重要的
fertilizer *n.* 肥料;使丰富者	**nutrient** *n.* 营养品;食物;促进生长的东西
abandon *vt.* 丢弃;放弃	**pollute** *vt.* 污染,弄脏
aeration *n.* 暴露于空气中;通气;充气	**bloom** *n.* 开花;开花期
in addition 另外,加之	**alga** *n.* [复] algae 水藻,海藻
nest *n.* 窝;穴;巢	**dispose of** 去掉,丢掉;清除;销毁
habitat *n.* (动植物的)生境,栖息地	**litter** *vt.* 使凌乱;乱扔东西于
enrich *vt.* 使土地肥沃	**inedible** *adj.* 不可食的,不适合食用的
earthworm *n.* 蚯蚓	**deprive** *vt.* 使不能享受,使不能做
digest *vt.* 消化(食物)	**smother** *vt.* 厚厚地覆盖
decompose *vt.* 分解	
第 8 段	
integral *adj.* 构成整体所必需的	**breeder** *n.* 饲养动物的人,饲养员
dairy farm 乳牛场	**entomologist** *n.* 昆虫学家
decade *n.* 十年	**specialised** *adj.* 专门的;专科的
a number of 若干,许多	**insect** *n.* 昆虫,虫
available *adj.* 可获得的	**competition** *n.* 竞争
private *adj.* 私人(用)的;私有的	
题目	
control *v.* 控制;支配	**preferred** *adj.* 优先选取的;更好的
established *adj.* 定居的;已移植生长的	**complementary** *adj.* 互为补充的;补充的
improvement *n.* 改进,改善	

考题解析

Questions 1–5

● 题型归类:YES/NO/NOT GIVEN

此类题型属于细节题,是雅思 A 类阅读中较难的题目,在大致看完本篇文章所有的题目后,可以得出这样一个推断,即后面图画题和表格题在答案定位和判断上都比这几道题容易,因此可以先完成后面的题目,最后再来完成这五道题目。

Y/N/NG 考查题目中细节信息是否与文章中完全对应。因此在解题时先要确保读懂题目,准确理解题目意思,然后根据题目定位词回原文中定位到相关内容后与题目进行对照判断。

● 题目解析:

题目编号	题目定位词	答案位置	题解
1	bush flies/ buffalo flies	第 2 段最后一句话(Australia's native dung...)和第 7 段第 1 句话(Dung beetles were...)	本题考点是两者比较关系,在原文中定位可以找到 bush flies 和 buffalo flies,但是在第一处(第 2 段)两者是并列关系,句子是说这两种 flies 都在牛粪中繁殖,而第 2 处只出现了 buffalo flies,文章其它地方没有提到这两者,所以无法根据文章判断题目中两者的比较关系是否存在,因此答案是 NOT GIVEN.

2	CSIRO/bring to Australia/数字	第3段第2句话（Between 1968 and,...）	本题考点是最初（initially）引进澳大利亚的金龟子的数量。题目提供的数字是4000种。原文提供的数字是50种左右（about 50 different species），数字不符，答案是NO。需要注意的是在T/F/NG题中一旦出现数字大多考查数字精确度，因此当题目中有数字时不要急着回文章直接去找数字，而应当在有数字的段落中先寻找其他定位词，然后再在相关定位词附近寻找数字。
3	CSIRO/年代	第3段第2句话（Between 1968 and,...）	本题容易误选NOT GIVEN。题目考点是CSIRO将金龟子引进澳大利亚的时间段。题目中说这一时间是“在14年间”（over a fourteen-year period），此处注意over的用法，在此处over指“在……期间”而不是“超过”，将over理解为“超过”的考生会发现文章虽然能够找到明确年代，但不能说明只在这一段时间引进了金龟子，同时没有明确的语言表明澳大利亚在什么时候停止引进金龟子，因此可能误选NOT GIVEN。所以准确理解题目意思是解答T/F/NG很关键的一步。在准确理解题意后在原文定位比较容易，题目和文章意思完全相符，答案是YES。
4	established in Australia/数字	第3段最后一句话（Of the 26...）	本题考点是已经在澳大利亚“定居”的金龟子数量，考查数字精确程度。题目提供的数值是至少有26种（at least twenty-six），回原文定位时题目中定位词在原文中是以近义词组的形式出现，原文中的表达方式是successfully integrated into the local environment，对这一词组的理解是解答本题的难点之一；原文26 species后面的定语从句说明这26种金龟子是“众所周知的已经成功地融入当地环境”，即题目中所说的“established”，题目与原文的意思完全相符，答案是YES。部分考生可能还会对该句后半句“only one,..., has reached its natural boundary”有所疑问，这一种是不是应当从前面说的26种当中减去。从句意来看，这一种也是包含在前面所说的已经成功融入当地环境的金龟子当中，所以后半句所说的内容不影响题目的意思。
5	an immediate improvement/cow pasture	第4段最后一句话（In time they...）	本题考点是金龟子是否会立即（immediate）引起农场的改善，仅凭定位词回原文定位时有一定难度，但在最初浏览全文了解文章结构的时候应当注意到有关这一细节的描写可能会集中在第4、7、8段（通过阅读各段首末句可大致了解文章结构）。在4段末句中明确说明要在三到四年间金龟子给农场带来的好处才会比较明显（within three or four years the benefits to the pasture are obvious），这一意思与题目中的immediate improvement直接抵触，因此答案是NO。

Questions 6–8

● 题型归类：picture

这类题型属于细节题，主要考查考生的读图能力，准确理解图画或图表的意思后需要在文章中寻找相应的描述语言来判断答案，这一类题目相关内容一般较为集中。相对而言，这一题型难度较低。

● 题目解析：

题目编号	题目定位词	答案位置	题解
6	20cm	第 5 段倒数第 2 句话（South African beetles...）	根据题目所提供的图画可以判断 6、7、8 题的答案不同在于三者距 cow pat/dung 的距离分别为 20 cm、30cm、10cm，这些数据将是定位时的重要依据，同时通过题目方框中提供的词可确定这三道题的答案应是（表示金龟子种类的）专有名词，因此回原文定位表示长度数据和专有名词集中的段落（第 5 段）寻找答案。第 8 题直接寻找稍有困难，无法找到 10cm，但文章中的 the shallowest tunnels 表现在图上就是第 8 题所表示的图形，因此可以判断该题答案。
7	30cm	第 5 段倒数第 3 句话（Some large species...）	
8	10cm	第 5 段倒数第 5 句话（The shallowest tunnels...）	

Questions 9–13

● 题型归类：table

Table 题属于细节题，大多考查某一类事物的相同点及不同点，答案在原文中的位置相对集中，同时相当一部分 table 题会涉及数字，因此回原文定位较为容易，同时回原文定位时可先定位大范围，如段落或某段落中的某几句话，然后在这些内容中寻找答案即可。此类题型在雅思 A 类阅读中属比较容易的题目。解题时需注意表格横纵轴的内容，特别是已填写完成的表格内容，可以为解题带来一定线索。

● 题目解析：

题目编号	题目定位词	答案位置	题解	
9 – 11	Spanish/1.25cm	第 6 段第 2 句话（In the cooler...）、第 4 句话（The latter, which...）	全部表格根据表格第一个横格中所填的内容（French/2.5cm）可以定位到文章的第 6 段。	第 9 题比较容易解答，在第 6 段直接定位于 Spanish 后寻找 climate 即可。10 – 11 题稍有难度，在第 2 句中并未提及后两项内容，但在接下来的这句话中说 The former（前者），如果清楚地知道这个单词的意思就会理解下面这句话说的是上面一句话中 the Large French species 的情况，而第 4 句话中所说的 The latter 就是指 Spanish species，从而在第 4 句话中寻找到 10 – 11 题的答案。（题目横轴中 start of active period = 文章中 multiply rapidly，题目横轴中 per year = 文章中 annually）
12 – 13	South African ball roller	第 6 段第 2 句话（The south African...）		直接定位后根据题目横轴定位词可直接找到答案。（题目横轴中 complementary = 文章中 works with）

参考译文

一种不平凡的甲壳虫

有些最不平凡的甲壳虫叫做金龟子，它们一辈子都住在粪堆里享受美味、生儿育女。

这种不平凡的小生物中有4000多个品种已有所进化并已适应了全球的不同气候和许多动物的粪便。澳大利亚的土生金龟子在灌木丛和林地中生活，它们专门从事处理有袋目动物的粗糙粪便，对松软的牛粪则敬而远之，而牛粪中繁殖有林蝇和水牛蝇。

上世纪60年代初期，当时任职于澳大利亚政府的高级研究机构——英联邦科学与工业研究组织(CSIRO)——的科学家George Bornemissza提出建议说，金龟子应该被引进到澳大利亚以便对畜粪中繁殖的苍蝇加以控制。在1968年至1982年间，英联邦科学与工业研究组织从亚、欧、非三大洲进口了约50个不同品种的金龟子，目的在于使它们能与澳大利亚各个不同的气候带相对应。在已知的成功融入当地环境的26个品种中，只有一个在澳大利亚北部放归自然的非洲品种生活在其相应气候带的自然边界内。

把金龟子引进牧场的过程很简单：大约有1500只金龟子被放归牧牛场上的新鲜牛粪堆中，每次释放一小部分。它们立即消失在粪堆下面又掘又挖地开凿起地道来了。如果它们能顺利地适应新环境的话，那么很快就会成为当地生态系统中一个永生不灭且自给自足的部分。到时候它们会成倍繁殖，不出三、四年时间，它们给牧牛场带来的好处就显而易见了。

金龟子是在牛屎堆里头工作的，所以它们受到庇护而免受肉食动物的捕食，如鸟类和狐狸等。大多数品种的金龟子会在土壤中打洞，并将牛粪埋在紧靠牛屎堆下面的地道里，而牛屎堆已被从中掏空。有些源自法国的大品种能在牛屎堆下面深挖地道约达30厘米。这些甲壳虫往往沿着地道打造形似香肠的幼仔屋。最浅的地道属于小小的西班牙种群，它们将牛粪装入小屋内，这些小屋就好像悬挂在梨树的枝条上面的果实一样。南非甲壳虫则在牛屎堆的表面下开挖约20厘米的狭窄通道。有些居住在地表的甲壳虫，包括一个南非种群，能从牛屎堆中切割出一个个滚瓜溜圆的粪球来，然后将它们就地滚开，并使之依附于植物的基部。

为了在春、夏、秋三季取得最大量的畜粪埋藏量，农民们需要多种多样的种群在时间上互有重叠地展开活动。在更为凉爽的维多利亚州的环境中，大型的法国种群(2.5厘米长)与较小的(小一半那么长)、温带气候的西班牙种群相配合。前者从冬寒季节中恢复较慢，而且从晚春到秋季这段时间中只能繁殖一到两代的子孙后裔；后者由于早春季节是生育高潮期，可年产两代到五代的子孙。作为亚热带甲壳虫的南非滚球一族，它们偏爱澳洲北部和沿海的新南威尔士州的气候，并经常在那里同南非的地道掘进一族一起工作。在较为温暖的气候条件下，许多种群都在为当年提供更长时间的服务而积极努力。

金龟子最初是在20世纪60年代晚期引进的，其目的是要通过在一、两天内把牛粪清除掉以防止蝇类繁育的办法进而对水牛蝇加以控制。不过，其他方面的好处也已经开始凸显。一旦甲壳虫的幼虫结束了化蛹期，其残留的余渣便是头等的肥料来源。甲壳虫所遗留下来的地道为植物的根系产生了高级的充气效应，同时也为其提供了水渠的功能。此外，当新一代的甲壳虫离开其窝巢时，被遗弃的洞穴对为土壤增肥的蚯蚓来说，便成了诱人的新居了。这些洞穴里的被消化过的牛粪也是蚯蚓的高级食品供应源。这些“食品”经过蚯蚓的进一步分解之后，可为土壤提供必需的营养成分。如果没有金龟子的存在，那么化肥和畜粪在未能被坚硬的土地吸收之前，就会被雨水冲刷而流入江河、溪流之中，从而污染水道并致使蓝绿藻开花。如果没有甲壳虫来对畜粪加以处理，牛粪堆会散落到牧场的各处致使牧草不宜为牛群食用、土壤得不到阳光的照射。澳大利亚的3千万头牛每头日产10个—12个牛粪堆，这相当于17亿吨一年，数量之大足以覆盖110000平方公里的牧场(半个维多利亚州的面积)，并致其窒息死亡。

在过去几十年中,金龟子已经成为对澳大利亚牛奶场进行有效管理工作中的一个不可或缺的部分。大量的种群可以从联邦科学与工业研究组织(CSIRO)或者私人养殖户那里取得,后者中的大多数原先都是CSIRO属下的金龟子研究机构的昆虫学家,他们利用自己的关于昆虫方面的专业知识,开设了小规模的企业,参与了同他们昔日的老板的直接竞争。

READING PASSAGE 2

文章结构

体　　裁	说明文	
主要内容	本文主要说明农业给环境保护带来了很大的影响,而政府的补贴性政策加剧了这一影响的结果。	
结　　构	A:提出政府在环境管理方面必须发挥作用,并指出废除那些对开发自然资源具有补贴性的政策会带来什么样的好处。	
	B:用事实和数据说明农耕活动对地表产生了极大的影响,然后集中说明农业使粮食产量增高。	
	C:进一步说明上段末尾提出的可使农作物高产的措施会破坏环境,进而侵蚀土壤,威胁土地生产力。	
	D:	第1段:用具体数据说明政府政策加剧了农业对环境的破坏。
		第2段:用具体事例说明政府为削减农业补贴所做的努力。
		第3段:说明在欧盟和中等文明国家中主要做法是削减农业补贴或新设一些补贴来鼓励农民根据环保要求善待土地,同时指出执行这种政策可能面临的问题。
	E:用数据和事实说明在贫穷国家政府政策使农民陷入了破坏环境的恶性循环。	
	F:指出世界贸易谈判乌拉圭回合可能使世界粮食生产由西欧转向发展中国家或前社会主义国家,以及这一结果在正反两方面的影响。	

词汇注释

文　章	
A	
role *n.* 作用;任务	**mining** *n.* 采矿,矿业
inescapable *adj.* 逃避不了的;不可避免的;必然发生的	**scrap** *vt.* 废弃,抛弃
harmful (to) *adj.* 有害的,致伤的	**two-fold** *adj.* 双重的;两倍的
subsidise *vt.* 给…补助,资助	**bonus** *n.* 额外给予的东西;红利
exploitation *n.* (资源等的)开发,开采	**efficient** *adj.* 效率高的
consumption *n.* 消费;消耗	**hand in hand** 同时并进地;密切关联地
protection *n.* 保护,防护	**confront** *vt.* 勇敢地面对;正视;使面对
coal *n.* 煤	**vested interest** 既得利益
B	
affect *vt.* 影响	**shape** *vt.* 使成形;塑造;形成
surface *n.* 地面;表面	**count** *vt.* 把…算入

proportion *n.* 比例,比
output *n.* (尤指一个特定时期的)产量
yield *n.* 产量,产物
cultivation *n.* 耕种,耕作,耕耘
plough *n.* 犁
irrigation *n.* 灌溉
breeding *n.* (植物的)培植;生育,生殖
pesticide *n.* 杀虫剂,农药
fertiliser *n.* 肥料(尤指化学肥料)

C

impact *n.* 影响;作用
deforestation *n.* 滥砍滥伐
contaminate *vt.* 弄脏,污染
intensive *adj.* 精耕细作的
intensive farming 集约农业
abandonment *n.* 放弃,抛弃
fallow *adj.* (耕地)犁过而未播种的,休闲的
tend(to) *vi.* 易于,往往会
exacerbate *vt.* 使加深,使加剧,使恶化
erosion *n.* 腐蚀;侵蚀
monoculture *n.* [农]单作
accompany *vt.* 伴随,和…一起发生(或存在)
disappearance *n.* 消失,不见;灭绝
insurance *n.* 安全保证;预防措施
threaten *vt.* 威胁;对…构成威胁
measurement *n.* 测量,量度
topsoil *n.* 表土;(来自)表土中的壤土
likely *adv.* 很可能
diminish *vt.* 减少,减小,缩减
productivity *n.* 生产能力;生产率
subsequently *adv.* 随后,后来;接着
embark (upon) *vi.* 从事,着手,开始工作;发动
convert *vt.* 使转变,使转化
crop *vt.* 在…上播种(或耕种)
meadow *n.* 草地,牧场
vanish *vi.* 逐渐消散;消灭

D

compound *vt.* 增加,加重
drive up 迫使…上去;迫使…上升
immense *adj.* 巨大的,广大的;无限的
acre *n.* 英亩
option *n.* 选择
readily *adv.* 无困难的,容易地
available *adj.* 可获得的
input *n.* (资金、材料、劳动力等的)投入;投入物;成本
apply *vt.* 应用;使用
frequency *n.* 频率;次数
application *n.* 应用;实施
effort *n.* 努力
dramatic *adj.* 引人注目的;给人深刻印象的
scrap *vt.* 废弃,抛弃
study *n.* 研究;调查
conduct *vt.* 进行;实施
decline *n.* 下降;减少
commodity *n.* 商品;货物
removal *n.* 消除;排除;移去
over-stock *vi.* 进货过多,存货过多
principal *adj.* 首要的;主要的;最重要的
diversify *vi.* 多样化;从事多种经营
subsidy *n.* 津贴,补贴;补助金
enlightened *adj.* 文明的;有知识的,摆脱偏见(或迷信)的
trend *n.* 趋势,趋向
rather than 与其…不如…;不是…而是…
eliminate *vt.* 根除;排除,消除
payment *n.* 支付,付款
treat *vt.* 对待;处理
existing *adj.* 目前的,现行的
incentive *n.* 鼓励,奖励;刺激
dislike *vt.* 不喜爱,厌恶
fuel *n.* 燃料
replacement *n.* 代替品,替换品
petrol *n.* 汽油
ethanol *n.* 乙醇
biomass *n.* (在一个单位面积或体积内的)生物量
carbon dioxide 二氧化碳
absorb *vt.* 吸收(液体、气体等)
therefore *adv.* 因此,因而,所以
likely *adj.* 可能的
contribute to 促成,有助于;是…的部分原因
greenhouse effect 温室效应(地球大气吸收太阳热的一种效应,大气起着如温室一样的作用)
rarely *adv.* 不常,难得
competitive *adj.* (价格等)有竞争力的
fossil *n.* 化石

E	
aggravate *vt.* 加重,加剧;使恶化	**weed** *n.* 杂草,野草
artificial *adj.* 人工的,人造的	**poison** *n.* 毒药;毒物
institute *n.* 组织,机构;学会	**lethal** *adj.* 致死的;会致死的
pest *n.* 害虫	**as for** 至于,关于
resistant *adj.* 抗…的;防…的	**developing countries** 发展中国家
pest-resistant *adj.* 防虫的	**overuse** *n.* 过多(或过度)的使用
moderate *adj.* 适度的;一般的,普通的	**rotate** *vt.* 使轮流,使轮换
treadmill *n.* 繁重的劳动;令人厌倦的工作	**in turn** 转而,反过来
bug *n.* 虫子	
F	
negotiation *n.* 谈判,洽谈	**habitat** *n.* (动植物的)生境,栖息地
reduction *n.* 减少,削减	**farmland** *n.* 农田;耕地
region *n.* 地区;地带;区域	**desirable** *adj.* 值得想望的;值得拥有的
non-existent *adj.* 不存在的	**intensity** *n.* 强度
former *adj.* (两者中)前面的;在前的	**decline** *vi.* 下降;减少
communist country 共产主义国家	**suited** *adj.* 合适的;适当的;适宜的
environmentalist *n.* 环境保护论者;人类生态学者	**sustainable** *adj.* 能保持的;能持续的;能维持的
outcome *n.* 结果;结局;后果	**run** *n.* 一段时间
undoubtedly *adv.* 无庸置疑地;肯定地;无可争辩地	**effectively** *adv.* 生效地;起作用地
pressure *n.* 压力;压迫	**efficiently** *adv.* 效率高地
题目	
suitable *adj.* 合适的,适当的	**diversification** *n.* 经营多样化
agreement *n.* 协议	**refer(to)** *vi.* 提到,谈到,指称
prospect *n.* 前景;预期	**disapprove** *vt.* 不赞成;不同意
degraded *adj.* 降级的	**replace** *vt.* 代替,取代;接替
severe *adj.* 严重的,危险的	**recognize** *vt.* 明白,认识到
significant *adj.* 重要的,相当数量的,不是微不足道的	**forward** *adj.* 向前的,前进的

考题解析

Questions 14–18

● 题型归类:Lists of Headings

此类题型属于结构题,考查考生对文章整体结构的把握。解答此类题型首先要分析题目中给出的选项,确定各选项的主要内容和相似选项之间的区别,接着要了解段落基本构成方式,准确寻找段落的主题句(通常集中在段落的首句和末句),如果主题句较难寻找,需要迅速浏览全段后总结段落中心意思。

● 题目解析:

题目编号	段落主题句	题解
14	The role of governments in environmental management is difficult but inescapable.	段落首句明确表明全段的主要内容,只有选项 v 指 governments 和 environmental management 两者之间的关系。此题较容易。

15	No activity affects more of the earth's surface than farming.	段落首句作为主题句阐述 farming 对 the earth's surface 的影响巨大,但究竟产生什么样的影响是在段落的扩展句中具体说明的。首先通过主题句可以缩小选项范围,正确的选项应当包括 farming,只有 ii,iii 和 vii 这三个选项符合要求,而迅速浏览段落时会发现 farming 的影响主要集中在一个方面,即段落中反复出现的一个概念:粮食产量(world food output/increases in yields/higher yields),而 ii 和 iii 选项中的 environmental impact 和 soil erosion 在本段中均没有提及。因此排除其他两个选项选择 vii。
16	All these activities may have damaging environmental impacts.	主题句说明段落主要内容是 all these activities 对环境造成了影响。有关影响的选项比较多,所以必须确定 all these activities 是什么。根据代词的使用方法可以确定,all these activities 只能指上文中出现过的内容,上段末句是说采用一些措施以获得高产,这些措施包括"增加灌溉面积、改良育种技术以及成倍增加杀虫剂和化学肥料的使用量",这些均是农业行为,因此在有关影响的选项中再选择与农业行为有关的选项即可,这样就可以排除其他选项而选择 ii 了。此题还有可能误选 iii (farming and soil erosion),此类题型中混淆选项通常是段落中没有展开阐述的细节信息,选择 iii 的考生可能注意到此段中的确提及 soil erosion 的内容,但 List of Headings 考查的是段落的主要内容,不是段落中的细节。
17	Government policies have frequently compounded the environmental damage that farming can cause.	段落首句表明此部分描写是政府政策对环境的影响。表示政府政策影响的选项有 3 个,其中 vi 已经做为例题答案出现过,可以排除(此处需注意,此类题型的同一个答案不被两次以上选为正确答案)。而 viii 概括政府政策主要影响了粮食产量,段落中虽然提及了粮食产量,但并不是段落主要内容,因此排除。最终选择 iv。这道题还有另一种解法:读题时注意到 Section E 做为例题已经给出答案 vi,而这一选项与 iv 只有一个词不同(poor/rich),从写作角度判断,这两个选项所表示的段落可能会在一起,做为一种对比描写,而 F 部分的主题句比较明显,与选项 iv 无关,因此 E 部分应当选 iv。
18	A result of the Uruguay Round of world trade negotiations is likely to be a reduction of 36 percent in the average levels of farm subsidies paid by the rich countries in 1986-1990.	主题句明确表明该段主要内容,即乌拉圭回合这一新的国际谈判的结果,与选项 i 完全吻合。

Questions 19－22

● 题型归类：Table

Table 题难度较小，考查文章细节，解题时注意横轴、纵轴提供的定位信息。

● 题目解析：

题目编号	题目定位词	答案所在位置	题解
19	deforestation	Section C 第 2 句（For example, land...）	读题时应注意到 instruction 中已经明确指出本题的范围是 in sections B and C，因而在寻找答案时可直接在这两部分中寻找。此外，还需注意到此题已经提供选项，在原文中寻找到答案后还需要与选项对应方可做答。 19 题根据 deforestation 可直接定位到 Section C 的第 2 句，同时会发现这句话共有 4 个不同的例子，每个例子之间用分号分开，本题也恰好是 4 组因果关系，相互对应。解答其他 3 道题只要分清因果即可。需要注意所给选项可能会与文章表述稍有不同。
20	water supply		
21	intensive farming		
22	monoculture		

Questions 23－27

● 题型归类：Multiple Choice

此类题型属于细节题型，解答此类题目时可以先不看选项，根据题干中的定位词找到答案所在的句子后再查看选项判断正确答案，但在区分混淆选项时常常要继续浏览相关段落以确定最终答案。

● 题目解析：

题目编号	题目定位词	答案位置	题解
23	1982/ the United States soil erosion	Section C 第 4 句话（The United States, ...）	由年代 1982 可以迅速定位到答案所在句子，仔细阅读后理解句子意思是"有 1/5 耕地的表土正在流失，其流失的速度很可能酿成土壤肥力的锐减"，然后阅读选项发现 A、C 选项均提到数字变化，误选 A 是因为没有完全理解答案所在的句子特别是 likely 的意思，likely 在这里表示一种可能，而不是比较。因此 C 选项符合原文意思，是正确答案。B、D 选项的内容在该段其他句子中出现，但和题干意思不符。
24	mid-1980s/ Denmark	Section D 第 1 段倒数第 2 句话（Fertiliser use doubled...）	根据年代词 mid-1980s 回原文定位时可以预测到原文中可能有两种重现方式，一种是 mid-1980s，另一种可能是 1985 等具体表达 80 年代中的方式，找到近似的年代表达后，再在附近寻找 Denmark，最后选定答案所在的句子。句子说明"在 1960 年至 1985 年间，肥料的使用在丹麦就翻了一番"，四个选项中，只有 B 选项表达了这一意思。其它的三个选项中，A 选项在原文中找不到 Denmark 和 Dutch 两国的比较。C 选项比较容易被误选，因为在原文答案下面一句话中的确提到化肥使用频率的增加，但句

			中也明确说明是比 1981 年以来的三年内有所增加,不是和 1960 年相比,在时间这一细节上和原文不符,因此是混淆答案。D 选项中的化肥用量 doubled 不是和 3 年内比较,因此不选。
25	after 1984/New Zealand	Section D 第 2 段第 2 句话(The most dramatic...)	本题难度较大,因为根据定位词回原文定位后发现这句话并没有提供选项中的任何内容,因此需要迅速浏览句子所在段落寻找正确答案。题目问 1984 年后新西兰增加的内容,迅速浏览发现四个选项中 A、C 在原文中没有出现,所以排除,而 B 选项内容在原文中是减少了(a fall in fertilizer use),因此正确答案是 D。
26	‘less enlightened’	Section D 第 3 段第 1 句话(In less enlightened...)	本题和 25 题一样,根据定位词只能确定答案所在段落,需要迅速浏览全段寻找答案。这一类的题目采用排除法解题比较容易。在浏览过程中首先排除 D 选项,因为该段第一句话内容与 D 选项完全相反,同样排除 A 选项,因为同一句话中说明农民休耕(leave it fallow)也会得到补贴。B 选项内容与原文也有出入,原文指出 new fuel crops 在环保方面比燃料具有优势,因为它们不仅释放较少的二氧化碳,同时在生长时还能吸收二氧化碳,而 B 选项是说 new fuel crops 和它们所取代的燃料一样有害,排除 B 之后就剩下正确答案 C 选项。如果要直接在原文中寻找正确答案,需要通读全段后对段落内容进行归纳,并不能直接找到相对应的原文,这样解答的难度比排除法大得多。
27	the Uruguay Round agreements	Section F 第 1 句话(A result of...)	本题也可以用排除法解答。用定位词先确定答案所在段落。C 选项首先被排除,因为原文中只说会有更大的压力迫使自然栖息地转变为农田,并没有说是在富国或穷国,细节信息不符。B、D 选项均在原文中找不到对应的比较内容,因此被排除。正确答案是 A,该答案虽然在原文中也有相关对应(in ways that are sustainable in the long run),但也需要一定的阅读后进行归纳。

Question 28

● 题型归类:The Best Title

此类题型属于主旨题,在雅思 A 类阅读中如果出现没有题目的文章,通常最后会有一道题目要考生选择最适合文章的题目或类似的主旨题。这类题目应当放在整个文章最后解答,注意避免选择表示某一段落细节的选项,最后选取的答案应能概括整个文章的内容。

● 题目解析：

题目编号	题解
28	在解答完其他题目后，考生事实上已经反复浏览过本文，对文章的主要内容已经有大致了解，因此不需再重新阅读文章，可以先通览所有选项，看是否有可以直接排除的选项，本题中 B、C、D、E 四个选项都可以直接排除，因为 C、D、E 选项都是对文章部分细节的表述，这也是此类题中混淆选项的主要特征，而 B 选项的内容在文章中没有提及。只有 A 选项可以概括文章的全部内容。

参考译文

政府要在环境管理方面发挥作用虽然困难但也责无旁贷。有时，国家试图管好它所拥有的资源，可有点力不从心，甚至政府行为往往会造成更大的损害。他们实际上对自然资源的开发与消费实行补贴。从对农产品价格的支持到对采煤业的保护等一整套的政策，对环境造成了损害，而且在经济上也往往是毫无意义的。废除它们可带来双重利益：一个干净整洁的环境和一个效率更高的经济。经济增长与环境保护二者在实际上是可以并行不悖的，如果政界人士有勇气面对补贴给他们创造的既得利益的话。

农耕活动对地表影响之大是其他任何活动所难以企及的。它对这个星球的 1/3 的土地施行过整形术（南极是例外），而这个比例还在不断提高。上世纪 70 年代和 80 年代之间，世界人均食品产量提升了 4 个百分点，这主要来自原有耕地的增产效果，但部分也是由于扩大耕地的缘故。在 70 年代和 80 年代，农作物的高产是通过以下措施取得的：增加灌溉面积、改良育种技术以及成倍增加杀虫剂和化学肥料的使用量。

所有这些活动都可能会产生破坏环境的影响。比如，开荒种地便是破坏森林的罪魁祸首；化肥和杀虫剂会污染水源；过多的精耕细作及土地休耕期的废除导致土壤侵蚀的恶化现象；单作制的普及、高产作物品种的选用招致一些传统的粮食作物品种的消失，而这些传统品种本来就可能具有抵御未来的病虫害侵袭的能力。土壤侵蚀不论在富国还是穷国，都会威胁到土地的生产力。1982 年在美国（那里曾进行过最详细的测算），曾经发现有 1/5 耕地的表土正在流失，其流失的速度很可能酿成土壤肥力的锐减。于是该国接着就启动了一项退耕还林（牧）的工程，即将其耕地的 11% 转建为牧场或是林区。在印度和中国，表土的流失比在美国的要快得多。

从事农业本身会对环境造成破坏，但政府的政策却常常加剧了这种破坏。在富裕的国家中，对种植农作物的补贴和对农产品价格的保护都促进了地价的上扬。这些补贴的年支出总额的价值是巨大的：大约 2500 亿美元，或是比世界银行在上世纪 80 年代的全部贷款还要多。为了增加农作物的亩产量，对农民来说最简单的选择便是多多使用最为现成的各种投入：肥料和杀虫剂。在 1960 年至 1985 年间，肥料的使用在丹麦就翻了一番，在荷兰则增加了 150%。杀虫剂的使用量也增加了：比如在 1975 年至 1984 年间的丹麦就增加了 69%；自 1981 年以来的 3 年中，在杀虫剂的使用频率上也上升了 115%。

在上世纪 80 年代后期和 90 年代初期，政府曾经为了削减农业补贴而作出过努力。1984 年，新西兰政府取消了大部分的农业资助基金而成为一个最引人注意的例子。1993 年进行的一项对环保效果的研究发现，随着化肥补贴的终止而出现的是化肥使用量的下降（世界商品价格的下跌也导致了这一下降趋势，农业收入也因之而减少）。随着补贴被取消，开荒（地）毁林、过度放牧等现象也终止了，这些过去是造成土壤侵蚀的主要原因。于是农场开始搞多样化经营。有一个补贴项目取消后似乎对环境并无好处，那就是用于控制土壤侵蚀的补贴项目。

在欧盟及中等文明国家里，共同的趋势是削减补贴而不是取消补贴，还增设新的支出科目以鼓励农民根据环保要求善待其土地，或是予以休耕。像这方面的支出费用如果不高于目前用来奖励农民播种粮食作物的补助金的话，那就会令人感到奇怪了。然而农民是不喜欢不劳而获、无功受禄的。有些国家的农民，对使用从庄稼的残渣中提炼燃料的可能性很感兴趣；这种燃料可作为石油（代替乙醇）的代用品，也可作为发电站的燃料（用作生物量）。这一类燃料在燃料过程中所释放的二氧化碳比起煤炭和石油来，要少之又少，而在它们生长过程中却一直在吸收二氧化碳。因此，它们不太可能会助长温室效应。但是它们很难与矿物燃料相竞争，除非是在得到补贴资助的情况下；而且种植这些作物对环境造成的损害也不见得比其他作物能小多少。

在贫穷国家里，政府加剧了其他方面的破坏。由于使用农药（杀虫剂）和化肥可领取政府补贴，农民就不顾实际需要而超量使用，以期取得最高的经济作物产量。国际水稻研究所对东南亚地区的农民使用农药情况所进行的研究发现，有了抗虫害的水稻品种，连农药的适量使用都往往会使农民入不敷出。如此这般的浪费陷农民于化学品使用的繁重劳务中：害虫与杂草产生了抗药性，因而次年的农药必须提高其毒性，使之更易致命。为此付出的代价之一是人类的健康。每年约有一万人死于农药中毒，他们几乎全部都生活在发展中国家，另有 40 万人重病缠身。至于各种人造肥料，它们在全球的普遍使用使每个单位农田的用量增加了 40%，这是上世纪 70 年代中期和 80 年代晚期之间大部分发生在发展中国家的情况。肥料的过度使用会使农民停止轮种作物，或是不让土地休耕。这种做法反过来又会导致土壤侵蚀的进一步恶化。

世界贸易谈判乌拉圭回合的一个结果很可能是，削减由富裕国家在 1986 年至 1990 年间支付的农业补贴平均水平的 36%。世界粮食生产的某些部分将从西欧转移到补贴较低或没有补贴的地区，比如前共产主义国家及发展中世界的部分地区。有部分环境保护论者担心会出现这样的结果。这无疑会意味着将有更大的压力来迫使自然栖息地转变为农田。不过那也会带来不少人们所希望的环保效果：富裕地区农业生产的强化手段应有所缓和；化学药剂的投入量将有所减少；农作物将更有可能在适合它们的自然习性的环境中播种；贫困国家中将有更多的农民获得资金和动力以便做到以高瞻远瞩的眼光对农田作好长期持久的治理。上述各点都很重要。要喂饱一个日甚一日忍饥挨饿的世界，农民需要更多的鼓励与刺激，使他们在利用土壤和水源时能做到效果与效率并重。

READING PASSAGE 3

文章结构

体　　裁	说明文
主要内容	本文主要内容比较抽象，主要说明角色理论中的一些相关概念，但是从文章结构和各部分内容来看，文章结构十分清晰，各部分黑体小标题已经充分说明本部分的主要内容。文章分别解释了三个角色理论中的相关概念，即角色丛、角色的定义和角色模糊。

<table>
<tr><td rowspan="10">结　　构</td><td rowspan="2">Role set</td><td>第 1 段:解释“角色丛”的概念。</td></tr>
<tr><td>第 2 段:一句话段落,说明“角色丛”的范围。</td></tr>
<tr><td rowspan="6">Role definition</td><td>第 3 段:说明角色应是各成员对焦点角色所抱有的“角色期望值”的综合,而这些期望值往往从职业角度来阐述。</td></tr>
<tr><td>第 4 段:说明必需的角色行为具有明显的强制性。</td></tr>
<tr><td>第 5 段:说明“角色标记”的重要性。</td></tr>
<tr><td>第 6 段:具体解释衣着如何作为“角色标记”。</td></tr>
<tr><td>第 7 段:解释另一种“角色标记”——地点,以及角色转化仪式。</td></tr>
<tr><td>第 8 段:列举其他“角色标记”,同时说明无标记角色会带来什么样的后果。</td></tr>
<tr><td rowspan="2">Role ambiguity</td><td>第 9 段:指出当焦点人物或其“角色丛”成员对其在某特定时段所任角色的确切定义存有疑惑时就会出现角色模糊,并进一步指出这样的角色模糊对焦点人物会造成什么影响。</td></tr>
<tr><td>第 10 段:说明角色模糊对角色丛其他成员有什么影响。</td></tr>
</table>

词汇注释

文　　章

第 1 段

concept *n.* 概念;观念
role *n.* 角色(心理学术语,指在人们期望中具有一定社会或身份的个人所应有的行为)
theory *n.* 理论,学理,原理
role-set *n.* (心理学术语)(由相互角色关系组成的)角色丛
individual *n.* 个人,个体
occupy *vt.* 居(某种地位);担任(职务)
in relation to 有关,关于,涉及
particular *adj.* 特定的,特指的,某一的
concern *vt.* 涉及,对…有关系,有关于
analysis *n.* 分析;分解
focal *adj.* 焦点的;(集中)在焦点上的
regard *vt.* 把…看作,认为;对待
interact *vi.* 相互作用;互相影响
for instance 例如,比如
figure *n.* (书本中的)插图;图表,图解

第 2 段

include *vt.* 包括;包含
trivial *adj.* 不重要的;琐碎的
interaction *n.* 相互作用;相互影响

第 3 段

definition *n.* 定义;释义
combination *n.* 混合(体);联合(体)
expectation *n.* 期望;期待
occupationally *adv.* 职业引起地;职业地;工作地
define *vt.* 解释;使明确;使清楚
legally *adv.* 从法律上解释地;符合法律条文地
lawyer *n.* 律师
fairly *adv.* 相当;还;尚
cultural *adj.* 文化(上)的;人文的
term *n.* 专门名词,名称,术语

第 4 段

escape *vt.* 逃脱;逃避;避免
behaviour *n.* 行为
constrained *adj.* 被约束的;被迫的
eventually *adv.* 终于,最终
personality *n.* 人格;(显明的)个性
hence *adv.* 因此,所以;由此
likelihood *n.* 可能,可能性
accountant *n.* 会计人员;会计师
alike *adj.* 同样的;相像的
blonde *n.* 白肤金发碧眼的女人
force *vt.* 强迫,迫使

第 5 段

particular *adj.* 特殊的，特别的；独特的
given *adj.* 规定的，特定的
means *n.* 方法，手段
obviously *adv.* 显然地，明显地
uniform *n.* 制服；制服式样
stripe *n.*（军装、警服等上面表示等级等的）条纹
pip *n.*（英国军官肩章上表示等级的）星
precise *adj.* 准确的，确切的
certain *adj.*（只作定语）某，某一，某种，一定的
prescribe *vt.* 规定，指定；限定

第 6 段

circumstance *n.* 环境，条件，情况
indicate *vt.* 表明；暗示
formality *n.* 正式（性质）
gathering *n.* 集会；聚会
occasionally *adv.* 偶然，偶尔，间或
status *n.* 地位，身份
present *adj.* 出席的，在座的，在场的
current *adj.* 现时的，当前的，进行中的
trend *n.* 趋势，趋向
blur *vt.* 使（视线、感觉、形状、界线等）模糊不清
democratic *adj.* 民主的；民主主义的
insecure *adj.* 不安全的；有危险的

第 7 段

behave *vt.* 使（自己）举止；使…（自己）表现得…
location *n.* 位置；场所；地点
indeed *adv.* 实际上，其实；甚至，而且
outward *adj.* 表面的；外表的
subordinate *n.* 部属，下级
significant *adj.* 重要的，重大意义的
e. g. <拉> exempli gratia（= for example）例如
bachelor *n.* 单身男子；单身者
obvious *adj.* 显然的，明显的
ritual *n.* 仪式；老规矩；习惯
decline *n.* 下降；减少
emphasis *n.*（对事物、意义、重要性等的）强调
indication *n.* 暗示；象征
therefore *adv.* 因此，因而，所以

第 8 段

furniture *n.* 家具
perquisite *n.* 特殊待遇，特权
frown（upon） *vi.* 表示不悦（或愤怒、不赞同）
lead（to） *vi.* 导致
confused *adj.* 困惑的；混乱的；弄糊涂的
differ *vi.* 相异，有区别，持不同看法

第 9 段

ambiguity *n.* 含糊不清；不明确；模棱两可
uncertainty *n.* 不确定；不确信
as to 关于，至于
crucial *adj.* 至关重要的；决定性的，关键性的
ability *n.* 能力
shape *vt.* 使成形；塑造；形成
desire *vi.* 渴望，热望，想望
stress *n.* 压力，重压
later on 以后
virtue *n.* 优点，长处
lessen *vt.* 使变小，使缩小；使减少
unfortunately *adv.* 遗憾的是，令人失望的是，可惜的是
description *n.* 说明；形容；描写
seldom *adv.* 不常，很少，难得
subtle *adj.* 微妙的，难以捉摸的
informal *adj.* 非正规的，非正式的
uncomfortable *adj.* 不舒服的，不安的
unsaid *adj.* 未（高声）说出的；（想到而）未讲出口的
i. e. <拉> id est = that is to say 那就是，即
heighten *vt.* 增大，增加；增强
sense *n.* 感觉

第 10 段

point of view 观点，看法；观察角度
clarity *n.* 清晰，明晰
insecurity *n.* 不安全，无保障
irritation *n.* 激怒，恼怒，生气
identify *vt.* 确定；识别
executive *n.* 经理；管理人员
planner *n.* 策划者；设计者
controller *n.* 控制者；制约者
reward *n.* 奖赏；奖品
punishment *n.* 惩罚；处罚
counsellor *n.* 顾问
operational *adj.* 实施时的；操作上的
react *vi.* 作出反应，反应
appropriate *adj.* 适合的，恰当的

题目	
contradict *vt.* 与…抵触,违背	graduation *n.* 毕业
specify *vt.* 明确说明;详细指明	ceremony *n.* 典礼;仪式
reverse *vt.* 使反向,使倒转	wig *n.* 假发
remove *vt.* 消除,去掉,除掉	court *n.* 法庭
eliminate *vt.* 排除,消除;根除	guide *n.* 指南;要览
enlarge *vt.* 扩大,扩展	critical *adj.* 批判的;评论(性)的
carpeting *n.* [总称]地毯	

考题解析

Questions 29 – 35

● 题型归类:YES/NO/NOT GIVEN

细节题,解答时可在 36 题 – 39 题之后做,因为 40 题属于主旨题,应当在全部题目的最后做。由此提醒考生,雅思 A 类阅读并不要求考生严格按顺序做题,在浏览题目时可以自己判断,先完成难度较低的题。解答此类题一定要准确理解题目的意思,然后再回原文相关部分定位阅读判断答案。

● 题目解析:

题目编号	题目定位词	答案所在位置	题解
29	the role definitions of soldiers	第 7 段第 5 句话(In very significant...)第 5 段第 4 句话(The number of...)	根据题目中的定位词 role definitions 可以首先将答案的搜索范围缩小到 2 段 – 8 段,即小标题 role definitions 所包含的段落。然后再在其中搜索有关 soldiers 的内容。第一处可以定位到第 7 段第 5 句话,此处出现的 soldier 只是作为一种角色转换的例子,并没有表明是否应当将士兵的角色定位更加清晰的意思。接下去再搜索时可以定位到第 5 段的第 4 句话,因为 strips(军装、警服等上面表示等级等的条纹)和 pip(英国军官肩章上表示等级的星)这两个词都是明显的士兵服装的特征。但在这句中也无法与题目中的内容相对应。在 role definitions 的其他部分无法寻找到有关 soldiers 的内容,因此答案确定为 NOT GIVEN。
30	accountants	第 4 段最后一句话(Hence, there is...)	accountants 特指一种人,用它作定位词在文章中较好搜索,在第 4 段最后一句中明确指出"所有会计人员有很大的可能会趋于雷同",同时指出原因:"这种结果完全是他们的角色期望值所逼出来的",也就是说由于相同的工作导致了相同的角色期望值,因此会计很有可能趋于雷同。这与题目叙述的内容完全重合,题目也包括两方面的意思:一是所有的会计有可能雷同,二是这种雷同的原因是会计的工作相同。答案选 YES,本题较容易。

31	dress	第6段第2句话(The current trend...)	本题稍有难度,因为在原文中不是直接和题目进行对应,而是需要进一步的理解。本文中有关 dress 的段落比较多,但是根据文章结构可以直接到第6段定位,因为这一段主要讲 dress 如何作为 role sign。题目的意思比较好理解,是说即使在今天(nowadays),保留衣着作为一种角色标记可能是个好主意。在第6段首先会发现第2句话前半句指出,目前着装所体现的角色标记有渐趋模糊之势。如果只读到这里,答案很可能会误选 NO,但需要注意文章这句话只是一种事实描述,而题目是一种态度判断,需要在原文中寻找确定文章有没有体现出这样一种态度。这句话的后半句很明确地表示"但是这种趋势也使一些人感到缺乏安全感",这是一种轻微的否定,接下去的一句话是反问句,使用反问句是为了加强语气,从这里更明确地看出文章对上面所说的趋势的态度,从而完全对应了题目的内容,因此答案选 YES。
32	marriage ritual	第7段倒数第2句话(It is interesting...)	本题比较好定位,在第7段中 ritual 是斜体字,而 marriage ritual 是 ritual 的一个具体内容,在它附近寻找即可。找到 marriage ritual 所在的句子后发现它在其中只是一个例子,说明存在对婚礼仪式的重视有减弱趋势的事实,但并没有说明是否要逆转这一现象,和题目中的 should be reversed 无法对应,而文章的其他部分没有再提到 marriage ritual,因此答案确定为 NOT GIVEN。
33	furniture/dress	第8段第2句话(These and other...)	定位时也可根据文章结构直接到第8段寻找。题目是对家具所扮演的角色和衣服一直扮演的角色的对比,说两者是完全一样的。furniture 出现在第8段首句,句中并未提及衣服,而接下来的句子中明确说明"他们可以用来像某种制服一样在民主社会中发挥作用"(they may serve a purpose as a kind of uniform),句中的他们指代的就是第一句话中的 office signs and furniture,这一句中将家具的角色与衣服角色进行了对比,意思与题目完全一样,因此答案选 YES。
34	role ambiguity/remove	第9段第3句 – 5句(If his occupation...)	本题定位时很容易先将范围缩小到9段 – 10段,由于这两段都是描写 role ambiguity 的,题目主要内容是认为消除角色模糊是个好主意,因此解题关键是寻找文章中是否有内容和题目中消除角色模糊的部分相对应,迅速浏览第9段会发现有一句问句非常醒目:Is it bad 而问句前一句话结尾的词是 role ambiguity,根据语法判断 this 指的正是上句话中的 role ambiguity,因此只要看对这句话的回答就可以知道文章表达的对 role ambiguity 的态度了。问句接下来的回答很明确:not necessarily,由此可以判断文章对 role ambiguity 的态度正好和题目中的意思相反。因此答案选择 NO。

35	job descriptions	第 9 段第 6 句（The virtue of...）	本题较容易解答。定位时一样在 9 段 - 10 段寻找，第一种 job descriptions 出现的句中就明确说明 job descriptions 的好处在于可以减少（lessen）角色模糊，而不是题目中所说的消除（eliminate）角色模糊，这两个动词的意思完全不同，答案为 NO。

Questions 36 - 39

● 题型归类：Sentence Completion

这类题目属于细节题，只要定位准确，比较容易解答，解答时首先要准确理解题意，而且需要特别注意空格处的语法成分以及题目中的字数要求。

● 题目解析：

题目编号	题目定位词	答案所在位置	题解
36	office/carpeting	第 8 段首句（In organizations, office...）	读题后明确空格处需要填写名词或名词性短语。根据 carpeting 可以应该在第 8 段寻找答案，因为第 8 段讨论 furniture 作为角色标记的作用，而 carpeting 正是 furniture 的一种。题目意思是：一个扩大办公室并在其中放置昂贵地毯的新校长是把办公室当作……。在第 8 段首句中，organizations 指一切机构，学校也包含在内，句中的 furniture 是被用作角色标志（used as role signs）。题目正是对这句话的举例，using... as 的结构也与文章中 be used as 重合，因此答案比较容易确定，应当填写 role sign。（注意此处应当用单数，因为空格前有不定冠词 a）
37	graduation ceremony	第 7 段第 5 句话（In very significant...）	本题稍有难度，需要对文章部分内容准确理解，只靠定位词寻找无法找到答案。因为全文都是和角色的三个概念有关，首先确定 graduation ceremony 和哪一个概念有关，角色丛和角色模糊似乎都没法与毕业典礼建立关联，因此先将范围缩小到角色定义（3 - 8 段），然后根据 3 段 - 8 段的主要内容再将范围缩小到第 7 段进行快速浏览，因为毕业典礼意味着学生将进入社会，角色发生变化，只有第 7 段集中讨论这一内容。题目意思可以简化为：毕业典礼是一种重要的……。7 段中用其他例子表示角色转化，从士兵到军官，从单身汉到已婚之夫。而从学生进入社会的角色转化与这些例子类似，所以对这些例子最后的总结性词语就是本题的答案。文章中说这些例子都要有一个非常明显的标志，因此就有了“仪式”（hence rituals）。ritual 这个词就是对这些例子的一个总结，因此也是本题的答案，同样需要注意这里填写的应该是单数。

38	wig/court	第6段首句(In social circumstances...)	本题的解法和36题一样,选定题目定位词后可以直接到谈dress的段落去定位正确答案,因为wig(假发)是dress(着装)的一部分,在第6段无法直接找到定位词,但可以推断题目的意思是对文章所表述内容的一个例证,因此找到dress的作用即可。答案较好判断,role sign。
39	parents of students	第1段-2段	题目问学生家长是校长……的一部分,考查两者之间的关系,有关不同个体关系的解释只在文章最开始的两段出现过,而头两段只解释了一个概念role set,特别是文章中的图表更加明确地表示了这个概念,因此答案很容易判断,是role set。

Question 40

● 题型归类:Multiple Choice

本题属于特殊的多选题,其实质是考查文章主旨,类似the best title题,因此在解答时也应放在最后。雅思A类阅读的主旨题经常以这种形式发问,即问文章有可能是从哪一种文体的什么文章中选摘。

● 题目解析:

题目编号	题解
40	这种题目用排除法解答较容易。首先排除选项A、B,因为文章的中心话题是role,而这两个选项中均未出现这一单词。接下来排除D,因为此选项中的role changes只是其中一个段落出现的细节,不能体现整个文章的意思,这是干扰选项的典型特点。如果从文体的角度去解答这道题,难度就相当大了,大部分考生对各种文体的区别还不是掌握得很清楚。

参考译文

角色理论的概念

角色丛

处于任何情况下的任何一个人,都会根据自己与其他人的关系而担当起一定的角色。你所关心的某一特定个人在对任何情况进行分析时往往被称为"焦点人物"。他具备"焦点角色"的条件,并且可以被视为总是在一群人中间就坐的人,在这种场合,他会以某种方式与大家互动沟通。这么一群人就称为他的"角色丛"。例如,在家庭的情景中,个人的角色丛就如图6所示。

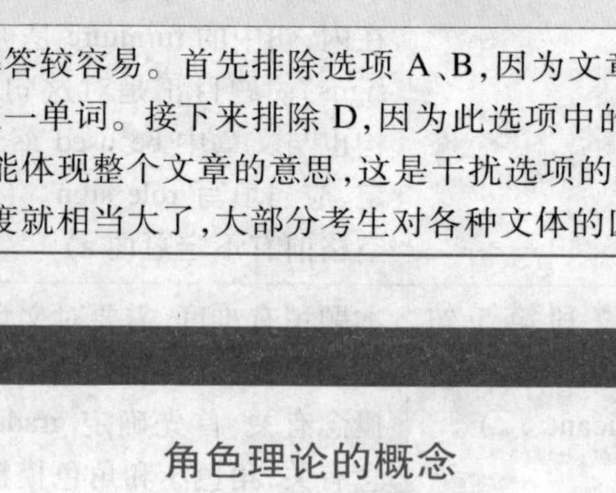

图6

角色丛应包括所有与个人具有不一般交往的人们。

角色的定义

在任何情况下,任何一个人角色的定义将是该角色丛各成员对焦点角色所抱有的"角色期望值"的综合。这些期望值往往是从职业的角度来阐述的,有时甚至用法律的观点加以界定。律师和医师的角色定义,无论从法律的视角或是文化的视角来看,都是相当明确的。例如电影明星或是银行经理,他们的角色定义从文化视角来看也是相当明确的,或许可以说是太明确了。

人们常会有这样的感觉,要想摆脱文化传统所赋予他们的角色往往是很难如愿的。必需的角色行为具有明显的强制性,这不仅体现在律师和医生身上,如果你长期担任此角色,那么它最终也将成为"你"的一部分,就是你个性的一部分。于是便有了很大的可能性:所有会计人员将趋于雷同,或全部的金发碧眼女郎会彼此相似而近乎一个模样——这种结果完全是他们的角色期望值所逼出来的。

在一个特定阶段,你要搞清楚你的特殊角色是什么,这一点非常重要。做到这一点的方法,叫做"角色标记",这个称谓直白易懂。角色标记中最简单的形式便是制服。你制服袖上的条纹数或是肩章上有几颗星星,都是极其确切的角色定义,它们允许你在某些情况下去履行某些明确规定的职责。可以想象一下:在你没有穿上带有角色标记的警服的情况下,又是在半夜时分,你正在一条昏暗的街上盘问一个陌生人,会是什么样子!

在社交环境中,衣着常被当作角色标记使用,借以表明集会的性质与规格标准,偶而还可表示出与会者的社会地位来。时下,由着装所体现的角色标记有渐趋模糊之势,这或许是民主风气使然,但这也使某些人感到缺乏安全感。如果没有角色标记,谁又能知道谁是什么角色呢?

地点是另一种角色标记。经理们在办公室内与办公室外的行为表现往往大相径庭,即便是面对同一个人也是这样。他们利用地点的转换来表现角色的转换,比如说吧,从老板转换成朋友。的确是这样,如果你希望转换角色,你必须设法显示出某种表象,表明你正在身体力行,否则你将难以获准——你的下属将一如既往地继续听命于作为老板的你,不管你付出多少努力要争取成为他的朋友。在意义重大的角色转换的例子中,例如:从普通一兵到军官、从单身汉到有妇之夫,这种角色的转换必须伴有非常醒目的标记,因此,就出现了这样那样的仪式。比如向来受到重视的结婚仪式,其重视程度已有所减弱,对这一现象作一深入观察,倒也不乏其趣。因为这可以被看作是一种迹象,它表明在从单身汉到有妇之夫的角色转换过程中,再也不会有如此巨大的变化存在了,当然也无须为了"标记"而举行公开的角色转换仪式了。

在机构、单位里,办公室的牌子和家具陈设常用来作为角色标记。这些以及其他表示身份、地位的特权,人们往往不屑一顾,但可以用来像某种制服一样在民主社会中发挥作用;无标记的角色常常导致对焦点人物角色的期望值趋于混乱或分歧。

角色模糊

当焦点人物或其角色丛成员对他在某特定时段所任角色的确切定义在思想上存有疑惑时,就出现了角色模糊。形成角色定义的若干关键性期望值之一便是对那位焦点人物个人的期望值。如果他担任的角色不明确,或是与角色丛其他成员的不一致时,将会产生一定程度的角色模糊性。这有什么坏处吗?那倒不一定,因为塑造自己角色的能力就是许多人希望得到的若干自由权利之一。但是其模糊性会引发角色压力,这将留待以后再来讨论。职务说明的好处是可以消除一定程度的角色模糊性。可惜的是,职务说明极少能成为完整的角色定义,除了最低级别的以外。在中级和更高级别的管理层次上,常常是以表格形式将种种职务与职责罗列其中,而有关对角色所抱有的更为微妙琐碎的随意期望却很少涉及。于是其结果等于是给了有关个人一种不舒服的感觉,认为还有些话欲言又止、尚未和盘托出,也就是说,角色变得越发模糊不清了。

从另一方面来看角色模糊性,即从角色丛各成员的观点出发,焦点人物的角色缺乏清晰度会在角色丛的成员中间引发一种不安全感、缺乏信任感、气恼甚至愤怒的感觉。一份关于一位经理所担任的角色的表格确认了他具有以下身份：经理、策划人、决策者、专家、奖罚评判人、顾问、朋友、教师。如果通过这样、那样的角色标记，还不清楚哪一个角色是目前正在操演中的。那么另一方就不会作出适当的反应——举个例子，如果焦点人物以教师的身份来同我们讲话而我们是把她当作经理来洗耳恭听的，我们实际上听到的可能是另一类信息。

WRITING

WRITING TASK 1

范文

范文1

When considering the amount spent on six consumer goods, including personal stereos, tennis racquets, perfumes, CDs, toys, and photographic film in Germany, Italy, France, and Britain, Britain consistently spent the most and Germany most often spent the least. On all the abovementioned goods, Britain's spending was always the highest, however it did not exceed other countries spending by much in the case of tennis racquets and personal stereos. In the case of photographic film, Britain spent at least 25% more than the lowest spender, Germany. For most goods, Germany was always the lowest spender, excluding tennis racquets and perfumes, which both showed France as the lowest spender.

France and Italy were middle spenders; they spent equal amounts on toys, with Italy spending more on personal stereos, tennis racquets, and perfumes, while France spent more on CDs and photographic film. This chart clearly indicates that there are some significant differences in spending habits within European countries. Some statistics are even a little surprising, for example, the French are famous for their production of many famous perfumes, but they have a lower consumption rate than the British.

当虑及包括个人音响、网球拍、香水、CD、玩具和胶卷在内的六种商品在德国、意大利、法国、英国的消费额时，英国一如既往是消费力最强的国家，而德国通常是消费力最弱的。在所有以上提及的商品中，英国人的花费一直是最高的，但在网球拍和个人音响方面的消费却没有超过其他国家。在胶卷方面的消费英国至少比此项商品消费力最低的德国高25%。对于大部分商品来说，除了网球拍和香水两项法国是最低消费者外，德国总是最低消费者。

法国和意大利是居中的消费者，他们在玩具上的花销差不多一样，意大利在个人音响、网球拍和香水上的花销较多，而法国在CD和胶卷上的花销较多。此表清楚说明了欧洲国家之间存在显著的消费习惯差异。有些统计数字甚至令人有些许惊讶，例如法国以许多出名的香水产品著称，但是在此项上的消费却低于英国。

范文2

The four countries included in the bar chart are: Germany, Italy, France and Britain, and the six consumer goods covered are: personal stereos, tennis racquets, perfumes, CDs, toys and photographic film. Britain outspent the other three countries in all categories, ranging from a low of over 1.5 million pounds sterling for personal stereos and tennis racquets to 1.6 million pounds sterling for perfumes and over 1.6 million pounds sterling for CDs and toys to a high of over 1.7 million pounds sterling for photographic film.

Germany spent almost the same amount for all six consumer goods, ranging from just below to just above 1.5 million pounds sterling. Italy spent the most on toys and photographic film, both nearly 1.6 million pounds sterling, with the rest around 1.5 million pounds sterling. France had the biggest variation in spending among the six goods, ranging from a low of just over 1.4 million pounds sterling for tennis racquets to a high of nearly 1.7 million pounds sterling for photographic film. Ironically, France had the lowest spending in perfumes, something for which it is famous, perhaps because perfume is cheaper in France.

此柱状图中的四个国家分别是:德国、意大利、法国和英国;六种消费品包括:个人音响、网球拍、香水、CD、玩具和胶卷。在所有类别的消费品中,英国人的消费高于其他三个国家,幅度从较低的超过150万镑用于购买个人音响和网球拍,160万镑用于购买香水,超过160万镑用于购买CD和玩具到较高的超过170万镑用于购买胶卷。

德国人在全部六项消费品上的花销基本上是一样的,范围从略低于150万镑到略高于150万镑。意大利人在玩具和胶卷上的花销最多,几乎都接近160万镑,其余的各项消费大概在150万镑左右。在六种消费品的花费上法国的变化最大,范围从较低的刚过140万镑用于购买网球拍到较高的近170万镑用于购买胶卷。具有讽刺意味的是,法国香水很有名,而法国在香水上的花销最少,也许是因为在法国香水比较便宜的缘故。

谋篇布局

1. 题目分析:

这是一道典型的柱状图题。

2. 描写原则:

我们基本有两条思路:第一,每组柱子内部的比较,哪一根多,哪一根少。第二,不同组中相同属性的柱子连起来(比如在本题中把表示德国的六根柱子连起来),这些柱子多少的变化。

3. 本题分析:

(1) 上面讲的两条思路中,采取第二种思路比较容易把文章写得有变化。同样是第二条思路,还有两种变化。

第一,绝对数量的变化。德国从 personal stereos 到 photographic film 的消费钱数的变化。意大利、法国和英国的变化。范文2的主体就写了这些绝对数量的变化。其实,按照这种思路,这六组柱子可以转换成四条曲线(横坐标是六种不同消费,纵坐标是钱数,四条曲线代表四个国家)。

第二,相对排序的变化。英国在哪一个项目上在四个国家中花钱最多,多多少。德国在哪些项目上在四个国家中花钱最少,在哪些项目上花钱次少。法国和意大利的情况。范文1用的就是这种思路。但是,这两篇范文存在的一点小问题是:在描述排序的时候,最好把绝对数值一起交代出来。比如我们可以这样写德国的情况:德国人在所有消费品上的花销基本持平,并不存在任何一个比其他消费品更受欢迎的情况,大概是150万磅左右。

(2) 此外,还可以写实际情况与预期的是否相同。比如说两篇范文都提到法国以生产香水出名,但香水的消费量却是最少的。

(3) 必须指出的是,一定不要尝试去解释"为什么法国的香水消费不是最高的"。因为图表作文的要求是描写,而不是解释。

WRITING TASK 2

范文

范文1

When a country develops its technology, the traditional skills and ways of life hopefully will not completely die out. Trying to keep them alive is a very valuable effort, for two main reasons. First, traditional aspects of a culture are part of its history and should be maintained to a certain degree from the perspective of a national cultural identity. Second, traditional methods may prove economically valuable in the future.

Traditional skills and ways of life are often maintained for hundreds of years with few alterations. These types of skills may include weaving cloth, embroidery, agricultural methods, and celebratory customs with music and special costume. We often consider these traditions as the core culture of a country, after electric looms, tractors, and CD players have replaced all the traditional instruments. Industrialization inherently means a loss of uniqueness, as faceless machines become the producers for society. Therefore, people in industrialized countries should create new aspects to their culture, in addition to maintaining a representation of their traditional skills and ways of life.

Whereas newly industrializing nations may be very eager to push away their old traditional ways entirely, some of the oldest industrialized nations are in many ways moving back toward their traditional heritage. Take organic food for example, which has become a major industry in both Canada and the US. Organic food must be grown with no added chemical fertilizers or pesticides, much as was done before chemical fertilizers or pesticides were invented. Now many farmers have reverted to traditional farming methods, referring to their ancestors' ways to handle specific pest or disease problems.

Traditional skills and ways of life are an integral part of a nation's culture and should not be brushed aside just because of advancing technology. Traditional skills and ways of life are not necessarily economically worthless and should be kept alive, as illustrated by the example of growing organic food with traditional methods.

当一个国家发展科技的时候,传统技艺和生活方式有希望不完全消失。试图使它们继续发展是一种很有价值的努力,主要有两个理由:首先,一种文化的传统方面是其历史的一部分,并且从一个国家文化特性的角度来看,它应该被一定程度地保留。其次,传统的方法也许可以在未来被证明有经济价值。

传统技艺和生活方式通常被保留几百年而只有极少的改变。这些技艺可能包括织布、刺绣、农耕方法以及伴随着音乐和特殊装束的节庆习俗。在电子织布机、拖拉机和CD机取代全部这些工具之后,我们通常会把这些传统当作一个国家文化的核心。工业化生来就意味着独特性的消失,正如没有个性的的机器变成了社会的生产者。因此,在保留传统技艺和生活方式的代表的同时,工业国家的人们必须创造他们文化中新的方面。

新兴工业化进程中的国家也许更渴望彻底摒弃他们的老传统,然而一些老工业化国家则以多种方式回归他们的传统文化遗产。例如绿色食品,这已经变成了加拿大和美国的一项主导工业。绿色食品的种植就像化肥和农药发明之前那样,一定不能添加任何化肥和农药。现在许多农民返回传统的种植方式,参照他们祖先的方式去处理各种特殊的害虫和灾害问题。

传统技艺和生活方式是一个国家文化的有机组成部分,绝不能因为先进技术的出现而丢弃它们。传统技艺和生活方式正如用传统方法种植绿色食品的例子所诠释的那样,并非绝对毫无经济价值,而是应当继续保留它们。

范文2

I agree with the first sentence, but not with the second. When a country develops its technology, it is inevitable that traditional skills and ways of life die out, as they are replaced by the new technology and no longer needed. However, this need not be, and is not always, the case. Sometimes a craft will be handed down from generation to generation, kept alive for the few people able and willing to pay a higher price. For example, some pieces of furniture are still made without using any nails or screws, with the pieces all hand carved and fitting together perfectly. There are actually quite a few things still made by hand, not replaced by mass production, whether it is the handcrafted belt, shoe, hat or small decorative items for the home.

Similarly, the traditional ways of life die out, but sometimes not completely. In the "good old days" people used to write letters by hand, both for personal and for business purposes. Then the typewriter came along and replaced hand writing for business. Mailing letters in turn was replaced by using the fax machine, which has largely been replaced by using email. This too, is being replaced by SMS (short messages sent by cell phone) for personal communication. All of these have had an impact on our way of life. Nonetheless, hand-written letters will never completely die out.

It is not pointless, however, to try to keep the old traditions alive in some fashion. Many places have restored old towns to their original architecture and way of life to be a "living museum". One of the most famous of these is Colonial Williamsburg in Williamsburg, Virginia. Here, an entire town has been meticulously restored to the way it was several hundred years ago, to represent life as it used to be in the colonial times. It is a very popular tourist destination, especially for families, as it brings history alive for the children.

我同意第一句话的观点,但是我不同意第二句话的观点。当一个国家发展自己的科技时,传统技艺和生活方式的消亡是不可避免的,因为他们都被新的科技所取代而不再必不可少。但是不需要非得这样,也不会总是这样。有时候一种手工技艺薪火传承而存活下来是因为仍有少数的人能够并且愿意付高价。例如一些家具的构件就仍然不用任何钉子和螺丝来制造,每个部分都用手工刻槽,并且能严丝合缝。有很多东西实际上还是用手工制作的,并没有被大规模生产所取代,无论它是手工皮带、鞋、帽子还是家居小装饰。

与此类似的是,传统生活方式虽然消亡了,但是有的时候并不彻底。在"过去的好日子"里,无论是个人信件还是商业信函人们都用手书写。随后打字机出现了,取代了手写商业信函。邮寄信件依次又被传真机的使用所取代,传真机后来又大量被电子邮件取代。而作为个人交往手段的电子邮件后来又被手机短信取代了。所有这些都对我们的生活方式产生了巨大的影响,可手写信件却依旧没有完全消失。

然而,尝试以某种方式来保留老传统并非毫无意义。许多城镇都重建了他们的传统建筑并恢复了他们的传统生活方式,使之成为所谓的"活生生的博物馆"。这其中最著名的一个就是位于弗吉尼亚威廉姆斯堡的威廉姆斯殖民堡。整座塔一直被小心翼翼地按照几百年以前的样式重建了,用来代表殖民时代的生活。它是一个非常受欢迎的旅游目的地,尤其是对家庭来说,因为它为孩子们展示了活生生的历史。

谋篇布局

1. 读题:

这篇文章的中心事物是 traditional skills and ways of life。题干的评价是:it is pointless to keep。我们作一个两分法("好"还是"不好")的判断,结果是 traditional skills and ways of life 不好。题干

的理由是 When a country develops its technology, the traditional skills and ways of life die out.

2. 写提纲：

(1) 我们构思分论点的总体思路是：因为中心事物的本质和后果，所以我们对它的评价是好（不好）。

从本质上来讲，传统技术和生活方式是历史的一部分，是一个民族区别于另外一个民族的标准，所以传统文化要保持（见范文 1 的第 2 段）。

从后果上讲，传统的技术和生活方式还可以给人们带来经济效益，所以传统文化要保持（见范文 1 的第 3 段）。

(2) 如果你不同意题干的观点，我们还有另外一条思路：可以反驳题干给出的理由，指出题干对事实判断的失误。题干给出的理由是 the traditional skills and ways of life die out，你的分论点可以是"传统技术和生活方式没有消失"。

我们在这里再多作一点分析：如何把"传统技术和生活方式没有消失"拆分成两个分论点。这里有一个很重要的分论点思考的技巧。

我们先来看一个数学上的概念。

我们的任务是全集 I 有 X 性质。

我们可以将全集 I 分成两个子集 a 和 b。

我先证明 a 有 X 性质，然后证明 b 有 X 性质。

最后我就可以得到结论 I 有 X 性质。

同样的，为了证明"传统技术和生活方式没有消失"，

我可以先证明"传统技术没有消失"；然后证明"传统生活方式没有消失"；

这样也就证明了"传统技术和生活方式没有消失"。（见范文 2 的 1 段和 2 段）

(3) 范文 2 还提供了一种思路（分论点）：即使传统的东西消失了，在某些的时候也会恢复。（见第 3 段）

3. 首段的写作：引出要讨论的内容 + 表达你的观点

(1) 范文 1 和范文 2 都直接表达了作者的观点，没有任何的迂回曲折。这是西方人写文章的风格。

(2) 中国人写文章的风格是先要说说现在的科技发展是如何迅速，传统的东西如何被逼得退除了历史舞台。其实，如果语言表达得精彩，这样写也未尝不可。但是篇幅一定不能太长，一句话足够。

4. 中间段落的写作：分论点的论证

(1) 范文 1 的第二段用了解释论证。先具体解释什么是传统技术和生活方式，然后解释传统的东西如何对一个民族的内凝力起作用。

(2) 范文 1 的第三段以及范文 2 的全部段落都用了举例论证。

SPEAKING

I = Interviewer C = Candidate

范例 1

PART 1

I: Good morning, my name is John. Could you tell me your full name, please?

C: My full Chinese name is Jiang Wen, but you can call me Richard.

I: And where are you from, Richard?

C: I'm from Hangzhou, in Zhejiang province.

I: Ok, and may I see your identification please?

C: Sure, here you are.

I: Good. I'd like to start our interview today by asking you some questions about the important festivals in China. Can you describe some to me?

C: **Certainly.** I always like talking about Chinese festivals. The most important one, of course, is Spring Festival, also called the Chinese New Year. It usually occurs in January or February. Chinese people all try to go home to be with family during this festival. I think it is sort of like Christmas for western people.

I: What do you and your family do together during Spring Festival?

C: Well, eating is always an important part of the holiday. On the evening before the first day of the New Year the whole family has a very important meal. Traditionally, families always ate a big feast at home, but nowadays more and more people also go out to restaurants to eat.

I: What do you enjoy most about this holiday?

C: I think I really enjoy just being with my family. Since I'm in university far away, it's one of the few times I can see my parents and grandparents. Also, I have some good friends from middle school in my hometown.

I: Tell me, do you think festivals are important for a country, and why?

C: I certainly do believe festivals and holidays are very important for every country. Everyone is busy working or going to school, and needs to have some time to spend with their families or to relax and even to travel. Also, festivals have long traditions, and they are to celebrate important events in history. For instance, our October 1 holiday is very important to us, because it celebrates China becoming a new country, under a new government, in 1949.

[From part one to part two]

I: Ok, great. Now I'm going to give you a topic and I'd like you to talk about it for one to two minutes. Before you talk you'll have one minute to think about what you're going to say. You can make some notes if you wish. Do you understand?

C: Yes.

I: Ok, here is your topic, and here is some paper and a pencil for making notes. I'd like you to describe a film or TV program which has made a strong impression on you.

PART 2

Candidate's Notes on Paper

What film/TV program	Lord of the Rings
When saw	early this year
Story	return a gold ring
Why impressive	photography, use of high tech

I: Alright? Remember, you have one to two minutes for this so don't worry if I stop you. I'll tell you when the time is up. Can you start speaking now, please?

C: Sure. Not long ago, earlier this year, I went with my friends to see the Lord of the Rings, Return of the King. This film should be called a **fictional** film, because it's based on a **fantasy novel**. Because I didn't see the first two films, I was a bit confused by the story. As far as I could tell it was about some young people who were supposed to return a very important gold ring back to a special place. This ring was supposed to be magic in some way. On the way to return the ring the two young men ran into a lot of **difficulties and hardships**. They had a very funny **creature** who acted as their guide. This creature was not very **honorable**, wanted the gold ring for himself, and tried to take it. There was a very **wise** old man who had a lot of power, and a king who was afraid to go to battle to defend his city. There were also some brave young men and some beautiful women. Of course there were also several big battles, with lots of men and horses and very odd creatures. There was one creature that looked like a very big bird, which would attack the people on horses.

I thought the **photography** was very **impressive.** Nowadays they can do such magical things with the computer, and make things look very real. I think it deserved many of the **Oscars** that it won. The main idea of the story was that it was the **good forces** against the **evil forces**. And, of course, just as one would guess, in the end the good forces won, though they made it exciting because sometimes you couldn't be sure they would win. The thing that **impressed** me the most was the photography and the use of **high technology.**

I: Why do you think this film was so popular all over the world?

C: I think because it is interesting to people of all ages and they could enjoy watching it. Young people **for sure** liked it, and even older people could be interested. For example, my parents, who almost never go to movies, also went to see it.

PART 3

I: Ok, we've been talking about films and TV programs. I'd like to discuss with you one or two more general questions relating to this topic. First, let's **consider cinema-going habits**. Do you think the cinema has increased or decreased in popularity in recent years?

C: I definitely think it has increased in popularity in recent years. One reason is that there are more and better films than in the past. The number of foreign films allowed into China is still **limited**, but there are more films coming in from HK and Taiwan, and better films being **produced** by Chinese people.

I: Any other reasons?

C: Yes, people have more **spending money** than before, so they can **afford** to go to the movies more often.

I: In your opinion, will this **trend** continue into the future?

C: Yes, I think it will. There will always be many people who watch movies at home on their DVD player, because it's much cheaper and more convenient. But young people especially enjoy going out and going to the movies with their friends. It's a nice **social** thing to do.

I：What are the advantages and disadvantages of making films of **real-life events**?

C：I think the advantage is that people can relate to the story, because it's real-life. For instance, *Cell Phone*, a recent popular movie, was supposed to have been based on a real story, and I think most people watching it could **relate to** the story. The disadvantage of basing a movie on real-life is that it could be too **common**, too boring to people. People go to the movies to be entertained, and **get away from real life.**

I：Well, if a film is based on a true story, then how important do you think it is for a film-maker to **remain true** to the original story?

C：I personally don't think it makes that much difference if the story is exactly the same, or if the story is somewhat different. The important thing is for the movie to be interesting, and, if changing the story **here and there** makes it more interesting, then I think that's ok.

I：One final topic. I'd like to ask you about **censorship**. Should films and television be censored or should we be free to choose what we see?

C：Basically, I believe people should be free to choose. But I can see why it may be a good thing to have some kind of censorship. Some films may just have too much violence or other **unacceptable** scenes. I think the best thing is to have a **ratings system**, like in the U. S., to **prevent** young people from seeing certain films.

I：How do you think censorship laws will change in the next 20 years?

C：I guess the trend is to become freer, more **liberal.** So, in that case, the censorship laws will also be freer, and more **relaxed.**

I：That's the end of the interview. Thank you.

C：Thank you.

范例 2

PART 1

I：Good morning, my name is Barbara. Can you tell me your full name please?

C：My full name is Zhang Hong. You can call me Jane.

I：Okay, Jane. Can I see your identification please?

C：Sure, here you go.

I：I'd like to start by asking you some questions about festivals in your country. Tell me about the most important festival in your country.

C：The biggest festival in China is the Spring Festival, which usually **falls** in January or February. This festival celebrates the beginning of a new year and the new **growing season.**

I：What special foods and activities are **connected with** this festival?

C：On the **eve** of Spring Festival, we make **dumplings** and stay up all night watching CCTV's **TV special.** At midnight, we go out and set off **firecrackers.**

I：What do you enjoy most about Spring Festival?

C：Well, it's a tradition that the members of the older generation give the young children in the family **red envelopes** filled with money. I think this is my favorite part. All the children like to compete to see how much money they can get!

I：Do you think festivals are important for a country?

C：Yes, I think so.

I：Why is that?

C： Because they are events that **connect** one generation to the next. They also provide opportunities for relaxing and celebrating with family and close friends. This is really important to me because my **extended family** gets together only once a year at this special time.

[From part one to part two]

I： Ok, great. Now I'm going to give you a topic, and I'd like you to talk about it for one to two minutes. Before you talk you'll have one minute to think about what you're going to say. You can make some notes if you wish. Do you understand?

C： Yes.

I： Ok, here is your topic, and here is some paper and a pencil for making notes. I'd like you to describe a film or **TV program** which has made a strong impression on you.

PART 2

Candidate's Notes on Paper

kind	music com., dram.
when	5 年 15 岁
about	family, governess, love
why impressive	romance, history

I： Alright? Remember, you have one to two minutes for this so don't worry if I stop you. I'll tell you when the time is up. Can you start speaking now, please?

C： Okay. One of the films I have seen that made a big impression on me is *The Sound of Music*, with Julie Andrews. This film is a **musical comedy**, although it has some **dramatic elements** as well. I first saw this movie five years ago, when I was fifteen years old.

The film is about a large family in **Vienna** that gets a **governess** from England. The family has eight children, and a father who uses the same **military discipline** with his children as he does with **his men**. The governess, played by Julie Andrews, is sent to the family from the **convent** where she was living. The children respond very well to her kindness and gentleness, and especially like the songs she sings and games she plays. Even though he seems serious and **disapproving**, the father falls in love with the governess, Maria. She is very shy and still thinks of herself as a nun, but discovers that she loves him and the children and they eventually marry. The final scenes of the movie show the family's escape from the **Nazis** in Vienna. They travel into **the Alps** on foot, where they finally reach freedom.

The film made an impression on me for two reasons. One was that the simple romantic relationships—between Maria and the father, and between the oldest daughter and her boyfriend—were **ideal models** of romance for a young girl. They all seemed to **fall in love** so easily, and that is what I think all girls hope for. The other reason was that the movie **took place** in a European country during a time in history about which I knew very little. Seeing how the father **determined** to **escape persecution** by the Nazis and seeing the **aggressive** behavior of the **German** soldiers made me aware that there is much about **human nature** and history that I have yet to learn.

I： Did you learn anything from the movie?

C： Yes. I learned that it is important for members of a family to work together to achieve their goals. I also learned about the lives of people who are persecuted in wartime. I had never really studied any European history, and watching that movie **stimulated** my interest.

I: One of my favorite parts was the music.

C: Yes, I also enjoyed the music, especially the way the governess used music with the children she was caring for. Actually, learning those songs is a good way to practice English!

PART 3

I: Ok, we've been talking about films and TV programs. Now I would like to ask you some more general questions, still on the topic of media and movies. Do you think **the cinema** has increased or decreased in popularity in recent years?

C: I believe the cinema has definitely increased in popularity in recent years. One of the reasons for this is that movies are **available** now on DVD, making them **affordable** for many more people. Also, there is much more money being spent on making films, not only in China, but in America and India as well.

I: In your opinion, will this **trend** continue into the future?

C: **I am certain** that this trend will continue into the future. There is always a **desire** for **leisure activities** that provide a view of situations and places that are new to us. **To put it simply**, there is such a **huge investment** in this industry that it couldn't possibly do anything but get bigger.

I: What are the advantages and disadvantages of making films of **real-life events**?

C: Hmm... The advantage of making films of real-life events is that they provide information and opinions about real historical and **current events**. The disadvantage of **realistic** movies is that because of **the nature of human interactions**, there is a lot of violence in these movies. In general, I think the advantages outweigh the disadvantages. After all, we can always stop the movie if it becomes too violent for us, and it is usually **beneficial** to learn about past events.

I: How important do you think it is for a **filmmaker** to remain true to the original story?

C: I think it depends on the vision of the filmmaker and what he wants to tell us through the film. I don't think it is entirely necessary to **adhere strictly** to the original story, as movies are both **visual** and **auditory**, and details may have to be added or **altered**. Sometimes the filmmaker can provide some important **insight** into a story. Other times, the filmmaker can turn an important historical event into a movie with both historical accuracy and great **emotional impact**, like ***Schindler's List***, for example.

I: Should films and television be **censored** or should we be free to choose what we watch?

C: I do not believe there should be an official body to censor what is available on TV. Adults should be **capable** of deciding the quality of what they watch. They should also be capable of deciding for their children what is **acceptable** viewing material. I think the current system of **rating** movies is helpful to parents in deciding what their children should watch. I don't think children should **be exposed** to violence at a very young age because they may develop violent **tendencies.**

I: How do you think censorship laws will change in the next 20 years?

C: Because China is opening up and becoming more liberal, I believe there will be less and less censorship. I believe that this function will move from the government to the individual, and I know that there are already tools to **restrict** what is available to children on the family TV. Censorship will always exist, and that's a good thing, but I believe the public has a right to know what is happening around them, both locally and abroad.

I: Thank you, that was very interesting. It was nice talking to you. That's all for the interview.

词汇表

范例 1	
certainly 当然	limited 受限制的
feast 盛宴	produce 制作、生产
fictional 虚构的	spending money 个人零用钱
fantasy novel 奇幻小说	afford 付得起
difficulties and hardships 艰难困苦	trend 趋势
creature 演员	social 社交的
honorable 光彩的	real-life events 现实事件
wise 睿智的	base on 基于
photography 摄影	relate to 涉及
impressive 吸引人的	get away from real life 脱离现实生活
Oscar 奥斯卡奖	remain true to 忠实于
good forces 正义的力量	here and there 到处
evil forces 邪恶的力量	censorship 审查制度、审查机构
impress 给…深刻印象	unacceptable 不被接受的、禁止的
high tech 高科技	ratings system 分级系统
for sure 确实	prevent 阻止
consider 考虑	liberal 宽松的、自由的
cinema-going habits 看电影的习惯	relaxed 不严格的、宽松的

范例 2	
fall 来临	determine 下决心
growing season 耕种季节	escape persecution 逃离迫害
connect with 与…有联系	aggressive 侵略性的
dumplings 饺子	German 德国人
TV special 特别节目	human nature 人性
firecrackers 鞭炮	stimulate 激起
red envelopes 红包	the cinema 电影院
connect 连接	available 可用的
extended family 数代同堂的大家庭	affordable 买得起的
TV program 电视节目	trend 趋势
musical comedy 音乐喜剧	I am certain 我肯定
dramatic elements 戏剧元素	desire 渴望
Vienna 维也纳	leisure activities 休闲活动
governess 女家庭教师	to put it simply 简单地说
military discipline 军纪	huge investment 巨额投资
his men 他的士兵	real-life events 现实的事件
convent 修道院	current events 最近的事件
disapprove 反对	realistic 现实主义的
Nazis 纳粹	the nature of human interactions 人的交际本能
the Alps 阿尔卑斯山	beneficial 受益的
ideal models 完美典范	filmmaker 制片人
fall in love 相爱	adhere strictly to 严格忠实于
take place 发生	visual 可视的

auditory 可听的	acceptable 合适的、满意的
alter 改变	rating 分级的
insight 见识、洞察力	be exposed 被暴露于
emotional impact 情感影响	tendency 倾向
censor 审查	restrict 限定
capable 有能力的	Schindler's List 辛德勒名单

补充词汇及句型

Part 1: Festivals

Common Chinese Festivals	
Spring Festival/Chinese New Year	The Lantern Festival
The Dragon Boat Festival	May Day/Labor Day/International Worker's Day
Mid-Autumn Festival/The Moon Festival	National Day
Festival Activities/Food	
setting off fireworks/ firecrackers	eating together
visiting relatives	dumplings
parades	mooncakes
flag-rasing ceremony	zongzi
red envelopes filled with money	

Festivals give people a time to celebrate. They also help to express and carry on a country's culture.

Part 2: Film or TV Program

Types of Films/TV Programs	
comedy	action
situation comedy (sitcom)	reality show
horror	romance
drama	romantic comedy
musical	

Part 3: Cinema-going habits, drama of real/fictional events, censorship and freedom

The cinema has...	
increased in popularity because...	decreased in popularity because...
people have more spending money.	more people have DVD players at home.
movies are getting better and better.	the quality of movies is declining.
less people like to read books.	people download movies on their computers and watch them at home.
Films of Real-Life Events	
Advantages	Disadvantages

interesting learn about real-life events audience relates to story	invasion of privacy distort the truth sometimes violent
Films and television...	
should be censored because... ...children might imitate what they see on TV. ...people shouldn't be exposed to sex and violence. ...society shouldn't glorify sex and violence.	shouldn't be censored because... ...we should all be free to watch what we want. ...parents should be responsible for what their kids watch. ...children shouldn't be shielded from the real world.

口试要点聚焦

问题听不懂怎么办?

雅思口试中,学生们面对的最麻烦的问题之一就是听不懂考官的提问。事实上,这种现象在面试中屡见不鲜,可很多学生还是不知如何应对。他们变得紧张不安,或者沉默不语,或者不懂装懂。说实话,不懂装懂麻烦最大了,因为它最终常常是答非所问。

那么,如果听不懂考官的提问该怎么办呢?通常,你要让考官知道你没有搞懂他的问题,这样你才能够与他继续正常交流。问题听不懂时,你可以这样说:

- I'm sorry?
- I beg your pardon?
- Excuse me?
- I'm sorry; I didn't catch what you said. Could you please repeat the question?
- I'm sorry, I don't quite understand. Could you please say that one more time?

考官会如何反应随口试阶段不同而不同。

在第一阶段,考官一般来说会逐字重复该问题,但通常只重复一遍。如果重复之后你还不懂,他往往会接着问下一个问题。别紧张!保持镇静、集中精神回答下一个问题。事实上,这对你有利,说不定下一个问题你更有把握呢。在第一阶段,考官不会解释问题中某些具体的词或把问题换个方式提出来。

在口试第二阶段,如果确实有必要,你可以要求考官解释卡片上你不懂的某个词。然而,你要知道,卡片上的问题设计得很周全,即使英语水平很差的学生也应该能懂。所以如果你连卡片上某个词的意义还要问,考官由此可以看出你水平很差。大多数情况下,考官不会解释该词的意义。

在第三阶段,由于话题较为复杂,所以考官常常会解释某些词的意义,或者把整个问题换个方式重述一遍。因此,在这一阶段,除了上面提到的句子,下面的表达方式也很有用。

- Could you rephrase that?
- What do you mean by...?

事实上,如果考官发现你没听懂或答不出某个问题,不用你请求,他们也常常会换个方式把问题再说一遍的。

重要的是要记住你可以请求考官重复或解释问题,事实上这比胡乱猜测或坐在那儿不知所措好得多。如果你每个问题都要求考官重复,这当然会影响到你的成绩。但要求重复一两次不可能对你的分数产生实质性的影响。

Test 3

LISTENING

SECTION 1

谈话场景：活动日程安排场景。
人物关系：同事之间。
谈话话题：讨论圣诞晚宴的安排。

词汇注释

sort out 弄清楚，分析明白
hang over （不愉快的事情）逼近，威胁
definite *adj.* 肯定的，明确的，确定的
work out 计算出，设计出
straightforward *adj.* 明确的，简单的，直接的
book *v.* 预定
hopeless *adj.* 没有希望的，绝望的
be bound to 一定…的，应该会…
pack *v.* 塞满，挤满
back-up *n.* 候补，后援，支持
reliable *adj.* 可靠的，可信赖的
ring *v.* 打电话
decent *adj.* 像样的，不错的，得体的
vegetarian *adj.* 素食的；*n.* 素食者
non-smoking *adj.* 禁烟的，无烟的
remind *v.* 提醒，使想起
onion *n.* 洋葱
soup *n.* 汤
roast *adj.* 烤肉的，烘烤的
lentil *n.* 兵豆，扁豆
curry *n.* 咖喱饭
tasty *adj.* 美味的，可口的
unusual *adj.* 不普通的，非同寻常的
dessert *n.* 甜点，饭后点心
plum *n.* 葡萄干
pudding *n.* 布丁
plus *prep.* 加上
deposit *n.* 押金，定金
confirm *v.* 确认
confirmation *n.* 确认
in advance 提前
guarantee *v.* 保证，确保
café *n.* 咖啡馆
notice board 布告栏
newsletter *n.* 业务通讯，时事剪报
bet *n.* 打赌，赌注

交际与语言表达

1. 本段对话为两个同事讨论公司圣诞晚餐的安排，所用语言非常口语化，而且西方人的幽默通过简单的对白呼之欲出，考生在口语练习时完全可以借用其中的表达和词句。
2. Let’s try and get it sorted out today so we don’t have it hanging over us. 我们尽量今天就搞定这事，就不用老想着它了。hang over 的意思很多，此处指一些不愉快的事情或者未完成的工作总是积压在心里，时不时地总得想着还没做完。
3. . . . which is going to be pretty difficult to book at Christmas so we’d better think of two or three places just to be on the safe side. 圣诞期间很难预定到（位子），我们最好想出两三个地方以防万一。
4. We ought to go for something more expensive, ’cos you. . . you get what you pay for. 我们应该找个更贵的地方，因为物有所值。口语中经常用’cos 代替 because。

5. The new Indian restaurant is supposed to be excellent. 那家新的印度餐厅应该不错。be supposed to 应该,想来。
6. It's bound to be packed. 那里肯定很挤。be bound to 的意思很多,此处接近 be sure to,表示肯定语气。
7. I think you'll find some people won't be able to go that high. 我觉着有些人不愿意出那么高的价。这句话的理解一定要根据上下文去分析,而不能单独猜测它的意思,本段对话中有很多这样的例子。
8. And a non-smoking section! You know what the boss is like. 还得是在非吸烟区!你知道我们老板什么样子。从上下文推断,他们的老板应该很讨厌吸烟。
9. I found Rajdoot's number straight away and they can fit us in. Their Christmas menu sounds great. 我马上就找到了 Rajdoot 餐馆的号码,他们还有空座。他们的圣诞菜单听起来相当棒。
10. I said I'd check with the staff first. But they did say they'd hold the booking until next Wednesday anyway. And if we go ahead, they'd like a £50 deposit. 我说我得先回去跟我们的员工商量一下,但他们说他们怎么着都会把我们的预定保留到下周三。如果我们的确要预定,要交 50 英镑的押金。
11. The newsletter is probably your best bet. 业务通讯可能是你最好的选择。bet 本意是指赌注,打赌。口语中说你最好的赌注是什么,也就是说是你最好的选择。

考题解析

Questions 1–10

这 10 道题目从做题的角度来说,没有任何技巧,只要把握空格前后处的单词,答案应该没有问题。例如第一题考查一个一个字母的拼写,第四题是考查一个一个数字的拼写,都是最简单的基本功。第 2 题、第 3 题和第 6 题有一定难度,虽然每个答案都念了两三遍,但让考生填写的内容非常生僻,要么是一个考生不熟悉的专有名词,却不告诉考生如何去拼写,要么是考生一辈子都可能接触不到的某种食物。这种情况在真正的雅思考试中出现得不多。如果出现,考生应尽量根据所听到的语音去推测该词的拼写。

SECTION 2

谈话场景: 运动设施情况说明会。
人物关系: 说话者为体育中心负责人,听众为学生。
谈话话题: 介绍体育中心的构造和运作。

词汇注释

facility *n.* 设施	**discount** *n.* 折扣,打折
membership *n.* 会员资格	**session** *n.* 学期,期间
entitle *v.* 给…以权利	**volleyball** *n.* 排球
annual *adj.* 每年的,年度的	**badminton** *n.* 羽毛球
register *v.* 登记	**aerobics** *n.* 增氧健身法(指跑步、散步、游泳等加强心肺等循环功能的运动)
passport *n.* 护照	
photograph *n.* 照片	**dance studio** 舞蹈排练场
issue *v.* 发放	**intimate** *adj.* 亲密的,私密的
allow *v.* 允许	**ballet** *n.* 芭蕾
opening hours 开放时间	**martial arts** 武术

separate *adj.* 分开的，单独的，分隔的	**court** *n.* 球场
park *n.* 停车场	**fitness room** 健身房
squash *n.* 壁球	**appeal** *n.* 呼吁

交际与语言表达

1. 本段文章尽管是一段独白，但应该把它与第二套题第一部分的对话放在一起学习，因为无论从说话的语气上，还是从出题的方式上，这两个部分都非常接近，一起复习有助于找出共同的规律。
2. All students at the college are entitled to become members of the Sports Center. 所有在校生都有权成为体育中心的会员。entitle sb. to do sth. 授予某人做某事的权利。后文中有一句用法相同：We also have an arrangement with the local tennis club, . . . , entitling our students to use their courts on weekday mornings in the summer。
3. We can't issue your card unless you bring all three. 我们不会把卡发给你，除非你把三样东西都带来。
4. For those of you who are up and about early in the morning, we are introducing a 50 per cent 'morning discount' this year. 对于你们中那些早上很早就起来走动的人，我们今年实行了一种50%的"晨练折扣"。
5. This is our newest facility, only completed in the Spring, but it is already proving to be one of the most popular. 这是我们最新的设施，今年春天才建成的，但已经成为最受欢迎的设施之一。completed 引导的分词短语是做 facility 的后置定语；prove to be sth.（被证明）成为……。
6. As well as all these facilities available here on the campus, we also have an arrangement with the local tennis club. 除了在校园这里可以使用的设施，我们还与当地的网球俱乐部有合作安排。as well as 表示（在……之外）"也，又"，可以引导从句或词组。

考题解析

Questions 11–12

这两道题不少考生会做错，原因是听力原文念得比较快，两个答案在一秒钟内迅速读过。试卷表格中是让考生填£ ________ per ________，可以判断前面是一个数字，而后面是单位。原文中很快读过的那句话是 **an annual fee of £** 9.50。**annual** 表示每年的，年度的，所以 per 后面应该填 **year**。**£** 9.50 在原文中读作 **nine pounds fifty**，这种读法很多考生以前并不熟悉，要注意货币的读法。

Questions 13–16

这几道题中有好几道答案不断重复，做题时应紧紧抓住空格前后的提示词，有的答案如16题完全可以根据上下文先行预测，然后核对所听和所预测的即可。

Questions 17–20

17题–20题是地图题，首先应分析图中的已知地名有哪些，大概判断各题号所代表的地名与已知地名的关系，并根据听力原文确定讲话者现在何处。

讲话者首先提到 **this room we are in at the moment is called the Main Hall**，暗示了听众所处的地方就是 **Main Hall**，而且后面的地点很可能是以这个地点为参照的。

Questions 17–18

介绍 **Main Hall** 之后，讲话者提到 **on the other side of the reception area there is the dance studio**。结合前句，可以判断 Main Hall 是在 reception area 的 this side，而图中跟 Main Hall 相关的地点只有17题，而17题的地点又紧挨着18题，所以这一句话提供了两个答案，即17题为 **reception**，而18题为 **dance studio**。

Question 19

考生在看题阶段应该确定19题与旁边的car park有很大的关系，听力原文中提到：**on the other side of the car park... there are the squash courts**，明确地给出了答案。即使这句话没有完全听清，后面马上补充**six of them**，可以帮助考生确定答案为**squash courts**。

Question 20

19题完了之后讲话者提到**at the far end of the building a fitness room**，用一个独立主格结构带出了要找的最后一个地名。

SECTION 3

谈话场景：课外讨论场景。
人物关系：师生关系。
谈话话题：讨论比赛申请表格的填写。

词汇注释

entry *n.* 进入，登录	**length** *n.* 长度
electronic *adj.* 电子的	**width** *n.* 宽度
engineer *n.* 工程师	**depth** *n.* 深度
competition *n.* 比赛	**approximate** *adj.* 大约的，大概的
jigsaw *n.* 拼图玩具	**main** *n.* 电线，干线
beeper *n.* 传呼机	**battery** *n.* 电池
designer *n.* 设计者	**feature** *n.* 特色，特征
electronics *n.* 电子学，电子设备	**educational** *adj.* 有教育意义的
surname *n.* 姓	**electrics** *n.* 电路，电灯
puzzle *n.* 难题，迷宫游戏	**brilliant** *adj.*（口语中）极棒的，非常好的
visually *adv.* 视力上地	**comment** *n.* 评论
handicap *v.* 加障碍于，妨碍	**envisage** *v.* 设想，预见
handicapped *adj.* 残疾的	**plastic** *adj.* 塑料的
equipment *n.* 设备	**range** *n.* 系列，范围

交际与语言表达

1. 本段对话是地道的口语表达，两个人在说话的时候都有针对前文的省略语，很多地方必须理解上文某人说的话才能理解下文另一人所说的话，这在口语中很常见。
2. I just wondered if you could help me with this entry form for the Young Electronics Engineer competition. 我就想问问您能不能帮我填写这份青少年电子工程师比赛的表格。当礼貌地请别人帮助自己的时候，就可以用这个句型：I just wondered if you could help me with...。
3. Too long. Just say blind puzzle, that'll do.（你说的）太长了，就叫作盲人拼图，肯定没问题。do在这里指“发挥作用，起作用”。
4. It's the next bit that I'm really not sure what to put. 就是下个部分我真不知道该填什么。这个句子是强调句型，所强调的内容为**the next bit**，后面用that连接。原句可以写成：I'm really not sure what to put in the next bit. 但这样的表达太平淡，没有强调句有力。

5. Special features means, what is really new about this, you know, suitable for the group you made it for. 额外的特色是指这个东西有什么地方真的很新颖,对它的使用对象很合适。you know 在口语中可以位于句子前面或后面,本身没有任何特定的含义,一般与某种解释相连,有时起到提示或强调的作用,有时仅仅是一个人的口头禅。说话的时候,如果过于频繁使用 you know,会被人认为缺乏清楚表达的能力。
6. There you are, you've done it. Anything else? 没问题,你已经做到这一点了。还有别的吗? **There you are** 在口语中经常表示认为对方已经到达了其目的地,或已实现了最初的目标。
7. What do they mean by other comments? 他们所说的"其他意见"是指什么? sb. mean... by sth. 某人所提及的某物是……这个句型常用来解释一些抽象的概念。
8. We've got a lot of work on at the moment and we want to get it as good as we can. 我们现在手头还有很多事情要做,我们想尽可能地做到最好。on 这里表示工作正在进行的状态;as good as we can 与我们能做到(的最好的)一样。
9. Why not say that? 干嘛不定那个(日期)呢? why not 句型表示一种肯定的建议。
10. Glad to be of help. Very best of luck to you both. 很高兴能帮助你,祝你们两个好运。在口语中,这种祝福、寒暄之类的话经常省略主语。be of help = be helpful, 对……有帮助的。

考题解析

Questions 21–22

这两道题对所有考生都比较简单。21 题答案在听力原文中是一个一个字母拼出来的,22 题题干已经标明是填年龄,听的时候应注意数字。

Question 23

这道题答案出现之前,老师先问 what have you called the design? 此时考生应该集中注意力听后面出现的名称。男生回答了一长串的 **jigsaw puzzle design for the visually handicapped** 后,老师说 too long. Just say **blind puzzle**。考生这里填写 **blind puzzle** 或者 **jigsaw puzzle** 都可以,但关键是考生是否知道这些词的拼写和含义。

Question 24

这道题的难点在于 3 个数字一个都不能错,而且必须是按照宽度、长度和深度的顺序填写。听力原文本身并没有难度,都是很直白地读出宽、长和深各是多少,所以考生唯一要加强的是对英语数字的熟悉程度。

Questions 25–30

这几道题目只要把握好试卷上空格前后的文字,答案不会有太大问题,除非考生的词汇量不够。一个细节问题是 28 题应该注意答案是 **electrics**,而不是 **electric**。

SECTION 4

谈话场景：学术报告场景。

人物关系：主讲者为动物养殖专家。

谈话话题：介绍鸵鸟的养殖前景和注意事项。

词汇注释

rear *v.* 饲养，培养
poultry *n.* 家禽
livestock *n.* 家养动物
concentrate *v.* 集中注意力，专心做某事
domesticated *adj.* 驯养的，教化的
ostrich *n.* 鸵鸟
association *n.* 协会，理事会
breed *v.* 养育，饲养，繁殖
supermarket *n.* 超市
feature *v.* 以…为特色，特写
beef *n.* 牛肉
lamb *n.* 羊肉
pork *n.* 猪肉
kangaroo *n.* 袋鼠
slightly *adv.* 稍微地
tough *adj.* 硬的，艰苦的
crocodile *n.* 鳄鱼
pale *adj.* 颜色苍白的
tender *adj.* 嫩的，温柔的
fashionable *adj.* 时髦的，流行的
fatty *adj.* 含脂肪的，肥胖的
increasingly *adv.* 日益增加的
texture *n.* 质地，质感，结构，构造
feather *n.* 羽毛
tribal *adj.* 部落的
ceremonial *adj.* 正式的，仪式上的
export *v.* 出口
decorate *v.* 装饰，修饰
out of fashion 过时的，不再流行的
hide *n.* 兽皮，皮革
square meter 平方米
leather *n.* 皮革，皮制品
delicate *n.* 细致优雅的
stuff *n.* 东西，事物
biltong *n.* 晒干的肉条
recognize *v.* 承认，认可
protein *n.* 蛋白质
cholesterol *n.* 胆固醇
hindquarter *n.* 后臀及后腿
climate *n.* 气候
embark on 从事，着手，启动
mature *adj.* 成熟的
fertilized *adj.* 受精的
capital *n.* 资本，资金
incubator *n.* 恒温箱，孵化器
dependent *adj.* 依赖的
minder *n.* 照看者，照管者
intensively *adv.* 集中地，加强地
calf *n.* 牛仔，小牛
lay *v.* 产（卵）
hatch *v.* 孵化
nourish *v.* 滋养，使健壮
initial *adj.* 最初的
outlay *n.* （用于某特定目的的）花费，开支
profit margin 利润空间

交际与语言表达

1. Today I'd like to introduce Ted Hunter, who used to rear sheep and poultry but who is here to tell us about a rather unusual type of livestock that he's been concentrating on in the last few years. 今天我要向大家介绍 Ted Hunter。他过去养殖过绵羊和家禽，不过今天在这里他要给我们讲讲他这几年一直专心研究的一种不寻常的动物。sb. has been doing sth. 现在完成进行时，表示某一个动作在此前的一段时间一直持续在做，未曾间断。此外考生还应该比较一下前后几套题中主持人是如何介绍演讲者的。

2. When you look at international restaurant menus and supermarkets they all tend to feature the same range of meats-beef, lamb, chicken, pork, that sort of thing. 你看看全世界的饭店菜单或者超市，发现他们卖的肉类一模一样：牛肉、羊肉、鸡肉、猪肉，诸如此类。that sort of thing 置于句末，相当于 etc., and so on。
3. Now a third type of meat becoming increasingly available, and the one that I think is by far the nicest of the three, is ostrich. 现在越来越多的第三种肉类，也是我认为三种肉类中最好的，是鸵鸟肉。by far 用在比较级或最高级前面，起强调作用，没有什么实际含义。
4. However, it's much better for you than beef, as we'll see later. 但对大家来说，它比牛肉好得多，我们呆会儿就会明白这一点。as 此处引导的是特殊的定语从句，所代替的是前面整句话的内容。
5. A series of European taste tests found that 82% of people prefer ostrich to beef. 一系列欧洲味觉测试表明 82% 的人喜欢鸵鸟肉甚于牛肉。prefer sth. to sth. 喜欢前者甚于后者。
6. However, setting up an ostrich farm isn't something to **embark on** lightly. 但是，建立一个鸵鸟养殖场并不是件能轻易启动的事情。黑体字是考生应学习的词组，下同。
7. **In addition**, ostriches can't be intensively farmed—they need space and exercise. 此外，鸵鸟不能集中饲养，它们需要足够的空间和运动。
8. But in spite of this they make good farming sense. 尽管如此，鸵鸟还是很有养殖价值的。make a... sense 在……方面有意义。
9. This is very different from the situation in the wild, where the **vast majority** of chicks will die or be killed before they grow up into mature ostriches. 这与野生的情况大不一样，绝大部分野生鸵鸟在长大之前就死去或被猎食。
10. So, it's possible, once the initial outlay has been made, for the farmer to be looking at very good profit margins indeed. 因此，一旦最初的资金到位，养殖者的确有可能看到很好的利润空间。once 引导的从句插入到主句中，这种情况在书面语言中很常见。

考题解析

Questions 31–32

有的考生可能不知道 kangaroo 为何物，考试时不要管它，只要大概猜测该词的发音。听到这个词或类似的发音读出后，就要注意其后的内容。

It looks and tastes rather **like rabbit**, **though** it's slightly darker in color, **but** it is rather **tough**, **so** that's a **problem** for some people. 这句话中有很多提示性的关键词和重要的连词。注意 though 并不是跟后文的 but 连用，而是对前面一句的转折；而 but 引导的内容是对作为一个整体的前面两句的转折。

Question 33

在 31 题和 32 题之后，听力原文把鸵鸟肉和牛肉进行了比较；即使这个地方没有听到，后文念到的许多地方，甚至从试卷上的 37 题都可以判断出此处是 **beef**。

Questions 34–36

这几道题的关键是注意横纵轴和前后文的关键词提示，只要把答案的核心词写出来即可。如 34 题写出 fans 即可，但如果前面加上定语，要注意 ladies' 的拼写。35 题也只用写出 feather，尽管原文对它有许多修饰词语。36 题 meat 一词在原文中反复出现。

Question 37

分析题目时，要看到其中两个选项是鸵鸟肉与牛肉的比较，在听的时候就应特别注意有关内容。题目中的 protein 一词可能有考生不认识，但如果把握好原文中提到 ostrich meat is slightly **higher** in

protein than beef 这句话中黑体字的任何一个词，就能确定选 A。

Question 38

题干中的最关键的地方在于 problem，所以听的时候应该去抓关键的贬义词。原文中首先提到 mature breeding birds are very **expensive**，听到这句话，应该大致确定选项。即使没有听到到底是什么昂贵，就可以排除 A 项。后文紧跟着说 even a fertilized ostrich egg isn't **cheap**，可以最终确定答案为 C。

Question 39

这道题很多考生不知道题干是什么意思。此处 reared on farms 是过去分词作后置定语，被修饰的关键词是 **ostrich chicks**。原文首先提到 the young **chicks** are very **dependent** on human **minders**，后文进一步解释 **need** a lot of **attention** from the people **looking after** them. 很多的关键词提示考生选 C。

Question 40

首先注意题干的关键词是 **profitable**，那么要选的内容必须与此相关。原文先把母牛和鸵鸟的繁殖情况对比，随后又把家养的鸵鸟与野生的鸵鸟存活率对比，最终的即使没有听到对比的具体内容，也应该可以判断出正确的答案 C。

READING

READING PASSAGE 1

文章结构

体　　裁	说明为主
主要内容	人种史馆独特的收藏重点和意义。
结　　构	第 1 段：人种史馆简介。
	第 2 段：人种史馆收藏特点。
	第 3 段：具体收藏品。
	第 4 段：收藏品的意义。
	第 5 段：承接上段，收藏的价值意义。
	第 6 段：展望。

词汇注释

文　章	
第 1 段	
ethnography *n.* 民族志学，人种学	**extraordinary** *adj.* 非常的；特别的；非凡的
antiquity *n.* 古老；古代；古代遗物	**mundane** *adj.* 世界的；世俗的；平凡的
kingdom *n.* 王国；领域	**banal** *adj.* 平凡的；陈腐的；老一套的
significance *n.* 意义；重要性	
第 2 段	
approximately *adv.* 近似地；大约	**scholar** *n.* 学者
artifact *n.* 手工艺品	

第 3 段	
carry out 贯彻，执行；完成，实现	**assemblage** *n.* 与会者；集合；集会
anthropological *adj.* 人类学的；人类学上的	**herdsman** *n.* 牧者；牧人
collaboration *n.* 协作；通敌	**ritual** *adj.* 典礼的；宗教(仪式)的
institution *n.* 公共机构，协会，制度	**occasion** *n.* 场合；机会，时机
textile *n.* 纺织品	**acquisition** *n.* 获得；获得物
Bolivia *n.* 玻利维亚	**camel** *n.* 骆驼；(打捞用的)浮筒
Guatemala *n.* 危地马拉	**trappings** *n.* 服饰；马饰
Indonesia *n.* 印尼	**adornment** *n.* 装饰，装饰品
coracle *n.* 小圆舟	**evolution** *n.* 进展，发展，演变，进化
reed *n.* 芦苇	**ceremony** *n.* 典礼，仪式，礼节，报幕员
Arctic *n.* 北极，北极圈	**possess** *vt.* 拥有；持有
canoe *n.* 独木舟；轻舟	
第 4 段	
in terms of 根据，按照，在…方面	**ecological** *adj.* 生态学的；社会生态学的
absence *n.* 缺乏，没有	**constraint** *n.* 约束；强制；局促
draw on 利用；招来	**exceptional** *adj.* 例外的；异常的
ingenuity *n.* 独创性；机灵	**disposable** *adj.* 可任意使用的
第 5 段	
assume *v.* 假定，设想，采取，呈现	**advent** *n.* 出现；到来
assimilation *n.* 同化；同化作用；消化	**trading** *n.* 贸易
irrevocable *adj.* 不能取消的	**destruction** *n.* 破坏，毁灭
alter *vt.* 改变	**indigenous** *adj.* 本土的；本地的
realisation *n.* 认识；实现	**ritually** *adv.* 依据仪式上地，仪式上地
marginal *adj.* 边缘的；边际的	**invert** *vt.* 使颠倒；使转换
in spite of 不管；尽管	**utilitarian** *adj.* 功利的；实利的；功利主义的
integration *n.* 综合；整体	**aesthetic** *adj.* 美学的；审美的；有美感的
notoriously *adv.* 声名狼藉地	**category** *vt.* 分类为
第 6 段	
database *n.* 数据库；资料库	**responsibility** *n.* 责任，职责
anthropologist *n.* 人类学者；人类学家	**multicultural** *adj.* 多元文化的

考题解析

Questions 1–6

- 题型归类：TRUE/ FALSE/ NOT GIVEN
- 题目解析：

题目编号	题目定位词	答案位置	题解
1	twentieth-century, mainstream societies, US, Europe	第 1 段第 3 句	题目：20 世纪的收藏品主要来自于美国和欧洲等主流社会。 原文：尽管这包括了诸如非洲的复杂的王国、美洲的古老帝国，但其在 20 世纪的注意力焦点还是一直集中在小规模的社会群体上面。

2	modern societies	第 2 段首句	题目:人种史馆主要针对现代社会。 原文:人种史馆的收藏品中包括将近 30 万件人工制品,其中约有半数系本世纪的产品。 除了这句话外,本文其他许多地方都可以判断出人种史馆的主要收藏品不是现代社会的。比如文章后面提到的 canoes, textiles。机敏的考生注意本文配的图片也能猜出正确答案。
3	single, unrelated objects	第 2 段第 3 句话	题目:人种史馆注意收集单独的,不相关的,但有巨大价值的物品。 原文:为此目的,文物征集的重点往往不在个别、零星的文物上,而更重视成批发现的古物,因为后者能够大面积展示一个社会的文化面貌。
4	textile	第 3 段第 2 句	题目:人种史馆的纺织品收集是世界上最大的。 原文:收集到的材料包括著名的技术系列,例如,来自玻利维亚、危地马拉、印度尼西亚和西非地区的纺织品,或是类似小船之类的人工制品。
5	traditional, technology, inventive	第 4 段第 4、5 句话	题目:传统社会在技术上十分善于发明创造。 原文:事实上,传统的惯例是吸取并利用源源不断的技术创新的源泉。资源的局限性和生态环境的约束性往往被个人的技能所克服,所以在西方人眼中看来,这种个人技能简直是非同凡响的了。
6	small-scale, survive	第 5 段 1、2、3 句	题目:尽管面临不利的预测,许多小规模社会仍然生存下来并适应。 原文:随着亚非各国在 1945 年之后纷纷取得独立的形势发展,当时就出现这样的假设,经济的发展将很快导致许多小型社会的消亡或彼此同化。因此,人们认为博物馆应该征集对一个民族具有代表性的材料,因为该民族的艺术或物质文化、典礼仪式或政治结构正面临着不可逆转的变革。这种态度已随着以下的认识而有所改变,即边缘社区尽管已部分地融入了一个名声在外、变幻莫测的全球经济体系之中,但仍具有其生存能力和适应性。

Questions 7–12

● 题型归类:Matching

● 题目解析:

7	Technical series	第 3 段第 7 行	第 3 段第 8 行
8	Artifact types	第 3 段第 10 行	第 3 段第 10 行中 the latter 后者指的是 artifact types。
9	Field assemblages	第 3 段第 14 行	第 61 页第 4 行
10	Artifact types	第 3 段第 10 行	第 3 段第 13 行

11	Field assemblages	第3段第14行	第61页第3行
12	Social experience	第61页第6行	第61页第8行

参考译文

人种史馆藏品概况

人种史馆是作为大英博物馆的一个单独的机构于1946年设立的，它由古文物馆历经140年逐渐发展而来。该馆的业务范围涉及非洲、南北美洲、亚洲、太平洋及欧洲部分地区的居民。尽管这包括了诸如非洲的复杂的王国、美洲的古老帝国，但其在20世纪的注意力焦点还是一直集中在小规模的社会群体上面。根据馆内现存的收藏品来看，该馆专为各种用具的制作方法及其用途提供证明并记录在案；要了解这些东西对于它们的生产者来说所具有的重要性及其深刻含意。诸如此类的东西中，既有非凡的，也有平凡的，还有美丽脱俗的，更有乏味庸俗的。

人种史馆的收藏品中包括将近30万件人工制品，其中约有半数系本世纪（指20世纪—译者注）的产品。在为参观者和学者们提供有关非西方文化的信息方面，该馆大有发挥作用的余地。为此目的，文物征集的重点往往不在个别、零星的文物上，而更重视成批发现的古物，因为后者能够大面积展示一个社会的文化面貌。

最近的征集工作中的大部分是在野外进行的，有时是由从事普通人类学项目的博物馆工作人员会同各国政府和其他机构共同进行的。收集到的材料包括著名的技术系列，例如，来自玻利维亚、危地马拉、印度尼西亚和西非地区的纺织品，或是类似小船之类的人工制品。后者包括来自印度的小渔船、安第斯山脉的的喀喀湖的芦苇船、北极的独木舟、还有几个国家的挖空的独木舟等创作范例。诸如来自苏丹、马达加斯加和也门的野外集成艺术品，也包括代表一个民族的一整套物质文化。这可能囊括了一位非洲牧民或是阿拉伯农民在生活上所需要的一切日用品、礼仪用品、有时甚至还有机场工艺展品。其次，一系列的征集所得可以代表十年野外工作的成就，从而证实并记载了在社会上的所见所闻，这已在以下情况中得到了表现：来自各中东国家的花式多样、风格各异的服装款式和珠宝首饰、帐篷和骆驼用的饰品，和来自巴布亚·新几内亚的有关个人服饰风格的发展与欣赏视角的趋向。特别有趣的是，一系列的收藏品继续要以实证来说明礼节仪式和物质形态的演变过程，为此目的，该馆原有的早期（如果还算不上是最早的话）馆藏展品（形成于与欧洲人初次接触之后）可予佐证。

这些征集所得的展品，其意义远远超出这些物件本身。它们是以社会历史背景的见证人的身份走进这所博物馆的，如果其中含有摄影图片方面的记录资料的话，那就更理想了。它们本身具有多重意义。意义最为深远的是，它们为未来的发展变化提供了实物见证。大多数人在看待这些馆藏的代表的各种文化时，认为其不足之处是缺乏有关先进技术方面的内容。事实上，传统的惯例是吸取并利用源源不断的技术创新的源泉。资源的局限性和生态环境的约束性往往被个人的技能所克服，所以在西方人眼中看来，这种个人技能简直是非同凡响的了。很多东西人们原本以为该处理或丢弃的，却在别处又被回收利用了。这种废品回收的办法引起了人们越来越浓的兴趣。

随着亚非各国在1945年之后纷纷取得独立的形势发展，当时就出现这样的假设，经济的发展将很快导致许多小型社会的消亡或彼此同化。因此，人们认为博物馆应该征集对一个民族具有代表性的材料，因为该民族的艺术或物质文化、典礼仪式或政治结构正面临着不可逆转的变革。这种态度已随着以下的认识而有所改变，即边缘社区尽管已部分地融入了一个名声在外、变幻莫测的全球经济体系之中，但仍具有其生存能力和适应性。自从17世纪以来，贸易公司对北美和亚洲开始出口纺织制品，随之而来的便是大量廉价商品的进口，这就使本地的熟练工人和市场遭受了毁灭性的打击。一方面，现代进口商品可以用在日常生活方面；而在另一方面，则其他传统产品在举行重大的典礼、仪式时仍然是需要的。在这样的背景中，人们从事贸易与交换的态度发生逆转。对西方人来说是功利主义的东西，在其他文化背景中却可能是珍藏品（在经过当地的精巧技艺进行加工改造之后），主要是由于具备了审美价值。同样，西方从别的民族地区进口的商品，在某种情况下会被列入“艺术品”的范畴。

征集品就像永远在扩容的资料库似的，其服务对象不仅有学者和人类学家，而且还包括那些投入到教育和艺术事业全过程中的人们。这其中既有艺术设计院系的，也有普通大学和其他学校的。该馆不但要为设计师和艺术家，而且要为所有的参观者提供非西方的有关美学和技术方面的信息，这对于自身具有多元文化日趋明显的欧洲社会背景的展馆而言，其责任是越来越重了。

READING PASSAGE 2

文章结构

体　　裁	议论为主
主要内容	通过发现森林中居民的原始生活，讨论森林和人类居住活动的关系。最后得出结论：亚马逊河地区能支持更大的人类社会发展，如何有效地保护森林环境。
结　　构	A 段：发现西里奥诺人。
	B 段：一种观点阐述——亚马逊河地区不能支撑复杂社会。
	C 段：驳斥上段错误观点。
	D 段：进一步提出证据，驳斥 B 段观点。
	E 段：错误观点导致的后果。
	F 段：提出建议，正确处理问题的方法。

词汇注释

文　　章

A

doctoral *adj.* 博士的；博士学位的
venture *v.* 冒险；探险
jungle *n.* 丛林；生死关头
strikingly *adv.* 醒目地；引人注目地
thatch *n.* 盖屋的材料；茅草屋顶
hut *n.* 小屋；棚屋
perpetual *adj.* 永久的
manioc *n.* 树薯；树薯粉
starchy *adj.* 淀粉的，含淀粉的；拘泥的
plot *n.* 小块地
scour *vt.* 冲洗；急速走遍
promising *adj.* 有希望的；有前途的
deplete *vt.* 耗尽；使衰竭
handicapped *adj.* 残疾的；身体有缺陷的
bow *n.* 弓；弓形
crude *adj.* 天然的，未加工的；粗糙的
machete *n.* 弯刀

B

intervening *adj.* 其中的；介于其间的
endure *v.* 耐久；忍耐
epitomize *vt.* 摘要；概括
casual *adj.* 偶然的；不经意的；临时的
influential *adj.* 有影响力的；有势力的
regional *adj.* 整个地区的；地方的；地域性的
luxuriant *adj.* 丰产的；丰富的；肥沃的
ageless *adj.* 不老的；永恒的
unconquerable *adj.* 不可征服的；克服不了的；压制不了的

hostile *adj.* 敌对的,敌方的	**dismiss** *v.* 解散,消失
simplicity *n.* 简单,简易,朴素,直率	**abandon** *vt.* 放弃,遗弃
ecology *n.* 生态学,[社会]环境适应学,均衡系统	**decay** *v.* 腐朽,腐烂,衰减,衰退
proof *n.* 证据,试验,考验,[印刷]校样	**uncompromising** *adj.* 不妥协的,不让步的,强硬的
archaeological *adj.* 考古学的,考古学上的	**tropical** *adj.* 热带的,热情的
elaborate *adj.* 精心制作的,详细阐述的,精细的	
C	
enormously *adv.* 非常地,巨大地	**thrive** *v.* 兴旺,繁荣,茁壮成长,旺盛
consequential *adj.* 结果的,相因而生的	**evolutionarily** *adv.* 逐渐地;进化地
myth *n.* 神话,神话式的人物(或事物),虚构的故事,荒诞的说法	**retard** *vt.* 延迟,使减速,阻止,妨碍,阻碍
	prehistoric *adj.* 史前的,陈旧的
anthropology *n.* 人类学	**adaptation** *n.* 适应,改编
indigenous *adj.* 本土的	**barrier** *n.* (阻碍通道的)障碍物,栅栏,屏障
extensive *adj.* 广大的,广阔的,广泛的	**comparatively** *adv.* 比较地,相当地
earthwork *n.* 建筑;[建]土方(工程),[军]土木工事	**investigator** *n.* 调查人
D	
revise *vt.* 修订,校订,修正,修改	**tenable** *adj.* 可维持的
ecologist *n.* 生态学者	**evidence** *n.* 明显,显著,明白,迹象,根据,[物]证据,证物
tropical *adj.* 热带的,热情的	
ecosystem *n.* 生态系统	**inhabitant** *n.* 居民,居住者
equation *n.* 相等,平衡,综合体,因素,方程式,等式	
E	
challenge *n.* 挑战	**casualty** *n.* 伤亡,破坏
depict *vt.* 描述,描写	**struggle to** 斗争,奋斗,作斗争
occupation *n.* 职业,占有,占有(房屋等)期间	**implement** *vt.* 贯彻,实现,执行
oppose *vt.* 反对,使对立,使对抗,抗争	**legislation** *n.* 立法,法律的制定(或通过)
ironically *adv.* 说反话地,讽刺地	**apace** *adv.* 快速地,急速地
F	
clash *n.* 冲突,撞击声,抵触	**judicious** *adj.* 明智的
crucial *adj.* 至关紧要的	**long-buried** *adj.* 被长期渴望的

考题解析

Questions 13–15

- 题型归类:List of Headings
- 题目解析:

题目编号	段落主题句	题解
13	In 1942 Allan R Holmberg, and doctoral students in anthropology from Yale University, USA, ventured deep into the jungle of Bolivian Amazonia and searched out an isolated band of Siriono Indians. The Siriono, Holmberg later wrote, led a "trikingly backward" existence.	A 段通读,注意文章结构。注意 heading 中 "early"。

14	To casual observers, as well as to influential natural scientists and regional planners, the luxuriant forests of Amazonia seem ageless, unconquerable, a habitat totally hostile to human civilization.	注意 B 段第 4 句, could not—and cannot—的表达。注意 heading 中"Unable, complex"。
15	The archaeological evidence shows that the natural history of Amazonia is to a surprising extent tied to the activities of its prehistoric inhabitants.	注意 D 段第 2 句和末句,和段中 shape, escaped human influence, tied to the activities of its prehistoric inhabitants 等表达都在揭示答案。注意 heading 中"Influence, prehistoric"。

Questions 16–21

● 题型归类:YES/NO/NOT GIVEN

● 题目解析:

题目编号	题目定位词	答案位置	题解
16	simplicity, Indian, support	B 段第 7 行和 C 段第 5 行	题目:印第安人简单的生活方式的原因是由于亚马逊河地区不能支持一个更加复杂的社会。 原文 B 段中:印第安人单纯朴素的生活方式是众所周知的,这种单纯朴素已被认定为对森林的生态环境的一种逐步进化的适应,同时也生动地证明了亚马逊河地区过去不能、现在也不能支撑起一个更为复杂的社会。 原文 C 段中:但是亚马逊河地区过去 11000 年的人类历史已揭示那种观点不过是神话而已。近年来从人类学和考古学方面收集到的证据表明,该地区已支持过一系列的当地文化长达 1100 年之久,形成了一张广泛而复杂的社会网络——有的已拥有多达十万人口的规模——在这块土地上欣欣向荣地繁衍生息历经一千余年,然后才有欧洲人的身影在此出现。 所以 B 段的观点是错误的。
17	popular, conception	C 段首句和第 2 句	题目:关于亚马逊河地区人类历史有一个重要的,流行的,但是是错误的概念。 原文:对于亚马逊河地区及其土著居民的普遍看法如果情况属实,将会对今后产生极其重大的影响。但是……
18	similar ecosystems		题目:我们可以从世界的其他相似的生态系统中吸取经验教训。 原文只描述了亚马逊河地区是一个热带雨林生态系统,没有提及其他的 ecosystem。

19	ecologist, human settlement, shape	D段第2句	题目:大多数生态学家相信他们研究的亚马逊河地区受到人类居住的影响。 原文:生态学家们把研究的重点放在动植物的栖息地上,因为他们认为这是一片未受人类侵扰的净土。
20	Indians, well-being	F段第5行	题目:亚马逊河地区的原住印第安人对森林的维护来说是必需的。 原文:其实,印第安人的存在对森林的维护与延续具有关键性的作用。 理解定语从句,注意 in fact。
21	part, support, higher	F段倒数第2句	题目:亚马逊河地区的一些地区有可能支持更多的人口。 原文:考古学研究明确指出,只要采取明智而审慎的管理手段,该地经选择的部分地区有能力养活比任何人事先所预料的还要多的人口。

Questions 22-25

● 题型归类:Multiple Choice

● 题目解析:

题目编号	题目定位词	答案位置	题解
22	1942, Sirione	A段	第1段许多地方提到 primitive 原始,如:Their villages were little more than clusters of thatched huts. Life itself was a perpetual and punishing search for food. May be classified among the most handicapped peoples of the world.
23	discoveries, complex	C段第3句	discoveries of remains 在原文中的表达为:evidence gathered from anthropology and archaeology。
24	tropical ecosystem, natural forces	D段第2、3、4句	特别注意第4句:有考古发现表明,亚马逊河地区的自然历史在极大的程度上是与史前时期的居民活动联系在一起的。
25	new insights, past	F段倒数第2句	可以用排除法,A、B、D选项明显错。

参考译文

森林的奥秘

1942年,Allan R Holmberg,美国耶鲁大学人类学专业的博士生,冒险深入波利维亚的亚马逊河地区,在那里发现了一处与世隔绝的西里奥诺印第安人的营居群。西里奥诺人——Holmberg后来这样写道——过着一种"落后得令人吃惊的"生活。他们的村落不过是一簇簇的茅草屋。生活本身整个是一个无休无止、受苦受累的觅食过程:有些农户从森林中开辟出几块小园地用来栽种"木薯"和其他含淀粉的作物,而其他部族成员则在野外猎捕小动物并搜寻鱼群在深水中的栖身处。在当地的资源消耗殆尽时，该部族便会继续迁移。至于技术，Holmberg 提到，西里奥诺人“可以被列入世界上使用工具最低级的族群之中”。除了一些弓、箭和粗糙的挖掘用的棍棒之外，看来西里奥诺人所仅有的工具就是两把磨损到只有袖珍折刀那么大的砍刀。

虽然在过去的数十年间，西里奥诺人的生活已有所变化，但是作为石器时代遗物的形象却仍保留至今。西里奥诺人的确在许多方面集中体现了人们对亚马逊河生活状态的普通看法。亚马逊河地区茂密富饶的森林似乎是青春永驻、不可征服的，是与人类文明完全相克的居住地，这不仅是具有影响的自然科学家和地区规划者的看法，就是那些漫不经心的观察者们也持有同感。印第安人单纯朴素的生活方式是众所周知的，这种简单朴素已被认定为对森林的生态环境的一种逐步进化的适应，同时也生动地证明了亚马逊河地区过去不能、现在也不能支撑起一个更为复杂的社会。对远为复杂的各种文化进行考古而遗留的蛛丝马迹已被当作外敌入侵的遗迹而废弃了，听凭其在毫不留情的热带气候的环境中自生自灭。

对于亚马逊河地区及其土著居民的普遍看法如果情况属实，将会对今后产生极其重大的影响。但是亚马逊河地区过去 11000 年的人类历史已揭示那种观点不过是谬论而已。近年来从人类学和考古学方面收集到的证据表明，该地区已支持过一系列的当地文化长达 11000 年之久；一张广泛而复杂的社会网络——有的已拥有多达十万人口的规模——在这块土地上欣欣向荣地繁衍生息历经一千余年，然后才有欧洲人的身影在此出现。（确实，有一些当代部落，包括西里奥诺人，仍然居住在属于早期文化的泥土屋里。）史前时期的亚马逊河地区的人民所开发的技术与文化在当时的历史背景下也算得上是先进的，就是从进化论的角度来看，也决不能说是发展滞后了。如果说印第安人今天的生活看来还很“原始”的话，那么造成今天这种状况与其说是由于适应环境或生态障碍所致，倒不如说，那是针对几个世纪以来的经济和政治压力而在较近期间作出的一种应对调适姿态。那些持有异议的调查研究人员已在无意间将现状归咎于历史了。

对亚马逊河地区的观点加以修正的根据将会让很多人大吃一惊。生态学家们已作出假设，热带生态体系完全是由自然力量形成的；他们把研究的重点放在他们认为未受人类侵扰的地区。但是就像佛罗里达大学的生态学家 Peter Feinsinger 特别提到的，不把人的因素考虑在自然的均衡关系之内的研究方法再也站不住脚。有考古发现表明，亚马逊河地区的自然历史在极大的程度上是与史前时期的居民活动联系在一起的。

对问题的认识来得恰是时候。1992 年 6 月，来自世界各地的政治、环保方面的领导人在里约热内卢聚首讨论发展中国家如何才能在不损害自然资源的前提下促进各自经济的发展。这对于亚马逊河地区来说简直是一个严峻的挑战。由于热带森林已被描绘成从生态学观点看不适宜于人类大规模定居的地方，有些环保专家就表示反对进行任何形式的开发活动。具有讽刺意味的是，那种极端主义立场的主要受害者竟是环境本身。尽管决策者们在努力对相应的法规作出解释并予以执行，但极具破坏性的开发活动仍在广袤的土地上迅速蔓延。

环保科学家们提出的自然主义的另一主要受害者就是当地（亚马逊河地区）的印第安人，因为他们的狩猎、捕鱼以及刀耕火种的农耕习惯等等往往被说成是对栖息地的破坏。其实，印第安人的存在对森林的维护与延续具有关键性的作用，但他们处在环保卫士们与开拓勇士们的矛盾冲突之中，故苦不堪言，受害最深。然而对史前期亚马逊河地区历史的新的解读，却提示人们采取中间立场。考古学研究明确指出，只要采取明智而审慎的管理手段，该地经选择的部分地区有能力养活比任何人事先所预料的还要多的人口。深埋已久的过去，似乎在为未来提出希望。

READING PASSAGE 3

文章结构

体 裁	说明为主
主要内容	天气和人类情绪及工作表现之间的关系。
结 构	第1段:引出内容,科学家们正研究天气和人类情绪及工作表现之间的关系。
	第2段:闷热的天气里人的脾气会变得比平常急躁。
	第3段:天气寒冷如何影响人们的表现。
	第4段:褪黑激素的荷尔蒙水平随光照变化。
	第5段:动物行为和人类的情绪受到日照时间长短的影响,即随季节变化。
	第6段:天气变化——电场变化——复合胺的变化——人们情绪变化

词汇注释

文 章

第 1 段

hormone *n.* 荷尔蒙,激素
hence *adv.* 因此,从此
gloomy *adj.* 黑暗的,阴沉的,令人沮丧的,阴郁的
depression *n.* 沮丧,消沉,低气压,低压
spirit *n.* 精神,灵魂,幽灵,妖精,勇气,火力,热情,情绪
drastically *adv.* 非常地,激烈地,彻底地
amount *n.* 数量
fight back 抵抗
spectrum *n.* 光谱
lamp *n.* 灯
ultraviolet *adj.* 紫外线的,紫外的
fluorescent *adj.* 荧光的,莹光的
tungsten *n.* [化]钨
siesta *n.* 午睡,午休

第 2 段

temper *n.* (钢等)韧度,回火,性情,脾气,情绪,心情,调剂,趋向
muggy *adj.* 闷热的
riot *n.* 暴乱,骚动,(植物,疾病等)蔓延,放荡,暴动

第 3 段

frequency *n.* 频率,周率,发生次数
psychologist *n.* 心理学者
compare *vt.* 比较,相比,比喻 *n.* 比较
arithmetic *n.* 算术,算法
impair *vt.* 削弱
function *n.* 官能,功能,作用,职责,典礼,仪式,[数]函数
distract *vt.* 转移(注意力)
diver *n.* 潜水者

第 4 段

sceptical *adj.* 怀疑论的,怀疑的
optimistic *adj.* 乐观的
connection *n.* 连接,关系,接线,线路,亲戚
melatonin *n.* [生化]褪黑激素,N-乙酰-5-甲氧基色胺
pineal *adj.* 松球状的,松果腺的
gland *n.* [解剖]腺,[机械]密封管
peak *n.* 山顶,顶点,帽舌,(记录的)最高峰
trigger *vt.* 引发,引起,触发

第 5 段	
hamster *n.* 东欧或亚洲产的大颊的鼠类	**murky** *adj.* 黑暗的，阴沉的
injection *n.* 注射，注射剂，(毛细血管等的) 充血，(人造卫星，宇宙飞船等的) 射入轨道	**borne** *v.* bear 的过去分词
	suicidal *adj.* 自杀的，自毁的，自取灭亡的
第 6 段	
thunderstorm *n.* [气] 雷暴	**concentration** *n.* 集中，集合，专心，浓缩，浓度
irritable *adj.* 易怒的，急躁的	**particle** *n.* 粒子，点，极小量，微粒，质点，小品词，语气
moody *adj.* 喜怒无常的，忧悒的	**negative** *adj.* 否定的，消极的，负的，阴性的
positively *adv.* 断然地；肯定地	**claim** *vt.* (根据权利) 要求，认领，声称，主张，需要
serotonin *n.* 含于血液中的复合胺	**fluorescent** *adj.* 荧光的，莹光的
nervous *adj.* 神经紧张的，不安的，强健有力的	
aggressive *adv.* 好斗的，敢作敢为的，有闯劲的，侵略性的	

考题解析

Questions 26–28

- 题型归类：Multiple Choice
- 题目解析：

题目编号	题目定位词	答案位置	题解
26	divers, colder	第 3 段，重点看最后一句	潜水员进入冷水中表现差，这时他们在体温还没有明显下降，说明是感觉到寒冷分散了潜水员在执行任务时的注意力。
27	daylight hours	第 4 段倒数第 11 行	注意后面的 for example 中的 food consumption。另外第 5 段首句也可判断。
28	irritability	末段第 3 行	暴风雨即将到来的时候，一些人抱怨"闷"得慌、脾气急躁、情绪化而且感觉自己好像马上就要不行了。

Questions 29–34

- 题型归类：TRUE/ FALSE/ NOT GIVEN
- 题目解析：

题目编号	题目定位词	答案位置	题解
29	SAD, Russia	第 1 段倒数第 10 行	题目：SAD 防碍了俄罗斯孩子的教育。 原文：俄罗斯科学家声称小孩子在接触紫外线之后会学习得更好。
30	serotonin, aggression, essential	全文末段第 3、4 句	题目：复合胺是人们侵略性的关键因素。 原文：神经系统里某些区域的复合胺含量高会使人更积极、更容易对外界事物作出反应，还有可能使人更活跃、更激进。

31	weather, human mood	倒数第 2 段第 11 行	题目:科学证据表明天气所导致的愉快和人们的情绪相关。 原文:研究表明人类的情绪受到日照时间长短的影响。原文中最后一段结论是天气导致人们神经系统中复合胺的变化。
32	depression, the time of year	第 2 段第 2、3、4 句	题目:消沉压抑和一年中四季的变迁是有联系的。 原文:无疑"与犯罪人意愿相违背的犯罪现象"在天气较为炎热的夏天会上升,在天气较为寒冷的冬季会下降。
33	melatonin, times, increase	第 4 段最后两句	题目:褪黑激素水平在一年中的某段时期会增加。 原文:冬季成年牡鹿的食量大增,2 月、3 月时到达顶峰。5 月又跌落到一低点,接下来 9 月又升至顶峰,11 月又低至另一低点。这些变化似乎都由不断变化的褪黑激素水平所致。
34	positively charged ions, eating	最后一段最后一句	题目:正离子会影响饮食习惯。 最后一段没有提到。

Questions 35–37

- 题型归类:Multiple Choice
- 题目解析:

题目编号	题目定位词	答案位置	题解
35	rainy weather	最后一段首句和上一段末句	B
36	high serotonin	全文末段第 12 行	D
37	sunny weather	第 4 段首句	E

Questions 38–40

- 题型归类:Matching
- 题目解析:

题目编号	题目定位词	答案位置	题解
38	US, social tension	第 2 段第 7 行	Gets warmer
39	hamster weight	倒数第 2 段首句	The nights are shorter
40	Animal, food	倒数第 2 段第 9 行	The cycle of the seasons

参考译文

起起伏伏

荷尔蒙水平可能受到天气的影响,从而影响我们的情绪。天气阴郁可能导致人们的情绪低沉,而晴空万里似乎会使人情绪高涨。例如,英国冬天阴郁的天气极大地减少了人们与阳光接触的几率,这严重影响了一部分人。他们变得非常郁闷,无精打采,以至于这些人的工作和社交生活都受到了影响。这种现象已被赋予SAD这个名字,即季节性影响紊乱。受这类病症困扰的人可以通过充分利用冬季任何可获得的阳光以及每日在特制的、包含全部光谱的日光灯下度过几小时来得到治疗。这类灯比普通的荧光灯和钨光灯提供更多的紫外线和蓝绿光。一些俄罗斯科学家声称小孩子在接触紫外线之后会学习得更好。在气候温暖的国度里在安排工作时间时有意在一天中最热的时候安排工作人员休息一下,甚至睡个午觉。科学家们正致力于研究天气和人类情绪及工作表现之间的关系。

人们普遍认为在闷热、潮湿的天气里人的脾气会变得比平常急躁。无疑"非犯罪人本意的犯罪现象"在天气较为炎热的夏天会上升,在天气较为寒冷的冬季会下降。美国的一项研究已表明气温与街头骚乱两者之间的关系。随着天气变暖,骚乱发生的频率急剧增高,在气温达到27至30摄氏度时达到顶峰。但是这种影响是否真的是由热力导致的情绪变化引起的呢?一些科学家提出,天气热麻烦事儿增多仅仅是因为天气好的时候上街的人更多而已。

心理学家也研究了天气寒冷如何影响人们的表现。研究人员将在摄氏5度的冰水中工作的潜水员与在20摄氏度(大概是游泳池水温)水温中工作的潜水员进行了对比。冷水使潜水员在进行简单的算术运算和完成其他需要动脑的任务时表现较差。但重要的是他们一进入冷水中,表现就受影响,此后体温才有所下降。这表明温度低没有直接导致大脑运转速度减慢,而是感觉到寒冷这件事分散了潜水员在执行那些任务时的注意力。

心理学家的研究已表明艳阳高照时,人们变得没那么疑神疑鬼,也变得更加乐观。然而,这一点明显不仅仅由气温决定。一位美国心理学家研究了在一家温度受控制的餐厅里就餐的客人。太阳熠熠发光时,就餐的客人给很多小费,相反就给较少的小费,而餐厅内的温度保持不变。由于出现人们的行为与日光照射时间长短之间的关系的证据,人们也相信了天气与人的情绪之间存在联系。这一点反过来很可能涉及到大脑松果腺分泌的褪黑激素的荷尔蒙水平。接触太阳光越多,褪黑激素的数量就越少。研究表明褪黑激素对一些动物的季节性行为有很大影响。例如,冬季成年牡鹿的食量大增,2月、3月时到达顶峰。5月又跌落到低点,接下来9月又升至顶峰,11月又降至另一最低点。这些变化似乎都由不断变化的褪黑激素水平所致。

实验室里的仓鼠在夜晚逐渐变短的时候,褪黑激素水平下降,体重增加。另一方面,如果给他们注射褪黑激素,他们会完全停止饮食。看起来,不断变化的昼夜长短提供的时间暗示导致了动物行为的变化——这些变化是为应付季节的循环而必需的。研究还表明人类的情绪也受到日照时间长短的影响。抱怀疑态度的人可能说,接触日照时间越长,人们的心情越好,这是因为人们将日照与度假、自由等美好的情感结合在一起,而忘却了责任。然而,确信阴沉的雨天会让人们更不开心被比利时的一项研究所证实,这项研究表明一项电话心理咨询服务在雨天接到更多的带有自杀情绪的人的电话。

暴风雨即将到来的时候,一些人抱怨"闷"得慌、脾气急躁、情绪化而且感觉自己好像马上就要不行了。他们或许会对如下事实作出反应,大型的雷雨云生成导致的强烈电场时,空气中会带一些正电荷。正电荷会增加血液里的复合胺(复合胺是一种化学物质,参与神经系统发送信号的活动)的含量。神经系统里某些区域的复合胺含量高会使人更积极、更容易对外界事物作出反应,还有可能使人更富侵略性。如果吹起像法国南部的寒冷的西北风或者德国南部的焚风,人们的情绪也要受到影响——而且交通事故也会增加。这些风带有超出平常风里的正电荷分子的集结,或许这一点很重要。在英国每年要销售40万个离子发生器,这些离子发生器可以提高一个房间里空气中负电荷的数量。很多人说自己在呈现负电荷的空气里感觉更舒服。

WRITING

WRITING TASK 1

范文

范文1

In order to analyze the levels of participation in education and science, three factors could be considered, including the average years of schooling, the number of scientists and technicians per 1000 people, and the total amount of spending on research and development.

Between 1980 and 1990, the average number of years of schooling for developing countries went from 2.4 to 3.2. Although this is an increase, in industrialized countries, this number rose from 8.3 to 10.2, which shows that the length of education in industrialized countries is significantly longer.

As for the number of scientists and technicians, in industrialized countries, this number saw a jump from 41 people to 70 people per 1000 whereas in 1990 in developing countries, there were only 18 of such people per 1000, proving that there is a lack of trained manpower to promote technological progress in developing countries. In addition, spending on research and development actually fell in developing countries whereas in industrialized countries, this amount more than doubled.

This data shows that there are very large inconsistencies between the levels of participation in education and science in developing and industrialized countries.

为了分析教育与科学的参与程度,我们应当考虑三个因素:包括受教育的平均年限、每1000人中的科学家和科技人员的数量以及研究与发展方面的经费投入总额。

从1980年到1990年,发展中国家的受教育平均年限从2.4年提升到了3.2年。尽管这也是一种增长,但同期工业化国家的这项指标从8.3年升到了10.2年。这表明工业化国家的受教育年限明显加长了。

至于每1000人中的科学家和科技人员的数量,工业化国家中这个数字从41人激增到了70人,然而在1990年发展中国家每1000人中的科学家和科技人员的数量只有18人。这说明在发展中国家缺乏推动科技进步的经过专门训练的人力资源。此外,研究和发展经费在发展中国家被实际削减而在工业化国家却将它增长了一倍。

该数据显示发展中国家和工业化国家之间在教育和科学的参与程度上存在着极大的差别。

范文2

What is very obvious at a glance is that the industrialized countries far outstrip the developing countries in all three areas measured: Average years of schooling, scientists and technicians per 1000 people and spending on research & development, in both 1980 and 1990. What is disturbing is that not more progress was made during this ten-year period by the developing countries. In fact, in spending on research and development, it even decreased, going from around $50 billion down to around $30 billion.

In average years of schooling, the industrialized countries went from over 8 to over 10, while the developing countries were only able to increase from 2 + to 3 +. The latter did better in terms of scientists and technicians per 1000 people, going from around 11 to around 18, while the industrialized countries were able to increase from over 40 to around 70. The biggest disparity and growing gap was in the area of spending on research and development, which, while it decreased for the developing countries, more than doubled for the industrialized countries, going from $150 billion to $350 billion. In 1980, this spending was three times that of the developing countries; by 1990, it was ten times!

很明显,一看就知道,在全部三个方面,即受教育的平均年限、每1000人中的科学家和科技人员的数量以及研究与发展方面的经费投入总额,1980年和1990年工业化国家都远远超过了发展中国家。令人困扰的是在这十年期间发展中国家几乎没有太大的进步。然而事实上研究和发展方面的经费甚至在减少,从500亿美元左右滑落到了300亿美元左右。

在受教育的平均年限方面,工业化国家从8年多增长到了10年多,然而发展中国家只从2年多增长到了3年多。后者在每1000人中的科学家和科技人员的数量方面做得稍好一些,从11人增长到了18人,工业化国家却能够从40多人增加到了70人左右。最大的不同和日益加大的差距在研究和发展经费投入方面,发展中国家在此项上的削减使得工业化国家在此项上的经费超过了发展中国家的两倍,从1500亿美元增长到了3500亿美元。1980年的时候此项经费就变成了发展中国家的3倍,到了1990年就变成了10倍!

谋篇布局

1. 题目分析

这是一道多图题。每张图都是简单的柱状图。这些图由两组柱子构成。描写原则:我们先讲一种比较好操作的:分别描写三张图。

● 首先是第一张图。为了方便掌握,我们可以把两组柱子,转换成两条曲线(即发达国家的变化和发展中国家各自的变化)。这样,我们可以分别写两条曲线的变化趋势,两条曲线之间的落差(两条曲线相差的绝对值和差距的变化趋势:差距增大还是减少)。

● 然后再用同样的方法写其他两张图。

● 最后有可能的话写三张图的联系。

还有一种原则是:先写发展中国家在三方面的特点,然后写发达国家的特点,最后作比较。

2. 本题分析

我们先来看第一种描写原则:

● 先来看“平均受教育年数”这张图。发展中国家两根浅色柱子组成的曲线表示“发展中国家受教育的平均年数在增长,从两年多到三年多”;发达国家两根深色柱子组成的曲线表示“发达国家受教育的平均年数在增长,从8年多到10年多”。然后我们可以比较这两条曲线的落差:“发达国家受教育的年数要比发展中国家长的多,而且两者的差距在增大,从6年增大到7年”。

● 同样的,在“每千人中的科学家和技术人员”这张图中,我们可以看到:“发展中国家从10人增长到18人”,“发达国家从160人增长到350人”,“发达国家和发展中国家的差距依然有增无减”。

● 在“研发投入”这张图中,上面两张图的趋势在继续,而更显著的是“发展中国家在研发上的投入反而减少了”。

范文1就是按照这个思路写的。不过,范文1有一个缺点,就是在写“研发投入”的时候,没有把具体数值写出来。

范文2的第二段也是从三方面把发展中国家和发达国家作了比较。而第一段写了这三张图总体特征:“发达国家占优势”,“发展中国家在教育上的投入甚至在减少”。(我们在前面讲过,第一段除了交代图表“四要素”以外,有可能的话要描写图表的总体特征。)

WRITING TASK 2

范文

范文 1

In my opinion, there is nothing wrong with children engaging in paid work. This is a valuable experience, important for learning and taking responsibility. While working can bring many benefits to children, children can be very vulnerable to poor working conditions and low wages. Therefore their work conditions should always be supervised by their parents.

Some people might think that children should only engage in volunteer work until they have developed their work ethic and understand the responsibility that comes with earning money, but I think money management should start with the first paycheck. Volunteer work has its advantages, but it is not a true reflection of the working experience. Knowing there is a direct relationship between the quality of work and the amount of money earned is important for developing a strong work ethic. Children can start learning about punctuality, thoroughness, and how to deal with difficult employers while they are young; these skills will make them more valuable employees in the future.

As for the issue of working conditions, I would like to point out that there is a difference between a 12-year-old babysitter and a 12-year-old worker in a Nike factory. The difference is the working conditions and the working hours. In theory, a child could work, but under safe conditions and for a maximum of around four hours at a time. Perhaps the babysitter and the factory worker could learn some of the same lessons in taking responsibility, but children should not be too involved in a work environment; their main responsibility is still to play and have fun. Regarding wages, a babysitter in a developed country may earn $2/hour while a child factory laborer may earn $2/week for full-time hours. This is obviously an unacceptable usage of a child's time and energy.

In summary, children who work for pay definitely have a valuable learning opportunity, however the difference between the babysitter and the factory worker has to be considered. I believe engaging in paid work is acceptable if the conditions are safe, the hours are reasonable and the wage is fair.

在我看来，儿童参加有偿劳动没有错误。这是一种有价值的体验，对学习和培养责任感都很重要。工作能给儿童带来许多好处，然而儿童可能容易受到伤害而不能在恶劣的条件和极低的收入的情况下工作。因此他们的工作环境应该受到父母的监督。

有些人也许认为儿童只能承担较轻的工作，直到他们培养成了自己的职业道德并且理解赚钱同时负有的责任。但是我认为对钱的管理应该从第一次得到薪酬就开始。志愿者工作有它的长处，但并不是工作经验的真实反映。了解工作质量与薪酬数量有直接关系这一点对培养职业道德至关重要。儿童可以开始学习守时、完整性以及如何在他们很年轻时与那些难以相处的老板搞好关系。这些技巧会帮助他们在未来成为更有价值的员工。

至于工作条件的问题，我想指出的是一个 12 岁大的保姆与一个在耐克工厂工作的 12 岁员工之间存在很大的不同。差别在于工作环境和工作时间。理论上一个儿童是可以工作的，但是必须在安全的环境下并且一次最多工作 4 个小时左右。也许保姆和工厂职工在承担责任方面学到的是相同的东西，但是儿童不应过分处于工作状态中，他们的主要任务就是玩和获得乐趣。关于薪酬，在发展中国家一个保姆一小时可能赚 2 美元，然而一个工厂的儿童员工也许全职工作一周也就能赚 2 美元。很明显对一个儿童的时间和精力来说这是不可接受的分配方案。

总之，参加有偿劳动的儿童一定可以获得宝贵的学习机会，然而保姆与工厂职工之间的差别是应当被考虑的。我相信如果工作条件安全、工作时间合理、薪酬公平的话，儿童参与有偿劳动是合理的。

范文2

I believe that it is wrong for children to engage in any form of paid work, particularly below a certain age, and especially if it is to bring in additional income for a family.

There are some situations when older children can work on the side to earn money for themselves, but this should never replace or take them out of school. As a teenager, for example, I delivered newspapers in the morning before school and in the afternoon, right after school. This did not affect my performance at school and I did learn how to become responsible with the demands of the job and handling financial matters. But I never contributed a penny to my family, nor was I required to do this job by anyone. It was by my own choice and with the support of my parents. This is the only type of child employment that I think might be appropriate.

A child should never work to support his family or go to work instead of school. There are child labor laws that strictly prohibit this and those that attempt to put a child to work in a factory rob a child of his or her childhood. Their use of the argument that it teaches a child responsibility is only an excuse for greedy employers who want to reduce their bottom line to increase their profit at the expense of children.

The argument that poor children need to earn money for their family has also been proven wrong in that, since they sacrifice a proper education, they can never move forward to greater earning opportunities for the rest of their life.

我认为儿童参加任何形式的有偿劳动都是不对的，尤其是在一定年龄以下和为了给家庭增加额外的收入。

有很多大一点儿的孩子能够做兼职为自己赚钱的情况，但是这绝不能取代学校或者使他们辍学。比如说我，作为一个青少年，在早上上学前和下午放学后送报纸。这不会影响我在学校的表现，还使我学会了如何变得对工作的要求负责，以及如何解决经济问题。但是我从来不给家里贡献一分钱，也不受任何人要求去做这份工作，完全是我个人的选择，并且我的父母支持我。这是唯一我认为可能合适的儿童打工形式。

儿童不应为了支撑家庭或者辍学去工作。儿童劳动保护法严厉禁止此种辍学打工行为和那些企图让儿童去工厂劳动、剥夺儿童的少年时代的行为。使用教会儿童要有责任心这样的观点无非是那些企图压低在儿童劳动力身上的底线成本、牺牲儿童提高利润的老板贪婪的借口而已。

贫穷的儿童需要为家庭赚钱的观点因此被证明是错的，因为他们牺牲了正常的教育。在一生中未来的日子里他们再也不能获得赚取更多钱的机会了。

谋篇布局

1. 读题

这篇文章的中心事件是“孩子参加有薪工作”。题干出现两种评价：第一种评价认为这样做不好；另外一种观点认为这样做好。题干没有给出认为这样做不好的理由；但是给出了认为这样做好的理由：“工作经验”和“增加责任感”。我们可以同意其中任何一种观点，或者两边都同意。无论怎么写，最好在文章中提到“工作经验”和“增加责任感”。比如，如果你的观点是“孩子应该参加有薪工作”，你的分论点最好写“这样做是如何增加工作经验和增加责任感，以及有进一步的好处”。又比如，你的观点是“孩子不应该参加有薪工作”，你在分论点中最好要提到“其实这样的工作不能提高工作经验和责任感”，或者“孩子参加工作的危害要大于这些好处”。总之，要尽可能地利用题干中的信息。

2. 写提纲

我们构思两种观点:"同意孩子参加工作"和"不同意孩子参加工作"。

(1)我们先来想"孩子应该参加工作":还是老话,想本质和后果。孩子参加工作的后果是"对他们的将来有好处",这里可以顺带提到"工作经验"和"责任感"对将来的好处。范文1的第二段就是这样写的。在写完上面的内容后,我们也可以写"孩子参加工作的底限"。这样写既在逻辑上显得完整,又可以增加篇幅。比如我们可以写"孩子参加工作必须有一个比较好的工作环境",参见范文1的第三段。

(2)我们再来想"孩子不应该参加工作":从后果上看,"参加工作未必能积累经验和增加责任感"。范文2的表述是"这些仅仅只是工场主剥削孩子的借口"。

(3)还有一条折中的路:范文2很有特点,它抓住的是"孩子不应该参加带薪工作"中的"带薪"两个字,即"孩子可以参加工作,但不能参加带薪工作"。这样的论述集中而有效率。

3. 首段的写作:引出要讨论的内容+表达你的观点

(1)范文1开门见山,表达自己"同意孩子参加工作"。然后对这个同意作了限制,"工作条件必须保证"。这样的开头比较标准。

(2)范文2也很清楚地表达自己的观点:"孩子在任何情况下都不能参加为了增加家庭收入的带薪工作"。然后他又作了一点让步:"孩子可以为了自己参加一点带薪工作,但是不能影响学习。"

4. 中间段落的写作:分论点的论证

(1)强对比论证:为了论述中心事物,我们可以用一个跟它相反的事物作为强对比项。如果分论点是"中心事物是好的",那么写"它的强对比项是不好的"就是对分论点的有力支持。范文1就很好利用了这种论证方法。在第二段中,用"义务工作存在的问题"论证了"带薪工作好";在第三段中,用不同工作场合的强对比,论证了作者的观点。

SPEAKING

I = Interviewer C = Candidate

范例 1

PART 1

I: Good morning. My name is Maryann. Could you tell me your full name please?

C: My Chinese name is Chen Na, but you can call me by my English name, Jennifer.

I: That's a very pretty name. Who gave it to you?

C: My English teacher in high school helped me to choose it.

I: Jennifer, as you know, China has many tourists every year. What would you suggest a visitor should see and do in your country?

C: Well... there's so much to see, and it's hard to know where to start. I guess I would start by saying that every visitor to China must see the **Great Wall.** I think it must be on the top of every visitor's list of places to see. I've seen it three times already, and I never get tired of seeing it. The next place to see would be the **Imperial Palace** at **Tiananmen. Just in Beijing alone** there are so many places to see and so many things to do. Of course there are other famous places to see, like Xi'an, Guilin, Yunnan, Shanghai and so on.

I: Are there any traditional arts or music you would recommend?

C: I don't know that much about traditional arts and music, but I would recommend that visitors see a **Peking opera**, at least once. They won't understand it, of course, but it's such a part of China's musical and cultural history. As for traditional arts, I like **Chinese paintings** very much. One can go to any of the famous art museums to see this kind of traditional art.

I: Where can one go to see Peking opera?

C: I've heard that in Beijing there are some famous **teahouses** where you can sit and drink tea, and they also have the Peking opera shows. I think the prices are quite **reasonable**, and you get tea and **snacks**!

I: Tell me about the kind of foreign visitors or tourists who come to China.

C: Well, as far as I know, China gets all kinds of people. I mean, there are always lots of foreign students who come to China to study, or just to travel around. Then, of course, there are lots of business people who come to China to work and do business. There are also government officials from other countries, who travel to China to hold meetings with China's government. Then, I think there are **retired people**, who **have the time** and enough money, who just want to come to China to see what it's like.

I: In what ways has tourism changed your country?

C: I think it has helped to make tourism an industry. Look at all the new 4 and 5-star hotels built for foreign businessmen and travelers. They also spend money at the **fancy** restaurants and the expensive shops.

I: Ok, great. Now I'm going to give you a topic, and I'd like you to talk about it for one to two minutes. Before you talk you'll have one minute to think about what you're going to say. You can make some notes if you wish. Do you understand?

C: Yes.

I: Ok, here is your topic, and here is some paper and a pencil for making notes. I'd like you to describe a **memorable event** in your life.

One minute passes...

PART 2

Candidate's Notes on Paper

when	two years ago
where	senior middle school
what	talent contest
why memorable	won second prize

I: Alright? Remember, you have one to two minutes for this, so don't worry if I stop you. I'll tell you when the time is up. Can you start speaking now, please?

C: I can still **vividly** remember the **talent contest** I was in two years ago, in my second year of **senior middle school.** The school I attended was **a joint Chinese/Australian high school**, with many foreign teachers. Every year there was a talent contest for the junior and senior middle schools. At first, I didn't think about **entering** the contest, but several of my friends encouraged me to do so. I chose my favorite song, and practiced nearly every day in **the two weeks leading up to the contest.**
The day of the contest, I was quite nervous. There were eight of us in the contest from the senior

middle school. One person played the **piano**, another played the **violin**, another danced, and two others were also singing. I watched the other students, and they seemed pretty good to me. I thought there was no **chance** I would win. Oh, I forgot to say, the contest was held in the largest classroom in school. It could seat 500 students, and every seat was full that day. It was the first time I had ever entered a talent contest.

When it was my turn to go on to perform, I took several deep breaths, as my teacher had told me to do. When I got in front of all those 500 students, I smiled and, suddenly, I felt more relaxed. I told them what song I was going to sing. I then **pretended** I was with my friends on a Friday night, just having fun, and sang just as I would then. When I finished my song, I was so surprised at the loud **applause**, and thought to myself, "I think they liked my singing".

The reason this event is so memorable is that I never **expected** to win anything—I just entered the contest for fun. And when it was announced I won second prize, I was more surprised than anyone. Now, I'm really glad I did it.

I: Do you think the event would be just as memorable if you hadn't won?

C: Actually, yes, I think it would still be very memorable. I truly enjoyed singing in front of all those students. And it gave me a good feeling that they enjoyed my singing.

PART 3

I: Ok, we've been talking about memorable events. Now I'd like to ask you a few more questions of **a general nature** related to this issue. Let's talk first about **the role of ceremonies.** How important are ceremonies in our lives?

C: I personally like ceremonies, and I think they **play** an important role in our lives. For instance, at graduation time, there is always a ceremony, and I think this has a lot of importance for all the students, and for their parents.

I: Do you see the role of **private and public ceremonies** changing in the future?

C: I think that the **specific** ceremonies might change, as all things do over time, but I don't think the role of ceremonies is likely to **undergo** any **drastic** change.

I: What do you feel is the role of a ceremony?

C: I think it's to **emphasize** the importance of **certain** events that happen. Ceremonies give people a reason or an opportunity to get together to **recognize** these events. A ceremony can **mark** a happy occasion, like a birth, or a birthday. But ceremonies can also mark sad events, like **funerals.**

I: Ok, now let's talk about **attitudes** towards marriage. Have attitudes to marriage changed in recent years?

C: Yes, here in China, I think attitudes have changed among young people. It used to be that when young men and women got to a certain age they felt they should get married. It was expected of them—by their parents, by their families, by their friends. Nowadays, young people are getting married later, at an older age. Both men and women are more **concerned with** their careers.

I: In what ways do men and women feel differently about marriage, in your opinion?

C: Actually, I think that in China men and women generally view marriage more similarly than differently. They both feel that both of them should continue working after marriage, and after a child is born. Many—or, most—men also help out with the **housework**, including the cooking. If the husband gets home before the wife, he can start cooking dinner. Marriage is to raise a family, and to be **company** for each other.

I: Alright, one final topic. Let's talk about the way **the media covers** events. What sort of national events **make headlines** in your country?

C: The annual meetings of the **People's Congress** always make the headlines, that's for sure. Also, anything of national significance, for instance, like **SARS**. Last year during SARS there were **plenty** of headlines about that. Of course, last year when the first Chinese **astronaut** went into **space**, that made plenty of headlines. And whenever any Chinese sports team does well in international competition, that also **shows up** on the **front page.**

I: Does the media in your country pay more attention to global or national events?

C: That depends on what sort of media you're talking about. If you're talking about newspapers, for instance, then it depends on which newspaper. Some newspapers are **devoted** to international news, like the *Economic Times*, and some more to domestic news, like the *Beijing Times*. As for TV, there are certain **channels** that carry a lot of international news, like CCTV 9, 1, and 2, and others which focus more on national events, like BTV and other local channels.

I: Ok, thanks so much, that's the end of our interview.

C: Thank you for your time.

范例 2

PART 1

I: Good morning, my name is Richard. Can you tell me your full name please?

C: My full name is Zhang Bin. You can call me John.

I: Okay, John. Can I see your identification please?

C: Sure, here you go.

I: Thanks. Okay, first please tell me where you are from.

C: I'm from Tianjin. It's about two hours away from Beijing.

I: What would you suggest a visitor see and do in China?

C: If the visitor had limited time, I would suggest that he spend time in only two or three **major centers**; I would recommend Beijing, Xi'an, and Shanghai. Beijing has many of the country's **historical sights**, such as **Tiananmen Square**, **the Forbidden City**, **the Summer Palace** and many beautiful parks. The **Great Wall** is also easily **accessible** from Beijing on a **day trip**. Xi'an is best known for the **archaeological digs** that have **revealed** many of the 10,000 **life-sized clay warriors** that were **buried** with **Qin Shi Huang.** Shanghai is famous for **the Bund** and **European architecture** from **colonial times.**

I: Are there any traditional arts or music you would recommend?

C: I would definitely recommend seeing a **Peking opera concert**, even though you might think it sounds terrible. It is a very traditional **form of music** and storytelling in China. You could also see an **acrobatic** performance; you would definitely enjoy that. If you enjoy quiet activities, you might want to view or participate in a tea ceremony. There are many **ancient rituals associated with** drinking tea, and a very **elaborate** culture surrounding it.

I: Tell me about the kind of tourists who go to your country.

C: For a long time, most of the tourists we saw in China came in **large**, **organized tour groups**. These groups moved around Beijing with their tour guides in large buses because foreigners weren't allowed to travel on their own. Nowadays, lots of people still come on tours, but there is a growing number of **independent travelers** who make their own plans, even when they can't speak Chinese!

I: In what ways has tourism changed your country?

C: The most obvious way tourism has changed the country is that many Chinese **citizens** have now met people from other parts of the world. This has made us more aware of cultural differences and similarities. In general, I think tourists coming to China have brought many benefits, such as **boosting** the economy and supporting traditional culture.

I: All right, now I'm going to give you a topic and I'd like you to talk about it for one to two minutes. Before you talk you'll have one minute to think about what you're going to say. You can make some notes if you wish. Do you understand?

C: Sure.

I: Ok, here is your topic, and here is some paper and a pencil for making notes. I'd like you to describe a **memorable event** in your life.

One minute passes...

PART 2

Candidate's Notes on Paper

when	last July
where	Nankai
what	prizes, degree, party
why memorable	transition

I: Ok? Remember, you have one to two minutes for this so don't worry if I stop you. I'll tell you when the time is up. Can you start speaking now, please?

C: The most important and memorable event in my life so far has been my graduation with a **bachelor's degree** from Nankai University. I graduated in July of last year with a degree in **computer science.** I was so **proud of myself**! This event took place on the campus of Nankai University, in our largest **auditorium.** In the evening, all the students went to a **formal reception** at a five-star hotel, where we ate dinner and drank lots of beer and champagne.

The event started with the students **gathering** in a large hall, where we were given the **robes** and hats, which we wore during the ceremony. We **filed** into the auditorium in **alphabetical order** and **took our seats**. The first event in the ceremony was the presentation of prizes to students who had **excelled**. I was proud to receive **the highest recognition** for my work in mathematics.

After the prizes had been awarded, the presentation of degrees began. As their names were called, the students walked to the stage where they **shook hands** with the president of the university and accepted the **scrolls commemorating** their success. Most of us spent the early evening hours **resting up** for the party that evening. My classmates and I started and ended the evening with glasses of **champagne** and, in between, **feasted** on many delicious dishes and **toasted** one another with glasses of beer.

At the end of the party, several of my closest friends and I continued our celebration at two of our favorite **downtown** bars. After that, I finally went home to bed. This event was memorable for me because from a very early age I knew that I had a special talent for understanding the **theories and practices of mathematics**. I worked hard through high school to make the best of my special ability, and continued my university education **with a focus on** computer science. For a student, the end of the four years of university **marks** a major **milestone** in his life. In a way, it marks the **transition** from **childhood** to **adulthood.**

I: Do you have plans to attend graduate school?

C: Yes, my plans are to attend either Cambridge or Oxford in England. I have already received a **letter of acceptance** from both of these universities. All that remains is to complete this IELTS exam.

I: Well, I wish you luck with that.

C: Thank you.

PART 3

I: We've been talking about memorable events. Now I would like to ask you some more general questions about **ceremonies.** How important are ceremonies in our lives?

C: I think ceremonies are very important in our lives, and throughout our lives, from birth to death. Ceremonies mark important **stages** in our lives, beginning with the 100-day birthday party, which celebrates the health of a new baby. When we celebrate birthdays in China, we eat long noodles, which represent a long life to come. Weddings are one of the biggest celebrations in China. Many families spend **the equivalent** of a year's income to be able to invite **a large circle of family, friends and colleagues.** Marriage means **the joining** of two families and is viewed as a major event for both families. Ceremonies also help families and **communities** stay connected, as they usually involve gathering and group activities. Ceremonies are also a **reflection** of traditional culture, which many people think is important to **maintain.**

I: Do you see the role of **private and public ceremonies** changing in the future?

C: I don't believe there will be much change in the celebration of important events because they are usually based on tradition and therefore change very slowly, if at all. Many traditions in China began thousands of years ago and have changed very little since that time. Chinese people **place a lot of value on** celebrations and their traditional aspects.

I: Let's talk a little bit about marriage. Have **attitudes** to marriage changed in recent years?

C: It's funny because there are some attitudes about marriage that are the same, no matter what the time period. For example, people think there is **a right time** to get married; they give marriage kind of a **deadline**, like 30 years old. Most Chinese people think that if you're not married by age 30 then you have no hope and no future. This goes for both men and women. A new attitude towards marriage is that divorce is more common, so people take **the vows of marriage** less seriously, because they know they can **change their minds** in the future. A very common **trend** these days is for people to get married when they are in their mid or late twenties and then to get divorced in their early or mid thirties.

I: In what ways do men and women feel differently about marriage, in your opinion?

C: In my opinion, men sometimes feel **trapped** by marriage, whereas women feel **secure** and **content**. Sometimes my friends refer to their wives as their **ball and chain**, like a heavy weight that they have to **drag around** wherever they go. They feel that marriage is very **constricting** and their wives like to control everything they do, including everything they eat. Women, on the other hand, usually feel very satisfied when they get married. A lot of women tell me that after they get married, the hard part is over, meaning that finding a husband is a difficult job. The easy part is telling him what to do for the rest of his life.

I: Ok, now let's talk a little bit about the way **the media treats** events. What sort of national events make headlines in your country?

C: China tends to pay a lot of attention to events that support **national pride.** For example, if there is a festival, like National Day, or Spring Festival, or Labor Day, many **television stations** have special, **holiday-themed** programs, and all the newspapers' **headlines** have to do with the holiday. Also, the government has started publicizing more and more **corruption cases** and telling the public how the corrupt officials are going to be **punished**. These stories can help **deter** other people from being corrupt and **taking bribes**. Another common headline is about economic development and how China is **progressing** at **breakneck speed.** These types of headlines are very encouraging to citizens and make them **optimistic** about the future.

I: Does the media in your country pay more attention to global or national events?

C: **To tell you the truth, I would have to say that** the media pays more attention to national events. Actually, I think it's a natural phenomenon for people to be more interested in their own country than in other countries. In China, we get general coverage of major world events, like wars, but most people do not stay **up-to-date** with international news. Because China is so big, it is also hard to stay **informed** about **national affairs**, and most people are satisfied with news about their city or community.

I: Okay, that's all for the interview. Thank you very much.

词汇表

范例 1

the Great Wall 长城	a general nature 基本性质
outer space 太空	the role of ceremonies 仪式的作用
Imperial Palace 故宫	play 起(作用)
Tiananmen 天安门	private and public ceremonies 个人和公共的仪式
just in... alone 单就…来说	specific 具体的
Peking Opera 京剧	undergo 经历、遭受
Chinese paintings 中国绘画	drastic 剧烈的
teahouse 茶馆	emphasize 强调
reasonable 合理的	certain 特定的
snacks 小吃	recognize 认清
retired people 退休的人	mark 标志
have the time 有闲	funeral 葬礼
fancy 奇异的	attitude 看法
memorable event 值得纪念的事件	concerned with 对…关心
vividly 生动地	housework 家务
talent contest 才艺大赛	company 公司
senior middle school 高中	the media 媒体
a joint Chinese/Australian high school 中澳合资高中	covers 报道
encourage 鼓励	make headlines 成为头条新闻
the two weeks leading up to the contest 在比赛前的两周	the People's Congress 国务院
piano 钢琴	SARS 非典
violin 小提琴	plenty 大量的
chance 机会	astronaut 宇航员
pretend 假装	space 太空
applause 鼓掌	show up 炫耀
expect 期待	front page 首页
	devote to 专心于
	channel 频道

范例 2	
major centre 主要的中心	feast 享受
historical sights 古迹	toast 干杯
Tiananmen Square 天安门广场	downtown 市中心
the Forbidden City 紫禁城	theories and practices of mathematics 数学的理论与实践
the Summer Palace 颐和园	with a focus on 关注于
the Great Wall 长城	mark 标志
accessible 可到达的	milestone 转折点、里程碑
day trip 一日游	transition 转变
archaological digs 考古发掘	childhood 儿童时代
reveal 揭开	adulthood 成人期
life-sized 与原物一样大小的	letter of acceptance 接受邀请的信
clay warriors 陶俑武士	ceremony 典礼
bury 埋葬	stage 阶段
the Bund 外滩	the equivalent 相当于
European architecture 欧式建筑	a large circle of family, friends and colleagues 一大圈的家人、朋友和同事
colonial time 殖民时代	the joining 结合
Peking opera concert 京剧演唱会	community 社区
form of music 音乐形式	reflection 反映
acrobatic 杂技的	maintain 维持
ancient rituals 古典礼节	private and public ceremonies 个人和公共的典礼
associate with 与…有关	place a lot of value on 很注重
elaborate 精致的	attitude 看法
large, organized tour groups 庞大的、有组织团队	a right time 合适的时间
independent travelers 单独旅行的人	deadline 最终期限
citizen 市民	the vows of marriage 爱的誓言
boost 推动	change their minds 改变主意
memorable event 值得纪念的时间	trend 趋势
bachelor's degree 学士学位	trapped 被捕捉的
computer science 计算机科学	secure and content 放心满意
be proud of myself 为自己骄傲	ball and chain 累赘
auditorium 礼堂	drag around 拖着
formal reception 正式的招待会	constricting 受限制的、压缩的
gather 聚在一起	the media 媒体
robe 礼服	treat 对待
file into 涌入	national pride 民族自尊
alphabetical order 按字母顺序	television stations 电视台
take our seats 就座	holiday-themed 节日主题的
excel 胜过、优越	headline 头条
the highest recognition 最高荣誉	corruption 贪污腐败
shake hands 握手	corrupt officials 腐败官员
scrolls 荣誉证书	punish 抨击
commemorate 纪念	deter 阻止
rest up 休养	take bribes 向…行贿
champagne 香槟	

progress 进步	phenomenon 现象
breakneck speed 飞速	up-to-date 最近的
optimistic 乐观的	informed 见多识广的
to tell you the truth 说实话	national affairs 国内事件
I would have to say that 我不得不说	

补充词汇及句型

Part 1: Visitors

Things to See and Do in China (mind map)		
climb the great wall	see a Peking Opera	go to Tibet
visit the Terracotta Warriors	eat Peking Duck	
Traditional Arts and Music in China		
Chinese Opera	Traditional Chinese Painting	
Chinese Acrobatics	Calligraphy	
Types of Visitors		
tourists	students	(can also refer to age, nationality, etc.)
businessmen/women/people	backpackers	

Has tourism changed China for the better, or for the worse? Has it helped develop the economy, or destroyed the environment?

Part 2: Memorable event

Common Memorable Events		
wedding	birth of a child	meeting a famous person
graduation	winning/losing a game	trip
acceptance into university	first kiss	

Part 3: Role of ceremony, attitudes to marriage, events of national/global significance

Ceremonies are...	
very important because...	not so important because...
they mark the passage of important events.	they don't let people express real emotions.
they help us learn about our culture.	no one really cares about them anymore.
they honor important people.	people pay less attention to them than they used to.

Types of Ceremonies	
flag-raising ceremony	awards ceremony
wedding	greeting foreign leaders
funeral	

Men...	Women...
see marriage as a burden.	see marriage as a gift.
are afraid of marriage.	look forward to getting married.
prefer to get married when they are older.	would rather get married when they are young.

None of the above are set in stone! Maybe you think that men see marriage as a gift, and that women are afraid of marriage. Remember, the most important thing is that you express your opinions clearly.

Types of Events
political events
sporting events
natural disasters
scientific accomplishments

口试要点聚焦

大脑总动员

有效地调动大脑是提高第二阶段口试成绩的一个关键。在这一阶段你有一分钟的准备时间，而这一分钟对你的成绩影响重大。

在口试第二阶段，学生们最大的问题之一就是语言空洞，没有思想。事实上，他们绝大部分人都能做到不间断地说上一两分钟，但问题是言之无物。因此，在一分钟的准备时间内，你要做的很重要的一件事就是尽可能多想出些点子来，从而保证回答问题时有话可说。

大脑总动员是指要在短时间内想出尽可能多的点子。以下几点可以为你闯第二关打开思想的闸门。大脑总动员的一个方式是把想法全都记在大脑里。你只需集中精神、努力思考第二阶段的话题，想出的观点越多越好。这种办法的好处在于你不必花时间把观点写下来，但也有其不足，你可能忘记刚才脑海中闪现过的观点。

我们建议你使用监考人员提供的纸和笔，根据卡片要求列出你的观点。这种做笔记的方法可参见本书模拟口试部分。

另一种做笔记的方法是在大脑里画一张图。这比较费事，但总的来说更能激发起你的创造力。采用这一方法，你需要在一张纸的中间写上话题，从话题辐射出的射线指向你的各种观点。

练习一下两种方法，看哪一种更适合你。

Test 4

LISTENING

SECTION 1

谈话场景:礼物选择场景。
人物关系:关系亲密的同事。
谈话话题:讨论给同事和她刚出生的孩子送礼物。

词汇注释

detail *n.* 细节,详情
weigh *v.* 称重量为…
kilo *n.* 千,多指代千克
centimeter *n.* 厘米
mass *n.* 块,团,大量
curly *adj.* 卷发的
pick up 用车接…
refresh *v.* 使恢复,使清新
garage *n.* 车库,修车厂
last *v.* 持久,持续
pot plant 盆栽,盆景
water *v.* 浇水
chocolate *n.* 巧克力
shampoo *n.* 香波,洗发水
talcum *n.* 爽身粉,扑粉
toy *n.* 玩具

交际与语言表达

1. 本段对话是非常熟悉的朋友之间讨论事情,基本没有用太难的词汇和复杂的句型,文章内容本身对考生做题没有造成任何障碍,但雅思听力考试中的一个怪现象是,越容易的题目考生错得越多,主要原因是基本功不扎实。所以考生在备考阶段对这些简单表达构成的对话反而要给予足够的重视。
2. I've just had some good news. Susan has had her baby. 我刚得到好消息:Susan 生孩子了! 后半句话如果让同学们用英文表达,很多同学会用很复杂的词组和句型,而 native speaker 一句非常简单的话,言简意赅。
3. It sounds quite good, don't you think? 这个名字听起来相当不错,你觉得呢? 用 don't you think 而不用 doesn't it 提问,是希望对方给出肯定的答复。
4. What about tomorrow afternoon at around 1pm? 明天下午 1 点左右怎么样? 提出建议可以用 what about 或者 how about,后面直接跟名词性的词组。
5. Just refresh my memory. What's the address again? 我应该不会忘吧,你的地址再说一遍行吗? 说话人此时有可能还记得地址的一部分,或者可能已经忘了(从后文来看应该是忘了),但没有直说,而是用 just refresh my memory,让对方觉得她还记得,只是为了确认一遍。
6. You will pick me up at a quarter to one and we will be there at one easily. 你 12 点 45 来接我,我们就能轻轻松松地 1 点钟到那里了。注意 quarter 的最基本含义是四分之一,引申的含义比较多,如 1 刻钟(1 小时的四分之一),25 美分(1 美元的四分之一),1 季度(1 年的四分之一)等。
7. What do you think of something like baby shampoo or talcum powder? 你觉得像婴儿香波或爽身粉之类的怎么样? what do you think of... 也是向对方提建议的一种方式,有些类似于 what about...

8. If they're going to be from both of us, I would like to go shares. 如果是我们两个人一起送的话，我得跟你平分礼物的费用。

考题解析

Question 1

听力原文中女声首先提到 he weighed **four and a quarter kilos** when he was born，男声马上补充道：That does sound big, **four and a quarter kilos.** 两个人都提到了本题答案，但很多考生还是会写错，原因是很多考生可能对这种数词的读法不熟悉。答案可以写出英文单词，也可以直接写阿拉伯数字：4.25。

Question 2

这个数字也有很多考生会填错，大部分原因是上面一题的数字还没有写下来，这道题的数字就出现了，所以考生在平常要加强听写练习，尤其是数字的拼写。

Questions 3–5

这几道地图题的思路可以参照第二套题的6–10题和第三套题17–20题，先确定要找的地名与图中已知信息的关系，然后带着这个判断去听，准确率非常高。把握好 **next to**, **opposite**, **on the other street corner** 这样的关键字词与图中其他已知地名之间的联系就可以了。

Questions 6–7

这两道题目本身非常简单，因为答案在原文中分别提到了四五次，唯一要注意的问题是 **chocolates** 这个词的拼写，虽然简单，不少考生会拼错，另外注意是复数。

Questions 8–9

这两道题中大部分考生会做错第8题。在女声问 what about a teddy bear 后，男声说：I could get one early tomorrow **at the market**，也就是说先把第9题答案给出了。很多考生可能比较迷惑，心里在想刚才是不是错过了第8题答案呢？实际上后文男声才提到：I could probably **get the chocolates there too**。最关键的是一个很小的词"too"。

Question 10

这道题又是一个简单的数字，但要注意听力原文中 **$35 or so**, or so 放在数字后面表示在……左右。

SECTION 2

谈话场景：电视或收音机的导购节目。
人物关系：讲话者为擅长购物的居民。
谈话话题：讨论四种小商品是否值得购买。

词汇注释

exhibition *n.* 展览会	**household** *adj.* 家庭的，家常的
gadget *n.* 小器械，小装置，小设备	**vacuum** *n.* 真空
resident *n.* 居民	**flask** *n.* 暖瓶，热水瓶
investigate *v.* 调查	**contain** *v.* 包含，容纳

therefore *adv.* 因此	**button** *n.* 按钮
unbreakable *adj.* 打不破的	**keyhole** *n.* 钥匙孔
intent *n.* 意图,含义	**unpleasant** *adj.* 不舒服的
purpose *n.* 目的	**metal** *n.* 金属
stainless *adj.* 不锈的,无瑕疵的	**cushion** *n.* 座垫
steel *n.* 钢材	**masterpiece** *n.* 杰作
guarantee *v.* 投保	**gizmo** *n.* 小发明,小玩意儿
unfortunately *adv.* 不幸地	**squeeze** *v.* 挤压
recommendation *n.* 推荐意见	**handle** *n.* 手柄,把手
natty *adj.* 漂亮的,整洁的	**generate** *v.* 产生
device *n.* 设备,装置	**objection** *n.* 反对意见
whistle *n.* 口哨 *v.* 吹口哨	**decoy** *n.* 圈套,诱骗
holder *n.* 钥匙夹,钥匙串	**fake** *adj.* 虚伪的,假的
basically *adv.* 基本上	**scare** *v.* 吓唬
pitch *n.* 音高	**burglar** *n.* 窃贼
flash *v.* 闪光	**realistic** *adj.* 真实的
press *v.* 挤压,摁	**burglary** *n.* 行窃行为

交际与语言表达

1. 本段文章摘自某电视或收音机节目,开头是主持人的开场白和对访谈嘉宾的介绍,语言正式又不失风趣。
2. Good evening. Tonight's show comes to you from the Good Home Exhibition. 晚上好,今天的节目从好家庭展览会现场向您报导。
3. . . . to tell us which ones are worth buying and which will die a death. . . . 来告诉我们哪些值得买,哪些不值得。be worth doing 值得……;die a death 这种用法不常见,death 前面还能加形容词来进一步修饰。能这样用的词不多,还有 live a life, dream a dream。
4. I have been investigating four new household gadgets and sorting out the advantages and disadvantages and then really deciding what are 'must buys' what are 'Maybe buys' and what are 'Never buys'. 我一直在研究四种新的家用设备,分析它们的优缺点,最后决定哪些"必买",哪些"可买可不买",哪些"绝不能买"。口语中根据上下文可以用很简单明了的词组新造一些表达法,像这里的"**must buys, maybe buys, never buys**"。
5. On the down side, it really works out to be quite expensive and, much more surprisingly, it unfortunately leaves a strange taste. 弊端是,它实在是太贵,更让人吃惊的是,它会产生一种难闻的怪味。work out 在这里类似于 turn out,表示"结果是"。
6. Basically this is where you whistle and the key holder gives off a high pitched noise and flashes light so you can find it. 这个东西的基本原理是,你吹一下口哨,钥匙夹会发出尖叫声并闪光,这样你就可以找到它了。
7. On the weaker side, I did find the noise unpleasant, which I'm sure the designers could have done something about. 弱点就是我的确觉得尖叫声很刺耳,这一点设计者本来肯定可以改进的。**I did find. . .**, did 在这里强调 find;the designers **could have done** something about 虚拟语气,有时表示轻度的指责,本可以做但没有做。
8. But taken as a whole, I thought it was a masterpiece of design and would highly recommend it. 但总体上来说,我认为它在设计上不失为杰作,所以强烈推荐它。
9. It works by squeezing the handle to generate the power. 挤压把手发电,它就可以发挥作用了。

10. My main objection to it though was although it did work in these conditions，但是我对它的主要反对意见是尽管在这些条件下它的确能起作用……前半句的 though 位于主句句末，表示“但是”；后文的 although 引导从句，表示“尽管”。
11. However, burglary is such a major problem these days that it is worth the effort, so this gets my strong recommendation. 但是，入室盗窃现在是这么大的一个问题，安装一个仿真摄像机还是值得的。因此我强烈推荐它。

考题解析

Question 11

这道题目比较简单，因为试卷上题干部分与磁带原文使用的是一样的字句，contains no **glass**；后文接着解释它名称中的 unbreakable，也可反推出答案。

Question 12

题干中使用的词组是 **keep warm**，而磁带里读到的是 **maintain heat** for **18** hours，基本上是一模一样的意思。

Question 13

此处是要填缺点，听的时候要注意贬义词，转折词等。在提到该物 expensive 的缺点之后，讲话者提到 much more surprisingly，这时考生应集中注意力听后文的内容。紧接着她说 it **unfortunately** leaves **a strange taste**。Unfortunately 再次暗示答案的出现。

Questions 14-20

这几道题目考生只要把握好空格的前后处，注意优点和缺点之间的转折，优点多听褒义词，缺点多听贬义词、否定词即可。

SECTION 3

谈话场景：课外研究场景。
人物关系：师生关系。
谈话话题：讨论学生所写论文的修改。

词汇注释

draft *n.* 草稿	**approach** *n.* 思路，方法
anxious *adj.* 着急的，焦急的	**valuable** *adj.* 有价值的
chapter *n.* 章，节，回	**complex** *adj.* 复杂的
amazing *adj.* 令人吃惊的	**remove** *v.* 撤除，除去
dash *v.* 猛冲，冲撞	**chronology** *n.* 年表
par *n.* 常态，一般状况	**simplistic** *adj.* （偏贬义）简单化的
division *n.* 分类	**represent** *v.* 表示，描绘，讲述
heading *n.* 标题	**proof reading** 校对工作
margin *n.* 页边的空白	**laser** *n.* 激光
relevant *adj.* 相关的	**faculty** *n.* 全体教员，（大学）系

交际与语言表达

1. 本文是师生之间的对话，老师的措辞和语调中流露出为人师者的威严；而学生明显是“受制于人”，说话时语调比较温和，又想竭力“保护”自己的劳动成果，反映了她“有求于人”的心态。作为旁观者，考生可以体会本篇对话隐藏的幽默。
2. I was just anxious to hear what you think of it. 我正急着想听听你怎么看待它。be anxious to do sth. 急于做某事。
3. I had been interested in looking at Barings Factory. 我本来对 Barings 工厂很感兴趣。此处 had been interested in 表示一个原来准备要做但最终没有完成的动作，同样的表达还有 had thought, had hoped 等等。
4. I spent about two or three weeks reading and doing general research and then I dashed the writing off very quickly. 我花了两三个星期阅读资料，进行调查研究，然后非常匆忙地写完了草稿。spend ... doing sth. 花费……做某事；dash off 匆忙做完某事。
5. That's about par for the course. You've got a while yet to make the changes. 这段时间对于这个过程很正常。你还得花点时间进行修改。
6. As long as I don't have to remove them altogether. 只要我不用全部删除这个部分（就好了）。这句话是该学生“劫后余生”的感叹，与上下文联系起来理解的话，能够感受到其中暗含的幽默。
7. And then I think you need to think about ways of representing interview data. 然后我觉得你要想想怎么解释调查获得的数据。
8. When by, do you think? 您认为到什么时候截止呢？这句话言简意赅，用两个单词就表达了一个复杂的意思。
9. I think I'm all set now! 我想现在一切都搞定了！

考题解析

Question 21

女生先提到自己本来对工厂感兴趣，但老师马上说：I think the **hospital** was a much better choice，一锤定音，确定了本题答案为 B。

Question 22

老师先说 it **opens well** and the **first chapter** is fine，但马上转折说 but **the middle** section really **stood out** for me... **most interesting.** stand out 非常吸引人的注意力，其形容词形式为 outstanding。

Question 23

在老师夸奖后，学生谦虚地说 that's **amazing**（与题干中的 surprise 同义）because I really **didn't** find it **a bit easy** to write. not a bit 表示一点也不，不容易就是 difficult。

Question 24

老师此处指出，I can see why you put it there but it **really isn't relevant** to the approach you've taken. 与所采用的方法毫不相干，当然应该删除。后面学生很沮丧地说：I think I see what you mean. 进一步肯定了该删除的做法。

Question 25

老师的意见是 spend a bit of time **making the data** a lot **clearer**，花点时间使数据更清楚，也就是要改写。后面学生说“只要不让我全部删除就好”，也暗示是改写。

Question 26

此处老师毫不客气地说 my advice on that is to **take them out**,删除。

Questions 27-29

这几道题的答案原文都重复两遍,应该没有问题,但注意 Sight and Sound 和 Support Tutor 的大写问题。

Question 30

原文并没有直接给出 laser print 的具体时间,但暗示说 be careful because the computer **center closes on** 10 **July.** 打印肯定要在计算机中心关闭之前进行,所以 7 月 10 日就是这道题的答案。

SECTION 4

谈话场景:学术交流场景。
人物关系:主讲者为某环境课程的教师,听众为学生。
谈话话题:讨论噪声污染的影响。

词汇注释

environmental *adj.* 环境的
effect *n.* 影响
estate *n.* 房产
particularly *adv.* 尤其地,特别地
highway *n.* 高速公路
somewhat *adv.* 多少,有那么些
abate *v.* 减少,减轻
extent *n.* 程度
modification *n.* 改动,修整,修葺
significant *adj.* 值得注意的,重要的
developer *n.* 发展商
be about to do sth. 马上要做某事
outline *v.* 描述,勾画轮廓
desirable *adj.* 令人渴望的,可取的
background *n.* 背景材料
astray *adv.* 入歧途地
propose *v.* 建议
perimeter *n.* 周长,周边,四周
threshold *n.* 门槛,开端
decibel *n.* 分贝
construction *n.* 建筑
modify *v.* 修饰,修改,修葺
specialized *adj.* 专业的
glazing *n.* 上釉
acoustic *adj.* 听觉的,音响的
seal *n.* 密封
exterior *adj.* 外面的
hinge *n.* 铰链
adjacent *adj.* 附近的,毗邻的
density *n.* 密度
insulation *n.* 绝缘
ceiling *n.* 天花板
plaster *n.* 石膏,灰泥
mechanical *adj.* 机械的
ventilation *n.* 通风
install *v.* 安装
absorber *n.* 消音装置,隔音设备
air conditioning 空调
substantially *adv.* 实质上,本质上,巨大地
centimeter *n.* 厘米
millimeter *n.* 毫米
pane *n.* 窗户玻璃
essential *adj.* 重要的,必要的
minimum *n.* 最小值
take... into consideration 考虑…
layout *n.* 格局
interior *adj.* 内部的
laundry *n.* 洗衣房
block *n.* 街区
intersection *n.* 十字路口

交际与语言表达

1. Today we are going to look into the effects of noise on a planned housing estate in a particularly difficult part of the new Manchester Park area. 今天我们要探讨噪声对一处计划开发的住宅区的影响，该区位于曼彻斯特公园新区某个十分糟糕的角落。
2. By the time most of the students and workers have arrived back home in the evening during the week the noise will have abated to a fairly large extent. 工作日当中，大多数学生和上班族晚上回家之前，噪音会很大程度上减少。to a fairly large extent，在相当大的程度上 。
3. Of course modifications to houses will be necessary at a site like this and they come at a significant cost to the developer and home buyer. 当然像这样的地方修葺房屋是必要的，这对发展商和购房者都是一笔可观的开销。后半句使用拟人的手法，非常形象。
4. A bit of background would not **go astray.** 提些背景材料不会跑题太远。注意划线词组的用法，下同。
5. It's a particularly difficult one in terms of noise with the highway along the eastern perimeter and the Black town airport not 3 kilometers away to the north. 从噪音的角度来看，这个地区的确很难受——东边有高速公路，北边 3 公里外有机场。
6. Of course, those nearest the highway will be the worst hit, with heavy traffic noise **as well as** the noise from the light planes overhead. 当然，离高速公路最近肯定最惨，既要忍受大量的交通噪声，还要忍受头上的轻型飞机的噪声。
7. As you all know, the normal noise threshold for private housing is 55 decibels. 正如大家所知的，一个家庭所能承受的正常噪声的底线是 55 分贝。当提及一个众所周知但不得不提的内容时，可以用 as you all know，或者 as is known to all 来开头。
8. The construction of the houses has to be somewhat modified from houses in most areas. 这些房子的构造要进行修整，得与其他地方的房子略有不同。
9. Every house built on this site, not just those **adjacent to** the highway or nearest to the airport, will require high density insulation materials in the roof. 这个地方建的每栋房子，不仅是那些靠近高速公路或临近机场的房子，都要在房顶上安装高密度隔音材料。
10. Not only will all the roofs need insulating, the exterior walls will be required to be double brick. 不仅房顶需要隔音，外墙也要铺双层砖块。Not only 置于句首，句子需要倒装。
11. Coming back now to the double glazing I mentioned before. 现在回到我前面提到的上双层釉的问题。这种句型可以用于思维发散后回到所讨论的主题，或者再次提起前面已经讨论过的话题。
12. **It is essential that** the glass **be** thicker on the outside than on the inside and that the gap between the panes of glass **be** of a minimum of 7 centimeters. 外面的玻璃比里面的要厚，两扇玻璃之间间隔至少是 7 厘米，这几点很重要。It is essential that 后面跟的是虚拟语气，两个 be 前面都省略了 should。

考题解析

Question 31

看题时首先要注意问的是 **between** what times，后面的词中 **lightest** 这个最高级要格外注意。原文提到机场在晚 6 点到早 7 点关闭，很多学生误以为这就是答案，明显是没有注意到问题问的是 **road traffic**。后面的一个时间段是 traffic is somewhat reduced between **7. 30 pm and 5. 30 am**。写答案时一定要写 pm 和 am，否则可能会被误解称是早上的 7 点半到下午的五点半。

Question 32

注意题干问的是 **who**，又有一个最高级 **most**。听力原文提到 the **people most** affected by the noise will be **housewives**。

Question 33

这道题要考查 **which day of the week, least traffic**，这里肯定要填的是周一到周日的某一天。听力原文先说周六比平常的交通肯定会减少，后面提到 **even more so on Sundays**，周日减少得更多。答案当然是周日。

Question 34

题干中问的是 **extra cost**，首先当然要注意听数字，其次要听 **extra** 附加的东西。原文是说 will **add** about $25,000 to the **price**。问题还是在于考生是否熟悉数字的读法。

Question 35

这道题大部分考生都能做对，只要注意到题干中的 **at this site**，听力原文所说的是 **at this site** the levels have been recorded as high as **67 decibels**，答案应该不会错过。

Questions 36–38

这三道题目有相当大的难度，最关键的问题是部分考生不太了解建筑材料的意义，而且三个答案又鱼贯而入，很快读完，容易听混。这样的情况考生不要太多的去思考文章的内容本身，只用根据单词的发音去判断。

Questions 39–40

这两道题目看题时应迅速找到四幅图之间的相同点与不同点，以利于迅速排除答案。

比如 39 题 A、B 两项间隔都是 6cm，C、D 两项间隔都是 7cm，这样的思路很重要。即使看不懂图，甚至也可以用最简单的办法，原文中提到三个数字 7、8、6，图中只有 D 项符合。

40 题根据一句话 **bedrooms and living rooms** will have to be built towards the **back**. 就可以基本判断答案为 C，后文中又补充在房子前面的只能是 garage, laundry, kitchen, bathroom and dining room，进一步使考生确定答案。

READING

READING PASSAGE 1

文章结构

<table>
<tr><td>体　　裁</td><td colspan="2">说明文。</td></tr>
<tr><td>主要内容</td><td colspan="2">说明面对日益严重的空气污染，各地采取了各种方式解决这一问题，但由于空气污染与城市发展有关，空气污染问题在大城市尤为突出。</td></tr>
<tr><td rowspan="6">结　　构</td><td rowspan="6">Part One：各地采用各种方式解决日益严重的空气污染问题。</td><td>A 段：概括性地指出各地采用种种方式解决空气污染，但解决问题的关键还是解决污染的措施也跟得上城市发展的速度。</td></tr>
<tr><td>B 段：指出解决空气污染的几条战线及相关例子。</td></tr>
<tr><td>C 段：详细说明把造成污染比较严重的陈旧汽车从道路上清理出去。</td></tr>
<tr><td>D 段：伦敦采用新方法测试汽车污染。</td></tr>
<tr><td>E 段：尽管洛杉矶有世界最清洁的车，但更多的人不愿意与他人共用一辆车。</td></tr>
<tr><td>F 段：新加坡根据司机行驶的区域收费，但这一方法在英国剑桥未能实施。</td></tr>
</table>

	Part Two：联合国调查的大城市污染状况以及城市发展空气污染的关系。	第 1 段：联合国公布大城市的污染情况。
		第 2 段：联合国监控的六种污染物中最受人关注的是颗粒物质。
		第 3 段：重度污染空气会加速死亡。
		第 4 段：联合国预测城市会继续增长，给减少污染带来极大压力。

词汇注释

文 章

Part One

A 段

increasingly *adv.* 渐增地；越来越多地
focus *n.*（注意、活动、兴趣等的）中心，集中点；重点
citizen *n.* 平民，老百姓（区别于政府官员、军人等）
concern *n.* 关心；忧虑，担心
solution（to） *n.*（问题、疑难等的）解决，解答；解决办法；解释
propose *vt.* 提出；提议，建议
trial *vt.* 试验
implement *vt.* 实施；执行；履行
ever *adv.* 不断地；总是；永远
reduction *n.* 减少；下降
measure *n.*（常作～s）措施，步骤，方法
keep pace with（与…）齐步前进，（与…）并驾齐驱
urban *adj.* 城市的；居住在城市的
major *adj.* 主要的；较重要的
deteriorate *vi.* 恶化，变化；质量（或价值）下降
beyond *prep.* 可及

B 段

front *n.*（政治、经济等的）阵线
legislation *n.* 法律，法规
improve *vt.* 改进，改善；提高，利用
enforcement *n.* 实施；强制执行
innovative *adj.* 革新的，新颖的；富有革新精神的
technology *n.* 技术，工艺
regulation *n.* 规章，章程；条例；规定
manufacturer *n.* 制造商；制造厂（或公司）
ever *adv.* 不断地；总是；永远
title *vt.* 用称号称呼，把…称作
emission *n.*（光、热、电波、声音、液体、气味等的）发出，射出，散发
vehicle *n.* 机动车；车辆；交通工具
available *adj.* 可获得的
intend *vt.* 想要，打算，计划
make up 组成，构成，补足
authority *n.*（authorities）当局，官方
campaign *vi.* 参加（或发起）运动；参加竞选
enforce *vt.* 实施，使生效；强制执行
anti-pollution *adj.* 防止（环境）污染的，减轻（环境）污染的（尤指空气污染）
at present 现在，目前
tend *vi.*（to）易于，往往会
elsewhere *adv.* 在别处；到别处
rent *vt.*（out）出租，出借

C 段

automobile *n.* 汽车
monitor *vt.* 监测，检测
exhaust *n.*（排出的）废气；废蒸汽
offender *n.* 犯法的人；犯规的人
sizeable *adj.* 相当大的；大的
a number of 若干，许多
identify *vt.*（经考虑）确定；认出；识别
gross *adj.* 严重的；恶劣的；极端的，十足的
tune *vt.* 使能被容纳，使能被接受；使达到要求
scheme *n.* 计划，规划，方案
flat *adj.*（价格等）无涨落的，固定的，一律的
run-down *adj.* 停止走动的，（钟、表等）发条走完的，电耗尽的
remove *vt.* 去掉，除去；消除
decrepit *adj.* 用旧的，破旧的

D 段

environmental *adj.* 环境的;有关环境(保护)的
programme *n.* 计划,方案
council *n.* 委员会;理事会;顾问委员会;议会
infra-red *adj.* 红外线的;产生(或使用)红外辐射的
spectrometer *n.* 分光计,光谱仪,谱仪
gauge *vt.* 精确地测量;量,测
annual *adj.* 每年的,年度的
stationary *adj.* 稳定的,不变的
standard *n.* 标准;规范;准则
bounce *vt.* (经通信卫星等)反射;使反弹,使弹起
beam *n.* (X 射线、核粒子等的)束,柱;(日、月、灯等的)光线,光柱
block *vt.* 堵塞,阻塞;封锁
link *vt.* 串连,连接
video camera 摄像机
number plate (汽车的)牌照
automatically *adv.* 自动地;以自动装置完成的

E 段

clean up (把…)打扫干净;(把…)理整齐
tendency *n.* 趋势,倾向
car pool 合伙用车(一群有自备汽车的人安排好在上下班时每次合乘其中一人之车,并由其开车)
car-pool *vt.* (根据合伙用车协议)轮流用各人的车运送
arrangement *n.* (解决问题的)办法,约定,非正式协议
destination *n.* 目的地,终点
average *n.* 平均数,平均
freeway *n.* 高速公路,高速干道
steadily *adv.* 稳定地;持续地;有规律地
effective *adj.* 能产生(预期)效果的,有效的
ease *vt.* 解除,减轻(痛苦、忧虑等),减低……的强度(或速度)
congestion *n.* 挤满;拥塞;密集

F 段

while *n.* 一会儿,一段时间
badge *n.* 标记,标识,徽号
electronic *adj.* 电子的,电子器件的
innovation *n.* 新奇事物;创新,革新
sophistication *n.* 复杂(或精密)的产品;高级(或尖端)的产品
vary *vi.* 变化;有不同;呈差异
according to 根据,按照
and so on …等等
direction *n.* 方面;领域
network *n.* 网状系统;网状物
transmitter *n.* 传送者;发射机;发射台
charge *vt.* 收(费);要(人)支付(钱)
controversial *adj.* 引起争论的,有争议的
technique *n.* 技术,技能,工艺
vocal *adj.* 清晰激烈地表达意见的;喜欢畅所欲言的
ultimately *adv.* 最后,最终;终于
opposition *n.* 反对;反对意见

Part Two

第 1 段

scope *n.* (活动、影响等的)范围
immense *adj.* 无限的;无边无际的
the United Nations 联合国
World Health Organisation 世界卫生组织
conclude *vt.* 推断出,推论出;(最后)决定
sample *n.* 样本;样品;范例
megacity *n.* 大城市
likely *adj.* 可能的;有倾向的;看来要发生的
inhabitant *n.* 居民;住户;常住居民
exceed *vt.* 超过;胜过
deem *vt.* 认为,以为,相信
at least 至少
two-thirds 三分之二
guideline 标准,准则,指导方针

第 2 段

pollutant *n.* 污染性物质,有害物质(尤指工业废物、废气、放射性物质等)
carbon dioxide 二氧化碳
nitrogen dioxide 二氧化二氮
ozone *n.* 臭氧
sulphur dioxide 二氧化硫
lead *n.* 铅
particulate *adj.* 微粒的,颗粒的,粒状的
category *n.* 种类,类,类别
sub-category *n.* 亚类;子种类;子范畴
across *adv.* 从一边到另一边
implicate *vt.* 使牵连其中(in);涉及
conduct *vt.* 进行;实施
disturbing *adj.* 引起烦恼的;令人不安的
conclusion *n.* 结论,推论

第 3 段	
allergy *n.* 过敏性;变态反应	**vulnerable** *adj.* 易受伤的,脆弱的
asthma *n.* 气喘,哮喘	**acute** *adj.* 严重的,剧烈的
decade *n.* 十年,十年期	**stagnant** *adj.* 不流动的,呆滞的
lung *n.* 肺	**hasten** *vt.* 加速,加紧
grow up 长成,成熟	**fume** *n.* (常作 ~s)(有害、浓烈、或难闻的)烟,气,汽
destructive *adj.* 破坏性的;毁灭性的;消极的	**linger** *vt.* 继续存留,缓慢消失
第 4 段	
estimate *vt.* 估计	**established** *adj.* 已确定的;已建立的
corporation *n.* 市政当局	**trend** *n.* 趋势,趋向
reverse *vt.* 使反向,使倒转	**in proportion with** 与…成比例,与…相称
题目	
contradict *vt.* 与…抵触,违背	**resident** *n.* 居民,定居者
commuter *n.* (尤指市郊之间)乘公交车辆上下班者,月季票旅客	**subject** *n.* (动作的)对象;主题
mere *adj.* 只不过的,仅仅的	**urgent** *adj.* 急迫的,紧要的
currently *adv.* 现时,当今	**severely** *adv.* 严重地;严厉地
whilst *n.* = while, 当…的时候	**intense** *adj.* 强烈的,剧烈的;极度的
	sufferer *n.* 患病者;受害者

考题解析

Questions 1–5

● 题型归类:Matching

Matching 考查文章细节,此类题目通常难度不大,但由于需要在全文反复搜索相关内容而需要耗费大量时间,在解题时可以根据题目中某一组比较明显的定位词先在文章中定位,然后在定位词附近迅速搜寻正确答案。

● 题目解析:

题目编号	题目定位词	答案位置	题解
1	clearner cars	B 段第 2 句(In Los Angeles,...)	首先在文章中把城市名都圈出来,然后再在这些城市名附近寻找题目中的定位词,1、2、3 题都是以原文形式重现,第 4 题定位词在原文中稍有变化,原文中是 passing vehicles,而且定位词和答案需要的地名不在同一句话中,第 5 题也一样,在定位词所在的句子没有地名,这种情况下只需要找到离定位词最近的地名所在的句子简单阅读即可判断。
2	enforce anti-pollution laws	B 段第 3 句(Local authorities in...)	
3	charged/the roads they use	F 段第 3 句(Singapore is advancing...)	
4	moving vehicles/monitored/exhaust emissions	D 段第 2 句(It gauges the...)	
5	commuter/share their vehicles	E 段第 3 句(One solution is...)	

Questions 6–10

● 题型归类:YES/NO/NOT GIVEN

细节题,需要将题目中信息与原文中信息相对应后进行判断,难度较大。首先必须准确理解题意,在文章中定位找到相应信息后进行判断。同时注意到这五道题中没有答案选择 NOT GIVEN,这种情况在正式考试中也比较少见。

● 题目解析:

题目编号	题目定位词	答案所在位置	题解
6	British research/ twelve per cent/fifty per cent	C 段首句(When Britain's royal...)	本题较容易解答,根据题目中的数字定位词很容易在原文中找到相关语句,有关数字的题目通常考查数字精确性,题目中有两处数字:第一处指被检测的车辆百分比,第二处是这些被检车辆造成污染的比例。原文的表述基本一致,只有第二个数字在题目中是以百分比形式 over fifty per cent 出现,而文章中是 more than half,表达的意思完全一致。因此答案选 YES。
7	whilst they are moving	D 段第 2 句(It gauges the...)	本句中的定位词很容易和第 4 题联系起来,都是在讲 moving vehicles,所以可以直接定位到第 4 题所在的句子。本题题意是指一种可能性,即可以测量正在行驶的车辆所造成的污染,在原文中虽然是以叙述事实的形式出现,但与题目中的各个细节都完全相符,"已经实现"就表明可能性存在。因此答案选择 YES。
8	Los Angeles	E 段第 2 句(Los Angeles has...)	本题选择城市名比较好定位,然后再在城市名附近寻找题目中相关内容。文章中一共有三处 Los Angeles,第一处在 B 段第二句,在解答第一道题时已经知道这句话的内容和本题题意无关。第二、三处地名集中在 E 段。题目的关键在一个趋势,即 Los Angeles 的居民每年驾车出行的距离在减少,而在第二处地名所在的句子内容与此趋势完全相反,文章句子指出:尽管 Los Angeles 拥有世界上最清洁的车辆,但这些车辆行驶的距离正在持续增长(continues to grow);尽管句中没有题目中的居民(residents)和时间限定(yearly),但文章内容与题目最重要的因素——下降趋势——直接抵触,因此答案是 NO。如果对文章内容理解不透彻,还可以通读全段,因为本段主题句(首句)已经揭示本段的主要内容是如果对更多地驾车不加关注,只清除汽车对减少污染是无济于事的,Los Angeles 正是对此观点的一个例证,因此也可以判断文章的内容是和题目相悖的。
9	car-pooling/ Los Angeles	E 段第 4 句(However, the average...)	本题难度较小,定位时比较容易,但定位词所在的句子并不能是答案所在的位置,这种情况在雅思阅读考试中非常常见,只要根据段落中句子的安排或衔接词的提示适当地阅读上下文就可以找到正确答案。题目也是反映一种趋势,即近年在 Los Angeles 合伙用车这件事更加普遍了。文章中定位词所在的句子是解释什么叫合伙用车(car-pooling),接下来的衔接词 however 很明确地表

			达了对上文轻微否定的意思，句中指出，Los Angeles 每辆车里的平均人数只有 1.3，同时这个数字还在持续下降。持续下降（falling steadily）和题目中的更加普遍（more popular）在意义上是相反的，因此答案选择 NO。
10	Cambridge, England	F 段末句（When the local...）	题目的意思是说在 Cambridge，对驾车人进入城市一些区域收费的做法已经获得成功。回原文定位时比较容易找到地名所在的句子，同时可以想到第 3 题的内容已经说明 Singapore 正是这么做的。原文说 Cambridge 当局引进新加坡的技术，这里指的就是题目中所说的在部分区域收费的做法，接下来的半句话说明引进该技术的结果，是 vocal and ultimately successful opposition，即使不认识前几个形容词，这个短语的中心词是名词 opposition（反对），加上形容词 successful 的修饰，意思更加明确，是这一做法遭到反对，被否定掉了。这与题目的意思正好相反，所以答案选择 NO。

Questions 11–13

● 题型归类：Multiple choice

此类题型属于细节题，通常先在题干中寻找定位词，回原文定位后搜索，由于在其他考试中此类题型较为常见，因此相对而言难度较小，解题时可以较为灵活，也可采用排除法等方法解题。

● 题目解析：

题目编号	题目定位词	答案所在位置	题解
11	WHO/megacities	Part Two 第 1 段第 2 句（In 1992, the...）	本题较为容易，题干定位词十分明确，同时根据题干的提问方式和选项都可以判断本题考查数字精确度，需要注意题干中的修饰语，即“所有被研究的大城市中”。因为文章中对超标的城市有好几种分类方式，但对于所有在城市的超标情况在定位词所在的句子中已经明确指出是 at least one major pollutant。因此答案选择 A。
12	nitrogen dioxide/ozone/lead/particulate matter	Part Two 第 2 段第 1 句（Of the six...）	本题在定位时稍有所变通会更容易解题，在读题干时可以判断，所有选项在原文中均可能出现，而选项的词均为专有名词，比题干中的词更容易定位。这样一来，很容易就找到答案所在的句子，题干问哪一种是较紧急的研究对象（the subject of urgent research），在文章中会找到所有选项内容以列举形式出现，在列举后文章说：最后一种吸引了健康研究者最大的关注。因此列举中的最后一项 particulate matter，即 D 就是正确答案。
13	severely affected/intense air pollution	Part Two 第 3 段第 3 句（The ole and ill, ...）	这道题可以通过题干定位后判断正确答案，也可以通过选项定位后通过排除法解答。如果用第一种方法解答，在文章中定位时定位词稍有变化，题目中的 severely affected 在文章中是以名词短语 the acute effects 的形式出

			现,而题目中的 intense air pollution 则以 heavily polluted stagnant air 的形式出现,但这两组短语的基本意思都是一样的。这种情况在雅思考试中会对部分词汇量较小的考生造成解题困难。根据句子的意思,可以判断正确答案是 C。

参考译文

第一部分

空气污染正日益成为全世界政府和平民忧虑的焦点。从墨西哥城和纽约,到新加坡和日本,解决空气污染这一旧课题的新方案正以不断增长的速度被提出、试验和实施。令人担心的是,如果降低污染的措施不能与城市发展的持续压力相匹敌,许多世界主要城市的空气质量会恶化到难以想象的地步。

各地在新的立法,增加执行力度和科技创新这几条战线上都在采取行动。在洛杉矶,政府法律强制制造商出售更加清洁的汽车:第一批号称"零排放"的最清洁的汽车必须尽快上市,因为制造商想在 1997 年使其销售额达到总销售额的 2%。伦敦地方政府正在为当局获准强制执行反污染法而努力;目前只有警察有这一权力,但他们总是在其他地方忙得不可开交。在新加坡,把道路空间出租给使用者是未来的方向。

英国皇家汽车俱乐部检测了 60,000 辆汽车的排气,发现一半以上的污染是其中 12% 的车辆制造的。较老的车辆违规最为严重;尽管相当数量的新车也被视为重污染源,它们只是未能完全达标。加利福尼亚制定了一个计划来把那些重污染源清理出街道:他们为任何由车主开来的旧的、报废的汽车统一支付 700 美元,目标是把造成严重污染的最陈旧的汽车从道路上清除出去。

作为欧盟环保规划的一部分,伦敦委员会正在检测由科罗拉多丹佛大学提供的红外光谱仪。该光谱仪可以通过一束射入并从汽车排放物中反弹回来的红外线测量其中的阻塞物,从而精确测量一辆驶过的汽车造成的污染,这比英国现今的标准做法即每年固定检测更为有用。委员会下一步可能要把这一系统和由计算机控制的摄像机连接起来,这个摄像机可以自动读入车牌。

如果对汽车使用频率越来越高这一趋势视之不理,清理汽车的努力可能对减少污染无济于事。洛杉矶拥有世界上最清洁的汽车,这些汽车远比欧洲汽车好,但它们的总里程数在继续增长。一种解决方案是合伙用车,即要去同一地点的若干人共用一辆车。但是洛杉矶高速路上每辆车里的平均人数是 1.3,这个数字还在持续下降。增加每辆车里的人数是减少排放和缓解拥堵的有效手段。问题在于,洛杉矶人似乎喜欢独享他们的车。

新加坡在一段时间内实施了一个方案,如果汽车司机想到城市某一特定区域,就要被强制购买一个标识。有了电子领域的创新,电子产品就可能越来越精密:可以根据路况、时间段等情况调整价格。新加坡在这一领域取得进展,建立了一个全城范围的传输网络用来收集信息并在驾驶者超过一定的积分时收费。但这种道路收费方式颇具争议。英国剑桥的当地政府在引进新加坡的技术时就遭到激烈的反对,最终未能得以实施。

第二部分

地球上的城市面临着巨大的问题。1992 年,联合国环境署和世界卫生组织推论出:2000 年抽样调查的 20 个常住人口可能超过 1000 万的大城市,至少都有一种主要污染物超过了世界卫生组织认定的健康标准。其中三分之二的城市有两项超标,七个城市有三项甚至更多项超标。

世界卫生组织监测的六种有害物包括二氧化碳、二氧化二氮、臭氧、二氧化硫、铅和颗粒物质，其中颗粒物质引起调查者最多的关注。十万之一米长的 PM10 是颗粒物质的一种，仅在英国一年就会引发成千上万的死亡。在南加利弗尼亚两个县进行的调查得出类似的结论，这些令人不安的结论都和这种未被充分了解的污染物有关。

过去四十年间世界范围内过敏反应特别是哮喘病的增加目前被认为与空气污染加重有关。在污染空气中长大的儿童的肺部和大脑更加证明了空气污染的毁灭能力。然而当重度污染且滞留不去的空气造成严重影响时，老人和病人最容易受到伤害。重度污染空气的滞留的确能加速死亡，1991 年 12 月一大片废气在伦敦上空飘了一个多星期才慢慢散去，当时就产生了这种情况。

联合国预测在 2000 年将有 24 个大城市人口超过千万，还有 85 个城市人口会超过 300 万。公共官员、政府当局和城市居民承受压力要逆转现有空气污染的趋势，这种压力可能会和城市的发展成比例增长。情况虽然正在改善，然而问题还是没变：“我们的改变会够快吗？”

READING PASSAGE 2

文章结构

体　　裁	说明文。
主要内容	说明面对日益严重的空气污染，各地采取了各种方式解决这一问题，但由于空气污染与城市发展有关，空气污染问题在大城市尤为突出。
结　　构	第 1 段：直接点题，说明展览的主要内容。
	第 2 段：说明展览名字的由来及主要展示内容。
	第 3 段：介绍 WSPU 的组建及历史背景。
	第 4 段：介绍 WSPU 的迅速发展。
	第 5 段：介绍 WSPU 主办的报纸在宣传方面的作用。
	第 6 段：介绍 WSPU 主办的报纸在筹集资金方面的作用。
	第 7 段：介绍 WSPU 引进的颜色方案带来新的商机。
	第 8 段：介绍其他募捐活动。
	第 9 段：说明展览比较直观，介绍主要展示内容。
	第 10 段：介绍展览展示的明信片及其意义。
	第 11 段：介绍展览中使用的短片。
	第 12 段：展览所提示的女权运动的意义及成就。

词汇注释

文　章

第 1 段

suffragette *n.* 主张（或争取）妇女参政权（或选举权）的女子

movement *n.*（政治、社会、思想等方面的）运动；积极开展运动的团体

campaign *vi.* 参加（或发起）运动；参加竞选

associate (with) *vt.* 在思想上把…联系在一起；使有联系

militant *adj.* 激进的；战斗的；积极行动的

varying *adj.* 不同的，有变化的

violence *n.* 暴力（行为）

draw on 动用；利用；凭，靠

archive *n.* 档案；大宗记录

convey *vt.* 传递；表达，表示；传达

exhibition *n.* 展览，展览会

purple *n.* 紫色

Pankhurst 潘克赫拉斯特(夫人),1858 – 1928,英国女权运动领袖,创立妇女社会和政治联盟[1903],为争取女权进行长期斗争,议会于其死前通过全民代表法案[1928],终使英国妇女获得平等选举权。

第 2 段

reference *n.* 引文出处,引文

scheme *n.* 计划,规划,方案

create *vt.* 创造;创作;设计并完成

uniform *adj.* 统一标准的;始终如一的;一贯的

nationwide *adj.* 全国范围的;全国性的

project *vt.* 提出;表明庑的特性,使呈现特性;设计

corporate *adj.* 团体的;公司的

identity *n.* 个性,特性;一致

advanced *adj.* 超前的,先进的

strategy *n.* 战略;策略;行动计划

along with 一道,一起

organizational *adj.* 组织(上)的

commercial *adj.* 商业的

achievement *n.* 成绩,成就

第 3 段

campaigner *n.* 活动家

educated *adj.* 根据一定事实(或经验)的;根据对情况的分析的

suffrage *n.* 选举权,投票权

agenda *n.* 议事日程

enfranchise *vt.* 给…公民权(或选择权)

counterpart *n.* 对应的人(或物)

第 4 段

slogan *n.* 标语,口号

deed *n.* (与言论相对而言的)行为,行动

cohesion *n.* 内聚力,团结,结合

focus *n.* (注意、活动、兴趣等的)中心,集中点;重点

previously *adv.* 以前,先前

membership *n.* 会员数

desert *vt.* 离弃;抛弃

headquarters *n.* (企业、团体、机关等的)总部,总办事处;活动中心

establish *vt.* 设立,建立

in spite of 不顾,不管

communication *n.* 交流;通讯

minimal *adj.* 最小的;尽可能少的;最低限度的

branch *n.* (机构的)分部;分行;分馆

stretch *vi.* 伸展,延伸

第 5 段

vital *adj.* 必不可少的,极其重要的

invaluable *adj.* 非常宝贵的;无法估价的

inform *vt.* 通知,告知

march *n.* 游行抗议,游行示威

fund-raising *n.* 资金筹集(工作);募捐(活动)

第 6 段

profit *n.* 利益;(资产等的)收益

partly *adv.* 部分的,不完全的;在一定程度上的

department store 百货商店

jeweler *n.* 珠宝商,钟表商

like-minded *adj.* 志趣相投的;想法相同的

enterprise *n.* 企业单位,公司

sympathetic *adj.* 支持的,赞同的

cause *n.* 运动;(奋斗的)目标;事业

identify *vt.* 识别;(经考虑)确定;认出

第 7 段

money-making *adj.* 赚钱的,能赚钱的

exploit *vt.* (为发挥人或事物的效能而)利用;开发

playing card 扑克牌

board game 需用棋盘进行的游戏(如西洋跳棋、国际象棋等)

greeting card (生日、节假日等场合致亲友的)贺卡

countless *adj.* 无数的,多得数不清的

merchandising *n.* 新产品计划和开发;销售规划

concept *n.* 概念,观念

第 8 段

sufficient *adj.* 足够的,充足的

meet *vt.* 支付,偿付

numerous *adj.* 许多的,众多的

combine *vi.* 联合,混合

coffer *n.* (~s)资金;金库
war chest (为竞选等特定用途筹措的)专用资金,专款
notable *adj.* 著名的,显要的
take place 发生,进行,举行
ice-skate *vi.* 滑冰
rink *n.* (通常为市内人工的)溜冰场
equivalent *n.* 相等物,等价物

第 9 段

largely *adv.* 大半,大部分,主要地
visual *adj.* 视觉的,直观的,(教具等)产生视觉形象的
item *n.* 条,项
hum *n.* 连续低沉的声音(如嗡嗡声、营营声等)
banner *n.* 旗,旗职,横幅
photograph *n.* 照片,相片
display *n.* & *vt.* 展示,陈列
trinket *n.* 小装饰物

第 10 段

depict *vt.* 描绘;描述;描写
vivid *adj.* 生动的;逼真的;清晰的
self-proclaimed *adj.* 自称的,自命的
monster *n.* 怪物,怪兽;巨人
march 游行抗议,游行示威
uniform *n.* 制服;(特定阶层或团体等使用的)特种衣服(或服式)
frock *n.* 女式礼服,连衣裙
decorate *vt.* 装饰
accessory *n.* 附加物,(妇女的)装饰品
chalk *vt.* 用粉笔在…上做记号;用粉笔写(或画)
pavement *n.* 人行道
detail *n.* 细节,详情
forthcoming *adj.* 即将到来的;即将出现的

第 11 段

postcard *n.* 明信片
indicate *vt.* 表明(意向、原因等);指出
call on 呼吁,号召,要求
talented *adj.* 有天才的,有才干的

第 12 段

make up 由(部分)组成,构成(全体)
newsreel *n.* 新闻(短)片
reveal *vt.* 使显露,展现
mood *n.* 思想倾向;气氛
devise *vt.* 设计,策划
anti *n.* 反对者,持反对论者,反对分子
oppose *vi.* 反对
fierce *adj.* 凶猛的;残酷的;好斗的
harridan *n.* 形容枯槁(或脾气暴燥)的老妇人;名声不好的老泼妇
bully *vt.* 欺侮;威胁
abuse *vt.* [常用被动语态]虐待,伤害
original *adj.* (文献等)原件的;原版的;原来的,原先的
footage *n.* (影片的)连续镜头
race-course *n.* 赛马场

第 13 段

officially *adv.* 正式地
chart *vt.* 制订…的计划
graphic *adj.* 用图(或图表等)表示的
board *n.* 纸板,厚纸板
outline *vt.* 概述,概括
bill *n.* 清单;单子
enfranchisement *n.* 给…公民权(选择权)
adult *adj.* 成年的
populace *n.* 平民,百姓,民众
achieve *vt.* 完成,实现
demonstrate *vt.* 论证; 显示; (用实验、实例等)证明
shrewd *adj.* 精明的;敏锐的
skilful *adj.* 熟练的;显示技术的
image-builder *n.* 形象树立者(或物)
freedom *n.* 自由;独立自主
equality *n.* 平等;相等
illustrate *vt.* 表明,显示;(用图或例子)说明
intelligence *n.* 才智,智慧;聪颖
deem *vt.* 认为,视为
aspect *n.* 方面
access *n.* 接近(或进入)的机会;享用机会;使用途径
merchandise *vt.* 推销;销售
additional *adj.* 另外的
organ *n.* (党派、集团等的)新闻媒介工具(如报刊、电台等),喉舌
confine *vt.* 限制,使局限
gossip *n.* 小道消息,内幕新闻;闲言碎语的题材
Parliament *n.* (由上议院与下议院组成的)英国议会;议会两院
opponent *n.* 反对者;对手

misleading *adj.* 使人产生误解的；导致错误结论的	**informative** *adj.* 增进知识的；增长见闻的
exceptional *adj.* 独特的；罕见的	

考题解析

Questions 14–15

● 题型归类：Multiple choices

较为常见的细节题，注意题干和选项中的有用信息即可。

● 题目解析：

题目编号	题目定位词	答案所在位置	题解
14	the exhibition/ Museum of London/devoted	第2段末句(By doing so,...)	题干问展览展示了女权运动的哪一个主要方面，根据定位词可以在2段直接找到问题的答案。句子在语法上稍有难度，句子的具体解析可以参看难句突破。虽然答案不是直接以选项内容出现，但是可以根据句子的意思排除其他三个选项，正确答案是C。
15	WSPU/other suffrage groups	第4段第2句(Membership grew rapidly...)	本题解符号时稍有难度，题干问WSPU比其他女权组织成功的原因所在。用WSPU定位会发现文中多次出现这一专有名词，只能寻找有其他女权组织出现的语句进行判断。第4段第2句明确说很多妇女放弃其他less directed的组织加入WSPU(joined it)，意思是说WSPU比其他组织more directed，只有选项D与这一意思吻合，因此是正确答案。也可采用排除法解答本题，A、C在文中是客观陈述，并没有和其他女权组织进行对比，而B选项在文章中找不到对应内容。

Question 16

● 题型归类：Multiple choices

本题属于比较特殊的多项选择题，此类多选题大多考查文章中以并列、对比等形式出现的细节信息。

● 题目解析：

题目编号	题目定位词	答案所在位置	题解
16	年代/allowing British women to vote	第12段首句(Although the exhibition...)	题目考查年代这一细节，确定题干问的是允许英国妇女投票的法案通过的年份，回原文直接寻找出所有的年代，然后在年代前后寻找有关投票法案的定位词即可。本题较容易解答，需要注意的是在答案出现的句中一共有两组并列出现的年代，通过句子结构确定后一组是本题的正确解答，答案选D、E。

Questions 17–19

● 题型归类：Sentence Completion

本题属于细节题，虽然是以完成句子的形式出现，但是题目是对某一事件三个方面的综合陈述，即对部分内容的总结，在这一意义上本题类似 summary 题型。解答这种题目关键是依靠题目定位词确定答案的大致方位，然后根据定位词前后的语句判断正确答案。

● 题目解析：

题目编号	题目定位词	答案所在位置	题解
17	newspapers/ selling	第 6 段第 2 句 (This was partly,...)	根据题目最前面的总结性话语可以知道下面的三个空全是有关 WSPU 筹募资金的方式。根据文章结构首先把定位范围缩小到 6 段 – 8 段。然后再做相关搜寻。
18	merchandising activities/goods produced	第 7 段第 2 句 (The group began...)	17 题的结构说明空格处要填写有关报纸如何募集资金，根据文章结构定位在 6 段，首句已经指出报纸带来了利润(the newspaper returned a profit)。紧接着第二句解释报纸如何创造利润，主要是因为大的百货商店购买广告版面(because advertising space was bought in the paper by large department stores)，句中的 bought 与题目中的 selling 正好是反义词，对于百货商店是买，对于报纸就是出售，因此答案只要把句中 bought 的对象 advertising space 填写进去即可。
19	additional fund-raising activities	第 8 段末句 (The most notable...)	本题主要指销售各种产品，根据文章结构定位到 7 段，题目中空格在介词 in 之后，因此寻找类似介词结构即可，7 段中和产品有关的类似介词结构只有一个，即 in the purple, white and green colours. 但需要注意题目要求中明确指出答案不能超过三个字(NO MORE THAN THREE WORDS)，可以将此短语简缩成中心词 purple, white, green 或者 three colours，如果对文章内容比较熟，可以判断这三种颜色正是 WSPU 的 colour scheme，填写这三个答案都正确。 根据文章结构定位到 8 段寻找，因为题目要求填写一个其他集资方式的例子，8 段只提供了一个例子，即 the Woman's Exhibition.

Questions 20–26

● 题型归类：YES/NO/NOT GIVEN

较有难度的细节题，准确理解题意并在文中定位是解答此种题型的关键。需要注意不要根据文章意思做过多的逻辑推断后解题，只需将文章内容与题目内容进行简单对应后判断即可。

● 题目解析：

题目编号	题目定位词	答案所在位置	题解
20	1903/Australia	第 3 段末句 (New Zealand, Australia...)	本题较容易解答，题目中时间和地名使回原文定位非常容易，在第 3 段末句中文章指明，澳大利亚妇女已经获得投票权(Australia had already enfranchised women)，这与题目内容完全相反，因此答案是 NO。

21	WSPU/two newspapers	第5段首句(The newspapers produced...)	根据文章结构可以直接到第5段-6段寻找答案,题目指出两份报纸是WSPU的喉舌/宣传媒介(organ),5段首句说这两份报纸在交流中扮演了至关重要的作用(played a vital role in this communication),如果这里的意思还不够明确的话,下一句的举例更明确了这两份报纸的作用是对WSPU的各项活动进行宣传和报道,这就是题目中所说的喉舌作用。因此答案选YES。本题的难点主要在于对organ这一单词的理解。
22	London and the south	第4段末句(By 1906 the...)	题目内容是说WSPU的活动仅限于伦敦和南部,但根据文章结构定位到4段后文章内容明确说明WSPU的会员和支部已经发展到远达苏格兰的地方(stretching to as far away as Scotland),根据地理常识可以判断,这一例子完全超出了题目中的地理范围,因此答案选NO。
23	newspapers/society news and gossip		题目说WSPU报纸的内容主要有两部分:社会新闻和小道消息(society news and gossip),根据文章结构在5、6段中寻找相关内容,5段末句明确指出WSPU两份报纸的内容是通知会员活动的相关信息以及活动的近期新闻和观点(informing members of ... and the latest news and views on the movement),完全否定了题目中对报纸内容的界定,因此答案选NO。如果误选NOT GIVEN,原因在于没有理解此类题型的本质,如果文章中出现相关内容与题目陈述内容不符,答案就应该是NO,只有在文章中没有提及题目相关内容时才能选项NOT GIVEN,本题如果文章中没有介绍报纸的内容,就可以选NOT GIVEN。
24	Woman's Exhibition/1909/Parliament	第6段末句(The most notable...)	本题较容易,定位词非常明确,题目的前半句可以在文章中找到相关对应(The Woman's Exhibition in 1909),但题目的后半句(opposition from Parliament)在文章中找不到相关对应,当题目内容在原文中未提及时,答案是NOT GIVEN。
25	Museum of London exhibition/goods sold by	第11段首句(Windows display postcards...)	本题在定位时稍有困难,因为文章所有内容都是讲the Museum of London exhibition这个展览的,但题目意思是展览展出的物品,因此根据文章结构将搜寻范围缩小到9段-11段即可,根据18题可以得知女权运动出售一些商品,包括圣诞卡、贺卡等,而11段首句说明展览的橱窗中展出明信片和贺卡,这一例子正符合题目的意思,因此答案选择YES。
26	opponents/films	第11段第3句(The programme begins...)	题目定位比较容易,有关film的内容都集中在11段,题目意思是说女权运动的反对者制作了一部反对该运动的电影。稍有混淆的是文章最先提到的film是反映整个女权运动的电影,如果只看到这里可能会选NOT GIVEN,但文中紧接着说这个电影的开始是一个小的电影短片,而这个短片正是由反对女权运动的人所拍摄的,这个短片把女权运动者刻画成泼妇的形象。这一内容与题目内容是相符的。因此本题的正确答案应该是YES。

Question 27

● 题型归类：Multiple choices

本题实质上是一道主旨题，这种类型的题通常在原文中无法找到直接提供答案的语句，需要对文章有一个全面的理解后才能推断出正确答案。

● 题目解析：

题目编号	题解
27	本题题干问文章中表现出对这个展览的态度，如果直接去文章中寻找答案比较困难，可以利用排除法解答。A、C选项首先被排除，因为在文章中没有表现出来误导或令人失望的这种态度(misleading/disappointing)，而B选项的混淆性较大，展览所展示的内容(女权运动)的确是独特的，但题目问展览所体现出来的特性，而不是展示内容的情况，因此B也可以排除。文章本身就是对展览情况的一种客观描述，提供了大量的材料说明女权运动的情况，因此比较符合正确答案D的意思，即展览可以令人增长知识。

参考译文

妇女要投票

20世纪初为妇女争取投票权的女权运动通常都会和潘克赫拉斯特家族以及不同暴力程度的激进行为联系在一起。伦敦博物馆用其收藏的档案举办了名为“紫色、白色和绿色：1906 – 1914年伦敦的女权运动”的展览，展示出一幅鲜活的画面。

这个展览的名字来自妇女社会和政治联盟(以下译文中均简称WSPU)创造的颜色设计，这个设计赋予了该运动统一的全国性形象。通过设计此方案，WSPU成为首批表明团体特点的团体之一。此次展览专门展示的正是WSPU这一超前的市场策略和其他在组织和商业方面的成就。

WSPU由政治活动家潘克赫拉斯特·埃米琳夫人和她的两个女儿克丽斯特贝尔和西尔维亚在1903年组建。WSPU发动了一场启蒙运动，使妇女投票权被提上政治议程。在新西兰、澳大利亚和美国部分地区妇女已经拥有了投票权，越来越多的英国妇女也想拥有同样的权力。

WSPU提出“要实干不要空谈”的口号，又引入了颜色方案，这样就使运动具备了以前所缺少的凝聚力和工作重心。妇女们退出许多其他目标不太明确的团体加入了WSPU，因此WSPU的成员人数迅速增多。到1906年，WSPU在Charing Cross路建立了总部，命名为妇女印刷社。尽管当时通讯方式有限，既没有收音机也没有电视，电话也用得极少，信息还是传遍了全国，WSPU的会员和分支机构也已远达苏格兰。

WSPU出版了两份报纸，起初是《妇女要投票》，后来是《妇女权利》，这两份报纸在信息传递方面发挥了极其重要的作用。这两份报纸都在全国发行，向成员报道会议、游行活动、募捐活动以及近期有关运动的新闻和观点，是一种极其宝贵的传递信息的方式。

对于一个正处于上升阶段的政治团体而言，同样重要的是报纸还带来了收益。部分原因是报纸上的广告版面出售给了Sulfridges这样的大百货商店和Mappin & Webb这样的珠宝商。这两家也和其他观点相同的商业机构一样支持妇女运动，它们还很快发现这有一个可以触及庞大妇女市场的捷径，而很多妇女都有钱去消费。

颜色方案的创设提供了另一个赚钱良机，WSPU很快就开发利用了这一机会。她们开始出售扑克牌、棋盘游戏、圣诞卡、贺卡以及其他各种各样的产品，所有这些都是紫色、白色和绿色的。在1906年这种带有团体特点的产品销售还是一个全新的市场概念。

但是只靠报纸和产品销售还不足以提供能负担 WSPU 开支的经费，所以还要有其他大量的募捐活动来为运动注入资金。其中最著名的就是 1909 年在 Knightsbridge 市内溜冰场举办的妇女展览，在十天内共筹集了相当于现在 250,000 镑的资金。

伦敦博物馆的展览比较直观，其中展示了大量物品。伴着温和的街道背景噪音，《妇女权利》、运动的横幅和图片都被展示出来，还有潘克赫拉斯特夫人的一只鞋子和一些紫、白、绿三色小装饰品。

展示的图片描绘出女权运动生活的生动画面：在一个自称“怪物”的游行中，WSPU 的成员身着正式的白色连衣裙制服，上面点缀着紫、白、绿三色装饰物；妇女在街角出售《妇女权利》；还有妇女在人行道上用粉笔写满即将召开的会议的详情。

橱窗中展示了由女艺术家为运动设计的明信片和贺卡，这些作品的高品质表明在 WSPU 才华横溢的成员中可以利用的资源十分丰富。

参观者可以观看一部由过去的新闻片和电影素材编辑成的电影短片，这个短片清楚地反映了当时女权运动所处的政治氛围。影片一开始是由反对女权运动的“反对派”设计的一个短片，其中把女权运动者刻画成一个残暴的老泼妇，欺负她那可怜的被虐待的丈夫。原始新闻片还有这样的镜头：女权运动者艾米莉 · Wilding · 戴维森在一个著名的赛马场扑倒在乔治五世的马下。

尽管此次展览正式记录的时间是从 1906 年到 1914 年，图表展示板在表明运动所取得的成绩时还提供了 1918 和 1928 年的选举权法案的概况，这两个法案赋予英国成年女性平民投票权。展览展示了女权运动者在思想、运动的市场营销和敏锐熟练地树立形象这些方面有多么超前。展览还提示了女权运动者为自由平等而战的干劲和能力。展览充分展示了妇女的聪明才智，而在当时，有些政客还认为妇女“大脑太小，不知道怎么投票”。

READING PASSAGE 3

文章结构

<table>
<tr><td>体　　裁</td><td colspan="3">议论文</td></tr>
<tr><td>主要内容</td><td colspan="3">本文用具体的实验说明一个观点，即直接施压的管理方式虽然会带来短期的产量增加，但会消耗大量的组织资源。</td></tr>
<tr><td rowspan="13">结　　构</td><td rowspan="8">介绍实验的经过</td><td colspan="2">第 1 段：提出观点。</td></tr>
<tr><td colspan="2">第 2 段：说明设计实验的目的。</td></tr>
<tr><td colspan="2">第 3 段：介绍实验涉及的人员及分组方法。</td></tr>
<tr><td colspan="2">第 4 段：说明部门工作的内容决定只有减小部门规模才能提高生产率。</td></tr>
<tr><td colspan="2">第 5 段：说明四个部分被分为两组，成为两个项目。</td></tr>
<tr><td colspan="2">第 6 段：说明实验进行的时间。</td></tr>
<tr><td colspan="2">第 7 段：说明在“参与项目”中的部门做了什么样的改变。</td></tr>
<tr><td colspan="2">第 8 段：说明在“等级控制项目”中的部门做了什么样的改变。</td></tr>
<tr><td rowspan="5">分析实验的结果</td><td rowspan="5">生产率的变化
工作态度的转变</td><td>说明图 1 显示的直观结果。</td></tr>
<tr><td>分析图 1 的结果。</td></tr>
<tr><td>指出尽管实验在生产率方面的结果一致，但在工作态度上的结果却大不一样。</td></tr>
<tr><td>用图 2 的直观结果说明员工态度的转变。</td></tr>
<tr><td>进一步用图 3、4 的直观结果说明员工态度的转变。</td></tr>
</table>

词汇注释

文 章

performance *n.* 表现;履行;执行

第 1 段

clear-cut *adj.* 明确的,清楚的
supervision *n.* 监督;管理;指导
productivity *n.* 生产力,生产能力;生产率
achieve *vt.* 完成,实现
significant *adj.* 相当数量的;不是微不足道的
production *n.* 生产;产品;产量
short-term *adj.* 短期的
obtain *vt.* 得到,获得
substantial *adj.* 相当数目的,大量的,可观的
serious *adj.* 重要的,重大的

第 2 段

extent *n.* 范围,程度,限度
impressive *adj.* 给人深刻印象的;激动人心的
earnings *n.* 收益,赢利,利润
exploit *vt.* (为发挥人或事物的效能而)利用;开发
investment *n.* 投资;(精力、思考、时间等的)投入
plant *n.* 工厂,车间
division *n.* 部门(如部、处、科、系等)
suffer *vt.* 受损害,受损失
description *n.* 说明;形容;描写
conduct *vt.* 进行;实施

第 3 段

employee *n.* 受雇者,雇员,雇工
clerical *adj.* 职员(工作)的,办事员(工作)的;文书(工作)的
parallel *adj.* 类似的,相同的;并存而可相比拟的
division *n.* 分;分开
technology *n.* 技术,工艺
comparable *adj.* 类似的
aptitude *n.* 才能,天资;聪明

第 4 段

depend (on) *vt.* 视…而定,决定(于)
involved *adj.* 有关的,牵扯在内的;参与的
entail *vt.* 使成为必要,需要
account *n.* (尤指对上级的)陈述,交代;账单;(会计年度等的)交易结清单;(伦敦股票交易所的)定期结清
generate *vt.* 产生;造成,引起,导致;使存在
invoice *n.* 发票;发货清单
volume *n.* 量,额
considerable *adj.* 相当大(或多)的;很大(或很多)的
come along 出现;来到;发生;进展
consequently *adv.* 所以,因此

第 5 段

assign *vt.* 分配;给予;布置(作业)
experimental *adj.* 实验(性)的;试验(性)的
random *adj.* 任意的,任意选取的;无一定之规的
at random 随便地;任意地;胡乱地
historically *adv.* 在过去,以往
attempt *n.* 尝试,企图,努力
habitual *adj.* 习惯性的,惯常的,通常的
assistant *adj.* 助理的;辅助的
supervisor *n.* 管理人;指导者

第 6 段

beforehand *adv.* 预先,事先
devote 是(to) *vt.* 把…专用于
approximately *adv.* 约莫,大概
continuously *adv.* (在时间或顺序上)连续不断地,接连地
compute *vt.* 计算,推断,估算
attitude *n.* 态度,看法
supervisory *adj.* 管理(员)的;指导(者)的
staff *n.* 全体职员,全体雇员

第 7 段

detailed *adj.* 详细的,细致的,复杂的
general *adj.* 一般的;常规的;笼统的
clerk *n.* 办事员,职员;文书
in addition 另外,加之
leadership *n.* 领导才能;领导
endeavour *vt.* 试图;竭力做到

reference *n.* 参照,参考;查阅
label *vt.* 把…归类为,把…列为;用标签标明
participative *adj.* 参与的,参加的,分担的

第 8 段

by contrast 对比之下
call for 需要,要求
modify *vt.* 缓和;减轻;降低
so as to 为使,以便
closeness *n.* 限制,只限于少数人
hierarchically *adv.* 等级森严地;等级制度地
controlled *adj.* 受制的
extension *n.* 范围,广度
approach *n.* 方法,方式,途径
standard *adj.* 标准的,规范的;通常的
overstaff *vt.* 为…配备人员过多
transfer *n.*(职务等的)调动,调任
replace *vt.* 接替,代替,取代
dismiss *vt.* 解雇;开除;免…的职
accomplish *vt.* 达到(目的);完成(任务);实现(计划、诺言等)

第 9 段

figure *n.* 图形
reflect *vt.* 表明,显示
occur *vi.* 发生;存在;出现

第 10 段

bring about 导致,引起,使发生
participate *vi.* 参与,参加
aware(of) *adj.* [一般作表语]意识到的;知道的
seek *vt.* 寻找;探求;寻求
obviously *adv.* 显然地,明显地
eliminate *vt.* 淘汰;排除,消除

第 11 段

effect *n.* 结果,效力,作用
significantly *adv.* 重要地,不可忽略地
respect *n.* 着眼点,方面
accompany *vt.* 伴随,和…一起发生(或存在)
shift *n.* 转换;转移;交换
adverse *adj.*(方向上)逆的;不利的
factor *n.* 因素,要素
loyalty *n.* 忠诚,忠心耿耿
involvement (in) *n.* 卷入,牵连
opposite *adj.* 对立的,对应的

第 12 段

provide *vt.* 提供,给予
responsibility *n.* 责任;责任感,责任心
decrease *vt.* 减少,减小
absent *adj.* 不在场的,缺席的;不存在的
tend (to) *vi.* 易于,往往会

第 13 段

moreover *adv.* 而且,加之,再者,此外
likely *adj.* 更可能的,有倾向的
pull for 热情支持;给…帮助
solely *adj.* 仅仅,只
trend *n.* 趋势,趋向

题目

establish *vt.* 证实;确定;表明
identical *adj.* 完全相同的,一模一样的
pattern *n.* 模式,样式
randomly *adv.* 任意地;胡乱地
specific *adj.* 独特的,特定种类的
comprise *vt.* 包含,包括
calculate *vt.* 计算;估计
weekly *adj.* 每周的,一周一次的
completion *n.* 完成,结束,实现

考题解析

Questions 28–30

● 题型归类:Multiple choices

较常见的细节题，注意题干和选项中的有用信息即可。这几道题的题干提供的有用信息比较少，因此要注意选项的内容。

● 题目解析：

题目编号	题目定位词	答案所在位置	题解
28	designed to	第二段 1－2 句（To what extent...）	题干问设计实验的目的（介词 to 在此处表目的），根据文章结构可以直接到第二段寻找答案。根据问题的内容可以很容易地排除掉 B、C 选项，但 A、D 选项的混淆性较大，能否准确理解选项的意思就成了解答本题的关键所在。A 选项是说实验的目的是为了证实是否应不惜一切代价增加生产率，而 D 选项是说实验的目的是利用公司的人员结构来增加利润。文章的首段已经明确表明文章谈论的是提高生产率的问题，二段末句说设计这个实验就是为了回答前面的两个问题，两个问题中一个问多大程度上一个经理可以利用公司人员结构在短期内创造更多的利润，另一个问如果经理这么做，他的组织质量会受到多大程度的影响，实验需要对两个问题都进行回答，而选项 D 只回答了第一个问题，因此应当被排除，正确答案是 A，是对两个问题的一种概括。
29	four division	第三段 1－2 句（The study covered...）	本题较容易解答，尽管题干部分并没有提供太多有用信息，但利用题干内容可以把搜寻答案的范围缩小到第 3 段－4 段，根据 3 段首句排除选项 A，根据 4 段首句排除选项 B，选项 D 在文章中找不到相关内容，可以排除，正确答案是 C。如果准确理解选项中 identical（相同的）的意思，也可以直接做答，因为 3 段的第二句强调说分成的四组在各个方面都是相同的。
30	before the experiment	第六段第 2 句（Beforehand, several months...）	题干部分较短，但已经提供了足够的定位信息，确定句子后，发现在实验前主要做了两件事：planning and training，选项中只有 C 的内容与此相吻合（preparing for the study），其他的选项内容都与 planning and training 无关。

Questions 31–36

● 题型归类：Summary

本题型属于细节题，但由于题目内容是对文章部分内容进行了概括后缩写而成，因此文章的结构也有助于解题，有时某一个空需要对一段或一部分内容进行总结后才能得出正确答案。

● 题目解析：

题目编号	题目定位词	答案所在位置	题解
31	one year/a different method	第 7 段首句（Turning now to...）	本题难度较大，因为在原文中比较难定位，根据题目的意思，空格处要填写的是一年内分组的项目中采用了不同的什么方法。根据文章结构和时间限定，从第 6 段开始

			找起,但第6段说的是实验开始前的准备工作,第7段才是实验的实际内容。7段首句指出两组试图采用不同的管理方法(supervision)。再通过对7、8段的整体阅读可以得知两种分组最大的区别在于管理方法的不同,所以答案最终确定为supervision。
32	on a weekly basis	第6段第3句(Productivity was measured...)	本题由于定位词明显,解答较为容易。只是题目中的动词和文章中的动词稍有变化,以近义词的形式出现,文章中说 measured and computed,而题目中说 calculated。空格处缺少主语,应填写 productivity。
33	supervision of all workers	第7段首句(Turning now to...)	根据文章结构,33题和34题应在7段寻找答案。根据定位词比较容易找到答案,需要注意的是这一段中 supervision 出现次数比较多,需要确认其定语是否与题目吻合,最后选定在首句,空格处缺少谓语动词的一部分,根据句子意思确定为 reduced。
34	supervisory staff/training	第7段第3句(In addition, the managers,...)	题目定位较容易,在7段寻找 supervisory staff 时会发现文章中是以具体职位的形式来代替题目中的这一短语(the managers, assistant managers, supervisors and assistant supervisors),在该句中很容易找到题目所缺少的名词,即介词 in 后短语的中心词:leadership。
35	30%	第8段第5句(This showed that...)	这两道题都比较容易解答,百分比形式出现的数字在原文中很好定位,只要在相关句子中找到题目中所缺少的动词即可。答案分别是 overstaffed 和 cut。注意36题在原文中是主动形式,而在题目中是被动形式即可。
36	25%	第8段倒数第2句(The general manager...)	

Questions 37–40

● 题型归类:Matching

本题实质上是考查读图能力,即对图表意思的理解,原文中也有相关语句对每个图形进行解释,因此难度不大。

● 题目解析:

题目编号	答案所在位置	题解
37	第9段首句(Figure 1 shows...)	本题难度较小,文章中对每一个图表所表示的内容都作了详尽的解释,在选择选项时只要注意一些选项中的细微差别,避免不必要的粗心造成的错误即可。40题可能稍有难度,但运用排除法也可轻松解决,因为文章中明确指出这一图表是雇员的感觉(employees in the participative programme felt...),剩余的选项中有A、F、H,A选项内容与文章内容不符被排除,H选项中的 increased supervision 在原文和图中都没有表现出来,因此也可以排除。
38	第12段首句(For example, Figure 2...)	
39	第13段首句(As Figure 3...)	
40	第13段末(Moreover, as Figure 4...)	

参考译文

衡量组织行为

有确凿的证据表明,直接施压于生产率的监督、管理在至少一年内可以使产量大幅增长。但这种短期增长是以巨大、沉重的组织管理上的损失换取的。

利用公司在工厂或分部对人力组织的投资,一个经理短期内(1 年 – 3 年)能在多大程度上创造一份令人瞠目的赢利记录?其组织管理的效果会在多大程度上因此受到影响?下面所述是由社会研究院实施的一项重要研究,该研究是专为回答这些问题而设计的。

该研究涉及 500 名员工,分为类似的四个部门。每个部门用相同方式编组,使用同样的技术,从事相同的工作,员工的资质也所差无几。

所有四个部门的生产率都有赖于参与员工的人数。工作必须涉及财务流程和由此产生的发票的处理。尽管工作量相当大,但这份工作的特点是有工作交给你你才有事做。因此,提高生产率的唯一途径就是改变工作部门的规模。

四个部门被随意指派进入两个项目。每个项目随意分配给两个部门,其中一个以往生产率就很高,另一个生产率低于平均数。并没有刻意把哪个部门放在项目中,让这个部门最适合经理、经理助理、总监、副总监以往的管理方法。

员工层面的实验进行了一年。之前有几个月专门用于制定计划,还有大约半年的培训期。一年里每周都要持续测量并计算生产率,在这段时期前后都要评定员工和管理者对工作的态度。

现在来看研究的核心,其中两个部门尝试改变管理方式,以降低决策层面并减少对工人繁复的管理,同时引进更多对员工和管理者的常规监督。此外,这两个部门的经理、经理助理、总监、副总监分组接受领导方法的培训,并要在一年试验期间在能力允许的情况下尽可能多地使用这一方法。为了便于查找,这两个部门中实验性的变化将被标记为"参与项目"。

对比之下,在另外两个部门中,项目要求改进管理方式来增加管理的封闭性,并使决策层面上升。这一项目被标记为"等级控制项目"。在更大范围内应用科学管理手段使这些变化得以实现。例如,产生的主要变化之一是给工作计时和计算标准时间。这一做法显示两个部门有约 30% 的冗员。于是总经理要求这两组的经理裁员 25%。裁员通过调离人员完成,但不安排人接替离职者;之后没有人被解雇。

实验结果

生产率的变化

图 1 显示单位工作时间薪金的变化,反映了不同部门生产率的变化。可以看到,等级控制项目的生产率增长约 25%。这是总经理直接要求裁员 25% 的结果。直接压力带来了可观的产量变化。

参与项目的生产率也有 20% 的显著增长,但还是没有等级控制项目那么多。员工参与决策缩减工作团队的规模来达到增长。(他们当然知道在这些实验中管理者想要增加生产率。)显然,要淘汰一些人来减少工作团队的规模,这可能是工作团队最难做的决定之一。然而员工们还是这么做了。事实上,参与项目中的一个部门生产率增长和等级控制项目的两个部门一样多。另一个参与项目的部门表现的不太好,生产率只增长了 15%,这个部门以前在所有部门中也最差。

态度的变化

尽管两个项目在生产率上结果相似,但在其他方面却大相径庭。等级控制项目生产率增长了,但其他要素却朝反方向发展,如对工作的忠诚、态度、兴趣以及参与程度。但参与项目的情况却恰恰相反。

例如,图二表示部门提供了更多常规管理和更高的参与度之后,员工对工作的责任感也增加了。当管理者再离开时,员工继续工作。但等级控制项目中的责任感却减弱了,管理者不在时,工作就可能停滞不前。

如图3所示,年终时参与项目的员工觉得他们的经理和经理助理比年初更亲近。等级控制项目的情况则相反。此外,如图4所示,参与项目的员工觉得他们的管理者可能更关注他们,或者说关注公司和员工,而不是只对公司感兴趣。而等级控制项目中的趋势正相反。

WRITING

WRITING TASK 1

范文

范文1

This graph shows the unemployment rates in the US and Japan between March 1993 and March 1999. There is a general falling trend for the US, whose unemployment rate stood at 7% in 1993, however every year there was a temporary increase in the unemployment rate before it fell again. Between March 1995 and March 1996, there were two soft peaks marking an anomaly in the general falling trend. After March 1996 there were few marked increases and by March 1999, the unemployment rate had reached a plateau around 5%.

In Japan, the unemployment rate rose according to a similar pattern, with consistent rises and the occasional drop. The sharpest rise occurred between March 1995 and March 1996 and the sharpest drop occurred in July 1996. Between March 1993 and March 1998, Japan's unemployment rate rose from 3% to 4.6%.

By July 1998, the rates both plateau and are approximately equal. This phenomenon may indicate that 5% is a natural rate of unemployment and that before this period unemployment rates were abnormally high in the US and abnormally low in Japan.

此表显示了1993年3月到1999年3月之间美国和日本的失业率情况。美国的失业率总体呈下降趋势,在1993年保持在7%左右,然而每年在回落之前都有一次短暂的升高。在1995年3月到1996年3月期间出现了两次缓慢增长的峰值,这标志了整体下降趋势中的一个异常现象。1996年3月以后有少数几次升高,到1999年3月,失业率就达到一个5%的平稳状态。

在日本,失业率依照一种近似的模式升高,就是持续的升高伴随偶尔的下降。最高点发生在1995年3月到1996年3月之间,最低点发生在1996年7月。在1993年3月到1998年3月之间,日本的失业率从3%升到了4.6%。

到1998年7月,美国和日本的失业率都达到一个平稳状态而且基本持平。这种现象也许说明5%是一个失业的自然比率,在这个平稳时期以前,美国的失业率反常地高而日本则过分走低。

范文2

What is very obvious, at a glance, is that the overall unemployment trend, during this 6-year time period from March 1993 to March 1999, went down for the US, whereby at the same time, it went up for Japan. Another very stark and obvious fact is that, though the US had a high unemployment rate of 7%

in March 1993, and Japan had a low of 2.5%, by March 1999, the two were essentially the same at around 5%.

Of course there were year-to-year fluctuations, ups and downs, but these were not strong enough to change the very strong overall downtrend for the US, and uptrend for Japan. The most dramatic change for both were the one year period from March 1993 to March 1994, when the US rate dropped by a full percentage point to reach 6% and Japan's rate increased by more than 1% to reach 3.75%. By March 1996, the US rate was just over 5%, and Japan's just under 4%. By spring of 1998, the two rates were the same, around 5.25%. The US rate fell slightly below Japan's towards the end of 1998, then went very slightly above by March 1999, at around 5%.

一看就很明显,从1993年3月到1999年3月这个6年的周期里整个的失业趋势在美国是下降的,然而同期在日本则是升高的。另一个明显的事实是尽管在1993年3月有高达7%的失业率,日本只有2.5%的低失业率,到1999年3月,双方就基本持平了,都在5%左右。

当然每年都存在浮动,或者升高或者降低,但是都不足以改变美国强劲的下降势头和日本强劲的升高势头。双方最戏剧性的变化在1993年3月到1994年3月的一年时间里。那时候美国的失业率下降了整整一个百分点,达到了6%,而日本则升高了一个多百分点,达到了3.75%。到1996年月,美国的失业率刚好超过了5%,而日本刚好低于4%。到1998年春天,双方的失业率相同,都在5.25%左右。到了1998年底,美国的失业率轻微下降,低于日本,然后到了1999年3月又轻微上升,围绕在5%左右。

谋篇布局

1. 题目分析:

这是一道曲线图。在这张曲线图中,有两条曲线。描写原则:

(1)两条曲线的总体特征。

(2)分别描写两条曲线上升/下降/保持不变的趋势。

(3)两条曲线的相同点和不同点。

2. 本题分析:

(1)两条曲线的总体特征是一条上升,一条下降。参见范文2第一段。

(2)范文1的第一、二段把两条曲线各自的趋势描写的很好。

(3)最后要写两条曲线的相同点和不同点。参见范文1第三段。

WRITING TASK 2

范文

范文1

I agree that the governments of richer nations should take more responsibility for helping the poorer nations in such areas as health, education, and trade, but they should not be expected to take full responsibility.

There is competition between nations just as within every nation there is competition between individuals. The basic principle governing this competition is survival of the fittest, meaning that the strongest thrive and the weakest die out. Granted, some nations have been endowed with more natural resources and clever citizens who help to put resources to best use, but this inequality is a given and cannot be avoided. Richer nations should show compassion to poorer nations and try to ensure that all humans enjoy basic rights such as clean food and water, shelter, security, and basic education. Often, implementing this type of basic infrastructure just takes initiative, and does not require a lot of time or money. As the saying goes, give a man a fish, feed him for a day; teach him to fish and feed him for life. Simply giving poorer nations money does not solve any problems.

On the other hand, richer nations should not have to take full responsibility for poorer nations because the welfare of its citizens is the primary responsibility of each nation's government. In many cases, the government does not live up to its expectations but that does not mean richer nations should take over and bear the responsibility. For example, some African countries receive aid from developed countries, but because of their government systems, this aid often does not reach the people, the people in power claim it. This is a terrible cycle of the rich getting rich and the poor getting poorer.

To summarize, I do believe that some support should be given to poorer nations, especially directed towards women in the areas of health and education, with as few middlemen as possible to avoid the misuse of funds.

我同意较富裕国家的政府应当在诸如医疗卫生、教育和贸易等领域负有更多的责任帮助较贫困的国家,但是不能期待让他们承担全部的责任。

就像每个国家内部存在个人竞争一样,国家之间也存在竞争。控制这种竞争的基本规则就是适者生存,这意味着强者生存而弱者被淘汰出局。当然,有些国家被赋予了更多的自然资源和能够帮助国家最合理地利用这些资源的聪明的公民。但这种不平等是既定的、不可避免的。较富裕国家应该对较贫困的国家显示出同情,并且尽力确保所有的人都享受到诸如干净的食物、水、栖身之所、安全和基础教育之类的基本权利。通常实现这样的基础条件只需要采取主动就行,不需要花很多的时间或是钱。正如俗谚所说的:"给人一条鱼,可以养活他一天;教会他捕鱼,可以养活他一生。"只给较贫困国家钱不能解决任何问题。

另一方面,较富裕国家没有必要对较贫困国家承担全部的责任是因为国民的福利是每个政府的基本责任。在许多情况下,政府达不到人民的期望,但这并不意味着较富裕国家应当接替和承担他们的责任。例如,一些非洲国家从发达国家收到了援助,但是由于政府的体制问题,这些援助根本到不了老百姓手里,而是被当权者领走了。这就成了一个富人愈富、穷人愈穷的恶性循环。

总的来说,我坚信对较贫困的国家应当给予一定的支持,尽可能减少中间环节,从而避免基金的滥用。

范文2

I agree with the statement that improvements in health, education and trade are essential for the development of poorer nations. But I disagree that governments of richer nations should take more responsibility for helping the poor nations accomplish this because poorer nations need to learn how to become self-sufficient and capable on their own, taking responsibility for their own actions and people.

There are numerous examples in Africa, in particular, where corrupt governments do nothing to improve the plight of their people in terms of health, education and trade even as they beg richer nations for handouts. These handouts are then stolen by corrupt government officials and sold on the black market for their own profit. The poor people in need of aid are actually never reached. Richer governments also usually expect something in return for their help and this results in huge levels of debt for poorer nations that they can never repay, remaining instead forever bound like a slave to the richer nation.

I believe that the only action of rich nations should be the withholding of aid so that corrupt governments fall and the people of each nation rise to take care of themselves in a responsible manner. This may seem harsh, but the alternative of keeping poor nations in slavery to debt and the authority of corrupt officials who are actually criminals, thugs and bullies is much worse.

When the true people of a poor nation take control and try to improve the condition of their country on their own, rich governments should help when they can, but not give handouts that might corrupt the new leaders of the people. Poor nations that improve their condition by themselves will then become a proud, capable and confident people.

我同意在医疗卫生、教育和贸易等方面的改善对较贫困国家的发展来说是必不可少的,但是我不同意较富裕国家的政府应当为帮助较贫困国家完成这一切而过分承担责任。

较贫困国家需要变得自给自足,对他们自己的人民负责,因为这是他们赢取一定自尊的唯一途径。尤其是在非洲,有无数这方面的例子。腐败的政府在改善人民在医疗卫生、教育和贸易等方面的状况上无所作为,甚至去祈求富裕国家的施舍。这些无偿的援助随即就被腐败的政府官员偷走,并且为了一己之私在黑市上出售。那些急需援助的人们则根本见不到这些无偿援助的东西。较富裕国家也期待对他们援助的回报,这却导致了较贫困国家债台高筑,他们永远保持欠较富裕国家的债款数额。

我认为较富裕国家应当采取的唯一的行动就是收回那些援助以使腐败政府垮台,并且使每个国家的人民更加以一种负责的方式来照顾自己。这看起来也许很尖刻,但是一边陷于债务的束缚之中,一边是罪恶、凶残、欺凌弱小的腐败官员,这样的情况才是更糟的。

当一个贫困国家真正的人民掌权并试图靠自身改善他们国家的生活条件时,较富裕的政府在他们可以的时候应当给予帮助。但是不能给予施舍,因为这会腐化新的人民的领导。较贫困的国家依靠自身的力量改善生活条件将会使他们变成一个自尊、自强、自信的民族。

谋篇布局

1. 读题:

这篇文章的中心事件是 the governments of richer nations take more responsibility for helping the poorer nations in such areas. 题干对这个事件的评价是正面的:should。题干还提到一个信息:Improvements in health, education, and trade are essential for the development of poorer nations. 这个信息是中心事件的相关内容。但因为题干用了 however,所以这个信息不是题干给出的正面评价的理由。

2. 写提纲:

这道题思路应该是比较清晰的:如果你同意发达国家应该多承担帮助穷国的责任,那么你可以从这个事件的本质和好的后果两方面来构思分论点;如果不同意,那么你也可以从这个事件的本质和不好的后果两方面来构思分论点。

所谓本质,其实可以包含两个方面的内容:一,一个事物本身的属性;二,一个事件发生以前的情况导致这个事件发生的合理/不合理。这里,第二个方面的内容很好写成分论点:"因为富国在以前造成了穷国的贫困,所以富国应该承担起帮助穷国的责任"或"富国之所以富,完全是优胜劣汰的结果,所以它们不必帮助穷国"。

而要写这个事件好的或者不好的后果就更容易了。这里我们可以抓住这个事件中的几个参与者:这个事件对富国的后果,对穷国的后果,对富国和穷国加起来(也就是这个世界)的后果。比如:"对于富国来说,因为穷国的贸易结构规范了,所以它们可以在国际贸易中获得更多的利润"。

范文 1 的第二段,从本质上说一个国家怎么样才能发展;第三段从实际后果来说富国帮助穷国并没有什么好的结果。

范文 2 的第三段用了我们以前讲过的思维:既然我们不同意这种做法,那么接下来我们就可以写一段:"我们究竟应该怎么做"。

3. 首段的写作:引出要讨论的内容 + 表达你的观点

范文 1 很简洁:"同意这个事件,但是不完全同意"。(其实是不同意)

范文 2 其实表达的是不同意这样做。注意,这里第一句话同意的是题干第一句的背景信息。

4. 中间段落的写作:分论点的论证

范文 1 的第三段是一个很经典的先具体解释后举例说明的段落。

SPEAKING

I = Interviewer C = Candidate

范例 1

PART 1

I: Good morning, my name is Stuart. Could you tell me your full name, please?

C: My full name is Su Zheng. You can call me by my English name, Susan.

I: Great. Susan, may I please see your identification?

C: Sure, here you are.

I: Thanks. Let's get started by talking about your **daily routine.** What would you like to change in your daily routine?

C: Well, it seems my daily routine is full of classes, and, if I'm not in class, then I'm at the library studying. So, if I could change something, I would really like to have fewer classes. That way I could spend less time studying. Then I'd have a bit more free time to exercise, play sports, or improve my English.

I: Are all your days the same?

C: Well, during the week, they are nearly the same. Three days a week—Monday, Wednesday and Friday—I have classes from 8:00 a. m. to 4:30 p. m. On Tuesdays and Thursdays I finish by 2:30 p. m. Of course, on the weekends I have more **variety** and **flexibility** in my schedule.

I: Tell me about your **typical weekday**?

C: Well, on a typical weekday I get up at 6:30 a. m. in order to get ready, and go to the **cafeteria** to eat breakfast around 7:00. Then at 7:30 I go to my first class, which starts at 8:00. I like to get there early in order to spend 30 minutes **or so** studying before class. I have classes all morning, and one hour for lunch before class starts again at 1:10 p. m. Evenings are spent in the library, or sometimes in my room, preparing for the next day's classes. So, you see, during the week, it's mostly classes and studying.

I: What about a **typical weekend**?

C: Well, on a typical weekend I usually study Saturday morning then go out in the afternoon to buy **needed supplies and so forth**. I usually have dinner in some restaurant with my friends, then we may go to some local bar for a beer. Sunday mornings I like to sleep in, and the rest of the day may be spent studying.

I: What is the **balance** of work/study and free time in your normal day?

C: Well, I've never added up the hours, but let's see... I have classes from 8:00 to 12:00 everyday, from 1:10 to 4:30 three days each week, and then until 2:30 two days a week. That's about five to seven hours of classes per day. Then, I usually study at least four to six hours a day. **Frankly speaking**, during the week, there's hardly any free time at all. I try to play **basketball** a couple of times a week, and that cuts my study time down by one and a half hours for those days. There's no work time, **as such**, as I'm a full-time student. Weekends, I usually have at least a half day of free time, sometimes one full day.

I: Ok. Now I'm going to give you a topic and I'd like you to talk about it for one to two minutes. Before you talk you'll have one minute to think about what you're going to say. You can make some notes if you wish. Do you understand?

C: Sure.

I: Ok, here is your topic, and here is some paper and a pencil for making notes. I'd like you to describe something you own which is very important to you.

PART 2

Candidate's Notes on Paper

Where got it	**pendant** from best friend
How long	since **senior middle school**
What use	brings me good luck
Why so important	reminds me of friend

I: Ok, your time is up. Now, remember, you have one to two minutes for this so don't worry if I stop you. I'll tell you when the time is up. Can you start speaking now, please?

C: Can you see the **pendant** I am wearing now? It was given to me by my best friend from senior middle school. Her name is Bess. We have known each other since we were in **primary school**, third grade. Even though we had known each other for so many years, we didn't become good friends till middle school. And, it wasn't until senior middle school that we became best friends. I guess that as we got older we seemed to have more **common interests. Let's see**, she gave it to me for my birthday in my second year of senior middle school, and now I'm in my second year at university, so that means I've had it for three years. During this time, I have worn it every day. I never take it off, even when I'm **taking a shower** or sleeping.

I think I've become a bit **superstitious** about this pendant. I think it brings me good luck. I remember the day she gave it to me—it was my birthday. I had hoped for a new watch from my parents. But, as the watch was quite expensive, I thought my parents would wait until my **senior year** to give it to me. So it was a very happy **surprise** when I got the watch that day. Also, it just seems to me my life has been happier ever since I started wearing the pendant. Sometimes I'm not sure if it's the pendant that actually brings me good luck, or just my thinking that does it. I read that our thoughts are very powerful, so if we think a certain way, then certain things can actually happen to us.

The pendant is one of my most **prized** possessions, because it was given to me by my best friend. **To this day**, she's still my best friend, though we don't see each other much, since we're in different universities in different provinces. Whenever I see the pendant around my neck, or whenever I touch it, it always reminds me of my good friend. I feel happy when I think of her. I think in life it's so important to have at least one good friend. And, as I mentioned before, I think the pendant brings me good luck.

I: So, what would you do if you ever lost your pendant?

C: Well, I certainly hope that never happens! I don't think it can, because I never take it off. But, if ever I lost it, then I think I'd replace it with another one, since I'm now so used to wearing something around my neck.

PART 3

I: Ok. We've been talking about things we own, and now I'd like to ask you some questions about how **values** change. What kinds of possessions show **status** in China?

C: Well, China's society has changed so **rapidly** in the past few years, especially in the past three to five years. This is especially true for large cities, like Beijing and Shanghai, where people's **incomes** have **risen sharply.** It seems like everyone can now afford to buy an apartment. I mean, even people with **fairly modest** incomes can afford to buy an apartment by **borrowing** money from the bank. So, owning your own apartment is definitely a **sign** of status, to show you have enough money to do so. Another possession which shows status is a car. As you can see, there are more and more cars on the roads in Beijing. Not just more cars, but better and more expensive cars. It used to be that a Mercedes or BMW would be quite rare, but now **no one takes a second look** at them on the road.

I: Do you think it was different for your grandparents?

C: It was very different for my grandparents. Not only for my grandparents, but also for my parents. In my grandparents' day, almost everyone was quite poor, and it was already something to own a nice bicycle. Also, to own a nice watch was quite special. Very few people even had black and white TVs. In my parents' day, it would show status to own a **refrigerator**, a color TV and your own telephone.

I: Now let's talk a little bit about **consumer society.** Modern society is often called **'Materialistic'.** Why do you think this is?

C: I think the very **term** 'modern' **implies** there are more **tangible goods**, for example the refrigerator, the **washing machine**, the **microwave**, DVDs and so on. With more and more people owning more tangible goods, then everyone has more what we call **'material goods'.** But the word 'materialistic' has a bit of a **negative image.** I think it implies an **overemphasis** on material goods, and the **neglect** of other **matters**, like relationships and so on.

I: Do you think **consumerism** is a **positive or a negative development**?

C: I think it has both good and bad effects. It's good for people to have the convenience and the enjoyment of consumer products. It also helps the economy when people buy things. But, at the same time, too much **emphasis** on material goods is not healthy. One needs to balance this with time with family and friends, taking care of one's health and so on.

I: What is the role of advertising?

C: One of the main roles should be to **inform** people about new products, and about the products' features. Of course, the **aim** is to get people to buy the products. That's ok, if what the advertisement says is entirely true, and not **misleading** people.

I: How do you think the Internet will affect buying patterns in the future?

C: Well, from what I know, quite a few people in the U. S., for example, already shop using the Internet. This of course saves people a lot of time. People are busier and busier, and the Internet can give them a lot of product information.

I: Great, thank you, Susan. That's the end of the interview.

C: Thank you for your time.

范例 2

PART 1

I: Good morning, my name is Frank. Can you tell me your full name please?

C: My full name is Ma Wei.

I: And what can I call you?

C: Please call me Mario.

I: Okay, Mario. Where are you from?

C: I'm from Beijing.

I: Can I see your identification please?

C: Sure, here you go.

I: Thanks. I'd like to start of by asking you some more questions about yourself. Let's first talk about your **daily routine.** Tell me about your **typical weekday** and your **typical weekend.**

C: All right. On a typical weekday, I get up at 6:30 a.m. I wash my face and have breakfast, and then I read an English **passage** out loud for 30 minutes. This is a habit my mother **instilled** in me when I was in high school. Classes start at 8:00 a.m. and go to 4:00 p.m. If I have any **spare time** during the day, I go to our study hall to do homework. This way, I can have more time to relax in the evening. In the evening, I either do homework or watch TV or play **video games**, depending on my **workload** and how much I got done during the day.

I: Are all your days the same?

C: Yes, pretty much the same. I have **a set number** of classes to attend and they all have to fit in somehow. The weekends have a little more variety. I like to get out for a bit of exercise, like playing basketball with friends or going window-shopping. I enjoy browsing bookstores and **computer markets** as well.

I: What would you like to change in your daily routine?

C: It would not be possible to change much in my daily routine. University classes are so busy and require the students to memorize so much that if I studied less, my grades would **drop**. Ideally, I would like to have more time for physical activity during the week because I think that really helps me study, but if other students see you outside playing, they will **accuse** you of being lazy. I think everyone needs quiet time to themselves as well, just to read, write, or sleep a little extra.

I: What is the balance of study and free time in your normal day?

C: I would say more than 90% studying and less than 10% free time. I try to get most of my work done during the week so I can have more free time on the weekend. Most students are in a similar situation—all work and no play. University is very competitive, and the **job market** is getting more and more competitive, so no one dares to **slack off.**

I: I see. Now, I'm going to give you a topic and I'd like you to talk about it for one to two minutes. Before you talk you'll have one minute to think about what you're going to say. You can make some notes if you wish. Do you understand?

C: I do.

I: Ok, here is your topic, and here is some paper and a pencil for making notes. I'd like you to describe something you own which is very important to you.

PART 2

Candidate's Notes on Paper

where	gift, family
how long	graduation
use	portable, research, reports
why important	special gift, useful

I: Okay, one minute is up. Remember, you have one to two minutes for this so don't worry if I stop you. I'll tell you when the time is up. Can you start speaking now, please?

C: The most valuable object I own is my **laptop computer**, which was given to me by my family when I graduated from high school. It is a **top-of-the-line** machine with every feature that I imagine I might need, and is special to me because it is **portable** and comes with me to university, on vacation, and wherever else I happen to go.

The computer is important to me, first of all, because it was a gift given to me on a very special occasion, and also because it will be very useful to me in my future. I was very **touched** to receive this gift, and I know that my parents must have planned and saved for years in order to be able to afford such an **extravagant** gift. The computer has a DVD player, a large screen and the finest **sound, video, and communication cards** available on the market today.

It has allowed me to use my time in a much more efficient way, not only during my study hours, but also during the **leisure time** I allow myself. I use the computer to **conduct** research on my major, which is **international economics**; to organize material that I need for my studies and for writing papers; and to **produce** professional looking reports exactly the way I want them. My computer also helps me keep in contact with my Chinese friends who are going to schools abroad, and who are in distant parts of China. It has added a new element to my **recreational activities**. I have a small **addiction** to computer games, but I think that is normal for young men my age. In the future, I know that the computer will help me in my search for **employment**, and in keeping **up to date** with new ideas and **trends** in my field.

I: So, your computer is already two years old. Do you feel it is a bit **outdated**?

C: No, it's not outdated yet. It was such a fine machine when it was purchased, that it is **capable** of doing everything I need it to do. However, the computer is **expandable**, so I can **upgrade** any of the **components** as required.

I: Have you ever taken any **computer literacy** courses?

C: Yes, both at high school and at university we had to take basic computer classes. I have also taken some extra courses at private schools.

PART 3

I: We've been talking about things we own. Now I'd like to ask you some questions about a few more related topics. First, let's talk about **values** and how they change. What kinds of possessions show **status** in your country?

C: In China, cars are the most common **status symbol** for older people. It has been reported that thousands of new cars appear on the streets in China's **major centers**. The **models** that represent the highest status are the large American and European cars, such as **Mercedes Benzes**, **BMWs**,

Buicks, and various **SUV's**. For **middle-income families**, a home computer is a symbol that the family is becoming more **affluent**. Computers are proudly displayed and **demonstrated** to visitors and **discussed at length** with **colleagues** and friends. Another smaller, but more common, status symbol is the mobile phone. Most people in China have a mobile phone, but people compete over having the latest model with the latest features.

I: Do you think it was different for your grandparents?

C: It absolutely must have been different for my grandparents. Science and technology have advanced so quickly in the past 20 or 30 years. A status symbol recognized by my grandparents' **generation** would have been a new bicycle or maybe a **radio**. In my grandparents' generation, there was less competition about possessions. People didn't have very much during that time, and most goods were **rationed**, so most people were all at the same level of **poverty.** I think when my grandparents talk about how good things used to be, they are referring to this lack of competition over **meaningless** status symbols. To tell you the truth, many young people do waste a lot of time comparing themselves to other people.

I: Modern society is often called 'materialistic'. Why do you think this is?

C: In my view, in modern society, relationships between two people are becoming less important than relationships between people and things. Especially in business, people often use **dishonest techniques** in order to **benefit materially at the expense of others. Teenagers** now prefer spending time with the TV set or their computer rather than with their friends. Children are rewarded for their successes with gifts rather than with praise and encouragement from their parents. In all the media, including print, TV, and movies, we are shown **a vast array** of material goods which we come to desire ourselves. I think media plays a huge role in our materialistic attitudes. They have **convinced** us that we want everything they put in front of us.

I: Do you think **consumerism** is **a positive or a negative development**?

C: In my opinion, consumerism cannot be viewed in an entirely positive or negative **context**. Consumerism has caused our standard of living to rise by **literally** creating the economy, by providing people with goods to buy and many **forums** where we can spend our money. On the other hand, consumerism has caused **alienation** by taking the focus off people and putting it onto things. We may eventually learn to put commercialism in its **proper place**, which is to **fulfill** our **physical needs**, and not our **emotional needs**, but there is not much evidence of this happening yet.

I: What is the role of advertising?

C: The role of advertising is to inform consumers of available products and to convince them that these products are good and that they should buy them. Advertising is not generally done for the benefit of the consumer, but for the profit of the business. Advertising is often done to **differentiate** between brands of different products. For example, many companies sell bread, so if a particular company wants to promote bread, it uses advertising to **set its own brand of bread apart** from all the other brands that can be found on the **shelf**. Nowadays, many types of products are advertised by famous people, especially sports superstars. Nike uses many athletes to promote its clothing and shoes, and is rewarded by huge **annual sales.**

I: How do you think the Internet will affect buying patterns in the future?

C: The Internet gives us access to much more information in a much shorter time than is available with **conventional** shopping methods. Because all specific details about products are available **instantaneously**, Internet shoppers can compare models and brands and reach a more **informed decision** about the **manufacturer** that can best meet their specific needs. They will also be able to shop for the best prices to be found. Many things can be bought online cheaper than in a storefront shop because the **overhead costs** are lower. The consumer is able to save both time and money by shopping online, therefore I believe that more and more people will rely on their computers to do more of their shopping.

I: Okay, our interview is now over. Thank you very much.

词汇表

范例 1	
daily routine 日常事务	rapidly 迅速地
variety 多样性	income 收入
flexibility 机动性、弹性	rise sharply 急剧增长
typical weekday 典型的平日	fairly modest 非常适度的
cafeteria 自助餐厅	borrowing 借款
typical weekend 典型的周末	sign 征兆
needed supplies 生活必需品	no one takes a second look 没人看第二眼
and so forth 等等	refrigerator 冰箱
balance 平衡	consumer society 合作社
basketball 篮球	materialistic 唯物主义的
as such 同样地	term 术语
pendant 垂饰	imply 暗示
senior middle school 高中	washing machine 洗衣机
primary school 小学	microwave 微波炉
common interests 共同的利害关系	negative image 负面印象
let's see... 让我们来看	overemphasis 过分强调
take a shower 冲澡	neglect 忽视
superstitious 迷信的	matter 事务
senior year 高年级	consumerism 用户至上主义
surprise 吃惊	positive/negative development 正向/反向发展
prized 珍视的	emphasis 强调
to this day 到今天	aim 目标
value 价值观	mislead 误导
status 地位、状况	

范例 2	
daily routine 日常事务	drop 下降
typical weekday 典型的平日	accuse 谴责
typical weekend 典型周末	job market 劳务市场
passage 文章	slack off 偷懒
instill 逐渐灌输	laptop computer 笔记本
spare time 空闲时间	top-of-the-line 一流的
video game 电子游戏	portable 便携式的
workload 工作量	extravagant 奢侈的
a set number of 一系列的	sound, video, communication cards 声卡、显卡、网卡
computer market 电子市场	leisure time 课余时间

conduct 进行	poverty 贫穷
international economics 国际经济	meaningless 毫无意义的
produce 制作	materialistic 唯物主义的
recreational activities 娱乐活动	dishonest technique 骗术
addiction 上瘾	benefit materially at the expense of others 以他人的代价赚取实际利益
employment 职业	teenager 青少年
up to date 最新的	a vast array of 大批的
trend 倾向、趋势	convince 确信
outdated 过时的	consumerism 用户至上主义
capable 有能力的	positive/negative development 正向/反向发展
expandable 可扩展的	context 上下文
upgrade 升级更新	literally 字面意义地
component 构件	forum 论坛
computer literacy 计算机能力	alienation 疏远、转让
value 价值观	proper place 适当的位置
status 状况、地位	fulfill 履行
status symbol 社会地位的象征	physical needs 生理需要
major center 主要中心	emotional needs 情感需要
model 代表	differentiate 区分
Mercedes Benz 梅赛德斯奔驰	set its own brand of bread 用自己的面包品牌
BMW 宝马	shelf 架子
middle-income families 中等收入家庭	annual sales 年销售额
affluent 富裕的	conventional 惯例的、常规的
demonstrate 展示	instantaneously 瞬间地;即时地
discuss at length 详细讨论	informed decision 高明的决定
colleague 同事	manufacturer 厂商
generation 代	overhead costs 营业间接成本
ration 配给	

补充词汇及句型

Part 1: Daily routine

Possible Changes	
Get up earlier. Watch less TV. Spend less time studying.	Spend more time with my family. What else?
Provide some details!!	
Do you spend too much time working? Maybe you have so much free time that you don't know what to do with yourself. Or maybe you have achieved a healthy balance of work and free time in your life.	

Part 2: Something important you own

Possible Important Things	
a ring a computer a cell phone	a car a T-shirt a pen/pencil lots of other things!

Possible Reasons for Importance
It is useful. It was a gift. It reminds you of someone/something.

Part 3: How values change, consumer society, consumer market

Possible Possessions	
car house clothing	jewelry computer

Consumerism is a...	
positive development because it helps the economy. it makes it possible for people all over the world to have access to goods. the desire for material goods encourages people to work harder.	negative development because relationships suffer. too much attention is paid to material things. it encourages people to be selfish.

Advertising...
helps us decide which products to buy. is a way for corporations to sell their products. is a way that companies can communicate with potential customers.

The Internet...
will allow people to do more "impulse buying", because they can buy things with just one click from the comfort of their home. might allow people to make more informed decisions about their purchases, because they can do research online. is likely to increase the amount of money that people spend on computer products.

口试要点聚焦

重在交流

雅思口试考查的与其说是你运用哪些词汇和句型,不如说是你能否与考官交流。虽然考官会注意到你的发音和语法错误,但在诸多方面中最重要的是他对你英语总体水平的感觉。因此,要记住口试中关键是注重交流。

注重交流的办法之一是口试中要保证充分放松。如果你精神太紧张,就可能过分担心自己的语音、词汇和语法,这会影响到你与考官的交流。如果你能够消除紧张,相对放松,你就能谈吐自然,充分发挥。

重在交流的办法之二是交谈时注重所表达的观点而不是语言本身。把精力和思想放在你想表达什么,而不是如何表达上。这样你的语言就是一种自然流露,从而给考官留下表达流利的印象。

你学英语已有多年,雅思可能也准备了好几个月。如果你在口试中注重交流,再加上你以前的努力,一定能给考官留下表达流利的印象;如果忽视交流的重要性,过分担心词汇、语音和语法方面的细节,与考官的交流就会受到影响,最终成绩比注重交流可能要低。

General Training: Reading and Writing

Test A

READING

词汇注释

Section 1

A 段

intensive *adj.* 强烈的，透彻的
commence *v.* 开始，着手
Mandarin *n.* 普通话
Cantonese *n.* 广东话
Thai *n.* 泰国话
Vietnamese *n.* 越南话

B 段

hospitality *n.* 好客，宜人，盛情

C 段

picturesque *adj.* 风景如画的
situate *vt.* 使位于，使处于
Mediterranean *adj.* 地中海的
imaginable *adj.* 可想象的，可能的
hostel *n.* 宿舍，旅店
module *n.* 模式，模块
optional *adj.* 可选择的

D 段

intermediate *adj.* 中等水平的

E 段

facility *n.* 设施，设备，工具

Section 2

non-returnable *adj.* 不可退回的
deposit *n.* 保证金，押金
registrar *n.* 登记员，注册主任
confirmation *n.* 确认；证实
invoice *n.* 发票
certificate *n.* 证明，证明书
transfer *v.* 移动，转移
balance *n.* 余额
interview *vt.* 面试；接见
assessment *n.* 评价；评估
accompany *vt.* 陪伴；伴随
incur *v.* 招致
refundable *adj.* 可偿还的
non-transferable *adj.* 不可转移的；不可转换的
charge *n.* 费用
reduction *n.* 减少
forfeit *vt.* 丧失；没收
determine *v.* 测定；决定
guarantee *vt.* 保证；担保
enroll for 入学；登记
linguistic *adj.* 语言上的；语言学的
option *n.* 选项；选择权
welfare *n.* 福利；福利事业
diverse *adj.* 不同的，变化的
spoil *v.* 破坏；扰乱
rugged *adj.* 波涛汹涌的
surfing *n.* 冲浪
superb *adj.* 极好的；华丽的
ski *n.* 滑雪
hiking *n.* 徒步旅行
co-ordinator *n.* 协调者
arrange *v.* 安排；排列

Section 3

A 段

account for 解决;占
awareness *n.* 认识;知道
sustainable *adj.* 持续的;可以忍受的
extract *vt.* 提取;吸取
critical *adj.* 危急的;批评的
rehabilitate *v.* 使复原;使恢复名誉
devote *vt.* 应用于;投身于,献身于
emission *n.* 散发;发射;喷射
status *n.* 地位;身份;情形,状况

B 段

target *vt.* 使成为…靶子;使成为…目标
critics *n.* 批评家;评论家
phenomenon *n.* 现象
temperature *n.* 温度
tropospheric ozone 对流层臭氧
methane *n.* 甲烷;沼气
natural *adj.* 自然的;普通的
build-up *adj.* 内建的
enhance *vt.* 提高;增强
relation *n.* 关系;联系
concentration *n.* 浓度;专心
compound *adj.* 复合的,混合的
predict *vt.* 预知,预言,预报
stabilize *v.* 稳定
take place 发生
associated *adj.* 联合的,关联的
emission *n.* (光、热等的)散发,发射,喷射
attain *vt.* 达到,获得
sustainable *adj.* 稳定的,可以忍受的,足可支撑的,养得起的
carbon dioxide *n.* 二氧化碳
nitrous *adj.* [化]氮的,含氮的,硝石的
CFC *n.* chlorofluorocarbon 氟氯化碳
contributor *n.* 贡献者,捐助者,投稿者
refrigerator *n.* 电冰箱,冷藏库
plastic *n.* 塑胶,可塑体,塑料制品,整形
allocate *vt.* 分派,分配
extensive *adj.* 广大的,广阔的,广泛的
capture *vt.* 俘获,捕获,夺取
dramatically *adv.* 剧烈地,戏剧地,引人注目地
combustion *n.* 燃烧
gasification *n.* 气化
demonstration *n.* 示范,实证
stage *n.* 舞台,戏剧,活动场所,发展的进程,阶段或时期,驿站
avenue *n.* 林荫道,大街,方法,途径,路
conversion *n.* 变换,转化

D 段

investigation *n.* 调查,研究
ultraclean *adj.* 超净的,特净的
pulverize *v.* 研磨成粉
defendant *n.* 保护,被告
temporary *adj.* 暂时的,临时的,临时性
monitor *vt.* 监控
rehabilitate *v.* 使(身体)康复,使复职,使恢复名誉,使复原
minimize *vt.* 将…减到最少,最小化
immediate *adj.* 直接的,紧接的,紧靠的,立即的,知觉的
spray *v.* 喷射,喷溅
stockpile *vt.* 储蓄,贮存
runoff *n.* 流走之物,决赛,决定性竞选
sediment *n.* 沉淀物,沉积
troll *vt.* 使旋转,轮唱,放声高唱,钓
modify *vt.* 更改,修改
insulation *n.* 绝缘,绝缘物
enclosure *n.* 围住,围栏,四周有篱笆或围墙的场地
temporary *adj.* 暂时的,临时的,临时性
superior *adj.* 较高的,上级的,上好的,出众的,高傲的
simultaneously *adv.* 同时地
cattle *n.* 牛,家养牲畜
graze *v.* 放牧,吃草,擦伤,擦过
reservoir *n.* 水库,蓄水池
urban *adj.* 城市的,市内的
disruption *n.* 中断,分裂,瓦解,破坏
stringent *adj.* 严厉的,迫切的,银根紧的
approval *n.* 赞成,承认,正式批准
exclusively *adv.* 排外地,专有地
rehabilitation *n.* 复原
core *n.* 果核,中心,核心
analyze *vt.* 分析,分解

subsoil *n.* 底土，下层土，天然地基	**reshape** *vt.* 改造，再成形，采用新方针
topsoil *n.* 上层土，表层土	**drainage** *n.* 排水，排泄，排水装置，排水区域，排出物，消耗
strip *vt.* 剥，剥去	**stable** *adj.* 稳定的
stockpile *vt.* 储蓄，贮存	**erosion** *n.* 腐蚀，侵蚀
prior *adj.* 优先的，在前的	**permanent** *adj.* 永久的，持久的
cease *v.* 停止，终了	**fertilize** *vt.* 施肥，使丰饶，使受精，使肥沃，使多产
disturb *vt.* 弄乱，打乱，打扰，扰乱	

考题解析

Questions 1–8

● 题型归类：Matching

● 题目解析：

题目编号	题目定位词	答案位置	题解
1	up-to-date	广告 B 第 8 行	题目：最新式的教学系统 原文：最新的教学方法
2	established, for a significant time	广告 E 第 3 行	题目：这个机构已经成立很久时间 原文：TESOL 中心拥有 24 年以上的经验
3	examination classes	广告 E 第 5 行	题目：考试班级 原文：备考
4	activities outside class	广告 C 第 9 行	题目：可以安排课外活动 原文：可进行所有的体育活动
5	school students	广告 D 第 12 行	题目：提供专门针对学校学生的课程 原文：高中生速成班
6	special purposes	广告 B 第 10、11 行	题目：特殊目的的语言教学 原文：商务用语、日常寒暄、旅游用语
7	wide variety	广告 A 中列举的 11 种语言；广告 B 倒数第 3 行	题目：可选择多种语言 原文：中文普通话 广东话 泰语 越南语 韩语 印度尼西亚语 英语 西班牙语 意大利语 德语 俄语（广告 A）；9 种语言供您选择（广告 B）
8	evening	广告 B 倒数第 6 行；广告 D 第 6 行和第 10 行	题目：晚上班 原文：白天上课 + 晚上上课（广告 B） 白天班或晚上班任您选择（广告 D）

Questions 9–13

● 题型归类：TRUE/FALSE/NOT GIVEN

● 题目解析：

题目编号	题目定位词	答案位置	题解
9	close, two days, re-open, Monday	第 1 段第 3 行	题目：道路将关闭两天，周一重新开放。 原文：从 8 月 12 日（星期六）早 6 点到 8 月 13 日（星期日）晚 6 点之间关闭

10	as far as Little Street	第 1 段第 2 行	题目:一直走到 Little 大街,道路都将是开放的。 原文:Little 大街和 Denning 大街之间的梅因大街将关闭。
11	continue, each weekend for the next month	第 2 段	题目:下个月的每个周末都将进行道路施工。 原文:我们希望这段时间之内可以完工,不会进一步妨碍交通。
12	temporary traffic lights, intersection	第 1 段第 4 行	题目:梅因大街的路口将安置临时的红绿灯。 原文:Little 大街和 Denning 大街与梅因大街的交口处不受影响。
13	bus service, university, weekend	第 4 段第 2 –4 行	题目:整个周末会有通往大学的公交车。 原文:在盖顿路、镇中心和大学之间 566 号公交线路和 45 号公交线路会提供服务。

Questions 14 – 19

● 题型归类:TRUE/FALSE/NOT GIVEN

● 题目解析:

题目编号	题目定位词	答案位置	题解
14	overseas students, deposit	第 1 段第 1 –2 行	题目:海外留学生必须在申请就读大学课程时交付保证金。 原文:请填写好申请表格,与数目恰好的保证金(保证金不退回、数目见下)将其寄送到以下地址……
15	outstanding fees, first week	上半部分第 8 条	题目:课程开始第一个星期结束前要将未付款项付清。 原文:学生付清未结清的课程费用和住宿费
16	ability level	上半部分第 7 条	题目:按照能力水平分班。 原文:学生抵达米德海文,参加考试、面试以及分班。
17	break, between	下半部分中间 Conditions 第 1 段	题目:每节课之间有休息。 原文:每小时包括 50 分钟教学及 10 分钟休息。
18	change courses	Conditions 部分未提及	题目:一个学期的任何时候学生都可以换课程。
19	any student, holiday, 12-week	右下脚第 1 段 Student Holidays	题目:在 12 周的课程里,任何学生都被允许休假一周。 原文:除考试准备课程外,参加其他长期课程的学生每 12 周休息一周。

Questions 20 – 26

● 题型归类:Summary

● 题目解析:

题目编号	题目定位词	答案位置	题解
20	local students, apply for a room	第 1 大段倒数 1、2 行	原文:可以和当地居民一起生活,也可以和新西兰学生一起住大学学生公寓。

21	minimum, enroll	第1大段第2、3行	原文:全年均开设每期四个星期的高强度英语课程,并且学生想参加几期课程均可。
22	class size	第1大段第7行	原文:班级人数少,一般为10至12人,最多15人。
23	member, Language Institute, join	第1大段第8、9行	原文:在语言学院学习英语的同学自然成为Waikato学生会的国际学生成员。
24	city, lies, either side	第2段第2-3行	原文:新西兰最长的河流Waikato河流过市中心。
25	views and enjoyable walks	第2段第3-4行	原文:新西兰最长的河流Waikato河流过市中心,给整个城市提供了一个风景如画的、公园一般的河畔散布的场所。
26	activities coordinator, organize, planning	第3段第2行	原文:目前正在安排学生旅行,也可得到他们的帮助。

Question 27

● 题型归类:Multiple Choice

● 题目解析:

题目编号	题目定位词	答案位置	题解
27	coal, environment	第1段	原文:据说煤炭将继续在全世界的能量需求里占有约27%的比例,然而,随着全世界人民对于环境的压力以及达到能源资源可持续性发展的意识的日益增强,获得这一资源的方式、运输手段以及使用方法变得异常重要。

Questions 28–31

● 题型归类:List of Headings

● 题目解析:

题目编号	段落主题句	题解
28	Such measures are helping coal to maintain its status as a major supplier of the world's energy need.	注意heading中"energy source",A部分第1段第1句,第2段最后一句。原文:据说煤炭将继续在全世界的能量需求里占有约27%的比例……这些措施都有助于煤炭保持其作为世界能量的主要来源的地位。
29	However, the greenhouse effect is a natural phenomenon involving the increase in global surface temperature due to the presence of greenhouse gases...	注意heading中"enhanced greenhouse effect",B部分第2段第3-4行。原文:这种额外的气体集结及其预知的结果已被称为温室效应加强。

30	The world-wide coal industry allocates extensive resources to researching and developing new technologies and ways of capturing greenhouse gases.	注意 heading 中"research and development",C 部分第 1 段第 1 行。原文:全世界的煤炭业花费大量资源用于研究和开发新的获取温室气体的技术和方法。
31	By carefully pre-planning projects, implementing pollution control measures, monitoring the effects of mining and rehabilitating mined areas, the coal industry minimizes...	注意 heading 中"environment protection measures",D 部分第 1 段第 3 – 5 行。通读 D 部分,重点阅读第一段——如果事先做好项目计划、执行污染控制措施、监控采矿影响以及修复采矿区域,那么煤炭业就会将其对附近居民区、周围环境和土地生产能力的影响降到最小。下文是具体的措施描述。

Questions 32 – 36

● 题型归类:Multiple Choice

● 题目解析:

题目编号	题目定位词	答案位置	题解
32	increase, greenhouse gases, attribute	108 页最后一段第一句话	原文:温室效应气体来源广泛,而且这些气体的集结在很大程度上与人口增加、生活水平提高以及生活方式的改变等复杂因素有关。
33	proportion, greenhouse gases, create, coal	109 页 4 – 5 行	原文:煤炭对温室效应气体排放造成的总影响约占 18%……
34	increase, efficiency, coal	C 部分第 1 段 2 – 4 行	原文:通过目前仍处于试验和示范阶段的氧化和气化技术,这方面的工作效率有可能得到巨大提高,由此将减少二氧化碳的排放。
35	clean coal	C 部分第 2 段第 1 句	原文:纯净炭是另一种提高燃料转化效率的方法。
36	control dust	D 部分第 2 段第 2 – 3 行	原文:包含沉积物和盐的排放水可以在处理之后在压尘中进行再利用。

Questions 37 – 40

● 题型归类:YES/NO/NOT GIVEN

● 题目解析:

题目编号	题目定位词	答案位置	题解
37	coal industry, abandon, damage	B 部分第 1 段第 2 行"However"	原文:煤炭业一直以来是批评家攻击的对象,说它是造成温室效应的主要来源。然而,温室效应是一个自然现象,它包括由于大气中造成温室效应的气体的存在导致的地球表面温度的升高……如果没有温室效应的话,地球表面平均温度要比现在低摄氏 33 度到 35 度,即摄氏零下 15 度。正如我们所知,那样地球上不会有生物。

38	threat to environment, gases, support standard of living, growing population	108 页最后一段第 6-7 行	原文:与辅助人口增长相关的活动,尤其是生产人口增长所需的能源和食物将会进一步导致温室效应气体排放的增加。
39	world population, exceed, 8 billion	B 部分第 3 段第 4 行	原文:(联合国预言)21 世纪全球人口将稳定在 80 亿至 140 亿之间。
40	CFC emission, reduce	109 页第 1 段第 2 行	原文:CFC 是唯一一种导致温室效应、但不是自然产生的气体,它来自致冷、塑料和制造生产等渠道。

参考译文

Questions 1–8

***A*:**

国际语言中心

理工学院

法语 & 日语

暑假语言强化班

亦在 1997 年 1 月开课

中文普通话　广东话　泰语

越南语　韩语　印度尼西亚语　英语

西班牙语　意大利语　德语　俄语

请联络以下地址获取进一步信息

悉尼南区 2000 布莱大街 5 号 招生咨询办公室

电话:295 4561

传真:235 4714

***B*:**

全球语言学习中心

全球最棒的语言学校之一现落户悉尼

10 到 20 个星期学习一门新语言

最新的教学方法

白天课程 + 晚上课程

商务用语、日常寒暄、旅游用语

9 种语言供您选择

电话预约:938 0977

C:

想换个地方学英文?
那就来西澳的首府—风景入画的佩思吧

地处美丽的天鹅河,佩思拥有:

* 地中海式气候
* 美妙的印度洋海滩
* 可进行所有的体育活动
* 多元文化社会
* 政府所有技术教育和继续教育学院
* 高标准设施及员工
* 灵活性最高
* 校外学生宿舍或居住在当地居民家

英语强化课程开课

* 每年五次招生
* 10 星期课程
* 多元文化班级
* 选修项目
* 学费:每 10 周 2000 澳币

学习体验

英语课程、文化课程、旅游课程

请联络以下地址获取进一步信息:

西澳 佩思 6000 米尔大街 1 号 5 楼
国际技术教育以及继续教育
电话:619 320 3777

D:

法语暑假课程
1997 年 1 月

成人速成班 1 月 9 日至 19 日

每天3或4小时强化授课
白天班或晚上班任您选择
30小时课程250澳币
(只招收初学者和中低水平的学生)

成人标准班1月9日至3月4日
从初学者到高级水平的学生划分为10个等级
每周两次课 —— 两个小时早上班或晚上班
每周一次课 周六上午9点——下午1点半
32小时278澳币

高中生速成班1月11日至25日
每天3小时强化课程 下午1点至4点
8年级至12年级学生
24小时200澳币
1997年1月11日星期三开始授课

法语俱乐部
悉尼克莱尔大街27号
电话:227 1746

E:
堪培拉大学
在澳大利亚首都学英文
●为海外留学生提供高质量的语言培训,TESOL中心拥有24年以上的经验
●备考并使继续学习变为可能
●可使用堪培拉大学的诸多设施
●在堪培拉大学授课,学生有机会与澳大利亚学生交友

Questions 9–13

梅因(Main)大街 盖顿(Gatton)再发展

道路拓宽影响周末交通以及通往大学校园的公交服务

下一阶段再发展盖顿镇的道路要将Little大街和Denning大街之间的梅因大街从8月12日(星期六)早6点到8月13日(星期日)晚6点之间关闭,Little大街和Denning大街与梅因大街的交口处不受影响。

我们希望这段时间之内可以完工,不会进一步妨碍交通。

司机应注意:梅因大街在周末上述时间内关闭。

大学公交车不许穿过Little大街和Denning大街之间的区域。但是,在盖顿路、镇中心和大学之间566号公交线路和45号公交线路会提供服务。

对于道路扩建过程中带来的不便,交通道路局深表歉意。

Questions 14–19

艾史伍德(Ashwood)学院

海外学生如何注册——

请填写好申请表格,与数目恰好的保证金(保证金不退回、数目见下)将其寄送到以下地址:米德海文(Midhaven) 格劳塞泊(Glossop)大街20号　艾史伍德学院

海外学生注册处主管(收)

电话:01423—968075

传真:01423—968076

1. 学生寄送申请表以及保证金到艾史伍德学院,课程保证金100英镑、课程+住宿保证金200英镑
2. 艾史伍德学院验证课程及住宿有空位
3. 艾史伍德学院寄给学生

——确认信

——保证金发票

——注册证明

——转机请求表格

4. 如有要求,学生返回填充完整的机场转机表格
5. 艾史伍德学院确认转机
6. 学生确认抵达当地居民家或艾史伍德学院的时间
7. 学生抵达米德海文,参加考试、面试以及分班
8. 学生付清未结清的课程费用和住宿费

米德海文当地的学生如何注册——

我们邀请您来拜访我们,参观校园。评估之后,您可以在即将开课的课程保留一个位置。我们在米德海文有两个中心。

支付保证金

1. 注册表格必须与100英镑的保证金一起寄到,如果您通过学校预订住宿,需交纳课程及住宿保证金200英镑。
2. 开课第一天前所有课程费用和住宿费用必须全部付清。
3. 汇款给艾史伍德学院过程中银行征收的费用应由学生支付。
4. 保证金和其他费用不退款、不转款。
5. 更改预订要交纳20英镑。

条件:

时间表:

每小时包括50分钟教学及10分钟休息

公共假日和学校假日:

除圣诞节两个星期的假日之外,上课期间若囊括公共假日,不减少课程费用。

年龄:

上述艾史伍德学院不接收16岁以下的学生。

出勤：
我们希望学生能够按期、定时上课。若学生迟到、早退或缺勤，授课费概不退费。

学生假日：
除考试准备课程外，参加其他长期课程的学生每12周休息一周，休息的这个星期不计授课费。
上课地点及课程时间
艾史伍德学院拥有两个中心全年运行，一个位于米德海文的暑假中心。入学之前，学生要先参加入学考试，然后决定他们在哪一个等级的班级就读。尽管我们尽全力安排学生在他们选定的时间里在中心学习，但是对于上课的时间和上课地点，我们不能给您任何许诺。

Questions 20–26

新西兰托泰拉(Totara)语言学院

与来自多国的学生在国立大学学英语

- 4星期一组课程
- 每天5小时授课
- 备考
- 大学入学(达到适当的学术要求和英语要求)

所有学生选择住宿——住在当地居民家或者和新西兰学生一起住学生公寓

托泰拉语言学院属于新西兰北岛汉密尔顿(Hamilton)市的Waikato大学的一部分。全年均开设每期四个星期的高强度英语课程，并且学生想参加几期课程均可。每天课程为五个小时，每星期一至五上课，包括备考几个国际英语语言考试。任课老师都非常称职，其中很多老师还在语言学院教授第二语言教学和应用语言学的研究生课程。班级人数少，一般为10至12人，最多15人，通常学生来自很多不同的国家。在语言学院学习英语的同学自然成为Waikato学生会的国际学生成员。如果学生选择了Waikato大学的某项课程并达到了该课程在学术水平和英语语言方面的要求，可以直接在该大学就读。语言学院向学生提供支持、福利还有活动服务。学生在抵达奥克兰机场时有专人在机场迎接，其后可以和当地居民一起生活，也可以和新西兰学生一起住大学学生公寓。

汉密尔顿是新西兰发展最为迅速的城市之一，如果您想参与各种各样的休闲文化活动，这里可谓一个理想去处。新西兰最长的河流——Waikato河流过市中心，给整个城市提供了一个风景如画的、公园一般的河畔散步的场所，也塑造了若干个天然的花园。Waikato地区的农产品多种多样，拥有多处历史古迹，艺术品、工艺品、温泉、土著森林、山脉、河流也数不胜数。保存完好的海岸线近在咫尺，未被开发的西海岸海滩崎岖不平，以冲浪闻名，东海岸的度假胜地更加祥和，距离汉密尔顿很近，开车只要很短的时间。更远的地方有北岛中部的山脉，这里要开车3小时才能抵达，冬季提供极好的滑雪设备，夏季这里是非常好的远足去处。

语言学院的活动协调人可以协助学生安排各种各样的体育运动以及休闲活动，还可以帮助学生安排未来的旅游。持有访问签证或工作许可的学生可以最多学习3个月。持续时间更久的课程需要学生持有学生签证，其签发有效时间与学习时间等同。

Questions 27–40

A 据说煤炭将继续在全世界的能量需求里占有约27%的比例，然而，随着全世界人民对于环境的压力以及实现能源资源可持续性发展的意识的日益增强,获得这一资源的方式、运输手段以及使用方法变得异常重要。

大多数现代煤矿里,很多控制污染的设备和做法都已经到位,并且人们花费大量资源用以将一些煤矿恢复为土地。此外,人们正在进行很多重要的研究和发展项目用来提高效率、减少煤炭使用过程中产生的造成温室效应的气体的排放。这些措施都有助于煤炭保持其作为世界能量的主要来源的地位。

B 煤炭业一直以来被批评者斥为是造成温室效应的主要来源。然而,温室效应是一个自然现象,它包括由于大气中造成温室效应的气体的存在导致的地球表面温度的升高,这些气体包括水蒸汽、二氧化碳、对流层臭氧、甲烷和一氧化氮。如果没有温室效应的话,地球表面平均温度要比现在低摄氏33度到35度,即摄氏零下15度。正如我们所知,那样地球上不会有生物。

有人担心这种自然现象正在被更多的人类活动产生的气体集结所改变,或许这种气体集结还导致了大气变暖以及地球气候的变化。这种额外的气体集结及其预知的结果已被称为温室效应加强。然而,温室效应加强存在很多不确定因素,尤其是关于将来全球气温升高到什么程度,什么时间升高都无法确定。

温室效应气体来源广泛,而且这些气体的集结在很大程度上与人口增加、生活水平提高以及生活方式的改变等复杂因素有关。以现在全世界人口50亿为基础,联合国预言21世纪全球人口将稳定在80亿至140亿之间,其中超过百分之90的人口增长均发生在发展中国家。促进人口增长的相关活动,尤其是生产人口增长所需的能源和食物将会进一步导致温室效应气体排放的增加。因此,我们目前面临的挑战就是在人口、经济增长和环境之间达到可持续性的平衡。

人类活动产生的主要温室效应气体有二氧化碳、甲烷和一氧化氮。含氯氟炭(CFC)是唯一一种导致温室效应、但不是自然产生的气体,它来自致冷、塑料和制造生产等渠道。煤炭对温室效应气体排放造成的总影响约占百分之18,其中一半煤炭的消耗用于发电。

C 全世界的煤炭业花费大量资源用于研究和开发新的吸收温室气体的技术和方法。通过目前仍处于试验和示范阶段的氧化和气化技术,这方面的工作效率有可能得到巨大提高,由此将减少二氧化碳的排放。

纯净炭是另一种提高燃料转化效率的方法。目前正在对超级纯净炭(3% -5%的灰烬)和超超级纯净炭(灰烬低于百分之1)进行调查研究。超级纯净炭有可能提高传统的粉碎燃料电厂的燃烧率。超超级纯净炭将可能使煤炭被应用于例如煤炭燃烧的气体涡轮机等高级的电力系统里,这种气体涡轮机在组合好的工作循环中运行其工作效率有可能大幅度提高。

D 采矿业的支持者指出,从环境角度讲,煤炭开采有两个重要的优势。它仅仅暂时使用土地,并且采矿不产生有毒的化学废物。如果事先做好项目计划、执行污染控制措施、监控采矿影响以及修复采矿区域,那么煤炭业就会将其对附近居民区、周围环境和土地长期生产能力的影响降到最小。

尘埃水平可以通过在路面洒水和囤积得到控制,将洁净的排放水和采矿过程中产生的包含沉积物和盐的排放水仔细分开,可以控制水污染。包含沉积物和盐的排放水可以在处理之后在压尘中进行再利用。更换设备、使用绝缘材料和在机器上罩上吸音物质控制噪音。

由于采矿仅暂时使用土地，实行大量土地修复措施保证采矿结束后土地生产能力达到适当的、大众满意的标准，这种标准在一些情况下要高于采矿前土地的自身条件。如果采矿是在地下进行的，那么地上区域还可以同时用来造林、养牛、种植农作物，甚至可以建水库，进行城市发展，对现在的土地使用造成很少、甚至不造成任何负面影响。在任何情况下，采矿都需要有严格的控制以及审核过程。

然而，如果进行露天采矿，土地只能用来采矿，但是一般来讲土地修复措施与煤矿的开采一起进行。提取核心样品来评估某处煤炭的质量及数量，同时也分析评估其土壤或下层土壤质地种植植被的能力。采矿前就铲掉顶层土壤、将其贮存起来，以备采矿后进行土壤修复时将这些土壤散布开来。一个地方的露天开采结束后，该地就恢复原状。仔细设计好开采地内外的排水装置，使得新的土地表面的结实程度达到当地环保的要求：通常会建水坝来保护这一地区不受土壤侵蚀，同时水坝也是永久性的水源。基于土壤的要求，这块土地的肥力和再种植能力都得到很好的保证。

WRITING

WRITING TASK 1

范文

范文 1

Dear Mr. Jones:

I am writing to let you know that, due to a medical condition, it is unlikely I will be able to start my new job next week. For quite a few days my eyes have been tearing and bothering me. Today, I woke up with both my eyes swollen and feeling sore, so I went to see an eye doctor.

The doctor said my eyes are infected, and prescribed antibiotic drops. He told me I cannot wear my contact lenses for a week, and should not wear my glasses either, to simply let my eyes rest. If I do not wear my contacts or my glasses, I cannot see well enough to read, so it seems it would not be worthwhile for me to come to work.

Assuming the eye drops work, and I am able to let my eyes rest, I trust I will be able to wear my contact lenses or glasses after a week, at which time I will be able to report to my new job. This means I will start my job a week later than originally planned. Thank you for your understanding.

亲爱的琼斯先生：

我想写信告诉您出于健康方面的原因下周开始我的工作不大可能了。我的眼睛一直流眼泪，这种情况困扰我都好几天了。今天早上醒来的时候我的眼睛肿了，觉得很疼，所以我去看医生了。

大夫说我的眼睛感染了，给我开了抗生素滴眼液。他说一周之内我不能带隐形眼睛，也不能带眼镜，只能让我的眼睛休息。如果我不带隐形眼镜或者普通眼镜的话，我什么都看不清楚，并且不能阅读。所以看起来让我工作是没有意义的。

要是滴眼液有效并且我可以让我的眼睛休息，我相信一周后我就能带隐形眼镜或者普通眼镜，那时候我就能够开始新工作了。这意味着我比原定计划要晚一周开始工作。感谢您的理解。

范文 2

Dear Mr. Jones,

I am writing to inform you that I will not able to start work this week because of several reasons. First, my car broke down yesterday and it is in the shop right now being repaired. It should be ready on Thursday. Second, I haven't yet found childcare for my daughter. I have several places to visit on Thursday and Friday once my car is repaired. My final reason is that I need to dedicate several days this week to completing the consulting job I told you about in our meeting. I will do this while my car is being fixed.

Once my car is repaired, my daughter is in daycare and my consultant job is completed, I will be 100% ready to begin work. I really look forward to this and hope you can understand my predicament.

I should be able to start next Monday, a week later than we discussed. If I encounter further problems I will let you know. Thanks for your understanding and patience.

亲爱的琼斯先生：

我想写信告诉您由于好几个原因这周我不能开始工作了。

首先，我的车昨天坏了，现在正在修理场修理，应该在周二修好。其次，我还没有给女儿找到幼儿园。一旦我的车修好，周二和周五我会去几个地方看看。我最后的原因是这周之内我需要抽出几天的时间来完成咱们见面时我告诉您的顾问工作。修车期间我将做这个工作。

一旦我的车修好，我的女儿入托，我的顾问工作做完，我100%准备好开始工作。我真的期待着这一天，并且希望您能够理解我的困境。

下周一我应该能够开始工作，比我们商量好的晚了一周。要是碰巧我遇到更麻烦的问题的话，我会告诉您。感谢您的理解与耐心。

谋篇布局

1. 书信类文章的结构题干已经给你组织好了，你自己不必太费心。

   这道题你需要表达三个意思。我们不妨把两个 sample 的表达方法并列起来，看看这些任务是怎么完成的。

2. Explain your situation:
   - **I am writing to let you know** that, due to a medical condition, **it is unlikely I will be able to start my new job** next week.
   - **I am writing to inform you** that **I will not able to start work** this week because of several reasons.

3. Describle your problems:
   - For quite a few days my eyes...
   - First, my car... Second, I haven't yet found childcare for my daughter... My final reason is that I need to dedicate several days this week to completing the consulting job...

4. Tell him/her when you think you can start:

   (1) 既然是跟老板请假，我们不妨客气一点，写写"希望你能理解我的苦衷"：

   Thank you for your understanding.

   I really look forward to this and hope you can understand my predicament... Thanks for your understanding and patience...

   (2) 然后写何时可以上班：

   Assuming the eye drops work, and I am able to let my eyes rest, I trust I will be able to wear my contact lenses or glasses after a week, at which time I will be able to report to my new job. This means I will start my job a week later than originally planned.

Once my car is repaired, my daughter is in daycare and my consultant job is completed, I will be 100% ready to begin work... I should be able to start next Monday, a week later than we discussed.

5. 最后,如何比较客气,我们可以写"希望不会因为请假影响我的工作":

I hope this situation will not jeopardize my position at Microsoft, as I am enthusiastic and fully prepared to immerse myself in my new job.

不过,也可以表现得"横"一点"如果还有什么情况,我会让你知道的":If I encounter further problems I will let you know.

WRITING TASK 2

范文

范文1

I completely agree with the statement that children's leisure activities must be educational, otherwise they are a complete waste of time; however, I would like to clarify the meaning of "educational". Many people think that books and facts are the only methods of education, therefore if a child is not reading, memorizing, or performing a science experiment, they are not engaging in educational activities. However, according to my understanding, some activities that most would consider to have little educational value, I would qualify as being very useful and educational.

First consider the example of a child playing in the mud. Is this educational? Many would argue that it is not. However, I assert that playing in the mud is a very educational activity. It teaches a child about ratios and textures when he adds more water to the mud to make it thinner; he can also observe evaporation and drainage as the mud dries out over time and becomes dirt again the next day. He may not know the words "ratio", or "evaporation", but he has witnessed these phenomena and has absorbed the practical knowledge.

The same can be said for running around and spinning in circles, a total waste of time to onlookers. But remember this child is learning how his muscles work and how to control them, and also about balance and velocity and gravity as he loses balances and is pulled towards the ground. I would also agree that baking a cake is an educational activity, as the child can observe how different raw ingredients mixed together react to heat and then become a delicious snack!

In my opinion, watching TV or playing video games very quickly loses its educational appeal. TV may convey some educational material and video games may exercise a child's strategic thinking, but most kids don't exclusively watch documentaries and can become addicted to video games, so I believe that these are two of the few non-educational activities to be avoided.

我完全同意儿童的休闲活动必须有教育意义,否则就是完全在浪费时间;但是我要澄清"有教育意义的"一词的含义。许多人认为书本和事实是教育的唯一的方法,因此要是孩子不读书、不背诵或者不做科学试验,他们就没有融入教育活动中。然而,按照我的理解,一些被认为几乎没有什么教育价值的活动,我会认定它们非常有用并且有教育意义。

首先来看儿童在泥巴地里玩耍的例子。这样的活动有教育意义吗?很多人会说没有。然而我确信在泥巴地里玩是一项非常有教育意义的活动。当孩子往泥巴里加水让它变得更稀时，这样的活动就教会了孩子关于比例和质地的知识。当泥巴随着时间变化而变干，在第二天再次成为泥土，孩子可以观察到蒸发和排水的现象。他也许不知道“比例”或者是“蒸发”这样的词，但是他能够见证这些现象并且吸收实际的知识。

同样值得一提的是绕圈跑步和转圈，对于旁观者来说完全是浪费时间的活动。但是要记住，这个孩子正在学会如何让他的肌肉活动以及如何控制它们，并且当他们失去平衡倒向地面的时候可以了解到平衡、速率和重力。我也赞同烤蛋糕是一项有教育意义的活动，因为孩子可以观察到不同的生的原料是如何混合在一起互相反应，在加热后会变成美味小吃的！

在我看来，看电视或者玩电子游戏会很快地失去它的教育吸引力。电视节目也许提供了很多教育材料，电子游戏也许可以训练孩子的战略思维，但是大多数的孩子不会只看纪录片，而是会变得对电子游戏上瘾。因此我认为这是应当被避免的少数毫无教育意义的活动中的两种。

范文 2

I disagree with people who believe that children's leisure activities must be educational or they are a complete waste of time. Childhood is for playing, not for preparing for college entrance exams.

Childhood is a precious time during which a child should have the freedom to play, explore and discover life on his or her own terms. Guidance is good and beneficial if done correctly, but not if it is done to the exclusion of free play. Imposing structure and a constant focus on education during leisure time means that it is no longer leisure time. Pressuring children to always be learning also casts a heavy burden on them to be productive in a manner that makes them fit into a certain mold that is best suited for adults. But every child is not alike. Free leisure time allows them to be who they truly are.

Forcing education on children during leisure time has the negative effect of creating little adults before they are ready. Numerous studies show that such pressure results in the early onset of common "adult diseases" in children such as stress, headaches, depression and emotional exhaustion. These then show up in their lives in the form of violence, bullying, and a refusal to attend school. They are, in effect, worn out on life too early.

Why? Because someone thought that they should get a head start, not waste their time with play and start preparing for a career at the age of three. These people need to lighten up and, as is so often said by adults these days, get back in touch with their inner child. How should they do this? Go out and play!

我不同意那些认为儿童的休闲活动必须要有教育意义或者干脆认为它们就是完全在浪费时间的那些人的观点。童年时代就是用来玩的，不是用来准备大学入学考试的。

童年时代十分宝贵，在那时儿童就应当有自由以他们自己的方式来玩耍、探索和发现生活。正确的指导是好的，也是有益的。但是如果这些指导剥夺了孩子的自由，那就是有害的了。在休闲时间给教育强加条条框框和对教育持有固定不变的关注意味着它不再是休闲时间。强迫孩子一直学习，以一种使他们适合于一种适于成人的特定的最佳模式的方式来使他们变得很有能力，也给他们带来了沉重的负担，但是每个孩子不一样。自由的休闲时间可以让他们做真正的自己。

在休闲时间给儿童强加教育会起到一种在他们准备好以前就创造出“小大人”的负面作用。无数的研究显示这样的压力会导致诸如压力大、头疼、沮丧和情绪萎靡之类的儿童中常见的“成人病”过早地发作。这一切会以暴力、欺凌弱小者、拒绝上学等形式表现在他们的生活中。他们过早地被生活弄得很疲惫。

为什么？因为有人认为他们应当早点开始，不要浪费时间去玩或者开始从 3 岁就开始为一生开始做准备。那些热衷于让儿童劳动的人应当放松一些，而且正如最近常常被成年人说到的，回到内心中你的童年。他们怎么做呢？出去玩吧！

谋篇布局

1. 读题：

这篇文章的中心事件是“孩子的平时活动应该有教育意义”。题干支持这种说法。理由是：“否则，将是浪费时间”。

2. 写提纲：

(1) 如果你同意，那么你可以从“孩子的平时活动有教育意义的好的后果”或“其他活动确实浪费时间”来构思分论点。

(2) 如果你不同意，那么你可以从“孩子的平时活动有教育意义的没有好的后果”或“所有的活动都不是浪费时间”来构思分论点。

(3) 从以前的文章分析我们可以看到，还有一种做法是对题目中的某一个词进行再定义。这里的范文1就在第一段重新定义了什么叫“有教育意义的活动”，然后就在下面段落中写“有教育意义的活动有什么好的后果”以及“没有教育意义的活动有什么不好的后果”。这里，这种强对比的思维也是很重要的。我们谈论“一个事物或事件很好”的时候，论述“跟它相反的事物或事件很不好”就是一个强有力的支持。

范文2着重讲了“只让孩子参加所谓有教育意义活动的危害”。尤其是第二段值得我们学习：把孩子和成年人作强对比（有些东西适合大人却不一定适合孩子）。

General Training：Reading and Writing Test B

READING

SECTION 1

文章结构

体　　裁	应用文
主要内容	说明某药物的具体使用方法。

词汇注释

文章	
direct *vt.* 指示,命令	**contact** *vt.* 与…取得联系
shake *vt.* 摇,(猛力)摇动;摇匀	**dizziness** *n.* 头昏,头晕,眩晕
dose *n.* (药物等的)(一次)剂量;一剂	**vomiting** *n.* 呕吐
midday *n.* 中午	**blurred** *adj.* 模糊的
instruction *n.* [~s] 用法说明;操作指南	**vision** *n.* 视力,视觉
empty *adj.* 空的	**available** *adj.* 可获得的
stomach *n.* 胃,肚子,腹部	**prescription** *n.* 处方,药方
immediately *adv.* 立即,马上	**suitable** *adj.* 合适的,适宜的
lie down 躺下;躺在床上休息(或睡眠)	**otherwise** *adv.* 以另外方式;别样;除此之外
occur *vi.* 发生;存在;出现	**period** *n.* 时期;阶段
discontinue *vt.* 停止,中断,终止	**expiry** *n.* (期限)终止;满期
题目	
eyesight *n.* 视力	**affect** *vt.* 影响

考题解析

Questions 1－4

● 题型归类：YES/NO/NOT GIVEN

雅思阅读 G 类和 A 类的 YES/NO/NOT GIVEN 题型有很大的区别,由于 G 类前两部分的文章难度较低,此类题经常是要考生根据文章中的标准判断题目中的情况是否正确,而不是像 A 类考试中单纯地进行题目内容与文章内容的对应。

● 题目解析:

题目编号	段落主题句	答案位置	题解
1	lie down	Instructions 第 1 条	定位后确定文章内容说在躺下休息之前不能吃药,与题目内容相反,因此选择 NO。

2	eyesight	Instructions 第 2 条	题目定位词在文章中稍有变化，eyesight is affected = blurred vision，内容相符，选择 YES。
3	stop taking the medicine	Instructions 第 4 条	第四条明确指出一旦开始服用就要一直吃光，除非医生建议停止。题目说感觉好了就可以不吃，两者意思相违背，选 NO。
4	a person of any age	Instructions 第 3 条	文章中对服药年龄有明确限制，题目内容与文章相违背，选 NO。

参考译文

使用说明

- 本品须按说明服用。
- 用时摇匀。
- 用量：午饭和晚饭后服用，每天两次，每次 50ml。

注意事项

- 本品不可空腹服用，不可在睡前服用。
- 如出现以下症状，请停止服用本品并与医生联系：眩晕、呕吐、视力模糊。
- 本品为处方药，5 岁以下儿童禁用。
- 开始服用本药物后，如没有医生建议，须服用完整瓶药物。
- 6 个月为一疗程。
- 有效期至：2004 年 2 月 16 日

文章结构

体　裁	应用文
主要内容	一份要求客户退还有问题产品的通知。

词汇注释

文章

inform *vt.* 通知，告知
metal *n.* 金属
curry *n.* 咖喱菜肴，咖喱
spicy *adj.* 辛辣的
batch *n.* 一批生产量；一批
jar *n.* 罐子，坛子
involved *adj.* 有关的，牵扯在内的
bottom *n.* 底部，底层
preferable *adj.* 更可取的，更好的，更合意的(to)
unopened *adj.* 未打开的
supermarket *n.* 超级市场
purchase *vt.* 买，购买
retailer *n.* 零售店
payment *n.* 支付，付款
empty *adj.* 空的
retailing *n.* 零售业
hear from 收到…的来信
consume *vt.* 吃光；消耗
in particular 特别，尤其
affect *vt.* 影响
reward *n.* 奖赏；酬金；奖品
lead(to) *vi.* 导致
conviction *n.* 定罪，判罪
guilty *adj.* 有罪的；证明(或判决)有罪的
contact *vt.* 与…取得联系

题目	
contaminate *vt.* 污染，弄脏	**maximum** *n.* 最大量，最大值

考题解析

Questions 5 – 9

● 题型归类：Short Answer Questions

此类题型属于细节题，注意题目的提问方式及问句中的定位信息。在 G 类考试中这类题目可以通过简单定位得到正确答案。

● 题目解析：

题目编号	段落主题句	答案位置	题解
5	batch number	第 1 段末句（The batch number...）	本题较易解答，基本通过简单定位就可以解决。5 题问罐头数字印刷的位置，定位 batch number 即可。6 题和 9 题根据提问方式均可判断与金钱有关，文中出现两组金钱符号，再确定问句中的具体内容即可。7 题需要寻找一个人名或相应专有名词作为答案，在文章中只有一处出现可以回答 whom 问题的职务名称。第 8 题问吃过咖喱鸡罐头的人要提供什么样的信息，答案比较容易定位。
6	how much/ opened jar	第 2 段末句（Fancy Foods will...）	
7	the batch numbers listed/ whom	第 3 段第 2 句（However, the company...）	
8	Chicken Curry you ate	第 3 段末句（In particular, it...）	
9	maximum reward	第 5 段首句（Fancy Foods will...）	

参考译文

重要通知：回收产品

幻想食品告知公众：在部分幻想咖喱鸡肉（辣味）罐头中发现金属条。罐头生产批号为 J6617 至 J6624，批号均印在罐头底部。

如已购买上述生产批号的罐头，请将其退回所购买的超市，退回的罐头最好尚未开封。也可将其退回厂家（布莱克镇幻想食品零售部）。尚未开封的罐头将退款 $10，已开封的退款 $5。

空罐恕不退费，亦无须退回。如有顾客已经吃过上述生产批号的罐头，本公司零售经理非常愿意收看他们的来信，如能提供购买地点的相关信息将尤为有助。

幻想食品的咖喱鸡肉（椰子味）和咖喱鸡肉（芒果味）不受此次事件影响，无须退回。

悬　赏

幻想食品公司悬赏 $10000 至 $50000，寻找可以判定任何在其产品中投放金属条的人的犯罪信息。如有相关信息，请与布莱克镇幻想食品零售部公共关系经理联系。

文章结构

体　　裁	应用文
主要内容	某家具商店关于其信用卡的推广广告。

词汇注释

文章

fabulous *adj.* 惊人的，难以置信的；传奇式的
furniture *n.* 家具
bedside table 床边小几，床头柜
credit card 信用卡
straight *adj.* 直接的，直截了当的
unlike *prep.* 不像…，和…不同
interest-free *adj.* 无息的
period *n.* 时期；阶段
purchase *vt.* 买，购买
in this case 既然是这(那)样，假使这(那)样的话
interest *n.* 利息
spread *vt.* 把…分期完成；使延续
charge *vt.* 收(费)；要(人)支付(钱)
initial *adj.* 最初的，开始的
application *n.* 申请，请求
absolutely *adv.* 完全地；肯定地；绝对地
annual *adj.* 每年的，年度的
fee *n.* 费(如会费、入场费、手续费等)
administration *n.* 管理，经营
fill in 填写，填充
application form 申请表
process *vt.* 使接受处理(或检查、审议)
promptly *adv.* 及时地，迅速地
approve *vt.* 批准，核准
major *adj.* 主要的；较重要的
local *adj.* 当地的；地方性的
telephone directory 电话(号码)簿

题目

option *n.* 选择；选择自由；选择权
furnish *vt.* 为(房间等)配备家具
location *n.* 位置；场所；地点
apply *vi.* (尤指以书面形式)申请；请求
order *vt.* 定购，预定
range *n.* 范围

考题解析

Questions 10–13

● 题型归类：List of headings

对于雅思 G 类阅读来说，这种类型的题目如果出现在前两个 Section，通常都比较容易解答，因为前两部分的文章通常篇幅较短，文章结构比较清晰，虽然也属于结构题，但比 A 类阅读中的此类题型要容易解答。

● 题目解析：

题目编号	题解
10	由于文章各段较短，找准段落的中心句即可顺利解答题目。Section C 末句指出“你可以剩余更多的钱去买别的东西”，意味着用这种方式购买可以省钱，而如何省钱在前面的具体解释中说的很清楚，用这种信用卡可能有 60 天的免息还款期(interest-free period)。与选项 ii 内容吻合。
11	Section D 的内容表达方式已经部分地表达了段落内容，是对某一件事物若干方面的一个列举，再看列举的具体内容，一个是说可以在 60 天内付清全款，另一个是说可以在更长的时间内付款。与选项 i 的内容相符。

12	Section E 的首句提示了整段的内容是和 application 有关的，选项中 application 有关的只有 vi。
13	Section F 主要告知如何查询各地店铺的 addresses，在选项中只有 v 中的 location 能表达这个意思。

参考译文

精品家具

想买张床头小几？或者买张可供 20 人晚餐的餐桌？您想要的这里应有尽有！精品家具拥有澳大利亚最多的家具供您选择。

前往精品家具店，使用精品家具信用卡便可立即拥有您喜欢的家具。想买什么可以直接提货后付款。

精品家具信用卡有别于大多数信用卡，无论何时购买，每件精品家具均可享受 60 天的免息付款期，省下更多的钱购买其他东西吧。

● 你可以在 60 天内付清全款，此种方式可免付利息。

● 你可以选择在更长的时间里分期付款。此种方式在最初 60 天的免息期后须收取利息。

绝对免费申请！无须交纳任何年费或管理费。只须填写申请表，将它交至离你最近的精品家具店即可。申请将会及时处理，一旦申请获准，即可开始使用。

我们在各大城市均设有分店，你绝不会离精品家具店太远。本店地址请查询当地电话号码簿。

SECTION 2

文章结构

体　　裁	应用文
主要内容	大学学生协会招收新成员的广告

词汇注释

文章	
club *n.* 会；社；俱乐部；（趣味相投的）一伙人	**urgently** *adv.* 紧迫地；急迫地
society *n.* 社团；会社；协会	**contact** *vt.* 与…取得联系
desperate *adj.* 极想望的，极需要的	**religious** *adj.* 宗教的
common *adj.* 共同的	**discussion** *n.* 讨论，谈论
A 段	
frequent *adj.* 时常发生的，频繁的	途径
realize *vt.* 知道，明白，了解	**activity** *n.* 活动
share *vt.* 分享，分担	**barbecues** *n.* 户外烤肉餐
membership *n.* 会员身份（或资格、地位），会籍	**function** *n.* 重大聚会，宴会
access（to） *n.* 接近（或进入）的机会；享用机会；使用	

B 段	
association *n.* 协会,社团	**campus** *n.* 大学;大学校园;学校校园
debate *vt.* 辩论,争论	**link** *n.* 联系,关系,连接部分
non-political *adj.* 非政治性的,不关心政治的	**agency** *n.* (一国政府内或联合国辖下的)专业行政部门
unbiased *adj.* 无偏见的,公正的	**include** *vt.* 包括,包含
aim *vi.* 旨在,目的在于	**guest speaker** 特邀演讲者
promote *vt.* 促进,增进,发扬	**model** *n.* 模型
awareness *n.* 意识,觉悟	**General Assemble** 联合国大会
C 段	
discuss *vt.* 讨论,谈论	**competition** *n.* 竞争
personal *adj.* 个人的,私人的	**compete** *vi.* 竞争,对抗
experience *n.* 经历,经验,阅历	**nationally** *adv.* 在全国范围内;全国性地
feminism *n.* 男女平等主义	**verbal** *adj.* 口头的
D 段	
on the other hand 另一方面	**direct** *vt.* 导演
reward *n.* 奖赏;奖品	**put down** 写下
put on 上演,演出	**president** *n.* (学会等的)会长
题目	
appreciation *n.* 欣赏,鉴赏	**drama** *n.* 戏剧

考题解析

Questions 14–17

● 题型归类:List of headings

虽然此类题型属于结构题,但在 G 类阅读的前两个 Section 中出现此类题型时难度都不会太大,因为这两个部分的文章通常篇幅较短且结构明显。

● 题目解析:

题目编号	题解
14	本题实际是问各段落所描述的协会名称。除了文章内容之外,文章中的插图也为解题提供了线索。A 段反复出现 movies,题目中有关的选项只有 iii。
15	B 段选择时稍有困难,很容易错选 viii,因为第一句话中有 has many opportunities to debate。但首句中的后半句指出该组织的目的是促进校园中的国际意识,这与 debate 的关系不大,同时段落旁边的插图也给出暗示 viii 可能不是正确选项。段落最后一句通过协会的活动内容确定了协会与 UN 有关。因此答案选择 ix。
16	C 段首句也出现 debate,根据这句话也可以判断上一题的答案不能选择 viii,因为不可能两个段落选择同一个答案。段落中再次出现的 debate 和旁边的插图都明确表示这个协会是与公众讲话有关,相关的选项只有 viii。
17	如果对西方文化比较了解,可以根据插图直接选择 iv,因为插图中的画像就是 drama 的象征。通过阅读段落也可以得出正确答案。

Questions 18 – 19

● 题型归类：Short Answer Questions

此类题型属于细节题，注意问句中的定位信息和提问方式即可。

● 题目解析：

题目编号	题目定位词	答案位置	题解
18	CAS president	文章最后的黑体部分	这两道题比较容易解答，只要准确理解题干意思，回原文很好定位。18 题问方式，19 题问时间频率，原文表述十分清楚。
19	CAS Ball		

参考译文

学生社团

渴望找到兴趣相投的朋友？

渴望与其他学生进行交往？

渴望获得不同的文化和宗教体验？

渴望进行有益的讨论？

无须再四处寻找！

加入学生社团，享受快乐！

本协会最初只是一群喜欢看电影的朋友。当电影之旅越来越频繁，我们意识到一定还有其他人一样热爱电影。这个协会就是为热爱电影的人而建。会员还可参与其他活动，比如篮球、足球、户外烧烤以及其他社交活动。我们并不只是喜欢电影。

本协会有很多辩论的机会。我们是一个没有政治偏见的国际组织，旨在促进校园内的国际意识。我们与联合国相关部门及其他国际组织建立了联系。协会今年的计划包括分组讨论、嘉宾讲座、以及建立联合国大会的模型。

无论是为了寻求乐趣，还是为了获得辩论体验，我们讨论各种事情，从个人经验、社会的未来到女权主义。今年我们计划举行内部竞赛、每周辩论、入门课程，并提供在国内辩论的机会。本协会不仅可以改善口头表达，还能提高社交技能！

想成为电影明星？那还是到其他地方去吧！但想要让付出有所回报而拼命工作吗？那就来加入我们协会吧，在这里可以制作有趣的戏剧作品。我们通常每年上演三部作品。如果你喜欢写作、绘画、表演、导演或在剧场中做任何事情，写下你的名字，加入我们。

有兴趣参加以上任何一个协会的同学，请把信息留在学生会楼 CAS 办公室的学生会主席处。

别忘了还有一年一度的 CAS 舞会！

今年舞会日期：12 月 22 日！

文章结构

体　　裁	应用文
主要内容	有关申请学生贷款的说明。

词汇注释

文章

loan *n.* 贷款
fund *vt.* 为…提供资金,资助
scheme *n.* 计划,规划,方案
available *adj.* 可获得的
top up 给…装满盛器
standard *adj.* 标准的,规范的;通常的
grant *n.* 授予物(如土地、权利、补助金等)
intend *vt.* 想要,打算,计划
supplement *vt.* 增补,补充
eligibility *n.* 有条件被选中,有资格当选
restrict *vt.* 限制,约束,限定
maintenance *n.* 生活资料(或费用),生计;维持费
eligible *adj.* 有资格当选的,有条件被选中的
resident *n.* 居民,定居者
attend *vt.* 参加(会议等);上(大学等)
postgraduate *adj.* 研究生的;研究生课程的
certificate 证书,(学习)结业证书
provided *conj.* 以…为条件,除非;假如,若是
full-time *adj.* 专职的,全日制的
at least 至少
academic *adj.* 学校的,学院的,大学的
include *vt.* 包括;包含
sandwich course 工读交替制课程
combine *vi.* 联合,混合
offer *vt.* (主动)给予,提供
grant-aided *adj.* <英>受公费补助的
publicly *adj.* 由公众(或政府);以公众名义
institution *n.* (教育、慈善、宗教性质的)社会公共机构
in general 一般(或总的)说来;大体上;从总体上看
equivalent *n.* 相等物,等价物
authority *n.* 当局,官方
tuition *n.* 学费
circumstance *n.* 条件,情况
means test (对申请补助者所作的)经济情况调查
credit *n.* 信用,信贷,借贷
vet *vt.* 检查,审查
income *n.* 收入,所得,收益
take into account 考虑到,估及;体谅
previous *adj.* 以前的,先前的
spouse *n.* 配偶(指夫或妻)
partner *n.* 配偶(指夫或妻),合伙人,股东
relative *n.* 亲戚,亲属
consideration *n.* 考虑;要考虑的事
apply (for) *vi.* (尤指以书面形式)申请;请求
readiness *n.* 准备就绪状态
entry *n.* 进入,进入权,进入许可
onward *adv.* 向前

题目

cookery *n.* 烹饪;烹饪术
private *adj.* 私立的,私营的
catering *adj.* 承办酒席的,提供饮食及服务的
diploma *n.* 毕业文凭,学位证书
foundation *n.* 基础;基本原理
actual *adj.* 现行的,现时的
scholarship *n.* 奖学金
earn *vt.* 赚得,挣得;获得
owe *vt.* 欠
pay back 偿付,归还
disqualify *vt.* 取消…的资格,使不适合
couple *n.* 两三(个),(几)个,一些
withdraw *vt.* 取消,撤消,撤回
half-way *adv.* 在中途,半路上
keep up (使)保持良好状态

考题解析

Questions 20–27

● 题型归类：YES/NO/NOT GIVEN

雅思 G 类阅读中此类题型的难点在于通常是文章提供某些准则，而题目是这些规则的实例，判断时有一定难度。特别注意本题的所有题目都是先陈述一种情况然后对这些情况进行提问，如果忽略或没读懂问句会给解题带来麻烦。

● 题目解析：

题目编号	题目定位词	答案位置	题解
20	a private catering college	Eligibility 部分第一段	题目假设条件：参加一个月的厨师课程，私营学校，非脱产课程，有证书。 问题：是否可得到学生贷款？ 文章得到学生贷款条件之一：参加全日制的高等教育课程。题目条件与文章内条件不符，答案选 NO。
21	foundation course/fees... paid for by my Local Authority	Eligibility 部分第三段	题目假设条件：九月参加全日制、为期一年的 foundation course，课程由政府付费。 问题：是否可得到学生贷款？ 文章得到贷款条件之一：任何由政府付款的课程（any other courses for which your Local Authority will pay your tuition）。符合条件，选 YES。
22	Postgraduate Certificate/Local Authority	Eligibility 部分第三段	题目问题：政府是否会为课程付款？ 由于全文谈论的都是学生贷款的问题，唯一出现政府付款的地方是 21 题答案所在句子中，而且是为了说明获得学生贷款的条件，文章中其他地方没有提及政府付款的问题，因此答案是 NOT GIVEN。
23	48	Eligibility 部分第一段	题目假设条件：母亲已经 48 岁，要参加全日制为期一年的课程。 题目问题：母亲是否年龄太大而不能获得学生贷款？ 题目只关注一个问题，即获得学生贷款的年龄界限，文章中明确的年龄界限是 50 岁以前（before your 50th birthday），因此答案是 NO。
24	scholarship	Your financial circumstances 第一条	题目假设条件：已经有小额奖学金。 题目问题：是否还可获得学生贷款？ 文章条件：生活补助和学费补助不会影响申请贷款。题目假设条件符合文章内容，答案选 YES。

25	staying with my aunt	Your financial circumstances 第四条	题目假设条件：和亲戚(aunt)住在一起。 题目问题：学生贷款公司是否要知道亲戚的收入情况？ 文章条件：亲戚的收入不在审查范围内。 题目条件与文章条件完全吻合，因此回答这个问题的答案是NO。
26	owed the bank a lot of money	Your financial circumstances 最后一条	题目假设条件：以前欠银行钱，银行不再提供贷款。 题目问题：这种情况是否会使其没有资格获得学生贷款？ 文章条件：以前的经济记录不在审查范围内。 题目条件与文章条件吻合，因此不影响获得学生贷款，答案是NO。
27	withdraw half-way	Your financial circumstances 第三条	题目假设条件：以前获得过学生贷款，中途取消。 题目问题：是否可以申请第二次贷款。 文章条件：以前的学生贷款不在审查范围内。 题目条件与文章条件吻合，因此不影响再次申请学生贷款，答案是YES。

参考译文

学生贷款

政府自1990年9月起为接受高等教育的学生贷款计划提供资金。

此项贷款是对生活补助的补充，包括但不仅限于已获得生活补助的学生。

是否申请贷款由贷款人自己决定。

贷款条件

申请学生贷款须符合以下条件：英国居民；参加硕士以下全日制高等教育课程，或授予教育学硕士证书的课程；入学时年龄未满50岁。全日制课程时间不少于一学年，包括半工半读的课程。

可提供符合条件的课程的学校包括：学院、大学，苏格兰公助学校和其他提供高等教育课程的公立学校。

总体而言，符合条件的课程包括大学本科课程或类似课程，以及任何其他由当地政府负担学费的课程。

经济条件

申请贷款的学生无须接受"经济情况调查"或"信用审查"，所有合格的申请者都可获得贷款。

细则：

- 生活补助和学费金额不计在内。
- 其他收入不计在内。
- 任何以前的学生贷款不计在内。
- 父母、配偶、伴侣或其他亲属的收入不计在内。
- 以往的经济记录不计在内。

申请时间

准备2003年秋季入学的学生如需要更多相关信息，请于2003年6月后与学生贷款公司取得联系。

在读学生可在学年的任何时候申请贷款。

SECTION 3

文章结构

体　　裁	说明文。
主要内容	说明制服已经转变成一种市场营销方式及该行业的近期发展。
结　　构	A 段：说明制服的传统意义。
	B 段：指出制服已在过去 30 年里转变成新的市场营销方式。
	C 段：说明用服装作为有效市场营销方式不好把握，并具体举例说明不同的服装会传递不同的信息。
	D 段：用具体数据说明制服市场的运营情况。
	E 段：说明成功的制服需要满足两方面的需要。
	F 段：说明制服公司的发展情况。
	G 段：预测制服公司市场前景乐观。

词汇注释

文　　章	
A 段	
impression *n.* 印象；影响，效果	**intend** *vt.* 想要，打算，计划
traditionally *adv.* 传统地，守旧地	**impress** *vt.* 给…深刻的印象
uniform *n.* 制服；制服式样	**terrify** *vt.* 使害怕，使恐惧
manufacture *vt.*（尤指大量）制造	**denote** *vt.* 表示，是…的标志
likely *adj.* 可能的；有倾向的；看来要发生的	**hierarchy** *n.* 等级制度，等级森严的组织
symbolic *adj.* 象征性的，作为象征的	**chef** *n.*（餐馆等的）厨师长；厨师
military *n.* 军人；军方；陆军	**flour** *n.* 面粉
originally *adv.* 起初，原先	**supervise** *vt.* 监督，管理，指导
B 段	
emphasis *n.*（对事物、意义、重要性等的）强调	**corporate** *adj.* 团体的，公司的
project *vt.* 提出；表明…的特性，使呈现特性；设计	**employ** *vt.* 雇用
workforce *n.*（工厂等在职的）工人总数，职工总数	**ambassador** *n.* 大使
homogeneous *adj.* 同种类的；同性质的；相同特征的	**behave** *vi.* 表现；以某种态度对待
particularly *adv.* 特别，尤其	**terribly** *adv.* 非常，很
retailing *n.* 零售业	**identify** *vt.* 确定；识别
workwear *n.* 工作服	**channel** *n.* 途径；门径
emerge *vi.* 出现，出来，显露	**communication** *n.* 交流；通讯
C 段	
visual *adj.* 视觉的，直观的，（教具等）产生视觉形象的	**aura** *n.* 气氛，氛围
cue *n.* 暗示，信号	**authority** *n.* 权威
subtle *adj.* 微妙的，难以捉摸的	**pastel** *n.* 柔和的淡色彩
wittingly *adv.* 故意地，有意地，蓄意地	**approachability** *n.* 可亲近，可接近性，可通达性
unwittingly *adv.* 不知不觉地，不知道地	**conservatism** *n.* 保守主义，守旧性
subliminal *adj.* 潜意识的，意识下的	**neatness** *n.* 整洁，简洁

efficiency *n.* 效率,功效	**obsession** *n.* 着迷,困扰
overdo *vt.* 把…做得过分;过分使用;过于夸张	**innovative** *adj.* 革新的,新颖的;富有革新精神的
spill over 大得无法被容纳	**subliminally** *adv.* 潜意识地
indicate *vt.* 表明;暗示	**consultant** *n.* 顾问
D 段	
philosophy *n.* 宗旨;哲学	**fraught** *adj.* 使人忧虑的;忧虑的
brand *vt.* 加商标于…;标明…与众不同,使显得独一无二	**according to** 根据,按照
	supply *vt.* 提供(所需物品),供给,供应
uniformity *n.* 统一(性);一致(性);相同(性)	**account (for)** *vt.* 提出理由;作出解释,作出说明
E 段	
balance *vt.* 使平衡,使均衡	**strategy** *n.* 战略;策略;行动计划
key *adj.* 主要的,极重要的,关键性的	**respect** *n.* 着眼点,方面
set *n.* (互相关连的东西构成的)一套	**perception** *n.* 感知,认知;看法
staff *n.* 全体职员,全体雇员	**size up** 估计;品评
uncomfortable *adj.* 不舒服的,不安的,不自在的	**attitude** *n.* 态度,看法
element *n.* 要素;成分;基本组成部分	**invest** *vt.* 投(资);投入(时间、金钱、精力等)
pointless *adj.* 无意义的,不得要领的;没有目的的	
F 段	
in addition 另外,加之	**inventory** *n.* 存货清单;财产目录
rental *adj.* 租赁(业)的;供出租的	**budget** *n.* 预算,预算案
specialization *n.* 专业化;专门化;特殊化	**distribution** *n.* 分发;分配;分送
marketplace *n.* 市场	**individually** *adv.* 各自地;分别地,各个地
predict *vt.* 预料,预计;预言	**amass** *vt.* 把…聚成堆,堆积;积累
consolidation *n.* 巩固,加强;联合,统一	**assurance** *n.* (人寿)保险
increasingly *adv.* 渐增地,越来越多地	**accreditation** *n.* 信托,委托;任命
supplier *n.* 供应者;(协作件等的)供应厂商	**package** *n.* (需一并考虑或施行的)有关联的一组事物;一揽子交易(或计划、建议等)
complex *adj.* 由部件组成的,组合的;复杂的	
reliable *adj.* 可靠的;可信赖的	
G 段	
potential *adj.* 潜在的;可能的	**survey** *n.* 调查
wardrobe *n.* (为某个季节或某种活动用的)全部服装	**identity** *n.* 个性,特性;一致
题目	
original *adj.* 起初的,原来的,原先的	**smart** *adj.* 整洁的,整齐的
popularity *n.* 普及,流行,大众化	**negative** *a.* 负面的,消极的
significance *n.* 意义;含义	

考题解析

Questions 28–33

● 题型归类:List of Headings

本题的形式是 Matching,但实质上是 List of Headings 题,即考查段落大意的结构题,因此解题时依旧可以先阅读各段的主题句判断段落大意后在各题题干中寻找相关内容。

● 题目解析：

<table>
<tr><th>题目编号</th><th>题目定位词</th><th>题解</th></tr>
<tr><td>28</td><td>purchasing agreement</td><td rowspan="6">A 段首句说传统的制服是为了保护工人，表明制服的目的所在，与 29 题题干内容吻合。
B 段末句指出制服不再是单纯的判断谁是雇员的方法，制服已经成为市场交流的一种新途径，表示制服角色的变化，与 32 题题干内容相符。
C 段用大量例子说明不同的制服代表不同的意思，与 33 题题干内容一致。
D 段已作为例题出现，可直接跳过。
E 段首句指出成功的制服需要平衡两种关键需求。其中之一就是职员对制服的感觉。有关职员的题目只有 31 题，而 30 题的 staff 是 uniform 的修饰语。
F 段首句说制服公司可以提供租赁服务，同时段落后继续描述可以提供的其他服务方式，与 28 题题干内容相符。
根据排除法则，G 段可以直接作为 30 题的答案，文章中也可找到解题依据，G 段末句说最近的调查发现 90% 的员工对可以反映公司特性的制服表示欢迎，这与 30 题题干内容基本一致。</td></tr>
<tr><td>29</td><td>original purposes</td></tr>
<tr><td>30</td><td>popularity rating</td></tr>
<tr><td>31</td><td>involving employees</td></tr>
<tr><td>32</td><td>changing significance</td></tr>
<tr><td>33</td><td>perceptions of different types</td></tr>
</table>

Questions 34–40

● 题型归类：YES/NO/NOT GIVEN

雅思 G 类阅读第三篇中的此类题型与 A 类中基本一致，需要准确理解题目意思，回原文定位后进行判断。

● 题目解析：

题目编号	题目定位词	答案位置	题解
34	carefully made		题目是对一种比较关系的判断，即以前的制服比现在的制服制作精良。在文章中寻找不到有关制服制作的内容，因此选择答案 NOT GIVEN。
35	employees/part of a team	B 段首句（The last 30 years, ...）	本题有一定难度，题目说制服的作用是可以让雇员感觉自己是团队的一部分。定位词并不典型，在文章中较难找到。但可以根据文章结构将搜寻范围缩小到谈论制服作用的 A、B 两段。由于定位词在原文中以近义词的形式出现，给定位和理解增加了难度。文中 workforce 等同于题目中的 employees，a homogeneous unit 等同于题目中的 a team，原文指出在过去的三十年里，制服在两方面的作用得到强调，其中一个就是将全体员工联合起来成为一个统一的整体（in uniting the workforce into a homogeneous unit），这一意思完全符合题目内容。因此答案选 YES。
36	marketing tool	C 段首句（Truly effective marketing...）	本题题目意思是说将制服用作市场手段需要特别谨慎。文章第三段首句提示段落主题是用制服等视觉暗示达到有效市场营销是一门很微妙的艺术（a subtle art）。

			subtle 的意思是说很难以把握，这个词在本句中很好地表达了 require great care 的意思。如果在阅读这一句时有词汇障碍也不影响解题，因为从文章结构上讲本题的答案应当集中在 C 段，通读 C 段会发现段落中举了若干实例来证明段落主题。答案选 YES。
37	too smart	C 段第 5 句（Neatness can suggest...）	本题比较容易解答，题目句子意思表达的是一种否定意思，即太整洁会给顾客带来负面影响。C 段中的举例明确指出，如果整洁过头（it is overdone）就会弄巧成拙，表示对权力的过分关注。句子的后半部其实就是对题目中 a negative impact 的具体说明。题目意思和文章意思完全吻合，答案选 YES。
38	business that supply company clothing/successful	D 段末句（Of these, 22...）	题目说大多数提供公司服装的企业是成功的。回原文定位根据文章结构将搜索范围缩小到 D 段，D 段第二句首先指出用合适的制服表达公司理念这一过程不一定总会成功。先从概括的角度对题目意思进行否定。紧接着在这一段的末尾又提供了具体的数据，在现有的 1000 家提供制服的企业中，22 家的销售收入占总收入的 85%，再次证明取得成功的只有极少数。因此答案选 NO。
39	marketing consultants		此题比较容易判断，题目说最好由市场顾问来选择制服。文章虽然谈到制服和市场营销的关系，但没有谈到由谁来选择制服的问题，在文章中也寻找不到句中的定位词。所以答案选 NOT GIVEN。
40	financial services/ in the future	F 段第 4－5 句（Increasingly, the big suppliers...）	此题稍有难度，可能会误选 NOT GIVEN，因为如果在文章中寻找 financial services 是寻找不到的，题目意思是说服装公司计划在未来提供金融服务，那么应该首先回原文寻找服装公司未来的发展情况。根据文章结构这部分内容应该集中在最后两段，在 F 段中可以看到大的供应商会逐渐成为“管理型的代理机构”，这是服装公司未来的方向，具体会做些什么呢，在下面的解释中说的很清楚，会包括：提供可靠信息、管理存货、控制预算、向总部或每个职员配送服装。这里并不包括提供金融服务，其中的控制预算并不等同于金融服务，它只是一揽子服务中的一项内容，也是和服装有关。这里的意思已经不符合题目的内容，可以直接选择 NO。如果看到 5 句中的 amassing quality assurance accreditations 可能会感到迷惑，assurance accreditations 指保险信托，这是属于金融范畴，根据两个词的内容答案是否可以选择 YES。不能选的原因在于本句是说在这些方面进行了投资，并没有说未来计划这么做，题目意思和文章意思并不完全相符。

参考译文

第一印象会起作用

传统意义上，制作制服是为了保护工人，在一些行业依旧如此。最初设计制服时，也可能所有的制服都具有象征意义。例如，军队制服最初是想要给敌人留下深刻印象甚至恐吓他们，其他的制服则是一种等级的象征——厨师们因为和面粉打交道所以身穿白色，但大厨要头戴黑色帽子来表示他是管理者。

但是，过去的三十年里，制服在表现公司形象和团结员工两方面的作用增强了，特别是在要“面对客户”的产业里，尤其是金融服务业和零售业。制服和工装演变成了“企业衣着”。UK一家主要的零售企业的经理彼得·格里芬说，“员工就是你的大使，他们的外表和言行举止都极其重要。”结果看待企业工装有了全新的视角，制服不再简单地用来分辨谁是企业的员工，它正在演化成一种市场流通的新途径。

但是要通过制服这样的视觉信号进行真正有效的市场营销，这是一门相当微妙的艺术。我们的外表有意无意的在向其他人传递各种强烈的潜意识信息。深色给人权威感，而较浅的柔和色彩则具有亲和力。一些服装式样会产生保守的感觉，另一些则显示对新事物的开放态度。整洁意味着高效，但如果整洁过了头，就会弄巧成拙，显示出对权力的过分沉溺。“色彩之家”的形象顾问经理林恩·Elvy指出，“如果公司销售的是产品质量，那就必须有优质的制服。如果销售的是时尚，制服就必须时髦。如果想表现出创新，每个人就不能看上去完全一样。我们会下意识地注意到这些事情。”

但是要把企业宗旨正确地体现在颜色、式样、创新和正式程度的混合之中，这个过程会令人忧虑，而且这么做也不见得总会成功。据《公司服装》杂志所言，在工装和企业服饰市场中共有1000家公司，1994年其中22家的销售额是三亿八千万美元，占总销额的85%。

一套成功的制服需要平衡两种需求：一方面，如果员工觉得制服不舒服或者不好看，制服就不会起作用。由穿制服的人做决定已经成为引进和管理企业服饰的关键因素。另一方面，如果制服无法表现企业的市场策略也会变得毫无意义。在这一方面最大的挑战就是时间。第一印象对于人类感知的确会起作用。顾客会在几秒钟内就对员工的外表做出评价，就是那几秒钟从那一刻起就会影响他们的态度。这几秒钟如此重要以致于大公司要花好几年时间和成百万的英镑来确保这几秒种不会出问题。

此外，一些制服公司还提供租赁服务。UK一家大银行的客服经理Blyth先生预测道：“专门化市场正在增长”。过去的两到三年已经见证了统一的趋势。大的供应商会逐渐成为“管理型的代理机构”，这意味着他们会把有关公司制服的整个复杂流程打包处理，提供一整套的服务——包括提供可靠信息、管理存货、控制预算、向总部或每个职员配送服装。他们已经对新系统、信息技术和积累优质的保险信托经验等进行了大量投资。

企业着装的确有长足发展的潜力。一些银行已经引进了全套的企业服饰；警察正在研究21世纪的全新面貌。现在许多员工可以接受企业制服。对员工的一次近期调查发现90%的员工对可以反映企业特性的服装表示欢迎。

WRITING

WRITING TASK 1

范文

范文1

Dear Sir/Madam:

I oppose the proposed plan to expand the airport and to increase the number of flights. I believe this would definitely be detrimental to all the people who live and work within a five-mile radius of the airport. I live only 2 miles south of the airport.

The current flight schedule of the airport is acceptable to the residents within this area, as the first plane takes off at 6 a.m. and the last plane lands by 8 p.m. However, once the expansion is complete, the number of flights will be greatly increased with early departures extended to the weekends and the last flight to 11 p.m. This will disturb the sleep and peace of mind for all residents, as well as for the people who work, within a five-mile radius of the airport.

The property values will drop, as this area becomes a less desirable place to live or work. Once the property values drop, the tax base will shrink, making it necessary to cut back on needed services, further contributing to a decline in our community.

The expansion of the airport will only benefit the airlines, but will have an adverse effect on the residents and the community.

亲爱的先生/女士：

我反对那项被提议的机场扩建和增加航班数量的计划。我认为此举无疑将有害于居住和工作在半径5英里范围内的所有的人。我住在机场南部距机场只有两英里的地方。

机场最近的航班起降时间对这个地区的居民来说还可以接受，因为首航班起飞时间是早上6点，末航班的降落时间是晚上8点。然而，一旦扩建完成，航班数量将会极大增加，早上航班的6点起飞将会延伸到周末，末航班的降落时间将会延长到晚上11点。这会影响所有居民的睡眠和打扰他们精神上的安静，工作在半径5英里范围内的人也会受到影响。

当这个地区变成一个让人不想在这里生活和工作的地方时，固定资产价值将会降低。一旦固定资产价值贬低，税收基础就会萎缩，削减必需的服务成为必然，在更远的未来还会造成社区衰落。

机场的扩建只会使航空公司受益，但是带给社区和居民的则是相反的效果。

范文2

Dear Sir/Madam,

I am writing to voice my concern about the new airport expansion.

I live near the airport, 4 blocks south of the western runway, and it is already quite an emotional strain with the current flight load. The problem, as I see it, is that airport expansion and more flights will negatively affect the local economy. This will happen because more land will be used for the expansion and the increased number of flights will create more noise. No one wants more noise from an airport. When all of this occurs people will start leaving the area, property values will decrease and the local economy will be negatively affected. This means that there will be fewer jobs in the area, a decline in the quality of life and a decline in business opportunity. The only people who will benefit from the expansion are the rich owners of the airport and the rich owners of the airport companies. None of these people live in this area and none of them could give a damn about how our lives are negatively impacted by their expansion.

I therefore strongly protest this expansion and urge others to join me.

亲爱的先生/女士：

我写信在这里表达我对机场扩建的关注。

我住在机场附近，就在机场西跑道南边的四个街区。近期航班数量的加载已经导致我的精神过度疲劳了。正如我所见的，问题在于机场的扩建和更多的航班将会给地方经济带来负面的影响。更多的土地被占，用于机场扩建，以及航班数量的增加制造的更多噪音会使这种负面影响发生作用。没有人愿意从飞机场听到更多的噪音。当这一切都发生的时候，人们就会开始离开这个地方，固定资产价值就会下降，并且地方经济会受到负面影响。这意味着该地区工作的机会越来越少，生活质量将会下降，商业机会也将减少。唯一会从扩建中受益的人就是富有的机场老板和航空公司老板。这些人没有一个住在这个地区，他们中没有一个人谴责机场扩建给我们的生活带来的负面影响。

因此我强烈抗议这项扩建并且呼吁其他人加入到我抗议的队伍中来。

谋篇布局

1. 英文写作的习惯是开门见山，所以一开始，最好就让别人明白你想干什么。所以我们可以把"描述问题"这个任务放到最前面写。
   (1) I oppose the proposed plan to expand the airport and to increase the number of flights. I believe this would definitely be detrimental to all the people who live and work within a five-mile radius of the airport.
   (2) I am writing to voice my concern about the new airport expansion.
2. 这里还有两个任务。首先是说明住址。
   (1) I live only 2 miles south of the airport.
   (2) I live near the airport, 4 blocks south of the western runway, and it is already quite an emotional strain with the current flight load.
3. 最后一个任务是说明原因：在这里，有一种写法可以学习，即把机场扩建以前和以后的情况作对比。
4. 最后还可以表达不达目的，誓不罢休的决心：
   I therefore strongly protest this expansion and urge others to join me.

WRITING TASK 2

范文

范文1

Families are definitely not as close as they used to be. As our society has progressed and accepted technology, the family unit has slowly broken apart. Fortunately, with a few changes, families can become close again.

One of the major reasons why this change has happened is the increased influence of TV. TV has become the center of many households and has turned many people into couch potatoes. Other reasons include the fact that in most families both parents now work, leaving young children in daycare centers during the day and often in thc hands of hired help or other family members at night. Children also have more on their plates, with constant activities like soccer, karate, violin, or drawing. In the summer during school vacation, many children go to summer camps instead of going on summer trips with their families.

Families could be brought closer together simply by reversing some of the factors that have caused them to split apart. They could start by turning off the TV. Watching TV could be replaced with other activities like talking, reading, simple sports or games, walking the dog, anything that allows for interpersonal interaction. Many parents insist that they could not possibly afford to live on a single income, but with some slight adjustments, often it is possible for one parent to stay home with the children, allowing for a more bonded household. Paring down some of the more expensive extracurricular activities with more simple, family oriented activities can not only save money but also bring families closer.

While we may feel that our standard of living is continually rising, due to many reasons, there has been a slow deterioration of the nuclear family. By resisting some of the temptations of modern technology, especially the TV, modern families can become bonded units again.

家庭成员确实是不再像过去那样亲密了。由于我们社会的进步和现代科技的发展,家庭的单位逐渐地分裂了。幸运的是,如果稍微做一些改变的话,家庭成员就可以再次恢复往日的亲密。

发生这种变化的一个主要原因就是电视的影响增加了,它变成了许多家庭的中心,把许多人变成了将军肚。另一个原因包括这样的事实:大部分家庭的父母都工作,白天把孩子留在幼儿园,通常晚上再雇人或者请其他的家人来帮忙照看。孩子们也有很多事情要做,例如踢足球,练空手道,拉小提琴或画画。在暑假,许多孩子去参加夏令营而不是跟家人一起旅行。

仅仅通过改变一些使家庭成员疏远的因素就可以使他们更亲密地聚在一起。他们可以从关掉电视开始做起。可以用诸如谈话、看书、简单的运动或者游戏、遛狗之类的任何人际互动活动来代替看电视。许多父母坚称一个人赚钱不可能维持一家人的生活。但是稍做调整的话,一般一个家长在家与孩子在一起是可能的,而且可以使关系更紧密。缩减一些较奢侈的业余活动,多组织以家庭为主的活动,不仅可以省钱,还可以使家庭成员更加亲密。

也许当我们感到生活水平在不断提高时,出于许多原因,核心家庭出现了缓慢的退化。抵制一些现代科技的诱惑,尤其是电视,现代的家庭是可以再次成为团结紧密的整体的。

范文2

Families are generally not as close as they used to be because of the changes in and requirements of our modern, industrialized culture.

In days of old families used to live and work together because society was more agrarian. Parents raised their children in the family trade, children cared for their parents in their old age, and local economies were capable of supporting themselves with little interaction from abroad. Industrialization changed everything. The family unit was destroyed when parents lost their farm and were forced to work long hours in factories while their children were hustled into public education. Children grew up during this age to not respect their families, but to only be concerned with their own individual welfare. They sought every chance to leave home and make it on their own in the new global economy that stressed upward mobility and self-gratification, not the concept of moderation.

The only way for families to be brought closer is for them to spend more time together. This can be done by forming a family business, by returning from the big, anonymous city to the betterment of the local economy and by the sacrifice of the ever-present fantasy of "getting rich". I know many "rich people", none of them are happy. This "get rich" fantasy needs to go and we all need to learn to get by with just what we need. Then we'll be able to rebuild our family unit and return to the relationships that matter the most, those within our family.

家庭成员普遍不像过去那样亲密是由于我们现代的、工业化的文化发生了变化,有了新的要求。

在过去,家庭成员一起生活,工作,这是因为社会还处于农耕时代。父母靠家庭贸易养育子女,子女在父母年迈的时候照顾他们,地方经济在与外界几乎隔绝的情况下就足以支撑他们的生活。然而工业化改变了一切。当父母失去了土地被迫到工厂长时间劳动而他们的孩子涌入公立学校的时候,家庭的单位就被破坏了。这个时代长大的孩子不尊敬家人,而只是关注自己的利益。他们寻找一切机会离开家,在新的全球经济中发展自己,而这种全球经济强调向上和自我满足,而不是有节制。

使家庭成员更加亲密的唯一途径就是更多地与他们在一起。这可以通过组建一个家庭事业,从大城市或者超级城市回归到地方经济或舍弃经常出现的富裕梦来解决。我认识许多"有钱人",他们中没有一个人快乐。我们都需要放弃这种变富的幻想,学会按需所取。那样我们就可以重建我们的家庭单位,重新拥有对我们至关重要的家庭关系。

谋篇布局

1. 读题:

   (1) 本题是典型的找原因并且给解决方法的题。这样的题目比较简单,只要想出一些原因,并且根据这些原因给出对策就可以了。

   (2) 当然写原因和解决方法的篇幅可以由自己决定。

2. 写提纲:"家庭关系的疏远"可以从三个方面找原因:首先是家长的原因,其次是孩子的原因,最后是社会环境的原因。解决方法也要从这三个方面入手。

剑桥雅思

真题全解 4

Test 1

LISTENING

SECTION 1

谈话场景:咨询旅游事宜场景,电话交谈。
人物关系:学校社会活动咨询员和学生。
谈话话题:咨询学校组织的旅游线路,旅游费用和旅行地点。

词汇注释

historical *adj.* 历史的
pattern *n.* 模式;典范
refund *n.* 退款,偿还金额
schedule *n.* 计划(表),日程安排(表)
optional *adj.* 随意的,任选的,可选择的,非强制的
etcetera *n.* 等等之人(或物)
available *adj.* 可利用的,可获得的
minibus *n.* 中客车,小型公共汽车(我国俗称面包车,乘员10人左右)
coach *n.* 长途公共汽车

考题解析

Question 1

1-10题为填空题,最大的特点是"所听即所得",也就是说,答案内容几乎一字不差地来自于考生所听到的原文,往往侧重考查考生对相关场景单词的熟悉程度。一般来说,听题前,考生应该仔细审题,观察已知信息,大致判断对话的场景,划出关键词。

在听题前观察这一部分要填表格,可以得知对话是关于学校的社会活动,尤其是旅游活动的一些注意事项。此题前面给出的文字里很明显地提到了参观地点将有的特征,所以对话一提到其第一个特征"historical interest",考生就应该注意后面接下来马上要提到的特征。可以说,给出文字"historical interest"是一个提示语,告诉我们下面的信息应该是要记录的信息了。

此题中variety一词应该予以注意,意为"多样性,种种,品种,种类",读为[vəˈraiəti]。短语"a variety of"意为"各种各样的",如:"She made the children glad in a variety of ways. 她用各种方法使孩子们高兴。"

Question 2

很明显,此题和上一题一样,也是参观地的有关特征。需要注意的是,如果写成"guide tour"是没有分的。"guided tours"意为"配备导游的线路"。

另外,考生应该牢记,由于第一部分内容和题型相对简单,所以对答案格式和形式的要求比较严格。考生在听到相关答案的同时,更要注意答案的正确拼写和格式要求,如:名词单复数、动词时态语态、形容词最高级比较级等等情况。

Question 3

此题前面给出的信息里提到了"special trips",所以听到这个词就应该注意其后的信息。此题考查的是数字。注意所填信息应该是"more than 12"或"over 12",而不能仅仅填一个"12"。

Question 4

此空考查的是日常生活用词。"notice board"意为"公告牌"。注意,此空中"board"考生很容易写

成“broad”。另外，此空后给出的文字“in advance”意为“提前”，如：“You must pay for the book in advance. 你必须预先付书的钱。”

Question 5

做题之前观察表格，可以发现5－10题要求填入的是一些周末游线路的有关信息，依次为：地点、日期、可供选择的其他线路。那么在填空前就应该要清楚，地名首字母一定不要忘记大写，月份词首字母也一定要记住大写。可见，听题前观察题目非常重要，可以给我们很多提示。

此题考查的是日期的英文写法。值得注意的是，如果按中文习惯全部写成阿拉伯数字，如“2、13”，那么肯定不会得分。考生平常要加强对日期和数字的敏感性的练习。

Question 6

此题考查的是地名，需注意此空中所填的单词中除介词外，其他的单词首字母都要大写。

Question 7

此题考查的还是地名，同样需要注意大写的问题。应该说，这一空非常简单，对话者已经把单词一个字母一个字母地念了出来，所以对英文字母的反应也应该很敏锐。

关于人名和地名在雅思考试中的拼写是经常出现的考点。其中的人名和地名一般都是逐个字母拼读出来，考生应一字不差地听写出来，拼写的任何一个错误，哪怕是极小的错误，都会导致该题目不得分。

Question 8

此题考查的情况和第6题类似，注意大写的情况。

Question 9

此空中要求填入的“student newspaper”意为“校报”。

Question 10

此题考查人名，也比较简单，文中已经把每个字母都读了出来。同样需要注意大写的情况。

5－10题中几乎都考查了英语单词的大写情况，但是有关大小写方面的错误层出不穷，这是考生的一个弱点。一般来说，大写规则有以下几条，考生应该牢记：

①英语句子第一个词的第一字母要大写。如：My name is Li Ping.

②国家、城市、乡、镇等名称的首字母要大写。如：China（中国），Shanghai（上海）

③表示语言、某国人等首字母要大写。如：Chinese（中国人，汉语），English（英语）

④姓名中指姓的词和名的词首字母要大写。如：John Smith（约翰·史密斯），Wu Hongjun（吴洪军）

⑤一些专有名词的首字母要大写。如：Grade Two（二年级），Marx（马克思）

⑥文章的标题、书名、报刊的名称等，第一个单词及每个实词的第一个字母一般要大写。如：Lesson Two（第二课），An Express Way to English

⑦表示节日、星期、月份的第一个字母要大写。如：Tuesday（星期二），January（一月），Children's Day（儿童节）

⑧表示职务或称呼的词首字母要大写。如：Mr Green（格林先生），Dr. Wang（王大夫，王博士）

⑨直接引语中，开头字母须大写。如：Polly says, “Sit down.”波莉说：“坐下。”

⑩表示“我”的字母“I”和“OK”等，永远大写。

SECTION 2

谈话场景:旅游场景。
人物关系:演讲者为导游,听众为游客。
谈话话题:介绍 Riverside 工业村的有关情况,其历史、特点以及工业产品。

词汇注释

roam *v.* (漫无目的地)随便走,漫步
manufacturing *adj.* 制造业的,制造的,生产的
ore *n.* 矿,矿石,矿砂
water wheel *n.* (水力推动的)水轮,水车
forge *n.* 锻造车间,铁匠工场,铁匠铺
bend *n.* (河流等的)弯曲处
water mill *n.* 水磨
entrance *n.* 入口,进口
furnace *n.* 火炉,熔炉
smelt *v.* 熔炼(矿石),炼取(金属),精炼(不纯净金属)
cast *v.* 浇铸,铸造
sharpen *v.* 削尖,磨尖,磨快
antique *adj.* 古时的,古老的
cottage *n.* (乡村、农舍等处的)小屋,村舍
stable *n.* 厩,马厩

考题解析

Question 11

做题前观察已知信息,得知此段话语是关于 Riverside 工业村的情况介绍,先确定会话主题。此题前提到了 Riverside 工业村能很好地开展工业生产的原因,并提到了"water, raw material and fuels",很明显,会话开始部分提到这几个单词的时候要特别注意。已知信息中的"such as"和录音中提到的"like"显然是一个意思,应该抓住这个信号词。同时,考生还应该注意这两个单词的读音和意思及其拼写。"coal"意为"煤,煤块",读为[kəul];"firewood"意为"木柴,柴火",读为['faiəwud]。

Question 12

此题较难。题前给出的信息在文中并没有一模一样的字眼提到,也就是说,此题给出的信息是对原文的相关信息的改写,所以要求考生的听力理解能力稍高。但是,也不是无据可循。观察已知信息,不难发现此空要求填入的是人名或一类人,因此只要抓住文中提到的人就可以。而文中只有一个地方提到了类似信息,可见,做题时应该学会充分利用已知信息来定位。此空中"craftsman"意为"工匠,手艺精巧的人,艺术家",读为['krɑːftsmən]。原文中"local craftsman"后提到的"iron forge"(铸铁)即意味着这是金属制造工业的开端。

Question 13

此题考查数字的填写,非常简单。考生对于数字应该特别敏感,平常要多多加强对于数字的练习。

Question 14

14–20 题为地图题,对地图题来说,最重要的是要注意所找地名与图中已知信息之间的关系,以及说话者所提到的第一个地名。在做题时,要根据已知信息来定位未知信息。此题相对来说比较容易,因为文中明显提到了"bottom"一词,比较容易定位。注意:此题所填单词为地名,首字母要大写。

Question 15

此题考查的仍是地名,注意大写情况。此题在听题时,要抓住信号词"to our right"。

Question 16

此题需抓住信号词“to the left”。

Question 17

此题做题时一定要注意不要把目光局限在15、16题周围，思路要随着文章的叙述变化而变化。说话者并没有按顺序来介绍地点，而是很快提到了“at the top”，需要紧紧抓住这个线索词。

Question 18

此题做题时要注意信号词“in the top right-hand corner”（右上角）。

Question 19

此题的介绍角度又有所不同。文中先介绍左上角的“Grinding Shop”，然后再说其一边是“The Engine Room”，这是已知信息，接着再提到另一边是“The Café”。考生需要熟悉地图题的介绍角度，思路要灵活多变，充分利用已知地名来定位。注意此空中“Café”一词的写法。该词是由法语转化而来的一个英语单词，所以比较特别，不能写成“Coffee”。

Question 20

此题做题时需要抓住信号词“on the left”。注意此空考查单词“cottages”的拼写，并且一定要用复数。“cottage”一词意为“村舍，小别墅”，读为[ˈkɔtidʒ]。另外，该词并非专有地名，并不需要大写首字母。

SECTION 3

谈话场景：作业场景。

人物关系：教授与学生。

谈话话题：学生向教授请教问题，以及由于种种原因作业没能完成，希望找到解决办法。

词汇注释

extension *n.* 延长；放宽的期限，延期

compassionate *adj.* 有同情心的，（深表）同情的；照顾性的

submit *v.* 提交，呈递

journal *n.* 日报，杂志，期刊

methodology *n.* （学科的）一套方法；方法论，方法学

relevant *adj.* 有关的，切题的，确当的，适宜的

essential *adj.* 必不可少的，绝对必要的，非常重要的

proximity *n.* 接近，邻近

考题解析

Question 21

此题解题时要注意关键词“a really big assignment due in for another course.”考生很容易错选B，因为文中出现了“big assignment”这样的字眼，但是这是断章取义，不符合题干所给出的内容。同样，选项C也是干扰选项，需要捕捉到前文的信息“I've been to the library several times, and all books are out.”（我去了好几次图书馆，但是书已经借出了。）所以问题不在于没去图书馆，而是图书馆的书已经借完了。

Question 22

此题首先就要理解题干。题干中“extension”一词意为“（作业、论文等）的延期”。解答此题需要注

意转折信号词"but"后面的有关信息。一般来说,"but" 一词是很多考点的提示词,所以考生在听题时一定要特别注意该词后面的信息。文中提到的原因是"medical or compassionate reasons",意为"生病或是出现了其他值得人同情的原因",所以选项 C 很好地表达了这个意思。注意"compassionate" 一词的意思,意为"富于同情心的",读为[kəmˈpæʃənit]。

Question 23

23 – 27 题相对来说比较简单。考生首先要看清楚提问"Dr. Johnson 对于阅读期刊文章有什么建议呢?"。所以文章提到这一点的时候要特别留心。接下来依次提到了人名,所以只需要注意相关人名后面的信息就可以了。

此题原文中出现的是"research methodology",选项中改为了"research methods",稍微作了一些变化。注意"methodology" 一词,意为"方法学,方法论",读为[ˌmeθəˈdɔlədʒi]。

Question 24

此题很简单,听到就选。

Question 25

此题选项与原文也稍有变化。原文提到"I won't bother with Morris",意思实际上就是"我不会去读 Morris 的文章"。

Question 26

此题和上题一样,也是稍有变化。原文提到"the last part",实际上指的就是"conclusion"。

Question 27

此题原文提到"It's not that bad and could be of some help, but not that much."(也没有那么糟,肯定会有用,但是用处不大),这其实就是选项 C 所提到的"limited value"(价值有限)。

Question 28

28 – 30 题为图表题。已知信息表明,此图表主要是关于更换居住处的人口学调查。28 – 30 题实际上都涉及到同义替换的问题,只要紧跟对话线索,不难找到相应的替换词汇。

此题原文中提到"the people living nearby disturbing them."(住在附近的人打扰了他们)其实就是选项 D"noisy neighbours"(嘈杂的邻居)的另一个说法。注意单词 disturb 的含义,意为"弄乱,打乱,打扰,扰乱",读为[distəːb]。

Question 29

此题与上文相同。原文为"the owner is not helpful"(房主不肯帮忙),当然实际上就是说"uncooperative landlord"(房东不肯合作)。单词 uncooperative 意为"不合作的,持不合作态度的",读为[ʌnkəuˈɔpərətiv]。

Question 30

此题的原文中所提到的"neighbourhood" 在这里实际上指的就是"environment",考生需要注意灵活替换。

SECTION 4

谈话场景:环境知识讲座。
人物关系:讲话者为园林绿化专家。
谈话话题:介绍植被在调节城市气候方面所起的作用,以及如何更好地利用植被来美化环境。

词汇注释

landscape *n.*（陆上）风景，（陆上）景色
vegetation *n.* [总称]植物，草木，【植】植被
humid *adj.* 微湿的，潮湿的，湿润的
shady *adj.* 成阴的，背阴的，多阴的
mechanism *n.*【生】机制，机理
evaporate *v.* 使蒸发，使挥发
humidify *v.* 使潮湿，使湿润
property *n.* 特性，性质，性能，属性
filter *v.* 过滤；使漏过，使漏出
gust *n.* 一阵强风，一阵狂风
intensify *v.* 加强，增强，使尖锐
belt *n.* 带状物
frequency *n.* 频率
branch *n.* 树枝

考题解析

Question 31

观察已知信息，可以知道文章的总体脉络非常清晰。文章先提到将要谈到的两个方面，然后阐明了树木的大范围影响和小范围影响，最后把书目和建筑物的相关信息作了比较。做题前的观察往往有利于更好地听题，使听题时不至于很盲目。

此题空前给出文字里提到“plan”一词，因此，在听原文时，注意“plan”这个信号词至关重要。另外，此题一定要填复数“cities”，否则不给分。

Question 32

此题需注意的是空前的“more or less”其实就相当于原文中的“a bit less”。另外，此题所填空中“windy”一词不能写成“wind”，否则不给分。

Question 33

此题较为简单，“humid”一词意为“充满潮湿的，湿润的，多湿气的”，读为[ˈhjuːmid]。

Question 34

注意此题应该填“shady”或“shaded”，为形容词，否则不给分。

Question 35

此题同样需要注意“dangerous”一词的拼写。“dangerous”意为“危险的”，读为[ˈdeindʒərəs]。

Question 36

此题前给出文字里提到的“evaporate”一词意为“（使）蒸发，消失”，读为[iˈvæpəreit]。另外，此题应注意填复数名词。

Question 37

此题较为简单，注意原文中的“windier”其实就相当于此空前的“more wind”。此处实际上是出题者故意设置一个思路转换问题考查考生。

Question 38

此题有多种填法，但是一定要注意每空只能填两个以内的单词的限制。原文中“filter”一词意为“过滤，渗透，用过滤法除去”，读为[ˈfiltə(r)]。“considerably”一词意为“相当地”，读为[kənˈsidərəbəli]。

Question 39

此题较为简单，听到就写。

Question 40

此题中“room”一词意为“空间”，相当于“space”，所以填“room”或者“space”都算对。

READING

READING PASSAGE 1

词汇注释

frequently *adv.* 经常地，频繁地
confront *v.* 面临；遭遇
alarming *adj.* 使人惊恐的，令人担心的
rate *n.* 比率，率；速率，速度
tropical rainforest 热带雨林
graphic *adj.* 图（或图表、图解、曲线图等）的；用图（或图表等）表示的
illustration *n.* 说明，图解；插图，图表
readily *adv.* 迅速地，敏捷地；无困难地，容易地
relate *v.* 讲述，叙述；发生共鸣，认同
estimate *n.* 估计，估计数；看法，评价
destroy *v.* 破坏，毁灭
equivalent *adj.* 相等的，相同的
duration *n.* 持续，持续期间
normal *adj.* 正常的；标准的
in the face of 在…面前
vivid *adj.* 生动的，逼真的
media *n.*（medium 的复数）新闻媒介，传播媒介（指报刊、广播、电视）
coverage *n.* 新闻报道；新闻报道量（或范围、质量）
endanger *v.* 危及，使遭危险；危害
independent of 不依赖…的；独立于…以外的；不管，不顾；除了…之外
tuition *n.*（某一学科的）教学，讲授；指导
harbour *v.* 心怀，怀藏
misconception *n.* 误解，错误想法；错误印象
curriculum *n.* 课程；（学校等的）全部课程；（获得学位、资格或证书的）必修课程
isolated *adj.* 分离的；孤立的
incorporate *v.* 把…合并，使并入
multifaceted *adj.* 多方面的
conceptual *adj.* 概念的
framework *n.* 框架；体系
component *adj.* 组成的，构成的
erroneous *adj.* 错误的，不正确的
robust *adj.* 强健的，健全的；坚定的，坚强的
accessible *adj.* 可（或易）接近的，可（或易）进入的
modification *n.* 修改，改变
peer *n.* 同等地位的人；同龄人
refine *v.* 提炼，精炼；使变得完善，使变得精妙
extensive *adj.* 广泛的，全面的
destruction *n.* 破坏，毁灭
strategy *n.* 策略，计谋；行动计划，对策
displace *v.* 取代，替代
survey *v.* 全面考察（或研究）；概括论述（或叙述）
questionnaire *n.*（通常用于收集信息或意见的）一组问题；调查表
self-evident *adj.* 不言而喻的
damp *adj.* 潮湿的，湿气重的
location *n.* 为止，场所，地点
the Equator 赤道
dominant *adj.*（在数量、分布等方面）占首位的，主要的
habitat *n.*（动植物的）生境，栖息地
indigenous *adj.*（尤指动、植物分布）当地的，本地的；土生土长的
observation *n.* 观察，观测；观察资料，观测数据
consistent *adj.* 一致的，符合的
previous *adj.* 以前的，先前的
conservation *n.*（对自然资源的）保护
sympathetic *adj.* 同情的，表示同情的
intrinsic *adj.* 固有的，本质的
identify *v.* 认同
personalize *v.* 使针对个人，使个人化
logging *n.*（木材）采运作业
acid rain 酸雨（指因排入大气的硫、氧化氮等污染物质在雨滴中生成硫酸、硝酸而导致的酸性雨）
proportion *n.* 比例
factor *n.* 因素，要素
embrace *v.* 接受；信奉；包括，包含
reduce *v.* 减少，削减
atmospheric *adj.* 大气的，空气的
incompatible *adj.* 不能和谐相处的，合不来的；不协调的，不相容的
majority *n.* 大多数

survive *v.* 活下来,幸存	**complexity** *n.* 复杂(性),错综(性)
contribute to 有助于,促成;是…的部分原因	**appreciation** *n.* 重视,赏识;评估,评价
issue *n.* 问题	**complex** *adj.* 复杂的,错综的
predominate *v.* 占主导地位,占绝大多数	**conflicting** *adj.* 冲突的;抵触的
ecosystem *n.*【生】生态系(统)	**arena** *n.*(喻)竞争场所,活动场所
volunteer *v.* 自愿提供(或给予等)	**essential** *adj.* 必不可少的;绝对重要的
appreciate *v.*(充分)意识到;体会,领会	

考题解析

Questions 1–8 True/False/Not Given

1. 要认识该题考点词汇 ignore(忽视)。定位词为 media,回原文找 media 一词的出处,在第 1 自然段第 7 行:In the face of the frequent and often vivid media coverage... 题干中 ignore 一词和原文中 frequent、often 驳斥。
2. 第 1 段第 7 行:In the face of the frequent and often vivid media coverage, it is likely that children will have formed ideas about rainforests... 和第 2 段第 5 行:These ideas may be developed by children absorbing ideas through the popular media. 都驳斥了题干中的 only 一词。
3. 原文出处为第 2 段首句:Many studies have shown that children harbour misconceptions about "pure", curriculum science. 其中,shown 对应题干中的 suggested;harbour 对应题干中的 hold,curriculum 对应题干中的 study at school。
4. 难题,易选 NG。定位词 framework,原文出自第 2 段第 2 句。该题考查建立在正确分析句子语法成分后对该句的理解,请参考该文中文翻译。原文中:... making it... more robust but also accessible to modification. 对应题干中:... means that it is easier to change them. 下划线单词成 3 组对应。
5. 题干中 yes/no questions 与原文中第 4 段第 3 行 open-form questions 驳斥。
6. 题干中定位 rainforests' destruction,原文第 7、8 段中描述。无 Girls 和 Boys 的比较。
7. 难题,主要是理解题干。题干中出现了 The study 和 a series of studies 要区分,the study reported here 指文中主要的研究,是第 4 段提到的包括 5 个 open-form questions 的 study。而 a series of studies 第 6 段第 2 句:These observations are generally consistent with our previous studies of pupils' view about the use and conservation of rainforests. 该句的表达和题干一致。
8. 题干中 a second study 原文中没有提到。

Questions 9–13 Matching

9. 第 4 段中"43%"对应题干中 most frequent response。
10. 较难,易错选 F。第 5 段第 2 行,"64%","provide animals with habitats"。
11. 第 7 段"59%","human activities"。
12. 较难。第 9 段首句:... the majority of children simply said that we need rainforests to survive. 其中 need 对应 P 选项中 depend on;survive 对应 P 选项中 continuing existence。
13. 第 9 段第 2、3 句。注意 global warming 对应 J 选项中 gets warmer。

Question 14 Multiple Choice

14. B 选项中包含了 Children、Rainforests、Course design 三个文中的关键点。

参考译文

成人和孩子们都经常听说热带雨林的流失速度是惊人的。比方说,孩子们可能会很容易提到一个图表,这个图表估计,热带雨林遭破坏的速度相当于每 40 分钟毁掉 1000 个足球场——大约就是一堂正常的课的时间。在频繁而且经常是很生动的新闻报道面前,很可能孩子们已经对热带雨林有了一些了解——热带雨林是什么、它们在哪里、它们为什么重要、是什么威胁着它们——根本不需要正式教育。也有可能他们的一些想法是错误的。

许多研究表明,孩子们对"纯"课程科学有一些错误想法。这些错误想法不会一直是孤立的,而是会合并到一个复杂却有序的概念体系当中去,从而使这个概念体系及构成这个体系的思想——其中一部分是错误的——更加健全,同时也更加容易得到修正。这些思想可能是孩子们通过吸收大众媒体的一些观点形成的,有时候这种信息可能是错误的。学校似乎不会给孩子们提供机会让他们重新表达自己的想法,所以就让老师们和他们的同龄人使这些想法得到检验和提炼。

虽然大众媒体对热带雨林的破坏进行了广泛的报道,究竟孩子们对这个问题怎么看正式报道却不多。现在这项研究的目的就是开始提供一些这样的信息,帮助老师设计他们的教学方案,以正确的思想为基础,去掉错误想法,在他们的学校开设环境研究课程。

这项研究全面调查孩子们的科学知识以及他们对热带雨林的看法。中学生们被要求填一个调查表,上面有5个开放式问题。对第一个问题最常见的回答是根据"热带雨林"这个不言自明的术语进行描述,有些孩子在描述中用了"潮湿"、"湿"或者"热"这样的字眼。第二个问题是关于热带雨林的地理位置,答得最多的是洲或者国家:非洲(43%)、南美洲(30%)、巴西(25%),有的孩子还给出了更大的范围,比方说赤道附近。

第三个问题的答案涉及热带雨林的重要性。64%的学生都认为热带雨林为动物提供栖息地,认为为植物提供生境的学生人数则少一些,提到热带雨林土著居民的学生就更少了,更多的女孩(70%)认为热带雨林是动物的栖息地,持此观点的男孩占60%。

同样地,但总的比例要低一些,更多的女孩(13%)认为热带雨林为人类提供栖息的地方,而男孩的比例是5%。这些观察数据与以前的研究基本一致,关于对热带雨林的使用和保护问题,女孩子显得对动物更有同情心,她们的观点对非人类动物生命似乎有一种固有的重视。

第四个问题是关于热带雨林遭受破坏的原因。也许鼓舞人心的是,超过半数的学生(59%)认为热带雨林的破坏是人类活动造成的,有的学生用"我们是"这样的表达法把责任个人化,大约18%的学生特别提到了木材采运活动。

大约10%的学生表达了一个错误的想法,那就是酸雨应该对热带雨林的破坏负责;相同比例的学生说污染正在破坏热带雨林。在这里,孩子们把热带雨林的破坏与被这些因素破坏的西欧森林混在了一块儿。尽管五分之二的学生认为热带雨林提供氧气,在某些情况下,这种回答也包含了一种错误的想法,那就是对热带雨林的破坏会减少空气中的氧气,使空气不适合地球上的人类生活。

在回答最后一个关于保护热带雨林的重要性问题时,大多数孩子只是简单回答我们的生存需要热带雨林,只有少部分学生(6%)提到热带雨林的破坏可能是全球变暖的原因之一。从媒体对这个问题连篇累牍的报道来看,这是很令人吃惊的。有一些孩子认为保护热带雨林并不重要。

本次研究的结果表明,有些想法在孩子们对热带雨林的看法中占有主导地位。学生们的回答表明,他们对热带雨林生态系统的基本科学知识有一些错误想法,比如他们对热带雨林作为动植物及人类栖息地的理解,对气候变化与热带雨林的破坏之间的关系的理解。

从学生们的回答中看不出他们已经意识到破坏热带雨林的原因的复杂性。换句话说,他们既没有显示出对热带雨林的重要范围的重视,也没有显示出对那些复杂的社会、经济和政治因素的重视,这些因素促使人们从事一些破坏热带雨林的活动。一件鼓励人的事情是,关于其他环境问题的类似研究的结果表明,大一点的孩子似乎能获得重视、评价和评估相冲突的观点的能力。环境教育提供了一个活动场所,这些能力可以在这里得到发展,这对这些作为未来决策者的孩子们来说是非常重要的。

READING PASSAGE 2

What Do Whales Feel?

词汇注释

whale *n.* 鲸(海洋中的哺乳动物,俗称鲸鱼)
cetaceans *n.* 鲸目动物(如鲸、海豚等)
mammal *n.* 哺乳动物
dolphin *n.* 海豚
porpoise *n.* 鼠海豚(尤指大西洋鼠海豚)
terrestrial *adj.* 陆地的,陆生的
species *n.* (单复同)【生】种
baleen *n.* & *adj.* 鲸须(的)
functional *adj.* 官能的,机能的;有功能的,在起作用的
speculate *v.* 推测,猜测
blowhole *n.* (鲸等的)鼻孔
migrate *v.* 迁移,移动
neural *adj.*【解】神经的,神经系统的,神经中枢的
pathway *n.*【生化】途径
sacrifice *v.* 牺牲
taste bud【解】味蕾
degenerate *v.* 衰退,退化
rudimentary *adj.* 未成熟的;已退化的
captive *adj.* 被俘虏(或猎获的);被关押的;受控制的
free-ranging *adj.* 自由放养的
calf *n.* (复 calves)(象、鲸、鹿、河马等大哺乳动物的)仔,幼兽
subgroup *n.*【生】亚群
courtship *n.* 求婚,求爱;(动物的)求偶
ritual *n.* (宗教等的)仪式;程序,礼制
vision *n.* 视力,视觉
at close quarters 接近地
grey whale【动】灰鲸
right whale【动】露脊鲸
humpback whale【动】座头鲸
moderately *adv.* 一般,中等
stereoscopic vision 立体视觉,体视
freshwater *adj.* (生在)淡水的
by comparison 比较起来
bottlenose dolphin【生】宽吻海豚
keen *adj.* 敏锐的,敏捷的
airborne *adj.* 升空的,在空中的,在飞行中的
interface *n.* 界面,分界面;结合部位,边缘区域
preliminary *adj.* 初步的,起始的
experimental *adj.* 试验(性)的,实验(性)的
accuracy *n.* 准确(性),精确(性)
leap *v.* 跳,跳跃
anecdotal *adj.* 轶事的,趣闻的;含轶事的,多轶事的
variation *n.* 变化,变动;【生】变异,变种
habitat *n.* (动植物的)生境,栖息地
inhabit *v.* 居住于,栖息于
turbid *adj.* 浑浊的,污浊的
slit *n.* 狭长的口子;裂缝,狭逢
intensity *n.* (电、热、光、声等的)强度
deteriorate *v.* 下降,退化
compensate *v.* 补偿,弥补
acoustic *adj.* 听觉的
vocal *adj.* 嗓音的;(用嗓子)发声的
vary *v.* 变化;有不同,呈差异
forage *v.* 搜寻
echolocation *n.* 回声定位
frequency *n.* 频率
repertoire *n.* 全部本领,全部功能
notable *adj.* 值得注意的,显著的;可查觉的,有相当分量的
chorus *n.* 合唱;齐声说的话(或发出的喊声)
bowhead *n.*【动】北极露脊鲸,弓头鲸
complex *adj.* 组合的;复杂的
haunting *adj.* 萦绕于心头的;给人以强烈感受的;使人不安的
utterance *n.* 发声;表达;说话方式
spectrum *n.* 系列;范围;幅度
sperm whale【动】抹香鲸
monotonous *adj.* (声音)单调的;单一得令人厌倦的
click *n.* 咔哒声,喀嚓声
complicated *adj.* 复杂的,难懂的
communicative *adj.* 通信的;交际的
speculation *n.* 思考,思索;推测,猜测

考题解析

Questions 15–21 Table

15. 定位 taste→nerves→underdeveloped，原文为第 1 段第 7 行... have taste buds, the nerves serving these have degenerated...要理解 these 指代 taste buds。
16. 定位 vision→stereoscopic→not，原文第 3 段第 6 行。
17. 定位 vision→stereoscopic→dolphins, porpoises，原文第 4 段首句。
18. 定位 vision→stereoscopic→forward and upward，原文第 4 段第 2 句。
19. 定位 vision→bottlenose→air-water，原文第 4 段第 3、4 句。注意文中 extremely keen 对应题干中 exceptional。
20. 定位 hearing→large→repertoire，原文第 6 段第 5 行。
21. 定位 hearing→song-like→and，原文第 6 段第 6 行。

Questions 22–26 Short Answer

22. 难题。题干中 mating（交配）一词文中似乎找不到。有考生注意到全文最后一句话中的：communicative, social life 等词，思考 mating 是其中一种，误填 hearing。要记住雅思考试不会设置这种似乎相似的答案，正确的答案是很严谨的。原文真正出处在第 2 段倒数第 3 行有 courtship 一词，court 一词多义，既指“法庭、宫廷”，又指“求爱、追求”。最后注意答案应该填写名词形式 touch，如填写 touching 是一个动作，答非所问；如填 stroking or touching 同样也算错。
23. 定位题干中 upside down while eating，原文中第 4 段第 3 行 upside down while feeding。
24. 定位题干中 bottlenose, follow，原文第 4 段第 5 行开始：Judging from the way it（bottlenose dolphin）watches and tracks airborne flying fish...其中 track 对应题干中 follow。
25. 定位题干中 habitat, good visual，原文第 5 段第 1、2 句。
26. 定位题干中 cetaceans, best developed，原文第 6 段第 3 行。

参考译文

鲸鱼有什么感觉？

一项对鲸目动物感官功能的研究，这组哺乳动物包括鲸鱼、海豚和鼠海豚。

一些我们及其他陆地哺乳动物认为理所当然的感官在鲸目动物身上要么减少或缺少，要么在水里不能充分发挥作用。比方说，从它们的大脑结构来看，齿鲸好像没有嗅觉；另一方面，长须鲸似乎有着某些相关的大脑结构，但它们是否起作用却不得而知。据推测，随着鲸鱼鼻孔的进化并移至头顶，为嗅觉服务的神经途径几乎全被牺牲掉了。同样地，尽管至少有些鲸目动物有味蕾，为之服务的神经却已经退化或者还未发育成熟。

触觉有时也被描述得很弱，但这个观点也许是错误的。训练已经捕获的海豚或者小鲸鱼的人常说，他们的动物对抚摸或者按摩有反应。无论是已经捕获，还是自由放养，所有种类的鲸目动物（尤其是成年和幼仔，或者同一个亚群中的成员），似乎都会有频繁的接触。这种接触也许有助于保持一个小组里的秩序。在大多数鲸目动物中，抚摸或者触摸是求偶的一种表示。鼻孔周围也特别敏感，捕获鲸一般会强烈反对摸那个地方。

不同的鲸目动物视觉发展得也不同。在水下受到近距离研究的长须鲸——尤其是一只捕获了一年的灰鲸仔以及在离阿根廷和夏威夷海面上研究和拍摄到的自由放养的露脊鲸和座头鲸 k——明显用水下视力跟踪过物体，很显然，它们无论在水下还是在空中都具有一定的视力。然而，由于眼睛的位置，长须鲸的视野受到限制，它们也许没有体视。

另一方面，大多数海豚和鼠海豚的眼睛位置表明它们有前体视和下体视。淡水海豚经常在吃东西的时候侧着或者倒着游泳，它的眼睛位置就表明它有前体视和下体视。比较起来，宽吻海豚的水下视力非常敏锐，从它观察和跟踪飞到空中的鱼的方式来看，它显然能通过空中与水面交界处看得相当清楚。尽管初步的实验证据显示海豚的空中视力较差，但它们能跳起来准确地从训练师手里取走小鱼，这为相反的结论提供了有趣的证据。

毫无疑问，这种变异可以通过鲸目动物的生长环境来解释。比方说，和那些生活在浑浊的河流和洪水泛滥的平原的鲸目动物相比，视觉对生活在清澈、开放水域的鲸目动物显然更加有用。比方说，南美的 boutu（一种鲸目动物）和中国的 beiji（一种鲸目动物）似乎就视力有限，印度的 susus（一种鲸目动物）根本看不见，它们的眼睛变成了眯缝眼，这也许只能让它们感觉光的方向和强度。

虽然触觉和嗅觉似乎已经退化，水中视力好像不能断定，鲸目动物发育良好的听觉对这些缺陷给予了充分的补偿。大多数鲸目动物都有很好的发音能力，尽管他们发出的声音各有不同，而且许多鲸目动物用回声定位的方法搜寻食物。大的长须鲸主要是使用低频率，它们的全套本领一般都十分有限。值得注意的例外是，弓头鲸会在夏天发出跟唱歌差不多的合唱声，座头鲸会发出复杂而吓人的声音。和长须鲸相比（尽管抹香鲸显然能发出一系列单调的高能咔嚓声，其他声音基本不会发），齿鲸一般会更多地使用频率范围，发出的声音种类更多。有些更为复杂的声音明显具有交际性，但是它们在鲸目动物的社会生活和“文化”中可能会起什么作用，这与其说是一个具体的科学问题，不如说是一个大胆的推测。

READING PASSAGE 3

Visual Symbols and the Blind

词汇注释

visual *adj.* 视力的，视觉的
symbol *n.* 象征，标志；符号，记号
appreciate *v.*（充分）意识到，觉察；对…做正确评价，鉴别
outline *n.* 轮廓画；草图，平面图
perspective *n.* 透视画法，透视图；透视效果，透视感
arrangement *n.* 排列方法，排列形式
surface *n.* 表面；（喻）外表，外观
literal *adj.* 用字母（或文字）表达的
representation *n.* 表示，表现，表述；说明，陈述
initiative *n.* 主动的行动
spin *v.* 旋转
motion *n.* 动，运动，移动
trace *v.* 勾画出…的轮廓，草拟
curve *n.* 曲线，弧线
be taken aback 吃一惊，被弄糊涂
illustration *n.* 说明，图解，图示
scholar *n.*（尤指人文学科的）学者
trend-setting *adj.*（在思想、服装式样等方面）创新风的
cartoonist *n.* 漫画家；动画片画家
subject *n.*（事物的）经受者，（动作的）对象
rendition *n.*（物体在视觉中的）再现
spoke *n.* 辐条，轮辐
metaphorical *adj.* 比喻的，比喻意义的
majority rule 多数裁定原则（指半数以上的人有权做出全体必须服从的决议或裁定等）
wavy *adj.* 波状的，波浪式的
for that matter 就此而言；（用于补充或语气递进的陈述）而且
apt *adj.* 恰当的，适当的
idiosyncratic *adj.*（表现手法、风格等）特有的，独特的
sighted *adj.*（人）看得见的，不盲的，有视力（或视觉）的
interpret *v.* 理解，了解
raised-line *n.* 凸起线条
depict *v.* 描画，描绘；雕出
perimeter *n.*【数】周，周长
volunteer *n.* 自愿参加者，志愿者
assign *v.* 指派，选派
wobble *v.* 摇晃，摇摆；抖动，颤动
steadily *adv.* 平稳地，稳定地

jerk *v.* 猝然一动	**doctoral** *adj.* 博士的,博士学位的;有博士学位的
brake *v.* 用闸,刹车	**symbolism** *n.* 象征作用,象征意义
control group (用作对照实验比较标准的)对照组	**square** *n.* 正方形,四方形
undergraduate *n.* 大学本科生	**deem** *v.* 认为,相信
distinctive *adj.* 特殊的,特别的,有特色的	**ascribe** *v.* 把…归属(于)
signify *v.* 表示,表明	**reveal** *v.* 使显露,显示
instance *n.* 例子,实例;情况,场合	**shallow** *adj.* 浅的
consensus *n.* 一致同意,一致(或多数人)意见	**resemble** *v.* 像,与…相似;类似于
evidently *adv.* 明显地,显然	**score** *v.* (考试等中)得(分)
metaphor *n.* 比喻;象征	**opposite** *adj.* 对面的;截然相反的;对立的

考题解析

Questions 27–29 Multiple Choice

27. 难题。A 可明显排除,但 B、C、D 三个选项都较难区分。原文出处为第 1 段首句。参考中文译文理解句意。C 选项说:盲人能认出(recognise)一些惯例,比如透视图,和原文表达一致。B 选项中 can draw outlines of different objects 第 1 段没有;而 D 选项 can draw accurately 又太笼统,不准确。
28. 题干中 surprised 一词对应原文第 1 段第 7 行:I was taken aback.
29. B、C、D 选项可轻易排除,A 选项是 Part 1 的中心内容再现。读 Part 1 的最后一段。

Questions 30–32 Matching

30. 定位原文第 4 段第 5 行。
31. 定位原文第 4 段第 6 行。注意原文 quickly 一词对应 C 选项中 rapid。
32. 较难。定位原文第 4 段第 2 行。要区别 curve 和 wavy 两个词的含义,才能区别 A 和 D 选项。如果留意到文章首段中已经出现过 curve 一词,并有示意图,即可猜测 A 选项。* 请注意《剑桥雅思 4》中第 29 页 32 题图中有一条 spoke 轮辐画错了弯曲的方向,容易导致考生想到 wavy。

Questions 33–39 Summary

33. 首先定位 Part 2,然后在 Part 2 中第 2 段首句。
34. 较难。需要理解该实验是将成对单词和正方形和圆形这样的抽象形状进行配对。定位 symbolism,原文出处在 Part 2 的第 1 段末句。
35. 首先找到原文最后一段首句:All our subjects deemed the circle soft and square hard. 那么该题转化为 our subjects 到底是哪种人?往回找实验开始时对实验对象的定义,即原文倒数第 2 段首句中 sighted subjects。
36. 定位"51%",原文最后一段找到仍然在描述 our subjects,即 sighted subjects。和 35 题相同。
37. 定位"51%",原文最后一段第 6 行。
38. 定位到原文最后一段第 7 行。
39. 定位到原文最后一段第 9 行,注意原文中 closely resembled 对应单词 similar。

Question 40 Multiple Choice

40. 注意文章首句和末句,轻松选出 B。

参考译文

视觉符号与盲人

第一部分

最近一些研究已经清楚表明,盲人能够理解为描述物体排列和在空间中的其他表面所使用的轮廓图和透视图。而图的含义不会局限在表面。这个事实引起了我的极大关注,因为在我做一项调查时,一位盲人妇女主动提出要画一个转动着的轮子,为了体现动感,她在一个圆圈中画了一条曲线(如图1),这让我大为吃惊。动感线条,比如她用的弧线,在图示历史上是很新的发明。的确,正如艺术大师 David Kunzle 所说,19 世纪创新风漫画家 Wilhelm Busch 直到大约 1877 年才开始在他广受欢迎的人物身上使用动感线条。

当我要其他几个盲人调查对象画转动着的轮子时,一种特别聪明的再现方法反复出现了:有几个调查对象用弧线表示轮辐。我问他们为什么用弧线,他们都说它们是表示动感的比喻手法。多数裁定原则可能会说,这种方法不管怎样都能很好地表示动感,但与其他线条相比,比如说虚线或者波浪线,它的动感效果就更好吗?答案不得而知,所以我决定检测一下到底是这些表示动感的线条适合表示动感,还是它们只是风格独特的符号。此外,我还想弄清楚盲人和有视力的人对动感线条的理解到底有没有区别。

为了找到这些答案,我创作了 5 幅不同轮子的凸起线条画,用不同的线条表示轮辐:弧形、弯形、波浪形、虚线形和在轮子周长之外延伸形,然后请 18 位盲人志愿者先摸轮子,之后把下面的运动状态和每个轮子对号入座:抖动、快速转动、匀速转动、猝然转动和刹车。我的对照组是从多伦多大学挑选出来的 18 名有视力的大学本科生。

除了一个盲人外,其他受试者都能把有特色的运动状态和轮子对起来。大部分人猜测弧形表示轮子在匀速转动;他们认为波浪形表示轮子在抖动;弯形则被认为是表示轮子在猝然转动。受试者们认为,轮辐延伸至轮子周长之外表示正在刹车,而虚线形轮辐则表示轮子在快速转动。

此外,在每一种情况下,有视力的人最喜欢的描述和盲人最喜欢的描述是一样的。更重要的是,有视力的人达成的一致意见几乎不比盲人高。由于盲人不熟悉转动方法,我给他们的任务涉及到一些解题问题。但是,那些盲人显然不仅弄明白了每种动感线条的意思,而且作为一个小组他们一般情况下得出的相同意思至少经常和有视力的人一样。

第二部分

我们发现,盲人还能理解其他类型的视觉比喻。一位盲人妇女在一颗心里画了一个小孩儿——之所以选择这个符号,她说,是想表示孩子被爱包围。我已经开始和来自中国的博士生 Chang Hong Liu 研究盲人对各种没有直接意义的形状的象征意义的理解,比如说心形。

我们给有视力的受试者 20 组词,让他们从每组词中选出跟圆形密切相关的词和跟正方形密切相关的词。例如,我们问:什么跟柔软相配?圆形还是正方形?什么形状跟坚硬相配?

所有受试者都认为圆形配柔软,正方形配坚硬;高达 94% 的人把快乐而不是悲伤和圆形联系起来;其他组词的一致性则低一些:79% 的人分别把快和慢、弱和强组成对,只有 51% 的人把深和圆形、浅和正方形联系起来。(如图 2 所示)当我们用同样这组词测试 4 名全盲志愿者时,我们发现他们的选择与有视力的人选择很相像。其中有个一出生眼睛就看不见的盲人拿到了相当好的分数,他只有一组词和大家的意见不一样,他把“远”跟正方形、“近”跟圆形配成了对。事实上,只有刚刚过半数的有视力的受试者——53%——把远和近的对象反了过来。因此,我们的结论是:盲人对抽象形状的理解和有视力的人一样。

与圆形/正方形有关系的词	受试者的一致意见(%)
柔软/坚硬	100
母亲/父亲	94
快乐/悲伤	94
好/坏	89
爱/恨	89
活/死	87
亮/暗	87
轻/重	85
热/冷	81
夏/冬	81
弱/强	79
快/慢	79
猫/狗	74
春/秋	74
安静的/喧闹的	62
行走/站立	62
单数/双数	57
远/近	53
植物/动物	53
深/浅	51

图2　受试者要指出每组词哪个适合圆形、哪个适合正方形，图中比例显示有视力的受试者意见的一致水平。

WRITING

WRITING TASK 1

这是考官准备的一篇优秀范文(原文在《剑桥雅思4》第162页)，请注意答案可以千变万化，下面只是其中之一。

本表对1999年澳大利亚的各种贫困家庭进行了分析。

平均来说，家庭总数的11%，差不多是200万人，生活在贫困之中。但是，单亲家庭或者独生身生活的人几乎是这个比例的两倍，分别为21%和19%。

结了婚的家庭一般生活不错，没有孩子的夫妻贫困水平相对较低(7%)，有孩子的则相对较高(12%)。可以看出，两种有孩子的家庭当时的贫困人数都超出了平均水平。

老年人生活贫困的可能性较小，虽然老年夫妻的情况(只有4%)同样比独居老人的情况(6%)更好。

总的来说，本表表明单亲家庭和有孩子的家庭比由夫妻组成的家庭更有可能生活在贫困之中。

WRITING TASK 2

This model has been prepared by an examiner as an example of a very good answer.

Media play an important part in every individual's life. No matter what the medium is, information is disseminated on a daily basis to billions of people throughout the world. There are of course some forms of media that are, for obvious reasons, better suited to this monumental task than others. I have chosen three types of media I think have both advantages and disadvantages.

First, television is probably one of the most efficient ways of delivering news and other types of information. One of the main advantages of television is that it is easily accessible to most people in developed countries and can deliver breaking news within minutes. A disadvantage is that it is considered a relatively new technology in developing countries and is not as accessible as other forms of media.

Secondly, radio runs a close second to television but is far more accessible to a larger population. It is cheaper and easier to purchase and the only thing lacking is the visual. It is also far more portable than TV. I often see older people out for a walk with their radio in hand listening for the latest news. The only disadvantage that I can think of would be the quality of the broadcast signal. In larger cities this may not be a factor, but in the countryside, it would definitely be a consideration.

Thirdly, books are probably the most accessible and most affordable of the three I have chosen, which is the obvious advantage. The major disadvantage would be the time it takes to compose, edit and publish. It takes some time for books to reach the consumer thus the information is often out of date. There is also the consideration of the literacy rate within a specific country.

In conclusion, I would say television, though not fully accessible to all, is probably the best way of conveying information.

(311 words)

参考译文

媒体在每个人的生活中都起着重要作用。无论通过什么媒体，信息每天都在传播给世界各地数十亿的人们。当然，有些形式的媒体比其他媒体更适合完成这一重大任务，其中的原因很明显。我选了三种媒体，我认为它们各有利弊。

首先，电视可能是传播新闻和其他信息最有效的途径之一。电视的主要优势之一是发达国家的大多数人很容易就能看到，重大新闻在几分钟之内报道出来。美中不足的是，在发展中国家，电视相对来说还是一门新的技术，其覆盖率不如其他形式的媒体。

其次，收音机仅次于电视，但其受众要大得多。它更便宜，人们更容易买得起，唯一的缺陷是它没有视觉效果。它比电视更易于携带。我常常看到一些老人外出散步时手里拿着收音机听最新消息。我能想到的唯一不足是广播信号的质量问题。大城市可能还好，但在乡下，这个问题无疑就值得考虑了。

再者，书籍是我所选择的三种媒体中最容易得到、最能买得起的，这是它的明显优势。它的主要缺点在于书的创作、编辑和出版需要很长时间，书到达读者手里也需要一段时间，书中提供的信息往往会有些过时。具体到一个国家还要考虑到人们的识字能力。

总之，我认为尽管电视的普及率不变，但它仍可能是传递信息的最佳途径。

SPEAKING

Band 9 Speaking Test Scripts

E: = Examiner C: = Candidate

PART 1

E: Let's talk about your friends.

C: OK.

E: Are your friends mostly your age or different ages?

C: Most of my friends are the same age as I am but I do have some older friends who are mostly foreign.

E: Why?

C: Do you mean why do I have older friends?

E: Yes.

C: Because when I was growing up in Beijing, I lived on campus because my dad was a professor so I met a lot of his graduate students over the years and we became friends. Anyway, I think that I grew up quicker than some of my younger friends.

E: Do you usually see your friends during the week or on the weekends?

C: Ah, usually on the weekends because I don't have that much free time during the week.

E: The last time you saw your friends, what did you do together?

C: We went to the Den to dance and have a few beers. Didn't like it much though because it was too loud.

E: In what way are friends important to you?

C: They provide some sort of stability in my life. You know, I always have someone other than my parents I can use as a sounding board. They're always around if I need help. Of course I'm there for them too. It works both ways.

PART 2

C: All right. I would like to tell you about the Silk Road. It's an ancient trading route opened up by the Han Dynasty. Silk merchants from the second century AD used it until its decline in the 16th century; now the Silk Road is open in parts to tourists who want to explore its heritage. This long string of caravan trails, oases, roads and mountain passes, stretched from northern China, through the desert and mountainous regions to ports on either the Caspian Sea or Mediterranean Sea, and was the conduit for goods and ideas passing between ancient China and the West. The Mongols later used the Silk Road to bind their vast empire, as Marco Polo found when he traveled it in the 13th century. The two main routes are split into the north route and the south route. The Silk Road was a major highway for the spread of Buddhism into East Asia, and later for the growth of Islam, and consequently many ruins dating back to the early centuries can still be seen. Within China the main sights are found in Xinjiang Province, including the Buddhist grottos at Dunhuang, and ancient relics at Turpan, such as the ruins of the city of Jiaohe. Travel along the Silk Road can be quite difficult because of the climate and lack of developed infrastructure. I just think historical places like this are so interesting because you can imagine what life was like for people so long ago.

PART 3

E: How do people in your country feel about protecting historical buildings?

C: I think that they're pretty apathetic. I don't really think they care one way or another. All people think about these days is money and how to get ahead. They don't seem to care about the past, which of course is our heritage, and we will never be able to rebuild what we tear down or cover in water.

E: Do you think an area can benefit from having an interesting historic place locally? In what way?

C: Yes, because if you maintain it you can charge money for entrance and the local economy can benefit from the tourists who come to visit. Restaurants, hotels and all the other businesses can make money that decreases unemployment and increases local wealth.

E: What do you think will happen to historic places or buildings in the future? Why?

C: If Beijing is any indication, I don't think there will be many historic buildings left. They can make more money off the property where these buildings presently stand by tearing them down and allowing developers to put up office buildings, apartments and hotels. It's a matter of finance. As for the historical places like the Summer Palace, the Forbidden City and so on, they will always be around because they are world famous and generate enough income to maintain the fabric of the sites.

E: How were you taught history when you were at school?

C: We were taught the usual way, by memorizing the text so we could pass the exams. Nothing was really explained to us. We were taught to listen, and not to Question the teacher. I really liked history, though, so I did a lot of reading about history on my own. I particularly enjoyed reading historical fiction.

E: Are there other ways people can learn about history, apart from school? How?

C: Yeah, just like I said before, you can read about in your spare time or actually go to places like the Forbidden City and ask people there about what went on. There are DVDs about history; especially some of the emperors like the guy who had all the terracotta warriors made in Xi'an. I can't remember his name right now.

E: Do you think that history will still be a school subject in the future? Why?

C: Yes, because we all learn from our mistakes and all of those have been made in the past. If we didn't we would be fools. You can look at history and see where people went wrong and avoid going there again.

Test 2

LISTENING

SECTION 1

谈话场景:旅游场景。
人物关系:两个旅行者,两个朋友。
谈话话题:谈论关于参观某地的问题,包括当地的名胜古迹,当地的风味小吃。

词汇注释

chilled *adj.* 冷却的,冷冻的	**cathedral** *n.* 大教堂
cash *v.* 把…兑现	**botanical** *adj.* 植物的
temporarily *adv.* 暂时地,临时地	**spectacular** *adj.* 壮观的,壮丽的,蔚为奇观的
transaction *n.* (一笔)交易,业务	**picnic** *n.* (自带食物的)郊游野餐
architect *n.* 建筑师	**swan** *n.* 天鹅

考题解析

Question 1

1–5 题为选择题,并且都给出了问题和选项。对于这类题,考生一定要注意先预测选项,看清楚问题,并浏览选项。带着问题去听对话,往往能很快抓住问题的答案。对于这一部分题,正确选项一般是对原文的改写,所以要注意同义替换的情况。

此题主要考查"chilled mineral water"一词的含义。"chilled"意为"冷冻的",读为[tʃɪlds],如:chilled meat 冷藏肉。另外,"mineral water"就是"矿泉水"的意思。所以在这里,"chilled mineral water"指的实际上就是"a cold drink"。

Question 2

此题的考查角度同样是同义替换。原文中提到的"the computer system was temporarily down"的意思是"电脑系统出毛病了",与选项 C 的意思实际上是一致的。在这个句子中,考生需注意短语"something is down"等于"something is broken down",意为"某物出毛病了,出故障了"。另外,选项 A 中提到的"the exchange rate was down"(汇率下降),与原文中提到的"the exchange rate was looking healthy"(汇率看起来还不错)的意思是不一致的,所以不能入选。

Question 3

这个题目相对来说比较简单,因为原文中提到了"a tourist, from New York",表明跟 Peter 说话的人是一个"纽约来的人",那么也就是说是个美国人。但是,选项 C 也很容易被错选,因为原文中提到了"he's moving on to Germany tomorrow"(他明天准备去德国),如果考生没有看清题目就选的话,很容易犯这样的错误。可见,看清问题相当重要。

Question 4

此题还是考查同义替换,原文提到的是"the bus system"(公交系统),实际上就是选项 B 中提到的"the bus routes"(公交线路)。此处,"route"一词意为"路线,路程",读为[ruːt]。

Question 5

此题实际上是考查较难单词的含义。原文提到“a snack and a drink”,此处的“snack” 意为“小吃,快餐”,读为[snæk]。

Question 6

6-8题较难。观察所给信息,考生可以发现实际上要填的是关于旅游点的一些信息:整天开门的地方,星期一不开门的地方,不要钱就可以进去的地方。所以在听题的时候,一定要特别注意所提到的每个旅游点的这方面的信息。

此题原文提到的是“Cathedral itself is open morning and afternoon”,实际上就是说 Cathedral 整天都开门,考生在听题的时候一定要注意这一点,一个简单的同义替换。

Question 7

这一题相对来说简单一些。原文提到“We can see other places on Mondays, you know. But I don't think the Markets will be open then, they only open on Thursday.”(我们可以在星期一去看其他地方。但是我认为 Markets 在星期一的时候不会开门,那儿只在星期四开门。)所以原文实际上是委婉地提到了“Markets 在星期一的时候不开门”,考生一定要注意这一点。

Question 8

此题考查转折词。原文提到“there's a charge for all of them except the Botanical Gardens”(所有地方都要钱,植物园除外),考生需注意此处的转折词“except”,一般来说,表示转折的连词后面一般埋伏着考点。另外,此题前给出信息里提到的“free entry” 表示的意思是“免费项目”。

Question 9

此题要填的是 Peter 和 Sally 第一个想要参观的地方。原文中提到“We'll go to see the painting you like first”(我们将先参观你所喜欢的一些绘画作品),这里提到的“绘画作品”应该在 Art Gallery(美术馆)展出。此处同样是作者提到的委婉和隐含的信息。

Question 10

此题很简单,原文中直接提到了“I really want to do at the Cathedral is climb the tower”(我在 Cathedral 最想做的事情就是爬上高塔),此题中,所听即所选。

SECTION 2

谈话场景: 学校生活场景。

人物关系: 主讲者为学校学生咨询处的老师,听众基本上是留学生。

谈话话题: 介绍学生咨询处所负责的有关学生学习生活方面的问题,包括课程咨询,个人问题咨询等等。

词汇注释

counselling service *n.* 咨询服务

chase up 为某一目的而寻找;不断要求得到(某人的注意等)

adjust *v.* 适应

unfamiliar *adj.* 不熟悉的,不常见的,陌生的

mount *v.* (在数量上)增加,增长,(在程度上)加剧

creep *v.* 不知不觉地到来

trigger *v.* 引起,促使

interrupt *v.* 中止,打扰,打断

unmotivated *adj.* 动机(或目的)不明确的

chaplain *n.* （军队、监狱、医院、船舰等的）牧师，祭司，犹太教教士	**sympathetic** *adj.* 同情的，有同情心的，表示同情的，出于同情的
self-esteem *n.* 自尊（心）	**dietary** *adj.* 饮食的，有关饮食的
resit *v.* （尤指考试不及格后）再参加（笔试）	**dietician** *n.* 饮食学家，膳食学家
anthropology *n.* 人类学	**appeal** *v.* 呼吁，吁请，恳求

考题解析

Question 11

此题也是考查对原文的概括和改写。原文提到"We can chase up your tutor if you're not getting proper feedback on how you are getting on in your subject."（如果你在该门课上的进展情况没有得到来自导师的及时反馈，我们可以出面联系敦促你的导师），与选项 C 的意思是一致的。注意原文中"feedback"一词的意思，该词意为"反馈，反应"，读为［ˈfiːdbæk］。

Question 12

此题较难，考查的依然是对原文的理解和把握。题干里提到了"stress"一词，所以听到这个词的时候应该特别注意。原文提到了"You'll have to start adjusting to teaching and learning methods that may be unfamiliar to you, as well as the mounting pressure as the deadline of that first assignment creeps up to you."（你必须开始调节自己，使自己适应陌生的教学和学习方式，以及第一次作业最后上交日期渐渐来临的压力。）在这一句里，说话者提到的压力有三个方面：教学方法压力、学习方式压力，以及交作业时间的压力。此句中有几个词语值得考生注意："adjust to" 意为"调整；调节；使适合；使适应"，如："He adjusted himself very quickly to the heat of the country. 他使自己很快适应了这个国家炎热的气候。"；"creep up" 意为"渐渐出现，慢慢来临"。

Question 13

此题考查对原文的准确把握。原文提到"You have to cope with all this without your usual social network—you know, the social contacts, family and friends you could normally rely on for help."（你必须自己来应付，而不是通过你平常所习惯的那些社会网络，也就是说，那些社会关系——你通常所依靠的家人和朋友。）这句话其实也就是说"缺乏了家人和朋友的支持与帮助"。注意题干中的"handle"一词实际上就相当于原文中的"cope with" 一词，听文章时抓住这个线索词比较重要。另外，此题还要注意不要错选选项 C，该选项的意思是"他们发现很难合群，很难和人交往"，但原文的意思并不是说"他们很难和人交往"，说的应该是"缺乏了家人朋友的帮助，缺乏了以往的社会关系"，强调的侧重点是大相径庭的。

Question 14

此题相对来说较为简单。题干中提到"personal crisis"（个人危机感）一词，所以在听题的时候要特别注意这个线索词后面的内容。原文提到的"interrupted personal relationships"（被打断了的个人关系）实际上就相当于选项 D 中所涉及到的内容"disruptions to personal relationships"（破坏个人关系）。在这里，"disruptions" 一词意为"中断、破裂"，读为［disˈrʌpʃən］。考生应特别注意要避免选择选项 B，这个选项的意思是"学生自己国家的商业问题"，这和原文中所提到的"unfinished business"（未竟事业）完全是两个概念。

Question 15

此题主要考查对于短语的把握。原文中提到的"drop out of a course"（退课），其意思就相当于选项 B 中提到的"没有完成一门功课"。另外，此题题干中的"self-esteem" 一词意为"自尊，自重"。

Question 16

此题在做题时较难把握。原文中提到"the local food is not to your liking"（当地食物不合你的胃口),意思就是选项 C 中所提到的"他们不吃当地食物"。此题题干中提到了"学生应该咨询 Glenda Roberts,如果……",一般来说,听题时注意人名 Glenda Roberts 就可以了,这个人名后面的信息应该就是要考信息。但是此题的正确答案在人名 Glenda Roberts 出现之前,所以说此题较难把握。不过,考生如果能在听题前充分预测选项,要找出正确选项还是不难的。

Question 17

此题较为简单。原文提到"full-time students can get a low-interest loan of up to six hundred dollars to buy books and for similar study-related expenses."(全日制学生可以申请一笔高达六百美元的低息贷款,来买书籍以及其他类似的学习有关花费。),这其实也就是选项 A 所提到的"帮助买书"。值得注意的是,选项 C 中所提到的"no-interest loan"(无息贷款)和原文中提到的"low-interest loan"(低息贷款),两者意思是完全不一样的,考生在听音时要注意分辨鼻音和非鼻音的区别。

Question 18

原文提到,"when you move into a flat, starting-up expenses, including furniture for it, can be covered by a loan"(当你搬进公寓,一些开始时的基本建设花销,包括买家具的花销,你都可以贷款。),也就是说,学生如果需要买家具,同样是可以申请贷款的,与选项 B 的意思相吻合。注意题干中的"available"一词,意为"可用到的,可利用的",读为[ə'veiləb(ə)l]。

Question 19

此题非常简单,仅仅是考查考生对数字听写的能力。注意分辨"fourteen"和"forty"两个词的读音差别。

Question 20

此题考查文章的结尾。原文提到"not too bad for an understaffed service"(员工缺乏情况下的服务也不错),意思就相当于选项 A 中提到的"尽管员工缺乏,工作效率还是很高"。考生在做题时,要充分理解原文,并找到同义替换的选项。

SECTION 3

谈话场景:作业场景。
人物关系:同学之间。
谈话话题:谈论如何写论文,如何收集数据,以及查阅参考书。

词汇注释

queue *n.* (排队等候的)一队人
questionnaire *n.* 用问题单进行的调查
time-consuming *adj.* 耗费时间的,旷日持久的
reckon *v.* 以为,认为,想
reliable *adj.* 可靠的,可信赖的
drawback *n.* 缺点,欠缺,不利条件,障碍
departmental *adj.* 部(或部门、系、科等)的
tutorial *n.* 大学导师的个别指导时间,大学导师的辅导课

考题解析

Question 21

观察已知信息,得知对话内容是关于某项作业的详细信息的。已知图表表明,作业分为三个部分:小

论文、小规模调查以及调查报告。需填信息也很明确:小论文的题目及要求字数、小规模调查的数据收集范围,以及调查报告的字数。所以考生在听题时,实际上对对话的内容已经大致了解,带着问题去听题相对来说就容易多了。此题很简单,所听即所选。需要注意的是,不能直接写成"collect data",因为在介词"of" 后面,所以要用动名词"collecting"。

Question 22

此题考查数字的听写。英文中,写千以上的数字时,最好用分割符号隔开。

Question 23

此题很简单,考查数字的听写。

Question 24

此题同样考查数字的听写。考生要注意的是,不能写成 "3 - 4,000",这样的话完全错误。

Question 25–Question 26

此题做题时需要注意两点:首先,要注意题目要求从给出的五个选项中选出两个选项,是一个多选题;其次,题干中提到的"disadvantage"一词实际上就是原文中提到的"drawback"(缺点、障碍),把握这一点非常重要。此题中,选项 B 即原文"response rate... is too low"(反馈率太低)的改写;选项 C 即原文"tends not to reveal anything unexpected"(可能不会反映没有预料到的情况)的改写。考生在听题时,只要能抓住原文中的"drawback"一词,不难选对正确选项。

Question 27

观察所给表格,可知需要填的信息分别是:作者名字、书籍名字、出版商名字,以及出版年月。所以,在听题时,要时时刻刻注意与已知信息相应的一些其他相关信息。此题考查对字母听写的速度。注意,由于是人名,该词首字母一定要大写。

Question 28

此题需注意的是,由于是书籍名称,所以每个单词的首字母都要大写。另外,所填"survey"一词的意思是"测量,调查",读为[se'vei]。

Question 29

此题同样要注意大小写的情况。专有名词的首字母需要大写。

Question 30

此题考查数字的听写,较为简单。

SECTION 4

谈话场景:学术报告场景。
人物关系:主讲者为犯罪行为学专家。
谈话话题:介绍(公司)集团犯罪的定义、研究现状、成因,以及社会影响。

词汇注释

preoccupation *n.* 全神贯注,入神
in accordance with 与…一致,依照,根据
quote *v.* 引用,引述
unquote *v.* 结束引文
embezzlement *n.* 盗用,挪用(公款),侵吞(财物)
fraud *n.* 诈欺,诈骗
excusable *adj.* 可原谅的,可辩解的,可免除的
serial *n.* 连载小说(或剧本、图画等)

victim *n.* 牺牲者，受害者，受骗者	**oil tanker** 油船，油轮
assess *v.* 对…进行估价	**subsequent** *adj.* 随后的，后来的
dilute *v.* 稀释，冲淡	**blame** *n.*（过错、事故等的）责任
carton *n.* 纸（板）盒，纸（板）箱，（硬蜡纸制的）液体容器，一纸板盒的量	**deliberately** *adv.* 故意地，蓄意地
deception *n.* 欺骗，诓骗，蒙蔽；诡计，骗术	**intentional** *adj.* 有意的，故意的
deprive *v.* 夺去，剥夺，使丧失	**tragic** *adj.* 悲惨的，可悲的，可叹的
undermine *v.* 暗中破坏，逐渐损害（或削弱）	**innocent** *adj.* 无辜的，清白的，无罪的

考题解析

Question 31

此文由于是学术报告，所以包含了较多的专业术语。但是考生做题的时候不能被较难的专业术语所吓倒，仔细观察已知信息，带着问题去听文章，很快就能找到问题的答案。此题不难，考查的是开头所提到的（公司）集团的定义。实际上，考生顾名思义也能把正确答案选对。

Question 32

此题首先要注意题干中的"not"一词，题干的意思是"（公司）集团犯罪不包括的方面"；其次，原文直接提到了"so crimes like theft by employees... are excluded according to this definition"（所以诸如员工偷盗之类的罪行并不算在内），与选项 A 的意思完全相同；再次，从第 31 题可知，所谓的（公司）集团犯罪肯定与传统意义上的犯罪有所区别，所以在选项中选出传统意义上的犯罪的选项就可以了。此题提示我们，考生在做题时要注意举一反三，而且一篇文章的前后应该是连贯的，是有逻辑联系的，所以要注意利用一切已知信息来做题。

Question 33

仔细观察所给图表，可以发现文章分为三部分：（公司）集团犯罪被忽视的方面、原因以及影响。考生听题时应该在脑袋里勾画出这个轮廓。此题不难，抓住题干中"been ingored by"（被忽视）一词，所以文中听到这个线索词的时候要特别留意。"mass media"一词意为"大众传媒"，需要注意"media"一词的读音[miːdiə]，该词意为"媒体"。

Question 34

此题解题时同样需要抓住线索词"been ignored by"。注意，此题"circles"一词一定要用复数。"academic circles"意为"学术界"。"academic"意为"学术的，学院的"，读为[ækə'demik]。

Question 35

此题所听即所选。"specialist knowledge"意为"专业知识"。

Question 36

此题较为简单。原文提到了"the third reason"（第三个原因），所以考生听题时应该引起注意。

Question 37

此题要填的信息是（公司）集团犯罪的经济影响的一个方面：对于什么人/方面来说，其经济影响并不重要。考生听题时要紧紧抓住这个线索。注意"customers"一词要用复数。另外，"individual"一词要注意拼写，意为"个别的，个人的"，读为[indi'vidjuəl]。

Question 38

原文提到的"massive illegal profit"（极大的非法所得利润），"massive"一词实际上就相当于题干中所提到的"large"一词，考生需要注意这个同义替换。"illegal"一词意为"违法的，不合规定的"，读为[iˈliːg(ə)l]；"profit" 一词意为"利润，得益"，读为[ˈprɔfit]。

Question 39–Question 40

这两个题较难把握。首先要注意所给六个选项中有两个是正确选项。其实观察所给选项，可以发现，选项 A 和 B 显然都不合适，因为说话者举的例子很明显是为了说明什么叫作"（公司）集团犯罪"，而这两个选项与原文相背离。另外，原文中提到"Now this illustrates two points to do with corporate crime. First of all, that it does not have to be intentional."（这样，这个例子就说明了（公司）集团犯罪的两个特征。首先，这种类型的犯罪可能并不是人为故意的），这样，选项 C 显然应该排除。接下来，原文又提到"The main crime here was indifference to the human results rather than actual intention to harm anyone, but that didn't make the results any less tragic."（这个例子中，主要的罪行是对人员后果的漠不关心，而不是有意要去伤害什么人，但这样一来，后果也是非常惨痛的），可见选项 D 和 E 比较好地阐释了这句话。

READING

READING PASSAGE 1

Lost for Words—Many minority languages are on the danger list

词汇注释

minority *n.* 少数；少数民族

native *adj.* 土生土长的，本地的，当地的 *n.* 土生土长者，本地人，当地人

Navajo *n.* 纳瓦霍人（散居于新墨西哥州、亚利桑那州及犹他州的北美印第安人）；纳瓦霍族；纳瓦霍语

sprawl *v.*（懒散地）伸开四肢躺（或坐）；（城市等）无计划地扩展（或延伸）

linguist *n.* 语言学家

vanish *v.* 消失

generation *n.* 代，一代（约指 20 至 30 年）；一代人，同代人

linguistic *adj.* 语言的；语言学的

diversity *n.* 多样性

shrink *v.*（shrank 或 shrunk；shrunk 或 shrunken）变小，减少

dominate *v.* 支配，统治；在…中占首要地位

evolutionary *adj.* 演变的，演化的；【生】进化论的，依据进化论的

mass *adj.* 大量的，大规模的

extinction *n.* 消亡，灭绝

rebound *v.* 弹回，跳回；重新跃起，回升

isolation *n.* 隔离，孤立

breed *v.* 养鱼，培养；酿成，惹起

pepper *v.*（撒胡椒面般地）在…上洒；使布满

endangered *v.* 危及，使遭危险

critically *adv.* 严重地

reject *v.* 咀嚼，排斥

crisis *n.*（复 crises）危机

confidence *n.* 信任；信心，把握

alongside *prep.* 在…旁边；沿着…的边

faith *n.* 新人，信心，信念

teens *n.*（年龄）十几岁（指 13 至 19 岁）

induce *v.* 引诱，劝

voluntary *adj.* 自愿的，志愿的

promote *v.* 增进，促进；发扬，提倡

reservation *n.*（美）（加拿大）（印第安人）居留地

chair *v.* 担任（会议、委员会等的）主席，担任（宴会等的）主持人

deadly *adj.* 致死的，致命的；极有害的，破坏性的

globalisation *n.* 全球化；全球性

adapt *v.* 适应

socio-economic *adj.* 社会经济（学）的；涉及社会和经济因素的；社会和经济地位的

comparison *n.* 比较，对照

intimately *adv.* 密切地

bound up with 与…有密切关系

preserve *v.* 保护
shift *v.* 转移,移动;改变位置(或方向)
deprive *v.* 夺去,剥夺;使丧失
mount *v.* (在数量上)增加,增长
physiological *adj.* 心理的,精神的;心理学的,心理学家的
perception *n.* 感知,感觉;认识,观念,看法
pattern *n.* 模式,模型;形式,方式,风格
identity *n.* 身份,本身;个性,特性
dire *adj.* 可怕的,使人感到痛苦的;预示灾难的,不祥的
prediction *n.* 预言,预计
foster *v.* 培养,促进;养育
ancestral *adj.* 祖先的;祖先传下的
tongue *n.* 语言,方言,土语
dominant *adj.* 占优势的;主要的
survive *v.* 活下来,幸存
bilingualism *n.* 熟练地讲两种语言的能力;双语制,两种语言的使用
erosion *n.* 腐蚀,侵蚀;减少,损害
Maori *n.* (新西兰的)毛利人,毛利语
rekindle *v.* 再点燃,重新燃起;重新激起
Polynesian *adj.* (中太平洋岛群的)波利尼西亚的,波利尼西亚人的,波利尼西亚语的
apprentice *n.* 学徒,徒弟;初学者,生手
indigenous *adj.* (尤指动、植物分布)当地的,本地的,土生土长的
pair up with 成对,成搭档
weave *v.* 织,编,编制
exclusively *adv.* 仅仅,专门地
sufficiently *adv.* 足够地,充分地
fluent *adj.* 说话流利的,熟练自如的
jar *n.* 罐子,坛子
revive *v.* 使复兴,振兴;使重新流行
essential *adj.* 必不可少的,绝对必要的,非常重要的
revival *n.* 复苏,复活;复兴,重新流行

考题解析

Questions 1–4 Summary

1. 较难。定位题干中6800, variety, as a result of。原文第2段首句出现6800,答案在此后寻找。第3段首句:Isolation breeds linguistic diversity... 其中 diversity 对应 variety;breeds 对应 as a result of。
2. 较难。定位 government。原文第5段中出现。43页第8行:有人认为比 government policy 更严重的因素(deadliest weapon),是 economic globalisation。
3. 原文第7段第2句:But a growing interest in culture identity may prevent... 其中 prevent 一词对应题干中:ensure... do not die out 的表达。
4. 定位词 apprentice schemes, teach people。原文倒数第2段倒数第12行中:to learn a traditional skills... 其中 learn 对应 teach。

Questions 5–9 Matching

5. 定位词 more than one language。原文第7段第11行:Most of these languages will not survive without a large degree of bilingualism.
6. 较难。定位词 not in itself a satisfactory goal。原文第7段倒数第3行:Preserving a language is more like preserving fruits in a jar... 其中 more like 对应 not in itself。
7. 原文第6段倒数第9行:Your brain and mine are different from the brain of someone who speaks French...
8. 定位词 young people。原文第4段倒数第4行:When the next generation reaches their teens, they might not want to be induced into the old traditions.
9. 定位词 culture。原文第6段第1、2句。

Questions 10–13 Yes/No/Not Given

10. 原文第3段第8行:Navajo is considered endangered despite having 150, 000 speakers.
11. 原文第3段第10行:What makes a language endangered is not just the number of speakers, but how old they are.
12. 定位词 government。原文第5段中出现 government,说政府为了提高全国的统一性,政策上对少

数民族语言有不利的影响。对这一做法,作者没有评论,更没有提到政府应该保护。

13. 原文中多处提到语言学家们正在努力,后果难料,当然不是 inevitable。比如第 2 段最后一句;第 7 段第 1、2 句;最后一段首句。

参考译文

语言的消失

许多少数民族语言已被列入危险名单

在美国西南部横跨 4 个州的土著民族纳瓦霍人当中,纳瓦霍语正在消失,因为大多数说纳瓦霍语的人不是中年就是老年。虽然有许多学生学纳瓦霍语,学校里教课都是用英语。街上的标牌、超市里的货物、甚至他们自己的报纸都是用英语。毫无疑问,语言学家们怀疑一百年以后还会有土生土长的人讲纳瓦霍语。

像纳瓦霍语这种情况决不只一家。世界上 6,800 种语言当中有一半将在两代人的时间内消失——相当于每 10 天少一种语言。地球上的语言多样性以前还没有以这样的速度减少过。"目前,我们正在朝 3、4 种语言统治世界的方向走,"里丁大学进化生物学家 Mark Pagel 说,"这是一种大规模的消失,我们能否挽回这种局面现在很难说。"

隔离带来语言多样性;最后的结果是,世界上到处都是只有少数人讲的语言。只有 250 种语言使用者超过一百万,至少有 3,000 种语言使用者不到 2,500 人,而即将消失的却不一定是这些少数语种。说纳瓦霍语的人尽管有 15 万,却也被认为是濒临灭绝。使语言濒临灭绝的不仅是使用人数,而且是它们的历史。如果孩子们说这种语言,那它相对来说比较安全。据位于费尔班克斯的阿拉斯加土著语言中心主任 Michael Krauss 讲,受到严重威胁的那些语言都只有老人们在说。

人们为什么会拒绝父母们的语言呢? 首先是因为信任危机,因为一个小的社区发现自己旁边就是一个更大、更富裕的社会,巴斯英国濒危语言基金会的 Nicholas Ostler 说。"人们会对他们的文化丧失信心,"他说,"等到下一代人长到十几岁,他们可能不想被劝到古老的传统里去。"

这种变化并非总是自愿的,很多时候,政府会想办法消灭一种少数民族语言,其做法是禁止在公共场使用或者不许在学校使用,全都是为了提高全国的统一性。比方说,美国以前曾实行过用英语开办印第安居留地学校的政策,结果就有效地把纳瓦霍语之类的语言送上了濒危名单。但是芝加哥大学语言学系主任 Salikoko Mufwene 说,最致命的武器还不是政府的政策,而是经济的全球化。"土著美国人还没有对自己的语言丧失信心,可他们不得不适应社会和经济带来的压力,"他说。"如果大部分商务活动都用英语,他们就不能拒绝说英语。"语言值得抢救吗? 至少,对语言及其发展的研究少了一些资料,因为对语言及其发展的研究有赖于语言之间的比较,无论是活的语言,还是死的语言。一旦一种既没有文字又没有记录的语言消失掉,那它就永远从科学里消失了。

语言同时与文化密切相关,因此不保护其中一个可能会很难保护另外一个。"一个人从纳瓦霍语改说英语,他们会失去一些东西,"Mufwene 说。"此外,多样性的丧失还可能使我们无法用不同的方法看世界,"Pagel 说。越来越多的证据显示,学一种语言会使大脑产生心理变化。"比如说,你的大脑和我的大脑与某个说法语的人的大脑是不一样的,"Pagel 说,而这种不一样会影响我们的思想和观点。"我们从不同的概念中得出的模式和联系也许是靠我们社区的语言习惯形成的。"

因此,尽管语言学家们不遗余力,下个世纪许多语言将会消失。但是对文化特征的兴趣的日益增加可能会阻止最可怕的预言的实现。"培养多样性的关键是让人们不仅学习占主导地位的语言,同时也学习祖先们传下来的语言,"Doug Whalen 说,他是康涅狄格州纽黑文濒危语言基金会创始人及会长。"没有很大程度的双语制,这些语言大部分都无法幸存,"他说。在新西兰,给孩子们开设的课程已经放慢了毛利语的受损速度,并且重新点燃了对毛利语的兴趣。在夏威夷采取的类似措施在过去几年带动大约 8,000 人加入了说波利尼西亚语的行列。在加利福尼亚,"学徒"计划为几种当地语言提供了生命保障。志愿者"学徒"从那些活着的能讲一种土著语言的人中挑出一位成为搭档,学习一门传统手艺,比如说编制篮子,教学用语只用那种濒危语言,经过大约300个小时的培训,他们基本上能说一口流利的当地语,足以把这种语言传给下一代。但是Mufwene说,不让一种语言死掉不同于通过每天使用给它新的生命。"保护一种语言更像是保护一个坛子里的水果,"他说。

不管怎样,保护能把一种语言从死亡线上拉回来。一些语言通过文字形式得以幸存,后代们使它重新流行,这样的例子已经有过。但文字形式对这项工作很关键,所以只要有重新流行的可能,许多说濒危语言的人都会想办法建立以前不曾有过的文字系统。

READING PASSAGE 2

ALTERNATIVE MEDICINE IN AUSTRALIA

词汇注释

alternative medicine 另类医学,另类疗法
therapy *n.*【医】疗法,治疗
acupuncture *n.* 针刺,针刺疗法,针刺麻醉
theory *n.* 理论
be based on 以…为基础
healing *adj.*(可)使愈合的;有疗效的
regulate *v.* 管理,控制;调整,调节
pathway *n.*【生化】途径
reflect *v.* 反应,表明,显示
struggle *n.* 斗争,搏斗;努力,挣扎
acceptance *n.* 接受,接纳
establishment *n.* 建立的机构(如军队、军事机构、行政机关、学校、医院、教会)
conservative *adj.* 保守的,守旧的,传统的
lecturer *n.*(英)(大学或学院的)讲师
public health 公共卫生(学);公共卫生措施
loath *adj.*(用作表语)不愿意的,厌恶的
pretender *n.* 伪装者,冒充者
industrialized *adj.*(实现了)工业化的
orthodox *adj.* 正统的,正宗的;传统的,符合社会习俗的
glove *n.* 手套
prescribe *v.*(医生)开(药),为…开(药)
herbal *adj.* 草本植物的;药草(制)的
remedy *n.* 治疗,治疗法
account for(在数量、比例方面)占
turnover *n.*(一定时期的)营业额,成交量
pharmaceutical *n.* 药剂,药物,药品
therapist *n.*(特定治疗法的)治疗专家
disenchantment *n.* 不再着迷,不再抱幻想,醒悟
popularity *n.* 普及,流行,大众化
chiropractor *n.*【医】按摩技士,手治疗者,用手法治疗者
naturopath *n.* 自然疗法医士
osteopath *n.* 按骨医生,整骨医生
acupuncturist *n.* 针灸医生,针疗医生
herbalist *n.* 草药医生
prior to 在…以前;先于;优先于
consultation *n.* 征求意见,咨询;(磋商)会议;会诊
colleague *n.* 同事
disillusion *v.* 使醒悟,使不再着迷,使不再抱幻想
skeptical *adj.* 惯于(或倾向于)怀疑的,表示怀疑的
empirically *adv.* 以经验为依据地,经验主义地
standing *n.* 级别,地位,名声
erode *v.* 腐蚀,侵蚀;削减,损害
consequence *n.* 结果,后果
rather than 与其…(不如);不是…(而是)
herbalism *n.* 药草学;草本植物学
incentive *n.* 刺激,鼓励,奖励;动机
bottom line 基本意思(或情况),概要
general practitioner(非专科)普通医师
potential *adj.* 潜在的,可能的
clientele *n.*(总称)顾客,主顾
attend *v.* 出席,参加(会议等)
chronic *adj.*(疾病)慢性的;(人)久病的
relief *n.*(痛苦、紧张、忧虑、负担等的)缓解,减轻,解除
comment *v.* 评论
holistic *adj.* 全盘的,全面的;【生】整体主义的
impersonal *adj.* 没有人情味的,冷淡的
feature *v.* 起重要作用;作为主要角色
exodus *n.*(大批的或成群的)出去,离开
clinic *n.*(医院等的)门诊部;私人(联合)诊所;(学校、机关等的)医务室
couple *v.* 并提,把…联系起来
relevant *adj.* 有关的;相关联的

inadequacy *n.* 不适当,不够格,无法胜任;弱点,缺陷	**emotional** *adj.* 感情(上)的,情绪(上)的
mainstream *adj.* 主流的	**respiratory** *adj.* 呼吸(作用)的;呼吸器官的,呼吸系统的
concur *v.* 同意,一致(with);赞同(in)	**candida** *n.* 念珠菌
bedside manner 医生对病人的态度;同情关怀的态度	**respectively** *adv.* 各自地,分别地
preventative *adj.* 预防的,防止的;防病的	**maintenance** *n.* 维修;养护,保养
musculo-skeletal *adj.*【解】肌(与)骨骼的	**complementary** *adj.* 补充的,补足的;互为补充的
complaint *n.* 抱怨,发牢骚,诉苦;(方)受苦,生病	**adjunct** *n.* 附属物,辅助物
digestive *adj.* 消化的,有消化力的	**seek** *v.* (sought)寻找;寻求,追求

考题解析

Questions 14–15 Multiple Choice

14. 原文正文第 1 段首句中 unusual 对应题干中 differed 一词。第 2 句中:... they are pretty loath to allow... 其中 loath 对应 C 选项中 reluctant。
15. 定位词 1990。原文正文第 1 段倒数第 3 行。

Questions 16–23 Yes/No/Not Given

16. 定位词 20 years。原文第 2 段首句。
17. 定位词 1983 and 1990。数字从 1.9% 增长到 2.6%,不是增长了 8%。
18. 定位词 550,000。原文第 2 段第 5 行。
19. 定位词 higher opinion。原文第 2 段最后一句。
20. 定位词 retraining。原文第 3 段第 3 行:... taking courses...
21. 定位词 salary。原文第 3 段第 4 行:Part of the incentive was financial... 主要说潜在客户的市场再转移,哪里的商机比较多。没有提到工资。
22. 难题。定位 1993 和 289,原文第 4 段首句。因为该句中没有 acupuncture,所以易错选 NG。注意到第 4 段第 3 行 a wide range of alternative therapies... 针灸只是 alternative therapies 中的一种。驳斥了原文的 a wide range of。
23. 定位词 1993。原文第 4 段第 3 行:Those surveyed had experienced chronic illnesses... 其中 chronic 对应题干中 long-term。

Questions 24–26 Table

24. 首先观察图表,确定答案在原文倒数第 2 段内。用 24 题上方单词 digestive 定位,原文倒数第 2 段第 3 行:12% suffer from digestive problems, which is only 1% more than those suffering from emotional problems. 所以比 digestive problems 稍微少一点就是 emotional problems。
25. 同理定位 candida。原文倒数第 2 段第 5 行:Headache sufferers and those complaining of general ill health represent 6% and 5% of patients respectively... 那么 6% 对应 headache。
26. 同上题,5% 对应 general ill health。

参考译文

澳大利亚的另类医学

1994 年初,澳大利亚首批大学水平的学习另类医学的学生在悉尼技术大学开始为期 4 年的全日制课程。他们的课程涉及多种疗法,其中包括针刺疗法。他们学习的理论基于中国对这种古老的治疗方法的传统解释:它能通过体内途径调节"气"或者精力的流动。这门课程反映出一些另类疗法在争取被医疗机构接受的奋斗过程中已经走了多远。

据悉尼大学公共卫生学讲师 Paul Laver 博士介绍，澳大利亚在西方世界一直有些与众不同，因为它对自然或者另类疗法持非常保守的态度。“我们的传统医生医术高明，我想他们非常不愿意让任何冒充者进入他们的领域。”在许多其它工业化国家，传统医学和另类医学已经“相安无事”了好多年。在欧洲，只有传统医生才能开草药。在德国，植物治疗法占全国药物销售量的10%。1990年，美国人看另类治疗专家的次数比正规医生要多，而且每年他们花在没有经过科学测试的治疗方法上的钱大约是120亿美元。

由于对传统医学不再抱幻想，澳大利亚的另类疗法在过去20年知名度稳步上升。在1983年做的一次全国健康调查中，1.9%的人说他们在调查前两周接触过按摩技师、自然疗法医师、按骨医生、针灸医生或者草药医生。到1990年，这个数字已经上升到了总人口的2.6%。据 Laver 博士和参加1993年《澳大利亚公共卫生杂志》创作的同事讲，1990年的调查报告中找另类治疗专家进行的55万次咨询占找合格医生咨询总数的1/8。“一群受教育程度更高、接受程度更低的人总的来说对专家们已经不再抱幻想，他们对科学和靠经验得来的知识越来越怀疑，”他们说，“其结果是，专业人员的崇高地位，其中包括医生，已经受到了损害。”

越来越多的澳大利亚医生，尤其是年轻医生，不但不反对或者批评这种趋势，反而和另类治疗专家联手开起了诊所，或者自己学习有关课程，特别是针刺疗法和药草学。部分动机是经济方面的，Laver 博士说。“基本情况是大部分普通医师都是生意人，如果看到潜在顾客去了别处，他们可能会希望能提供类似的服务。”

1993 年，Laver 博士和他的同事发表了对289名悉尼人的调查报告，这些人参加过8位悉尼另类治疗专家的治疗活动，这些治疗活动提供了范围很广的、来自25名治疗专家的另类疗法。接受调查的人得过慢性病，传统医学对他们的病无能为力。他们意见是，他们喜欢另类治疗专家的整体疗法以及他们受到的友好、热情和无微不至的关怀。传统医生在调查中的主要特点是态度冷淡、没有人情味。越来越多的病人离开他们的诊所、加上这次和其它许多次在澳大利亚进行的相关调查，所有这些都指向传统医生的严重失职，使得主流医生们自己也承认，他们能从另类治疗的人性化风格中学到一些东西。普通医师皇家学院院长 Patrick Store 同意这种观点，认为传统医生可以从另类治疗专家那里学到很多东西，比如医生对病人的态度、给病人提出一些预防疾病的建议。

根据《澳大利亚公共卫生杂志》，18%的看另类治疗专家的病人之所以找他们是因为他们得了肌与骨骼方面的疾病；12%是因为消化系统的问题，而有消化系统方面的问题的人只比受感情问题困扰的人多1%；患呼吸道疾病的人占7%，感染念珠菌的人也是这个比例；患头痛的人和主诉全身都有毛病的人分别占6%和5%，还有4%的人看治疗专家是为了常规的身体保健。

调查显示，替补医学这个名称也许要比另类医学好一些，因为另类医学似乎是一种辅助手段，在传统医学好像提不出解决方案时就会在不再抱幻想的情况下寻找这种解决办法。

READING PASSAGE 3

PLAY IS A SERIOUS BUSINESS

词汇注释

engrossed 全神贯注的，专心致志的
make-believe *adj.* 假装的，虚假的，虚伪的；虚幻的
cub *n.*（狐、狼、熊、虎、鲸等的）幼兽
kitten *n.* 小猫；幼小动物（如小兔）
tease *v.* 戏弄，逗弄
a ball of string 一团线
carefree *adj.* 无忧无虑的，轻松愉快的
exuberant *adj.* 生气勃勃的，兴高采烈的

adulthood *n.* 成人
juvenile *adj.* 少年的;【生】幼(态)的
fur seal 【动】海狗
pup *n.* (小狐、小狼、小海豹等)幼小动物
spot *v.* 发现,看出
predator *n.* 捕食者
approach *v.* 接近,靠近
cavort *v.* 跳跃,欢腾;寻欢作乐,嬉戏
figure *n.* 数字
developmental *adj.* 发展的,生长的;发育的;促使生长的
hiccup *n.* 暂时的下降(或中断、停顿)
evolve *v.* 演化,发展;成长,发育
intelligent *adj.* 有才智的,理解力强的,聪颖的
mammal *n.* 【动】哺乳动物
indulge *v.* 沉溺,纵容自己;让自己享受一下,使自己高兴一下
unique *adj.* 独一无二的,独特的
tailwagging *n.* (狗)摇尾巴
superficially *adv.* 表面上地
resemble *v.* 像,相似
earnest *n.* 严肃认真,诚挚
hunt *v.* 打猎;(兽类等)猎食
mate *v.* 成配偶;(鸟、兽)交配
socialize *v.* 焦急,交流
respiratory *adj.* 呼吸(作用)的;呼吸器官的,呼吸系统的
endurance *n.* 忍耐,忍耐力
permanent *adj.* 永久的,永远的
benefit *n.* 好处,益处;帮助
rapidly *adv.* 很快地,快速地
optimum *adj.* 最优的,最佳的
advantageous *adj.* 有利的,有助的,有益的
peak *v.* 达到最高峰 *n.* 顶点,顶峰
suckling *adj.* 哺乳的,未断奶的
stage *n.* 时期
hypothesis *n.* (复 hypotheses)假设,假说
at first glance 乍一看
complex *adj.* 复杂的,错综的
manoeuvre *n.* 策略,花招
inspection *n.* 检查,审视
reveal *v.* 显示
interpretation *n.* 理解
simplistic *adj.* (把复杂问题)过于简单化的
behavioural *adj.* (关于)行为的;行为方面的;行为科学的
ecologist *n.* 生态学家
predatory *adj.* 掠夺(性)的,掠夺成性的;故意破坏的,损人利己的
prowess *n.* 英勇,无畏;杰出的才能(或技巧),高超的本领
positive *adj.* 有事实根据的,无可怀疑的;真是的,实在的
measurement *n.* (量得的)尺寸,大小
converse *n.* 相反的事物;反面说法
stimulus *n.* (复 stimuli)刺激(物),促进(因素)
mould *v.* 塑造,使成形
plot *v.* 规划,计划
devote *v.* 将…献给;把…专用(于)
pattern *n.* 模式,模型
associate with 在思想上把…联系在一起
brief *adj.* 短暂的,短时间的
modify *v.* 修改,改造,改变
opportunity *n.* 机会
activate *v.* 使活动起来,使开始起作用
coyote *n.* 【动】丛林狼,郊狼
involve *v.* 使陷入,使卷入,牵涉
markedly *adv.* 明显地;引人注目地
variable *adj.* 易变的,多变的,反复无定的
unpredictable *adj.* 不可预测的,无法预言的;不定的,易变的
liken *v.* 把…比作(to)
kaleidoscope *n.* 万花筒;(形势、色彩、景致、事物等)千变万化,变化多端
context *n.* 背景,环境
predation *n.* (动物的)捕食行为;掠夺,掠夺行为
aggression *n.* 侵犯,侵略;侵犯行为,侵略行为
reproduction *n.* 生殖,繁殖
stimulation *n.* 兴奋(作用),刺激(作用),刺激(作用)
suspect *v.* 怀疑;推测,猜想
cognitive *adj.* 认识的,认识过程的,认识能力的
enormous *adj.* 巨大的,极大的
assessment *n.* 评价,估计
playmate *n.* 游戏伙伴,玩耍的同伴
reciprocity *n.* 相互性,相关性;相互关系,相互作用,相互依存
specialized *adj.* 专门的;专科的
flexibility *n.* 灵活性
potential *n.* 潜在性,可能性;潜力,潜能
bout *n.* 较量,比赛;一段,一阵,一次,一场
chemical *n.* 化学(制)品
nerve cell 【解】神经元,神经细胞
extent *n.* 范围,程度,限度

activation *n.*【化】活化(作用),激活	**interact** *v.* 互相作用,互相影响
light *v.* 点燃;照亮	**peer** *n.* 同辈,同事,同龄人
link-up *n.* 连接,联系;连接物,连接因素	**schooling** *n.* 学校教育;培养,训练
enhance *v.* 提高(价格、质量、吸引力等),增加	**exam-orientated** 以考试为目的的,重视考试的
component *n.*(组)成(部)分	**look-in** *n.* 成功的机会;参加的机会;受到注意的份儿

考题解析

Questions 27–32 Matching

27. 难题。定位词 unusual connections, beneficial。H 段最后一句:By allowing link-ups... not normally... play may enhance creativity. 下划线分别对应题干定位词。
28. 定位词 how much time。F 段首句、第 2 句。
29. 定位词 physical hazards。A 段第 4、5 行。
30. 难题。定位词 mental activities,和 H 段首句、第 2 句中:cognitive processes, cognitive involvement 相对应。
31. 难题。定位词 effect, reduction, human。I 段最后两句话。其中 schooling beginning earlier and becoming increasingly exam-orientated... 都表示孩子们玩的时间减少。
32. 难题。要理解题干含义。B 段中第 3 行:Playfulness, it seems, is common only among mammals, although a few of the larger-brained birds also indulge.

Questions 33–35 Multiple Choice

33. A 选项出自 B 段倒数第 4 行:A popular explanation...
34. C 选项出自 C 段第 2 句,其中 build muscle 对应 build up strength。
35. F 选项出自 E 段第 2 行:positive link between brain size and playfulness... 其中 brain size 对应 F 选项中 organ growth。

Questions 36–40 Matching

* 难题,耗时。注意在人名附近寻找。

36. E 段最后一句。其中 environmental data 对应 B 选项中 input, physical surroundings。
37. G 段最后两行。
38. C 段倒数第 2 行:But it doesn't work like that.
39. E 段第 1、2、3 句。
40. H 段第 6 行:Siviy studied how bouts of play affected the brain's levels of a particular chemical...

参考译文

玩是一件严肃的事情

玩能帮助长出更大、更聪明的大脑吗? Bryant Furlow 就此做了一些调查

A 玩是一件严肃的事情。孩子们全神贯注于虚幻的世界、小狐狸玩打架或者小猫戏弄一团线不纯粹是为了好玩。玩可能看起来是长大成熟、辛勤工作之前一种无忧无虑、兴高采烈地打发时间的方式,但是其中的含义远不止于此。首先,玩甚至能使动物丢掉性命。小海狗 80% 的死亡是因为玩耍时没有发现捕食者的靠近。从能量的角度来说,玩的代价也是非常之高的。小动物玩耍时欢腾跳跃要耗掉大约 2 ~ 3% 的能量,而在孩子身上,这个数字可能接近 15%。"即使 2 ~ 3% 也是一个巨大的比例,"爱达荷大学 John Byers 说,"你很难发现动物会那样浪费能量,"他补充说。这背后一定是有原因的。

B 但是如果玩不是简单的发育暂停，正如生物学家曾经认为的那样，那它是怎样演变过来的呢？最新的观点认为，玩的演变是为了让大脑长大。换句话说，爱玩耍使你变聪明。爱玩耍似乎只在哺乳动物中常见，尽管少数大脑大一些的鸟也喜欢玩。动物玩耍时经常使用一些独特的动作——比如狗摇尾巴——说明表面上像成年动作的活动其实不是认真的。对玩的一种大众化解释是：它有助于小动物们掌握长大以后需要的技巧，像猎食、交配和交际。另外一种解释是，通过提高它们的呼吸系统的耐力，玩能让小动物们为成年生活准备一幅好身体。这两种观点近年来都遭到了质疑。

C 来看看运动理论。如果玩的演变是为了强身健体或者作为一种耐力训练，那么你会希望看到永久的好处。但是 Byers 指出，只要训练停止，增加运动量带来的好处就会马上消失，因此小时候通过玩耍提高的耐力长大后有可能会丧失。"如果玩的作用是变得身强体壮，"Byers 说，"玩耍的最佳时间就要看什么时候对某种特定的小动物最有利，但玩并不遵循这个规律。"在所有动物当中，玩的高峰大约在哺乳期的中间，之后就会下降。

D 接下来是技能训练假设。乍一看，玩耍的动物真的像是在练习长大后需要的各种复杂的技能。可是更仔细的观察表明，这种解释也过于简单化。在一项研究中，加利福尼亚大学的行为生态学家 Tim Caro 观察了小猫玩的掠夺游戏以及它们长大后的掠夺行为，结果发现猫的游戏方式对它们长大之后的猎食本领没有太大的影响。

E 今年早些时候，加拿大莱斯布里奇大学的 Sergio Pellis 报告说，在哺乳动物中，大脑的大小与玩耍之间总的来说存在着很强的实实在在的联系。通过对 15 种哺乳动物大脑大小的比较，他和他的小组发现，大一点的大脑（对于特定的身体大小来说）与玩得更多是有关系的，相反的情况也发现是真的。达勒姆大学 Robert Barton 相信，由于大一点的大脑比小一点的大脑对成长刺激更为敏感，它们需要更多的玩耍来帮助自己长大成熟。"我的结论是这与学习有关，与大脑发育过程中环境资料的重要性有关。"他说。

F 根据 Byers 的观点，对幼小动物玩耍时期时机的掌握对到底发生着什么提供了很重要的线索。如果你在小动物的发育过程中每天安排一段时间让它玩，你会发现一个典型的与一段"敏感时期"有关系的模式——一个短暂的发育窗，在此期间，大脑实际上是可以改变的，而这种改变在此之前或者之后都是不可能的。想想孩子们吸收语言相对来说是很容易的——婴儿和成人就没有这种能力。其他研究者们发现，猫和老鼠玩得最起劲的时候正好是这个"机会窗"到达顶峰的时候。

G "人们对玩耍激活的大脑数量还没有给予充分的注意，"科罗拉多大学 Marc Bekoff 说。Bekoff 研究了小丛林狼的玩耍过程，发现它们的行为显然比成年丛林狼的行为更加变化多端、无法预测。这些行为激活大脑许多不同的部分，他说。Bekoff 把这种情况比作一个行为万花筒，玩耍的动物会在各种活动之间快速地跳来跳去。"它们会使用许多不同环境里的动作——捕食、侵略、繁殖，"他说，"它们正在发育的大脑接受着各种各样的刺激。"

H 玩耍不仅涉及的大脑数量比猜测的要多，而且还好像能激活更多的认知过程。"玩耍涉及大量的认知活动，"Bekoff 说。他指出，玩耍经常涉及对玩伴的复杂评估、互惠互利的想法以及特殊动作和规则的使用。他相信，玩耍能创造出更加具有行为灵活性、今后更加具有学习潜力的大脑。这个观点得到了葛底斯堡大学 Stephen Siviy 研究成果的支持。Siviy 研究了一次次玩耍如何影响大脑那些与刺激和神经细胞发育有关的某种化学品的水平，结果他对大脑的激活程度感到吃惊。"玩耍会把一切都调动起来，"他说。通过让正常情况下相互不交流的大脑区域连接起来，玩耍可以提高创造力。

I 进一步的实验对今天多种社会养育孩子的方式可能会有什么启发呢？我们已经知道，那些不给机会玩耍的小老鼠脑成分会长得小一些，与同伴交往时它们不会具备使用社会规则的能力。随着学校教育的越来越早并且变得越来越重视考试，玩耍受重视的程度甚至可能会更低。谁知道这会带来什么样的结果？

WRITING

WRITING TASK 1

This model has been prepared by an examiner as an example of a very good answer.

The graph illustrates the daily number of units of electricity used in England during both summer and winter. The pie chart indicates the percentage of typical uses of the electricity.

First, the graph indicates that the amount of electricity used in the winter is double that used in the summer. In winter, usage rises between 00:00hrs and 02:00 hrs, from 35 thousand units to 40 thousand followed by a decrease between 02:00hrs and 07:30hrs to 30 thousand units. Usage rises from 07:30hrs to 12:00hrs then evens out at 40 thousand until it peaks at 22:00hrs, to 45 thousand units.

Heat and other daily items consume 85% of the electricity and 15% is consumed by items used irregularly such as blenders, vacuums, etc. in both summer and winter.

In the summer, usage starts at 16 thousand units at 00:00hrs and drops steadily to 15.5 thousand at 07:30hrs. Usage rises to a peak of 20 thousand units at 13:30hrs, then drops of to a steady 15 thousand units until it peaks again at approximately 23:00hrs to just under 20 thousand units.

It is worth noting that the low and high usage periods in both winter and summer are similar except between 00:00hrs and 02:00hrs.

(201 words)

参考译文

曲线图显示出英格兰在冬夏两季每天的用电量,饼状图表明各种典型的用电比例。

首先,曲线图表明冬天的用电量是夏天的2倍。在冬天,0:00至2:00的使用量从3.5万度上升到4万度,接着从2:00至7:30降到3万度。从7:30到12:00用电量有所增加,然后保持在4万度,直到22:00到达最高峰4.5万度。

在冬夏两季,取暖和其他日常使用消耗了85%的电量,15%的电量用于搅拌器、吸尘器等非常规用途。

在夏天,用电量从0:00的1.6万度稳步下降到7:30的1.55万度,到13:30到达2万度的高峰,接着降到1.5万度并保持稳定,直到大约23:00再次到达将近2万度。

值得一提的是,除0:00点至2:00以外,冬夏两季的用电高峰和用电低谷时段差不多。

WRITING TASK 2

这是考官准备的一篇优秀范文(原文在《剑桥雅思4》第165页,请注意答案可以千变万化,下面只是其中之一。

幸福的定义很难下,因为它对不同的人有不同的含义。有的人把幸福与财富和物质成功联系起来,其他人则把感情和人与人之间的相亲相爱看作幸福,还有人认为只有精神之路——既不是物质世界也不是与别人的关系——才能通往幸福。

由于人们为自己对幸福作出了如此多不同的解释,所以很难给幸福下一个大家都认可的定义。

但是,既然人的幸福各有不同,那么获得幸福的第一步就是有一定的自知。一个人要知道自己是谁,然后才知道什么东西会让自己幸福。

当然,相亲相爱、身体健康、谋生能力和环境安定之类的因素也都是幸福的原因,但这决不是说没有这些条件人就得不到幸福。

总的来说,我认为在生活中能够保持清醒头脑对获得幸福更为重要。我的意思是说,明确知道生活中什么重要(家庭幸福、关系好坏、使别人幸福,等等),什么不重要(工作不顺心、为琐事烦恼,等等)。

在生活中保持清醒头脑和具有自知一样难以做到,但我认为这两点对获得幸福来说是最重要的。

SPEAKING

Band 9 Speaking Test Scripts

E: = Examiner C: = Candidate

PART 1

E: What kinds of food do you like to eat?

C: I'll eat almost anything. I like Chinese food of course because I was brought up eating it, but I also like fast food like pizza and KFC, and I like Western restaurants. I used to eat at MacDonald's until I watched the movie *Supersize Me*, now I don't! I should add, there are certain things in China I won't eat like insects and some other internal animal organs. I don't like the thought of it.

E: What kind of new food would you like to try? (Why?)

C: I would like to try African food, but I haven't found any restaurants that serve it yet. I have a couple of African friends who tell me it's very good but they can't get the ingredients they need here in China. When they do, I will definitely try it.

E: Do you like cooking? (Why/why not?)

C: Yes I like cooking because I can control the amount of salt and spices I put in it and it's an art. I'm not that fond of really spicy food or lots of salt and MSG, so when I have time I prefer to cook my own food. Unfortunately, I don't really have a lot of time.

E: What was the last meal you cooked?

C: I invited some friends over to my parents' place about a week ago and I cooked some couscous with lamb and it went great with beer.

E: Do you prefer home-cooked food or food from restaurants?

C: I think I already answered that question. I prefer to eat at home so that I can control what ingredients go into the food. But sometimes I do like to go out to restaurants.

PART 2

E: Describe an interest or hobby that you enjoy.

C: I enjoy studying genealogy, which refers to family history and descent. The basic objectives of genealogical research are to identify ancestors and their family relationships. At a basic level you can identify and record the following for each individual in your family tree: date and place of birth; names of, date and place of marriage of parents; names of children; date and place of death. But in China, this can sometimes be difficult because a lot of records were destroyed during various wars and military campaigns. You can, however, get a lot of information from your parents and grandparents, aunts and uncles and others that can at least help to try and figure out who your long lost relatives were. It's just interesting to know. I think that a lot of people think that they probably have some sort of relationship with famous Chinese writers, emperors, even Genghis Khan. You never know and that's what makes it so fascinating.

After you get some information together, you start to build a family tree that is kind of like an upside-down pyramid and you would be the point at the bottom. This is a kind of ancestral pyramid. But to this date, I haven't gotten too far with it. Some people spend years studying this stuff. I have a friend from Scotland who tells me that his father is into genealogy and that he is in some way related to William Wallace, you know the guy Mel Gibson played in the movie, but who knows? I'm quite frankly hoping to find out that I am related to someone really wealthy. I might get lucky.

PART 3

E: Do you think having a hobby is good for people's social life? In what way?

C: Yeah, especially what I'm doing. It's a lot of fun to sit around and talk about who your ancestors may have been and what it was like in their time. It's sort of an icebreaker if you're meeting people for the first time. You know, you can just toss the Question out, "What do you guys do for fun or do you have any other interests other than school, girls and food?" and people will respond.

E: Are there any negative effects of a person spending too much time on their hobby? What are they?

C: Yes, then the hobby becomes an obsession and that's not good for anyone or his or her social life. Nobody wants to hear about your hobby all the time. You become a sort of social misfit.

E: Why do you think people need to have an interest or hobby?

C: Well, since you're not around people all the time, except of course at university where you really can't get away from them, you should have something else to focus on to relieve stress, something that you find relaxing. That's what other interests and hobbies are for.

E: In your country, how much time do people spend on work and how time on leisure? Is this a good balance, do you think?

C: People now in China, at least in the large centers, spend most of their time trying to make money and have very little leisure time. Although, having said that, the government has created a lot more holiday time for people, but that is primarily to get them to spend money—it's economic as opposed to a kind gesture. I don't think that the balance now is good at all, and we need to be careful. I've heard that in some countries people die at their desks working. It's crazy. I won' t being doing that.

E: Would you say the amount of free time has changed much in the last fifty years?

C: Yes, of course. As I just told you, people are now driven by money and the need to have it, and that basically discounts most leisure time except for weekends for some, not most. Fifty years ago people may have had a little more leisure time, but then most businesses were state-owned and there were very few foreign companies here.

E: Do you think people will have more or less free time in the future? Why?

C: Well, I think that they will have more, with the increase of concepts such as SOHO—small office, home office. A lot of people will be able to work from home and as long as they get the work done on time, it doesn't really matter when they do it so they will probably be able to go out more often and go on vacation more often because even if they're away, they can take the office with them on their laptop.

Test 3

LISTENING

SECTION 1

谈话场景：租房场景。

人物关系：租房中介咨询员以及租房者。

谈话话题：交流租房信息，房源、客户要求、客户信息以及房租等问题。

词汇注释

cousin *n.* 堂兄弟（或姐妹），表兄弟（或姐妹）　　**proportion** *n.* 部分，份儿

考题解析

Question 1

观察所给图表，可知此对话是关于住房申请的问题。需填信息分别为：在澳大利亚居住的时间、目前住址、目前课程，以及所需住房的时间段。

此题一定要注意题目要求。题目要求的是每空所填单词不得超过三个，所以在填空的时候，不能把原文一字不变地照搬下来。原文提到"a year in Adelaide and six months in Sydney"，实际上填空的时候，考生可以将其简化为"1.5 years 或 11/2 years"。

Question 2

此题考查对专有名词的把握。注意此题"Forest"一词首字母应该大写。同时，"Forest"一词有另外一个写法"Forrest"，都是对的。

Question 3

此题考查较难单词的写法。注意"Academic"一词首字母需大写，另外，该词的意思是"学术的"，读为[ækə'demik]。

Question 4

此题较为简单，考查日常用语的写法。注意"Thursday"一词的首字母需大写。

Question 5

此题考查对原文的把握与重写。原文提到"share a room with someone else"（和其他人共用一个房间），意思就是需要一个双人间，所以选择选项 B。选项 A 意为"单人间"；选项 B 意为"双人间"；选项 C 意为"三人间"。

Question 6

此题同样考查对原文的理解。原文提到"Do you have any women living alone, retired women?"（你认识退休了的，独自居住的女子吗？），这实际上就是说 Sara 喜欢和单身女子一起住，所以选择选项 B。

Question 7

此题不难。原文提到"Most of them live in flats, but that's not a problem for you, is it?"（她们很多都住在公寓里，但是我想那对你来说并不成问题，是吗？），接下来 Sara 马上说，"Not at all. I'm used to that."

(一点也不成问题,我都已经习惯了。),所以此题应该选择选项 A。"flat" 一词在此意为"公寓"。

Question 8

此题考查常用单词的拼写。"deposit" 一词意为"押金,保证金",读为[diˈpɔzit]。

Question 9

此题中,"monthly" 一词意为"每月的,每月一次的"。此题的意思是"她需要按月用现金或者支票来缴房租"。

Question 10

此题题干中的"her part of" 实际上就相当于原文中的"your proportion of"。"proportion" 一词意为"比例,部分",读为[prəˈpɔːʃ(ə)n]。另外,注意在此题中,填"telephone" 或者"phone" 都是对的。

SECTION 2

谈话场景:电台(或电视台)访谈场景。
人物关系:电台(或电视台)节目主持人和嘉宾。
谈话话题:介绍"夏季节日"活动的有关内容。

词汇注释

sensational *adj.* 激起强烈感情的,令人兴奋的,轰动性的
theatrical *adj.* 剧场的,演剧的,戏剧的
theme *n.* (文艺作品的)主题
circus *n.* 马戏,杂耍,马戏团,马戏演出
marquee *n.* (用于展览会、游园会等的)大帐篷,大营帐
canvas *adj.* 帆布制的
portable *adj.* 便于携带的,手提式的,轻便的
acrobatic *adj.* 杂技的,杂技演员的
purist *n.* 纯粹派艺术家
showcase *n.* (为引起普遍注意而设的)供亮相的地方(或媒介)
aerial *adj.* 空中的
puppetry *n.* 木偶剧演出(或创作)
puppet *n.* 木偶
puppeteer *n.* 演木偶剧的人
comedy *n.* 滑稽节目,喜剧
troupe *n.* (尤指巡回演出的演员、歌手等组成的)团,班,队

考题解析

Question 11

此题考查对原文的改写。原文提到"they've put it at the end of the month"(他们把活动的日期定在了月末),那么当然应该选 C 选项。

Question 12

题干问"今天评论者的重点将集中在什么地方?",所以听到原文中提到"today" 一词的时候要特别注意。原文提到"for today's report though, I'm looking at some of the theatrical events that you might like to see"(在今天的报道中,我想提及一些你们可能想看的戏剧表演节目),所以此题选 A。考生需要注意的是,要抓住题干中的信号词到原文中去定位,就能很快的找到正确答案。

Question 13

此题考查对原文的理解。原文提到"I'm going to tell you about two circus performances, but there are plenty of others in the programme."(我想跟你们谈两个马戏团的表演,但实际上,演出的有很多个马戏团),此题是出题人出的一个转折点,先提到"two" 这个概念,再提到"plenty" 一词,考生很容易被迷惑,所以此题千万不能错选 B。

Question 14

此题考查对较难单词的掌握情况。原文提到"in a marquee"(在大帐篷里),实际上就相当于"in a tent"。注意"marquee"一词的含义与读音,意为"大帐篷,大营帐",读为[mɑːˈkiː]。

Question 15

观察所给图表,可以知道原文应该提到了三个马戏团的表演,分别是:Romano 马戏团、Electrica 马戏团,以及 Mekong Water 木偶剧团。需要填的信息分别为:Romano 马戏团的"highlights"(保留节目)和观众类型;Electrica 马戏团及 Mekong Water 木偶剧团的演出地点和观众类型。所以仔细观察完图表之后,考生应该充分利用所给信息,带着问题去听题,就能迅速地找准正确答案。此题原文提到"the best part is the music and lighting"(最好的节目是音乐和灯光),实际上就是"highlights"部分为"music and lighting"。

Question 16

此题不难,原文提到"it's really for adult tastes"(真的适合成人观看),所以直接填"adult"一词即可。

Question 17

此题很容易,所听即所得。考生需注意的几个问题:一是,题目要求每空只能填三个以内的单词,所以不能把原文中提到的"at the Studio Theatre"全部写下来;二是,"Studio Theatre"这两个词由于是专有名词,所以首字母要大写;三是,"theatre"一词有两个写法,另外一个写法为"theater",都是对的。

Question 18

此题很简单,也是所听即所得。另外,此题有多种填法,"the whole family","the entire family","all the family","families"都是可以的。

Question 19

考生填题时需注意:"City Gardens"是地名,所以首字母要大写;另外,"Gardens"一词后面要加"s"。

Question 20

此题很简单,而且有多种填法:"young children / younger children / children"都可以。

SECTION 3

谈话场景:课程咨询场景。
人物关系:学校课程咨询员与学生。
谈话话题:咨询有关学期前预备课程的有关事宜,包括如何合理安排学习时间、如何制定学习计划、如何解决心理问题等。

词汇注释

semester *n.* 学期
seminar *n.* (研究班的)专题讨论会
motivate *v.* 激发…的积极性(或学习兴趣)
strategy *n.* 策略,行动计划,对策
tip *n.* 指点,指导,忠告
motivational *adj.* 激发积极性(或学习兴趣)的;动机的,有关动机的
enthusiastic *adj.* 满腔热情的,热心的,热烈的,极感兴趣的
overcome *v.* 克服

procrastination *n.* 拖延,耽搁	**essential** *adj.* 必不可少的,绝对必要的,非常重要的
sandwich *n.* 三明治	**consecutive** *adj.* 连续的

考题解析

Question 21

此题不难。原文提到"we run quite a few different short courses for students who are either returning to study or studying part-time."(我们有些不同种类的短期培训课程是专门为那些工作了之后再回来学习的人或者兼职工作的学生准备的。),所以此题应该选择 A。注意,选项 B 意为"研究生";选项 C 意为"商业经理人"。

Question 22

此题考查对原文的理解。原文提到"'Study for Success' seminar on the first and second of February."("成功之道"讨论课是在 2 月的 1 号和 2 号),出题者设计了一个考点,问"这门课程要持续多长时间",所以此题选 B。此题提醒考生注意:很多时候出题人会换一种角度来问问题,所以在听题时一定要把握住关键信息。

Question 23

此题考查对较难单词的把握。原文提到"build some techniques to help you write more clearly"(获得一些帮助你写文章更为清楚的一些技巧),与选项 C 的意思相同。注意选项 C 中"clarity" 一词的含义,意为"清楚,透明",读为 [ˈklæriti]。

Question 24

此题考查对原文的同意替换。原文提到"with reading ,there'll be sessions aimed at getting into the habit of analyzing material as you read it."(在阅读方面,将会有专门关于如何养成阅读时分析材料习惯的讨论会),实际上相当于选项 A 所提的信息。注意选项 A 中的"analytically" 一词意为"分析地,解析地";选项 C 中的"thoroughly" 一词意为"十分地,彻底地",读为[ˈθʌrəli]。

Question 25

此题相对应的原文提到"there's a range of motivational exercise that we do to help the students feel positive and enthusiastic about their study."(还有一些学习动机方面的练习,来帮助学生在学习方面建立积极和热情的态度),也就是说,这种练习主要是为了使学生在学习的时候有兴趣有信心,所以选择选项 B。此题同样考查对原文的理解和同义替换。

Question 26

此题较为简单。题干中提到"a key component of the course",所以听到原文中提到"key component of the course" 这样的字眼时,考生需要特别留心。原文提到"two of the key components of the course are time management and overcoming procrastination."(这门课程的两个主要组成部分是时间支配问题和避免拖延学习的问题),所以所谓的"time management" 实际上就是选项 A 所提到的"use time effectively"(有效利用时间)。在这里,"procrastination" 一词意为"延迟,推迟",读为[prəuˌkræstiˈneiʃən]。

Question 27

此题考查对日常用语的掌握情况。原文提到"it's essential that you book well ahead of time"(提前预订座位非常重要),实际上就等于选项 C 中所提到的"reserve a place in advance"(提前预订座位)。在选项 C 中,"reserve" 一词意为"预订","in advance" 为短语,意为"提前"。选项 A 中,"register" 一词意为"注册,登记",读为[ˈredʒistə(r)];"Faculty Office" 意为"系办公室"。选项 B 中,"Course Convenor" 意为"课程组织者,发起人"。

Question 28

此题考查对较难单词的把握。原文提到"'Learning Skills for University Study' is on three consecutive mornings starting on a Monday"("大学学习的艺术"这门课从每个星期一开始,连续三天的上午),所以实际上就是星期一、星期二、星期三的上午。此处,注意"consecutive"一词的含义与读音,意为"连续的,持续的",读为[kən'sekjutiv]。

Question 29

题干问"这门课程的一个特点是什么",所以考生在听题时一定要特别注意 A、B、C 三个选项所涉及的内容是否在原文中提到了。原文只提到了一个内容,即"stress management"(压力控制),所以选 B。

Question 30

此题较为简单。原文提到"I think I'd be better off starting from the basics"(我想从基础学起可能会更好),所以选择 B 选项。此处需注意词组"be better off",意为"(情况、境况)会更好"。

SECTION 4

谈话场景:报告项目进展场景。

人物关系:讲话者为学生会代表,听众为学校负责建筑的人员以及学生。

谈话话题:介绍学生会在学生中所做的关于新建筑的意见调查工作,以及此次意见调查的结果。

词汇注释

feasible *adj.* 可行的,行得通的
ultimate *adj.* 最后的,最终的
beneficiary *n.* 受益人,受惠者
option *n.* (供)选择的事物(或人)
submit *v.* 提交,呈递
questionnaire *n.* 调查表
approximately *adv.* 近似地,大约
consensus *n.* 一致(或多数人的)意见
crucial *adj.* 关键性的,至关重要的
outskirt *n.* 市郊,郊区
living quarter 住宅区
on the premises 在房屋内,在场所内
gym *n.* 体操馆,健身房
respondent *n.* (调查表、问题表的)答卷人
refectory *n.* (修道院、学校等的)食堂,餐厅
drama *n.* 戏剧
largish *adj.* 相当大的
minority *n.* 少数
elitist *adj.* 上等的,高级的,具有高人一等优越感的
security *n.* 安全
surveillance *n.* 监视,监督
reception *n.* 接待处

考题解析

Question 31

观察图表,可知原文是关于"New Union Building"的有关内容的。31–32 题主要是在学生中征求意见的步骤,主要三个步骤:学生以书面形式对新建筑的设计提出自己的见解;依据这些书面依据来确定以后的调查工作;收集数据,撰写报告。需要填的主要是第二个步骤,后来的调查工作以什么方式来进行,以及有多少被访学生提出了反馈意见,所以考生听题的时候要牢记这几个出题点。

此题考查对较难日常用语的把握。原文中直接提到了"questionnaire"(调查表,调查问卷)一词,所听即所得。考生需要注意该词的拼写。

Question 32

原文提到“approximately two thousand”（大约2,000），所听即所得。但是考生需注意：题目要求每空填词不得超过2个，所以只能用阿拉伯数字来表示数目。另外，如果对较难单词“approximately”没有把握，完全可以用“about”来表示。

Question 33

观察所给图表，得知33–37题主要要求填新建筑的候选地址的有关信息：各自的地址和优缺点。原文首先分别提到三个地址的地点，然后再分别提到三个地址各自的优缺点。考生在做题时需注意这个顺序。此题填空的时候需注意“Education”一词首字母需要大写。

Question 34

此题所填“halls of residence”意为“居住区”。首先注意“halls”一词需要用复数，另外，还要掌握“residence”一词的含义和读音，意为“居住，住处”，读为[ˈrezidəns]。

Question 35

此题所填的两个单词顺序可以颠倒。同时，由于所填空应该是名词，所以“parking”一词应该用动名词形式，考生应该特别注意这一点。“parking”意为“停车”。

Question 36

此题也很简单，所听即所得。需注意的是，“rooms”一词后一定要记得加“s”。

Question 37

此题原文提到“more room for a choice of facilities”（设备的选择余地更大），但是由于题目要求所填空不得超过三个单词，所以最好写成“（more）room for facilities”。此处，“facility”一词意为“设备，工具”，读为[fəˈsiliti]。

Question 38

此题需注意要选两个正确选项。考生在听此题时可以用排除法来做题。由于题目问的是学生要求新建筑里有哪些设施，所以不在大多数学生要求范围之内的选项可以去除。首先原文提到“there was a minimal interest in having a library”（很少有学生对图书馆感兴趣），所以选项A可以排除。接着又提到“we would like the current table games room to be replaced by a small gym.”（我们希望取消现在的乒乓球游戏室，代之以小型体育馆），所以选项B排除，而选项D入选，因为D选项提到的“a mini fitness centre”（微型健身中心）实际上就相当于原文提到的“small gym”。随即，原文又提到“a small swimming pool”（小型游泳池），所以E选项要排除。然后，原文提到“there was a large number of respondents in favor of a travel agent's and insurance center.”（有很多被调查者希望能有旅行社和保险中心），所以F选项入选。其他两个选项，C和G，原文都没有直接提到，属于干扰选项，考生要特别留心。

Question 39

此题考查对较难单词的掌握。原文提到“it is elitist and a waste of funds”（太高档，而且浪费金钱），与选项B意思完全相同。注意，“elitist”一词意为“上等的，高级的，具有高人一等优越感的”。

Question 40

此题同样要注意有两个选项是正确答案。题目问“学生们要求哪两项安全措施？”，所以考生需要特别注意原文中的信号词“security”。原文提到“video surveillance”（录像监控），以及“check Student Union cards on request”（按要求检查学生会证件），这两处与选项A和C意思一样。注意几个单词的意义和读音：“surveillance”意为“监视，监督”，读为[səːˈveiləns]；选项A中“closed-circuit TV”意为“闭路电视”；选项E中“permanent”一词意为“永久的，持久的”，读为[ˈpəːmənənt]。

READING

READING PASSAGE 1

Micro-Enterprise Credit for Street Youth

词汇注释

micro- 表示“小的”，“微小的”
enterprise *n.* 企业单位，事业单位；公司
credit *n.* 信贷，赊欠
youth *n.* [总称]（男女）青年们
bun *n.* 小圆（果子）面包；小圆糕点
decent *adj.* 过得去的，尚可的，还好的
confident *adj.* 有信心的，自信的
participant *n.* 参加者，参与者
initiative *n.* 主动的行动，倡议
opportunity *n.* 机会，时机；就业机会，良机
circumstance *n.* [～s]境遇，境况，经济状况
partner *n.* 伙伴，同伴
purpose *n.* 目的，意图
end up 结束，告终
due to 由于，因为
dearth *n.* 缺乏，不足
adequately *adv.* 足够地
breakdown *n.* 分离，分散，破裂
violence *n.* 暴力（行为），强暴（行为）
adventurous *adj.* 充满危险的，有危险的
exposed *adj.* 易受攻击的，无保护的
exploitative *adj.* 剥削的，榨取的
urban *adj.* 城市的
crime *n.* [总称]犯罪，犯罪活动
abuse *n.* 虐待，凌辱，伤害
labour-intensive *adj.* 劳动密集型的，劳动集约的
shine shoes 擦鞋
informal *adj.* 非正式的，非正规的
trading *n.* 贸易，交易，经商
pride *n.* 自豪，得意 take ～ in 以…自豪；对…感到得意
entrepreneurship *n.* 工商企业家（或主办者）的身份（或地位、职能、能力、活动）
independence *n.* 独立，自主，自立
flexible *adj.* 可变通的，灵活的
participate *v.* (in) 参与，参加
domestic *adj.* 家的，家庭的，家务的
innovative *adj.* 革新的，新颖的，富有革新精神的
courier *n.* （递送急件、外交信件的）信使
Sudan 苏丹[非洲东北部国家]
parcel *n.* 小包，包裹
take up 着手处理，着手进行
Bangalore 班加罗尔[印度南部城市]（卡纳塔克邦首府）
Dominican Republic 多米尼加共和国[拉丁美洲]（在西印度群岛海地岛东部）
purchase *v.* 买，购买，购置
facility *n.* [常作 facilities]设备，设施，工具
individual *adj.* 个人的
Zambia 赞比亚[非洲中南部国家]
joint *adj.* 与他人合作的
access *n.* 享用机会，享用权
emerge from 浮现，出现，出来
entrepreneur *n.* 企业家
ideally *adv.* 为取得最好结果，作为理想的做法
potential *adj.* 潜在的，可能的
essential *adj.* 必不可少的，绝对必要的，非常重要的
relevant *adj.* 有关的
determine *v.* 决定，规定
procedure *n.* 程序，手续，步骤
abide by 遵守（法律、决定等）；信守（诺言等）
enforce *v.* 实施，使生效
critical *adj.* 决定性的，关键性的，重大的；必不可少的
loan *n.* 贷款
tremendous *adj.* 巨大的，极大的
guardian *n.* 监护人
staff *n.* 全体职员，全体雇员
fixed *adj.* 固定的
asset *n.* [～s]资产
kit *n.* 成套工具；用品箱
stall *n.* （商场或集市上的）货摊，摊位
consideration *n.* 考虑
charge *v.* 要（价），收（费）；要（人）支付（钱）；收（税）
primarily *adv.* 首要地，主要地

modest *adj.* 不太大(或多)的,不过分的,适中的,适度的	**highlight** *v.* 使显著,使突出;强调
recognize *v.* 明白,认识到	**poverty** *n.* 贫穷,贫困
impoverished *adj.* 贫困的,赤贫的	**reject** *v.* 拒绝
seek *v.* [后接不定式]试图,设法	**employ** *v.* 雇用
fulfil *v.* 满足,使满意	**storage** *n.* 贮藏,保管
provision *n.* 供应,提供	**slightly** *adv.* 少量地,轻微地
ambition *n.* 雄心,志向,抱负	**aid** *n.* 帮助,援助,救助
quotation *n.* 引文,引语,语录	**ambitious** *adj.* 反映野心(或雄心)的;有野心的,有抱负的
exemplify *v.* 例示,举例证明;是(或作为)…的例证(或榜样、典型等)	**realistic** *adj.* 现实的,实际可行的
outline *v.* 概述,概括	

考题解析

Questions 1–4 Multiple Choice

1. 注意 exemplify 一词足矣。
2. 原文 Introduction 第 2 段首句中... to support the economic lives of street children. 不定式表目的。文章后面描述主要通过 business training 和 loans 的手段。
3. 原文 Background 第 1 段第 2 行中 demand for income at home 对应 poverty。
4. 较难,易误选 A。定位题干中 independent,原文在 66 页第 5 行中:Many children may choose entrepreneurship because it allows them a degree of independence... 要理解 entrepreneurship 一词指企业家,自己当老板。

Questions 5–8 Table

5. 定位词 courier service。原文 Street Business Partnerships 中第 3 行:... first started in the Sudan. 第 5 行中:A similar program was taken up in Bangalore, India.
6. 定位词 courier service。原文 Street Business Partnerships 中第 3 行:... were supplied with bicycles. 下划线对应 provision 一词。
7. 定位词 Dominican Republlic。原文 Street Business Partnerships 中第 6 行。
8. 定位词 Zambia。原文 Street Business Partnerships 中最后一行。

Questions 9–12 Yes/No/Not Given

9. 原文 Lessons learned 部分第 3 行:Being an entrepreneur is not for everyone.
10. 定位 family,原文中几处提到 family,但没有说到 family may need financial support from S. K. I.。而且 S. K. I. 主要是帮助孩子,而非孩子的家庭。
11. 原文 Lessons learned 部分第 14 – 16 行,先给 small loans,再给 increasing loan amounts。
12. 原文 Lessons learned 部分倒数第 3 行说到要 charge interest。

Question 13 Multiple Choice

13. 原文 Lessons learned 部分第 9 行:It is critical for all loans to be linked to training programs... 贷款只是整个项目的一部分。

参考译文

给街头青年小企业的信贷

"我家里穷,人又多,很多年我们都吃不上早饭。自从我加入国际拯救街童组织以后,我就让家人早饭吃上糖和小圆面包了。我还给自己买了相当不错的二手衣服和鞋。"

Doreen Soko

"我们有了做生意的经验。现在我有信心扩大经营。我学会了现金管理和保管资金的方法,所以我们可以存钱投资了。现在,生意是我们生活的一部分。而且,以前我们互相不认识——现在我们已经交了新朋友。"

Fan Kaoma

赞比亚青年技术企业项目的参与者

介绍

虽然小规模的商业培训和信贷项目在全球越来越普遍,但相比之下,需要把这样的机会给予年轻人还没有引起多大的关注。对流落街头或者身处困境的儿童的关心就更少了。

在过去的9年里,国际拯救街童组织一直和非洲、拉美和印度的合伙组织一起合作,给街头儿童提供经济上的支持。这篇文章的目的是和大家分享国际拯救街童组织和我们的合作伙伴取得的一些经验。

背景

一般来说,儿童流落街头的原因不止一个,而是多方面的原因造成的:缺少资金充足的学校、家里需要收入、家庭破裂和暴力。对儿童来说,街头也许很有吸引力,因为在那里可以找到冒险的感觉并能弄到钱。但是街头也缺少或者没有保护,有的孩子面临着打工剥削、城市犯罪和各种虐待。

在街头干活的儿童一般都是做一些不需要技术、劳动力密集、时间要求长的工作,比如说擦鞋、送货、看车、洗车和一些不正规的生意。有的也可能通过乞讨、行窃和其他非法活动挣到钱。与此同时,也有街头儿童因为能够自力更生并且贴补家用而感到自豪,他们往往喜欢自己的工作。很多儿童也许会选择自己当老板,因为这让他们有一定程度的独立性,受剥削的程度比很多其他形式的有偿劳动要低一些,而且有足够的灵活性让他们参加其他活动,比如接受教育和家务劳动。

街头商业伙伴关系

国际拯救街童组织与拉美、非洲和印度的合伙组织合作,为街头儿童开辟全新的赚钱机会。

- 国际拯救街童组织自行车信使服务首先在苏丹展开。这项事业为参与者提供自行车,他们用来送包裹和信件,自行车的钱要逐渐从他们的工资里扣。印度的班加罗尔也开始了类似的项目。
- 另一个成功的项目叫做擦鞋合作社,这是一个和多米尼加共和国的基督教女青年会的合作项目。这个项目借钱给参与者,让他们买擦鞋的箱子。他们还会得到一个安全的存放工具的地方,同时还给提供个人存款计划的设施。
- 赞比亚的青年技术企业项目是和红十字会的一个合作项目,参加基督教女青年会的街头青年可以获得支持做自己的小生意,支持的方式有商业培训、生活技能培训和让他们得到信贷。

取得的经验

下面是国际拯救街童组织与合作组织从合作项目中取得的一些经验:

- 并不是每个人都适合当老板,街头儿童也是如此。理想的情况是,项目的潜在参与者至少在项目里干六个月,这样,信任和相互之间的关系就有可能已经建立起来。
- 成员的参与对相关项目的发展至关重要。一旦儿童在决定程序中起到主要作用,他们就更有可能遵守并实施这些程序。
- 把所有贷款与包括发展基本商业和生活技能在内的培训项目联系起来是非常关键的。

● 如果有家长和监护人，让他们参与到项目中来会带来巨大的好处。家访为工作人员提供了了解情况的机会：参与者住在什么地方，每个人到底情况怎样。

● 小笔贷款开始是用来购买自行车、擦鞋工具箱和市场摊位需要的基本建筑材料之类的固定资产。随着承包者经验越来越丰富，生意可以慢慢扩大，可以考虑增加贷款的金额。国际拯救街童组织提供的贷款数额一般在 30 至 100 美元。

● 所有国际拯救街童组织的项目都对贷款征收利息，主要是为了让承包者习惯为所借的钱支付利息的概念。通常，利率都比较适中（低于银行利率）。

结论

对那些追求满足经济需要的贫困青年来说贷款机会是很重要的，认识到这一点很有必要。为年轻人提供小额贷款，支持他们当老板的梦想和年轻人的抱负，这可能是一种帮助他们改变生活的有效方法。然而，我们认为提供信贷必须和其他支持方法同时进行，不仅帮他们把生意做好，还帮他们获得重要的生活技能。

READING PASSAGE 2

Volcanoes—earth-shattering news

词汇注释

volcanic *adj.* 火山(性)的
eruption *n.* 喷发，爆发
relief *adj.* 救济的，救援的
unpredictability *n.* 不可预测性
shatter *v.* 使心烦意乱，使震惊
volcano *n.* 火山
ultimate *adj.* 无法超越的，最大的，最高的，决定性的
violent *adj.* 猛烈的，剧烈的，强烈的
scatter *v.* 使分散，使散布在各处
ash *n.* [有时作 ~ es] 火山灰
practically *adv.* 几乎，差不多
hurl *v.* 猛投，力掷
fragment *n.* 碎片，破片，碎块
stratosphere *n.*【气】平流层，同温层
cone *n.* 火山锥，锥状地形
bang *n.*（突发的）巨响，爆炸声
surge *n.* 波涛般的汹涌奔腾，浪涛般的轰鸣声 *v.*（浪涛等）汹涌，奔腾
molten *adj.* 熔化的，熔融的；灼热的，炽烈的
lava *n.*【地】熔岩
tiny *adj.* 极小的，微小的
process *n.* 过程，进程
rift *v.* 使开裂，使断裂
chain *n.* 山脉
topography *n.* 地形，地貌，地势
basalt *n.*【地】玄武岩
stable *adj.* 稳定的，牢固的，稳固的
atmosphere *n.*（包围地球的）大气，大气圈，大气层
cubic *adj.* 立方的
crust *n.* 地壳
crater *n.* 火山口
vapour *n.* 蒸气，汽，雾，烟雾
nitrogen *n.* 氮
carbon dioxide *n.* 二氧化碳
sulphur dioxide *n.* 二氧化硫
methane *n.* 甲烷，沼气
ammonia *n.* 氨，阿摩尼亚
hydrogen *n.* 氢
multiply *v.* 使增加，使成倍地增加
semi-molten *adj.* 半熔化的
mantle *n.* 地幔
brittle *adj.* 易碎的，易损坏的
yolk *n.* 蛋黄
squishy *adj.* 湿软的，黏糊糊的
crack *v.* 裂开，破裂 *n.* 裂缝，裂口，缝隙
bubble *v.* 汩汩地流；冒泡，起泡 *n.* 泡，水泡，气泡；泡沫
archipelago *n.* 群岛，列岛
treacle *n.*（尤指炼制蔗糖时产生的）糖浆，糖蜜
convection *n.* 对流；传送，传导，传递

fracture *v.* 使破裂,使断裂	**Giant's Causeway** 巨人岬(北爱尔兰安特里姆郡北海岸的柱状玄武岩岬角,由数千根大多为六角形的岩柱组成)
bump *v.* 碰,撞	**widen** *v.* 加宽,放宽;扩大…的范围,增加…的程度,扩大
grind *v.* 磨	**Atlantic** 大西洋
overlap *v.* 互搭,复叠	**earthquake** *n.* 地震
centimetre *n.* 厘米	**tectonic plate** (地壳)构造板块
zone *n.* 地带,带;层	**dramatic** *adj.* 引人注目的,给人深刻印象的
collision *n.* 碰撞,互撞	**ring of fire** 火环
occur *v.* 发生	**Krakatoa** 喀拉喀托火山[印度尼西亚西南部](即腊卡塔火山;苏门答腊岛同爪哇岛之间的一个活火山岛)
spot *n.* 地点,处所,场所	**Sunda Straits** 巽他海峡(在印度尼西亚的苏门答腊岛和爪哇岛之间)
liquid *n.* 液体,液态	**predictable** *adj.* 可预言的,可预料的,可预计的,可预报的
swiftly *adv.* 迅速地	**slop** *v.* 溢出
vast *adj.* 大量的,极多的	**rim** *n.* (尤指圆形物的)边,缘,边缘
magma *n.* 岩浆	**plug** *n.* 岩颈
inch *v.* 缓慢地移动	**block** *v.* 堵塞,阻塞
show through 显露,暴露	**irresistible** *adj.* 不可抵抗的,不可抗拒的,不能压制的
granite *n.* 花岗岩,花岗石	**survive** *v.* 活下来,幸存
extrusion *n.* 喷出,喷出物(如熔岩)	**fierce** *adj.* 猛烈的,激烈的
dyke *n.* 岩墙,岩脉	**dust** *n.* 灰尘,尘土,尘埃
squeeze *v.* 用力挤压,硬挤,硬塞	**cancel** *v.* 取消,撤销;删去,划掉
toothpaste *n.* 牙膏	**starve** *v.* 挨饿,饿死
horizontally *adv.* 水平地	**frost** *n.* 冰冻(期),严寒天气
plateau *n.* 高原	**potentially** *adv.* 潜在地,可能
slurp *v.* 出声地吃(或喝)	**especially** *adv.* 特别,尤其
boiling *adj.* 极热的,炎热的	**inactive** *adj.* 不活动的,不活跃的,无活力的
froth *v.* 起泡沫	**outcrop** *n.* 露头,出露,露出地表
lip *n.* (洞口、伤口等的)边缘	**emit** *v.* 发出,散出,散发(光、热、电波、声音、液体、气味等)
Mars *n.* 火星	
Jupiter *n.* 木星	
Uranus *n.* 天王星	
vulcanologist *n.* 火山学家	
blast *n.* 爆炸,爆破	
pumice *adj.* 浮石,浮岩	
crystalline *adj.* 结晶的,结晶体组成的	

考题解析

Questions 14–17 List of Headings

14. Section A 中第 5 行:Volcanism, the name given to volcanic processes, really has shaped the world. 第 9 行:Volcanoes have not only made the continents, they are also thought to have made the world's first stable atmosphere . . . 最后一句:We are alive because volcanoes provided the soil, air and water we need. 都在讲火山爆发对地形地貌的影响。
15. Section B 中用煮得半熟的鸡蛋会帮助理解地球内部的运动,最后两句:These fracture zones, where the collisions occur, are where earthquakes happen. And, very often, volcanoes. 总结地震火山的成因。
16. Section C 中第 2 段首句:Sometimes it is slow. . . 第 3 段首句 Sometimes the magma moves very

swiftly indeed. 说明不同的类型,对应 different types。

17. Section D 首句:But volcanoes are not very predictable. 对应 the unpredictability。

Questions 18–21 Short Answer

18. Section C 倒数第 6 行中:... what are called tectonic plates...
19. 定位 molten rock from the mantle,原文 Section C 第 5 行中。
20. 定位 Pacific Ocean,原文 Section C 倒数第 4 行。
21. 定位 Pinatubo,易误填 a decade。原文 Section C 倒数第 3 行,该句说 Pinatubo 在大约 10 年前爆发。题目问的是 Pinatubo 山在爆发前沉寂了多久。正确出处在原文 Section D 第 6 行。

Questions 22–26 Summary

22. 有难度。原文 Section A 第 3 段首句中有三个并列:the continents, atmosphere, the water。22 题本来可以填 the continents 或 the water,但 Summary 首句已经提到 land surface,对应原文中 the continents,所以此处只能填 the water。
23. 有难度。原文 Section C 第 5 行 Sometimes it is slow... 要判断 it 的指代。找到 Section C 第 8 行 sometimes... the magma rose faster... 在找到 Section C 第 3 段首句 Sometimes the magma moves very swiftly indeed. 可以判断 it 指代 magma。
24. 较难。定位词 Northern Ireland, Wales, South Africa 很好找,原文 Section C 第 2 段第 5 行中,但在该句中找不到其他的地名并列了。要注意到下一句话 In the Deccan Plateau in western India... 该句意思承接上句,仍然是 the magma rose faster 的一个例子,只不过该例子更加具有代表性,单独放在后面加深读者印象。
25. 定位 A third type→lava,原文 Section C 中第 3 段第 3 行:... it explodes with tremendous force. 其中 it 指代 the lava;with tremendous force 对应 25 题空格后 violently。
26. 较难。但如注意到 26 题空格后是单词 are,说明 26 题应会在原文处找一个复数名词,该题就简单了。Section C 中的复数名词直接应找到 gases,而且气体才能被 emitted。如果不靠语法知识的帮助,只有把原文相对应的几句话多读几遍理解透彻,请参考译文。

参考译文

火山——震惊地球的新闻

1991 年 6 月 9 日,皮纳图博火山突然爆发,以前和现在爆发的火山产生的威力再一次成了头条新闻。

A 火山是最大的掘土机械。一次猛烈的爆发能把山的最上面几千米掀飞,将细火山灰几乎驱散到整个地球,把碎石块抛到大气的平流层,使一个大陆之外的天空变黑。

但是最典型的喷发——锥形火山、巨大的爆炸声、蘑菇云以及汹涌奔腾的熔岩——从整个地球来讲只是故事的一小部分。火山爆发过程叫火山活动,真的是它把世界造就成了现在这个模样。火山爆发使大陆断裂,使山脉长高,使小岛形成,使地貌定型。整个海底以火山玄武岩为基底。

火山不仅造就了大陆,人们还认为它们造成了世界上最早的稳定大气,所有海洋、河流和冰盖的水都是它们提供的。目前大约有 600 座活火山。每年,它们给大陆增加 2 – 3 立方千米的石头。想像一下相同数量的火山在过去 35 亿年里不停地冒着烟。这些石头足以说明大陆地壳的成因了。从火山口喷出来的大部分是气体。这些气体 90% 以上是来自地球深处的水蒸气,这足以解释经过 35 亿年的时间之后海洋的水。剩下的气体包括氮、二氧化碳、二氧化硫、甲烷、氨和氢。这些气体的量同样在 35 亿年的时间里成倍增加,足以说明世界的大气之多。我们之所以活着,是因为火山提供了我们需要的土壤、空气和水。

B 地质学者认为地球有一个熔化的地核，周围包裹着半熔化的地幔和一层易碎的外壳。想想煮得半熟的鸡蛋会帮助我们理解，蛋黄是溏心的，蛋清虽然结实但又湿又软，蛋壳是硬的。煮蛋过程中蛋壳只要稍稍有一点破裂，白色的东西就会冒着泡鼓出来，像一座小山脉一样堆在裂缝上——就像夏威夷群岛那样的火山群岛。但地球要大得多，下面的地幔也要热很多。

尽管地幔岩石由于上面的压力作用一直保持着固态，它们还是可以像浓稠的糖浆一样慢慢地"流动"。这种流动被认为是一种对流，其威力足以使地壳这个"蛋壳"破裂成板块，并且使它们一直进行相互碰撞和摩擦，甚至以每年几厘米的速度重叠在一起。这些发生碰撞的断裂带是发生地震的地方，而且经常会有火山爆发。

C 这些地区是薄弱地带，或者说是热点。每次爆发都不一样，但用最简单的话来说，只要是薄弱地带，地幔深处的岩石只要热到1350℃就会开始膨胀和上升。在这个过程中，压力下降，体积膨胀，成为液体，而且以更快的速度上升。

有时候速度很慢：巨大的岩浆泡泡——来自地幔的熔化了的岩石——缓慢地向地表移动，逐渐冷却，以花岗岩喷出物的形式显露出来（就像在斯凯岛上，或者 the Great Whin Sill，熔岩岩脉就像牙膏一样往外挤，支撑起位于英格兰北部哈德良长城的一部分）。有时候——像在北爱尔兰、威尔士和南非的卡鲁——岩浆上升得更快，然后水平地流到地表，成为大片厚厚的岩席。在印度西部的德干高原上有超过两百万立方千米的熔岩，有的地方厚达2400米，历经50万年咕咚咕咚地爆发才得以形成。

有时候岩浆移动确实非常迅速。往上涌的时候它没有时间冷却，困在炙热的岩石里面的气体突然膨胀起来，熔岩热得发光，它开始起泡沫，然后就是剧烈的爆炸。接着，后面温度稍微低一点的熔岩开始从火山口边缘流出来。这种情况会在火星上发生，曾经在月球上发生，甚至在木星和天王星的一些卫星上发生。通过研究证据，火山学家可以了解过去的大爆炸的威力。浮石轻吗？是不是布满了小孔？这次爆炸规模巨大。那些巨大的结晶玄武岩、像北爱尔兰的巨人岬那样的石头重吗？那次喷发速度慢、威力小。

最大的火山喷发在海底中部最深的地方，新的熔岩猛地把大陆分开，每年大约使大西洋宽5厘米。看一看火山、地震以及像菲律宾和日本这样的群岛地图，你就可以看到所谓的构造板块的大致轮廓——那些形成地壳和地幔的板块。最引人注目的是太平洋"火环"，那里发生过最猛烈的爆发——马尼拉附近的皮纳图博火山、落基山脉的圣海伦斯火山和大约10年前的墨西哥的埃尔奇琼火山，像1883年在巽他海峡喀拉喀托火山那样的震惊世界的爆发就更别提了。

D 但是火山爆发不是很容易预测，那是因为地质时期不像人类的时间。在平静时期，火山用从火山口边缘溢出的熔化了的岩石形成强大的火山锥把自己罩起来；后来熔岩逐渐冷却，变成一个巨大的、坚硬的、稳定的塞子，不让火山继续喷发，直到里面的压力变得无法抗拒。就皮纳图博火山的情况来说，这个过程花了600年的时间。

有时候，只有一点点预兆，火山就把山顶炸开了。1902年5月8日早晨7点49分，马提尼克岛上的培雷火山就是这样爆发的，一个2.8万人口的小镇只有2人幸存。1815年，印度尼西亚的坦博拉火山突然爆发，把1280米的山顶都掀掉了。这次爆发如此猛烈，被抛到平流层的灰尘使天空一片黑暗，欧洲和北美洲那年都没有了夏季。由于六月下雪、八月霜冻，庄稼歉收，成千上万的人忍饥挨饿。火山很可能成为世界新闻，尤其是那些平静的火山。

READING PASSAGE 3

Obtaining Linguistic Data

词汇注释

linguistic *adj.* 语言的，语言学的
procedure *n.* 传统的做法；程序，手续，步骤
available *adj.* 可利用的
intensive *adj.* 集中的，密集的，深入细致的，透彻的
investigation *n.* （官方）调查，调查研究
casual *adj.* 不是安排好的；无计划的，无条理的，未经考虑的；随便的，漫不经心的
introspection *n.* 内省，自省，反省
tongue *n.* 语言，方言，土语
armchair *n.* 扶手椅
informant *n.* （为语言学调查）提供资料的讲本地话（或本国话）的人
native *adj.* 土生土长的，本地（或本国）出生的
utterance *n.* 言辞，言语，言论
analysis *n.* 分析
correctness *n.* 正确性
usage *n.* 使用，用法；【语】惯用法，习语，成语
linguist *n.* 语言学家
ambiguity *n.* 含糊不清，不明确，歧义，模棱两可，可作多种解释
acceptability *n.* 可接受性
property *n.* 特性，性质，性能，属性
intuition *n.* 直觉，直觉力，直觉行为；敏锐的洞察力
convenience *n.* 方便，合宜
approach *n.* （处理问题的）方式，方法；态度
norm *n.* 标准，规范
generative *adj.*【语】生成的
linguistics *n.* ［用作单］语言学
recourse *n.* 依靠，依赖，求助
unavoidable *adj.* 不可避免的
interact *v.* 互相作用，互相影响
identity *n.* 身份；个性，特性
influence *v.* 影响，对…起作用，左右，支配
conversation *n.* 谈话，会话，交谈
characteristic *n.* 特性，特征，特点，特色
social setting 社会环境
formality *n.* 正式（性质）
relevant *adj.* 有重大关系的，有意义的
consistency *n.* 一致，连贯
scrupulous *adj.* 细致的，一丝不苟的，严肃认真的
investigative *adj.* （官方）调查的，调查研究的
technique *n.* 手段，方法
tape-record *v.* 用磁带录（音或像）
enable *v.* 使能够，使可能，使可行，使实现
naturalistic *adj.* 自然的，模仿自然的
abnormally *adv.* 反常地
minimise *v.* 使减少（或缩小）到最低限度
paradox *n.* 自相矛盾的荒谬说法，似是而非的矛盾说法
ethical *adj.* 道德的，合乎道德的
anticipate *v.* 预期，期望，预料
alternatively *adv.* 或，非此即彼，如其不然
attempt *n.* 企图，尝试，努力
out of sight 在视程以外，在看不见的地方
stimulate *v.* 刺激，激励；促使，引起
locality *n.* 地区
audio *adj.* 音频的，声频的
ambiguous *adj.* 含糊不清的，不明确的，难以理解（或区分）的；引起歧义的，模棱两可的，可作多种解释的
supplement *v.* 增补，补充
participant *n.* 参加者，参与者
facial *adj.* 面部的
expression *n.* 表情
dramatically *adv.* 戏剧性地；引人注目地，显著地
alter *v.* 改变，更改，使变样
limitation *n.* 局限，限制因素，缺陷，弱点
transcription *n.* （录音资料的）文字本
benefit *v.* 得益，得到好处
commentary *n.* 评论
session *n.* （从事某项活动的）集会（或一段时间）
systematically *adv.* 系统地，有条理地
bilingual *adj.* 熟谙两种语言的，能说两种语言的
interpreter *n.* 译员，口译者
worksheet *n.* （记录初步考虑的问题、想法等的）备忘单；（学生做的）活页练习题
questionnaire *n.* （通常用于收集信息或意见的）一组问题，问题单，调查表
variable *n.* 易变的事物，可变性，可变因素
pronunciation *n.* 发音，发音法，读法

elicit *v.* 引起，使发出	**depend on** 视…而定，决定（于）
elicitation *n.* 引出，诱出，启发	**hypothesis** *n.* 假说，假设，前提
substitution *n.* 代替，代用，替换	**by contrast** 对比之下
frame *n.* 结构	**principle** *n.* 原则，主义，原理
stimulus *n.* 刺激（物），激励（物），促进（因素）	**inevitably** *adv.* 不可避免地，必然（发生）地
representative *adj.* 有代表性的，典型的	**coverage** *n.* 覆盖，总括，覆盖范围
compile *v.* 编辑，编纂	**derive from** 起源，衍生
corpus *n.* 语料库	**experimentation** *n.* 实验，试验
unbiased *adj.* 不偏袒一方的，无偏见的，公正的	**self-conscious** *adj.*（在他人面前）不自然的，忸怩的，怕难为情的
frequency *n.* 重复发生率	**convenient** *adj.* 省力的，方便的
accessible *adj.* 可（或易）使用的，可（或易）得到的	**rely on** 依靠，依赖
corpora corpus 的复数	
extract *n.* 摘录，选段，引文	

考题解析

Questions 27–31 Matching

27. 定位词 recording。D 段第 7 行：People talk abnormally when they know they are being recorded, and sound quality can be poor.
28. 定位词 notes, body language。E 段第 4 行：the recording has to be supplemented by the observer's written comments on the non-verbal behaviour... 其中 written comments 对应 notes；non-verbal behaviour 对应 body language。
29. 定位词 social situation, influenced。C 段第 10 行：The topic of conversation and the characteristics of the social setting are also highly relevant... 其中 highly relevant 对应 influenced。
30. 定位词 less self-conscious。D 段倒数第 1、2 句。
31. 较难。定位词 various methods。F 段中 structured sessions, translation techniques, a restricted set of questions 等，都是各种得到数据的方法。

Questions 32–36 Table

32. 定位词 convenient。原文 B 段 12 行 The convenience of this approach... 再往回看看 this approach 是指哪种方法，找到前面有 linguists act as their own informants 的表达。
33. 定位词 child speech。B 段末尾。
34. 定位词 recording→sound。原文 D 段第 9 行：... sound quality can be poor.
35. 较难。定位词 videoing。原文 E 段倒数第 5 行：Video recordings avoid these problems... 往前找 these problems 是哪些？E 段第 3 句说：如果只录音，就需要笔录下参加者的 non-verbal behaviour。第 4 句又说：录音同样没有办法记录 facial expression。意思是用 video 就没有这些问题。
36. 较难。原文 E 段最后一句：... but even they have limitations... 其中 they 指代 video recordings。

Questions 37–40 Summary

* 注意到题目描述：Complete the summary of paragraph G below.

37. 定位 comment objectively on。原文 G 段第 4 行：... unbiased statements about frequency of usage... 其中 unbiased statements 对应 comment objectively。
38. 定位 focus on。原文 G 段第 11 行：... deals only with a particular linguistic feature. 其中 deals only with 对应 focus on。
39. 定位 time, affect。原文第 12 行：The size of the corpus depends on... 原文和题干中通过使用不

同的因果关系表达（affect 和 depends on）使主语和宾语位置调换。

40. 定位 be gained from。原文倒数第3行：derived from the intuitions of native speakers... 其中 native speakers 对应题干中 those who speak the language concerned.

参考译文

获得语言资料

A 要获得一门语言的资料有很多种途径，从去国外进行计划缜密、深入细致的实地考查到坐在家中的扶手椅里对自己的母语做漫不经心的反思。

B 在所有的情况下，都需要有人充当语言资料的来源——即一个为语言学调查提供资料的讲本地话的人。提供资料的讲本地话的人（最理想的）是土生土长的讲这种语言的人，他们能为分析提供言语资料，还能提供有关这种语言的其他信息（例如，翻译、对正确性的评价或者是对用法的看法）。通常，在研究自己的母语时，语言学家会充当自己的提供资料的讲本地话的人，根据自己的直觉判断言语的多种解释、可接受性或其他属性。这种方法方便易行，因此被广泛使用，并被认为是语言学生成法的标准。但是一位语言学家的个人判断通常是捉摸不定的，或者与其他语言学家的意见相冲突，这个时候就需要用更加客观的方法进行研究，用非语言学家来充当提供资料的讲本地话的人。后面这种做法在研究外语或儿童说话时是不可避免的。

C 选择提供资料的讲本地话的人时必须考虑很多因素——研究对象是否是单个说话人（语言没有得到研究之前情况往往如此）、两个相互交谈的人、一组人还是一大批一大批的人。年龄、性别、社会背景和其他方面的特性都很重要，因为众所周知这些因素会影响使用的那种语言。谈话的话题和社会环境的特征（例如正式的程度）也有很大关系，就像提供资料的讲本地话的人的个人品质那样重要（例如流利程度和连贯性）。对于更大型的研究来说，使用的取样理论得到了极大重视，而且，在所有情况下，必须就使用哪种研究方法最好作出决定。

D 如今，研究者经常用磁带给提供资料的讲本地话的人录音。这就使语言学家关于语言的主张能够经受检验，并且提供使这些声明更加准确的办法（"难懂的"片断可以反复听）。但是获取自然、高质量的资料决非易事。知道自己的话被录音，人们说话时就不正常，声音质量也可能很差。为此人们设计了各种各样用磁带录音的方法，尽量减少"观察者的矛盾"（如何在人们不被观察的情况下观察他们的行为方式）。有的录音制作的时候说话人并不知情——这种做法获取的资料很自然，但必须预料到从道德上会遭到反对。还有一种选择方案，那就是可以想办法努力让说话人忘记录音的事，比如把录音机放在看不见的地方，或者使用无线麦克风。一种有用的方法是，提出一个很快让说话人参与进来的话题，激发出自然的语言表达（例如问年纪大一点的人他们家乡的日子是怎样改变的）。

E 然而，一盘录音磁带不能解决语言学家的所有问题。录到的话经常含糊不清、模棱两可。因此，只要有可能，观察者必须对录音进行文字补充，对参与者的非言语行为和当时总的环境做些点评。例如，面部表情可能会彻底改变话的意思。录像在很大程度上避免了这些问题，但就连它们也有局限（摄像机不能面面俱到），观察者提供的附注对文字材料总是有帮助的。

F 语言学家也充分利用安排好的见面活动，他们有计划有步骤地让提供资料的讲本地话的人说一些话描述某些动作、物体或者行为。如果研究对象能说两种语言，或者借助口译，翻译也是一种切实可行的办法（"桌子在你们的语言里怎么说？"）。使用会谈备忘单和调查表可以在很短时间涉及很多问题。通常，研究者只希望获得一个可变因素方面的信息，这样的话就可以用一组有限的问题：例如，可以通过让提供资料的讲本地话的人说一组规定的词，得出某个发音特点。直接推导法也有很多种：比如让提供资料的讲本地话的人在替换结构中填空（例如：*I see a car*），或者为他们提供错误的答案让他们改正（"可以说 *I no can see* 吗？"）。

G 一个为语言分析编写的具有代表性的语言样本就是所谓的语料库。语料库使语言学家能够对使用频率提出公正的说法,并且为不同研究者的使用提供可获得的资料。语料库的范围和大小各不相同,有的语料库试图把语言作为一个整体,从许多种文本中做一些摘录;其他的则进行了严格挑选,提供的资料只涉及某个语言学特征。语料库的大小取决于很多实际因素,比如可用来收集、处理和储存资料的时间:为几分钟的谈话提供一份准确的文本可能会花长达几个小时的时间。有时候一个小的资料样本就足以决定一个语言学的假设;相比之下,大的研究项目中的语料库包含的单词数量可达到数百万个。一个重要的原则是,所有的语料库,无论大小,其覆盖范围必然都是有限的,总是需要补充一些资料,这些资料来自土生土长说这种语言的人的直觉,获取途径要么通过内省,要么通过实验。

WRITING

WRITING TASK 1

这是考官准备的一篇优秀范文(原文在《剑桥雅思 4》第 166 页),请注意答案可以千变万化,下面只是其中之一。

此图表提供了 1999 年澳大利亚男性和女性在毕业后的继续教育方面获得不同层次文凭的信息。

首先我们可以看到,男性和女性获得不同文凭的比例存在巨大的差异。最大的性别差异存在于继续教育的最低层次,其中 90% 获得职业技术文凭的是男性,相比之下女性只占 10%。相反,获得本科文凭的女性(70%)要多于男性,而且获得其学位的女性也稍多于男性(55%)。

在较高水平的教育阶段,获得硕士文凭的男性明显多于相应的女性(分别为 70% 和 30%),而且硕士研究生中 60% 是男性。

因此我们可以看到,无论在较低还是在较高的教育层次上,获得文凭的男性都要比女性多;但是获得本科文凭的女性要多于男性。然而,在学士学位层次上性别差异是最小的。

WRITING TASK 2

This model has been prepared by an examiner as an example of a very good answer.

I believe that there are pros and cons to this statement but in general I would have to agree. Creativity is not something that anyone has the right to control except the artist, writer, producer or composer.

Take for example the impressionist movement that started in the late 19th century. When artists such as Monet, Van Gogh, and Renior first exhibited at the Louvre, there were riots in the streets of Paris. This was exactly what the movement needed. It was controversial and forced people to look at art in a different light.

More recently, according to Xinhua News agency, the German Gunther von Hagen developed a process called plastination, which preserves human bodies indefinitely. He held a show in Berlin and was met with cries of, "Is that art?" and "Is that moral?" His art consists of plastisized skinned human bodies in various poses. I believe that he has drawn attention to anatomy in a very unique way and that while some may not consider it art, he has the right to express his creativity in any way he wishes. All his pieces are crafted from bodies he has received permission to use. Certainly it is odd and controversial, but it sure makes you think. Curiosity is an odd thing.

There have been hundreds of books, films, art and music that have caused passionate anger, fear and a multitude of other emotions and reactions, but this I believe is what they were meant to do.

Finally, people like to be challenged and forced to face their fears and I think that all these media help to nurture creativity through the attention they spark in others. Art is not a passive activity. It requires the viewer to participate in some way or another and the government has no business in defining what artists may or may not do.

(309 words)

参考译文

我认为这种说法有利有弊,但总的来说我得表示同意。创造力不是任何人有权控制的,除了艺术家、作家、制片人或作曲家。

以19世纪晚期开始的印象派运动为例。当莫奈、凡·高和雷诺阿这样的艺术家开始在卢浮宫举办展览的时候,巴黎街头出现了骚乱。这正是印象派运动所需要的。由于颇受争议,这就迫使人们用不同的眼光看待艺术。

晚些时候,据新华社报道,德国的Gunther von Hagen发明了一种叫做塑化的方法,这种方法可以无限期地保存尸体。他在柏林举办了展览,招来一片声音:"那是艺术吗?""那样做道德吗?"他的艺术由姿态各异的剥皮塑化尸体组成。我认为他用一种独一无二的方法把注意力吸引到了解剖学上,虽然有人认为这不是艺术,他仍有权用他希望的任何方式表现自己的创造力。他的所有作品都是用获准使用的尸体精心制作的。这样做无疑有些古怪而且颇受争议,但它肯定会引发你思考。好奇心是个奇怪的东西。

有成百上千的书、电影、艺术品和音乐引起了强烈的愤怒、恐惧和很多其他情感和反应,但我相信这正是它们的用意。

最后,人们喜欢接受挑战,喜欢被迫面对恐惧,我认为所有这些媒介都是通过激起别人的注意力帮助培养创造力。艺术不是被动的活动,它要求观众以某种方式参与其中,艺术家可以做什么、不可以做什么根本就不关政府的事。

SPEAKING

Band 9 Speaking Test Scripts

E: = Examiner　　C: = Candidate

PART 1

E: Do you have any hobbies or interests? (What are they?)

C: Yes, I like collecting memorabilia from the Mao era. You know, like money, food stamps, pictures, books and a few other things. I think that in the future they could be worth something. I also like exercising when I have the opportunity.

E: How did you become interested in the Mao memorabilia?

C: Well, it's part of our history and I find the history behind it very interesting. I just like to be able to put things and events together. It makes the history more vivid and real.

E: How do you usually spend your holidays?

C: Holidays here are usually spent with family. I personally would prefer to travel around China and then outside of China, but I'll have to wait until I can afford it. Also, my grandparents are getting old and probably won't be around too much longer, so while they're still here I'll visit them.

E: Is there anywhere you would particularly like to visit? (Why?)

C: I have always wanted to go to the Ice Hotel in Sweden. Ever since I saw a National Geographic program on it, I have had this passion to visit the place just to see what it's like. I think it would be really cool.

PART 2

E: Describe a river, lake or sea which you like.

C: I'd like to talk about the Yangtze or Chang Jiang river, the longest river in China and Asia. It's about 5, 550 Kilometres long and starts in the Tibetan highlands, in southwest Qinghai province and flows through central China into the East China Sea at Shanghai. It's a major trade and transportation route. At the Sichuan basin it meets up with the Wu River and flows through the Chang Gorges where it's almost impossible to navigate, except for the locals. There are temples and pagodas perched on the hills along the gorge. In 1994 construction began farther upriver on the Three Gorges Dam, 50 km west of Yichang; the dam is scheduled to be completed in 2009. It will be the world's largest concrete structure and largest hydroelectric station filling a reservoir that will hold as much water as Lake Superior in Canada and the USA. I like the river because it is so large and majestic. To tell you the truth, I've never been there, but a dream of mine is to take a cruise along the Yangtze! I have a friend who took such a cruise, and he said it was one of the most incredible experiences of his life.

PART 3

E: What do people enjoy doing when they visit rivers, lakes or the sea? Why do you think these activities are popular with people?

C: I think that most people enjoy fishing, swimming, sailing or just sitting around and taking in the scenery because all these activities are relaxing in one way or another. I personally think that most people just like to get away from the noise and pollution of big cities.

E: What benefits do you think people get from the activities they enjoy in water?

C: As I said before, I think that the biggest advantage they get from these activities is relief from the noise, pollution and stress of living in mega cities.

E: What are the different advantages of going to the sea or to a swimming pool to enjoy yourself? What do you think the disadvantages are?

C: Well, the obvious advantages of the sea over a swimming pool again would be the congestion of the pool over the relative peace and quiet at the sea. You also have to contend with the chemicals and other nasty fluids in pools whereas the ocean is for the most part natural and beneficial for your health and to be quite honest I don't see any disadvantages in going to the sea other than the time it takes to get there.

E: How does water transport, like boats and ships, compare with other kinds? Are there any advantages/disadvantages of water transport?

C: Water transport is obviously going to be slower than say truck, train or airplane, but on the other hand is quite a cheap way of shipping goods. The majority of exports from China for example go by ship to save on costs. However, when you consider the number of goods that come from remote parts of China via water to Shanghai and other ports, barges and small ships also play an important economic role in domestic trade.

E: How important is it for a town or city to be located near a river or the sea? Why?

C: That would depend on whether or not the town or city was producing large quantities of goods that were to be transported elsewhere. Many of the towns and villages in China haven't reached that point of development yet. There are many cities, though, such as Shanghai, that clearly benefit from being near a river or the sea.

E: Have there been any changes in the number of jobs available in fishing and water transport industries, do you think? Why do you think this?

C: Yes, over the past 10 years the development of industry in China of both raw materials and finished products has risen exponentially and has necessitated a need for larger ports thereby creating more jobs of dockworkers and logistic companies. As for fishing, I don't know much about that industry but I would assume that there has also become a need for more seafood given the rise in popularity of tourism and foreign enterprises here now.

Test 4

LISTENING

SECTION 1

谈话场景:筹备告别会场景。
人物关系:关系亲密的同事。
谈话话题:讨论将给要离开的同事开告别会的有关事宜:时间、地点、邀请人员、礼物等。

词汇注释

venue *n.* (行动、事件等的)发生地点,举行场所
envelope *n.* 信封
handy *adj.* 便利的,方便的,近便的
plenty *adj.* 很多的,足够的
snack *n.* 快餐,点心,小吃
tape deck 磁带放送机

考题解析

Question 1

观察所给表格,可以预知对话内容是关于 John 的告别晚会的筹备问题。对话所涉及的内容将包括:举办告别会的地点、邀请人员、送邀请信的日期、大伙凑份子的数目、收份子钱的时间、考虑买什么礼物、请客人带的东西,以及请学生代表准备发言。并且,考生还应该注意到,关于"邀请"的问题主要是要听清楚 Tony 所说的话,而关于"礼物"的问题主要是听清楚 Lisa 所说的话。听题前先仔细观察已知信息,对对话内容进行大致猜测,考生能够更好地把握对话内容,从而更好地解题。此题题干中给出的单词是考查重点,该词"venue"一词意为"会议地点,集合地点",读为[ˈvenju]。考生需注意此题所填每个单词的首字母都要大写。

Question 2

此题较为简单,所听即所得。注意"staff"一词的意思为"全体职员",读为[stɑːf]。

Question 3

此题需注意"students"一词应该用复数形式。

Question 4

此题需注意不能只写日子"Tenth",要把月份和日期都写上才算对。其实要抓住月份很简单,表格前面的例子里就已经表明告别会是在"22nd December",所以此处的送邀请信的日期也应该为"December"。另外,考生还要注意月份的首字母是需要大写的。

Question 5

此题所填"coffee break"意为"休息时间,喝咖啡时间"。

Question 6

此题相当简单,填阿拉伯数字和英文单词都可以。

Question 7

此题也不难,问的是需要去查价格的礼物包括哪些。考生要注意题目要求每空所填单词不得超过三

个，所以不能按原文所说"a set of dictionaries"来填，可填"dictionaries / set of dictionaries"。

Question 8

此题需紧紧抓住说话者说话的线索。原文提到"Well, some music, because there'll be a tape deck there in the room, and we can have some dancing later on."（还有一些音乐磁带，因为房间里有音乐播放器，我们可以在稍后跳舞。），所以此题可填"some music / some music tapes / some tapes"。

Question 9

此题较为简单，注意需填复数单词。另外，"photos"和"photographs"都可以。

Question 10

此题非常容易，所听即所得。

SECTION 2

谈话场景：旅行社咨询热线的电话录音。

人物关系：说话者为电话录音者，听众为对该旅行社旅行线路感兴趣的顾客。

谈话话题：介绍旅行线路、服务质量，以及费用问题。

词汇注释

complaint *n.* 抱怨，诉苦	**cater** *v.* 满足需要，投合，迎合
discerning *adj.* 有识别力的，有眼力的，聪明的，精明的	**fitness** *n.* 健康
pride *n.* 自豪，得意	**communal** *adj.* 集体公用（或参加）的，公共的，共同的
guidance *n.* 引导，指导	**quiz** *n.* 智力竞赛，答问比赛
guarantee *v.* 保证，担保	**inclusive** *adj.* 包括一应费用在内的，一切项目包括在内的

考题解析

Question 11

题干中提到"to find out how much holidays cost, you should press button..."（要想知道每趟假日旅行线路的价格，请按...），所以当对话开头提到"旅行线路价格"之类的线索词的时候，考生应该特别注意。原文中提到"if you want to hear our latest price lists, please press two"（如果你想知道最新的旅游线路报价，请按2），所以此题选B。

Question 12

原文提到"We offer guided walking tours to suit the discerning travller in twelve different centres throughout the whole of Western Europe."（我们提供有导游的旅游线路，以适应整个西欧12个不同地区的旅行者），所以此题选A。

Question 13

原文提到"catering for all skills and fitness levels"（适应所有不同技术不同适应能力的人），其实就是选项A的另一种表达法。注意短语"cater for"意思是"迎合，适应"。

Question 14

原文提到"we guarantee that no single client will pay more"（我们保证所有单独的顾客都不会另外缴费），所以此题应该选A。注意"client"一词的意思和读音，意为"顾客，客户"，读为[ˈklaiənt]。

Question 15

原文提到“entertainment is laid on nearly every night”(几乎每个晚上都有娱乐活动),此处的“be laid on” 就相当于此题题干中的“be provided”,考生在听题的时候要抓住线索词“entertainment”。另外,考生还要注意不能选择 C,因为原文提到的是“几乎每个晚上”,而不是“每个晚上”,此处是出题人设计的一个干扰选项。

Question 16

观察所给表格,可知对话内容是关于不同时间长度的旅游线路的花费问题。有三种时间长度的旅游线路可供选择:3 天、7 天和 14 天。考生要填的是不同线路的每个人的费用,以及价格内所包括的特殊服务。此题很简单,考查数字的听写。注意由于题目要求每空所填单词不能超过三个,所以最好写阿拉伯数字。

Question 17

此题考查最高级的拼写。注意“nearest”一词的拼写。

Question 18

此题同样是所听即所得,注意“local”一词的意思和读音,意为“当地的,地方的”,读为[ˈləukəl]。

Question 19

此题还是考查数字的听写,同样要写阿拉伯数字以满足题目要求。

Question 20

此题在听题时抓住线索词“membership”较为重要。注意“walking”一词要用动名词形式。

SECTION 3

谈话场景:作业场景。
人物关系:同学之间。
谈话话题:讨论作业如何完成,如何设计实验,以及如何找参考资料。

词汇注释

primary school 小学,初等学校
hovercraft *n.* 气垫飞行器,气垫船
ambitious *adj.* 有野心的,由强烈欲望的,有抱负的
paperclip *n.* 回形针
copper sulphate 硫酸铜
dissolve *v.* 使溶解
crystal *n.* 结晶,结晶体
spinning *adj.* 旋转的
segment *n.* 部分,片,断片,切片
string *n.* 线,细绳
merge *v.* 合为一体,融合
principle *n.* 原理
elementary *adj.* 基础的,初级的
physics *n.* 物理,物理学
hand drill 手钻
bolt *n.* 螺栓;插销,闩
amplifier *n.* 放大器,扩音机,扬声器,喇叭
suitable *adj.* 合适的,适宜的,适当的
risky *adj.* 危险的,有风险的
tame *adj.* 不危险的,安全无害的
fortnight *n.* 十四天,两星期
babyish *adj.* 婴儿般的,孩子气的,幼稚的

考题解析

Question 21

观察已知图表,可知21–26题要求分别填5个实验的有关信息:实验装备和实验目的。考生在听题时按图索骥即可。此题不难,注意"balloons"一词要用复数表示。

Question 22

原文提到"it's supposed to demonstrate the importance of having fixed units of measurement."(这个实验是用来证明特定度量衡单位的重要性),所以此题可以按原文填为"units of measurement"。

Question 23

此题较为简单,原文即提到了"rock salt"(石盐,岩盐),所听即所得。另外,原文提到的"copper sulphate"意为"硫酸铜"。

Question 24

原文提到"so it basically teaches the kids about growing crystals"(所以这主要是要告诉孩子们有关晶体的增大的知识),所以此空填"crystals",并且要用复数。注意"crystals"一词的意思和读音,意为"晶体,结晶",读为[ˈkristəl]。

Question 25

此题前面给出信息里已经包括了两个必要的装备:"cardboard, coloured pens",所以考生在听到这两个词语时要特别注意,这两个词语后面的文字里必然会提到要填的信息。"a piece of string"意为"一根线"。

Question 26

此题虽然不难,但是考生要注意题目要求每空所填单词不超过三个,所以如果按照原文一字不落写下来"white light or ordinary light"(白光或者普通光)是不能得分的。考生可以填"white light"或者"ordinary light"。

Question 27

27–30题要求把方框内的每个实验的所存在的问题都对号入座,所以考生可以先观察方框内的选项,然后一边听一边在相应选项旁边做记号。选项A—H的意思依次分别为:太乱,太乏味,太难,太多设备,太长,太容易,太嘈杂,太危险。此题考查同义替换,原文提到"a bit risky"实际上就相当于选项H中提到的"too dangerous"。

Question 28

此题是出题人精心设计的。原文提到"I think it needs to be something a bit more active and interesting than that"(我认为应该比这更加活泼有趣),所以实际上这是说话者在抱怨这个实验不够活泼有趣,那也就是说太乏味,所以选B。考生在做题时一定不能断章取义,要全面考虑。

Question 29

此题考查对原文的精确把握。原文提到"we had to wait up to a fortnight"(我们必须等两个星期),所以实际意思是"等待时间太长",选E。注意,"fortnight"一词意为"两星期",读为[ˈfɔːtnait]。

Question 30

此题考查对原文隐含意思的理解。原文提到"don't you think it's a bit ambitious for this age group?"(你不认为这个实验对这个年龄段的人来说太野心勃勃了一点?),也就是说,对于这个年龄段的人来说这个实验有点难度,所以选C。注意"ambitious"一词,意为"有雄心的,野心勃勃的",读为[æmˈbiʃəs]。

SECTION 4

谈话场景：学术报告场景。

人物关系：主讲人为海洋动物专家。

谈话话题：介绍澳大利亚鲨鱼的有关信息，其长度、重量、觅食习惯等，以及澳大利亚政府为防止鲨鱼攻击人类所采取的措施。

词汇注释

shark *n.* 鲨鱼	**scavenge** *v.* 搜寻食物
breed *n.* 种，属	**prey** *n.* 被捕食的动物，捕获物
skeleton *n.* 骨骼	**acute** *adj.* 敏锐的
elastic *adj.* 有弹性的，有弹力的	**mesh** *v.* 用网捕捉
cartilage *n.* 软骨	**parallel** *adj.* 平行的
pliable *adj.* 易弯的，柔韧的	**metropolitan** *adj.* 大城市的，大都会的，属大城市的
scale *n.* 鳞片，鳞	**systematic** *adj.* 有系统的；有计划有步骤的
barb *n.* 倒钩	**authorities** *n.* 当局，官方
texture *n.*（皮肤的）肌理	**uneconomical** *adj.* 不经济的，浪费的，代价高的
sandpaper *n.* 砂纸	**rolling** *adj.* 起伏的，翻腾的，滚滚的
fin *n.* 鳍，鱼翅，鳍状物	**current** *n.* 潮流，流速

考题解析

Question 31

观察所给表格，可以预测到文章将会涉及到澳大利亚的鲨鱼的情况，要求填的是关于重量、水中游泳的方式，以及觅食习惯。所以考生听到类似的信息时要格外注意。此题考查数字的听写，考生写阿拉伯数字就可。

Question 32

原文提到"this is made possible by their fins, one set at the side and another set underneath the body, and the tail also helps the shark move forward quickly"（鲨鱼的鳍，一个在侧面，另一个在底部，使之成为可能；同时，鲨鱼的尾巴也能帮助鲨鱼更加快速地移动），所以此题填"tail" 就可以了。

Question 33

原文提到"mostly, they swim at the bottom of the ocean, scavenging and picking up food that's lying on the ocean floor. "（通常，它们在海底游弋，以躺在海底的腐烂食物为食），所以此题填"floor / bottom / bed" 均可。

Question 34

原文提到"they have a very acute sense of smell"（它们有着非常敏锐的嗅觉），所以此题填"sense of smell" 就可以了。

Question 35

首先注意此题题干中提到的"meshing" 一词的意思是"用网捕捉，落网"。原文提到"meshing involves setting large nets parallel to the shore"（用网捕捉包括在沿海岸线铺设大规模的鱼网），所以此题选 A。

Question 36

原文提到"The New Zealand authorities also looked at it, but considered meshing uneconomical—as did Tahiti in the Pacific. At around the same time, South Africa introduced meshing to some of its most popular swimming beaches."(新西兰政府也考察过,但是认为这种方法经济上不划算——太平洋上的塔希提岛也持同样观点。同时,南非把这种方法应用到了其游人最多,最受欢迎的一些海滩上。)所以,此题应该排除选项 B 和 C,要选择。

Question 37

此题较为简单,考查数字的听写。考生需注意区别"fifteen"和"fifty"两词在读音上的不同。

Question 38

原文提到"the majority of sharks are caught during the warmest months, form November to February"(大多数的鲨鱼都是在最温暖的月份被抓住的,从 11 月到 2 月),考生应该注意到南半球澳大利亚的夏天正是北半球的冬天,所以此题应该选 B。此题也是出题人故意设计的考点。

Questions 39–40

这个两个题要求考生挑出使"shark nets"减少作用的选项。原文提到"But meshing does appear to be less effective than some other methods, especially when there are big seas with high rolling waves and strong currents and anything that lets the sand move"(但是在某种程度上,比起其他方法来说,用网捕捉这个方法的效果并不那么明显,尤其是当有大浪和强流的时候,以及沙流动比较厉害的时候),所以应该选 B 和 E。

READING

READING PASSAGE 1

How much higher? How much faster?

词汇注释

limit *n.* 限度,极限,限制
performance *n.* 表现;成绩
in sight 看得见,被见到;在望,在即,临近
athletic *adj.* 运动的,体育的;运动员的,体育家的
steady *adj.* 稳定的,固定的;持续的,有规律的
improvement *n.* 改进,改善;增进,增值
athlete *n.* 运动员,体育家;<英>田径运动员
hurl *v.* 猛投,力掷
massive *adj.* 大而重的,大块的,厚实的
brief *adj.* 短暂的,短时间的
release *n.* 放出,排放,发放,释出,使逸出
sprint *n.* 短(距离赛)跑
endurance *n.* 持久(力),耐久(性)
dramatic *adj.* 引人注目的,给人深刻印象的,突然的
marathon *n.* 马拉松赛跑(全长 42.195 公里)
genetics *n.* (有机体的)遗传性,遗传现象
invoke *v.* 援引,(作为根据)提出
oft-cited *adj.* 常引用的
adage *n.* 谚语,格言
composition *n.* 组成,构成,成分,成分的性质
gene *n.* 基因
pool *n.* 【生化】库
appreciably *adv.* 相当可观地
participation *n.* 参与,参加
tempt *v.* 吸引,引起…的兴趣,使很想要(做)
complement *n.* 补充,补足物,互为补充的东西,配对物
sprinter *n.* 短跑选手,短跑运动员

talent *n.* 天才,天资,才干
emeritus *adj.* 荣誉退职的,退休后保留头衔的
impressive *adj.* 给人以深刻印象的,感人的,激动人心的,令人钦佩的
duplicate *v.* 重复,比得上
plyometrics *n.* 增强式训练
pioneer *v.* 当先驱,当先锋,开路
expend *v.* 用光,耗尽
devoted *adj.* (to)专用于…的
interval *n.* (时间、空间上的)间隔,间距,间隙,空隙
nutrition *n.* 营养,滋养
supplement *n.* 补给品
nutritional *adj.* 营养的,滋养的
coach *n.* (体育队的)教练,领队
deficiency *n.* 缺乏,缺少,不足
trace *adj.* 微量的
mineral *n.* 无机物
injury *n.* 伤害,受伤处,损害
focused training 专项训练
outstanding *adj.* 杰出的,出众的,著名的,显著的,重要的
assert *v.* 坚定地断言;主张,维护,坚持
left and right 一个接一个
even if 即使,纵然,虽然
methodology *n.* (学科的)一套方法
biomechanics *n.* [用作单或复]生物力学,生物机械学
motion *n.* 动,运动,移动
digitize *v.* 使(数据)数字化
joint *n.* 关节
limb *n.* 肢,臂,腿
dimension *n.*【数】维,维数度
Newton's laws 牛顿定律
take-off *n.* 开始,出发
high jumper *n.* 跳高运动员
to date 迄今为止
revolutionary *adj.* 革命性剧变的,大变革的,突破性的,完全创新的
bar *n.* (跳高架等的)横杆
contradiction *n.* 矛盾(性),对立(性),不一致(性)
received *adj.* 被普遍接受的,公认的,普遍的,一般的
wisdom *n.* 知识,学问
dub *v.* 授予…称号,给…起绰号,把…称为
flop *n.* 拍,扑,重坠
specialist *n.* 专家
comprehend *v.* 理解,懂,领会
complex *adj.* 复杂的,错综的,难懂的
unorthodox *adj.* 非正统的,非传统的,不保守的
mathematical *adj.* 数学的,数学上的
simulation *n.* 模拟,仿真,模拟法,模拟试验,模式
innovation *n.* 革新,改革,创新
cushion *n.* 垫子
pit *n.* (地面的)坑,洼
sawdust *n.* 锯末,锯屑,木屑
foam *n.* 泡沫材料(如泡沫塑料、泡沫橡胶);泡沫状物
humble *v.* 降低…的地位,使卑贱;消灭…的力量(或锐气),使威信扫地
resourcefulness *n.* 足智多谋,机敏,随机应变
vexingly *adv.* 令人恼火地,使人苦恼地,伤脑筋地
psychologist *n.* 心理学家
mundane *adj.* 单调的,例行的,平凡的
equation *n.* 等式
fundamental *adj.* 基本的,根本的
foreseeable *adj.* 可预见的
burst *n.* 爆发,迸发,突发,猝发,突然的显现
recognise *v.* 认出,识别
inadequate *adj.* 不适当的
diet *n.* 日常饮食,日常食物,平时营养
diverse *adj.* 多种多样的,形形色色的,多变化的
theoretical *adj.* 理论(上)的,纯理论的

考题解析

Questions 1–6 True/False/Not Given

1. 较难,易误选 NG。原文定位第 1 段首句:Since the early years of the twentieth century, when... 下划线中二十世纪早期即是题干中 about 1900 的同义表达。
2. 较难,易误选 F。虽然原文第 1 段第 5 行有:... there has been a steady improvement... 其中的 steady 一词和题干 little 驳斥,但还要看到题干中 before the twentieth century 的表达。原文首句是从二十世纪开始谈起,没有提起之前的情况。
3. 定位 intensive burst of energy,原文出自第 1 段第 14 行:explosive release of energy... 后说到提高 ten to twenty per cent。而后提到的 the endurance events 提高了 almost thirty per cent;可见 the

endurance events 是提高最大的，而非 the power events。
4. 定位找到第 2 段首句。文章其他各处也出现过相反的表达。
5. 定位 parents。原文出自第 2 段第 3 行：The athlete must choose his parents carefully. 这是一种调侃的说法，强调基因的重要性，并没有说："顶尖运动员的父母通常都是优秀的运动员"。有的父母有运动基因，但不一定是运动员。
6. 第 2 段后半部分都在表达该含义。如：... but with increasing global participation in athletics... can be identified early...

Questions 7–10 Sentence Completion

7. 定位 Yessis，原文第 3 段第 8 行开始... running on their genetics。
8. 较难。先定位 Soviet Union。原文第 3 段最后一句中... as well as plyometrics，后接同位语：a technique pioneered in the former Soviet Union. 所以题干中的 a training approach 即是 plyometrics。再找描述 plyometrics 的作用和目标的句子。出现在第 4 段首句：... plyometrics focuses on increasing power.
9. 定位 an inadequate diet，原文第 5 段讲 nutrition。该段最后一句... lead to injuries. 考因果关联。
10. 注意到题干中的 new records，定位到原文第 6 段。原文第 3、4、5 段都是 Yessis 在发言，但讲的是提高运动员表现。而第 6 段讲到破纪录：If we applied the Russian training model... they would be breaking record left and right.

Questions 11–13 Multiple Choice

11. 定位 Biomechanics films，原文第 7 段第 3 行：A biomechanic films an athlete in action and then digitizes her performance...
12. 应该定位选项中的 Fosbury flop。原文第 8 段第 9 行：That understanding took the later analysis of biomechanics specialists. 下划线单词对应 D 选项中 explain 一词。
13. 定位 John S. Raglin。原文最后一段倒数第 3 行中 fundamental 一词对应 B 选项 basic。

参考译文

高多少？快多少？

——人类运动成绩的极限仍然是个没有揭开的谜——

自从二十世纪早期国际田径联合会开始记录成绩以来，运动员跑步的速度、弹跳的高度和向空中投掷包括他们自己在内的物体的距离都有稳步的提高。对于所谓的力量型项目——那些能量释放要求时间相对更短、更快的项目，像 100 米短跑和跳远——时间和距离都提高了 10 – 20%。在耐力性项目中，成绩更加引人注目。在 1908 年奥运会上，美国队的 John Hayes 跑马拉松仅用了 2:55:18。1999 年，摩洛哥的 Khalid Khannouchi 创下的新的世界纪录是 2:05:42，几乎快了 30%。

没有一种理论能够解释成绩提高的原因，但最重要的因素是遗传。"运动员必须慎重选择自己的父母。"印第安那大学体育科学家 Jesus Dapena 说，他援引了一句常引用的格言。在过去一个世纪的时间里，人类基因库的构成没有发生显著的变化，但随着全球越来越多的人参加体育运动——越来越高的奖励吸引着运动员——具有独特的运动补充基因的人更可能被及早发现。"20 世纪 20 年代曾经有过像[短跑运动员]Michael Johnson 那样的人吗？" Dapena 问。"我能肯定曾经有过，但他的才能很有可能从来未被发现。"

发现天生有才的人只是第一步。Michael Yessis 是位于富勒顿的加利福尼亚州立大学体育科学荣誉退休教授，他主张"遗传只能决定运动员能力的三分之一，但是只要训练得当，我们就可以好好利用这三分之一，比目前走得远得多。"Yessis 相信，尽管美国的跑步运动员成绩惊人，但他们是在

"靠遗传跑步"。通过利用更加科学的方法,"他们会跑得快得多"。这些方法包括重复跑步比赛中的动作的力量训练以及前苏联开创的技术——增强式训练。

尽管大多数运动的目的是增加力量或提高耐力,增强式训练主要是增加力量——一个运动员耗尽体力的速度。Yessis 解释说,一个短跑运动员跑步的时候,她的脚和地面接触的时间只有不到十分之一秒,一半时间用于着地,另一半用于离地。增强式训练帮助运动员充分利用这个短暂的间歇。

营养是运动教练员没有充分发挥作用的另一个领域。"很多运动员都没有摄取最好的营养,即使有补品营养也不够。"Yessis 强调说。每项运动都有自己的营养要求。比方说,很少有教练明白缺少微量元素怎么能导致受伤。

专项训练对打破纪录也能发挥作用。"如果我们把俄国的训练模式用到我国的优秀运动员身上,"Yessis 断言,"他们就会接二连三地打破纪录。"然而,他不愿估计成绩提高的程度;"究竟极限在哪里不好说,但只要我们的训练继续完善,就肯定会有提高,哪怕只有百分之一秒。"

一种最重要的新方法是生物力学,它研究运动中的身体。生物力学研究者把运动中的运动员拍摄下来,然后把她的动作数字化,把每个关节和肢体的动作用三维记录下来。通过用牛顿定律分析这些动作,"我们可以说这位运动员跑得不够快;这位运动员起跑时手臂摆得不够有力,"Dapena 说,他用这些方法帮助跳高运动员。然而,迄今为止,生物力学对提高运动员的成绩作用并不大。

革命性的想法还来自运动员本身。比如说,在 1968 年墨西哥城的奥运会期间,有一位相对来说不太出名的跳高运动员 Dick Fosbury 通过背跃式过杆,获得了金牌,这与大家公认的跳高技术完全背道而驰,这个动作立即被命名为 Fosbury 跳高(即背跃式跳高)。Fosbury 自己都不知道他在干什么。为了做出解释,后来的生物力学专家进行了分析,对于理解这个过于复杂、有悖传统、用他们的数学模式根本无法创造出来的动作他们可是费了些功夫。背跃式跳高还需要另一个因素,这个因素是很多运动成绩提高的原因:运动器材的革新。在做背跃式跳高时,跳高运动员会落在垫子上。传统的做法是,跳高运动员落在填满锯屑的坑里。但到了 Fosbury 时代,锯屑坑被软泡沫垫所取代,这是一种理想的落地器材。

结果,大多数研究人类运动成绩的人被运动员的足智多谋和人体的力量挫伤了锐气。"一旦你研究体育运动,你就会明白这是一个令人伤脑筋的复杂问题。"印第安那大学体育心理学家 John S. Raglin 说。"核心表现不是简单的或者普通的更高、更快、更长,如此多的变量会进入这个公式,而我们的理解在很多情况下都是最基本的。我们还有很长的路要走。"在可以预见的将来,纪录将会屡创屡破。

READING PASSAGE 2

The Nature and Aims of Archaeology

词汇注释

nature *n.* 本质,性质
aim *n.* 目的,志向
archaeology *n.* 考古学
treasure *n.* 金银财宝,珍宝
analyst *n.* 分析者,善于分析者
imagination *n.* 想像,想像力,创造力
toil *v.* 苦干,辛勤劳动,辛苦从事(at, on, through)
excavation *n.* 开凿,挖掘,发掘
Inuit *n.* 因纽特人
sewer *n.* 污水管,下水道,阴沟
painstaking *adj.* 煞费苦心的,仔细的,精心的,十分小心的
interpretation *n.* 解释,说明,阐明;翻译,口译
conservation *n.* 保存,(对自然资源的)保护,避免浪费(或损坏)
heritage *n.* 继承物,遗留物,传统
loot *v.* 掠夺,抢劫
physical *adj.* 身体的,肉体的

intellectual *adj.* 知识的，智力的，理智的；用脑力的，需智力的
pursuit *n.* 实行，从事，职业，事务
detective *adj.*（关于）侦探的
vehicle *n.* 传播媒介；（用来表达思想、情感或达到某种目的的）工具，手段；（为展露演员等的才华而）特意编写的一出戏（或一部电影、一部音乐作品等）
fiction *n.*［总称］小说，（一部）小说
portrayal *n.* 描绘，描写，描述
quest *n.*（历时较久的）寻求，探求，调查研究
discipline *n.* 学科，科目
anthropology *n.* 人类学
responsibility *n.* 责任，指责，任务，义务
humanity *n.* 人类，［总称］人
characteristic *n.* 特性，特征，特点，特色
anthropologist *n.* 人类学者，人类学家
moral *n.*［～s］道德，品行，道德规范，伦理学
custom *n.* 习惯，习俗，风俗，惯例
capability *n.* 能力，才能，技能，力量
refer to 提到，谈到；指称
distinguish ... from ... 区分，辨别，分清
branch *n.*（学科等的）分科
ethnography *n.* 人种志，人种论，民族志
ethnology *n.* 人种学，民族学
set out 打算，试图
ethnographic *adj.* 人种论的，民族志的
contemporary *adj.* 当代的
artefact *n.* 人工制品，制造物（区别于天然物）；（代表特定文化或技术发展阶段的）手工艺品
constitute *v.* 组成，构成，形成
pot *n.* 罐，壶
dwelling *n.* 住处，住宅，寓所
square *adj.* 四方形的，方的
overlap *v.* 互搭，复叠
ethnoarchaeology *n.* 种族文化考古学，文化群落考古学
ethnographer *n.* 人种志（或人种论）学者，人种志（人种论）研究者，民族志研究者
specific *adj.* 明确的，确切的，具体的
purpose *n.* 目的，意图
weapon *n.* 武器，兵器，凶器
settlement *n.*（人口稀少地区的）小村落，小社区，小居民点
diminish *v.* 减少，减小，缩减，降低
span *n.* 持续时间，时间阶段
conventional *adj.* 普通的，常见的
historical *adj.* 历史的，历史科学的
draw *v.* 划清（界限等）
distinction *n.* 区分，辨别，分清
pre-history *n.*（有文字记载以前的）史前史，（人类进化的）史前阶段，史前学
convenient *adj.* 在合适时刻出现的，适合一时需要的，提供便利的
dividing *adj.* 起划分（或区分、分隔）作用的
oral *adj.* 口头的，口述的
humanistic *adj.* 人文学科的，人文主义（者）的
differ from 相异，有区别
fundamental *adj.* 基本的，根本的
in this respect 在这方面
conduct *v.* 进行，实施，经营
formulate *v.* 系统地（或确切地）阐述（或表达、说明）；构想出（计划、方法等）
hypothesis *n.* 假说，假设，前提
devise *v.* 设计，发明，策划，想出
model *n.* 假定的模型
summarise *v.* 总结，概述，概括
coherent *adj.* 一致的，协调的；（话语等）条理清楚的，连贯的，前后一致的
creativity *n.* 创造性，创造力，创作能力
investigative *adj.*（官方）调查的，调查研究的
ancient *adj.*（尤指公元 476 年西罗马帝国灭亡以前）古代的，属于古代的
realistic *adj.* 逼真的
document *v.* 用文件（或文献等）证明，为…提供文件（或证据等）
subdivide *v.* 再分，重分，把…分得更小
diet *n.* 日常饮食，日常食物，平时营养
determine *v.* 确定，查明，测定
deduce *v.* 演绎，推论，推断
domestic *adj.* 家的，家庭的，家务的，家用的
valuable *adj.* 有价值的，珍贵的，重要的，有用的

考题解析

* 文章抽象，难度大。

Questions 14–19 Yes/No/Not Given

14. 题干中 creativity 和 investigative 出现在文章首段第 1、2 句。

15. 定位题干中 translate,原文中首段第 3 行中:But it is also the painstaking task of interpretation... 原文较泛泛,没有像题干所说的"考古学家必须能翻译古代语言"这样绝对。
16. 定位 movies。原文第 2 段第 4 行:However far from reality such portrayals are... 和题干中 reality 驳斥。
17. 定位 culture。原文第 4 段第 5 行。
18. 较难。主要理解题干中 demanding 一词的含义。demanding 在这里指"费力的,耗精力的"。文中没有在这方面对人类学和考古学进行比较。
19. 定位 3000 BC。原文倒数第 3 段末句中:... around 3000 BC in western Asia, and much later in most other parts of the world. 由此理解欧洲历史的文献记载应大大晚于 3000 BC。

Questions 20–21 Multiple Choice

20. D 选项:It is subdivided for study purposes. 原文出处在第 4 段末句。注意下划线单词在原文中对应... broke down into three smaller disciplines...
21. E 选项:It studies human evolutionary patterns. 原文出处在第 5 段首句。注意下划线单词在原文中对应... how they evolved.

Questions 22–23 Multiple Choice

22. C 选项:deducing reasons for the shape of domestic buildings. 原文出处在第 7 段第 2 行:Why are some dwellings round and others square?
23. D 选项:investigating the way different cultures make and use objects. 原文出处在第 7 段第 5、6 行。

Questions 24–27 Summary

* 一定要看到题目说明:Complete the summary of the last two paragraphs of Reading Passage 2. 否则将没有头绪。

24. 定位 written records→but。原文倒数第 2 段倒数第 2 行:... the written word, but... 再看到后面的:... in no way lessens the importance... 对应 24 题空格后的 equally valuable. 即可知道答案就是 in no way lessens the importance... 后面的两个名词 information 和 oral histories 其中之一了。通过理解可以选出 oral histories,或注意到 oral 和前面的 written 并列,也可选出正确答案。
25. 注意到 25 题和 26 题要填两个名词,并且是并列结构。定位原文最后一段首句找并列结构。
26. 同 25 题。
27. 定位 compares to→that of a。原文最后一段第 6 行中:... is rather like that of the scientist...

参考译文

考古学的本质与目的

考古学一部分是发现历史珍宝,一部分是科学分析者细致的工作,一部分是发挥创造性的想像力。它是在中东的烈日下的辛苦挖掘,是在阿拉斯加的雪地里和活着的因纽特人一起工作,是对罗马人统治时期英国的下水道的调查。但它也是煞费苦心的解释说明,好让我们明白这些东西对人类历史意味着什么,它还是保护世界文化遗产免遭掠夺和无意伤害。

因此,考古学既是在野外的体力活动,又是在书房或实验室的脑力劳动。这只是它巨大魅力的一部分。由于它既充满危险,又颇具侦探性质,所以是小说家和电影制作者最完美的媒介,从 Agatha Christie 的《美索布达米亚谋杀案》到 Stephen Spielberg 的《印第安那·琼斯》。不管这种描述和现实相差有多远,它们都抓住了一个基本事实,即考古学是一种激动人心的研究——对我们自己和我们的过去的研究。

但考古学与人类学、历史之类同样和人类历史有关的学科有什么联系呢?考古学本身是一门科学吗？考古学家在当今世界背负着什么样的责任？

从最广泛的意义上来说，人类学是对人类的研究——我们作为动物的身体特征以及我们称之为文化的独特的非生物特征。从这个意义上来说，文化包括人类学家 Edward Tylor 1871 年总结的"人作为社会成员获得的知识、信仰、艺术、道德、习俗和其他任何能力和习惯"。人类学家也会从狭义上使用"文化"这个词指某个特定社会的"文化"，意指这个社会区别于其他社会的独特的非生物特征。因此人类学是一个范围极广的学科——广到通常被分为 3 个更小的学科：体质人类学、文化人类学和考古学。

体质人类学，或者也称作生物人类学，主要研究人类的生物和体质特征及其发展。文化人类学——或者社会人类学——分析人类文化和社会，它的两个分支是民族志（对现存的每一种文化做第一手研究）和民族学（通过使用民族志证据对人类社会得出一些普遍原则，对文化做出一些比较）。

考古学是"文化人类学的过去式"。文化人类学家通常把他们的结论建立在当代社区的生活体验上，而考古学家则主要通过残存的物质研究过去的社会——房屋、工具和其他人工制品，它们构成了我们所知的过去社会遗留的物质文明。

然而，今天的考古学家最重要的任务之一是知道如何用人类的语言来解释物质文明。这些罐子是如何使用的？为什么有的住处是圆的，而其他的则是方的？在这里考古学和民族志的方法是重叠的。最近几十年，考古学家发展了"种族文化考古学"，他们像民族志研究者一样住在当代社区里，但他们有一个明确目的，那就是了解这些社会如何使用物质文明——他们如何制造工具和武器，为什么在现在的地点建造村落等等。此外，考古学在资源保护领域可以发挥出积极的作用。对遗产的研究形成了一个正在发展的领域，人们意识到世界文化遗产是一种正在减少的资源，对不同的人来说有着不同的意义。

如果考古学研究的是过去，那么它和历史的区别是什么呢？从最广泛的意义上来说，就像考古学是人类学的一个方面一样，它也是历史的一部分——我们指的是从三百多万年前开始的整个人类的历史。的确，对于 99% 以上的这一大段时间来说，考古学——对过去物质文明的研究——是信息的唯一重要来源。传统的历史资料是在有了文字记录之后才开始的，那大约是公元前 3000 年的西亚，世界上其他大部分地区则要晚得多。

一般分史前史，即有文字记录出现之前的那段时期——和狭义上的历史，即用文字证据对过去进行研究。对研究所有文明和时期的考古学来说，无论有没有文字记录，历史和史前史的区别都是一条便利的分界线，它承认了书面文字的重要性，但一点也不降低口述历史中包含的有用信息的重要性。

由于考古学的目标是了解人类，所以它属于人文学科的研究，而且由于它研究人类的过去，它是一门历史学科。但它与对有文字记载的历史的研究有根本的区别。考古学家发现的东西不能直接告诉我们应该想到什么。历史记载不仅做出陈述，而且提供见解、作出判断。另一方面，考古学家发现的东西就其本身而言并不告诉我们什么。从这方面来讲，考古学家所做的工作很像科学家的工作，他们收集资料、做实验、提出假设、用更多的资料来检验假设，最后得出一个似乎最能总结从资料中观察到的模式的模型。就像科学家必须对自然世界形成一个前后一致的观点一样，考古学家必须要把过去画成一幅画。

READING PASSAGE 3

The Problem of Scarce Resources

词汇注释

impact *n.* 影响,作用
illusion *n.* 幻想,错误的观念
sustainable *adj.*【经】能保持一定速度的,能保持在一定水平上的
allocate *v.* 分配,分派
apportion *v.* 分派,分摊,(根据计划或规定)按比例分配
distribute *v.* 分发,分配,分送
disability *n.* 残疾,伤残
treatment *n.* 治疗,疗法,疗程
priority *n.* 优先,重点;优先权
in respect of 关于,至于,就…而言,在…方面
cost-effective *adj.* 有成本效益的,值得花费的,合算的,划算的
outlook *n.* 观点,看法
finitude *n.* 有限,限定,限度
clientele *n.* [总称]顾客,主顾
emerge *v.* (问题、困难等)发生,显露;(事实、意见等)暴露,被知晓
awareness *n.* 意识
provision *n.* 供应,提供
fossil fuel *n.* 矿物燃料
finite *adj.* 有限的
exhaustible *adj.* 会用完的,可耗尽的,会枯竭的
capacity *n.* (做某事的)能力,资格,力量
environment *n.* 生态环境,自然环境
sustain *v.* 保持,使(声音、努力等)持续不息;支撑,承受(压力或重量)
obvious *adj.* 显然的,明显的,无疑的
consciousness *n.* 意识,观念,觉悟
revelation *n.* 揭示,揭露,暴露,透露,展现,显示
incredible *adj.* 难以置信的,不可思议的
immediately *adv.* 紧接地
assume *v.* 假定,假设,想当然地认为,臆断
in principle 原则上,基本上,大体上;在理论上
invisible *adj.* 看不见的,视力外的;无形的;隐匿的
realisation *n.* 理解,认知,认识
character *n.* (事物的)性质,特性,特色
sink in 被理会,被理解
contrary *adj.* 相反的,对抗的
legal *adj.* 法律(上)的,属于法律范围的
institution *n.* 制度;制定
fundamental *adj.* 基本的,根本的
facility *n.* [常作 facilities]设备,设施,工具
autonomous *adj.* 自治的,有自治权的,独立自主的
be in a position to do sth. (由于客观或主观条件)可(能)做某事
liberty *n.* (行动、言论、选择等的)自由,(政治上的)独立自主
self-determining *adj.* 有自决力的,能自主的
poverty-stricken *adj.* 贫穷的,穷困的,贫乏的
deprive *v.* 夺去,剥夺,使丧失
context *n.* (人、事、物存在于其中的)各种有关情况,来龙去脉,背景,环境
autonomy *n.* 人身自由,自由,自主权,意志自由;自治,自治权
confusion *n.* 辨别不清,混淆
resistance *n.* 反抗,抵制,抗拒,阻力
formal *adj.* 形式(上)的,表面的,徒有其表的;正式的
generate *v.* 造成,引起,导致,使存在
obligation *n.* (法律上或道义上的)义务,责任
duty *n.* 责任,本分,义务
adequate *adj.* 能满足需要(量)的,足够的
purse *n.* 资金,财力,财源
recognise *v.* 承认,确认,认可
private *adj.* 私人(用)的,私有的,个人的
declaration *n.* 宣言,公告,声明(书)
attainable *adj.* 可以达到的,可以获得的
distinction *n.* 区分,辨别,分清
remark *v.* 说,评论说
liberal *adj.* 自由主义的
indispensable *adj.* 必不可少的,必需的
distribution *n.* 分发,分配,分送
stem from 起源于,基于,由…造成
dramatic *adj.* 引人注目的,给人深刻印象的,突然的
accompany *v.* 伴随,和…一起发生(或存在)
demographic *adj.* 人口的,人口统计的,人口学的
elderly *adj.* 较老的,过了中年的,近老年的(用于人时常带有尊敬意)

major *adj.* (数量、大小、程度等)较大的,较多的,较大范围的	**extrapolation** *n.* 推断,推知
consumer *n.* 消费者,顾客,用户	**project** *v.* 提出,阐释
predict *v.* 预言,预料,预计,预报	**administrator** *n.* 管理人,行政官员
proportion *n.* 比例,比	**ever-rising** *adj.* 不断增长的
current *adj.* 现时的,当前的,进行中的	**match** *v.* 使相称,使相配
figure *n.* 数字	**static** *adj.* 静止的,停滞的,稳定的,不变的
as a consequence 因此,结果	**acceptance** *n.* 赞同;接受;承认;相信
doomsday *n.* 【宗】最后审判日,世界末日	**guarantee** *v.* 确保
scenario *n.* 设想,方案	**link** *v.* 连接起来,联系在一起
analogous *adj.* 相似的,类似的,可比拟的	**evident** *adj.* 明显地,显然
similar *adj.* 相像的,相仿的,类似的	**have an impact on** 对…有影响
	underestimate *v.* 对…估价过低,对…估计不足,低估

考题解析

Questions 28–31 List of Headings

28. Section A 中第 2 句:Every health system in an economically developed society. . . 对应选项。
29. 注意到第 1 个 heading 中的 other human rights。Section C 中第 3 行:. . . that people have a basic right to. . . Like education, political and legal. . .
30. Section D 中第 4 行:It is also accepted that this right generates an obligation or duty for the state to ensure that ... The state has no obligation to ... but to ensure (the state 的作用). . .
31. Section E 第 3 行:The second set of more specific changes that have led to the present concern about. . .

Questions 32–35 Matching

* 要迅速解题需要先观察到文中年代出现的地方,最好作出标记:Section B 出现了 1950s, 1960s, 1939–45,Section D 出现了 1976,Section E 出现了 1960,1980s。

32. Section B 中第 9 行:The new consciousness that there were also severe limits to health-care. . . 是 in the 1950s and 1960s 时候的事。
33. Section E 中第 1 段后面部分数字增长:from 3.8% of GDP in 1960 to 7% of GDP in 1980。
34. Section B 中最后一句。注意 in the years immediately after the 1939–45 World War. . . 的表达。下划线中 the years 指的就是 1945 年世界大战结束后的几年,是属于 A 选项:between 1945 and 1950。
35. 注意题干中 the role of the state 的表达与第 30 题选出的 heading 相似,所以该题直接定位到 Section D 中,而 Section D 中只有 1970s 和 1976 的时间表达,轻松判断 B 选项。

Questions 36–40 Yes/No/Not Given

36. 定位词 liberty and independence。Section C 中最后 3 行已经提到,驳斥题干中 never 一词。
37. 定位词 the same time,比较时间。Section C 首句。
38. 定位词 OEDC, population。Section E 第 6 行,中 demographic 对应 population。
39. 定位词 OEDC, underestimated。Section E 中在 OECD 出现的附近没有看到 underestimated(政府低估)的说法。
40. 题干较难理解,解题很简单。注意题干中 make special provision 的表达,意思是"做特殊的准备"。题干其实暗示:社会的医疗保健资源不充分,老人们自己需要在医疗上做一些特殊的准备,比如自己买个保险什么的。定位词 elderly。原文 Section E 中第 7 行说:"这些变化意味着老年人是现在卫生资源的主要(而且相对而言非常昂贵的)消费者。"没有提到 special provision。

参考译文

资源匮乏问题

Section A 保健资源应该如何分配,从而达到最公正、最有效的分配,这个问题并不新鲜。经济发达的社会里每个保健系统都面临着需要决定(正式或非正式地)社会总体资源用在保健事业上的比例应该是多少;资源如何分配;哪些疾病、残疾以及哪种治疗应该给予优先考虑;就保健方面来说,哪些社会成员应该给予特殊考虑;哪种治疗是最合算的。

Section B 新鲜之处在于从20世纪50年代起,关于保健资源的享用者和这些资源的社会成本,人们的看法发生了一些具体的改变之外,同时,对总体资源的有限性、尤其是保健资源的有限性,人们的看法也发生了某些总的变化。因此,在20世纪50年代和60年代,西方社会开始意识到提供矿物燃料能量的资源是有限的而且有可能枯竭的,而且大自然或环境承受经济发展和人口的能力也是有限的。换句话说,我们开始意识到一个显而易见的事实,那就是"发展是有限的"。保健资源也有严格的限度这种新的意识是对显而易见的事实普遍发现的一部分。回顾过去,现在想想似乎很不可思议,1939-1945年世界大战之后,在很多国家出现的国家保健系统里,人们毫不怀疑地认为任何社会所有基本保健需要都能得到满足,至少从理论上来说是这样的;经济发展的"无形之手"会提供这个方便。

Section C 然而,几乎就在保健资源是有限的这个新认识刚刚被理解的同时,一种相反的观点也在西方社会逐渐形成:保健是人们的基本权利,是人类生活的一个必要条件。像教育、政治和法律程序及制度、公共秩序、通讯、交通和资金的提供一样,保健开始被看作是人们作为独立自主的人行使其它权利必要的基本社会设施之一。如果人们穷困潦倒、或者被剥夺了基础教育的权利、或者没有生活在法律和秩序的环境之中,人们就不可能有个人自由,也不可能独立自主。同样,基础保健是独立自主的一个条件。

Section D 尽管"权利"这个词有时候会引起混淆,但到了20世纪80年代末,大多数社会都承认人们有享受保健的权利(尽管在美国有相当多的人反对有正式的保健权这个概念)。大家同时也同意,这种权利也对政府产生义务和责任,确保用大家的钱包提供足够的保健资源。政府本身没有义务提供保健系统,但要确保能提供一个这样的系统。换句话说,基础保健现在被认为是"公共商品",而不是希望人们为自己购买的"私人商品"。正如世界卫生组织在1976年的宣言中写道:"享受能实现的最高标准的健康是每个人的基本权利之一,不分种族、宗教、政治信仰、经济或社会条件。"就像刚才所说的,在一个自由社会,基本健康被看作是行使个人自主权利必不可少的条件之一。

Section E 就在保健资源明显可能供不应求之时,人们提出了国家满足他们基本保健权利的要求。导致人们如今关注保健资源分配问题的第二组更加具体的变化是因为经济合作与发展组织的大多数国家健康消费的急剧上升造成的,此外还有大规模的人口和社会变化,这些变化意味着,举个例说,老年人是现在保健资源的主要(而且相对而言是非常昂贵的)消费者。因此,从整体来看,经济合作与发展组织国家的保健费用从1960年占国内生产总值的3.8%增加到了1980年的7%,据预计,保健费用占国内生产总值的比例将继续上升。(在美国,当前的数字是国内生产总值的12%,而澳大利亚占国内生产总值的7.8%。)

因此,在20世纪80年代,卫生官员、经济学家和政治家提出了一种世界末日方案(类似于关于能量需要、矿物燃料或者人口增长的世界末日的推断)。在这个方案中,他们把不断增长的保健花费与不变的或者正在减少的资源进行了对比。

WRITING

WRITING TASK 1

This model has been prepared by an examiner as an example of a very good answer.

These graphs represent the travel patterns of UK residents and their choice of country in 1999, the number of UK citizens traveling and the number of foreign visitors to the UK from 1979 to 1999.

The first graph indicates that the number of UK citizens traveling rose gradually from 12 million in 1979 to 20 million in 1984 and increased steadily from 20 million to 53 million from 1985 to 1999. It also indicates that the number of overseas visitors to the UK rose from 10 million in 1979 to 12 million in late 1985 and slowly increased from 12 million to 26 million in 1999. However, the number of overseas visitors traveling to the UK was approximately half the number of UK residents traveling abroad.

The second graph suggests that the countries preferred by UK travelers in 1999 were France and Spain at 11. 5 million and just fewer than 10 million respectively, both close to Britain. The USA, Greece and Turkey were 3rd, 4th, and 5th with fewer than 4 million UK travelers.

(173 words)

参考译文

这些图表显示1999年英国居民的旅游情况和他们对旅游国的选择、1979年至1999年英国公民的旅游人数和到英国的外国游客的人数。

第一幅图表表明英国公民的旅游人数从1979年的1200万逐渐上升到1984年的2000万，1985年至1999年从2000万平稳上升到5300万。从图表中还可以看出，去英国旅游的海外游客从1979年的1000万增加到1985年下半年的1200万，然后从1200万慢慢增加到1999年的2600万。但是，到英国旅游的海外游客大约只是去国外旅游的英国公民人数的一半。

第二幅图表说明1999年英国游客喜欢去的国家是法国和西班牙，分别是1150万和差不多1000万，这两个数字都接近想在英国旅行的人数。美国、希腊、土耳其分别排第三、第四、第五位，去这些地方的英国游客都不到400万。

WRITING TASK 2

这是考官准备的一篇优秀范文（原文在《剑桥雅思4》第169页），请注意答案可以千变万化，下面只是其中之一。

学生的不良行为似乎已经成为越来越普遍的一个问题。我认为，现代生活方式可能是引起这一问题的原因。

在很多国家，人口出生率都在下降，这样，孩子少了，家庭也变小了。这些孩子常常被父母宠坏，原因不在父母的关心和爱护方面，因为有工作的父母没有时间关爱孩子，而更多是在物质方面。父母们不计代价，孩子们要什么就给什么，还允许他们想怎么做就怎么做。这意味着孩子在成长过程中从不为他人着想，也不明白他们的幸福生活来自何处。

当他们长到上学年龄,还没学会自我控制或自律。他们不尊重老师,也不像父母那样遵守学校的规章制度。

老师们经常为这一问题而抱怨,必须采取措施改变这一局面。但是,我认为,问题的解决办法在于家庭,父母需要更加清楚宠惯孩子的后果。如果他们能把孩子培养成为体贴他人、善于交往、有责任心的人,这对整个社会都会极为有益。

也许需要开设家长课堂,以帮助他们来完成这一使命。还应该开办高质量的幼儿园,以便在培养下一代方面为父母提供更多的帮助。政府应该为此提供相应的资金支持,因为这不再是单个家庭,而是整个社会的问题。

SPEAKING

Band 9 Speaking Test Scripts

E: = Examiner C: = Candidate

PART 1

E: What place do you most like to visit?

C: I like to visit small parks where there are not too many people. I hate noisy amusement parks full of people. I like to be able to sit quietly and read or just sit and day dream. I find it very refreshing.

E: How often do you visit this place?

C: I visit as often as I can which is not that often these days. If I'm not working, I'm often running errands for my grandparents. But, when I can, I go.

E: Why do you like it so much?

C: I like it because it's quiet and you can travel to many other great places in your mind. I love daydreaming when I get the chance.

E: Is it popular with many other people?

C: Not where I go. If it were I wouldn't go. Like I said, I don't like noisy places with too many people.

E: Has it changed very much since you first went there? (In what way?)

C: No it hasn't changed much. They have added a few trees and cleaned up the pond, but for the most part it remains unchanged and I hope it continues that way.

PART 2

E: Describe a useful website you have visited.

C: I often visit MSN's Encarta online. It has an encyclopedia, dictionary, thesaurus, multimedia collection, and homework tools. It's very useful when you need to look something up in a hurry. You can type in your search criteria and in seconds you will have the information you need, whatever it may be. If you happen to use Hotmail, you can access your e-mail directly from their site. You can hook up to a chat line. Encarta also has something called the top ten. It is a list of archives where you can find information about almost anything. For example, it lists the top ten national parks in the world and so on. You can go shopping and read the Princeton Review. You can find pretty much anything you want there. A friend of mine actually recommended it when I was learning English as a resource several years ago and I've continued to use it. There are sections on new careers, games, online University courses and host of other things. Of course I visit many websites in a day, but this was the first English site I was introduced to and quite frankly it's more useful and cheaper than going out and buying a bunch of books.

PART 3

E: What effect has the Internet had on the way people generally communicate with each other?

C: People communicate far more frequently now than they did before. Now you can type out an e-mail and know that it will probably arrive anywhere from a minute to fifteen minutes later at any destination in the world. It is much easier and less expensive than posting letters. In fact, I can't remember the last time I handwrote a letter to anyone. I rarely do that unless the circumstances warrant it, like for a really private letter, because the Internet is not all that secure yet.

E: Why do you think the Internet is being used more and more for communications?

C: Because of it's speed and efficiency. Security is becoming better, but you still have to be careful, especially in business. It's important not to download stuff from sites that you are not familiar with.

E: How reliable do you think information from the Internet is? Why? What about the news on the Internet?

C: It's as reliable as any other information depending on the site you go to. If you want garbage, you can always find it. If you want good solid information, you can find that, too. Of course you always have to verify everything before you can rely on it, but in general it's as reliable as newspapers and television. Like I said before, there is a lot of garbage on the Internet, you just have to know how to weed it out.

E: Why do you think some people use the Internet for shopping? Why doesn't everyone use it in this way?

C: Maybe some people are just too lazy to get up and go out to buy things. On the other hand, some items come from overseas and it is much more convenient and cheaper to order online than to fly to the US to buy a book. The reason everyone doesn't use it is that we don't all have credit cards. That's the only drawback. You need a credit card.

E: What kinds of things are there to buy and sell online? Can you give me some examples?

C: You can buy almost anything you want online. Most large retail stores and smaller specialty shops have web sites and online order forms. Take Amazon. com for example. You can buy any book you can think of from them. If they don't have it, they will find it. You can buy cars online. You name it and you can probably get it. You can even do online banking now.

E: Do you think shopping on the Internet will be more or less popular in the future? Why?

C: I think that in the future the Internet will evolve and become even more popular as an add-on to your home entertainment centre. All you will have to do to buy groceries or whatever else you want, will be to click on touch sensitive screens on your television and an hour or so later everything will be delivered to your house. I believe that this is happening in some countries already. It's called interactive television. It's a great idea, but I personally don't think I would use it. I like to get out and see what's going on and talk to people in the store or whatever.

General Training：Reading and Writing

Test A

READING

SECTION 1

Questions 1–5

词汇注释

surroundings *n.* 周围的事物，环境
deliver *v.* 分送，投递
extra *adj.* 额外的，外加的
authentic *adj.* 真正的；可信的
Thailand 泰国
acre *n.* 英亩
scenic *adj.* 自然景色的，风景优美的
license *v.* 批准、许可（从事某行业或活动）；licensed 特许的，领有许可证的
bar *n.* 酒吧间
luxury *adj.* 豪华的，奢侈的
landscape *n.*（陆上）景色，（陆上）风景
cuisine *n.* 烹饪（术），菜肴，饭菜
classic *adj.* 第一流的，上等的
burger *n.* 汉堡包，牛肉饼
steak *n.* 牛排，牛肉饼
chips *n.* 油炸土豆条
vegetarian *n.* 素食者
menu *n.* 菜单；（端上来的）饭菜，菜肴
takeaway *adj.*（餐馆等）供应外卖食物的，（饭食等）供外卖的；*n.* 外卖餐馆
express *n.* 快递，特快货运
radius *n.* 半径，半径距离，半径范围
hygiene *n.* 卫生
delicious *adj.* 美味的，好吃的
anniversary *n.* 周年纪念，周年纪念日；结婚周年（日）
snack *n.* 快餐，小吃
light meals 清淡的饭菜
informal *adj.* 非正式的，随便的
premier *adj.* 首位的，首要的；最早的
chef *n.* 厨师长，厨师
ultra-modern *adj.* 超现代化的；超时髦的；最新式的
ample *adj.* 宽敞的；足够的
speciality *n.* 特制品，特色菜

考题解析

Questions 1–5 Matching

1. 定位 can't，Monday evening。B 中最后两行。
2. 定位 peaceful country surroundings。A 中：40 acres of scenic woodland，outside dining area，beautiful landscaped gardens。
3. 定位 Sunday night。
4. 定位 delivered，an extra fee。
5. 定位 dinner，stay the night。A 中 hotel，accommodation。

参考译文

A

真正的泰国风味
CHANGTOM
泰国饭店(餐饮、住宿)
中午12点至3点
下午6点至晚上12点(星期天除外)
· 坐落在风景秀丽的林区,占地40英亩
· 可户外就餐
· 用料保证新鲜
· 可用信用卡结账
· 可容纳50人就餐
· 酒吧可出售酒类
· 可租用小型会议室
· 拥有豪华套房
· 停车方便
· 可眺望风景如画的花园
饭菜质量上乘、服务一流

B

杰克饭店
传统的美国饭店
适宜家庭聚餐或其他特殊聚会

· 优选美国上等汉堡、牛排
· 供应鱼片和薯条,还有特为素食者和孩子们准备的饭菜
· 酒吧准许出售酒类
· 欢迎婚庆及聚会订餐
· 提供外卖服务

营业时间:
中午:星期二—星期六
晚上:星期三—星期六

C

莫卧儿菜快递
印度菜外卖

在家里尽情享受印度美食
每天开放,公共假日照常营业
停车方便
提供在4英里范围内的订餐递送服务,只收少量服务费

电话:诺里奇 420988/588980
连续两年荣获英国外卖及卫生、质量一等奖

D

玛丽娜饭店

全天开放
以当地价格享受世界美味佳肴
新鲜自制菜的花样不断翻新,只选当地上乘原料
※ 商务聚餐 ※纪念日和婚礼庆典 ※所有有特别意义的宴会
快餐及清淡食物,午饭和晚饭,酒吧可出售酒类,葡萄酒种类齐全
玛丽娜饭店富丽豪华,环境轻松惬意
欢迎品尝诺里奇一流饭店的美味佳肴
周一至周六,全天开放
对面有大型带摄像监控的停车场

E

北京饭店

饭店兼外卖

本店中国菜美味可口,质量上乘,名厨主灶,厨房设备独特、超现代

外卖免费递送,停车场宽敞

欢迎电话订餐

欢迎垂询我店名师特色菜

	中午	晚上
星期日	不营业	下午5:00-晚上11:00
星期一	不营业	下午5:00-晚上11:30
星期二	不营业	下午5:00-晚上11:30
星期三	不营业	下午5:00-晚上11:30
星期四	不营业	下午5:00-晚上11:30
星期五	不营业	下午5:00-午夜
星期六	不营业	下午5:00-午夜

诺里奇 (01603)571122

诺里奇女王大街40号

Questions 6-14

词汇注释

gear *v.* 调整,(使)适合;换档
atmosphere *n.* 气氛;大气;空气
unthreatening *adj.* 没有胁迫的,没有危险的
confidence *n.* 信心
initially *adv.* 最初,开头
apprehensive *adj.* 忧虑的,担心的,恐惧的;有理解力的
samba *n.* 桑巴舞;桑巴舞曲
percussion *n.* 打击乐器
workshop *n.* 研习会,讨论会;车间,工场
carnival *n.* (定期的文艺或体育等)表演会,(吃喝、化妆舞会之类的)狂欢作乐,欢宴;狂欢节
exotic *adj.* 异国情调的;外来的;奇异的
rhythm *n.* 节奏,韵律
story-telling *n.* /*adj.* 讲故事(的);说谎(的)
narration *n.* 讲述;故事,(一篇)叙述
poetry *n.* [总称]诗,诗歌;韵文;诗集
proverb *n.* 谚语
Scottish *adj.* 苏格兰的,苏格兰人的
essential *adj.* 基本的,不可缺少的;本质的
enthusiasm *n.* 热心,热情,激情
guarantee *v.* 保证;担保
choir *n.* 合唱团;(教堂的)唱诗班
rehearse *v.* 排练;排演
audience *n.* 听众,观众
participation *n.* 参与;分享
sight-read *v.* 即兴演奏乐曲;即兴演唱歌曲
choral *adj.* 合唱的;合唱队的;唱诗班的
desirable *n.* 可取的,有利的;值得向往的
intensive *n.* 集中的;加强的;密集的;
shade *n.* 阴影;(图画等的)阴暗部分
emotion *n.* 感情;情感
maximum *n.* 最高的;最多的;最大极限的
relevant *adj.* 有关的,相应的
cheer *v.* 使…快乐或振奋
guidance *n.* 指导,指引
overcome *v.* 战胜,克服

考题解析

Questions 6–14 Matching

6. C 中最后一句。
7. D 中最后一句。
8. B 中 Lift your spirits.
9. B 中最后一行:An event for all the family.
10. E 中 instruction, maximum attention for each student.
11. D 中 we are rehearing for a special concert with audience participation...
12. A 中 developing the confidence.
13. B 中 you'll be creating complex exotic rhythms in no time.
14. D 中 7:30 – 9:30 pm。

参考译文

A 里士满实验剧院

表演课程讲授全面的表演技巧。本课程尤其适合几乎没有或根本没有表演经验的学员。这里教学环境轻松自然;对最初有点胆小顾虑的人,重点培养他们的信心和能力。

B 世界文化日

巴西街头打击乐演奏

2:30 – 4:30

桑巴舞曲打击乐演奏学习班会令你情绪激昂、尽情狂欢。不管你是资深的音乐家,还是完全的初学者,这都无所谓,很快你就会创作出有异国情调的复杂旋律。

来自非洲的故事

3:45 – 4:45

以叙事体、诗歌和谚语的方式讲故事(主要来自加纳和尼日利亚)。这一传统充满神奇色彩,适宜全家人一起参加。

C 苏格兰舞蹈

有趣

很好的一种锻炼方式

· 设有适合不同程度的舞蹈者的学习班
· 以前有无舞蹈经历并不重要
· 你只需带来一双舞鞋和你的热情
· 可以在众多不同时间和地点报名上课
· 保证为你们提供热情的服务

D 文艺复兴歌手

特邀新歌手加盟我们合唱队,到剑桥演奏各类音乐。合唱队成立于 1993 年。我们每周三晚七点半到九点半聚会。本学期我们将在 11 月 1 日(星期六)排演一场有观众参与的特别音乐会。

能够即兴演唱和以前有过合唱经历的人可优先考虑,但这并非绝对条件。

E 水彩画

初学者的集中培训班

10 月 13 日(周六)至 14 日(周日)

本水彩画辅导班教学方法独特、高效。教学内容包括学习用颜料体现光与影,表达心情与感情。

小班教学(12 人)能保证给每个同学最大的关注。我们采用专业水平的学习材料,学费 95 英镑中包括此费用。

SECTION 2

Student Life at Canterbury College

词汇注释

atmosphere *n.* 周围情况,环境,气氛
environment *n.* 环境,周围环境
relationship *n.* 关系;联系
mutual *adj.* 互相的;彼此的
respect *n.* 尊敬,尊重
tutor *n.* 导师,辅导教师
accessible *adj.* 可以达到的,容易取得的
opportunity *n.* 机会,时机
Students' Union *n.* 学生会
automatically *adv.* 自动地;机械地
executive committee 执行委员会
elect *v.* 选举,推选
continuity *n.* 连续性,连贯性
academic *adj.* 学院的,大学的;学会的,(学术、文艺)协会的;教学的;学术的
representative *n.* 代表 *adj.* 典型的,有代表性的
affair *n.* [常用复] 事务,事态;事情
internally *adv.* 内部地;在内部
academic board 学术委员会
sub-committee *n.* 委员会的附属委员会,小组委员会
entertainment *n.* 娱乐活动,文娱节目;娱乐,消遣
coursework 课程作业
ample *adj.* 宽敞的;足够的
journal *n.* 杂志,刊物
cassette *n.* 盒式录音带;录音带盒
loan *n.* 暂借;暂借的东西;贷款
via *prep.* 经过,经由,取道;以…作媒介,通过
situate *v.* 使位于,使处于
variety *n.* 种种,各类;变化;多样性
word processing 文字处理
desktop *n.* [计] 桌面;台式电脑
stationery *n.* 文具;信笺
subsidy *n.* 津贴,补贴,补助金
reserve 预订,预约
refectory *n.* (修道院、学校等中的)餐厅,食堂
refreshment *n.* [~s] 茶点,点心;便餐;饮料
option *n.* 选择;选择权;选择自由;可选择的东西,任选项
normal *adj.* 正常的;正规的;平常的;通常的
snack *n.* 小吃;快餐
cuisine *n.* 烹饪,烹饪术;菜肴,饭菜
modest *adj.* 适度的,适中的
allocate *v.* 分派,分配
placement *n.* 工作安排,(人员的)安插
staff *n.* 全体职员,全体教员,全体雇员
nursery *n.* 托儿所

考题解析

Questions 15–20

15. 第 4 段中... many students have the opportunity of visiting and working in a European country...
16. Students' Union and SRC 部分中:... an Executive Committee elected by students in the Autumn Term. The president is elected every Summer Term...
17. Learning Resources Centre (LRC)部分中没有提到 staff。
18. 较难,易误选 NG。Children's Centre 部分中 Places are limited, so, if your are interested, apply early to reserve a place...
19. Refectory 部分中没有提到 fast-food。
20. 最后一段没有提到 for students only。

参考译文

坎特伯雷学院的学生生活

坎特伯雷学院一周只上四天课，留出一天独立学习。

整个学院有一种成人教育的环境，提倡学生和导师之间的互相尊重。

坎特伯雷是个学生城，有几所继续教育和高等教育学院。从坎特伯雷学院到市中心步行只需五分钟，午饭或课余的休息时间去那里很方便。

多年来，坎特伯雷学院已经与世界很多地方建立了稳定的联系。因此，许多学生在学习期间都有机会到某个欧洲国家参观和工作。

学生会和学生代表委员会

所有学生都自动成为坎特伯雷学院学生会的成员，可以参加其会议。学生会活动很多，由学生在秋季学期选出的执行委员会负责管理。主席在每个夏季学期选出，连任到下一学年。每个学科的代表组成学生代表委员会，它允许每个学生在学生会的事务中都有发言权。坎特伯雷学院学生会在校内的学术委员会中代表学生的利益，拥有学院公司的一个下属委员会，此外，它属于代表全国学生利益的全国学生联合会。学生会还安排、资助一些娱乐活动、体育活动和旅游。

学校设施

学习资料中心

在凯利学习资料中心很容易查到各种文字和音像学习资料，它们能帮助学生完成课程作业。这里既有宽敞的房间，适合安静地自习；又有地方进行小组活动。这里提供的资源包括书、杂志、音像带和CD光盘。通过英国图书馆可以在当地和全国范围内进行馆际借阅。所有学生都可利用位于一楼的开放取阅信息技术中心，它拥有各种各样的计算、文字处理和桌面出版软件。

书店

校园里有一家水石书店的连锁店，那里你可以买到各式各样的文具、绘画用具、艺术材料和书籍以及很多其他所需用品。

托儿所

有小孩的学生还可以把自己五岁以下的孩子送进学院的托儿所，有的还可以得到补贴。但名额有限，所以如果感兴趣，请尽早拨打学院电话，与琳达·贝克联系，申请预订。

餐厅

餐厅在8:30 – 19:00间提供一日三餐，除了热饭菜，还有茶点及饮料等。有健康饮食供您选择。

咖啡吧

咖啡吧在大学正常的工作时间都会开放，提供清淡快餐和饮料。咖啡吧的收入交给学生会。

地下餐厅

这是一家培训餐厅，这里饭菜可口，环境幽雅，价格合理。餐厅的开放日，欢迎你品尝技艺高超的学生们做的饭菜。订餐电话:01227511244

看得见小教堂的饭店

这也是一家培训饭店，创建它是为了提供快速服务，这里提供各种快餐和主菜，而且价格适中。

CANTERBURY COLLEGE
LIST OF COURSES

词汇注释

media *n.* 媒体
pursue *v.* 追求;追随;进行,从事
potential *n.* 潜能, 潜力
adaptability *n.* 适应性, 顺应性
thorough *adj.* 彻底的,完全的;详尽的,透彻的
grounding *n.* 基础;根基
comprehensive *adj.* 广泛的,全面的,综合的
workload *n.* 劳动负荷(量),工作负荷(量)
progression *n.* 前进,进步,发展
maintain *v.* 保持;维持;继续
salon(营业性的)厅,院,室,店;沙龙;客厅
duty *n.* 职责,职能;责任,义务
facial *adj.* 面部的
massage *n.* 按摩(术)
make-up *n.* 化妆品;化妆
lash *n.* 睫毛
brow *n.* 额;[常用复数]眉, 眉毛
artificial *adj.* 人工的,人造的
nail *n.* 指甲
pierce *v.* 刺入,刺;穿孔于
leisure *n.* 空闲, 闲暇;安逸
physical *adj.* 身体的;物质的
participant *n.* 参与者,参加者
colleague *n.* 同事,同僚
handle *v.* 运用;操纵;管理;处理
issue *n.* 问题,难题
foundation *n.* 基础;根据
career *n.* 职业;事业, 生涯
elderly *adj.* 上了年纪的;老年的
core *n.* 中心;核心
numeracy *n.* 识数,计算能力
graphic *adj.* 书写的;书法的;绘画的;图形的;用图表示的
visual *adj.* 视觉的, 视力的
composition *n.* 结构;构图;组织,织成;作文, 乐曲
photographic *adj.* 摄影的;照片的
alongside *prep.* 和…在一起;在…旁边
hands-on *adj.* 实习的;亲身实践的
presentation *n.* 介绍;陈述、描述;赠送;表达;呈现;展示
urban *adj.* 城市的,有关城市的,或居住在城市的
property *n.* 性质,特性;财产, 所有物, 所有权,
vocational *adj.* 职业(上)的;业务的
assignment *n.* 分配,分派,指定;任务;课题,作业
integrate *v.* 使结合(with);使并入(into);使一体化,使完全, 使成一整体
reputable *adj.* 著名的;名气好的
qualification *n.* 合格证明[证书],资格证明书;资格
employment *n.* 职业, 工作;雇用
spreadsheet *n.* 电子表格
database *n.* 数据库, 资料库
confidence *n.* 信心
appearance *n.* 外表,外貌
recommend *v.* 推荐;介绍
advertising *n.* 广告业;广告;总称 *adj.* 广告的总称
architecture *n.* 建筑; 建筑学
the disabled *n.* 残疾人
secretarial *adj.* 秘书的;秘书工作的;书记的
beauty therapy *n.* 美容院

考题解析

Questions 21–27 Matching

21. COURSE F 中:visual communication skills, picture composition, photographic processing...
22. COURSE A 中:performing arts, media
23. COURSE G 中:construction industry, Urban Environment, Materials
24. COURSE B 中:business, manage a heavy workload...
25. COURSE E 中:people with special needs.
26. COURSE H 中:office work, word processing, personal appearance...
27. COURSE C 中:salon, facial massage, skin care...

参考译文

坎特伯雷学院课程介绍

课程 A

本课程可以使学生们初步接触表演艺术和媒体。学生们有机会亲身经历，然后再决定是否希望在这一领域继续发展自己的兴趣，开发自己的潜力，提高适应性，从而在演艺公司做演员或技术工作。

课程 B

本课程旨在为学习商业有关的技巧和商务综合知识打下全面的基础。它为有过商业学习背景的学生而设计，他们能承受繁重的课业负担，其中包括进行较高水平的学术研究。

课程 C

本课程可使你全面提高水平。内容包括遵守职业标准，美容厅管理职责，还包括如何进行面部按摩、皮肤保养，如何化妆，如何修睫毛和眉毛，以及指甲美容和耳朵穿孔。

课程 D

设计此课程是为了提高休闲娱乐管理所需技能。它包括如何准备和进行体育活动，场地保养，与参与者和同事建立良好关系，操作、管理体育器材以及健康和安全问题。

课程 E

本课程为将来从事照顾儿童、老人和有特殊需求的人的工作奠定基础。它的核心内容是计算基础、交流、信息技术。工作实习是本课程的重要环节。

课程 F

本课程讲授图像和视觉通信技术的基础知识。学生们将学习图片结构分析、图像处理，图形设计因素，而且还可亲自进行桌面出版和演示。

课程 G

此课程简要介绍建筑业。讲授内容包括《热、光和声音》，《城市环境介绍》，《通讯过程和技术》和《材料的特性》。所有学生都可在知名大公司实习，并结合此工作经历写出实习报告。

课程 H

学完这门课后拿到的证书和学到的技能会为你找到一份办公室的工作打下良好基础。除了文字处理，本课程还讲授电子表格的制作，电算会计，数据库和桌面出版。所有学生都有机会发展自己的潜能，还可以得到有关找工作、面试技巧和个人外表方面的建议和信息。

SECTION 3

The History of Early Cinema

词汇注释

major *adj.* 重大的；主要的；较多的；

unparalleled *adj.* 无比的；空前的；（种类或质量方面）独一无二的

expansion *n.* 扩展，扩张；伸展，延长，发展

a handful of 一把；少数，少量

medium *n.* 传媒；新闻媒介

audience *n.* 听众，观众

entertainment *n.* 娱乐；消遣，乐趣；娱乐活动

finish up with 最后有…；以…告终

palace *n.* 宫，宫殿；宏伟的建筑物，华丽的娱乐场所

rival *v.* 与…竞争；与…相匹敌竞争

occasionally *adv.* 有时候，偶尔

supersede *v.* 代替；取代；占先于；接替

opera-house *n.* 歌剧院

opulence *n.* 富裕；豪华
splendour *n.* 光彩，壮丽；显赫，杰出
attraction *n.* 吸引，吸引力，吸引人的事物
a couple of 两个；几个
full-length feature 长片
dominate *v.* 支配，占优势；占支配地位
pioneer *n.* 开辟者；先锋，先驱；提倡者；创始人
credit *v.* 信任；归(功于某人)(to)；赞颂(with)；credit sb. with 认为某人[某事]具有…；认为某人[某事]能够…；把…归因于某人[某事]
exploitation *n.* (资源等的)开采；(为人物、影片、产品等所作的)宣传、广告
passionate *adj.* 热情的，热烈的
exporter *n.* 出口商；输出者
artistic *adj.* 艺术的；美术的
to take the lead *v.* 为首，带头
to play a part 扮演一个角色；参与，在…中起作用
remain *v.* 继续存在；保持
pursue *v.* 进行，从事；实行，推行；继续
vigorous *adj.* 有力的，强劲的
dominant *adj.* 支配的，统治的，占优势的；最有力的，有权威的
Hollywood 好莱坞(位于美国加利福尼亚洛杉矶城的西北)，美国电影业
studio *n.* 画室，照相室，工作室，(无线电或电视节目的)演播室，(制作电影的)摄影棚，(电影公司的)摄影场
flood *v.* 淹没；(洪水般地)涌进，涌满；充满
competitive *adj.* 竞争的，竞赛的；经得起竞争的
feature film 正片，故事片
spectacular *adj.* 引人注目的，壮观的；引人入胜的，轰动一时的
collapse *v.* 倒塌，崩溃，瓦解
Scandinavia 斯堪的纳维亚(半岛)(瑞典、挪威、丹麦、冰岛的泛称)
Swedish *n.* 瑞典人，瑞典语 *adj.* 瑞典的
glory *v.* 辉煌；繁荣，昌盛；光荣，荣誉
notably *adv.* 引人注目地，显著地；尤其；特别
epic *n.* 史诗 *adj.* 史诗的
comedy *n.* 喜剧；喜剧性事件；喜剧作品；喜剧因素
capable *adj.* 有能力的，能干的，有可能的，可以…的
commercial *adj.* 商业的；商品化的；商用的；以获利为目的的
isolation *n.* 隔绝，孤立，隔离
industrially *adv.* 产业上地
appeal *v.* 引起兴趣，有感染力
narrative *n.* 叙述，记事
impressive *adj.* 给人深刻印象的，感人的
dimension *n.* 特点，特性；方面，部分
innovation *n.* 创新，革新
survive *v.* 活下来，幸存，保存下来
correspond *v.* 与…一致；符合(to，with)
adventurous *adj.* 爱冒险的；充满危险的
deal with *v.* 安排；处理；涉及；做生意
primitive *adj.* 原始的，古老的；初期的，最早的；简单的
similar *adj.* 相似的，类似的
original *adj.* 最初的，原始的
slide *n.* 幻灯片
mixture *n.* 混合，混合物
comic *adj.* 喜剧的；使人发笑的；滑稽的；连环图画的
sketch *n.* 短剧[曲]；独幕剧
serial *adj.* 连续的，一系列的；连载的；连续广播的
episode *n.* (戏剧、电影、电视等的)连续剧的一出(或一集、一部分)；(小说、剧本的)插曲、片断；(连载小说的)一节
occasional *adj.* 偶然的；不定期的；临时的
trick *n.* 窍门；手法；技艺
animate *adj.* 动画的；动画片的
cartoon *n.* 卡通片，动画片；漫画
branch *n.* 枝，分枝，分部，分店，(学科)分科，部门，支流，支脉
newsreel *n.* 新闻片
slapstick *n.* 闹剧，趣剧
format *n.* 设计、计划、安排；(安排或表现的)样式，方式
thrive *v.* 兴旺，繁荣；茁壮成长
factual *adj.* 事实的，实际的；根据事实的
documentary *n.* 纪录片
acquire *v.* 获得，取得
distinctiveness *n.* 特殊性，独特性
avant-garde *adj.* 先锋派的(艺术) *n.* 先锋派
exclusively *adv.* 排外地，独占地；专有地，唯一地
maintain *v.* 保持；维持；继续
display *v.* 展现，展示；呈现
continuity *n.* 连续性；继续性；(电影、广播、电视节目的)连续
in spite of 虽然；尽管…仍
uncertainty *n.* 无常，不确定
pre-war *adj.* 战前的
explode *v.* 爆发；突发；激增，迅速扩大
scene *n.* 现场，场面；情景；舞台；活动范围
overshadow *v.* 遮蔽；使阴(暗)；使失色；使…相形见绌，超过

émigré *n.* 移居外国的人，移民
flee *v.* 逃走，逃避；消失，消散
escape *v.* 逃走，逃避，避免，
undistinguished *adj.* 未经区分的，听(看)不清的，普通的，平凡的
fame *n.* 声望，名气
Denmark 丹麦
proportion *n.* 相称，均衡；比例；比率 out of proportion 不合情理的
primarily *adv.* 最初，首先，原来；主要地，根本上
theatrical *n.* 戏剧表演（尤指业余演出）；戏剧表演艺术
influence *n.* 影响
plenty of 大量的，很多的
profitable *adj.* 有用的，有益的；有利可图的，可赚钱的
producer *n.* 生产者，制作者，演出人，（电影）制片人
responsible *adj.* 有责任的，可靠的，可依赖的，负责的
Soviet Union（前）苏联

考题解析

Questions 28–30 Multiple Choice

28. A 选项出自原文第 4 段第 4 行：... it had a great deal of money... 其中 money 对应选项中 capital。
29. D 选项出自原文第 4 段第 2 行：... because they had better-constructed narratives... 其中 better-constructed narratives 对应选项中 well-written narratives。
30. F 选项出自原文第 4 段第 2 行：... their special effects were more impressive... 其中 impressive special effects 对应选项中 excellent special effects。

Questions 31–33 Short Answer

31. 定位词 major studios。原文第 6 段倒数第 3 行中：cartoons... outside the major studios, and the same was true of serials.
32. 定位词 short, feature。原文第 7 段首句。
33. 较难。定位词 profitable, silent。原文第 7 段第 2 行出现“Silent Film” era，第 4 行：It was also at this time（指代上文说到的“Silent Film” era）that the avant-garde film first achieved commercial success... 其中 commercial success 对应 profitable。

Questions 34–40 Matching

34. 较难。定位词 helped other countries。原文第 2 段第 3 行：It was above all the French... the most passionate exporters... helping... 虽然原文也提到美国，但法国排第一，故选法国。
35. 该题考常识判断也可选出 USA。原文第 3 段。
36. 定位词 first, feature film。原文第 3 段第 7 行：The Italian industry, which had pioneered the feature film...
37. 定位词 creating stars。原文第 4 段讲述 Hollywood，第 3 行中 the star system。
38. 较难。定位词 money, avant-garde。原文第 7 段最后一句：... avant-garde film 首次获得商业上的成功，almost exclusively（这几乎要完全）归因于法国电影，occasional（偶尔）还有德国电影的发展。选法国。
39. 定位词 based more on own culture。原文最后一段倒数第 3 行：... Japan, where a cinema developed based primarily on traditional theatrical...
40. 定位词 silent, size。原文最后一段第 4 行... silent cinema quite out of proportion to their small population...

参考译文

电影早期发展史

电影在其发展史的头30年经历了重大的发展变化,这直到现在都是无与伦比的。电影这种奇特玩意儿首先出现在纽约、伦敦、巴黎和柏林等几个大城市,但作为新媒体它很快风靡全世界。不管它出现在哪里,都能吸引越来越多的观众,从而取代了其他的娱乐方式。随着观众的增加,电影放映场所也就增加,最后在二十世纪20年代出现了一些"大型电影院",其豪华和壮观能与当时的剧院和歌剧院相媲美,有时还会超过它们。同时,电影自身也从只持续几分钟的短片发展成了大型故事片,直到现在它在世界电影界都占着主导地位。

尽管电影被认为是法国、德国、美国和英国人发明的,但英国人和德国人在电影发展史上所起的作用相对较小。首先是法国人,紧随其后的是美国人(电影这一新发明最热情的传播者),他们帮助中国、日本、拉丁美洲及俄国开创电影事业。在电影的艺术制作方面还是法国和美国名列前茅,尽管在一战之前意大利、丹麦和俄国也起了一定的作用。

最后是美国发展成为(现在仍然是)最大的电影市场。通过保护自己的市场,推行灵活的出口政策,美国人在一战开始的时候就取得了在世界电影市场上的霸主地位。电影制作中心向西迁移到好莱坞,正是这些从好莱坞崭新的摄影棚里拍摄的影片一战之后源源不断地涌入世界电影市场,而且从此一发不可收拾。面对好莱坞的全面霸主地位,几乎没有几个国家的电影业能与之抗衡。开辟故事片先河的意大利电影业(曾拍摄巨片《暴君焚城录》(1913)和《卡比莉亚》(1914))也几乎垮掉。在斯堪的纳维亚,瑞士电影业曾以其英雄史诗电影和喜剧而著名,但也只是短暂的辉煌。甚至法国的电影业也处境维艰。在欧洲,只有德国的电影在商业上有所发展,但刚成立的苏联和日本电影的发展却远离商业的影响。

好莱坞电影在艺术上和产业上都占领先地位。它吸引人的原因在于其故事构思更巧妙,特技更具感染力,明星阵容又给银屏表演增添了新看点。即使好莱坞自己资源不够,但它拥有大笔资金,可从欧洲聘请艺术家、购买新的技术设备,以保证它目前和将来的霸主地位。

世界上其他电影业能够存活下去的部分原因是他们效仿好莱坞,部分原因是仍然有些观众喜欢适合自己口味的电影,而好莱坞并不拍这类电影。除了爱看流行大片的观众外,还有越来越多的观众喜欢看在艺术上更具探索性或涉及外层空间问题的电影。

没有技术支持所有这些都无法实现。作为一种艺术形式,电影有其独特性。刚刚起步那几年,这种艺术形式很原始,和法国十七世纪使用灯笼和幻灯片的最初做法很相似。早期的电影形式是个大杂烩,包括喜剧短剧、独立故事片、系列剧,偶尔还有滑稽剧或动画片。随着越来越多的人喜欢长篇故事片,其他类型的电影就变得不那么重要了。卡通片制作成为电影制作的一个分支,拍摄通常在大摄影棚外面进行系列剧也是一样,和纪录片一样,它们常常在放映之前作为短片在节目中播放。

在早期的电影中,只有美国的闹剧成功地发展为短片和长片两种形式。然而,在无声电影时代,动画片、喜剧片、系列剧和戏剧故事片,连同纪实电影或纪录片都不断蓬勃发展;随着时代的发展,这些影片都越来越需要有自己独特的风格。也正是在这个时期,先锋电影首次获得商业上的成功,这几乎要完全归因于法国电影,多少还有德国电影的发展。

在无声电影时期,有些国家发展并保持了具有自己鲜明特色的民族电影,其中最重要的有法国、德国和苏联。尽管法国在战争期间和战后经济很不稳定,但其电影的发展表现得最具连贯性。战前相对逊色一点的德国电影业在1919年迅速发展,登上世界舞台。然而,1917年革命之后的俄国电影发展迅猛,其势头盖过了前两个国家。苏联人抛开战前俄国的电影风格,但因避开革命而逃到西部的移民们却把它继承下来。

还有一些国家的电影也发生了巨大变化。英国在无声电影时期有过一段有趣但不显赫的历史;

意大利只是在战前在国际上名噪一时；在斯堪的纳维亚半岛国家，尤其是丹麦在无声电影的发展中起了重大作用，其作用之大与其人口之少，简直不成比例。日本电影主要是在传统戏剧表演和较小程度上其他艺术形式的基础上发展起来的，但它渐渐受到了西方电影的影响。

WRITING

WRITING TASK 1

This model has been prepared by an examiner as an example of a very good answer.

Dear Sir or Madam,

My name is Wang Li and I was in your store Wednesday last week. I would like to bring to your attention an incident that occurred while I was in your store.

I was browsing through the canned soft drinks and noticed a particularly good brand of almond juice. When I reached and removed a can to check the contents, the whole shelf collapsed, dumping at least 100 cans of various sorts onto the floor, me and other customers. In my opinion, this resulted entirely from the overloading of the shelves. As you can imagine, this was not only disruptive for the other shoppers but also extremely embarrassing for me. Luckily the injuries I sustained were minor. Unfortunately I cannot speak for anyone else as people dispersed fairly quickly to allow the staff to clean up the mess.

May I suggest that in future during regular maintenance the staff make sure that the display units are secure and when restocking, put out fewer products in order to prevent a similar accident from happening.

Yours sincerely,

(173 **words**)

参考译文

亲爱的先生或女士，

我叫王丽。我上周三曾去过你们商店，我想告诉你在你们商店发生的一件事，以引起你的注意。

当时我正在随意打量一些灌装软性饮料，后来发现了一种名牌的杏仁露。我伸手拿起一罐，想看一下产品的内容说明，这时整个架子就倒了。至少100罐各种各样的饮料都被倒在了地板上，我和其他几个顾客也被撞倒在地。我想，这完全是由于货架负荷过重造成的。可想而知，这不仅惊扰了其他顾客，也使我极为难堪。幸运的是，我只是受了点轻伤。遗憾的是，我找不到其他任何人来证明此事，因为人们当时很快散去了，好让工作人员收拾残局。

我建议，将来工作人员在常规检修中要保证货架的安全，上货时要少放些商品，以防止类似事件再次发生。

WRITING TASK 2

This model has been prepared by an examiner as an example of a very good answer.

There has been a change in the amount of work people are willing to do repairing their homes and fabricating their own clothing for a number of reasons, particularly in China.

In recent years, foreign companies have injected billions of dollars into the Chinese economy, allowing the local population to make more money than ever before. Graduates from universities often seek employment with foreign companies, which offer far better opportunities, wages and benefit packages than state or privately owned Chinese businesses. This has led to an increase in disposable income. Given this increase and the cheap cost of labor, people would much rather pay someone to repair their homes because they can afford it.

Social values have also changed more recently in China, giving rise to the "brand name" generation. Young people with good jobs or wealthy parents would much rather purchase brand name clothing than wear sweaters that grandma spent hours knitting. At least in the Eastern parts of China, people are becoming increasingly conscious of the social status of brand name clothing and being able to hire someone to decorate or repair their homes.

Part of the changing social situation in China can also be attributed to the lack of interest young people have in pursuing these kinds of activities. I think it is true in most cultures that as societies become more affluent, traditional values and activities tend to decline. Of course, there are always those who struggle to save the "culture" of the country, but they are quickly becoming the minority, which to my way of thinking is very unfortunate.

To conclude, China, like every other developing country in the world is facing a dilemma: do we change to become a better country and help our people to sustain life or hide and remain insular and ignorant to outside influences? I would choose the former.

(309 **words**)

参考译文

由于许多原因,尤其是在中国,人们在愿意自己修房子、自己做衣服的事情上已经起了变化。

近年来,外国公司给中国经济注入了大量的资金,从而让地方人口赚到的钱比以往任何时候都多。大学毕业生经常去外国公司求职,和中国的国有企业和私有企业相比,外企提供更多的机会、工资和福利待遇也更高,这就使可支配收入有所增加。由于工资的增加和劳动力成本的低廉,人们更愿意花钱请人修房子,因为他们出得起钱。

中国的社会价值观在最近几年也发生了一些变化,结果产生了所谓的"名牌"代。工作不错或者父母有钱的年轻人更愿意买名牌衣服,而不愿意穿奶奶花几个小时编制的毛衣。至少在中国东部,人们越来越意识到名牌服装的社会地位,他们能雇人装饰和整修他们的家。

中国社会环境的变化一部分还可以归因于年轻人对做这些事情缺乏兴趣。我认为大多数文化都是这样:随着社会变得更加富裕,传统价值观和传统做法会呈下降趋势。当然,总是会有一些人拼命想保住国家的"文化",但他们很快就成了少数,我认为这是很不幸的。

总之,中国像世界上其他发展中国家一样正面临一个两难境地:我们是改革、成为一个更强的国家、帮助人们过好日子?还是闭关自守、与世隔绝、不受外面的影响?我会选择前者。

General Training: Reading and Writing Test B

READING

SECTION 1

Questions 1–7

词汇注释

brochure *n.* 小册子;手册;简介材料
alternative *adj.* 两者择一的;选择的
cottage *n.* 村舍;小别墅
availability *n.* 可用性，有效性，实用性
reservation *n.*（旅馆房间、剧院座位等的）预订;保留[存]，备用，储备
suitable *adj.* 适合的;恰当的
provisional *adj.* 临时的，暂定的
reference number 参考编号
deposit *n.* 保证金，押金;存款
rental *n.* 租金总额;出租的财产
confirmation *n.* 确定，确立，证实;确认，批准;确认书
payable *adj.* 应支付的;可支付的
outstanding *adj.* 显著的，著名的;未付的;未解决的，未完成的
caretaker *n.* 管理者，看管者，看守者
sufficient *adj.* 足够的，充分的
property *n.* 财产;所有物(不可数)
delighted *adj.* 喜欢的，高兴的
pound sterling *n.* 英镑
linen *n.* 被单;床单;亚麻布;亚麻布制品
duvet *n.* 羽毛被褥
pillow case *n.* 枕套
towel *n.* 毛巾
query *n.* 疑问;问题
slightly *adv.* 轻微地;有一点;略
receipt *n.* 收到;收条，收据
majority *n.* 多数，大半

考题解析

Questions 1–7 True/False/Not Given

1. 定位词 February，属于原文 21st October to 30th March 部分：Saturday 9:30 a. m. to 4:30 p. m. 平时 weekdays 下午 5:00 关门。
2. 原文中：When we receive your booking form and deposit, your reservation will be confirmed—we will send you a Booking Confirmation... 而非打电话。
3. 原文 ARRIVAL 部分前一句：Outstanding balances on bookings made in the UK must be settled within 10 weeks of sending the deposit. 其中 settle 的意思在这里是“完结，付账”。对应 paid。
4. 原文 DEPARTURE 部分第一句。
5. 难题，易选 NG。原文 Last-minute Bookings 部分中第 2 段：If your reservation is made within 10 weeks of the holiday start date, full payment is due on booking. 请注意 within 10 weeks 就是指 last-minute，而 full payment 和题干中 lower 相斥。
6. 原文 ELECTRICITY 部分第一句。
7. 原文 LINEN 部分第 5 行：If you choose to hire linen... but will not include towels for swimming or beach use.

参考译文

预订韦塞克斯假日别墅

假日别墅预订方法

看过我们的手册、选中两三栋别墅后，请致电我们的假日预订办公室。

联系电话：01225 892299

3月31日——10月20日

星期一、二、三、五 上午9:00——下午5:00

星期四 上午9:30——下午5:00

星期六、日休息

10月21日——3月30日

星期一、二、三、五 上午9:00——下午5:00

星期四上午9:30——下午5:00

星期六上午9:30——下午4:30

星期天休息

我们将查看您选中的别墅是否空着，预订处的工作人员将帮您做出选择。如果您所选的别墅已经全部订出，我们将尽力向您推荐其他合适的选择方案。

一经做出暂行预订，就将保留七天。我们会给您一个参考编号，请您填写一份假日别墅预订单并寄回给我们，并随寄相当于别墅总租金三分之一的押金。

我们的通信地址是：威尔特希尔郡默尔克沙姆市韦塞克斯假日别墅预订处

邮箱：675号（邮编：SN12 8SX）

押金可在预订时用信用卡支付，也可采用支票付给韦塞克斯乡村别墅有限公司。

如果七天之内我们未收到您填写好的预订单和押金，很抱歉您的预订将被取消。

收到您的预订单和押金后，我们将对您的预订进行确定。我们将寄给你预订确认书，并告诉您如何到达假日别墅，以及当地的联系方式，以防您在离家前需要了解更多的细节。随确认书寄去的还有一个通知单，上面写着剩下的款项及交款时间。在英国，大额预订欠款应在交押金后的十周内付清。

到达

请不要在下午3:30前或7:00后到达假日别墅

离开

离开的那天上午，请您在10点前停止使用别墅物品，以便管理者有足够的时间为下一位客人整理好所需物品。请您物归原样，不要挪动家具，因为那样可能会对家具和物品造成损坏。

海外预订

我们欢迎海外预订，您可以打电话或发传真，号码是：+ 44(0)1225890227。所有费用请用信用卡或支票以英镑的形式支付。请注意：海外临时预订可保留14天。如果在规定日期内未能收到填好的订单和押金，预订将被取消。

紧急预订

如果您想做紧急预订，请致电假日订票处查询。

如果您在假日开始十周内进行预订，预订时就要将款一次付清。

电费

在绝大多数韦塞克斯的乡间别墅，除了其他假日费用，用电也是要付费的。假日旅行结束的时候，可能会要您查看电表，或额外收取一定的电费。屋内可能装有投币电表，这种情况在您预订时会向您说明的。在有些别墅，租金里就含有电费。不交电费的情况是极少的。

日用品

在大多数韦塞克斯别墅,您可以选择租用日用品,租金是每人每周6英镑。也可以自己带。有些别墅备有日用品,完全没有日用品的极为少见。如您选择租用,它会包括床上用品(褥单、羽毛被褥和枕头)、浴巾、手巾和台布,但不包括游泳或去海滩用的毛巾。不提供折叠床的床单。如有问题,请向假日预订处咨询。

Questions 8–14

词汇注释

charter *n.* (政府颁发的)特许状,凭照,许可证
v. 给予…特权;特许设立;chartered 特许的
accountant *n.* 会计师
auditing *n.* 查账,审计,审核
accountancy *n.* 会计工作;会计职务
taxation *n.* 征税;纳税;税款
garage *n.* 车库;汽车修理厂
mechanical *adj.* 机械的;与机械有关的
insurance *n.* 保险,保险单,保险业,保险费
respray *n.* 重新喷涂,重新油漆
restoration *n.* 恢复;修补,翻修,整新
breakdown *n.* 崩溃,破坏,断裂;故障
victim *n.* 受害人,牺牲品
fault *n.* 过错,缺点
solicitor *n.* 律师,(多用于英国)初级律师;法律顾问
compensation *n.* 补偿,赔偿
buffet *n.* 快餐;快餐部
cater *v.* 备办酒菜,承办酒席;提供食物(娱乐节目)
caterer *n.* 酒宴承办人
function *n.* 重大聚会,宴会;庆祝仪式
quote *n.* [口]引语,引文
stated *adj.* 规定的,确定的,固定的
budget *n.* 预算
town hall *n.* 市政厅
venue *n.* (行动、事件等的)发生地点,举行场所,会场
reliable *adj.* 可靠的,可信赖的
knight *n.* (欧洲中世纪的)骑士,武士;爵士;(人名)奈特
estate *n.* 地产,遗产,不动产,财产,产业;财产权
agent *n.* 代理人,代理商
Pascal *n.* 帕斯卡
surrounding *n.* (*pl.*)周围的事物,环境
brasserie *n.* 啤酒店
table d'hote (按规定菜肴的价格供应的)份饭,套餐
guarantee *v.* 保证,担保
commission *n.* 代办费,手续费;佣金
ensuite 成套地,构成一体地
licensed *adj.* 有官方许可的;有酒类专卖许可证的(亦作:licenced)
conference *n.* 协商,谈判;讨论会,协商会;会议
occasion *n.* 场合,时机,机会
interpret *v.* 口译
voice-over *n.* (电视等的)画外音;旁白叙述
editorial *adj.* 编辑的;社论的
localisation *n.* 定位,定域
analysis *n.* 分析,分解

考题解析

Questions 8–14 Matching

8. 定位词 car, broken, replaced。对应 B 中:mechanical, repair。
9. 定位词 at the bride's family's house, provide the food。对应 D 中:in your home, you supply the venue, we will supply the menu.
10. 定位词 lawyer, paperwork。对应 K 中 solicitors, legal services。
11. 定位词 Thai recipe book, help me understand。对应 L 中 translation, interpreting。
12. 定位词 somewhere to live locally。对应 G 中 estate and property agents。
13. 定位词 the weekend, somewhere for them to stay。注意和 12 题区分开。12 题要找长期的住宿地点 somewhere to live,13 题要找短期聚留的地点 somewhere to stay。对应 J 中:conference room available for meeting, wedding, parties & all other special occasions.
14. 定位词 tax, organise our finances。对应 A 中:accountants, taxation。

参考译文

A

史迪曼有限公司
注册会计师

提供所有专业服务,包括从小
企业到大公司的审计、会计和纳税。
随时提供个人咨询
伊利市教堂街 12 号
电话:(01353)562547/561331

B

圣保罗汽修部(伊利)
全方位机械及车身修理服务
由保险公司承保
重新喷漆和翻新
故障排除服务
剑桥郡伊利市河街 6 号
邮编:CB6 4BU
电话:伊利 552247

C

车祸受害者吗?

在车祸中受伤了吗?是别人的过失吧?
让咨询律师免费为您查明能否
要求索赔。

拨打
免费电话:0800 8760831 (24 小时)

国内事故求助热线

D

美罗斯快餐酒席承办
拥有 15 年酒席承办的专业经验
订餐之前请听我们的承诺:我们将在您规定的预算范围内提供最佳服务。无论宴会大小,我们都能承办:可以在您的家里、办公室、花园、市政厅、教堂,确切的说,任何您喜欢的地方。
"您提供地点,我提供美食"
——为您量身定做的佳肴
剑桥郡密尔顿市柏利路 28 号
电话:01223 640789

E

LM 大型轿车租赁

为婚庆或其他特殊活动
提供个人租车活动

约翰 & 苏·毕晓普

伊利市法尔街 12A 白宫
邮编:CB6 1AE
电话:01353 667184

F

机票速订

您通往世界的热线
如果您正为到世界某地订机票
犯愁,如果您在考虑周到的服务与
便宜的价格同等重要
请致电:0990 320321
赫兹赫特福德市
联合路 25 号
邮编:CM23 2LY

G

巴顿·希尔和奈特公司

地产和财产代理商
特许房产鉴定估价人

商业财产
家庭财产和艺术品拍卖
独立的财产服务，提供专家咨询

贝利 ST 埃德蒙兹
01284 800717

萨福克郡贝利 ST 埃德蒙兹市
迪斯路 15 号

H

帕斯卡饭店

法式饭店和啤酒店
允许酒类出售

在轻松的环境中享受新鲜美食
外加一杯葡萄酒

营业时间：
午饭——有啤酒供应——周一至周日
晚饭——三道菜的套餐，固定价位，
周三至周六

本饭店为无烟饭店
剑桥郡小港市沼泽路 2 号
01353 565011
请不要用信用卡

I

全球旅游

外币兑换业务
每周工作六天
$ 保障最佳兑换率 £
收取最低手续费

剑桥郡伊利市行进路 14 号
电话：01353 551136

J

花园之乡

· 设备完善，房间宽敞，家具成套，
包括彩电，茶具及咖啡自制设备
· 特许饭店和酒吧
· 为会议、婚礼、聚会和其他特殊活动
提供会议室

电话：(01440) 862581
哈弗里尔市快乐山

K

贝克，斯图尔特和杨律师事务所

提供广泛的法律服务

剑桥郡伊利商业街 2 号

电话：(01353)552918

L

FINE LINE 翻译有限公司

1984 年以来最杰出的语言学家
3000 多名专业翻译聚集于此
笔译和口译

笔译	桌面出版
口译	本地化
旁白叙述	媒体分析
编辑业务	

电话：+44 (0)1223 856732
传真：(0)1223 821588
剑桥郡城堡院 5 号，邮编：CBI 2PQ

SECTION 2

Questions 15–21

Courses Available at North Coast College Campuses

词汇注释

rural *adj.* 乡下的；农村的
renown *n.* 名声，传闻，谣传 *v.* 使有声望
module *n.* 模件，组件
macadamia [植]澳大利亚坚果
bushfood 丛林食品
veterinary *n.* 兽医 *adj.* 医牲畜的，兽医的
agristudy *n.* 农业研究
flexibly *adv.* 可变通地，能适应环境地
correspondence *n.* 通信，信件，函件
tutorial *n.* 个人辅导；受大学教育时间
session *n.* （从事某项活动的）一段时间，（一届）会议；会期
workshop *n.* 专题学术讨论会；讨论会会议录；专题研究小组
traineeship *n.* 受训练的情况（时间）；受训者的地位
fitness *n.* 健康，结实
theoretical *adj.* 理论的；理论上的
practical *adj.* 实际的，实践的，实用的，应用的
residential *adj.* 住宅的，与居住有关的
remedial *adj.* 治疗的；补救的；矫正的
clinic *n.* 诊所；门诊部
determine *v.* 决定；决心
impact *n.* 碰撞，冲击，冲突；影响，效果
degrade *v.* 降低；降级；退化
regeneration *n.* 再生，重建
pathway *n.* 路径，通道，轨迹
marine *adj.* 海的；海中的；海船的

参考译文

北海岸一些大学的可选课程

农业

北海岸大学的专业农业中心开设农业技术、牛肉制造、马的研究和农村管理等课程。伍伦巴农业研究院以其热带水果种植研究而著名，而且开设了澳大利亚坚果、丛林食品及咖啡加工方面的选修课程。塔里学院开设助理兽医和农业研究课程，通过函授，综合利用学生辅导、电话辅导、学习交流会和研讨会等手段，让学生们学得更灵活。马伦宾比开设当今流行的农村商业管理课程，这门课可通过函授学习。同时，格拉夫顿开设包括牛肉和乳品业方面的农业培训课程。

保健课程

通过在社区内不断宣传更加健康的生活方式，人们的健康意识增强了，对健身运动行业培训人员的需求也有所增加。特威德赫兹开设健身指导课程，教学生们如何组织和实施安全的健康计划。

利斯莫尔开设老年人照顾课程，麦考理港有婴儿护理课程。从这些课程中你既可学到理论技巧和知识，又能掌握实践经验。要在各种居民区和社区办的保健机构工作，就需要有这方面的培训。对于有志于从事医疗保健行业的学生，金斯克里福是所专门学校，那里可获得自然疗法文凭，而且校园里就有保健门诊部。

环境研究

北海岸学院开设的环境研究课程旨在帮助学生增强对环境问题的意识和了解，使他们能够明白这些问题对环境的影响。巴林纳学院开设环境实践课，其中包括海岸管理。

对恢复被毁自然森林感兴趣的同学，可选择北海岸学院。该学院在卡西诺开设了森林再造课程，这门课为学生们提供了在大学获得自然资源管理文凭的途径。在考夫斯港则开设了海洋业管理课程。

Questions 22–27

Information on Photocopying

词汇注释

photocopier *n.* 影印机，复印机
laser *n.* 激光
printer *n.* 打印机，印刷机
plastic *adj.* 塑胶的
initially *adv.* 最初，开头
purchase *v.* 买，购买 *n.* 买，购买
refund *n.* 归还，偿还额，退款
teller machine *n.* 自动柜员机
denomination *n.* （度量衡等的）单位，面额
lab *abbr.* 实验室，试验室（laboratory）
optional *adj.* 可选择的，随意的
allocate *v.* 拨给，分配，配置

考题解析

Questions 22–27 True/False/Not Given

22. 原文第1段中3个地方是：library，B Block，SRC。
23. 原文第2段第3行：students and other users will have to purchase a Prepaid Services Card from a teller machine located in the Library or B Block Computer labs.
24. 原文中没有提到最小数额，也没有$5的字样。
25. 原文中没有提到library fines。
26. 原文第4段最后一句：The SRC has a smaller, coin only, teller machine.
27. 易错。题目中说：当你购买卡时，PIN会分配好。原文中最后一段说：为了更加安全，你可以选择设置一个PIN。说明购买卡时是没有PIN的，你如果想更安全一点，可以自己设置密码，这项服务是可选的。

参考译文

复印须知

信息服务中心在图书馆安装了预付服务卡系统。学生和工作人员可持卡使用图书馆的复印机和相关设备，以及B楼内的激光打印机。学生代表委员会大楼内最近也安装了同样的系统，以便那里的复印机也可以使用。

此系统使用一个类似用户识别卡的塑料卡，这种被称为预付服务卡的卡片每张都有一个独一无二的能进入系统的六位数账号。首先，学生及其他使用者必须从安装在图书馆或B楼计算机实验室的自动柜员机上购买一张预付服务卡，每张卡2美元。千万要记住卡上面的账号，并签上你的名字，或者写上学生证号码。

使用者通过给预付服务卡充值享受图书馆、计算机中心和学生代表委员会的服务。此卡不能退款，所以最好用多少冲多少。预付服务或充值金额最多不能超过50美元。

学校已安装了两台纸币和硬币柜员机，一台在图书馆二层的复印室，另一台在B楼的计算机实验室。这些柜员机可识别50美元以内的纸币和硬币。学生代表委员会有一个较小的柜员机，只可使用硬币。

用户购买新卡时，图书馆和B楼的电子计算机实验室的柜员机会自动给用户开收据。但是，给现有卡加钱时，是否开收据你可以选择。

为了更加安全，持卡人可选择在预付服务卡中设置个人身份号码（PIN）。每次用卡时必须输入此号码。

SECTION 3

Questions 28–40

Understanding Bee Behaviour

词汇注释

tiny *adj.* 微小的；极小的	**waggle** *v.* 来回摇动，摆动
encode *v.* 译成密码(电码)；编(译)码	**semi-circle** *n.* 半圆形
complex *adj.* 复杂的，多元的，综合的，错综的	**particular** *adj.* 特殊的，特别的，独特的
amazing *adj.* 令人惊异的	**troop** *v.* 成群移动；群集、成群；成群地来去
behavioral *adj.* 行为的，关于行为的	**spiral** *n.* 螺旋 *v.* 盘旋
witness *v.* 亲眼看见，目睹；表明，显示	**sniff** *v.* 用鼻吸气；[非正式用语]寻找
arguably *adv.* 可论证地，正如可提出证据加以证明的那样；可能，大概	**downwind** *adj.* 顺风的 *adv.* 在下风
apart from 除…外	**come into play** *v.* 开始活动
decade *n.* 十年，十	**measurement** *n.* 测量，度量
pure *adj.* 纯粹的；纯洁的，纯净的；无错的，完美的	**hunch** *n.* 直觉；预感
unravel *v.* 拆开；(使某事物)变清楚或被解决	**actual** *adj.* 实际的，真实的
astonishing *adj.* 惊人的；令人惊讶的	**precise** *adj.* 精确的，准确的
award *v.* 把…奖给，授与	**indicate** *v.* 表明；显示；象征；暗示
derive *v.* 获得；起源于，出自(from)	**horizontal** *adj.* 地平的；水平的；平(坦)的；横的(与 vertical 相对)
syrup *n.* 糖浆	**entrance** *n.* 入口，进口
realise *v.* 明白	**platform** *n.* 台，平台，高出之地
pass on 传递	**vertical** *adj.* 垂直的；竖式的；直立的
spot *n.* 地点，场所，现场	**portion** *n.* 一部分，一分
scout *n.* 侦察员；童子军；侦察；搜索	**decode** *v.* 解码，译解
scamper *v.* 蹦蹦跳跳；奔逃，惊奔	**merely** *adv.* 仅仅，只，不过
alternate *v.* 交替，轮流	**inner** *adj.* 内部的；里面的
occasionally *adv.* 有时，偶而地	**gravity** *n.* 重力；(地心)引力；重量
regurgitate *v.* 吐出；(动物)反刍；使回流	**represent** *v.* 代表
chase *v.* 追赶，追逐	**remarkable** *adj.* 不平常的；值得注意的；显著的
sickle *n.* 镰刀	**revolutionize** *v.* 使变革
distinctly *adv.* 清楚地，显然	

考题解析

Questions 28–34 List of Headings

28. A 段中：For bees are arguably the only animals apart from humans which have their own language. 对应 the special position。
29. B 段最后一句，蜜蜂传递 messages，对应 communicate。
30. 注意 C 段讲到 three dance types。
31. D 段首句中：first two related types。

32. 重点注意E中的第2段。
33. F段第2行:outside;第5行:different directions。
34. G段首句:But by studying the dace on the inner wall of the hive...第3行:When inside the hive。

Questions 35–37 Short Answer

原文C段就提到了蜜蜂有三种舞蹈,但没有给出舞蹈的名字。D段首句中出现了两种:...the round and the sickle dances。第三种舞蹈的名称出现在E段第8行:...the third, quite different, waggle dance。

Questions 38–40 Sentence Completion

38. 原文D段和E段中三种舞蹈的不同和原因。所以应该在这两段里寻找答案,找到E段第4行:...he started gradually moving the feeding dish further and further away...
39. 定位词outside,应该在F段中找答案。F段倒数第2行:...the dance pointed directly to the food source...
40. 定位词angle, vertical。注意到G段中出现40°,是angle的标志,找到G段倒数第3句。

参考译文

蜜蜂行为揭秘

A 蜜蜂的大脑和一颗草籽一样大,但在这个小脑袋里却隐藏着一些人类看不到的最复杂、最惊人的行为模式。除人类以外,蜜蜂可以认为是唯一拥有自己语言的动物。本世纪早些时候,慕尼黑大学动物学教授Karl Van Frisch花了几十年进行"最纯粹的快乐的发现",从而揭开了蜜蜂行为的秘密。由于他惊人的成就,他获得了诺贝尔奖。关于蜜蜂之间说些什么,今天的大部分知识都来自于他的成果。

B 开始的时候很简单。Van Frisch从一位早期研究者的实验中发现,如果他在外面放一碗糖浆,蜜蜂刚开始可能不那么容易发现它,但糖浆一旦被发现,一小时内就会有数百只蜜蜂赶来争吃。Frisch明白,消息正传回蜂巢,消息说,"外边,就在这个地方,可以找到吃的。"

C 但这是如何发生的呢?为了观察蜜蜂,Van Frisch建造了一个四面都是玻璃的蜂巢。他发现,找到食物源的侦查蜂一旦回到蜂巢,就会跳三种舞中的一种。侦察蜂跳的第一种舞是圆圈舞。身体轮流向左或向右旋转着,偶尔停下来,给追随其后、兴奋不已的蜜蜂吐出些食物样品。第二种舞蹈明显是圆圈舞的引申版。她表演镰刀形的8字舞。第三种舞蹈明显不同,她先是笔直地爬一小段,身体左右摇摆着,然后沿半圆路线返回原地,之后就反复重复上面的过程。他还不时地停下来给那些讨东西的蜜蜂东西吃;很快其他蜜蜂就会兴奋地离开蜂巢去寻找食物。Frisch注意到,几分钟后,很多蜜蜂就会出现在糖浆碗边。

D 经过进一步的实验,Van Frisch揭开了前两种有关系的舞蹈(圆圈舞和镰刀舞)的秘密。他得出的结论是,这两种舞蹈都只是告诉蜜蜂一个信息,蜂巢附近就有值得去找的食物源。侦查蜂舞跳的时间越长,越兴奋,食物源可能就越丰富。对其他蜜蜂来说,她携带的食物样品及身上的气味就是一种信息:这种东西正是他们正在寻找的特别食物。之后其他蜜蜂就会倾巢出动,呈螺旋形飞起来,在风中"闻着"找侦察蜂许诺过的食物。

E 开始时,Van Frisch认为蜜蜂只是对食物气味有反映。但第三种舞蹈的意思是什么呢?如果蜜蜂只是对气味有反应,它们又如何能闻到离蜂巢数百米之外的食物呢?况且有时候这些食物还在它们的下风?出于直觉,他开始把喂蜜蜂的食物移得越来越远。在这个过程中,他注意到,返回的侦查蜂的舞蹈也开始起变化了。如果他把盘子移到九米以外,第二种舞蹈——镰刀舞——就开始上演了,但一旦把食物移到36米以外的地方,侦查蜂就会跳截然不同的第三种舞——摇摆舞。

他得出的结论是：蜜蜂对实际距离的测量也是很准确的。例如，要表示食物在 300 米远的地方，蜜蜂就会在 30 秒内完整地跳 15 次摇摆舞；如果把食物移到 60 米远的地方，它们跳舞的次数就会减到 11 次。

F Van Frisch 还有进一步的发现。当侦察蜂返回蜂巢把食物源告诉他们的姐妹们时，她们有时会在蜂巢外面的水平入口处的平台上跳舞，有时则在蜂巢内陡直的墙面上跳。而且，根据不同的跳舞地点，摇摆舞的笔直部分就会指向不同的方向。蜂巢外面的舞蹈很容易破解：笔直部分直接指向食物源，所以蜜蜂只需要解读出这种距离信息，然后就朝那个方向飞去寻找它们的食物。

G 但是通对蜜蜂在巢内墙上舞蹈的研究，Van Frisch 发现了侦察蜂的一个绝招——她能以太阳的位置为参照告诉姐妹们食物源的方位。在蜂巢内部，跳舞的蜜蜂无法利用太阳，于是她利用地心引力。蜂巢壁的顶端代表着太阳的方向。如果她笔直地爬上去，这就意味着食物源和太阳在同一个方向。但是如果食物源位于太阳偏左 40 度的地方，那跳舞的蜜蜂就沿垂直线偏左 40 度向上爬。这是 Van Frisch 众多重大发现的开始。不久他又对蜜蜂之间如何交流有了重大发现，从而在整个动物行为研究领域引发了一场革命。

WRITING

WRITING TASK 1

这是考官准备的一篇优秀范文(原文在《剑桥雅思 4》)第 172 页)，请注意答案可以千变万化，下面只是其中之一。

亲爱的 Jan：

你知道，我们很快就要搬新家了，有一些东西带不走。新房子要小一点，所以我得卖掉一些家具，不知道你感不感兴趣？

我特别想卖的是大餐桌。你记得吗——客厅里的那张？桌腿是木头的，桌面是灰色玻璃的，足够六个人用，有六把配套的椅子。

我知道你一直喜欢这个家具，所以我可以以优惠价给你。与其卖给一个陌生人，我宁愿卖给你！

为什么星期六不过来再看一看呢？我们整天都会在这里，也许我们可以一起吃中饭？

等你电话。

爱你的，
Shanda

WRITING TASK 1

考官范文翻译。这是考官准备的一篇优秀范文，请注意答案可以千变万化，下面只是其中之一。

如今，很多地方的小孩大概 6、7 岁开始上小学。但是，因为现在父母双方都工作的可能性越来越大，小孩很少有机会能一直呆在自己家里到这个年龄。他们可能很小就到托儿所去了。

虽然有的人认为这样会对孩子的发展或孩子与父母的关系造成伤害，但其实小时候有上学的体验好处很多。

首先,孩子会学会和很多各不相同的人打交道,有的孩子因此很早就学会了沟通。通常,他们比那些和父母一起呆在家里、不习惯陌生人或新环境的孩子更加自信、独立。这样的孩子到了 6 岁发现上学第一天非常可怕,这可能对他们的学习产生负面影响。

早上学的另一个好处是孩子在社交方面发展更快。他们结交朋友,学会如何与年纪相仿的孩子交往。这在家里是不可能做到的,因为他们是独生子女,或者因为他们的兄弟姐妹要么比他们大,要么比他们小。

因此,总的来说,我相信上学早对大多数孩子来说是有好处的。他们也有足够的时间和父母一起在家里,所以他们可以从两种环境中受益。

爱你的,
Shanda

剑 桥 雅 思

真题全解 5

Test 1

LISTENING

SECTION 1

谈话场景：旅游咨询，电话交谈。
人物关系：旅游公司接待员和客户。
谈话话题：寻找合适的旅游项目，咨询项目内容、价格和出发日期等。

词汇注释

（此处词汇释义指在本段文章中的特定含义，后文同）

interested *adj.* 感兴趣的 interested in sth. 对某事感兴趣	**view** *n.* 景色，风景
holiday *n.* 假期（这里指旅游公司的度假项目）	**cruise** *n.* 巡游，航行
offer *v.* 提供	**guide** *n.* 向导，导游
coast *n.* 海岸	**bushwalk** *n.* 灌木丛行走
operate *v.* 操作，运行	**national park** 国家公园
tour *n.* 旅行	**charge** *n.* 收费 extra charge 额外收费
particular *adj.* 特别的，特殊的	**fishing** *n.* 钓鱼（动名词）
whale *n.* 鲸鱼	**reptile** *n.* 爬行类动物
watch *v.* 观察，观看	**snake** *n.* 蛇
popular *adj.* 流行的，时兴的	**relax** *v.* 放松
beach *n.* 海滩	**tennis** *n.* 网球 tennis court 网球场
coach *n.* 大客车	**table tennis** 乒乓球
actually *adv.* 其实，实际上	**accommodation** *n.* 住宿，住处
minibus *n.* 面包车	**check** *v.* 检查，查找
personal *adj.* 私人的，个人的	**booking** *n.* 预定
peak *n.* 高峰 peak time 高峰时间	**avoid** *v.* 避免
sight *v.* 观看，观光	**cancellation** *n.* 取消 cancel *v.* 取消
facility *n.* 设施	**deposit** *n.* 定金，押金
Paris 巴黎	**credit card** 信用卡
	tango *n.* 探戈

交际与语言表达

1. 接听电话时，一般要自报家门，如果是公司的接待员要报公司的名称。这里通过旅游公司的接待员自报家门 Dreamtime Travel，可以了解电话涉及旅游业务。Can I help you? 是接待员或服务员常用的礼貌用语，如果在别人为了取得指路等帮助而对你说 excuse me 的时候，你也可以回答 Can I help you?
2. 顾客讲明了他想知道的旅游服务项目内容，要注意抓住句子中的重点词语 coast，这样就知道他对海岸旅游感兴趣。在下面关于旅游项目的咨询中，他们谈到了旅游项目的时间、地点、交通工具、组团人数等内容，听的时候也要注意抓住每句的关键词。

3. In particular 这里当“到底”讲，接待员说我们在运营(operate)好几个项目，你到底对哪一个比较感兴趣。
4. I like the sound of the holiday that mentioned whales. 我喜欢提到鲸鱼的那个度假项目。
5. Based in somewhere 也是英语中一个很有用的表达法，意思是“在……地方”，一般用于人在什么地方工作或者活动在什么地方举行。比如 I work for Nokia, and I am based in Beijing. 我在北京为诺基亚工作。
6. Four hours’ travel time each way from here. 从这儿到那里单程 4 小时。
7. By coach 乘坐大巴车，by minibus 乘坐中巴车，使用交通工具一般用 go to somewhere by sth. (bus, car, taxi)，但比较特殊的是坐飞机和坐船一般说 by air 和 by sea。
8. Keep those tours small and personal，保持这些旅行小规模和个性化(针对个人进行设计)。
9. There’s one in three weeks’ time which is April 18th，在两周多以后的 4 月 18 日有一次。In three weeks’ time 是指两周多不到三周的时间。
10. We don’t have one until June 2nd，直译为“我们在 6 月 2 日之前没有这类旅行”，其实意思是下一次旅行是 6 月 2 日。
11. Interested in either... or...，对某件事或者另外一件事感兴趣，注意 either... or 表示两者选一。
12. Prefer whales to snakes 更喜欢鲸鱼而不是蛇，注意 prefer sth. to sth. 的用法。
13. Get back to sb.，这是口语里一个比较常见的说法，意思是“回头再找你”或者“给你回音”，一般是某人问了你某个问题，或者请你做某件事，你当时无法回答或解决，就说 I will get back to you，我会再找你。
14. Provisional booking 暂时的预定。Provisional 表示是暂时的，往往是在某种前提实现的条件下才可以变成永久性的。这里是因为这位顾客还要和他的同伴商量一下才能决定最后的行程。
15. T for tango，这是英文通讯中为了使姓名等专有名词中的字母能够被对方准确无误地记录下来而使用的方法，就像我们在介绍自己的姓名时说“张丽，弓长张，美丽的丽”，同样英文中也说 A for apple 等。

考题解析

Question 1

答案应该是 by minibus，必须听清楚顾客曾经问是否 by coach，而接待员回答说 by minibus，不要把答案写成 by coach。

Question 2

答案应该是 fifteen people，这是旅行社预设的组团人数，不要跟接待员后来介绍时说的少则十二、三人混淆。

Question 3

答案应当是 April 18th，注意不要把再下一次旅行的时间 June 2nd 当成正确答案。

Question 4

注意要把那家旅馆的名字“The Pallisades”一个字母一个字母的记下来，如果拼写错误这道题没分。

Questions 5–6

这道题对考生的听力理解要求比较高，因为在接待员的介绍中，guided bushwalk and fishing trip 并列在一起，让人很容易产生这两个项目是免费的错觉。但实际上 fishing trip 和 reptile park 是要收费的，tennis 在谈话中没有提到，而 table tennis 包括在酒店住宿里，因此只有 bushwalk 和 table tennis 是免费的。

Question 7

答案应该是 280，接待员先说了一个 300，但她又查了一下，才说这个旅行项目是 280 美元。

Question 8

这里应该填 fourteen days 或者 two weeks，雅思考试中只要答案意思正确，与原文不同的表达法不扣分。

Question 9

这里要填 20%，不要被接待员所提到的违约金等其他数字迷惑了。

Question 10

这道题测试考生听力理解和记要点的能力，如果在听谈话之前没有来得及把题目浏览一遍，那么在听的时候一定要把所有名称的拼写和数字、电话号码等一一记录下来。

SECTION 2

谈话场景：生活常识类电视节目。
人物关系：主持人独白。
谈话话题：主持人向观众介绍怎样判断儿童床的优劣。

词汇注释

beware *v.* 谨防，小心 beware of 对…小心
programme *n.* 节目，项目
show *n.* 电视节目
tip *n.* 提示
wheel *n.* 轮子
wisely *adv.* 明智地，聪明地
cot *n.* 轻便小床，帆布床
budget price range 预算价格范围
feature *v.* 着重说明
verdict *n.* 判断，在法律用语中意为裁决
dangerous *adj.* 危险的
brake *n.* 刹车闸
negative *n.* 缺点，缺陷
side bar *n.*（床的）侧面栏杆
trap *v.* 使…陷入
satisfactory *adj.* 满意的
pick up 抱起来
wide *adj.* 宽的，广的
slight *adj.* 轻微的
niggle *n.* 不顺心的小事
hazard *n.* 危害
sharp *adj.* 尖锐的，锋利的
smooth *adj.* 光滑的
convenient *adj.* 方便的
be concerned with sth. 对…关注的
minor *adj.* 微小的，无关紧要的
discontinue *v.* 终止
obviously *adv.* 明显地
especially *adv.* 尤其
detach *vi.*（将连接的部分）分离，分开
comfort *n.* 舒适
convenience *n.* 方便
recommend *v.* 推荐
edging *n.* 边饰
wooden *adj.* 木制的
newborn baby 新生儿
label *v.* 标记
drop down 放下来

交际与语言表达

1. 从开场白中的 programme，show，today 等几个关键词可以判断出这是一期电视节目，内容是教人们如何识别商品优劣。所以在下面的电视解说中将谈到商品的种类、性能、优缺点等，考生要对相关内容做针对性的记录。
2. 在第一段的末尾，主持人提到将对每个商品的 good points，problems and our verdict 做着重的介绍，下面对三个商品的介绍都是依照这三方面进行的。

3. It has several good points to recommend it. 它有几个比较突出的优点。
4. easy to move around，容易移动，因为有四个轮子，儿童床能够很容易朝四面移动。
5. They didn't think that mattered too much，他们不认为那很重要。sth. matters or does not matter，一般当某事很重要或不重要讲。
6. Simple to put together，组装方便。put together 在这里当组装讲。
7. on the minus side，从负面因素考虑，下面就开始讲儿童床的缺点。考生在做听力时要擅于抓住语句中的关键词，帮助自己理解听力材料的要点。
8. label this one dangerous，把这种商品列为危险。
9. The base could be raised or lowered into two different positions making it safe as well as convenient. 底板可以升降到两个不同的高度，使它既安全又方便。注意这里 make 的现在分词用法，后面跟一个起形容词作用的从句。
10. be safe in every way，在各方面都安全。
11. make ... our best buy，这里 buy 作为名词当选购讲，把某物选为最佳购买品。
12. What features should you look for in a baby's cot? 你应当选购一个具有什么特点的童床呢？

考题解析

Question 11

有了前面 easy to 的提示，这道题的答案比较直接，为 move around。

Questions 12–13

这两道题的答案也比较清楚，分别是 brakes 和 fingers，在写答案的时候要注意用复数，不然会扣掉一半分数。

Question 14

这道题的答案是 satisfactory，作为对第一种童床的评价。如果在听力材料开始播放之前，快速地浏览一遍要回答的问题，会对解题有很大帮助。尤其是这样的表格，只要匆匆看一眼就知道需要填的几个大项。

Question 15

这里要填 put together，注意不要把不同童车的特点混淆，在边听边记笔记的时候，可以用符号把三种童车区分开来。

Question 16

在答这道题时只记住 wide 是不够的，作为这类童床必须点出 too wide，如果说 too big 或者 too large 也能得分。如果听漏了这一句话，也可以猜到应当是栏杆之间的间隔太大。

Question 17

第二类童床被列为 dangerous，要注意拼写正确。

Question 18

从对前两类童床可以看出它们存在的问题主要围绕是否可以移动调节以及是否有安全隐患这两个方面，那么第三类童床存在的第一个问题很可能是有关移动性的，这里要填 wheels。

Question 19

如果考生没有听清 best buy，可以试着填 best 或者 best choice，应当可以得一半分。

Question 20

考生在答这道题的时候一定要看清楚题目是 should not be，而不是 should be，所以应该填 sharp，而不是 smooth。

SECTION 3

谈话场景:招生咨询。
人物关系:问讯者和招生咨询员。
谈话话题:讨论学校提供的课程安排和学习模式。

词汇注释

management *n.* 管理	**quit one's job** 辞职
diploma *n.* 文凭	**keen** *adj.* 热衷于
prospectus *n.* (课程)说明书	**qualifications** *n.* 资质
course *n.* 课程	**obviously** *adv.* 显然地
content *n.* 内容	**unpaid leave** 停薪假期
confused *adj.* 困惑的	**afford** *v.* 负担,支付
intensive *adj.* 强度大的,密集的	**salary** *n.* 薪水
full-time *adj.* 全职的,专职的	**module** *n.* 模块
part-time *adj.* 兼职的	**essay** *n.* 学术论文
advantage *n.* 优势,好处,长处	**seminar** *n.* 研讨会
disadvantage *n.* 劣势,坏处,短处	**mixture** *n.* 混合物
financial circumstances 财政状况,经济条件	**assessment** *n.* 评估
administration *n.* 行政,管理	**workshop** *n.* 座谈会
section *n.* 部门	**involve** *v.* 与…有关
relevant *adj.* 相关的	**survey** *n.* 调查
focus on 专注于	**topic** *n.* 题目
personnel management 人事管理	**attractive** *adj.* 迷人的
current *adj.* 现在的,当前的	**expensive** *adj.* 昂贵的
flexible *adj.* 有弹性的,宽松的	**employer** *n.* 雇主
option *n.* 选择,选项	

交际与语言表达

1. I was told to come here for... 这是一种开门见山的寒暄方式,Andrew 并没有先做自我介绍,而是先说他来有什么事情,这样如果没找对地方,就可以赶紧出来,避免了许多麻烦。
2. Monica 在知道了对方的来意之后,做出了积极的回应 you've certainly come to the right place,并做了自我介绍。
3. confused with sth., Andrew 说他对课程的种类和学习模式感到困惑。他先肯定了课程的信息有用,再说出他的问题,这样显得比较委婉。
4. It really depends on you, 这完全取决于你。有时也用 it depends,意思是那要看情况,然后再具体说根据什么条件来决定这件事。
5. leave your current job,taking a year off,这里咨询员给出了两种选择,是辞职呢,还是请一年的假。take some time off,表示请假,时间可长可短,请一天假,也是 take a day off。
6. It would be better if I could do a course without taking too much time away from work, 最好我可以读一个不用耽误很多工作时间的课程。
7. It's also a question of finance,经济状况也是一个我考虑的问题。

8. ... which counts towards your final assessment,这将计入你最后的成绩。
9. 案例研究,是西方高等教育课程一般都会要求的一种研究方法,做案例研究通常是运用所学理论对一个具体的事件、人物或现象进行深入研究。
10. "modular" course, 模块化的课程,把一个学位分成几个模块,一个学期修一个模块。
11. It's up to you,这是另外一个非常有用的口语表达法,意思是由你自己来定。

考题解析

Question 21

Andrew 的第一份工作做了 2 年,而现在这份医院的管理工作做了 3 年。注意原文中的时态,Andrew 说 I' ve been working in... for the last three years,现在完成进行时既表示了 3 年以前就开始这份工作,又表示现在还在延续。

Question 22

正确答案是 A,这从原文 my office have agreed to pay the cost of course itself 可以看出来。另外还有 Andrew 提到 unpaid leave 以及 I don' t think I could afford to support myself with no salary for a whole year。

Question 23

答案中的几个时间都在谈话中出现过,关键在于听的时候要记录前面提到的课程模式。

Questions 24–25

要选对这道题的答案,需要建立在理解记忆的基础上。A case study 和 a survey 实际上在文章中是指的同一个项目,而 a study diary 没有出现过。因此应当是 an essay 和 a short report。

Question 26

注意这个表达法比较特殊,不是说学生在每个模块学什么,而是以 full-time 的形式学。

Question 27

这道题填 one term 或者 about twelve weeks 都可以得分。

Questions 28–29

注意 module 的拼写,可参照这段第一句话中的相同单词,考生在做题时遇到拼不出来的单词可以在题目和上下文中找一找,有时就会找到相同的单词。

Question 30

填出 a topic 对考生来说可能有一些难度,在一时无法想出正确答案时,不宜花太多时间思考,应当立即投入到下面一篇听力的准备当中。

SECTION 4

谈话场景:有关个人财务管理的讲座。
人物关系:讲话者为大学老师。
谈话话题:大学老师向听众介绍女性和男性在个人财务管理中采取的不同态度和储蓄方法等,并向女性推荐业余财务管理课程。

特别提示

雅思听力的第四部分经常是围绕某一学术选题展开的讲演和讨论，文章中会涉及一些程度较深的专业词汇。这些专业词汇一般不会影响考生理解题目和得出答案，但是丰富的词汇量和相关知识会对提高听力有所帮助。

词汇注释

save (money) *v.* 储蓄
aspect *n.* 方面
gender *n.* 性别
consider *v.* 考虑
issue *n.* 问题，论点
basically *adv.* 基本地
attitude *n.* 态度
George Bernard Shaw 萧伯纳（英国作家）
politics *n.* 政治
economics *n.* 经济
finance *n.* 财政，财务
unwilling *adj.* 不情愿的
accept *v.* 接受
essential *adj.* 实质的，基本的，精华的
instruction *n.* 指导
pretension *n.* 主张，自负
assumption *n.* 假设，假想
contain *v.* 包括，包涵
statement *n.* 陈述，声明
fundamental *adj.* 根本的，基本的
surprisingly *adv.* 令人吃惊地
household budget 家庭预算
priority *n.* 优先权
retirement *n.* 退休
earning *n.* 收入
disturbing *adj.* 令人担忧的，烦扰的
partner *n.* 伙伴，伴侣
nursing care 看护
spouse *n.* 配偶
divorce *n.* 离婚
create *v.* 造出，产生
poverty *n.* 贫穷
cycle *n.* 圆圈，（人际交往的）圈子
situation *n.* 情况
crisis *n.* 危机
pension *n.* 养老金
confidence *n.* 自信
properly *adv.* 适当地，完全地
inform *v.* 告知，通知 well-informed 充分知道的
initiative *n.* 主动
invest *v.* 投资
stocks and shares 股票证券
for instance 比如
advice *n.* 建议
advise *v.* 建议
low-risk investment 低风险投资
dependent *adj.* 依附的，附属的
independent *adj.* 独立的
proportion *n.* 比例
population *n.* 人口
consequence *n.* 结果，后果

交际与语言表达

1. 本文是一篇关于男性和女性个人财务管理状况的经济学分析，但是里面的经济学术语和统计数据并不多，主要是对一些比例、特点和趋势进行分析，篇幅有些长，但理解起来不应当非常费力。
2. 文章第一段的最后一句话对将要阐述的问题进行了概括：So if we consider gender issues we're basically asking whether men and women have different attitudes towards saving money, and whether they save money for different things. 如果我们把性别因素考虑进来，我们基本上想了解男人和女人对储蓄的不同态度和他们是否为不同的目的储蓄。
3. 第二段是英国作家萧伯纳对男女两性在求知方面的不同态度，根据第一段的指导，考生应当在听这段文章时特别注意记录关于男女两性不同态度和做法的描述。A man is supposed to understand politics, economics and finance and is therefore unwilling to accept essential instruction. 男人通常都

会知晓一些政治、经济和金融方面的知识，所以会不愿意接受有关这些方面最基本的指导。A woman, having fewer pretensions, is far more willing to learn. 女人由于在上述领域很少有自己的主张，所以她们更愿意去听别人的建议。

4. 第三段是关于北美妇女的一个调查所提供的男女两性为不同目的而储蓄的统计分析，女性更愿意为子女教育和购房而储蓄，而男性则为买车和养老而存款。
5. 第四段对第三段所提出的对男女在储蓄目的差异所做的分析，两个因素决定了女性更应该为养老做储蓄，一是女性的寿命普遍比男性长，二是北美的高离婚率造成离婚女性贫困，而她们还需要抚养孩子。
6. 接下来的第五段分析了女性疏于进行财务管理和计划的原因，并给女性提供财务管理的课程和建议。
7. At present for women it takes a crisis to make them think about their future financial situation. 现在女性只有在经历危机的时候才会考虑他们未来的财务状况。crisis 是危机的意思，这里指妇女只有在遇到经济问题时才会转变思想。
8. ... by getting themselves properly informed 通过让她们自己更加充分地掌握相关知识。

考题解析

Question 31
这道题有关男性应当了解的三个领域实际上按重要性的大小进行逻辑排列，所以 politics 排在 economics 和 finance 的前面。

Question 32
这里如果想不起来 learn，也可以填 know。

Questions 33 – 34
注意 children's education 用复数，而 car 的前面要加量词 a，如果自己拿不准，可参照考题中的提法 a house。英语中单复数的运用有时是约定俗成，很难说是遵循一个统一的规律，因此平时要多听多读，增加语感，记录一些比较常见的用法，这样对提高听力水平会有很大帮助。

Question 35
这里的难点在于听的时候一定要记住短语 nursing care，不要只说其中的一个单词，这样意思不准确。

Question 36
考题用了与文章中不同的句式来表达同样的内容，这就需要对原文完全理解（见交际与语言表达8），才能填对答案。

Question 37
这道题要注意 twenties 的拼写，写成 20th 或 twenty 都是错误的。

Question 38
这道题的难度比较大，必须在理解原文中... women avoid dealing effectively with their economic situation because of a lack of confidence. 以及接下来的两句话的基础上，才能给出正确答案。

Question 39
这道题不难，只要记住课程的名称，并把正确的拼法写出来就可以了。

Question 40
答这道题的时候要注意，不要漏掉 low-risk 中的连接符。一般英文将一个形容词和一个名词放在另一个名词前面做修饰时，前两个词之间要加连接符。

READING

READING PASSAGE 1

文章结构

体　裁	说明文
主要内容	本文主要描写18世纪出版的一本英语词典,详细记述了它的编纂过程、主要特点和历史意义。
结　构	文章基本按照词典编纂的前因、经过和后果的顺序展开。一、二、三段介绍了约翰逊词典出版之前的历史背景,四、五、六段记述字典的编纂过程,最后三段说明字典出版之后对其作者、对英语以及后世的影响。
	A段:约翰逊词典出版前,英语的用法和拼法处于混乱状态。
	B段:17世纪出版的一本英文小词典只收录了学者常用的词汇。
	C段:约翰逊做为当时文人的典范,在18世纪中产阶级鼎盛期出版词典顺理成章。
	D段:约翰逊与书商签约,独自承担了词典的编纂工作。
	E段:约翰逊租用了一个阁楼,雇佣了助手和抄写员编辑词典。
	F段:约翰逊借鉴了以前词典中的一些内容,用一种实用而细致的风格编写了他自己的词典。
	G段:词典出版以后被整个欧洲当成里程碑,并使英语更加受欢迎。
	H段:约翰逊克服了重重困难编成词典,使英语成为一个稳定的语言。
	I段:词典为约翰逊赢得了荣誉和一份国王颁予的退休金。

词汇注释

文　章	
A段	
century *n.* 世纪	**order** *n.* 顺序,秩序
dictionary *n.* 词典	**chaos** *n.* 混乱
publish *v.* 出版	**spelling** *n.* 拼写
language *n.* 语言	**provide** *v.* 提供
agreement *n.* 赞同,同意	**solution** *n.* 解决办法
B段	
compile *v.* 编写	**concentrate** *v.* 注重
table *n.* 目录	**scholarly** *adj.* 学者似的,学者的
alphabetical *adj.* 按字母顺序排列的	**enable** *v.* 使…能够做
usual *adj.* 通常的,常用的	**convey** *v.* 传递,传达
various *adj.* 不同的,各种各样的	**impression** *n.* 印象
tend *v.* 倾向于	**fine learning** 良好的教养
C段	
beyond *prep.* 在…之上	**middle class** 中产阶级
practical *adj.* 符合实际的,实用的	**anxious** *adj.* 焦急的,热切的
associate *v.* 联系	**define** *v.* 定义,限定

circumscribe *v.* 限制，划分
conquer *v.* 征服
lexical *adj.* 词汇的
commercial *adj.* 商业的
famous *adj.* 著名的
heyday *n.* 全盛期

D 段

poet *n.* 诗人
critic *n.* 批评家，评论家
common sense 共识
height *n.* 高度
genius *n.* 天才
approach *v.* 态度，方法
throughout *adv.* 遍及
intensely *adv.* 密集地，集中地
usage *n.* 用法
academy *n.* 学院
settle *v.* 解决
single-handed 独自，独立
contract *n.* 合同
bookseller *n.* 书商，出版商
breakfast *n.* 早餐
installment *n.* 分期付款
workshop *n.* 工厂，车间

E 段

biographer *n.* 传记作家
describe *v.* 形容，描述
garret *n.* 阁楼，顶楼
counting house 会计室
clerk *n.* 职员
station *v.* 布置，安排
rickety chair 摇椅
crazy *adj.* 疯狂的
assistant *n.* 助手
preparation *n.* 准备

F 段

immense *adj.* 宏大的，数量众多的
fill *v.* 填充
notebook *n.* 笔记本
definition *n.* 定义，含义
illustrate *v.* 证明，说明
meaning *n.* 意思，含义
quotation *n.* 引语
draw *v.* 吸取，引用
subject *n.* 题目，辞条
complete *adj.* 完整的
originality *n.* 原创
heroic *adj.* 英雄的，英勇的，雄壮的
synthesis *n.* 综合物
predecessor *n.* 前人，前任
treat *v.* 对待
shade *n.* 层次
adopt *v.* 收录，接受
common law 共同规律
precedent *adj.* 先例
seriously *adv.* 严肃地，认真地
rival *v.* 竞争

G 段

vicissitude *n.* 曲折，周折
instantly *adv.* 立刻地，立即地
recognise *v.* 承认，确认
landmark *n.* 地标，里程碑
noble *adj.* 高贵的
lexicographer *n.* 字典编纂者
perpetual *adj.* 永久的，永远的
monument *n.* 纪念碑
fame *n.* 名声，名望
author *n.* 作者
honour *n.* 荣誉
in particular 尤其
general *adj.* 总体的，笼统的
benefit *n.* 使…受益
republic *n.* 共和国，国度
letters *n.* 文字（这里指文人）
match *v.* 媲美，匹敌
celebration *n.* 庆祝，庆典

H 段

assistance *n.* 帮助，协助
(the) learned *n.* 有学问的人
patronage *n.* 庇护，赞助
great *adj.* 伟大的
obscurities *n.* 隐匿，偏僻
retirement *n.* 退休

shelter *n.* 庇护,遮挡
bower *n.* 荫蔽
inconvenience *n.* 不便
distraction *n.* 分散注意力的东西
sickness *n.* 疾病,不适
sorrow *n.* 悲痛,悲伤
fault *n.* 缺点,错误
eccentricities *n.* 古怪,偏离
masterpiece *n.* 杰作
orthography *n.* 正确拼字法
display *n.* 陈列,展示
analogy *n.* (语言)类推法
regulate *v.* 规定,规范
structure *n.* 结构
ascertain *v.* 确定,探知
signification *n.* 定义
achievement *n.* 成就
confer *v.* 授予,赠与
stability *n.* 稳定性

I 段

esteem *v.* 尊敬,敬重
prevail *v.* 战胜,超越
offer *n.* 提供
pension *n.* 退休金
folklore *n.* 民间传说

题目

contemporary *adj.* 当代的
completion *n.* 完成
ignore *v.* 忽视
subtlety *n.* 细微之处
excess *n.* 过度,超额
hail *v.* 向…欢呼,致敬
reward *n.* 奖赏,奖励
demand *n.* 需求,要求
survive *v.* 生存,幸存

考题解析

Questions 1–3

题目编号	题目定位词	答案位置	题解
1	contemporary texts	F 段第 13 行: John treated English very practically, as a living language...	文中没有说约翰逊词典没有收录任何学术词语,所以排除了A。然后文中 F 段倒数第三行说,约翰逊词典在其出版后的一个世纪没有任何词典能够比得过它,没有说此后 200 年都没有词典与他并列,因此 B 也不对。剩下 D 的对应内容可以从原文中 F 段的第 13 行中找到。它说约翰逊词典用非常实用的态度来对待英语,把它当成一个活的语言。这和 D 给出的 Contemporary texts 相符合。
2	time limit completion	F 段第 9 行: Working to a deadline, ...	题目 E 说它的完成有时间限制。在 F 段中相对应的是"为了在截稿日期之前编好这本词典,他……"这说明 E 的陈述是对的。
3	subtleties, meaning	F 段第 13 行: Johnson treated English... with many different shades of meaning.	题目 F 说"它忽视了所有以前词典编纂者的著作",这是不对的,在 F 段第 10 行:"他不得不汲取所有从前的词典当中最好的地方。"题目 H 说"它的定义以原创性著称"也不对,因为 F 段第 8 行:"他没有追求词典的原创性"。题目 G 说"它记录了词义的细微差异,"可以在 F 段 13 行开始的句子中找到相对应的内容:他……注意了不同层次的含义。

Questions 4–7

● 题型归类:Sentence Completion

● 题目解析:

题目编号	题目定位词	答案位置	题解
4	copying clerk	E 段第 5 行	“stood at a long central desk”是这段里的提示语句,到原文中 E 段第 5 行找到“copying clerks would work standing up”,就找到了正确答案。
5	library	F 段第 2 行	“did not have ... available to him” 和 “without a library to hand”意思基本相同。
6	stability	H 段倒数第 2 行	题目“was to bring ... to the English language.”意思是“为英语带来……”和文章中的“conferred stability on the language of his country”相对应,可以知道答案是 stability。
7	pension	最后一段第 4 行	文章中的“... King George III to offer him a pension”(乔治三世国王为他提供了一份退休金),在题目中动词变成了被动语态,“granted a pension by the King”。

Questions 8–13

● 题型归类:TRUE/FALSE/NOT GIVEN

● 题目解析:

题目编号	题目定位词	答案位置	题解
8	middle class 和 increased demand	C 段第 2 行	题目说“地位日益上升的中产阶级导致了对词典需求的增加。”这道题可以在 C 段的第 2 行找到相似的意思“词典的兴起与中产阶级的兴起关系密切。”
9	well known 和 death	I 段第 1 行	题目说“约翰逊在死后才变得有名起来。”这与文中所说“这本词典和他的其他著作使约翰逊变得非常有名和受人尊敬”不符,所以是错误的。
10	plan 和 several years	D 段	在文章的 D 段中可以找到约翰逊与书商签约以及他准备独自承担字典的编纂,并没有提及他为编写词典做了多年准备,因此本题选 NOT GIVEN。
11	academy help	D 段第 11 行	题目说“约翰逊成立了一个学院来帮助他编写词典”,这和 D 段第 11 行所述“约翰逊决定他不需要一个学院来帮他解决有关语言的争论”意思相反,因此选 FALSE。
12	payment completion	D 段倒数第 4 行	题目说“约翰逊只有等到词典完成才能得到报酬”,而实际上文章中说“他将分期收到 1575 英镑”,所以选 FALSE。
13	survive to see	E 段最后一句话	题目说“并不是所有的助手都活着看到了词典的出版”,这和文中所述“他助手中有两个人在编写的过程中去世”意思相符,因此选 TRUE。

参考译文

约翰逊词典

在约翰逊词典1775年出版前的18世纪，人们曾经担心英语的地位。那时没有标准的英语口语和书面语，也没有一个可以使混乱不堪的英语拼写变得有章可循的规则。但约翰逊博士解决了这个问题。

此前也曾有过几部词典，最早的一部是由一个叫罗伯特·考德瑞编写的一本约120页的小词典。这本词典的名称叫《英语常用词汇查询表》(按字母顺序)，出版于1604年。然而，像17世纪其他在它之后出版的词典一样，考德瑞的词典主要收编了学者用语中的词汇。这部词典的功能之一就是让使用它的学生能够给人留下受过良好教育的印象。

当时词典的出现并非出于乱中求序的实际需要，而是与英国中产阶级的出现有关。那时的中产阶级正急于划分和限定他们需要征服的从语言、社会到商业的不同领域。对塞缪尔·约翰逊这样一个典型的18世纪文人以及在当时和现在都很出名的人，他在中产阶级鼎盛期刚刚开始时出版词典是一件非常顺理成章的事情。

约翰逊当时是诗人兼批评家，他能够把常识提升到天才的高度。他对于17世纪晚期、18世纪初期作家们担心的一些问题采取了非常实用的态度。在他所处的年代，如果不成立一个学术团体来判断词汇用法的正确与否，编写这样一个大规模的词典几乎是不可能的。但是约翰逊决定不要学术团体来帮助统一语言的用法，他准备自己承担全部编写工作。1764年6月18日，约翰逊与书商罗伯特·多斯里在霍尔本(HOLBORN)酒吧附近的金锚客栈签定了出词典的合同。书商将分期付给他1575英镑。约翰逊用这笔钱租下了高夫(GOUGH)广场17号，在那里开办了他的“词典工作室”。

约翰逊的传记作家詹姆斯·波斯威尔形容约翰逊工作的顶楼“布置得像一个会计室，屋子中间有一张长长的桌子，而负责抄写的职员则在桌子两旁站着工作。约翰逊把自己安置在一张“古旧不堪的老板桌”后面的摇椅上，连人带桌椅都被包围在杂乱的借来的图书中。他还有6个助手，可是其中有两人在词典的编纂过程中去世了。

编词典的工作量是巨大的，他们填满了80个笔记本(身边没有一个图书馆可供使用)。约翰逊编写了40000个辞条，并用了114000个从伊利莎白时代到他自己年代英文文章中的引语来说明每个词的用法。约翰逊并没有打算让他的词典都是原创。为了赶上截稿时间，他不得不充分借鉴以前出版的词典中的有用部分，然后使他的作品成为一个创记录的综合产物。实际上，他的词典特点不仅仅包括这些。约翰逊与他之前的词典编著者不同，他把英语当作一个活的语言，并从实用的角度来解释英语。他根据前人的工作及人们对英语使用上的已有共识，对词汇进行了重新定义。他的词典在出版后的一个世纪都没有哪一本词典可以与其媲美。

这本词典在经历了许多曲折之后终于在1775年4月15日出版，并立即被整个欧洲当作一个里程碑式的著作。“一位意大利著名的词典编纂者写到：“这部高贵的著作将为作者，特别是他的国家带来永远的荣耀，同时也为全欧洲的文化界带来了很大益处。”由于约翰逊挑战了欧洲的学院派并且超过了他们(所有人都知道40个法国学者花了40年时间才编出了第一本法国国家词典)，因而使得英语的地位更为巩固。

约翰逊工作了9年才完成这项工作，“中间没有学问家的帮助，没有伟大人物的指导，没有退休带来的清静或者学院氛围的荫庇，只有许多不便和打扰，不时的病痛和忧愁”。无论有多少谬误和偏失，这部两卷本的词典是一部经典之作和里程碑。约翰逊自己形容这部作品是“设定了拼写法，展示了类推法，规定了语言结构，确定了英语词汇的含义”。它是标准英语的奠基石，用波斯威尔的话说，它是一项“赋予他祖国语言稳定性”的成就。

这本词典以及他的其他著作使约翰逊变得非常有名和受人敬重，他的朋友们最终说服了乔治三世国王为他提供一份退休金。此后，他又成为《约翰逊民间传说集》的编者。

READING PASSAGE 2

文章结构

体　　裁	说明文
主要内容	文章主要介绍一个行为心理学实验及其意义。
结　　构	第1段：几年前，耶鲁大学的研究员MILGRAM做了一个行为心理学实验，告诉每位被测试者他在参加一个具有高尚目标的教育实验。
	第2段：MILGRAM让每位被测试者在学生答错问题的时候，按动面前的按纽对学生进行电击。
	第3段：在被测试者不愿意继续对学生进行更高电压的电击的情况下，MILGRAM会设法说服他们继续。
	第4段：在进行实验前，精神病学家预测只有很少百分比的被测试者会对学生进行高电压的电击。
	第5段：实验却发现，有60%甚至更多的被测试者会使用高达450伏的电击。
	第6段：对实验的结果有一种解释是由于动物攻击性的本能。
	第7、8段：而对实验的另一种解释则是个人在制度权威之前会放弃自己的特性和道德。
	第9段：生物社会学关注的就是阐明所有行为中的生物学因素。

词汇注释

文　章

第1段

fascinating *adj.* 迷人的，引人入胜的
disturbing *adj.* 令人不安的，心烦的
experiment *n.* 实验
behavioural *adj.* 行为的
psychology *n.* 心理学
subject *n.* 对象
willingness *n.* 愿意
obey *v.* 服从
instruction *n.* 指令，指导
personal *adj.* 个人的
distaste *n.* 讨厌，厌恶
action *n.* 行动
perform *v.* 表演，表现
specifically *adv.* 具体地
noble *adj.* 崇高的，高贵的
cause *n.* 事业
design *v.* 设计
punish *v.* 惩罚
pupil *n.* 学生
mistake *n.* 错误
positive *adj.* 正面的，积极的
effect *n.* 结果
ability *n.* 能力

第2段

panel *n.* 面板，仪表板
switch *n.* 开关
label *n.* 标签
range *v.* 在…范围
electricity *n.* 电力
slight *adj.* 轻微的
shock *n.* 震动，惊讶，电击
severe *adj.* 严重的，强烈的
administer *v.* 管理，执行
successive *adj.* 连续的
supposed *adj.* 假想的
reality *n.* 现实

actor *n.* 演员
hire *v.* 雇佣
stimulate *v.* 刺激
receive *v.* 接收
emit *v.* 发出,放射
spectrum *n.* 光谱,频谱
groan *n.* 呻吟
scream *n.* 喊叫
writhe *n.* 翻腾
assortment *n.* 分类
statement *n.* 话语,陈述
expletive *n.* 咒骂
denounce *v.* 公开指责,谴责
govern *v.* 统治,主宰
situation *n.* 情况

第 3 段

unfold *v.* 展开
deliberately *adv.* 故意地
pose *v.* 摆姿势,假装
various *adj.* 不同的
electrical *adj.* 电的
punishment *n.* 惩罚
danger *n.* 危险
level *n.* 水平,标准
volt *n.* 伏特(电压的单位)
balk *v.* 停止
complaint *n.* 抱怨
reluctant *adj.* 不愿意的
proceed *v.* 进行
important *adj.* 重要的
for the sake of sth. 以…的名义
procedure *n.* 手续,过程
revulsion *n.* 反感

第 4 段

psychiatrist *n.* 精神病学家
predict *v.* 预测
ordinary *adj.* 普通的
population *n.* 人口
overwhelming *adj.* 压倒性的
consensus *n.* 共识
virtually *adv.* 事实上,实质上
refuse *v.* 拒绝
anticipate *v.* 预测
furthermore *adv.* 此外,而且
lunatic *n.* 疯子
fringe *n.* 边缘

第 5 段

result *n.* 结果
repetition *n.* 重复
account *v.* 占据(比例)
vast *adj.* 广泛的,广阔的
discrepancy *n.* 差距
calm *adj.* 平静的
rational *adj.* 合理的
knowledgeable *adj.* 有学问的
comfort *n.* 慰藉
pressure *n.* 压力
fluster *v.* 使慌张、激动
cooperative *adj.* 合作的
laboratory *n.* 实验室

第 6 段

inclination *n.* 倾斜,倾向
aggression *n.* 进攻,攻击
instinct *n.* 本能
activate *v.* 使…活动/活跃
follow *v.* 跟踪
genetic *adj.* 遗传的
discharge *v.* 卸下,放出
pent-up 被压抑的
primal *adj.* 最初的
urge *n.* 强烈欲望,迫切要求
core *n.* 核心
evolve *v.* (使)发展,(使)进化
advantageous *adj.* 有优势的
trait *n.* 显著的特征,特性
survival *n.* 生存,幸存
ancestor *n.* 祖先
struggle *n.* 挣扎
hardship *n.* 困难
cave *n.* 洞穴
ultimately *adj.* 最终地,最后地
remnant *n.* 残余,剩余

第 7 段	
alternative *n.* 替代物,替代选项	**evoke** *v.* 唤起,引起
notion *n.* 概念,想法	**isolation** *n.* 孤立
environment *n.* 环境	**evil** *adj.* 恶意的
behaviour *n.* 行为	**acquire** *v.* 获得,学到
psychological *adj.* 心理的	**completely** *adv.* 完全地
claim *n.* 要求,主张	**setting** *n.* 场面,场景
legitimacy *n.* 合法性,正统性,合理性	
第 8、9 段	
explanation *n.* 解释	**forgo** *v.* 作罢,放弃
merge *v.* 兼并,合并	**institutional** *adj.* 制度上的
unique *adj.* 独一无二的,独特的	**anthropologist** *n.* 人类学家
personality *n.* 个性,人格	**polar** *adj.* 两极的,对立的
moral *adj.* 道德的	**plausible** *adj.* 似是而非的
code *n.* 规范	**essence** *n.* 精华,要旨,实质
self-sacrifice *n.* 自我牺牲	**sociobiology** *n.* 生物社会学
discipline *n.* 纪律	**dictate** *v.* 独裁,控制
malevolent *adj.* 恶意的,恶毒的	**bias** *n.* 偏见
authority *n.* 权威	**interaction** *n.* 互动
radically *adv.* 激进地	**elucidate** *v.* 阐明,讲明
题目	
identity *n.* 身份	**contradict** *v.* 与…矛盾
statistical *adj.* 统计学的	**mechanism** *n.* 机制
outcome *n.* 成果,结果	**powerful** *adj.* 有力的
persuade *v.* 劝说,说服	

考题解析

Questions 14–19

- 题型归类:Multiple choice
- 题目解析:

题目编号	题目定位词	答案位置	题解
14	biological explanation, behaviour	F 段	题目"对被测试对象行为的一个生物学解释"可以在 F 段第 3 行中找到相应的"扮演教师的被测试者只是按照遗传学的需要通过施加电击将这种被压抑的原始的愿望发泄到学生身上"。
15	explanation, experiment	A 段	题目"MILGRAM 向被测试对象解释实验的目的"可以在 A 段的最后一句话找到对应内容。
16	identity, pupil	B 段	题目"学生的身份"可以在 B 段第 6 行找到对应的"实验中的学生实际上是 MILGRAM 雇佣的演员"。
17	expected, outcome	D 段	题目"预期的统计结果"在 D 段整段都是精神病学家对统计结果的预期。

18	aim, sociobiological	I 段	题目"生物社会学研究的总体目标"在 I 段里可以找到相对应的"the problem of modern sociobiology",这样就知道正确答案在哪里。
19	persuade, continue	C 段	题目"MILGRAM 采取什么方式说服被测试者继续"在 C 段第 5 行开始可以找到 MILGRAM 采取的几种手段。

Questions 20-22

- 题型归类:Multiple choice
- 题目解析:

题目编号	题目定位词	答案位置	题解
20	testing, whether	A 段	从题目"被测试者被告知他们是帮助测试是否……",从这儿可以判断答案是实验的目的,可以在 A 段找到。应当选"惩罚有助于学习"。
21	instruct	B 段	从题目"被测试者被要求"做什么事,可以找到 B 段中有关 MILGRAM 让被测试者采取的惩罚学生的方式,因此要选 D,"按照规则给予惩罚"。
22	before, psychiatrists	D 段	只要在题目中看到"精神病学家"就知道要到 D 段寻找答案,几个选项的表述有的比较复杂,比如 B"不能就被测试对象对知道如何反应达成一致"和 C"低估了被测试对象愿意遵守实验步骤的程度"。

Questions 23-26

- 题型归类:TRUE/FALSE/NOT GIVEN
- 题目解析:

题目编号	题目定位词	答案位置	题解
23	students, Yale university	A 段	题目"被测试对象中有一些是耶鲁大学学生",到 A 段中找到有关被测试对象的描述,只说了是"志愿者(volunteer)",没有其他进一步的说明,所以只能填 NOT GIVEN。
24	survival mechanism	F 段	题目"一些人认为被测试对象的行为可以解释为一种积极的生存机制",联想到有关实验的第一种生物学方面的解释,不难在 F 段看出这个陈述是对的。
25	personal value, authority	G 段	这道题与上面一道类似,只要看出这是关于实验的第二种社会学方面的解释,就可以在 G 段找到可以比对的内容,发现题目阐述的个人与权威的关系与原文中的阐述正好相反,所以选 FALSE。
26	solve question	I 段	MILGRAM 的实验到底有没有解决生物社会学的问题,文章里还是存在疑问的。要做对这道题,必须对文章的意思有一个整体的把握。实际上,关于实验结果在存在多种解释,因此不能说它解决了问题,选 FALSE。

参考译文

先天，还是后天？

几年前，在一个关于行为心理学的最吸引人、也最令人不安的实验中，耶鲁大学的 Stanley Milgram实验室测试了40个来自各行各业的人，测试他们在被要求做会使他们感到厌恶的事情的情况下，是否愿意服从“领导者”发出的指令。具体地说，Milgram告诉每个扮演“教师”角色的志愿者，实验是为了高尚的教育目的而设计的，主要是看惩罚学生所犯的错误是否会帮助学生提高学习能力。

Milgram的实验方案是将扮演“教师”的测试对象安排坐在具有三十个标示为以15伏为增幅、从“15伏电压”（轻微电击）到“450伏电压”（危险——剧烈电击）的开关面板前。他们被告知只要学生给出错误的答案，他们就按开关电击学生，其强度从最低级开始，并随着学生给出连续的错误答案而增加。实际上，假定的“学生”是Milgram雇用的演员，通过发出各种呻吟、尖叫和挣扎，以及谴责实验和实验者的咒骂声来模仿受到电击后的反应。Milgram告诉“教师”扮演者不要去管学生的反应，并让他们按照实验的规则来使用相应强度的电击。

当实验开始以后，学生会故意对教师提出的问题给出错误答案，引来各种电击的惩罚，甚至达到300伏或更高的危险电压。许多测试对象会在施加更高的电压前停下来，满脸疑问地转向Milgram，或是抱怨不该再把实验进行下去。在这些情况下，Malgram平静地解释说他们应当不理睬学生请求手下留情的喊叫，继续进行实验。如果对象仍不愿继续进行，那么Milgram就说对于实验而言坚持到底是非常重要的。他最后的回答是“你没有选择，你必须继续”。Milgram试图发现的是即使在对实验规则和条件具有强烈的个人和道德反感的情况下仍愿意施加最强电击的测试对象的人数。

在进行实验之前，Milgram向39个精神病专家解释了他的想法，并要求他们预测在普通人群中愿意施加最高电击450伏电压的平均百分比。压倒性的共识是所有的测试对象将拒绝服从实验者。精神病专家觉得多数对象将不会施加超过150伏的电击，他们还预期只有百分之四的人将施加高达300伏的电压。此外，他们认为只有大约千分之一的疯子才会施加最高的450伏电击。

实际结果是什么呢？超过百分之六十的测试对象一直服从Milgram，直到450伏的极限。在其他国家进行的重复实验中，服从的人数比例更高，有一个国家甚至达到百分之八十五。由此可见，那些知识丰富、处在冷静和理性状态下的人们，在正常学习环境下表现出来的行为，与这些在现实生活实验中处于压力、紧张状态下的“教师”们（尽管他们还算比较配合）所表现出的行为相差甚大。我们该如何解释这种巨大的差异呢？

第一种倾向是说一定存在某种通过实验激发出来的内在的动物攻击性本能，Milgram的测试对象只是按照生物的需要，通过施加电击将这种被压抑的原始的愿望发泄到学生身上。一位现代重要的生物社会学家甚至走得更远，他们声称这种攻击性本能是作为一种有利的特性而发展的，它来自我们祖先在平原上和山洞中生活时与艰难困苦做斗争的生存理念，并最终成为我们从远古动物进化到现在保留在基因中的生物遗存。

另一种对于通用设计概念的解释是将测试对象的行为视为实验所处的社会环境的结果。正如Milgram本人指出的，实验中的多数对象在认为实验会对社会产生良性的和有用的效果——是为了追求科学真理。心理学实验室具有强大的令人感到合理的效力，并进而使参加实验的人产生信任和信心。电击受害人的行为，孤立地讲是邪恶的，但在处于这种情形时却具有完全不同的涵义。

因此，在该解释中，对象将其自己独特的人格以及个人和道德的编码融入更大的制度结构之中，放弃了个性特点，例如忠诚、忘我和纪律，来服务于恶意的权威系统。

对于为什么会有那么多测试对象愿意因为制度上的权威者而放弃他们自己的个人责任，我们有两个完全不同的解释。对于生物学家、心理学家和人类学家来说，需要弄清的是这两种截然相反的解释哪一种更可信。这在本质上讲是现代生物社会学的问题——即去发现编排缜密的遗传程序在多大的程度决定人的行为，或者至少使人产生某种行为倾向，以及动物和人与其所属环境之间的互动。换句话说，生物社会学关注的是，如何阐明所有这些行为中的生物学因素。

READING PASSAGE 3

文章结构

体　　裁	议论加说明
主要内容	论证和说明有关环境污染被夸大的论点。
结　　构	A 段:环保主义者勾勒出一幅悲观的污染状况图景。
	B 段:但是实际情况不想他们想像的那么糟。
	C 段:有四个原因使人们产生环境污染日益恶化的印象。
	D 段:第一个原因是科研资金往往流入问题最多的领域，给人造成潜在问题比实际多的印象。
	E、F 段:第二个原因是环保主义者为了吸引公众注意力和捐款，有时会夸大环境问题的存在。
	G 段:第三个原因是媒体迎合公众更注意坏消息的习惯，总是报负面的环境新闻。
	H 段:第四个因素是个人理解能力的不足。
	I – K 段:为了控制全球变暖而降低二氧化碳排放量所造成的损失比全球变暖带来的损失要大得多。
	L 段:最重要的是我们要以事实为依据来为我们的未来做决定。

词汇注释

文　章

A 段

environmentalist *n.* 环保主义者
develop *v.* 发展
fear *n.* 恐惧
resource *n.* 资源
population *n.* 人口
species *n.* 物种
extinct *adj.* 灭绝的
vast *adj.* 广大的，众多的
polluted *adj.* 被污染的

B 段

abundant *adj.* 丰富的
starving *adj.* 饥饿的
disappear *v.* 消失
predict *v.* 预测
pollution *n.* 污染
exaggerate *v.* 夸张，夸大
transient *adj.* 暂时的，瞬时的
associate *v.* 联系
phase *n.* 阶段
industrialization *n.* 工业化
restrict *v.* 限制
accelerate *v.* 加速
phenomenon *n.* 现象
extend *v.* 延伸
impact *n.* 影响
devastating *adj.* 毁灭性的
inappropriate *adj.* 不恰当的，不适当的
response *n.* 回答

C、D、E 段	
opinion poll 民意测验	**potential** *n.* 潜力
nurture *v.* 培养	**exist** *v.* 存在
standard *n.* 标准	**mass media** 大众传媒
decline *v.* 下降	**overstate** *v.* 夸张，夸大
disjunction *n.* 分离，分裂	**argument** *n.* 论点
perception *n.* 观念，理解，感知	**issue** *v.* 发布
reality *n.* 现实	**press release** 新闻发布稿
lopsidedness *n.* 不平衡	**forest** *n.* 森林
impression *n.* 印象	
F 段	
overwhelmingly *adv.* 压倒性地	**degree** *n.* 程度
selfless *adj.* 无私的	**skepticism** *n.* 怀疑
folk *n.* 人们，亲属	**organization** *n.* 组织
nevertheless *adv.* 然而，不过	**weak** *adj.* 薄弱的
share *v.* 共享，分享	**instantly** *adv.* 立即地
characteristics *n.* 特点，特征	**altruistic** *adj.* 利他的，无私心的
lobby *n.* 游说	**impartial** *adj.* 公平的，公正的
apply *v.* 应用，适用	**control** *n.* 控制
G 段	
confusion *n.* 混乱，混淆	**tourism** *n.* 旅游业
attitude *n.* 态度	**allergy** *n.* 过敏
curious *adj.* 好奇的	**melt** *v.* 融化
broadcaster *n.* 广播公司	**ski-slope** 滑雪坡
public *n.* 公众	**bulletin** *n.* 公告，公报
significant *adj.* 至关重要的，重大的	**meteorological** *adj.* 气象学的
distortion *n.* 歪曲，扭曲	**society** *n.* 学会
perception *n.* 观念，概念	**damage** *n.* 破坏
encounter *n.* 遭遇，遇到	**estimate** *v.* 估计
El Nino 厄尔尼诺现象	**benefits** *n.* 利益，收益
climatic *adj.* 天气的	**estimate** *v.* 估计
phenomenon *n.* 现象	**reduce** *v.* 减少
accuse *v.* 谴责	**heating** *n.* 取暖
wreck *v.* 破坏，失事	**diminish** *v.* (使)减少，(使)变小
H 段	
throw *v.* 扔掉，丢弃	**output** *n.* 产出
dispose *n.* 抛弃	**double** *n.* 翻倍
waste *n.* 废物，垃圾	**rubbish** *n.* 垃圾
trash *n.* 垃圾	**entire** *n.* 完全的
I、J、K 段	
carbon dioxide 二氧化碳	**considerable** *adj.* 数量可观的
emission *n.* 排放	**intuition** *n.* 直觉
planet *n.* 星球	**drastic** *adj.* 激烈的
temperature *n.* 温度	**costly** *adj.* 昂贵的
rise *v.* 上升	**analysis** *n.* 分析

expensive *adj.* 昂贵的	**postpone** *v.* 推迟
radically *adv.* 激进地	**prevent** *v.* 防止，阻止
adaptation *n.* 适应	**sanitation** *n.* 卫生
model *n.* 模式	**measure** *n.* 措施
expect *v.* 预期，期望	**seriously** *adv.* 严重地
experience *v.* 经历	

考题解析

Questions 27-32

- 题型归类：YES/NO/NOT GIVEN
- 题目解析：

题目编号	题目定位词	答案位置	题解
27	pessimistic, reasons	A 段	题目“因为一些原因，环保主义者对世界的态度非常悲观”，需要找到 A 段第一句“对于许多环保主义者来说，世界正变得更糟糕”，下面列举的他们产生这种想法的原因，因此应当选 YES。
28	data, resources, since 1972	B 段	通过关键词找到在 B 段中相对应的部分，但是没有发现有与题目“有关地球自然资源的数据从 1972 年才开始收集”的陈述，因此选 NOT GIVEN。
29	starving people	B 段第 4 行	找到 B 段第 4 行说“处于饥饿中的人减少了”，与题目所述“世界处于饥饿的人数近年来越来越多”不符，因此选 NO。
30	extinct species, new species	B 段第 5 行	在文中相应位置找到有关叙述以后会发现，文章中说物种在减少，但速度没有预测的那么快，没有提到“新的物种替代灭绝的物种”，因此选 NOT GIVEN。
31	pollution, industrialisation	B 段第 8 行	题目“一些污染物问题准确地与工业化联系在一起”可以在文中找到相对应的内容，选 YES。
32	pollution problems, industrialization	B 段第 7 行	题目中说“最好的办法是试着减缓经济增长”，这与文中所述“为了减少工业化初期带来的污染，最好的办法是发展经济而不是限制经济的发展”不符，选 NO。

Questions 33-37

- 题型归类：Multiple Choice
- 题目解析：

题目编号	题目定位词	答案位置	题解
33	aspect, scientific research	第 4 段	这道题实际上是考第 4 段的段意，英文写作的手法往往把中心句放在段首，因此理解了第 4 段的第一句“科学研究存在不平衡的问题”，就基本上知道 C 是正确答案。

34	worldwide Fund for Nature	第5段	要找到第5段第2行所述"他们有时会夸大他们的论点"。
35	main point	第6段	仔细阅读第6段会发现,这段讨论的主要是环保组织比其他游说组织更拥有人们的认同,而因此不容易受到怀疑和批评。因此正确答案选C。
36	intend, expectations	第7段	如果理解了第7段的前两句话,这道题并不难。另外用一些常识也可以排除掉A和D,而C在文章中没有提到,只有B是正确的。
37	waste problem	第8段	题目"作者是怎样评述美国的垃圾问题的",这也需要对第8段有一个全面的理解。这段首先叙述了媒体对于美国垃圾问题的渲染,然后又用事实说明没有那么严重。因此,可以看出B是正确答案。

Questions 38–40

题目类型:Sentence Completion

题目解析:

题目编号	题目定位词	答案位置	题解
38	long-term	第2段第9行	注意原文中所说"一个会影响到我们的未来的现象",这说明是长期的,因此填E。
39	right way	第10段	这个答案可以用逻辑思维来排除其他选项,实际上只有"right"这个词填在句子中,句子才有意义。
40	urgent problem	第11段	这一段第3行,抓住"pressing"这个词,它的意思就是"urgent"。

参考译文

环境真相

对于许多环境保护主义者来说,世界似乎正在变糟。他们提出了一连串我们最担忧的事:自然资源枯竭、人口不断增长使得食物越来越少、物种大量灭绝,地球上的空气和水受到越来越严重的污染。

但是稍微地看一下实际情况,事实却显示完全不同的画面。首先,自从一些科学家在1972年发表"发展的极限"一书以来,能源和其他自然资源越来越丰富,至少不是那么少。第二,现在世界人口中平均每人所占有的食物比历史上的任何时期都多。挨饿的人越来越少。第三,尽管物种确实在逐渐减少,但是在未来的50年内只有大约0.7%会消失,而不是经常预测的25–50%。最后,大多数形式被夸大的或者转瞬即逝的环境污染都与工业化的初期有关,因此最好的解决方法不是限制而是促进经济增长。但是有一种形式的污染——导致全球变暖的温室气体排放——确实将成为影响到我们未来的现象,只不过它的总体后果不会成为毁灭性的问题。对全球变暖不恰当的反应却可能是一个更大的问题。

然而,民意测验表明许多人相信环境质量正在下降,有四种因素导致这种感觉与现实之间的偏差。

首先是科学研究重点的不平衡性。科研资金主要流入问题较多的领域。这是一种明智的策略,但是它也会造成潜在问题比实际问题更多的印象。

第二,环境组织需要吸引大众媒体的注意。他们还需要保持资金的来源。因此,不难理解他们有时过分夸张了他们的论点,例如在1997年,世界自然基金会发表了题为"世界上三分之二的森林已经永远消失"的新闻稿。实际情况却是不到20%。

尽管这些团体是由一些无私的人管理着,但是他们具有游说团体的许多特性。问题是民众对环保游说活动的怀疑程度往往低于对其他领域游说团体的怀疑。如果一个贸易组织为减少污染控制而争辩,会被立即认为是出于自身利益的考虑。然而,绿色环保组织反驳弱化污染控制的观点则被认为是为他人考虑,即使对问题公正的分析可能会发现他们这样做实际上弊大于利。

媒体的态度是造成混乱的第三个根源。公众对坏消息显然要比好消息更加好奇。于是报纸和广播公司就会去提供公众想要的东西。然而,这将导致明显的概念扭曲。一个例子是美国在1997和1998年遭遇了厄尔尼诺现象。这种气候现象被指责为旅游业滑坡、过敏症发作、滑雪坡融化并导致22人死亡的罪魁祸首。然而,根据美国气象学会公告中的文章,该现象造成的损失大约为40亿美元,而造成的收益为大约190亿美元。这主要来自于更高的冬季气温(挽救了大约850条生命,减少的供暖费用,减少了因融水导致的春季洪水)。

第四个因素是较差的个人理解力。公众担心不停增加的人类抛弃的废弃物将使世界用尽处置垃圾的空间。然而,即使美国和以前一样持续增加垃圾的输出量,即使美国人口在2100年翻一倍,美国在整个21世纪所生产的垃圾将只能够占据整个美国领土面积的1/12000。

那么全球变暖到底会造成什么后果呢?据我们所知,二氧化碳的排放导致地球变暖。最保守的估计是气温在本世纪将上升2-3度,将导致严重的问题,总计损失达50000亿美元。

尽管直觉是必须针对这种代价高昂的问题采取一些激烈的措施,但是经济学分析清楚地表明消减二氧化碳排放的代价远远高于为了适应气温升高而付出的代价。美国国家气候变化组的主要创始人之一建立的模型表明,在2100年预期达到的2.1度的气温升高将会减小为1.9度。或者换句话说,地球在2094年预期达到的气温将会推迟到2100年达到。

当然这不能阻止全球变暖,只是为地球赢得了6年的时间。然而降低二氧化碳排放的代价,仅就美国而言,将高于解决世界上唯一的、最紧迫的健康问题:在全世界提供干净的饮用水和卫生设施而付出的代价。该项措施每年可以避免200万人死亡,防止5亿人患上严重疾病。

至关重要的是我们着眼于如下事实,我们是否想为将来作出一个最佳决策。过度乐观将使我们付出昂贵的代价——但是过于悲观的代价将是更加昂贵的。

WRITING

WRITING TASK 1

a) Question analysis, including discussion of main features, comparisons that need to be made, and possible misinterpretations of the question. (审题)

"The graph below shows the proportion of the population aged 65 and over between 1940 and 2040 in three different countries. Summarise the information by selecting and reporting the main features, and make comparisons where relevant."

Points to note.(审题要点)

1. Type of graph. The graph is a line graph.(表格的类型。这是个曲线图。)

2. The horizontal axis shows years in the past and in the future.（横轴表明的是现在和过去的年份。）
3. There is information about three countries that must be analysed.（关于三个国家的信息必须要进行分析。）
4. It is acceptable to use "65 +" instead of "65 and over".（最好用"65 +"，而不是"65 或65 以上"。）
5. Don't worry about exact years given that the horizontal scale is quite small.（考虑到横轴的跨度很小，不用过分关注具体的年份。）

Main features and comparisons.（主要特点和比较）

1. All three countries begin, in 1940, with 5 – 9% of their population aged 65 +.（三个国家在 1940 年开始的时候，65 岁以上人口的比例都是 5 – 9%。）
2. All three countries end, in 2040, with 23 – 27% of their population aged 65 +.（三个国家在 2040 年结束的时候 65 岁以上人口的比例都是 23 – 27%。）
3. From 1940 to 1990, Japan and Sweden follow the same trend and have similar proportions of people aged 65 +.（从 1940 年到 1990 年，日本和瑞典的趋势是一样的，超过 65 岁人口的比例是相似的。）
4. From 1940 to 2000, the USA has a small proportion of people aged 65 + (3 – 5%)（从 1940 到 2000 年美国 65 岁以上人口的比例很小。）
5. All three countries are expected to have dramatic increases in the proportion of people aged 65 + after 2030, particularly the USA.（在 2030 年后三个国家的 65 岁以上人口都有望大幅度增加，尤其是美国。）
6. The proportion of people aged 65 + in Sweden rises substantially between 1990 and 2010.（瑞典 65 岁以上的人口比例在 1990 到 2010 年之间大幅度上涨。）
7. Although the overall trend is a rise in the proportion of people aged 65 + in all three countries, there are slight dips.（尽管三个国家 65 岁以上人口的比例整体呈上升趋势，但是也有小幅度的下降。）

Possible misinterpretations and problems.（审题误区）

1. Be careful not to confuse the lines, particularly those for Japan and the USA. Pay special attention to points where the lines cross each other.（注意不要将各条曲线混淆，尤其是代表日本和美国的。特别注意这些线相交的地方。）
2. The vertical axis shows percentages/proportions, not total numbers. Be careful to include the percentage symbol—%.（纵轴表示的是百分比或比例，不是整个数量。注意不要漏掉代表百分比的符号%。）
3. The graph contains a lot of information. This is good because it means that it should be easy to write at least 150 words about it. However, it also means that you should not include every piece of information for each 20-year interval. The examiner knows that you only have 20 minutes to write the report and will not expect all the details.（图表包含丰富的信息。这样很好，因为这意味着要写 150 字并非难事。但是，它也说明我们不能把所有的信息都按 20 年的间隔写下来。考官知道考生只有 20 分钟的时间来写出这篇报告因此并不期望大家把所有的细节都包含进去。）

***b) Suggested answer format, including contrast with possible unsuitable formats.*（写作思路）**

The introduction should consist of rewriting the sentence "The graph below shows the proportion of the population aged 65 and over between 1940 and 2040 in three different countries." The obvious changes are:

i) change "The graph" to "The line graph".

ii) change "three different countries" to "Japan, Sweden, and the USA".

iii) change the word order.

Most candidates will examine each country in turn. This is completely acceptable. However, given that Japan and Sweden follow the same pattern between 1940 and 1990, (and from 2030 to 2040), it is worth combining them. This will avoid repetition. Remember that the question specifically states that you should "make comparisons where relevant." So, for the model answer, we will examine Japan and Sweden in one paragraph. The USA follows a different trend to Japan and Sweden and so needs to be dealt with alone. Finally, by way of a 'conclusion', add a sentence giving the overall trend for the three countries.(很多考生会按次序论述每个国家的情况。这是完全可以的。但是,鉴于日本和瑞典在1940和1990年期间<以及2030到2040之间>趋势完全一样,因此可以将两者合起来讨论。这样可以避免重复。记住问题很明确地要求你必须"在相关的时候进行必要的比较。"因此,在范文里,我们会在一段中分析日本和瑞典。美国的趋势和日本与瑞典不同因此需要单独进行讨论。最后,在结论处我们可以增加一个句子将三个国家的整体趋势进行描述。)

c) *Model answer.*(参考范文)

The line graph shows the proportion of people in Japan, Sweden, and the USA aged 65 + from 1940 and the expected proportions up to 2040.

From 1940 – 1990, the proportions of people aged 65 + in Japan and Sweden are similar and follow the same trend. In 1940 the figures were 9% and 7% respectively, rising to 15% and 14% respectively in 1980, before dipping to 14% and 13% respectively in 1990. Thereafter, Japan's proportion of people aged 65 + leveled out and is forecast to remain at 14% until 2020, after which it is expected to increase to 23% in 2040. However, Sweden's proportion of people aged 65 + began to rise after 1990. This increase is forecast to continue until 2010 when the proportion is estimated to be 20%. Then, there is expected to be a slight drop to 18% in 2030, followed by a steep climb to 25% in 2040.

The situation in the USA differs considerably, with a fall in the percentage of people aged 65 + between 1940 (5%) and 1960 (3%). The percentage remained steady until 1985, whereupon it began to climb. This rise is projected to continue until around 2030, when the proportion of Americans aged 65 + is expected to reach 10%. Thereafter, within just a few years, the proportion is forecast to rise dramatically to 25%, with a less dramatic rise to 27% in 2040.

The overall trend is a rise in the proportions of people aged 65 + in the three countries between 1940 and 2040.

译文:

该曲线图表明日本、瑞典和美国在1940年65岁以上人口的比例以及到2040年的预计比例。

从1940年到1990年,日本和瑞典的65岁以上人口的比例相近而且发展趋势相同。1940年两国数字分别是9%和7%,1980年分别上升到15%和14%,然后1990年分别下降到14%和13%。此后,日本60岁以上的人口比例有所下降,到2020年将保持在14%,此后预计2040年将上升到23%。但是,瑞典的比例在1990年开始上升。预计这种上升将持续到2010年,届时预计比例为20%。然后,预计将会轻微下降至2030年的18%,到2040年,这个比例将会徒增至25%。

美国的情形与此大不相同,在1940(5%)和1960(3%)65岁以上人口的比例是一个下降趋势。该比例一直平稳保持到1985年,此后开始上升。预计这一上升将持续到2030年,届时美国65岁以上人口预计为10%。此后,在短短的几年之内,该比例将大幅上升到25%,此后上升幅度将不那么显著,2040年将达到27%。

三个国家65岁以上人口比例在1940到2040年之间的总体趋势是上升的。

d) Analysis of vocabulary and structures used in model answer, including possible mistakes made by candidates. **(语言分析)**

It is important to repeat words associated with describing trends as little as possible. Using the same words repetitively indicates a narrow vocabulary. The model answer uses the synonyms 'rise', 'climb', and 'increase'. Note that these words are used as both verbs and nouns, indicating to the examiner that the candidate knows they can be used in both ways. This technique is used again with the words 'dramatically' and 'dramatic'. The words 'projected', 'expected', 'estimated', and 'forecast' are used throughout the model answer as synonyms. (要尽可能少的重复和描述趋势相关的词汇,这一点很重要。反复使用同样的单词表明考生的词汇量贫乏。范文在不同地方变换使用一组同义词“rise”,“climb”和“increase”。记住这些词即被当作名词由被当作动词来使用,这样可以向考官表明考生明白这些词可以有多种用法。在使用“dramatic”和“dramatically”的时候所使用的技巧是相似的。范文中在不同的地方使用“projected”、“expected”、“estimated”和“forecast”这一组同义词也是为了突出词汇的丰富性。)

The graph shows figures for years in the past, giving candidates the opportunity to show that they know how to form the past tense. Although the graph shows years in the future, candidates shouldn't use 'will', as this indicates a high level of certainty. The figures for the future are only estimates, so the use of 'will' should be avoided. (曲线图显示了过去几年的数据,这样考生就有机会表明他们知道如何使用一般过去时。尽管曲线也描述了将来的情况,但是考生不应该使用“will”,因为这个词表示很肯定。而这里边的将来数据只是一些预测,因此一定要避免使用“will”这个词。)

When discussing Japan and Sweden, the model answer uses the word 'respectively'. Unfortunately, this word has to be used three times to save words when describing the fact that those two countries follow the same trend. (在探讨日本和瑞典的时候,范文使用了“respectively”这个词。不过,在描述这两个国家趋势相同这个事实的时候,这个单词只被使用三次以节省字数。)

Note the use of the gerund in the same sentence. This reduces the number of words that would otherwise be needed and allows the creation of one complex sentence rather than a few simple ones. "In 1940 the figures were 9% and 7% respectively, **rising** to 15% and 14% respectively in 1980, before **dipping** to 14% and 13% respectively in 1990." (注意,在同一的句子中对动名词的使用。这样可以减少单词的数量并且可以使用一个比较复杂的句式而不是使用更多的简单句子。"In 1940 the figures were 9% and 7% respectively, **rising** to 15%" and 14% respectively in 1980, before **dipping** to 14% and 13% respectively in 1990".)

WRITING TASK 2

a) Question analysis, including discussion of the points that need to be made in the essay, possible misinterpretations of the question. **(审题)**

"Universities should accept equal numbers of male and female students in every subject. To what extent do you agree or disagree?"

Possible misinterpretations and problems. (审题误区)

1. The question prompt clearly refers to universities. Answers that refer to schools, companies, etc., can expect to be penalized as irrelevant. (问题提示部分明确指出是大学。如果在文章中提到中小学

和公司等其他机构将被视为不相关而被扣分。)

2. The question prompt clearly says "in every subject", so answers cannot refer to certain subjects at the exclusion of others. (问题提示部分明确说的是"在每一个科目中",因此答案中不能只提到某些科目而将其他的排除在外。)
3. The question asks, "To what extent do you agree or disagree?" This means that you can take an extreme position or one somewhere between. However, taking a position somewhere between might be problematic since, even if you think it is a good idea for some subjects, you still disagreeing with the basic principle of having the same number of males and females on each course. (问题问的是"你在多大程度上同意或不同意?"这意味着你既可以持极端的态度也可以采取介于两种态度之间的中间态度。但是,采取中间态度可能会带来一些问题,因为即使你认为这种做法对某些科目是可行的,你实际上还是表明你不同意每一种科目的男女生人数相同。)

b) *Suggested answer format, including contrast with possible unsuitable formats.*(写作思路)

For this question, the essay format should involve an introduction, two or three main paragraphs, and a conclusion. The introduction should be short and may or may not include the writer's opinion. Each of the main paragraphs should focus on a particular argument. However, these main paragraphs can either focus on one side of the argument (as in model answer 1 below) or take into account the opposite point of view (as in model answer 2 below). The conclusion should be short and state the writer's opinion. (针对这个问题,文章的格式应该包括一个引论部分,两到三段主体以及一个结论部分。引论应该尽量简短可以包括也可以不包括写作者的观点。每一段主体段落应该尽终论述一个主旨。但是,三个主体段落及可以集中论述论点中的一面 <见范文 1> 或考虑对相反的论点进行批驳 <见范文 2>。结论部分应该简短并且说明作者的观点。)

The most important thing is to make sure that each of the main paragraphs focuses clearly on one argument. If several arguments are included in the same paragraph they could confuse the reader. It is also important that each argument be well developed, and having a separate paragraph for each will help the writer achieve this. (最重要的是确保每一段主体部分都应该清晰地集中描述一个论点。如果同一段落中包括几个论点可能对读者产生误导。每一段同样需要很好的发展,要做到这一点,考生最好一段论述一个论点。)

c) *Two model answers of around 300 words, each essay taking a different view.*(参考范文)

Model answer 1—Agreeing with the prompt.(范文 1,持赞同观点)

There has been some debate about the basis on which universities should accept students. In particular, the traditional system of accepting students purely on the basis of their grades needs to be re-evaluated. In this essay, I would like to point out the benefits of accepting an equal number of male and female students onto each university course.

The first benefit is that it would encourage young men and women to consider a wider range of careers. Many young people think that certain careers are "for men" or "for women" whereas a person can actually do any job provided that they get the right qualifications for it and work hard at it. Very often, the idea of "men's jobs" and "women's jobs" comes from parents and grandparents who are out of touch with today's job market. In this way, our society will develop more slowly than it should because of traditional preconceptions. If young women saw more women becoming successful in business, they would be encouraged to enter that field. If young men saw more men becoming nurses, they would consider that traditionally female area of work.

The second benefit is that women would more rapidly been seen as equal to men. At the moment, many women are discouraged from attending university. Many people still think that it is better for a young woman to find a well-off husband than to develop her own career. On the other hand, it is extremely rare for a man to be encouraged to marry a well-off woman rather than develop his career. If men and women were given equal opportunities to develop themselves, and contribute to society, there would be less sexism. The result would be a society where a person's gender was less important than their skills and personality.

To conclude, providing an equal number of places on university courses or young men and young women would encourage people not to think in stereotypes about what they can and can't do and would lead to sex equality.

译文：

关于学校应该根据什么标准来录取学生的问题一直以来都有争论。尤其是，传统的完全按照分数录取学生的做法需要我们重新考虑。在本文中，我将指出接受同样数量的男女学生会对大学课程带来的好处。

第一个好处是它将鼓励青年男女考虑范围更广的职业。很多年轻人认为某些职业仅适合"男人"或"女人"的，而实际上一个人只要具有相应的素质并且努力工作，他(她)可以从事任何工作。在很多情况下，"男人的工作"和"女人的工作"这样的观念来自于和现代职业市场脱节的父辈或祖父辈。如果按照那样的趋势发展下去，我们的社会将因为这些传统的偏见而发展缓慢。如果年轻的妇女看见更多的女人在商业领域获得成功，她们就会受到鼓励而投身于那一行。如果年轻的男人看见更多的男人成为护士，他们也会考虑进入这个传统的妇女从事的行业。

第二个好处是妇女会更快地获得和男人一样平等的地位。目前，很多妇女都被劝说不要读大学。很多人仍然认为年轻女人更应该嫁一个财产殷实的丈夫，而不是发展自己的事业。另一方面，很少有人鼓励男人不去发展自己的事业，而是去找一个家境较好的女人。如果男女都有同样的机会发展自己，并为社会做出贡献，那么性别主义就会减少。这样就会使我们社会里个人的技能和个性比性别更重要了。

总之，在大学课程中，为青年男女提供同样就读机会将鼓励人们不会带有偏见地去考虑谁到底能做什么和不能做什么，并最终实现男女平等。

Model answer 2—Disagreeing with the prompt.(范文2，持反对观点)

Although it is not a particularly widely discussed topic, there has been some discussion about the idea of having equal numbers of young men and young women accepted onto each course offered at each university.

The supporters of such a move have generally focused on two arguments. The first is that women are often not equally represented in particular professions which generally require a university education, such as law and scientific research. They argue that it is necessary to get more women onto these courses at university in order that they may proceed to develop careers in those fields. Whilst I would agree with this argument, I believe that it is not strong enough to overcome two objections. First, there is the argument that university places should go to those who deserve them, on the basis of university entrance tests. Second, there is the point that certain courses are simply more popular with young men than with young women (and vice versa!).

The second argument raised in favour of having equal numbers of young men and women on university courses follows from the first. The argument is that many young people choose particular courses at university because of stereotyping. For example, a young woman might think about studying law, but be put off by the idea that it is "a man's profession". Alternatively, she might never even consider a particular job because she doesn't have a role model. This leads to a vicious circle whereby few women study law, so few women see it as a suitable profession, and so on. Although I see the validity of this argument, I also know that people are moving into professions once dominated by the other gender. For example, it is no longer unusual to hear of a female police officer.

In conclusion, I would argue that it is not a good idea to force universities to accept equal numbers of male and female students onto each course. I believe that it is far better to let people choose which courses they prefer and to allow universities to accept students on their merits.

译文：

尽管这不是一个被广泛讨论的话题，但现在仍然有一些关于在每所大学里每个科目是不是应该接受同样数量的男生和女生的讨论。

那些支持这种做法的人一般会集中讨论两个问题。首先，妇女在某些特定的行业里并没有被平等地对待，这些行业一般要求有大学教育背景，比如，法律和科学研究领域。他们认为应该让更多的妇女进入大学学习这些科目，从而使这些女性能够从事这些行业的工作。尽管我同意这一论点，但是我认为这并不足以反驳人们的两个反对意见。首先，有人认为大学里的位置应该给那些通过了大学入学考试成绩，配得上上大学的人。其次，有人认为某些课程本来就是更适合年轻男性或年轻女性。

第二个支持大学应该接受同样数量男女同学的观点，是建立在第一个论点的基础上的。这一论点认为很多年轻人因为世俗偏见的缘故，在大学里选择某些特定的课程。比如，一个年轻的妇女可能考虑过学习法律，但是因为想到这是一个"男人的职业"而放弃了这个想法。另外，她可能因为没有一个职业榜样，就从来没有考虑过某一职业。这样会导致几乎没有妇女学习法律，从而很少有妇女认为这是一个适合妇女的职业，而且这就形成了一个恶性循环。尽管我认为这个观点有其合理性，但是我也知道人们现在已经开始进入一个职业性别互相渗透的时代。比如，现在听说一个女性当警官已经不是一件什么新鲜事了。总之，我认为强迫大学在每个科目接受同样数量的男性和女性不是个好主意。我相信让人们根据自愿选择科目并允许大学根据学生们的长处选择学生，会是一个更好的办法。

d) Analysis of vocabulary and structures used in model answer, including possible mistakes made by candidates. **（语言分析）**

"**There has been some debate about** the basis on which universities should accept students." Many Chinese candidates have been taught to begin by saying that the subject is "a hot topic" or "a controversial issue", when in fact it isn't. This subject is one example.（很多考生曾经被老师告知在文章开头要说这个问题是"一个热点问题"或"一个有争议的话题"，而事实上该问题并非如此。本话题就是一个这样的例子。）

"Many young people think that certain careers are "for men" **or** "for women" **whereas** a person can actually do any job **provided that** they get the right qualifications for it **and** work hard at it." Note the use of different connectors in one sentence to combine ideas and create complex sentences. Examiners are looking for the ability to do this.（注意在一个句子中使用不同的连词来连接观点并创造复杂句。考官实际上是在关注考生这方面的能力。）

"Very often, the idea of "men's jobs" and "women's jobs" comes from parents and grandparents who

are out of touch with today's job market." Examiners are looking for appropriate use of idiomatic English. Most Chinese candidates make the mistakes of using too many idioms or of using idiomatic English inappropriately.（考官很关注对习惯表达的合理运用。很多中国的考生因为使用过多的习语或不恰当的使用习语而犯错误。）

"At the moment, **many** women are discouraged from attending university." Many candidates would not include the word 'many' in this sentence, which would change the meaning significantly and also be untrue. Candidates should be very careful about making absolute statements. "At the moment, **many** women are discouraged from attending university."（很多考生不会把 many 这个词放在这个句子当中,这样会显著改变意思而且会导致不正确的表达。考生需要特别注意过于绝对的表达。）

"**They argue that** it is necessary to get more women onto these courses at university". Notice that the writer uses 'they' to refer to people he/she disagrees with. This is commonly done in academic writing in English.（注意这里作者使用了 they 来表示他不同意的人。这是一种在学术英语写作中常用的手法。）

"Whilst I would agree with this argument, I believe that it is not strong enough to overcome two objections." The writer is showing that he/she accepts the opposing argument, but feels that it is insufficient.（作者表明他接受反面的观点,但是感觉那种观点不够充分。）

"The argument is that many young people choose particular courses at university because of stereotyping." Examiners are looking for appropriate use of uncommon vocabulary. This doesn't mean that every sentence should contain uncommon words, because that would make the essay look contrived.（考官很关注对不太熟悉的词汇的恰当运用。这并不意味着每个句子都要含有不熟悉的单词,因为那样的话整篇文章会看起来矫揉造作。）

SPEAKING

a) *Question analysis, including possible misinterpretations of the questions.*

Which part of your country do most people live in?

The key point here is to describe the location of the **part** of the **country.** Many candidates confuse country, province, countryside, and city. The question asks about **most** people, not you personally!

Tell me about the main industries there.

This is a simple vocabulary question. Remember that the question relates to the previous one—**there.**

How easy is it to travel around your country?

This question asks about methods of transport and the efficiency of the transport network.

Has your country changed much since you were a child?

Many candidates will focus on the word 'child' and start talking off topic. Talk about changes. Given how quickly China has changed, this is an easy question for Chinese candidates. Remember to use the past tense and/or present perfect tense, as appropriate.

Describe a well-known person you like or admire.

'Well-known person' refers to someone who is known throughout your country. It does not refer to a person that you know well!

What kind of people become famous people these days?

Talk about the fields of life these people come from and why people from those fields are more likely to be famous.

Is this different from the kind of achievement that made people famous in the past? In what way?

Remember to use the past tense and/or present perfect tense, as appropriate.

How do you think people will become famous in the future?

Remember to use the future tense. You could also use modals (could, might) and words that express possibility (probably, possibly).

What are the good things about being famous? Are there any disadvantages?

The examiner will probably ask about disadvantages only if you give a short answer about the good things. Provide an answer that includes both.

How does the media in your country treat famous people?

The key word here is **treat.** Give examples if possible.

Why do you think ordinary people are interested in the lives of famous people?

Many candidates misinterpret this question as "Are people interested...?" The key word is why.

b) Shortlist of useful vocabulary that candidates could use in their answers to each question and brainstorming diagram for Part 2 questions.

Which part of your country do most people live in?

East, west, south, north, center, on (near) the coast, in coastal areas, along rivers.

Tell me about the main industries there.

Tourism, chemical, manufacturing, hi-tech, car, steel, mining, service.

How easy is it to travel around the country?

Quite easy, very difficult, trains, rail network, road network, highways, airports.

Has your country changed much since you were a child?

Got better/worse, stayed the same, great differences, not much different, richer, poorer, cleaner, dirtier.

Describe a well-known person you like or admire.

actor/actress, businessman/woman, politician, singer, musician.

tall, short, thin, slim, average build, broad shouldered, hair, eyes.

married, single, divorced, widowed.

great, charity work, speak out on issues.

What kind of people become famous people these days?

Is this different from the kind of achievement that made people famous in the past? In what way?

How do you think people will become famous in the future?

Actor/actress, sports stars, film stars, film directors, business people, politicians, scientists, environmentalists, supergirl, reality TV.

What are the good things about being famous? Are there any disadvantages?

Recognition, money, big house, interesting work, meet other famous people, media, paparazzi, little privacy, pressure, appointments, meetings, interviews.

How does the media in your country treat famous people?

Respect, disrespect, well, badly, hound, endless questions, breach privacy.

Why do you think ordinary people are interested in the lives of famous people?

Bored, interested, glamour, wealth, fashion, trend.

c) *Two model answers for each question.*

Which part of your country do most people live in?

Most people in my country live near the coast, because inland it is mountainous. Most people live in cities and large towns.

In my country, most people live in the north and west, where the climate is warmer and not so wet. The center of my country is a desert, so hardly anyone lives there.

Tell me about the main industries there.

Because most people live near the coast, the main industries are fishing and shipbuilding. There are some hi-tech industries in the cities and the capital is a major car manufacturing center.

In the north and west, the steel and chemical industries are very important. Many people work in service industries and there has been a lot of growth in the tourist industry in recent years.

How easy is it to travel around your country?

It's very easy to travel along or near the coast, but the mountains inland make traveling there quite difficult. There are a few highways going inland, but they are often jammed, particularly when many people go to the mountains on holiday.

Apart from the center, my country is covered by roads and a rail network, so it is fairly easy to travel around. There are also many large airports connecting major cities.

Has your country changed much since you were a child?

Yes, it has. Most of the cities have grown in size and places are better connected than when I was a child. There are many more industries than before, but the environment is still fairly clean. People are richer than they used to be and they have better housing.

I'm only 18, and my country hasn't changed too much in the past ten years. People are a little richer than before. The main thing that has changed is that the environment has become dirtier.

Describe a well-known person you like or admire.

I like the actress Shirley Bean. She has appeared in many films, the most famous being "Starbird", for which she won an Oscar last year. She is quite tall and slim, with long blond hair. I don't know her eye colour! She is married to the actor John Temple. They don't have any children, but Shirley has said that she would like two or three. They live in Hollywood, but Shirley is originally from Montana. I admire her for two reasons. First, she is a great actress. Second, she does a lot of work for charity, especially those that help children. She uses her fame and connections to raise money.

I admire the politician James Weaver. He is a member of the US Senate for Virginia. He is quite old—68, I think—and has grey hair. He is very tall and broad shouldered. He has two homes—one in Virginia and another in Washington, D. C. He is divorced and has four children, who are all successful in their careers. The reason that I admire him is that he speaks out on issues that the media doesn't report on very often. He is particularly active on the issues of poverty and crime. He seems to me to be the kind of person who wants everyone to have the chance to be as good as they can be.

What kind of people become famous people these days?

In my country, the most famous people are politicians and businessmen. You can see them on TV and read about them in newspapers. Sometimes, they even allow magazines to come to their homes and take photographs, so readers can see how they live and what furniture they have.

The people of my country are big sports fans. The most famous people at the moment are the members of our football team who played in the World Cup. They didn't win, but people really admire them and want to know everything about them. Actors and actresses from TV series are also very famous.

Is this different from the kind of achievement that made people famous in the past? In what way?

I think that politicians have been famous in my country for a long time, but I think that businessmen becoming famous is a new thing. Many people want to have their own business and are keen to find out how they became successful.

In the past, communications weren't as good as today, so it was more difficult to become famous. To be honest, I can't even name any famous people from my country's past, other than political leaders. In the past, you really had to do something special. That's sometimes true today, but often it's easy to become famous—at least for a short time.

How do you think people will become famous in the future?

I think that political leaders will always be famous. Perhaps other people will become famous for helping the environment, but more likely they will become famous for winning a competition on TV, like American Idol.

I think that people in the entertainment field will have the best chances of becoming famous. I know this is already true in America and other countries, but in my country the entertainment industry has only just stated to develop. I think we will have some international singing and acting stars in the future.

What are the good things about being famous? Are there any disadvantages?

I think the best thing about being famous is that you usually get lots of money, which you can use to buy a big house, nice car, and so on. The problem of being famous is that the media is constantly watching you. That puts them under a lot of pressure. Sometimes I think they hope you make a mistake, so that they can publicise it.

Being famous can be difficult, because you will probably have to go to many meetings and do interviews with the media. However, I think it must be great to know that so many people like you and respect what you have achieved. Everyone wants recognition for what they do.

How does the media in your country treat famous people?

I think that the media treats famous people very badly. They often seem to be looking for problems, particularly in famous people's private lives. I wish they would respect famous people's privacy. Sometimes, they even hound famous people's family and friends.

I think the media in my country treats them well. They don't ask too many personal questions. I heard that, in other countries, the media will ask friends of famous people for information, but the media doesn't do that in my country. The media doesn't often breach the privacy of famous people—at least, not yet.

Why do you think ordinary people are interested in the lives of famous people?

I think that they want to know what clothes they are wearing, which cars they drive, and things like that. Ordinary people think that famous people lead glamorous lives and have the best of everything. They want to know about these things.

I think that many ordinary people are bored with their own lives and reading about the lives of famous people allows them to fantasise a little. Very often, famous people set fashion trends, which women in particular like to try and follow. Famous people are often very wealthy and this attracts many people. I mean, most people would like to be wealthy.

d) Text boxes showing how sentences can be completed. For example:

	near the coast.
Most people in my country live . . .	in cities and towns.
	in the north and west.

My country hasn't changed too much	
Most of the cities have grown in size	. . . since I was a child.
My country has changed enormously	

	quite tall and slim.
She is . . .	married to an actor.
	in her 50s.

	does a lot of work for charity.
I admire her because she . . .	uses her connection to raise money.
	speaks out on issues.

	politicians	
I think that . . .	actors and actresses	. . . will always be famous.
	singers	

Test 2

LISTENING

SECTION 1

谈话场景:图书馆咨询,电话交谈。
人物关系:顾客和图书馆管理员。
谈话话题:顾客就怎样加入图书馆,能享受什么服务等咨询图书馆管理员。

词汇注释

library *n.* 图书馆
wonder *n.* 怀疑,惊讶
possible *adj.* 可能的
join *v.* 加入
minimum *n.* 最少量,至少
passport *n.* 护照
photo *n.* 照片
document *n.* 文件
driving licence 驾照
credit card 信用卡
address 地址
bank statement 银行通知
otherwise *adv.* 否则,另外
current *adj.* 目前的,现在的
steel *n.* 钢,钢铁
factory *n.* 工厂
expensive *adj.* 昂贵的
local *adj.* 当地的
range *n.* 范围
reference book 参考书
facility *n.* 设施
external *adj.* 外部的
borrow *v.* 借,借阅
fiction *n.* 小说
booklet *n.* 小册子
detail *n.* 细节
renew *v.* 续借
require *v.* 要求
telephone *v.* 电话
log on 登陆
nominal *adj.* 名义上的,象征性的
database *n.* 数据库
photocopy *v.* 复印
selection *n.* 选择,选集
creative *adj.* 创造性的,有创造力的

交际与语言表达

1. I was wondering if... 这是在向别人询问某件事时的一个礼貌用法,if 后面跟想询问的内容,意思是我想知道某件事是否怎样。在本文后面还有一种类似的用法,"another thing I was wondering about was if..." ,意思是我想知道的另外一件事是……
2. ... someone told me it was possible to join, even if I wasn't. 注意 even if 在这里当"即使"讲,"我听说即使我不是(本校学生)也可以加入"。
3. could you tell me 也是一种礼貌用法,用 can 的过去式来发问是为了使语气更加委婉,本文中还有许多类似的用法。
4. You'll need to come in to the library, 这句话也是以一种婉转的方式来告诉对方必须做的事情,这些考生都可以记下来,作为口语练习的积累。
5. Would that do? 那样成吗? 注意又是过去时,表示客气。

6. Otherwise 前面一定要有一个句子说明条件,后面则表示如果满足不了前面的条件,将会怎样。
7. I was at Westerley College until last year, 直到去年我还在 WESTERLEY 学院。注意 until 表示在这一时间之前所处的状态。
8. It's more expensive than I thought. More... than 这是一个有用的句式,另外 think 要用过去时,因为现在他已经知道这个事实了,所以只能同他以前知道的做比较。
9. We allow twelve items borrowed at any one time if you're a student... 如果你是学生,我们允许你任何一次都可以借 12 本书。注意 at any one time,意思是任何一次。
10. You can have both fiction and reference books for fours weeks... 无论是小说还是参考书你都可以借 4 星期。have sth. for some time,表示在某一时段保有某种东西。
11. free of charge 免费,也可以说 for free.
12. It's advisable,这样做比较合适。
13. in great demand, 需求量很大。
14. 文中图书馆管理员提到了几种英国报纸,*The Guardian* 卫报, *The Observer* 观察家报, *The Independent* 独立报, *The Times* 泰晤士报, *Sunday Times* 星期日泰晤士报。注意报纸的名字的首字母要大写,前面要加定冠词 the。
15. I assume you have photocopying facilities, 我想你们肯定有复印机。assume 也是口语中一个比较常见的用法,表示语气比较肯定的假设。
16. I'll be along later this week to join, 我本周晚些时候会有空来参加。To be along 是一个比较口语化的用法,表示在家或有空的意思。

考题解析

Question 1

这道题不难,但要注意照片要用复数,如果用了单数就会被扣掉一半的分。

Question 2

如果有国外生活经验的人都会知道 driving licence 和 bank statement 是比较常见的证明一个人身份的文件。希望考生能够通过学习语言多了解英国的社会文化背景,这样对以后出国留学会有帮助。

Question 3

这道题主要是要注意不要把几个价格混淆在一起,紧跟着 125 英镑的还有 25 英镑,这是有其他学校学生卡的价格。考生在听到数字的时候一定要记下来,并仔细辨明不同数字的不同含义。

Question 4

同样地,这道题也是考学生是否辨明了本校学生的借书数量和社会人员的借书量,后者应当是 8 本。

Question 5

这道题关键是在听的时候有没有听到 minimum fine 这个词组,考生在听材料的时候对有比较级的形容词和名词要特别注意,这些单词往往指示了考题的正确答案。

Question 6

对这道题的理解很重要,题目是说"计算机可以提前多少小时预定"而不是可以预定多少小时,所以答案应当是 48 小时。

Question 7

这道题填 local papers 当地报纸,注意复数。

Question 8

注意填这道题的答案时 card 前面要加量词 a,做题的时候每次都要注意量词和冠词的使用。

Question 9

这道题人名的拼写比较长,听的时候可以先记住音,再根据读音把名字拼出来,这需要一些语感。

Question 10

注意星期几的首字母也要大写。

SECTION 2

谈话场景:广播节目。
人物关系:志愿者组织代表的演讲。
谈话话题:介绍志愿者组织和如何向他们募捐。

词汇注释

pedal *n.* 蹬,踩
power *n.* 电力,力量
charity *n.* 慈善,慈善机构
contact *n.* 联络,联系
detail *n.* 细节
support *v.* 支持
Ecuador *n.* 厄瓜多尔
adventure *n.* 冒险
voluntary *adj.* 自愿的
organisation *n.* 组织
survey *n.* 调查
rural *adj.* 农村的
unusually *adv.* 不同寻常地,特殊地
successful *adj.* 成功的
radius *n.* 半径,范围
bicycle *n.* 自行车
skilled *adj.* 熟练的
collect *v.* 收集,采集
collection *n.* 收集,收藏
distribute *v.* 分配,分发
overseas *adj.* 海外
enormous *adj.* 巨大的,庞大的
expensive *adj.* 昂贵的
locally *adv.* 当地
continue *v.* 继续
operate *v.* 操作,运作
constant *adj.* 经常的
supply *n.* 供应
container *n.* 集装箱
Amsterdam 阿姆斯特丹(荷兰首都)
bill *n.* 帐单
situation *n.* 情况
fortunately *adv.* 幸运地
profile *n.* 形象,声誉;侧面,轮廓
standard *n.* 标准
donate *v.* 捐献
condition *n.* 条件
repair *v.* 修理
strip *v.* 剥去
consignment *n.* 交货,发货
public awareness 公众意识

交际与语言表达

1. I'd like to talk about... I'd like 是一个很有用的口语表达法,它和 I want 的意思相同,但是却令口气更加委婉,所以在说我想做什么事的时候,都可以采用这样的表达法。
2. I got the idea of exporting bicycles to developing countries while I was in Ecuador. 我在厄瓜多尔的时候想出了这个向发展中国家出口自行车的主意。
3. The project came to an end after five years. 项目 5 年后结束了。Come to an end 一般用来表示一个进行时间比较长的事情的结束,比如战争、婚姻、学业等,而且一般没有突然的人为干预。

4. My neighbour had the only bicycle in the village, whereas everyone else walked everywhere. 尽管在那个村里所有的人都走路去各处,我的邻居却拥有村里唯一的自行车。Whereas 在这里表示转折的语气,而且它后面所跟的从句所述的内容往往是前面部分的条件或者环境。
5. But in order to continue operating we need to have a constant supply of bikes which we send out every six months. 我们每6个月发货一次,因此需要一个固定的自行车供应源,才能保证持续的运行。In order to 本来应当跟在前提条件的后面,但是因为表达条件的句子太长,因此可以利用英语语句结构的灵活性,将 in order to 提到前面。
6. The local economy has developed so much, you wouldn't recognise it as the same place. 当地的经济发展得如此之好,你简直无法认出它还是原来那个地方了。如果是完整的句型在 you 之前应当有 that,是 so... that 的句型,但是这里省略了 that,意思也是清楚的。
7. Winning the award helped raise our profile, and the money enabled us to pay all our shipping costs, which represent our greatest expense. 得到这个奖项提高了我们的声誉,而奖金帮我们支付了我们最大的花销——海运费用。
8. Pedal Power changes lives—when someone gets a bicycle from us, they see a 14% increase in their income. 踏板力量改变人的生活——当某个人从我们这里得到一辆自行车以后,他们的收入会增加14%。
9. ... if we can't repair it, we'll strip it down for spare parts. 如果我们不能修好它,我们会把它拆掉,变成可以使用的零件。
10. Also, we're always interested to hear of other places that would benefit from receiving a consignment of bikes,... 同时,我们也希望知道有哪些地方会因为从我们这里收到自行车而获益。

考题解析

Question 11

原文中没有直接出现 voluntary worker 这个词,但是从这句话 I decided to join a voluntary organisation and was sent to Ecuador carry out land surveys 可以知道正确答案。

Question 12

解答这道题的时候要把题目和 Dan 的邻居拥有自行车联系起来,这样才会知道自行车使他到顾客那里去非常方便。

Question 13

考生在这里可能会不清楚 charity 指的是 Dan 的志愿者组织,然后回想听过的句子 we need to have a constant supply of bikes... 就知道正确答案选 A。

Question 14

在这道题中,A 所述的内容在听力材料里没有出现过,B 是错误的,因为文中说 Rivas 的自行车比阿姆斯特丹还要多。只有答案 C 在文中可以找到想对应的内容,即 the local economy has developed so much...。

Question 15

在这道题中,考生可能不知道 overhead 是"企业经济管理费用"的意思,因此用排除法比较合适。答案 B 和 C 都可以在原文中找到相反意思的语句,可以知道它们是错误的。

Question 16

这道题如果听清了听力材料中给出的数字就不难,要注意在数字前加上英镑的符号。

Question 17

这道题在原文中也可以很容易地找到相对应的地方,注意 computers 要用复数。

Questions 18–20

做这道题的时候一定要看清楚题目的要求是选出公众能够为这个慈善组织做的事情,因此像"组织自行车收集"、"修理捐献的自行车"等有慈善组织完成的事就应该被排除在外,其次象 D 和 E 这样似是而非,好像对又好像不对的选项要依靠考生对听力材料的透彻理解来进行判断,可以把拿不准的题目列一个次序,挑选最有把握的前三个选项填写在答卷上。

SECTION 3

谈话场景:老师给学生上辅导课。
人物关系:一位老师和两名学生。
谈话话题:讨论两个学生拍摄的一个电视短片。

词汇注释

video *n.* 电视,录像	**technical** *adj.* 技术的
tutor *n.* 辅导老师	**slang** *n.* 俚语
tutorial *n.* 辅导课	**enjoyment** *n.* 享乐,快乐
feedback *n.* 反馈	**benefit** *n.* 利益,福利,好处
session *n.* (一节)课	**cooperate** *v.* 合作
reflect *v.* 反映	**persuade** *v.* 劝说,游说
experience *n.* 经历	**edit** *v.* 编辑
camera *n.* 照相机	**experiment** *v.* 试验
operate *v.* 操作	**angle** *n.* 角度
result *n.* 结果	**focus** *n.* 焦点,聚焦
invite *n.* 邀请	**ambitious** *adj.* 有野心的,有雄心的
dinner *n.* 晚餐,主餐	**inexperienced** *adj.* 缺乏经验的
dish *n.* (一道)菜	**semester** *n.* 学期
practice *n.* 实践	**opportunity** *n.* 机会
compromise *v.* 妥协,让步	

交际与语言表达

1. to enjoy doing sth. 是一个固定用法,注意不要说 enjoy to do sth.。
2. ... you got a lot out of it, 你们从中收获很大。
3. I'd like to use this tutorial as a feedback session, where you reflect on the experience of doing the project. 我想把这堂辅导课用来收集反馈,你们可以说说你们对完成这个项目的经历的感想。
4. Well for me it was a very good chance to get to know students who are on other courses, 对我来说这是一个结识其他专业学生的好机会。Get to know 结识,on a course 读一个专业的课。
5. What was the most useful aspect of the project from the point of view of the English practice? 从练习英语的角度来说,这个项目最有用的方面是什么?
6. I think they speak at a natural speed, so it forces me to get used to it. 我觉得他们按自然的速度说话,这强迫我去适应这种语速。
7. ... we had to find ways of cooperating, erm, and compromising, and sometimes persuading people, when they don't agree with you. 我们必须设法去合作、妥协,有时当别人不同意你的意见时,要想办法说服他们。

8. I mean to put it another way, if you had to do it all over again, is there anything you'd do differently? 我的意思是换句话说,如果你们不得不重新再做一遍这件事,你们会做得有什么不同呢? I mean 是口语里比较常见的用法,一般用来说明自己前面说过的话。To put it another way, 换句话说,也是比较有用的短语。
9. I think we should have tried to experiment more with the camera. 在这里 should 后面加现在完成时表示一种对过去已经发生的事情的虚拟语气。
10. ... you'll have an opportunity to put into practice what you've learnt this time. 这次你们将有机会把你们学到的东西付诸实现。

考题解析

Question 21

在这里填 student's home 或者 home 都可以算对。

Question 22

答这道题时用吃饭的各种表达法都可以,比如 have dinner, go for dinner,或者 dinner。

Question 23

这道题中要理解 vocabulary 就是替换了听力材料中的 word,这样就不难找到答案了。

Question 24

这道题要注意 slang 不可数,这从前面 large amount of 可以判断出来,所以不要在词语末尾加 s。

Questions 25–26

这两道题并不难,关键要把 cooperating 和 persuading 拼写正确。

Question 27

在这道题里 editing 当剪接讲,再回忆起听力材料里关于片子长短和剪接的安排,就可以把题做对。

Question 28

这道题的关键是在听材料的时候,注意听动词以及跟在后面的名词和时间,这样有助于对谈话整体意思的把握。

Question 29

这里 experiment 当动词使用,但是后面必须加介词 with。

SECTION 4

谈话场景:科学家演讲。

人物关系:海洋生物学家向年轻听众演讲。

谈话话题:介绍南极洲的自然概况和科学探索。

词汇注释

remarkable *adj.* 不同寻常的,非凡的	**remote** *adj.* 偏远的
continent *n.* 大陆	**hostile** *adj.* 敌对的
Antarctica *n.* 南极洲	**uninhabited** *adj.* 无人居住的

permanent *adj.* 永久的	**enormous** *adj.* 巨大的,数量众多的
explorer *n.* 探险者	**previous** *adj.* 以前的
ultimate *adj.* 最后的,最终的	**crush** *v.* 倒塌
survival *n.* 生存	**architect** *n.* 建筑家
contest *n.* 竞赛	**platform** *n.* 平台
researcher *n.* 研究员	**extendable** *adj.* 可延伸的
remain *v.* 留下,剩下	**polar** *adj.* 两极的,极地的
intellectual *adj.* 智力的	**climate** *n.* 气候
challenge *n.* 挑战	**carbohydrate** *n.* 碳水化合物
wilderness *n.* 荒野,荒地	**ration** *n.* 配给量
extreme *n.* 极端	**fieldwork** *n.* 野外考察
contain *v.* 包含	**maximum** *n.* 最大量
technically *adv.* 技术上地	**compact** *adj.* 紧凑的,紧密的
unbelievably *adv.* 难以置信地	**presentation** *n.* 形式
category *n.* 种类	**diet** *n.* 食谱
desert *n.* 沙漠	**available** *adj.* 可用的,可以利用的
surrounding *adj.* 周围的	**insufficient** *adj.* 不充足的
ocean *n.* 海洋	**fascinating** *adj.* 迷人的,醉人的
freeze *v.* 冻结	**crucial** *adj.* 关键的,至关重要的
self-contained *adj.* 独立的,设备齐全的	**stability** *n.* 稳定性
community *n.* 社区,团体	**profound** *adj.* 深刻的,深的
gym *n.* 健身馆	**ozone** *n.* 臭氧
generate *v.* 发出,产生	**indicator** *n.* 标志物
electricity *n.* 电力	**radiation** *n.* 辐射
communicate *v.* 联络,联系	**pollution** *n.* 污染
satellite *n.* 卫星	**bubble** *n.* 气泡,泡沫
feature *n.* 特征	**atmosphere** *n.* 大气,气氛
supply *n.* 供应	**vacancy** *n.* 空缺,空位置
sledge *n.* 雪橇	**insight** *n.* 见识

交际与语言表达

1. Antarctica is a place of extremes—the highest, coldest and windiest continent and over fifty-eight times the size of the UK. 南极洲是一个拥有许多“之最”的地方,它是世界上最高、最冷和风最大的大陆,它的面积是英国的58倍。
2. ... but with low snowfall, most of the continent technically falls unbelievably into the category of “desert”! 但是由于降雪量很少,南极大陆的大部分按理论上讲都令人难以置信地属于“沙漠”的范畴!
3. ... while in winter half the surrounding ocean freezes over, which means its size almost doubles. 冬天的时候有一半环绕它的海洋会结冰,这会使它的面积增加一倍。
4. Here science and technical support have been integrated in a very cost-effective way... 在这里科学和技术支持都在成本合算的基础上制定出来的。
5. ... architects who finally came up with a remarkable solution. 建筑家们最终找到了一个不同寻常的解决办法。Come up with sth. 想出了某个解决办法,或者有了某个想法,这里的 sth. 一般是指需要智力活动的,有创造性的东西,比如 idea, plan, solution 等。
6. They need to provide maximum energy, but they must also be compact and light for easy transport. 它

们应当能提供最大限度的能量,但是它们又必须紧凑而轻巧以便运输。

7. Within this general field, surveying changes in the volume and stability of the ice-cap is vital, since these may have profound effects on world sea levels and on ocean currents. 在这个研究领域中,最关键的是对冰川的体积和稳定性的调查,因为这些可能会对世界海平面和洋流造成深刻的影响。
8. There are an increasing number of opportunities for young people to work for a period in Antarctica—not only as research assistants in projects like mine, but also in a wide range of junior administrative and technical positions including vacancies for map-makers. 对年轻人来说在南极洲工作一段时间的机会增多了——不仅仅是在我这样的项目中做助手,还有许多包括地图制作等一大批初级的管理和技术工作可以做。这句话比较长,在听的时候可能容易抓不住重点,这时最好把几个关键词记录下来,比如 young people, work, vacancies, research assistants, map-makers 等。

考题解析

Question 31

这道题本身不难,主要是要把数字记准确。

Question 32

这句话的句型比听力材料里的 fall into the category of 'desert' 更容易理解,在学习英语时要注意一个意思的不同表达方式,这样就可以丰富自己的英语表达。

Question 33

和上面一道题一样,这道题也是把句型变了一下,注意 science 要用名词,不要还象原文里一样用形容词。

Questions 34–36

这几道题都不难,但要注意根据题目前面的量词调节名词的单复数。

Question 37

这道题要注意不要把英国成年人每天消耗的卡路里数字与在南极工作的人每天消耗的卡路里数字搞混。

Question 38

这道题答 ocean currents 或是 currents 都可以得分,但前提是 currents 的拼写和单复数要准确。

Question 39

答案 pollution 前面应当加定冠词 the,但不加也不扣分。

Question 40

这道题几乎是一道送分的题,对应听过的内容,可以知道应当填 young。

READING

READING PASSAGE 1

文章结构

体　　裁	说明文。
主要内容	本文介绍了酚醛塑料的发明过程、制作工艺和流行历史。
结　　构	第 1 段:比利时科学家发明的酚醛塑料开创了现代塑料工业。
	第 2 段:对不同种类塑料的介绍。
	第 3 段:19 世纪发明塑料的动力。
	第 4 段:比利时科学家 Baekeland 发明酚醛塑料的经过。
	第 5 段:酚醛塑料的化学合成工艺。
	第 6 段:酚醛塑料的铸造工艺。
	第 7 段:酚醛塑料的流行历史。

词汇注释

文　章

第 1 段

Bakelite *n.* 酚醛塑料
Belgian *adj.* 比利时的,比利时人
discover *v.* 发现
patent *v.* 为…申请专利
revolutionary *adj.* 革命性的
synthetic *adj.* 合成物
enormous *adj.* 巨大的,数量众多的
technological *adj.* 技术性的
effectively *adv.* 有效地
launch *v.* 开创
plastic *n.* 塑料

第 2 段

mould *v.* 铸造
derive *v.* 起源
semi-synthetic *n.* 半化合物
chemical *adj.* 化学的
substance *n.* 物质,成分
entirely *adv.* 完全地
constituent *n.* 要素
thermoplastic *n.* 热塑性塑料
candlewax *n.* 蜡烛
reshape *v.* 重新成形
thermosetting *n.* 热硬化塑料
revert *v.* 回复
viscous *adj.* 粘性的
distinction *n.* 差别,区别

第 3 段

impetus *n.* 推动力
generate *v.* 产生,发生
factor *n.* 因素
immense *adj.* 巨大的
chemistry *n.* 化学
domain *n.* 领域
couple *v.* 伴随
acceptable *adj.* 可接受的
substitute *n.* 替代品
dwindle *v.* 缩小,缩减
luxury *adj.* 奢侈的
pragmatic *adj.* 实用的,实际的
tortoiseshell *n.* 龟甲
ivory *n.* 象牙

第 4 段

embark *v.* 着手,从事
phenol *n.* 苯酚,石碳酸

phenolic *adj.* 酚的，石碳酸的
resin *n.* 树脂
sticky *adj.* 粘的
aldehyde *n.* 乙醛
volatile fluid 挥发性流体
abandon *v.* 放弃，遗弃
photographic paper 相纸
amass *v.* 积累，积攒
formaldehyde *n.* 甲醛
preparation *n.* 配制品
commercial *adj.* 商业的
essential *adj.* 本质的，实质的

第 5 段

vacuum *n.* 真空
soluble *adj.* 可溶的
malleable *adj.* 有延展性的
shallow *adj.* 浅的
tray *n.* 碟子，盘子
grind *v.* 碾碎
woodflour *n.* 木屑
asbestos *n.* 石棉
cotton *n.* 棉花
strength *n.* 力量
moisture *n.* 湿度
resistance *n.* 抵抗力，阻力
catalyst *n.* 催化剂
ammonia *n.* 氨水
granular *adj.* 粒状的
hollow *adj.* 空的

第 6 段

earring *n.* 耳环
govern *v.* 统治，控制
design *v.* 设计
extract *v.* 提取
taper *v.* 逐渐变细
molten *adj.* 熔铸的
evenly *adv.* 平稳地
impractical *adj.* 不实用的

第 7 段

disdain *n.* 轻视，忽视
unparalleled *adj.* 无比的，空前的
popularity *n.* 流行，声望
expansion *n.* 扩张，延展
non-porous *adj.* 无孔的
heat-resistant *adj.* 耐热的
germ-free *adj.* 无菌的
sterilisable *adj.* 可消毒的
manufacturer *n.* 生产者，厂家
insulate *v.* 绝缘，隔离
property *n.* 特性，性质
relish *v.* 欣赏
dazzling *adj.* 令人眼花缭乱的
array *n.* 排列，编队
shades *n.* 图案
delighted *adj.* 高兴的
restrict *v.* 限制
drab *adj.* 单调的
despise *v.* 轻视
destroy *v.* 破坏，毁坏
renew *v.* 使更新，使恢复
appreciate *v.* 欣赏
originality *n.* 原创性
innovative *adj.* 创新的

题目

behave *v.* 表现
unique *adj.* 独特的，独一无二的
alternative *n.* 替代物
combine *v.* 联系，连接
intense *adj.* 剧烈的，强烈的
influence *v.* 影响
mention *v.* 提到，提起
facility *n.* 设施
limitation *n.* 限制
fashionable *adj.* 流行的，时髦的
immediately *adv.* 立即地

考题解析

Questions 1–3

- 题型归类：Sentence Completion
- 题目解析：

题目编号	题目定位词	答案位置	题解
1	plastics, melt, mould	第 2 段	本题考点是第 2 段提到了两种不同类型的塑料,这个题目中提到的是第一种塑料,即"热塑性塑料",它的特点是可以像蜡烛一样熔化,然后再重新塑形。要理解原文中的比喻内容,才能正确给出答案。
2	entirely, origin, thermosetting	第 2 段	本题主要考查考生对酚醛塑料特性的掌握情况,做对这道题需要对有关两种塑料特性的综合理解,才能得出酚醛塑料是属于第二种塑料,但是又是全人工化合物的结论。
3	advance, field	第 3 段第 4 行	这道题容易错答成 plastics,因为第 4 段有相类似的叙述,但是细读题目就不会出现判断错误。题目说"19 世纪进行的塑料研究有几个原因,其中最重要的是在某一个领域的巨大进步"。

Questions 4–8

● 题目归类:Table

● 题目解析:

题目编号	题目定位词	答案所在位置	题解
4	stage one, resin	第 5 段第 3 行	这组题难度比较大,必须是在透彻理解第 5 段的基础上才能够把题目做对。可以运用的解题技巧是按照工艺步骤的先后,依靠关键词的提示,到原文中的相应位置寻找答案。本题中就需要利用 stage one, resin等关键词找到 Novalak 这个词。
5	cotton, asbestos	第 5 段第 5 行	这是在进行第 2 道工序之前需要添加的辅料,根据题目给出的具体辅料名称棉花、木棉等可以知道需要填一个辅料的总称 filler。
6	ammonia, formaldehyde	第 5 段第 8 行	这道题的解题提示和思路与第 5 题相似,看到 ammonia 和 formaldehyde,就知道需要填 dexa。
7	stage two, grind, Bakelite	第 5 段第 10 行	从题目可以判断需要给出一个形容词,通过关键词定位,在文中找出 The resulting granular powder was raw Bakelite 这句话,就可以知道答案是 raw。
8	apply, heat	第 5 段第 12 行	这道题的表达方式与原文不同,考生需要理解 apply 是使用的意思,与原文中的 subject to 相对应,并由 heat 判断出应该填它的并列名词 pressure。

Questions 9–10

● 题型归类:Multiple Choice

● 题目解析:

题目编号	题目定位词	答案位置	题解
9	resin，fill，mould	第6段第7行	这一组多项选择是根据第6段酚醛塑料的铸造过程而编写的。要大概分析一下每个选项都是什么意思。A说物体将做什么用处，这在文章中没有提到，B说树脂能够被装到模具里面的容易程度，这与文中的模具要做得没有尖角等部分对应，因此可以选。
10	facility，remove，mould	第6段第3行	C说用什么样的设施可以使物体可以从模具中被取出来，这与文中的模具一般做成越向深处越细的形状，便于塑料被取出相对应，因此可以选。

Questions 11-13

● 题型归类：TRUE/FALSE/NOT GIVE

●考题解析：

题目编号	题目定位词	答案位置	题解
11	modern-day plastic，1907	第4段最后一句话	本题主要考查对第4段最后一句话的理解，题目只是把这句话稍加变化表达出来。
12	immediately	第7段第1行	本题的关键词immediately可以帮助检验题目是否真实。在原文中可以读到Baekeland的发明虽然在早期不被重视，但是后来却空前流行。因此题目说酚醛塑料立即因实用和多用途而受到欢迎是不对的。
13	colours	第7段第6行	题目说酚醛塑料只有有限的几种颜色，与文章中所说酚醛塑料具有令人眼花缭乱的色彩矛盾，因此要填FALSE。

参考译文

酚醛塑料——现代塑料的诞生

1907年，在纽约工作的比利时科学家Leo Hendrick Baekeland发现了一种革命性的新型合成材料，并申请了专利。这项被他命名为"酚醛塑料"的发明具有重大的技术意义，并有效地开创了现代塑料工业。

名词"塑料"来自希腊语的plassein，其含义是"铸造"。有的塑料来源于自然资源，有些是半合成的（化学反应作用于天然物质的结果），还有一些是完全合成的，即由煤或石油的成份经过化学加工制成。有一些是"热塑性塑料"，它们像蜡烛一样在受热时会融化，然后可以重新成形。其他的是"热硬化性的"，它们像鸡蛋一样不能重新恢复到初始的粘性状态，因此他们的形状是永远固定的。酚醛塑料是第一种完全合成的热硬化性塑料。

现代塑料的历史起始于19世纪中期，当时发现了一些半合成热塑性材料。发展这些早期塑料的推动力来自以下几个因素：伴随着广泛文化变化的化学领域的巨大科技进步，以及为供给日益减少的龟甲和象牙等"奢侈"材料寻找可接受的替代品的实际需求。

Baekeland 对塑料的兴趣始于 1885 年，当时作为比利时的青年化学学生，他开始研究酚醛树脂，即苯酚（石碳酸）和乙醛结合在一起时生成的粘性物质族。他很快放弃了这项研究，但却在几年之后又继续研究。在 1905 年，他已经是一个富有的纽约人，因为发明了新型相纸而获得大量财富。当 Baekeland 正在忙碌地积累金钱时，在开发塑料的过程中出现了一些进展。1899 和 1900 年出现了能够进行工业生产的第一种半合成热硬化性材料的专利。如果用纯粹的科学语言来描述，Baekeland 对该领域的主要贡献实际上并不是发现了由他命名的材料，而是发现了控制苯酚和甲醛之间化学反应的方法，并使配制品的商业化成为可能。在 1907 年 7 月 13 日，Baekeland 获得了描述该配制品的著名专利，其主要特征现在仍在使用。

原始专利概述了三个阶段的工艺，其中苯酚和甲醛（来自于木材或煤）最初在巨大的蛋形罐内，在真空条件下化合在一起。生成物是被称为 Novalak 的树脂，该树脂在受热时是可溶解和可延展的。树脂可以在浅槽中冷却直至硬化，然后打碎，并研磨成粉末。之后加入其他物质：包括填充物，例如可以增加强度和耐潮性的木屑、石棉或棉花，催化剂（一种可以加速两种化学材料之间的化学反应却不参加化学反应的物质）和 hexa，一种可以为形成热硬化性树脂提供额外甲醛的氨和甲醛的化合物。然后对该树脂进行冷却和硬化，并再次研磨成粉末。获得的颗粒状粉末是初始酚醛塑料，可以用于制作各种产品。在最后阶段，加热的酚醛塑料灌注到具有所需形状的空心模具中，并经受高温和高压，由此永久地“确定”其形状。

酚醛塑料产品，包括从耳环到电视机的所有设计在很大程度上受到铸造工艺技术要求的限制。产品的设计不能使产品卡在模具中，难以取出。通常的规则是产品沿着指向模具最深部分的方向逐渐变细，如果需要，产品可以分片铸造。必须仔细设计模具，使得融化的酚醛塑料均匀地、充分地流入模具。尖锐的拐角是不实用的，应当避免，这导致了 20 世纪 30 年代光滑的流线型风格的流行。模具壁的厚度也是非常关键的：较厚的壁需要更长的时间进行冷却和硬化，这是机器设计者必须考虑的一个因素，从而使机器得到更加有效的使用。

Baekeland 的发明，尽管在早期未受到重视，但却在整个 20 世纪前半叶获得了空前的流行。它成为工业化扩张的新世界的神奇产品——“具有上千种用途的材料”。作为无孔耐热材料，酚醛塑料厨房用具因为无菌和可消毒受到欢迎。电器制造商利用了它的绝缘性能，各地的消费者却对它令人眼花缭乱的形状大加赞赏，很高兴他们终于不用再像没有塑料的时候那样忍受木头质地和单调的棕色了。之后到了 20 世纪 50 年代，塑料又因失去人们的宠爱而大量被忽视和销毁。然而最近它又经历了一次“复兴”，在收藏品市场出现了对最初的酚醛塑料产品的需求，而博物馆、研究学会和一些爱好者又重新开始欣赏这种新材料的风格和原创性。

READING PASSAGE 2

文章结构

体　　裁	说明文。
主要内容	介绍有关大脑对幽默反应的研究。
结　　构	第 1 段：笑这种行为似乎不具有明显生物目的。
	第 2 段：亚里士多德关于笑话的理论得到了许多理论学家的认同。
	第 3 – 4 段：计算语言学家给出了笑话为什么引人发笑的一种解释。
	第 5 段：另一种解释是笑是社交安抚的一种形式。
	第 6 段：认知型的笑可能是更加复杂的大脑活动的结果。
	第 7 段：一位心理学家用扫描仪监测大脑在处理笑话时的活动。

	第8段:他发现了与眼睛活动有关的脑皮层参与了笑话的处理。
	第9段:这个大脑皮层为更复杂的思想过程提供了情感信息。
	第10段:对于处理笑话的脑部活动的认识使我们明白了笑话是否好笑还取决于每个人的观念。
	第11段:笑话也许会帮助我们理解大脑的工作原理。

词汇注释

文　章

第1段

funny *adj.* 可笑的
review *v.* 评论
punchline *n.* (戏剧,小说,笑话中的)妙语
silly *adj.* 愚蠢的
fitting *adj.* 适合的,适宜的
tempt *v.* 诱惑,引诱
strike *v.* 打动
mysterious *adj.* 神秘的,离奇的
pointless *adj.* 无意义的
dub *v.* 授予称号
reflex *n.* 反射,反映
apparent *adj.* 显然的,明显的
biological *adj.* 生物学的
purpose *n.* 目的

第2段

theory *n.* 理论
humour *n.* 幽默
ancient *adj.* 古老的,古代的
pedigree *n.* 血统,家族
Plato 柏拉图
superiority *n.* 优越,高傲
rely *v.* 依靠,依赖
psychic *adj.* 精神的
tension *n.* 紧张
puncture *v.* 标点
ludicrousness *n.* 滑稽,可笑
theorist *n.* 理论家
version *n.* 版本
Aristotle 亚里士多德
reaction *n.* 反应
resolution *n.* 坚定,决心,决议
incongruity *n.* 不调和的,不适宜的
nonsense *n.* 胡说,废话

第3段

computational *adj.* 计算的
linguist *n.* 语言学家
Edinburgh 艾丁堡
linguistic *adj.* 语言学的
machine *n.* 机器
format *n.* 格式,式样
revolve *v.* 旋转,考虑
conceptual *adj.* 概念上的
comedian *n.* 戏剧演员
unexpected *adj.* 想不到的,意外的
interpretation *n.* 翻译,解释
apt *adj.* 敏捷的,灵巧的

第4段

mental *adj.* 精神的,智力的
buzz *n.* 嗡嗡声
creative *adj.* 创造性的
leap *v.* 跳跃
perspective *n.* 观点,看法
semantic *adj.* 语义的

第5段

appeasement *n.* 缓和
crucial *adj.* 至关重要的
mammal *n.* 哺乳动物
rat *n.* 老鼠
ultrasonic *n.* 超声波
squeak *n.* 尖叫声
prevent *v.* 阻止,防止
scuffle *n.* 混战
nasty *adj.* 污秽的,肮脏的,不堪的
chimpanzee *n.* 黑猩猩
accompany *v.* 陪伴,伴随
pant *v.* 喘气

signal *n.* 信号	**instinctual** *adj.* 本能的
mutate *v.* 变异	**marker** *n.* 标记
trigger *v.* 引发,引起	**fairground** *n.* 露天市场
cognitive *adj.* 认知的	**amused** *adj.* 愉快的,开心的
第 6 段	
expressive *adj.* 表现的,表达的	**circuit** *n.* 电路
machinery *n.* 机器总称,机械	**vocalization** *n.* 发声法
emotion *n.* 感情	
第 7 段	
psychologist *n.* 心理学家	**track** *v.* 追踪
investigate *v.* 调查	**process** *n.* 过程
magnetic *adj.* 磁的,有磁力的	**comprehend** *v.* 领会,理解
resonance *n.* 共鸣,回声	**development** *n.* 发展
oxygenate *v.* 氧化处理	**snapshot** *n.* 快照,简单的印象
scanner *n.* 扫描仪	
第 8 段	
evidence *n.* 证据,迹象	**consistent** *adj.* 一致的,协调的
widespread *adj.* 分布广泛的,普通的	**attempt** *n.* 努力,尝试
prefrontal *adj.* 额叶前部的,前额的	**spring** *v.* 弹出,跳起
cortex *n.* 脑皮层	**orbital** *adj.* 轨道的
temporal *adj.* 暂时的	**evaluate** *v.* 评估,估计
lobes *n.* 圆形突出部	**tuck** *v.* 打摺,缩拢
第 9 段	
assessment *n.* 估价	**positive** *adj.* 肯定的,积极的
extremely *adv.* 极端地	**negative** *adj.* 消极的,否定的
demanding *adj.* 过分要求的,苛求的	**candidate** *n.* 候选人
arousal *n.* 觉醒,激励	**connection** *n.* 联系,关系
retune *v.* 重新调整	**apparatus** *n.* 设备,仪器
blink *n.* 眨眼	**metabolic** *adj.* 代谢作用的,新陈代谢的
abrupt *adj.* 突然的,陡峭的	
第 10 段	
constant *adj.* 不变的,持续的	**pleasurable** *adj.* 愉快的,快乐的
complicated *adj.* 复杂的,难解的	**evaluation** *n.* 估价,评价
emotionally *adv.* 在情绪上	**disgusting** *adj.* 令人厌恶的
surrounding *n.* 围绕物,环境	**frightening** *adj.* 令人恐惧的
shudder *v.* 颤抖	**outlook** *n.* 见解,前景
题目	
consider *v.* 考虑	**diagram** *n.* 图表
above-average 在…之上,超出	**activate** *v.* 激活
intelligence *n.* 智力,智能	**instantly** *adv.* 立即地
nervous *adj.* 神经的	**subjective** *adj.* 主观的,个人的
ignore *v.* 忽视	**ancestor** *n.* 祖先,祖宗
artificial *adj.* 人工的	

考题解析

Questions 14–20

● 题型归类：TRUE/FALSE/NOT GIVEN

● 题目解析：

题目编号	题目定位词	答案位置	题解
14	laughter, biologically important	第1段	只有第1段里有 Arthur Koestler 对笑的观点，因此不难发现他认为笑没有特别的生物学目的，因此要填 FALSE。
15	above-average intelligence	第2段	对照第2段第二句话，我们可以知道柏拉图认为幽默仅仅是认为比别人优越的一种高兴的感觉，并没有说是智力超过平均水平的标志，因此要填 NOT GIVEN。
16	kant, release, energy	第2段	这道题目的考点在于对第2段的理解，其实题目 Kant 认为一个成功的笑话涉及对神经能量的有控制的释放概括了第2段的一个重要内容，是正确的。
17	current thinking, ignore, Aristotle	第2段	把题目中的 ignore 和原文中 settle on 对照起来，就知道题目的叙述是错误的。
18	artificial intelligence	第3段	第3段集中叙述了计算语言学家将笑话和计算机处理语言和进行逻辑思维联系起来，因此题目所述“Graeme Ritchie 的工作把消化和人工智能联系起来”是正确的。
19	comedian, personal situation	第3段最后一句话	第3段中所述“喜剧演员采取的表演形式是表现一种情形，并随后给出一个意想不到却很切题的解释”，并没有提到题目中的内容，因此选 NOT GIVEN。
20	particular noise	第5段第4行	解答这道题时，可将题目中的内容放在第5段的相应位置，看看意思是不是一样。

Questions 21–23

题目编号	题目定位词	答案位置	题解
21	right prefrontal cortex	第8段	考生在做这道题时不要因为有一些不认识的专业术语就产生畏难情绪，实际上只要仔细阅读第8段，即使不知道大脑解剖学的一些部位名称，也可以正确解题。这道题在第8段第3行可以找到相对应的内容。
22	active	第8段	在第8段第5行可以找到相对应的内容，另外，根据画面中所示脑部的不同位置也可以辅助解题。
23	orbital prefrontal cortex	第8段	这道题的解题思路可以借鉴上面一道题，要注意 evaluating 要用现在分词的形式，才能与题目的语法同步。

Questions 24–27

● 题型归类：Sentence Completion

● 题目解析：

题目编号	题目定位词	答案位置	题解
24	most difficult	第 9 段第一句话	题目"大脑最困难的任务之一是"，根据前半句可以排除 A、C、E 以外的所有答案。如果再读 25 题"由于他们发展了语言，人类"，还可以排除 A。这是如果有一点对文章的记忆就会想起，第 9 段第一句话所述"无论对动物和人类来说，快速地对当前发生的事件做出情感评估都是一件非常费脑力的事"，因此选 C。
25	language	第 10 段第 2 行	解题思路见上题。
26	response, humour	第 10 段最后一行	这道题不太难，关键要找到第 10 段最后一行所述"一个笑话是会引起愉悦还是痛苦也取决于每个人的见解。"
27	Peter Derks	第 11 段引语	题目"Peter Derks 相信幽默"，从语感的角度来判断后面最有可能跟 may 引导的句子，再回忆一下在文章中读过的内容，不难判断 D 是正确答案。

参考译文

什么事这么可笑？

—John McCrone 最近关于幽默研究的评论

笑话通过耳机传递过来："狗的哪一面长着大部分的毛？左面"。不，一点儿也不可笑。再试一次。"狗的哪一面长着大部分的毛？外面"。哈！这个妙语虽然有点蠢但是恰到好处，试图引起微笑，甚至是大笑。笑对大家来说是非常神秘的甚至可以说是无意义的。作家 Arthur Koestler 把它称为奢侈的反应："它独一无二，因为它没有明显的生物学目的"。

关于幽默的理论具有古老的渊源。柏拉图认为，幽默仅仅是一种因自己比他人优越而感到高兴的感觉。Kant 和 Freud 觉得讲笑话依靠的是建立一种精神的紧张，而这种紧张可以通过妙语的滑稽之处而被释放。但是多数现代幽默理论学家承袭了亚里士多德的观点，认为笑话是当妙语是一句胡闹的话，或者看起来很愚笨却有另外一层聪明意思的时候，人们对不协调氛围的一种反应或解决。

爱丁堡的计算语言学家 Graeme Ritchie 专门研究笑话的语言学结构，其目的是不仅理解幽默，而且用机器进行语言理解和推理。他说尽管对于笑话而言没有单一的形式，但是许多笑话都是以突然的令人惊讶的概念转换为中心的。喜剧演员采取的表演形式是表现一种情形，并随后给出一个意想不到却很切题的解释。

因此即使笑话中的妙语听起来无聊，但是听众可以看出其中聪明的语义上的巧合，而那声在脑海里浮现的"阿哈！"正是使人发笑的启动开关。从这个角度看，幽默仅仅是一种创造性的洞察力，一种向新观念的突然跳跃。

然而，同时也存在另外一种作为社交安抚的笑声，理解这种笑声也十分重要。游戏对于多数年轻的哺乳动物是其发育的关键部分。老鼠发出超声波一般的吱吱声，以防止它们的混战变得过于激烈。黑猩猩具有"游戏面孔"——一种伴随着"哈，哈"喘气声的类似打呵气的表情。在人类中，这些信号则变异为微笑和大笑。研究人员相信社会情景，而不是像笑话这样的认知事件，会引发这些本能的游戏或安抚的标记。无论高兴还是不高兴,人们都会在露天游乐场或者被咯吱时开怀大笑。

社会和认知型的笑声都会触动我们大脑中的同一表达机制以及情感和运动的神经回路,使我们发出笑声或者兴奋的声音。然而,如果认知笑声是更一般的思考过程的产物,那么它就应当是更加复杂的大脑活动的结果。

心理学家 Vinod Goel 利用新技术"单次事件"功能磁响应成像(fMRI)研究幽默。一台磁响应成像扫描仪能够利用磁场和无线电波追踪与智力活动相伴的血液载氧量的变化。直到最近,磁响应成像扫描仪还需要几分钟的运转时间,因此不能追踪快速的思考过程,例如领会笑话。现在最新的科学进展可以对各种类型的推理和解决问题的脑部活动进行半秒钟的"快照"。

尽管 Goel 觉得在大脑扫描仪中不是评价笑话的理想场所,但是他发现理解一个笑话包括广泛的神经转换。他的扫描图显示,在笑话的开始阶段,听众的前额叶皮层发光,特别是被认为与解决问题相关的右前额叶。但是头部两侧颞的圆形突起部(通常与尝试回忆存储的知识有关)和在脑部的其他区域也有相应的活动。然后当听到妙语的时候,大脑中的一个新的区域——与眼睛有关的前额叶皮层也突然活跃起来。这部分隐藏在眼窝后面的大脑组织的活动往往与评估信息有关。

无论对动物和人类来说,快速地对当前发生的事件做出情感评估都是一件非常费脑力的事。在眨眼之间,大脑可能就需要对能量和觉醒度进行重新调整。这些突然的改变可能会带来积极的情绪,也可能带来消极的情绪。在 Goel 的实验中变得活跃起来的与眼睛有关的皮层似乎是把这些情感传送给更高层次的思维程序的最佳选择,因为它与大脑亚皮层的觉醒装置和控制新陈代谢的中枢都有非常紧密的联系。

所有暖血动物都会经常根据外界的变化对自己的觉醒度做出调整,但是人类由于拥有语言而发展出了一套更加复杂的内部活动机制,从而不但对他们的环境,也对他们自己的思想做出情绪反应。每当一个被寻找的答案突然出现的时候,人类都会因为高兴的认同而战栗。有创造力的发现会令人愉快,人类早就学会了滋养这种自然反应的方法。笑话能够触动我们的总体评估机制,可以用来解释为什么可笑与可憎,可笑与可怕之间仅有毫厘之差。一个笑话是会引起愉悦还是痛苦也取决于每个人的见解。

也许幽默是奢侈品,但是它背后的作用机理却不是进化的偶然事件。正如弗吉尼亚州 WILLIAN 和 MARRY 学院的心理学家 PETER DERKS 所说:"我喜欢把幽默当作头脑的镜子。它富有创造力,有知觉,具有分析性和表达性。如果我们弄清楚了头脑是怎样处理幽默的,那么我们将会为研究头脑怎样工作找到一个很好的突破口。"

READING PASSAGE 3

文章结构

体　　裁	说明文
主要内容	讲述科学英语的诞生和发展过程。
结　　构	第 1 段:英语是全球最流行的科学语言。
	第 2 段:文艺复兴时期,欧洲国家将英语带到别的国家。
	第 3 段:英格兰是最先狂热地接受并发表哥白尼的思想的几个国家之一。
	第 4 段:原始的科学文章直到 17 世纪下半叶才用英语写作。
	第 5 段:用拉丁文写作的第一个原因是它更适宜国际读者。
	第 6 段:用拉丁文写作的第二个原因是为了保密。
	第 7 段:用英语写作科学文章被延迟的第三个原因是英语在语言学上的不充分性。

	第 8 段:皇家社团的成员为推广英语做了大量的工作。
	第 9 段:《哲学学报》成为第一份国际化的英语科学杂志。
	第 10 段:直到 19 世纪,科学英语才再次获得迅速发展。

词汇注释

文 章

第 1 段

dominate *v.* 统治
global *adj.* 全球的
international *adj.* 国际的
prominence *n.* 突出,显著
surprising *adj.* 令人惊讶的
intellectual *n.* 知识分子

第 2 段

the European Renaissance 欧洲文艺复兴
revival *n.* 苏醒,复兴
classical *adj.* 古典的
scholar *n.* 学者
emergent *adj.* 新兴的
extend *v.* 延伸
competitive *adj.* 竞争的
exploration *n.* 探索
magnetism *n.* 磁力,吸引力
compass *n.* 指南针
cartography *n.* 绘图法
planet *n.* 行星
star *n.* 恒星
Copernicus 哥白尼

第 3 段

adopt *v.* 接受
publicise *v.* 推广,宣扬
enthusiasm *n.* 热情,热心
royal *adj.* 皇家的
society *n.* 学会
empirical *adj.* 经验主义的,完全依据经验的

第 4 段

arise *v.* 出现,发生
initial *adj.* 最初的
tradition *n.* 传统
encyclopaedia *n.* 百科全书
mathematical *adj.* 数学的
treatise *n.* 论文,论述
property *n.* 特征

第 5 段

audience *n.* 观众
popular science 科普

第 6 段

perversely *adv.* 倔强地
concern *n.* 关注
secrecy *n.* 秘密,保密
danger *n.* 危险
preliminary *adj.* 预备的,初步的
exploit *v.* 开拓,开发
author *n.* 作者
reflect *v.* 反应
feature *n.* 特征
humanist *adj.* 人文主义的
notion *n.* 观念,概念
rational *adj.* 理性的,合理的
distinction *n.* 区别,差别
mathematician *n.* 数学家
proof *n.* 证明
cipher *n.* 密码
obscure *adj.* 朦胧的,晦涩的
precisely *adv.* 精确地
restrict *v.* 限制
cling to 依靠,坚持

第 7 段

linguistic *adj.* 语言学的
inadequacy *n.* 不充分
equip *v.* 装备,配备
argument *n.* 争论,论点
vocabulary *n.* 词汇,词汇量
grammatical *adj.* 语法的

impersonal *adj.* 非个人的	**hypothetical** *adj.* 假设的,假定的
complex *adj.* 复杂的	**entity** *n.* 实体
第 8 段	
possess *v.* 拥有	**curator** *n.* 馆长,管理者,监护人
engage *v.* 从事,参与	**describe** *v.* 描述
establish *v.* 建立,设立	**microscope** *n.* 显微镜
committee *n.* 委员会	**narrative** *adj.* 叙述性的
improve *v.* 完善,改进	**transcript** *n.* 手稿,抄本
foster *v.* 培养,鼓励	**demonstration** *n.* 示范,演示
encourage *v.* 鼓励	**lecture** *n.* 演讲,讲座
monograph *n.* 专论,专著	
第 9 段	
journal *n.* 杂志	**inaugurate** *v.* 创立
philosophical *adj.* 哲学的	**genre** *n.* 种类
transactions *n.* 学报	**particular** *adj.* 特别的,特定的
第 10 段	
formative *adj.* 形成之中的,正在形成的	**lexical** *adj.* 词汇的
momentum *n.* 动力,要素	**specialized** *adj.* 专门的
estimate *v.* 估计	**professional** *adj.* 专业的,职业的
substantial *adj.* 实质的	**discipline** *n.* 学科
题目	
emerge *v.* 出现	**privileged** *adj.* 特权
allow *v.* 允许	**desire** *n.* 愿望,期望
communicate *v.* 联络,交流	

考题解析

Questions 28－34

● 题型归类:Sentence Completion

● 题目解析:

题目编号	题目定位词	答案位置	题解
28	language choice	第 1 段最后一句话	题目"最初,科学语言一直是选用什么语言",从原文第 1 段可以找到在 17 世纪之前人们不会用英语写作科学文章,而一直用拉丁语,因此填 Latin。
29	communicate, mathematicians	第 6 段最后一句话	这道题与数学家并列的使用拉丁语的医生在原文中相隔比较远,但都在第 6 段里,只要理解的文章的意思,找出医生并不难。
30－31	neither... nor	第 7 段	题目中出现的并列否定的选择形式,提示考生要在原文中找到不利于英语使用的因素,根据文章中 first 和 second 两个表示并列原因的词,可以找到正确答案。注意答案的次序可以调换。
32	develop English	第 8 段	这道题不是很难,根据对文章的记忆可以判断出答案的大概位置,注意专有名词首字母要大写。

33	English, overtaken	第 10 段	这道题需要考生通过对第 10 段提供的数字进行比较,自己得出结论,因为德语期刊的种类最多,所以德语超过了英语。
34	19th Century, direct result	第 10 段最后一句话	这道题需要考生抓住第 10 段最后一句话的主要意思,不要被很长的句子难倒,长句往往在开头或者末尾有对中心意思的提示,这句话的中心在句首。

Questions 35–37

- 题型归类:TRUE/FALSE/NOT GIVEN
- 题目解析:

题目编号	题目定位词	答案位置	题解
35	competition, scientists	第 2 段	题目"欧洲文艺复兴时期科学家之间的竞争激烈",仔细阅读原文第 2 段会发现是各国之间存在贸易等方面的竞争,因此选 Not Given。
36	most important, magnetism	第 2 段	形容词,尤其是最高级形容词是最好的定位词,在文中第 2 段我们可以知道 most important 是哥白尼的天文发现,不是指南针,因此要选 FALSE。
37	17th century, leading thinkers, express ideas	第 8 段	解答这道题需要对第 8 段的意思有一个全面的把握。找到 1664,可以与题目中的"17 世纪"对应起来,另外可以找到皇家学会的成员为改善英语写作所做的努力,因此选 TRUE。

Questions 38–40

- 题型归类:Table
- 题目解析:

题目编号	题目定位词	答案位置	题解
38	science, original	第 5 段	表格类型的题目要注意全面地领会题目给出的提示词,这里要求填出科学的种类,前面已经给出了 original 原创性科学,那么相对应的就应该是科普或者通俗科学,popular science。
39	example	第 4 段	文中只有第 4 段出现了 17 世纪用拉丁文写作的著作,这道题可以填 Principia,注意首字母一定要大写,也可以填 Newton's Principia, mathematical treatise。
40	audience international	第 5 段	根据题目中的提示"国际读者",可以在文中第 5 段找到相对应的地方读者 local audience,也可以只写 local 或者 more local。

参考译文

科技英语的诞生

当今,科学界经常使用的语言只有少数几种,其中主要有日语、德语和法语。但是,只有英语是全球最流行的科学语言。这不仅仅是因为英语国家,例如美国,在科学研究领域的重要作用;许多非英语国家的科学家发现他们需要用英语写作他们的研究文章才能获得广泛的国际读者。尽管当今科技英语有如此显著的作用,但令人惊讶的是在17世纪之前没人真正知道如何用英语写作科学文章。在此之前,拉丁文被认为是欧洲知识分子的通用语言(lingua franca)。

欧洲文艺复兴(14-16世纪)有时被称为"学习的复兴",对古典时期"迷失的知识"的兴趣复兴时代。然而同时,学者还开始检验并扩展这些知识。欧洲新出现的国家对探索世界和发展贸易具有强烈的兴趣。将英语向西带到美洲、向东带到印度的这种扩张是由科技发展所带动的,例如磁力的发现(由此发明了指南针)、绘图学的进步以及——可能是它们当中最重要的科学革命——哥白尼(1473-1543)发展的天文学和地球相对于行星和恒星运动的新理论。

英格兰是最先热情接受并宣传哥白尼的思想的几个国家之一。他们当中的一些学者,包括两个对语言感兴趣的学者——John Wallis 和 John Wilkins,在1660年为促进经验主义的科学研究创立了皇家社团。

在整个欧洲,类似的学院和学会逐渐兴起,并衍生出新的本国科学传统。在科技革命的初期,大多数用母语写作的出版物都是流行的著作、百科全书、教材和译文。原始的科学文章直到17世纪下半叶才用英语写作。例如,牛顿用拉丁文创作了被称为"Principia"的数学论文,但是后来关于光的性质的著作"Optiks"则是用英语发表的。

原始科学文章一直用拉丁语写作的原因有多个。首先是读者的问题。拉丁语适用于国际上学者间的交流,而用英语则可以与社会上更广泛的读者交流。因此,科普文章通常是用英语写的。

用拉丁文写作的第二个原因可能是出于保密的考虑。将还没有被"作者"彻底研究的初步想法公开发表在公众领域具有危险性。逐步增强的关于知识产权的观念是那一时期的特点——它反映了各个有理性的通过个人的智力劳动进行发明和发现的科学家的人文主义主张以及原创科学和商业开发之间的日益增长的联系。在懂得拉丁文的"学者和绅士"与缺乏正统教育的商人之间存在一定的社会差别。在17世纪中叶,对于数学家来说,利用密码、难解的语言书写他们的发现和证明或者以私人信件的方式放置在皇家社团的密封盒子内,以便对其进行保密是非常盛行的做法。一些科学家还觉得利用拉丁文写作更加舒服,只是因为其读者尽管是国际的,但社交圈子毕竟不同。至今,医生仍坚持用作为"内部语言"的拉丁文书写大部分处方。

科技英语没有及时盛行的第三个原因,是与现代早期英语语言方面的缺陷有关。英语不太适合于进行科学论证。首先,它缺少必须的技术词汇。第二,它缺乏一种客观的、非个人的方式描述世界的语法结构功能,因此在讨论复杂和假设的实体之间关系时,例如因果关系时,显得不足。

幸运的是,皇家社团的几个成员对语言感兴趣,并从事了各种语言学项目。尽管1664年提出的建立改进英语委员会的提议没有最终结果,但是社团成员做了大量工作,促进了用英语写作科学出版物、鼓励规范的写作风格。皇家社团的许多成员还用英语出版专著。这样做的第一个人是Robert Hooke,社团的第一个实验管理人,他在*Micrographia*(1665)中描述了利用显微镜进行的实验。这项工作主要是叙述性的,主要内容来自口头演示和讲座的手稿。

1665年,一份新的科学杂志《哲学学报》创刊了。它也许是第一份国际化的英语科学杂志,它鼓励一种崭新的科技写作风格,即对某个特定实验进行简洁和重点的描述。

17世纪是一个科技英语的建立和发展时期。在随后的一个世纪,由于德语成为欧洲主要的科技语言,这一势头暂时消失了。据估计,在18世纪末期,有401种德语科技杂志,而相应的只有96种法语科技杂志和50种英语科技杂志。然而,在19世纪,随着工业革命对技术词汇产生新的需求,科技英语再次获得实质性的词汇增长,新的、专门化的专业社团成长起来并开始在新的学科领域推广和出版英语读物。

WRITING

WRITING TASK 1

a) *Question analysis, including discussion of main features, comparisons that need to be made, and possible misinterpretations of the question.* (审题)

"The charts below show the main reasons for study among students of different age groups and the amount of support they received from employers. Summarise the information by selecting and reporting the main features, and make comparisons where relevant."

Points to note. (审题要点)

1. Type of graph. The graphs are bar charts. (图表类型。这里的图表是柱状图)
2. The horizontal axis of each chart shows age groups. (各图的横轴代表的是年龄群体。)
3. There is information on two separate issues that must be analysed. (两个不同问题的信息需要进行分析。)
4. The vertical axis of each chart shows percentages, not total numbers. (各图的纵轴代表的是百分比例,不是总数。)

Main features and comparisons. (主要特征和比较)

1. The percentage of students who study for career reasons drops as people get older. (随着年龄的增长,出于涉及职业的原因进行学习的学生比例下降。)
2. The percentage of students who study out of interest rises as people get older. (随着年龄的增长,出于兴趣方面的原因进行学习的学生比例上升。)
3. The percentage of people who get employer support decreases, then rises, as people get older. (随着年龄的增长,得到雇主支持的学生比例先是下降,然后上升。)

Possible misinterpretations and problems. (审题误区)

1. Be careful not to confuse the two different reasons in the first chart. (不要弄混了第一个图表中的两个不同的原因。)
2. The graph contains a lot of information. This is good because it means that it should be easy to write at least 150 words about it. However, it also means that you should not include every piece of information for each 20-year interval. The examiner knows that you only have 20 minutes to write the report and will not expect all the details. (图表中包含了很多的信息。这意味着要写出至少 150 词的短文难度应该不会太大。不过这也意味着你不应该包括关于每一个 20 年时间段的信息。测试人知道你只有 20 分钟来写出这份报告,他们不会要求在文中看到所有的细节。)

b) *Suggested answer format, including contrast with possible unsuitable formats.* (写作思路)

The introduction should consist of one or two sentences saying what the charts show by rewriting the Question prompt. The obvious changes are:

i) change "The charts" to "The first (second) bar chart".

ii) adding "for career reasons" and "out of interest".

iii) adding "in the form of time off and/or help with costs".

Most candidates will examine each chart in turn. This is completely correct, because the charts show different things. Therefore, the report will have two main paragraphs.（大部分考生会依次对每个图进行分析。这样做是完全可以的，因为各图显示了不同的信息。因此，考生写出的报告应该包含两个主体段。）

Finally, by way of a 'conclusion', add a sentence or two giving the overall trend for the two bar charts. This will involve comparing the charts using the age groups.（最后应该通过“作结论”的方式，加入一两个句子说明两个图中体现的总体的变化趋势。这中间会涉及到通过年龄群体对比两个图表。）

c）Model answer.（参考范文）

The first bar chart shows the percentage of students of various ages who study for career reasons and out of interest. The second bar chart shows the percentage of students of various ages who receive help from their employers, in the form of time off and/or help with costs.

From the first chart, we can see that the percentage of people who study for career reasons declines from 80% in the under 26 age group to a little under 20% in the over 49 age group. The decline is fairly even. Conversely, the percentage of people who study out of interest increases from 10% in the under 26 age group to 70% in the over 49 age group. The rise is steady until the 30-39 age group, but then the increase is faster, from 25% in the 30-39 age group, to 40% in the 40-49 age group and then to 70% in the over 49 age group.

From the second chart, we can see that the percentage of people under 26 receiving some kind of support from their employers is 65%. This falls to 50% for the 26-29 age group. The 30-39 age group receives the least help. Just over 30% get support from employers. This percentage rises to almost 40% for the 40-49 age group. The percentage of people aged over 49 getting support is about 45%.

To sum up, as people get older they study more out of interest than because of their career and people aged under 26 are most likely to get support for their studies from employers whereas those aged 30-39 are least likely to receive it.

译文：

第一个柱状图表现的是不同年龄段的学生分别出于涉及职业的原因或是出于兴趣进行学习的百分比例。第二个柱状图表现的是不同年龄段的学生得到雇主支持的百分比例，支持的形式有给予休息时间和帮忙承担开支。

从第一个图我们可以看出在低于26岁的年龄段里，以涉及职业方面的原因进行学习的学生占到了80%；而在高于49岁的年龄段里，这个比例降到了略低于20%。下降的趋势相当均匀平稳。

与此不同的是，在低于26岁的年龄段里，出于兴趣进行学习的学生的比例是10%，；而在高于49岁的年龄段里，这个比例增加到了70%。比例随年龄上升的趋势在30-39岁年龄之前一直很平稳，随后上升速度加快，从30-39岁年龄段的25%到了40-49岁年龄段的40%，然后到高于49岁段的70%。

从第二个图我们可以看到在低于26岁的年龄段，得到来自雇主的某种支持的人所占的比例是65%。在26-29岁年龄段，该数字跌落到了50%。30-39岁年龄段得到的帮助是最少的，只有略高于30%的人可以得到。到了40-49岁年龄段，得到帮助的比例有上升到了差不多40%，而在高于49岁的年龄段，得到帮助的比例大约是45%。

总的来讲，随着人们年龄的增长，人们更多的是出于兴趣在学习，而不是出于职业方面的原因。此外年龄低于26岁的人们最有机会得到来自雇主的对他们学业的支持，而在30-39岁年龄段的人得到支持的机会最少。

d) Analysis of vocabulary and structures used in model answer, including possible mistakes made by candidates. **(语言分析)**

It is important to repeat words associated with describing trends as little as possible. Using the same words repetitively indicates a narrow vocabulary. The model answer uses the synonyms 'rise' and 'increase' and 'decline' and 'fall'. Note that these words are used as both verbs and nouns, indicating to the examiner that the candidate knows they can be used in both ways. The words 'help' and 'support' are used throughout the model answer as synonyms.(有一点很重要的是应该尽可能少的重复使用与描述趋势有关的词汇。重复使用几个相同的词表明你的词汇有限。范文当中用到了同义词"上升"和"增加"以及"下降"和"跌落"。注意这些词可以用动词和名词两种方式使用,这可以向考官展示考生知道这些词汇可以以两种用法使用。此外在范文中,"支持"和"帮助"一直被作为同义词使用。)

Note that the correct phrasing for the reasons why people study are "for career reasons" and "out of interest".(注意说明人们学习的原因的正确说法分别是"出于涉及职业的原因"和"出于兴趣"。)

Note that your figures do not have to be exact. The writer uses 'a little over 20%', 'just under 30%', and 'about 45%'. Similarly, the writer describes the decline in the number of people studying for career reasons as 'fairly even'.(注意你提到的数字不需要很确切。范文作者使用了"略低于 20%","略高于 30%",以及"大约是 45%"。类似的,在描述以涉及职业方面的原因学习的人数下降的趋势时,作者的说法是"相当均匀平稳"。)

In the conclusion, the writer uses the phrases 'most likely' and 'least likely'. Many candidates would make incorrect statements suggesting that employers do or don't support employees of certain ages. Be careful when making absolute statements!(在结论部分,作者使用了"最有机会"和"机会最少"等说法。而有很多考生会写出错误的句子来表示雇主会或者不会支持某些特定年龄段的雇员。在写表达绝对意义的句子时一定要小心。)

WRITING TASK 2

a) Question analysis, including discussion of the points that need to be made in the essay, possible misinterpretations of the question. **(审题)**

"In some countries young people are encouraged to work or travel for a year between finishing high school and starting university studies. Discuss the advantages and disadvantages for young people who decide to do this."

Possible misinterpretations and problems.(可能产生的曲解和问题)

1. The Question prompt clearly refers to a year off studying between high school and university. Answers that refer to part-time jobs, starting a career without any intention of attending university, etc., can expect to be penalized as irrelevant.(题干明确提到了是介于高中和大学之间不学习的一年。所以如果考生回答时谈论兼职工作,开始职业生涯而不作上大学打算等等,可以被视为偏题并失分。)
2. The Question prompt asks candidates to "Discuss the advantages and disadvantages", so both sides of the argument must be examined.(题干要求考生"讨论这样做的好处和弊端",因此考生应该分析争论的两个方面。)
3. The Question prompt doesn't actually ask you to give an opinion, but most candidates will and this is acceptable. However, candidates that do not express an opinion will not be penalised.(题干并没有真

的要求你给出一个观点，不过大多数考生会这样做而且这也是可以接受的。不过如果考生没有给出观点的话，也不会失分。）

***b*）*Suggested answer format, including contrast with possible unsuitable formats.*（写作思路）**

For this question, the essay format should involve an introduction, two or three main paragraphs, and a conclusion. The introduction should be short and may or may not include the writer's opinion. Each of the main paragraphs should focus on a particular argument. However, these main paragraphs can either focus on one side of the argument or take into account the opposite point of view. The conclusion should be short and may or may not state the writer's opinion.（在答这个题目的时候，文章中间应该包括一个引入部分，两到三个主体段，以及一个结论段落。引入段应该很简短，可以包含考生的观点，也可以不包含。各主体段应该分别着重讨论一个讨论的点。不过各主体段可以选择只是着重分析讨论点一方的观点，也可以选择同时考虑对立一方的观点。结论段应该很简短，可以包含作者的观点，也可以不包含。）

The most important thing is to make sure that each of the main paragraphs focuses clearly on one argument. If several arguments are included in the same paragraph they could confuse the reader. It is also important that each argument be well developed, and having a separate paragraph for each will help the writer achieve this.（最重要的问题是要保证每个主体段清晰地集中关注一个讨论点。如果在同一个段落中出现了多个讨论点，那么读者会困惑不解。此外关于每个讨论点的分析应该很有组织的展开，如果采用一个独立的段落来讨论每个点对此会很有帮助。）

***c*）*Two model answers of around 300 words, each essay taking a different view.*（参考范文）**

Model answer 1—Focusing more on the advantages.（范文 1，侧重 advantages）

In recent years, taking a gap year between secondary school and university has become increasingly popular in my country. In this essay, I will look at the advantages and disadvantages for young people who take one.

The main advantage is that young people can take a year to consider their futures. They can do this in different ways. If they already favour working in a particular field, they can take the year to get some work experience in that area to see if they are truly suited to it. A friend of mine was accepted to university to study law. She decided to take a gap year and work as a clerk in a law firm. Although she earned little money, she discovered what it was like to work in the legal field. She learnt a lot of things that helped her in her studies. When she finished university, she had no problem finding a job because the same law firm hired her.

Another way that young people can use a gap year to think about their futures is if they have no real idea what they want to study. They can use the gap year to see what options are open to them. Some people go to work in foreign countries on aid projects or to teach English. This can inspire them to take particular subjects at university that wouldn't have normally considered.

However, there can be disadvantages. Some young people might simply waste their gap year if they have no direction, though I think this is only likely to happen in a minority of cases. Something that is more likely to happen is that a young person will get out the study routine and find it harder to adjust than someone straight out of secondary school when they finally go to university.

To sum up, I believe that the advantages of taking a gap year generally outweigh the disadvantages, though each person should make a decision based on what they know of themselves.

译文：

近年来在我们国家，选择在完成中学学业和开始大学学业之间度过一个间隔年的做法越来越流行。在本文当中，我将分析这样做对年轻人有什么好处和弊端。

这样做主要的好处在于年轻人可以花一年时间来考虑他们的未来。他们可以通过不同的途径达到这个目的。如果他们已经倾向于从事某个领域的工作，他们可以利用这一年得到在这个领域的工作经验，考察自己是不是真的适合这个工作。我有一个朋友本来被一所大学录取了去学习法律，但她决定先过一个间隔年，并且在一家法律事务所里做职员。尽管挣钱不多，但是她知道了在法律领域工作是怎样的状况。她学到了很多对她的学业有帮助的东西。后来她大学毕业的时候，很容易就找到了工作，因为原来那家事务所又雇了她。

如果年轻人并不真正清楚自己想要学习什么，那么选择度过一个间隔年也可以帮助他们考虑自己的未来。他们可以利用这一年来了解自己都有哪些机会。有些人会到国外去工作，比如参加援助项目或是教英语。这可能会鼓励他们到大学里选学他们可能本来不会考虑的学科。

然而，这样做也会有不好的一面。如果没有选定方向的话，有些年轻人可能会浪费这一年时光（尽管我认为这只会在很少的情况下发生）。更有可能发生的情况是，有些年轻人会在一年以后去上大学时发现自己脱离了原来中学里形成的学习的常规习惯，比那些从中学直接进入大学的人更难调整和适应大学的学习状态。

总的来说，我认为选择过一个间隔年的做法总体带来的益处要超过弊端，不过每个人都应该根据对自己的了解作出决策。

Model answer 2—Focusing more on the disadvantages.（范文 2，侧重 disadvantages）

Taking a year off studying between high school and university is becoming more popular in my country. Although I can see some advantages, I think that taking a gap year is usually not a good idea.

The main disadvantage is that young people who intend to go to university might lose some of study skills during the year off. This means that, when they finally go to university, they will spend some time getting back into the habit of studying. They might even forget some relevant information they learnt at high school and need to spend time relearning it.

Another disadvantage is that they might not use the gap year productively. It is almost impossible to get a decent job immediately after graduating from high school, and this likelihood is going to be further reduced when a potential employer discovers that the young person is only going to be working for them for a year at most. I believe that it is far better to go to university first and then start one's career after graduation.

As I said, there are advantages of taking a year off. One is that a student may not know exactly what they want to study at university and so might want to get some work experience before making a decision. However, nowadays, studying a particular subject does not necessarily restrict a person to working in a particular area. For example, my boss studied English literature at university and he now a logistics manager.

To conclude, I believe that the disadvantages of taking a gap year outweigh those of taking one, particularly because a young person might take a year off studying for little gain.

译文：

在我们国家，选择在完成中学学业和开始大学学业之间度过一个间隔年的做法越来越流行。尽管我可以看到这样做的一些好处，但我还是认为这样做通常来说不是太好。

这样做主要的坏处在于打算去上大学的年轻人会在这个间隔年中丧失一些学习的技能。这就意味着在回到大学的时候,他们会需要花一些时间来找回原来学习的习惯。他们甚至于可能会忘记一些在中学学到的相关信息,而要在大学里花时间重新学习这些东西。

另外的一个弊端是有些人可能这一年会过得不是特别有收获。在刚刚高中毕业的情况下,要找到一份不错的工作几乎是不可能的。而当潜在的雇主发现一个年轻人最多只会为他们工作一年的时候,这种可能性还会进一步降低。我认为先上大学然后在毕业之后开始职业生涯要远远好于选择过一个间隔年。

正如我说过的,过一个间隔年也有它的好处。其中一条就在于有的学生可能不知道自己在大学里想学什么,因此可能想要在作出决定之前先得到一些工作经验。然而现在,学习某一个特定的学科并不一定把一个人局限在某个特定的领域。比如说,我的老板在大学里学的是英语文学,但是现在他是一位物流经理。

总的来说,我认为过一个间隔年的弊端要超过益处,很大程度上是因为年轻人可能会在收获不大的情况下度过这一年。

d) *Analysis of vocabulary and structures used in model answer, including possible mistakes made by candidates.*（语言分析）

"In recent years, taking a gap year between secondary school and university has become increasingly popular in my country." Many candidates will refer to a debate between two opposing arguments. This introductory sentence demonstrates that this is not always necessary. ("近年来在我们国家,选择在完成中学学业和开始大学学业之间度过一个间隔年的做法越来越流行。"很多考生会谈到两种对立观点之间的争论。这里的这个引入句展示了其实不是总是需要这么做。)

"In this essay, I will look at the advantages and disadvantages for young people who take one." Notice that the writer has decided not to give an opinion at the beginning of the essay. This is acceptable. It might also mean that the writer has not yet come to a decision about which side of the argument to support. In this essay, it is not necessary to hold an opinion, since the Question prompt only asks candidates to discuss both sides of the issue. ("在本文当中,我将分析这样做对年轻人有什么好处和弊端。"注意这里作者决定在文章开始的时候先不给出观点。这样做是可以的。这也有可能说明作者还没有决定到底应该支持争议中的哪一方。在这篇文章中,考生并没有必要去持有一个观点,因为题干只是要求考生去讨论争论的两个方面。)

"A friend of mine was accepted to university to study law." Examples like this are acceptable. You can make up examples, but make sure that are realistic. ("我有一个朋友本来被一所大学录取了去学习法律。"这样的例子是可以采用的。你可以虚构例子,但是要保证是实际可信的。)

"**Although** she earned little money, she discovered what it was like to work in the legal field." Using 'although' to show a positive point and a negative one in one sentence is a common strategy. ("尽管挣钱不多,但是她知道了在法律领域工作是怎样的状况。"利用"尽管"来在一个句子里说明一个正面观点和一个反面观点是很常见的一个策略。)

"She **learnt** a lot of things that **helped** her in her studies. When she **finished** university, she **had** no problem finding a job because the same law firm **hired** her." Using an example like this also gives you the chance to use the past tense, demonstrating to the examiner that you can do that! ("她学到了很多对她的学业有帮助的东西。后来她大学毕业的时候,很容易就找到了工作,因为原来那家事务所又雇了她。"使用一个这样的例子也给了你一个使用过去时的机会,向考官展示你可以做到这一点。)

"**Some** young people **might** simply waste their gap year". This sentence is another good example of how to make an argument without using absolutes. The writer does not say that if you take a gap year, you **will** waste it. Instead he/she is pointing out the possibility. ("有些年轻人可能会浪费这一年时光"。

这句话是一个很好的例子，说明了可以如何在不使用绝对表达的情况下表明一个观点。作者并没有说如果你选择过一个间隔年，你就"<一定>会"浪费这一年。他所做的只是指出了这种可能性。)

"Something that is more likely to happen". By saying this the writer is pointing out that he/she thinks that something happens in more cases and is therefore a stronger argument than the suggestion that young people will waste a gap year. ("更有可能发生的情况是"。通过这个表达，作者指出了他/她认为这是一个发生得更多的情况。因此比起暗示年轻人<一定>会浪费间隔年，这个说法更加有力。)

"I think that taking a gap year is usually not a good idea." The candidate is stating his/her view without suggesting that it is always correct. ("我还是认为这样做通常来说不是太好。"作者表明了自己的观点，但是又没有说它总是对的。)

"This means that". The candidate is pointing out a result of an action or decision. ("这就意味着"。这指出了一个行动或决策的结果。)

It is almost impossible to get a decent job immediately after graduating from high school". Notice that the writer doesn't say 'a job', but instead says 'a decent job', thereby expressing his/her exact meaning. ("在刚刚高中毕业的情况下，要找到一份不错的工作几乎是不可能的。"注意作者说的不是"一份工作"，而是说的"一份不错的工作"，这样就说明了自己的确切意思。)

"However, nowadays, studying a particular subject does not necessarily restrict a person to working in a particular area. For example, my boss studied English literature at university and he now a logistics manager." Notice how the example is directly connected to the first sentence—the argument. ("然而现在，学习某一个特定的学科并不一定把一个人局限在某个特定的领域。比如说，我的老板在大学里学的是英语文学，但是现在他是一位物流经理。"注意这个例子是如何直接与第一个句子联系在一起的——作者的论点。)

SPEAKING

a) *Question analysis, including possible misinterpretations of the questions.*

What's your favourite colour? Why?

This Question shouldn't present any problems. Many people have no particular reason for liking a colour.

Do you like the same colours now as you did when you were younger? Why? Why not?

Remember to use the past tense when talking about the past.

What can you learn about a person from the colours they like?

Try to use words and phrases like '(quite) a lot', 'a little', 'a great deal' to quantify how much people can learn.

Do any colours have a special meaning in your culture?

You could even make up an answer to this question, but make it sound realistic! Be sure to talk about **your** culture, not other cultures!

Describe a song or a piece of music you like.

This is a fairly simple question, but candidates should be careful not to talk about a type of music that they like or a singer/musician/group that they like.

What kinds of music are popular with young people in your culture?

This is a vocabulary question, but don't just list all the types of music you know. Talk about how **popular** they are—very, quite, not very. Note that the Question asks about young people, but you can extend your answer to include older people.

What do you think influences a person's taste in music?

There could be many reasons for this. Although the Question asks 'what', you can add 'who' to your answer.

How has technology affected the kinds of music popular with young people?

The problem that many candidates will have with this Question is that they will hear the word 'technology' and start talking about computer games, scientific research, the development of society, and so on. This Question is an excellent example of why candidates must listen to the **whole** question! Notice that the Question still focuses on young people, but can be developed to include older people.

Tell me about any traditional music in your culture.

Here, candidates can discuss the type of music, melody, and instruments.

How important is it for a culture to have musical traditions?

As with any Question asking "How important...?", use words like 'not very', 'quite', etc.

Why do you think countries have national anthems or songs?

This is fairly easy question, but be sure to focus on anthems, not on traditional music or folk music as many candidates do.

b) Shortlist of useful vocabulary that candidates could use in their answers to each Question and brainstorming diagram for Part 2 questions.

What's your favourite colour? **Why**?

Light, dark, best, attractive, the colour of.

Do you like the same colours now as you did when you were younger? **Why**? **Why not**?

I've always liked, don't know why, used to, change one's mind.

What can you learn about a person from the colours they like?

Nothing, a lot, a little, quite a lot, very much, personality, pessimistic, optimistic, outgoing, introverted, dark, light, bright, sad, happy, feel.

Do any colours have a special meaning in your culture?

Romance, wedding, death, purity, symbolic, associated with, stand for, mean.

Describe a song or a piece of music you like.

Music/songs are by singers/musicians/groups.

Type of music—techno, jazz, folk, slow, fast, romantic.

Why you like it?

Fast, energetic, romantic, slow, relaxing.

How it makes you feel?

Happy, alive.

Instruments—guitar, piano, drums, violin, keyboard, sax, flute, er hu.

What kinds of music are popular with young people in your culture?

Folk music, pop music, rock, dance, jazz, techno, hip-hop, romantic, trend, prefer.

What do you think influences a person's taste in music?

Friends, family, change, musical tastes, radio, TV, Internet, bars, clubs, lend, make copies.

How has technology affected the kinds of music popular with young people?

Download, Internet, other cultures, instruments, techno, DJ, mix songs, distribute.

Tell me about any traditional music in your culture.

Traditional instruments, er hu, drum, guitar, slow/fast rhythm/beat, singing, dancing, high-pitched.

How important is it for a culture to have musical traditions?

Very/quite important, distinctive, unique, feel part of a group, pass down traditions and stories, diversity, forget, remember.

Why do you think countries have national anthems or songs?

United, nation, different, connection.

c) Two model answers for each question.

What's your favourite colour? Why?

My favourite colour is blue. I'm not sure why I like it. Maybe because it is the colour of the sky and the sea.

I like black best. Some people think that it is a depressing colour, but I think it can make a person look a little mysterious.

Do you like the same colours now as you did when you were younger? Why? Why not?

Yes, I've always liked blue. As I said before, I don't really know why.

As I said, I like black now, but I used to like white. When I was a little girl, I used to wear white clothes as often as possible. I don't know why I changed my mind. Maybe because you can see dirt on white clothes easily.

What can you learn about a person from the colours they like?

I've heard of this idea before, but I don't think you can tell anything about a person from the colours they like. For example, people say that if you like black you are pessimistic, but my best friend likes black and she is very optimistic.

I think that people who like bright colours are generally more outgoing than people who like dark ones. However, it's not always true. Sometimes, I wear bright colours when I'm sad to try and make myself feel happier.

Do any colours have a special meaning in your culture?

Yes. Red symbolizes romance. Women often wear red on their wedding day.

Yes. White is symbolic of purity, so many women wear a white dress on their wedding day. Black is often associated with death. People wear black to funerals.

Describe a song or a piece of music you like.

My favourite song is *Ride* by DJ Speedy. It is a techno song with very few words—just a fast beat and modern, electronic sound. The reason I like it that it is so fast and energetic. When I hear it, it makes me feel happy and alive. I first heard it at a disco last year. I didn't dance to it at first—I just listened to it. I asked a friend the name of the song and the artist. The next day, I went to look for it in the shops. I found the album with it on quite easily and bought it. I like the other songs on the album too, but not as much as *Ride*. I don't think that the song or the words have any real meaning or story, like many songs, but they are just meant to make a person want to have fun and be happy.

My favourite song is *Still* by Jane Creedy. She's an American country and western singer. The song is slow and romantic—just Jane singing and playing the guitar. I like romantic songs—I guess I'm a romantic person! The song is a story. It tells of a woman remembering her lover who has gone away. She remembers him and is waiting for him to return. I heard the song when I was on holiday in the United States last summer. I wanted to buy some typical country and western music, so I bought a CD with it on. I also bought another CD by Jane Creedy, who is now my favourite singer.

What kinds of music are popular with young people in your culture?

In my culture, young people generally like folk music, but pop music from other countries is becoming more and more popular. I think that this trend will continue, but that many young people will still prefer their own folk music.

Young people in my country usually like pop music, rock music and dance music. However, some like jazz and this seems to getting more popular. There are several new jazz clubs in my city and they are often full at the weekends.

What do you think influences a person's taste in music?

I think that a lot of people are influenced by their friends. You know, friends will say to each other "Oh, I like this song. Listen to it!" I think that a person's taste in music can change quite quickly, depending on their mood. Most people I know have CDs with different kinds of music—from slow romantic songs to fast beats.

I think that people's musical tastes are often influenced by what they hear on the radio and at bars and clubs. After all, you can't like a song until you've heard it! I think that friends also influence what music people like. Friends lend each other CDs or even make copies for each other. I know that's illegal, but it's what many people do.

How has technology affected the kinds of music popular with young people?

I think the fact that young people can download a lot of music for free from the Internet—both legally and illegally—has allowed them to explore music that they might otherwise never have listened to. I think that's wonderful. We can find out what people from other cultures are listening to.

Without modern technology, there wouldn't be music like dance or techno or hip-hop. Technology has allowed DJs to mix songs and create their own styles. Technology also allows music to be distributed around the world very quickly, so people are influenced by music from other countries.

Tell me about any traditional music in your culture.

In my culture, there are only a few traditional instruments. One is a drum. Another is similar to a guitar. The music generally has quite a slow rhythm and is accompanied by singing and dancing.

I think that most of the traditional music in my culture is high-pitched, as is the singing that goes with it. The best known instrument is probably the er hu, which is a small stringed instrument. Most foreigners will recognize the sound of the er hu if they listen to Peking opera.

How important is it for a culture to have musical traditions?

Music is a very important part of any culture. The instruments used each have distinctive sounds and the singing that goes with the music can help people to feel part of a group. In some cultures music and song is still an important way of passing down traditions and stories.

I think that it is quite important. After all, each culture has music that is different to that of other cultures and it is important to keep this diversity. However, if people decide that they prefer music from another culture or if they decide to create their own style, I don't think we should accuse them of forgetting their musical traditions. Often, you can hear traces of old styles in new musical styles.

Why do you think countries have national anthems or songs?

That's easy. It's to make people feel united as one nation. It can be a little dangerous, because people will see themselves as different or separate from others.

I think that national anthems are used to make people feel a connection with their country and culture.

d) Text boxes showing how sentences can be completed. For example:

Black ...	is my favourite colour.
	can make a person look mysterious.
	is a depressing colour.

I don't think you can tell anything	... about a person from the colours they like.
I think you can know a lot	
I think you can find out some things	

I like it because it is ...	so fast and energetic.
	slow and romantic.
	a reminder of my girlfriend.

In my culture/country, young people ...	generally like folk music.
	pop music from other countries.
	usually like pop music, rock music and dance music.

I think that a lot of people are influenced by ...	their friends.
	what they hear on the radio.
	other people's tastes in music.

Test 3

LISTENING

SECTION 1

谈话场景:售车中心购车咨询场景。

人物关系:售车中心工作人员与购车客户。

谈话话题:购买合适的汽车,讨论车况细节以及客户信息。

词汇注释

advice *n.* 建议,意见	**reasonable** *adj.* 公平的;不过分的;适度的
particular *adj.* 特别的,特殊的	**colleague** *n.* 同事
make *n.* 产品出处;牌子	**arrangement** *n.* 计划;安排
make up one's mind 下定决心	**part-exchange** *n.* 部分抵价交易(用旧物抵一部分价款购买较昂贵同类物品,如将旧汽车作价)
various *adj.* 不同种类的,各种各样的	
model *n.* (产品的某种)设计,型号	**valuation** *n.* 估计;(尤指专业人员的)估价
litre (US **liter**) *n.* 升(液量单位)	**postcode** *n.* 邮政编码
detail *n.* 细目;细节;详情	**get hold of** 与某人联系;找到某人
gear *n.* (机动车辆的)传动装置,排档	**message** *n.* (以书面、口头、无线电等形式向某人传送的)信息
presume *v.* 假定(某事物)是事实;认定(某事物)	
manual *n.* 手册;指南	**mileage** *n.* 英里数
automatic *adj.* 自动;自动调整的	**roughly** *adv.* 大概;大约
chart *n.* 示意图	**metallic** *adj.* (似)金属的
shade *n.* 颜色,色度	**describe** *v.* 描述;形容
assume *v.* 假定;假设;设想;以为	**call in** 拜访;去某人家等
finance *n.* (个人、公司或国家)可动用的钱,财源,财力	**mart** *n.* 贸易中心
in the region of 大约(某数量、重量、价格等)	**customer** *n.* 顾客
credit *n.* (银行等的)借款;贷款	**enquiry**(also **inquiry**)*n.* 问讯;调查

交际与语言表达

1. 本篇文章主要讨论购车咨询过程中的细节问题,这也是雅思生活场景听力试题中经常涉及的内容之一,考生要对一些常用的买车购车以及汽车的词汇和表达法要耳熟能详,并且还要了解填写顾客情况调查表时所涉及的一般常用问题。
2. 在售车中心,或者在一般性商场,工作人员或者是销售人员都会主动向顾客问好,并且通常会说:How can I help you? 或 Can I help you, Sir/Madam? 或者是 Is there anything I can do for you? 考生在听到这一问题后,应首先反应到下面的对话应该是属于买家与卖家的对话。
3. Had you got any particular **make** in mind? 您心里是否已经有了特别钟意的(汽车)牌子了? 许多考生可能不知道、或者没有留意到 make 这个词在这句话的实际意思,但该词直接影响到第一题的答案。事实上,如果我们事先注意到题目的设置,我们就会知道 make 在这里是指“汽车牌子”。
4. Any idea? 您有什么想法/意见吗? 该句是地道的口语表达,两个人在说话的时候都有针对前文的省略语，很多地方必须理解说话人上句话才能理解下一句，这在口语中很常见，所以考生一定要对这种省略语倍加注意。这句话如果补充完整应该是：Do you have any idea of the engine size? 下文中 a 1.4 should do 和 I don't think I need a 1.6 or anything 以及 Mileage? Roughly? 都是如此。

5. I **presume** you'd want a manual? ... but I **assume** that'd be OK? 这两句问句都是售车人员在征求顾客的意见，其中 presume 和 assume 都等于 think，但售车人员在问这两句话时一般都是期望得到顾客肯定的答复。
6. Have you given that any **thought**? 您是否考虑过这一点？give thought to sb./sth.：考虑某人或某事。
7. I think I'll **go for** that. 我想我还是选择那个吧。go for sth.：选择某事物，这里的 go for 等同于 prefer。
8. The cash price is going to be somewhere **in the region** of seven and a half thousand. 现金支付的话大约是 7,500 英镑。考生要注意该句中出价的表达方法和黑体部分，这句话可以简单地表达为 The cash price is going to be about 7,500。下句 Are you in a **position** to pay cash，您是否愿意现金支付，同样可以简单地表达为 Are you going to pay cash? 注意这两种表达方式的区别。
9. Could I have your full name? 请问您的全名是什么？这样的问法要比 What's your name? 有礼貌的多。类似的说法还有 Is there any possibility that I can have/get your name?
10. And is that Mrs... Miss... Ms...? 那么是该称作夫人，小姐还是女士？西方国家很重视对人的称谓（Title），对人称谓的错误通常被视为对人不尊重，尤其是对女性而言。并且，如果对方是 Doctor（博士、医生），他/她会很乐意你使用这个称谓。
11. and then I'll **get back to** you when I can. 我收到（信息）后就给您回过去。该句是电话用语，西方国家经常会使用电话语音留言的功能。
12. I'd probably **describe** it **as** reasonable. 我可能会说车况尚可。describe sb./sth. as... 将某人/某物形容为，as 通常后接形容词，describe 可以用 think，deem，consider 等词代替。

考题解析

Question 1

这道填空题考查考生对细节的把握与辨别能力。当考生听到售车人员问到 engine size 的时候都会留意具体的数字。但购车人的回答中出现了三个不同却又相互关联的回答，这就需要考生细心甄别。1.2 liters 是购车人以前的 engine size，1.6 liters 又太大，所以只有 a 1.4 适合（should do）。另外，填空时还需要注意两点：1）liters 与 litres 两种拼写均可；2）注意 liters 是复数，虽然原文中是单数，但那是作状语修饰 engine，liter 作为量词时是可数的。

Question 2

此题较为简单，考生只需清楚汽车自动档（automatic）与手动档（manual）的拼写与区别即可正确填出空白，因为购车人说得很明白：I'd want automatic。

Questions 3–4

在谈到车的颜色及付款方式时，购车人都清楚地表明了自己的态度：I think I'll go for that (Sky)；以及 I'd like **credit** provided the terms are reasonable。需要注意的是，1）购车人对售车人提出的两种颜色——Royal 和 Sky——表示了兴趣，但更倾向于后者，考生要对其态度准确把握；2）Sky blue 要比 Royal blue 颜色更轻一点，所以空白 3 也可填上文章中出现过的 light 一词。

Questions 5–6

第 5 题与下面的第 7 题一样，难度不大，但需考生细心听写。要注意西方人念字母或数字时出现的 double 一词。正如上面"交际与语言表达"第 10 项所说的，空白 6 应该填上 Doctor，或者其缩写形式 Dr.。

Question 7

本题不难,只是稍微拐了一个弯,这也提醒考生注意西方人姓名拼写"音同字不同"的现象。售车人拼错名字时,购车人及时更正过来。考生答题时要注意名字拼写的细节。

Question 8

购车人在提供电话号码之前,已经给出一个前提条件,即:I can give you a number just for messages,这里的 just 等同于题干出现的 only,考生只需把握住这一点,了解 message 的意思是信息、留言就能填对。但需要注意的是,这里的 messages 是复数形式,所以考生在答题时,一定要注意名词的单复数问题。

Questions 9-10

购车人在说出她正在使用的车的名称时,特地在 lion 后面加了一句注释:like the animal,所以考生应该能轻松填对空白;如果考生清楚 describe sb./sth. as...(将某人/某物形容为)的用法,那么第 10 题也就迎刃而解了。

SECTION 2

谈话场景:留学某英国大学情况介绍会。

人物关系:讲话者为校方发言人。

谈话话题:介绍学校教研水平及留学生在校学习生活情况。

词汇注释

excellent *adj.* 优秀的,卓越的

combination *n.* (两个或两个以上事物或人)结合,混合,联合,合并

physical *adj.* 自然规律的;按自然法则的

geographical *adj.* 地理(学)的

advantage *n.* 优势,长处

rural *adj.* 乡村的;在乡村的

capability *n.* 能做某事的素质;能力

assessment *n.* 评价;看法

engineering *n.* 工程;工程学

geography *n.* 地理学

individually *adv.* 单独地;个别地

take a sip of 小口喝一下

application *n.* 申请;请求

confirmation *n.* 证实;证明;肯定

process *n.* 程序;过程

occasionally *adv.* 偶然地;不时地;有时

reference *n.* (有关某人品格或能力的)证明文书,介绍信

referee *n.* (愿为求职者提供证明的)证明人,推荐人

reassure *v.* 消除某人的恐惧或疑虑;使某人放心

liaise *v.* (infml 口)做联络人;联络

concern *n.* 对某人来说是重要的或感兴趣的事物

objective *adj.* 客观的;中肯的

opinion *n.* 意见;看法

academic *adj.* 学校的;学院的

atmosphere *n.* 气氛

facility *n.* 能够或易于做某事的环境,设备等;辅助物

awful *adj.* 很坏的;糟糕的

pack *v.* 将某物装入(箱、盒等)(尤指装入衣箱)

environment *n.* (影响人们生活的)情况;环境等

norm *n.* 标准;规范

adjust to (使)适合,适应(新环境的)

surroundings *n.* 周围的物体、条件等(可为有影响力的);环境

accommodation *n.* 房间(尤指作居住用者);住所

priority *n.* 优先权

allocation *n.* 配给;分配

residence *n.* 居住

category *n.* 种类;类别;范畴

procedure *n.* 程序;手续

snap up 抢购一空

afford *v.* 为(某目的)有足够的钱	**make allowance for**(因某原因需区别对待而)体谅、照顾某人
in advance 事先;预先	**audience** *n.* 听众;观众
available *adj.* 可用的或可得到的	**afterwards** *adv.* 后来;然后;以后
get in touch with 联系上	
on sb.'s behalf 做某人的代表;为某人之利益	

交际与语言表达

1. 本文是英国 Rexford 大学校方负责人介绍本校教学研究情况及外国留学生在校学习生活的各方面情况,相信会对准备雅思考试的考生有所启发。
2. ... something **that** will certainly be of interest to you is **that** Rexford is just 35 minutes from London Airport. 有一点你肯定会感兴趣,那就是 Rexford 距离伦敦机场只有 35 分钟的路程。这一句话有三点需要我们注意:1)第一个 that 作为关系代词引导后面的限定性定语从句,修饰 something,that 不能省去;2)第二个 that 引导后面的名词性从句用作宾语,that 可以省去;3)Rexford is just 35 minutes from London Airport. 这句话可以这样理解:It takes only 35 minutes (to drive, walk, etc.) from Rexford to London Airport. 请注意这样的表达方法:somewhere is xx minutes (away) from somewhere。
3. We came 7th **out of** 101 universities in last year's research assessment. 在去年的研究评估中,我们在 101 所大学中排名第 7 位。该句中的 out of 意为"在……之中,从(若干)中",而不是字面意思的在"……之外"。
4. 说话人在 one further point 后加了一句很长的插入语,然后才接着说完这句话。这在口语中很常见,考生遇到这种情况时一定要注意摆脱插入语的干扰。一般说话人在准备加上插入语时,都会稍稍停顿一下,考生要留意连接上插入语后面的主句谓语动词。
5. Anyway that's enough **sales talk** from me... 好了,我就不再自卖自夸了。这句话带有自嘲的意思,sales talk 原为"推销货物的说辞",在这里是指说话人一直在宣传自己学校的优势。
6. 这段介绍文字句子中间夹杂了很多插入语,如 I mean, shall we say, anyway, hopefully, if possible, in most cases 等等,另外还有一些稍长的句子也作为插入语。这符合英国人的说话习惯,他们说插入语时一般停顿很短,或者没有停顿,这也给我们做听力题时造成了一定困难。因此,考生需要熟悉这些插入语,并要学会掌握他们的用法。
7. **That way** you can get an objective opinion of... 这样的话,你就能对……有一个客观的认识。这句话开头省略了介词 in,考生要注意口语中经常会省略介词。
8. You will be in an environment **where** independent learning is the norm. 你将会处在一个崇尚独立学习的环境中。这句话包含了一个以关系副词 where 引导的限制性定语从句,该从句充当地点状语。
9. It is the University's policy to **give priority** in the allocation of residence places to three categories... 大学的政策是:将给予三类学生住房分配优先权。这一句话有两点需要我们注意:1)句子中包含的带 to 的不定式在句中作主语,但在实际使用中,特别是在口语中,人们常常用 it 作形式主语来代替作主语的带 to 的不定式,而将不定式移到句子后面;2)give priority to sb./sth. 意为给某人或某事物优先权。
10. Demand **exceeds** supply. 需求大于供应/供不应求。(exceeds = is greater than)这是一句很好的反应供需关系的句型,考生可以说 supply exceeds demand,就是供大于求了。
11. **What** you can't do is leave it until a few days before the start of term. 你不要等学期开始了才开始着手这件事。该句有两处需要我们注意:1)句子主语是以 what 引导的名词性从句;2)句子的宾语实际上是一个 to 引导的不定式,leave 前面的 to 可以省略。
12. **I'm afraid** the lecturers will make **little** or no allowance for the presence of non-native speakers in

the audience. 我想讲课老师大概不会对听众中的非英语母语学生特别照顾。西方人说话时一般不会特别绝对,会留有余地,特别是在说否定的事情时。这句话的意思其实就是说老师不会对外国留学生特别照顾,但说话人不会说:the lecturers will not make allowance for the non-native speakers.

考题解析

Questions 11–12

这两道选择题考查考生的归纳以及对细节的把握与辨别能力。在解答 11 题时,有的考生可能会选择 B 选项,因为说话人提到 Rexford 大学紧邻 central London,但是并没有提到与伦敦有 good transport links,该选项偷换了概念,具有一定的迷惑性;第 12 题的答案距离上道题的答案有点远,但细心的考生会留意到说话人以 one further point 引出该题的答案。虽然说话人又在答案之前加了一句很长的插入语,但只要我们清楚 close relationships 等同于 good links,就能做出正确选择。总之,这两道题具有相当的迷惑性。用同义词更换原文中的关键词语,而这也是雅思出题常见的套路。

Questions 13–15

题目中的表格内容实际上是对话中提到的 application process(申请流程),考生只要紧跟说话人的逻辑顺序,就能顺利填出 13–15 题的空白。第 13 题有两处需要注意:1)考生要知道 hold-up 等于delay,雅思出题时经常会使用原文的同义词作题干;2)references 是复数形式,少写 s 就会导致扣分。第 14、15 题较为简单,只是说话人在给出 15 题的答案 weather 之前还说了一个连词 whether,并且二者相隔不远,考生听到这里时可能会一时间反应不过来。其实,说话人在这里使用了"双关语(pun)"的修辞手法,以达到一种幽默的效果。

Question 16

该题同样是使用原文中关键词的同义词作为题干,原文中,说话人提到 you will be in an environment where independent learning is the norm。出题人把 learn 换成了 work,但意思不变,所以考生平时准备考试时,要灵活掌握词汇。

Question 17

该题可以用排除法做题。选项 A、B 中的 undergraduates, postgraduates with families 并不属于说话人所说的享有住房优先权的三类人群,只有 C 选项的 new postgraduates 是符合学校的标准的。

Question 18

该题考查考生对细节的把握与辨别能力。考生要做出正确选择,除了要深入了解文章内容,并且还需作一个小小的计算。说话人提出 in other words, if you're starting in October you need to be thinking about it in June or at the very latest July,十月与六月、七月相差几个月(several months),所以选择 A 选项。

Question 19

该题不难,考生只要知道 on your behalf 的意思就是选项 B 中的 for students 就能做出正确选择,而其他两项说话人并没有提到。

Question 20

文章中的最后一段是在强调加强英语口语联系的重要性,说话人明确指出讲课老师不会因为非英语母语学生听不懂就会特别照顾,因此选项 A 可以排除。问题就出在选项 B 与 C 上,说话人提出:Some extra practice before you arrive is worth more than... for example private lessons afterwards,说话人的态度不是很明显,他使用了 worth 一词来表明自己的观点,但恰恰是许多考生没有听清楚这个词,导致无法在 B 与 C 之间做出选择。

SECTION 3

谈话场景:课外讨论场景。
人物关系:同学关系。
谈话话题:商量如何填写教学反馈表。

词汇注释

feedback *n.* 反馈信息
fill in 填写;加入必要内容使某事物完备
code *n.* 代码
comment *n.* 评论;意见
aspect *n.* 方面
organization *n.* 组织性;系统性;条理性
outline *n.* 要点;大纲;纲要
session *n.* (进行某活动连续的)一段时间
load *n.* 负荷物,载荷物(尤指沉重的)
even *adj.* 均匀的;有规律的;均衡的
delivery *n.* (在讲课中的)讲话方式;风度;态度
suppose *v.* 认为;以为;猜想
standard *n.* 标准
material *n.* (讲课用的)材料,资料
handout *n.* 教师分发给学生的讲义等
website address 网站地址
reserve *n.* 储备(物);储备量
evaluation *n.* 评估;评价
assignment *n.* 指定给某人的任务或职责
mark *n.* 评定某人的工作或操行用的数字或字母符号
oral *adj.* 口头上;口述的
presentation *n.* 出席;发言
criterion *n.* (pl. **-ria**)(评判的)标准,尺度
clarity *n.* 清楚;明晰;清澈
stressful *adj.* 有压力的
pass *n.* 及格

交际与语言表达

1. 本段对话是地道的口语表达,两个人在说话时候都有针对前文的省略语和替代,很多地方必须理解上文某人说的话才能理解下文另一人所说的话,这在口语中很常见。
2. If you **want**, we can **do it** together. 如果你愿意的话,我们就一起填这个表。这句话有一处省略,一处替代。want 本来是及物动词,后面须加上宾语或者带 to 的不定式,但这里省去了后面的宾语成分;do it 很明显是替代前面所说的"填写反馈表",在口语中,说话者经常会用 do 这个含义丰富的词代替前面的动作。
3. CB16 **something**, CB162, isn't it? 是 CB16 什么来着,CB162,对吗?在口语中,我们经常会用 something 这个比较模糊的词来表达"不清楚、不确定"的意思,比如:She's writing a dictionary **or something.** 她在编写字典之类的书。
4. My birthday's on May 4th and it was the day after, it **must have been** May 5th. 我的生日是 5 月 4 号,这门课开始时间是它的后一天,(所以)一定是 5 月 5 号。"情态动词 must + have + 过去分词"是表示对过去行为的比较肯定的推测,意为"一定;想必"。这位女生在推测课程开始的日期时,是以自己的生日为参照,所以比较肯定。如果说话者对自己的推测不是那么肯定的话,可以使用"情态动词 may/might + have + 过去分词"。
5. Ok, **anything else** for course organization? 好了,关于课堂组织方面你还有什么要说的吗?这句话有两点需要考生注意:1)这句话实际上包含了一个"there be"句型,它的完整形式应该是"Is there anything else for course organization?"。口语中为了简练起见,省去了 is there;2)在口语中,说话者在问"还有什么(要补充的)吗?"时,一般会简单地说"anything else?",而不会把省去的成分都补充完整。

6. Yeah, I **suppose** so. 是的,我认为是这样。I suppose so 是口语中经常被用来表示说话者赞同对方的观点,给予对方的问题以肯定的回答,等于 I think so. 当给与对方问题以否定的回答时,一般会说 I' m afraid not,或者是 I don' t think/suppose so.
7. **What about** suggestions for improvement? 那改进意见该怎么写呢? what about/how about 句型一般被用来征求对方关于某事物的意见,观点等。比如说 what about/how about Wednesday? 周三怎么样? 这在口语中很常见,考生要注意掌握这个有用句型。
8. You have to wait **ages** to get one. 你得等很长时间才能拿到一份。这句话我们需要注意两点:1)ages在这里不是"年龄"的意思,在口语中它通常指 very long time(很久;极长的时间);2)在日常对话时,说话者常常会使用一种很常见的修辞手法:exaggeration(夸张)。实际上,这位女生说 wait ages to get one 本身就是一种夸张说法。类似的还有前面一句话:I mean at the beginning it seemed dead easy. 我的意思是刚开始的时候它(课程)容易得要死。
9. It' s hard to say **until** we' ve got our written assignments back. 在拿到我们的书面作业之前,这还很难说。这句话包含了 3 个语法点:1)带 to 的不定式在句中作主语。但当作主语的不定式短语太长,谓语动词是连系动词或被动语态时,通常用 it 代替作主语的带 to 的不定式;2)it' s hard to say 已经演变成一个习语,即使 say 后面没有宾语;3)该句实际上是一个"it + be 动词 + 否定词…… + until"的句型,因为 hard 本身就带有否定意义。

考题解析

Questions 21–22

这两道填空题按道理来说不是很难,只需把听到的日期填上即可,但出题人在答案附近设置了不少迷惑项,比如第 21 题,说话人接连给出两个相似的数字,而 22 题则给出三个相邻的日期,这给考生带来一些麻烦。其实,考生只要冷静下来,细心辨别这几个日期的关系就能写出正确答案。值得注意的是,第 22 题因为说话人把日期具体到星期几,所以可以把 Friday 也写上,只要注意 Friday 拼写正确。当然,多一事不如少一事,不写也没有关系。

Questions 23–25

这篇听力文章不难,考生只要跟着说话人的思路和逻辑就能迅速定位答案:两个学生商量完教学某一项具体方面的 Good points 之后,紧接着就会转移到 Suggestions for improvement 上面去,并且一方说完一点之后,通常会问对方"anything else? (还有什么要补充的吗?)",所以,考生在做题时一定要紧跟着这些"路标"。23 题的答案可以加上谓语动词 was,也可以省去,因为题干中给出的例子就没有谓语动词;24 题的答案可以加上冠词(a 或者 the),同样也可以省去;25 题也是同样的道理,定冠词可要可不要。

Questions 26–27

这两道填空题的答案同样是"所听即所写",只需把听到的内容原封不动地搬上即可。值得注意的是,如果考生没有听清,或者拿不准如何拼写文中的 standard 和 group 时,可以将这两个词省去不写,对于这两道题来说都是可以接受的。

Questions 28–30

考生在回答这几道题时,一般不会出错。容易出错的地方是 29 题的 handouts 是复数形式,考生不要忘记 s;在填写 29 题的时候考生也可能会比较迷惑:两位学生在谈到 Testing and evaluation 的时候,从 Good points 到 Suggestions for improvement 中间并没有明显的过渡,只用了一个转折连词 but 就引出这方面的不足,所以考生可能会措手不及。这提醒我们不论在做阅读还是听力的时候一定要关注以 but 为代表的转折连词。

SECTION 4

谈话场景：课堂发言介绍调研结果。
人物关系：讲话者为调研小组的学生代表。
谈话话题：介绍英国生活垃圾回收利用情况。

词汇注释

project *n.* （学校的）科研习作项目，课题
household *n.* （attrib 作定语）家庭的
recycle *v.* 回收（废旧材料）；（利用废旧材料）再造（原始成品）
shocked *adj.* 感到震惊的
figure *n.* 数字
dramatically *adv.* 戏剧性地；非常大地
target *n.* 目标
carbon dioxide 二氧化碳
emission *n.* （烟、气）排放
achieve *v.* （通常藉努力、技巧、勇气等）获得或达到（某事物）
virgin materials 原始材料
greenhouse 温室
landfill site 垃圾掩埋点
incineration plant （垃圾）焚烧厂
survey *n.* （对部分人的行为、意见等的）调查
bale *v.* 将某物打成包或包装成捆
container *n.* 容器（如箱、瓶等）
plastic *n.* 塑料
toughened *adj.* （经过硬化更）坚韧的
temperature *n.* 温度
oddly *adv.* 奇怪地；不寻常地
import *n.* & *v.* 进口；输入
fiberglass *n.* 纤维玻璃
manufacture *n.* & *v.* 生产；制造
filtration *n.* 过滤
crushed *adj.* 被压碎、碾碎的
amazing *adj.* 令人惊异的
stationery *n.* 文具
in terms of 在某事物方面
soil conditioner 肥料
ban *v.* 明令禁止（某事物）
alternative *adj.* 可用以代替其他事物的；其他的
bumper *n.* （机动车辆前后的）保险杠
scheme *n.* 计划；方案
vending *n.* 出售；销售
polystyrene *n.* （attrib 作定语）聚苯乙烯
variety *n.* 多样性；变化
business card 名片
sum up 总结，概括（某事物）
lack *n.* 缺少；不足
utilize *v.* 利用；使用

交际与语言表达

1. 本文讨论如何实现垃圾回收利用，中间夹杂部分术语和专有名词，可能会对考生造成一定麻烦，这也再次提醒我们准备雅思考试时，尤其是学术类的，一定要尽可能地扩大自己的知识面与涉猎领域。
2. ... by 2008 we must **reduce** our carbon dioxide emissions **by** 12.5%, **compared with** 1990. ……到 2008 年，与 1990 年相比，我们必须将二氧化碳排放量降低 12.5%。这句话有两点需要我们注意：1）"（某事物）降低或增长多少"的表达方法是 reduce or increase by...，请注意介词 by 的用法，by 表示度量、单位或标准；2）"与……相比较而言"的表达方法是：compared with... 可直接用在句首，用作状语。
3. ... people **don't think** it's easy to recycle their waste. 人们认为回收利用他们的垃圾并不容易。这句话实际上是"转移否定"，即句中的否定虽然出现在主句谓语动词部分，否定范围却不在主语谓语动词本身，而转移到句子的宾语、状语或其他成分上。转移否定多用于表示思维活动，如判

断看法之类的动词 believe, expect, hope, suppose, think 等。如:I don't think that it's going to rain tomorrow. 我认为明天不会下雨。

4. One problem is that there aren't enough "drop-off" sites, **that is**, ... 问题是:并没有足够的垃圾投放点,也就是说……。在口语中,人们经常会对上一句话做进一步的解释说明,这就需要短暂的插入语来引出下面的解释说明性文字。这样的插入语有文中的 that is (to say),还有 in other words, to put it more (simply), i. e. 等等。考生一般听到这些插入语时,就应该知道下面的文字是对上文的进一步阐释,这也说明,上文提到的内容比较重要,也是出题的重点。

5. One problem here is taking out everything **that** shouldn't have been placed in the recycling containers. (面临的)一个问题是:人们把许多本来不应该放在垃圾回收箱的垃圾也全部拿出来了。这句话有两点需要我们注意:1) taking out everything 构成动名词结构短语(动词 + ing 形式),它在该句中作主语补足语,对主语所表示的内容(one problem)作进一步的说明;2) 句中的 that 引导一个限定性定语从句,修饰 everything,请注意:当先行词是 everything, something, anything 等时,关系代词通常不用 which,而用 that。

6. **Another difficulty** is that toughened glass used for cooking doesn't fully melt at the temperature required for other glass. 另外一个难点是在其他玻璃熔解要求的温度下,钢化玻璃并不能充分熔解。该句开始的 another difficulty 应该被视为上一句 one problem 的对应,这提醒考生:1) 当一段话中出现 one、another 时,我们应该明白这是一种并列关系;2) 英语语言与汉语不同,讲究善于变化(variation),通常用不同的词来说明同一意思,前面的 problem 与这里的 difficulty 应该被理解为是近义词,都是在阐述垃圾回收利用时所面临的问题。

7. For recycling paper, Britain **comes second** in Europe with 40%, behind Germany's amazing 70%. 在回收利用纸张方面,英国的利用率为 40%,排在第二位,仅次于德国令人称奇的 70% 的利用率。在谈论"取得第 x 名、排第 x 名",我们经常会用到下列表达法:come/rank + 序数词,或者 take/in + 序数词 + place,如:He finished in third place. 他取得了第三名。注意这里的序数词前面不加 the。

8. ... and Martin's, **based** in South London, produces a range of office stationery which is 100% recycled, costs **the same as** normal paper and **is of equally high quality.** 还有总部设在伦敦南部的马丁公司,生产一系列使用 100% 回收利用材料的办公文具,与普通纸张价格相同,并且质量同样很好。这句话比较复杂,中间夹杂多种语法现象,有几点值得我们注意:1) based in South London 从语法上看,是属于-ed 分词短语作定语修饰前面的 Martin's,由逗号和其要修饰的词分开,实际上,它还可以被看作是省略的非限制性定语从句,省去了前面的 which is;2) 如果两件事物完全相同,可以用 the same as 表示,其前还可用 exactly, virtually, nearly 等修饰;3) "be + of + 抽象名词"用作表语或定语,修饰前面的名词,如:Your help is of great value to us. 你的帮助对我们很有价值;of great importance/consequence:很重要。一般 of 后面的抽象名词都要加上表程度的形容词修饰。

9. Over a third of the waste paper that comes in can't be used in the recycled paper, leaving the question of **what to do with** it. 有超过三分之一的收集来的废纸不能用来制造可再生纸,如何处置它成了一个难题。what to do with sb./sth. = how to deal with sb./sth. 如何处置某人/某事物。

10. ... and the company is looking into the **possibility** of alternative uses. 那家公司正在调查是否可能找到其他可替换的用途。look into sth. 调查或观察某事物;与汉语语言相比,英语语言倾向于使用抽象名词表达法,在汉语中一般是用其他形式,如动词或形容词结构来表达的。比如上文所说的"be + of + 抽象名词"形式,汉语完全可以用形容词结构来表达,本文的 possibility 就是possible 的抽象名词表达。

11. Well, to sum up, there seems to be plenty of research going on into how to reuse materials, ... 好

了，总结来说，看起来关于如何回收再利用垃圾还有许多研究等着我们去做…… 英文行文讲究首尾呼应，结尾处一般要总结全文、呼应首段。本文是一篇比较正式的课堂发言，所以会出现 to sum up 这样比较正式的说法，但开头的 well 依然是口语常用的口头语。当考生听到 to sum up，或者 let's have a conclusion 之类的话时，一定要知道这段话即将结束，中间可能会有总结全文内容的出题点。

考题解析

Questions 31–35

第 31–35 题都是考查考生对细节的辨别和掌握能力，并且题干都基本上是对原文的改写，这是雅思出题、特别是填空题的重要思路。

第 31 题出题人把原文中的动词 reduce（减少）换成题目中的形容词 lower，但意思不变，考生只需把听到的数字填进去即可。

第 32 题几乎是对原文的重现，但是许多考生因为对 **incineration plant**（垃圾）焚烧厂这个词组不熟悉而出现拼写错误。

第 33 题把原文中的 there aren't enough 换成了名词词组 a lack of（缺少、缺乏），考生只要熟悉这个词组就能很轻松地填对。

第 34 题有些难度。首先，出题人把原文中的 used for 换成了难度较大的 utilized for，并且还把原文语句中暗含的逻辑结果提到题目中，造成许多考生无所适从。原文中只是说钢化玻璃在一般玻璃熔解的温度下不能溶解，并没有直接提到钢化玻璃因此不能与其他玻璃一起回收利用。所以考生必须熟悉新单词 utilize 和文章中蕴含的逻辑关系才能正确填写答案。

第 35 题较为容易，考生只需把相继出现的 3 个数字区分开来即可。雅思听力考数字时，一般不会直接给出一个单一数字让考生填写，肯定是给出一连串互相关联的数字让考生选择，以前的题目也印证了这一重要出题思路。

Questions 36–40

第 36–40 题是表格填空题，这类题型同样考查考生对细节的辨别和掌握能力，以及在芜杂的信息中挑选有用信息的能力。第 36–40 题所涉及的表格里，把原材料分为 3 类，又按照不同公司分为 6 类，因此考生要注意说话人的停顿及每段话的承上启下的首末句，跟着说话人的逻辑填空。

第 36 题难度不大，因为在玻璃回收利用方面，只有 CLF 一个公司，并且该公司的产品也只有一类：roads。考生注意 roads 的复数形式即可。

纸张的回收利用有两家公司在做，一家制出高质量的办公文具，一家利用不能回收利用的纸张做成肥料卖给农民。所以在做第 37 题时，考生一方面要把握住第二家公司的名字，另一方面要把题目中的 on farms 与听到的 farmers 联系起来。

第 38 题具有一定的难度，因为说话人并没有像对别的公司一样，对 Pacrite 这家公司加以任何说明，而是直接列出它在塑料回收利用方面的做法，这使得许多考生没有反应过来。所以这也提醒考生做题之前一定要争取看题目，尽快熟悉题目中出现的像公司名称这样的专有名词，做到心中有数。

说话人在介绍第 38、39 题 Waterford 和 Johnson & Jones 这两家公司及其产品时，都是一句话带过，并且对它们的介绍集中在一个句子中，这使得考生在填写答案时来不及写全，只能记下要点；另外，在表达“制造”这个动词时，说话人分别用 turn sth. into sth. 和 develop 来代替 make，考生要灵活掌握近义词的用法。

READING

READING PASSAGE 1

文章结构

体　　裁	说明文
主要内容	本文论述了新西兰政府对儿童早期教育重要性的科学认识，注意从以往的几次儿童早期教育试验项目中吸取经验教训，认识到不仅要重视儿童早期教育，而且要同样重视父母对儿童的教育。
结　　构	A 段：Introduction 从新西兰政府专门负责儿童早期教育的工作组报告谈起，指出儿童早期教育的重要性。
	B 段：一项长达 13 年的研究项目指出：3 岁之前的阶段是人类获取基本技能和知识的最重要时期。
	C 段：1965 年美国实施一项名为“领先”的项目，旨在提高来自贫穷家庭的儿童的教育水平。但是由于文中所述的两个原因，项目最终未能达到预期目标。
	D 段：美国实施“密苏里”项目，不仅重视儿童早期教育，同样重视家长对儿童的教育。该项目把重点放在后者。
	E 段：“密苏里”项目产生良好效果，在该项目中受教育的儿童不管家庭背景如何，在学习各方面明显优于其他同龄人。
	F 段：总结全文：新西兰政府从上述试验项目中得出结论，要重视儿童 0 – 3 岁期间的教育，同时重视家长在这期间对儿童的教育。

词汇注释

文　章	
A 段	
childhood *n.* 童年；幼年时代	**funding** *n.* 专款；基金
argue *v.* 争论；争辩	**institution** *n.* 慈善机构；社会福利机构
enhance *v.* 提高；增强（某人、某事物的优点）；使（某人、某事物）看起来更好	**unquestionable** *adj.* 无可争辩的；无疑的；确实的
equity *n.* 公平	**normal** *adj.* 正常的；常态的
access (to sth. /sb.) *n.*（使用某物或接近某人）的机会或权利	**miss out** (infml 口）失去获得利益或获得兴趣的机会
B 段	
study *n.* 研究科目；课题	**suppress** *v.* 压制；压抑
development *n.* 发展；成长	**dramatically** *adv.* 戏剧性地；非常大地
potential *n.* 潜力；潜能	**claim** *v.* 声称；宣称
ordinary *adj.* 平常的；正常的；普通的	**personality** *n.* 个性；人格
conversation *n.* 谈话；交谈	**form** *v.* 形成
furthermore *adv.* 此外；再者；而且	**expand** *v.* 使（某事物）变大，扩大；扩展
curiosity *n.* 好奇心	**existing** *adj.* 现有的；存在的

C 段

acknowledge *v.* 承认(某事物)属实
background *n.* 背景;出身
tend to 倾向于;趋向于
observe *v.* (常用在被动语态)看到,注意到(某人、某事物)
attempt *n.* & *v.* 试图;企图;尝试
overcome *v.* 战胜;克服(某事物)
nationwide *adj.* 全国范围的
programme *n.* (US **program**) 活动安排;行动方案
launch *v.* 使(某事物/某人)行动;使开始
pour into (大量)涌入;注入
substantial *adj.* 数目大的;可观的
disappointing *adj.* 令人失望的
explanation *n.* 解释;说明
peer *n.* (usu. pl. 通常作复数)同龄人
measurable *adj.* 可量度的;可测量的;可衡量的
intelligence *n.* 学习、理解和推理的能力;智力;脑力
involve *v.* 包含,包括,牵扯,牵连(某人/某事物)
disadvantaged *adj.* 社会地位低下的;贫困的
environment *n.* (影响人们生活的)情况、环境等

D 段

evidence *n.* 证据;根据
pilot *adj.* 试验性的;试点的
focus on 将(注意力等)集中(于某事物)
predicate *v.* (esp passive 尤用于被动语态) ~ sth. on sth. 使某事物依据于另事物;使某必需的事物成为另事物的结果
bypass *v.* 绕过或避开(某人/某事物)
effective *adj.* 有效的;产生预期结果的
start *n.* 起始时的领先(程度);起始优势
be about to 即将、正要(做某事)
represent *v.* 代表;作为…典型
status *n.* 身份;地位
configuration *n.* 某物的构造、结构、布局
information *n.* 信息;消息
guidance *n.* 引导;领导;指导
foster *v.* 培养;鼓励;促进
intellectual *adj.* 智力的;理智的
periodic *adj.* 定期的;周期的
check-up *n.* 全面检查
sensory *adj.* 感觉官能的;感觉的;感受的
detect *v.* 发现、察觉或查出(某事物)
handicap *n.* 生理上或智力上的缺陷;残疾;智力低下
interfere *v.* 干涉;介入;干预
professional *n.* 具有某专业资格的人;从事某专业的人;专业人士
locate (esp. passive 尤用于被动语态)将(某物)设置在某处;使坐落于

E 段

evaluate *v.* 评价;估计,评估(某人/某事物)
range *n.* 成套或成系列的东西;种类
random *adj.* 随便的;任意的;胡乱的
sample *n.* 货样;样品;样本
phenomenal *adj.* 非凡的;格外的;了不起的
advanced *adj.* 高深的;高等的
stride *n.* & *v.* 大步行走
average *adj.* 平均的
auditory *adj.* 听觉的;关于听觉的
comprehension *n.* 理解(力)
verbal *adj.* 词语的;言语的;文字的
bear relationship to 与(某事物)有关
regardless of 不理会(某人/某事物);不顾
child abuse 虐待儿童
virtually *adv.* 几乎
eliminate *v.* 消除,清除,排除(尤指不必要或不需要的人或事物)
affect *v.* 影响
stress *n.* 精神上或肉体上的痛苦、困难的情况等(所造成的压力或忧虑)
lead to 导致;引起
interaction *n.* 一起活动;合作;配合

F 段

perpetuate *v.* 使(某事物)永久、永存
initiative *n.* 为解决困难而采取的行动
outline *v.* 概述(某事物)
cycle *n.* 循环,周期
concept *n.* 概念;理念
markedly *adv.* 显著地,突出地
institutionalize *v.* 使(某事物)制度化
similar *adj.* 相似的
vital *adj.* 极重要的,必不可少的
indicate *v.* 指出;显示
inequity *n.* 不公平

考题解析

Questions 1–4

● 题型归类：Short-answer Questions

● 题目解析：

题目编号	题目定位词	答案位置	题解
1	family types, education programme	D 段 第 3、4 句	题目：参加一项教育活动的家庭类型的细节。 文中具体描述的教育活动只有两个：Headstart 和 Missouri，集中在 C、D、E 三段。我们从文中了解到，Headstart 的失败就在于没有重视家庭的因素，所以排除 C 段；而 E 段主要描述 Missouri 活动的成功，只有 D 段对参加这次活动的各类家庭的情况作了详尽的说明。
2	reasons, child's early year, important	B 段	题目：为什么儿童的早期这么重要？ 该题不难，因为作者为了阐述儿童早期教育，在文章的开始就交待了儿童早期、特别是 3 岁之前是最重要的时期。A 段只是提出问题，引出下文。
3	education programme, failed	C 段 第 2 小段	题目：为什么一项教育活动失败了？ 从文中看，两个不同的教育活动一正一反，效果相反。失败了的活动是 Headstart，所以只能在 C 段；另外，考生还要抓住一个关键句：It is thought that there are two explanations for this. 两个原因解释它的失败。
4	positive outcome	E 段	题目：对一项教育良好效果的描述。 此题正好是第 3 题的对照，要求考生能找到成功了的 Missouri 活动的信息。考生同样需要抓住一个关键句：The results were phenomenal。但是即使不熟悉 phenomenal 这个形容词，考生如果看到 E 段中多次出现的积极性形容词，也能填上正确答案。

Questions 5–10

● 题型归类：Matching

Matching 考查考生对文章细节的把握和辨别能力。此类题型一般难度不大，但由于需要在全文反复搜寻相关内容而可能耗费大量时间。因此在解题时，考生可以根据题目某一组比较明显的定位词先缩小搜寻范围，然后在定位词附近迅速搜寻正确答案。

● 题目解析：

题目编号	题目定位词	答案位置	题解
5	a variety of, families	D 段 第 3、4 句	考生可能不理解题目中出现的 administered（实施、执行），但是只要看到 a variety of（一系列的）就知道又是在谈论参与家庭众多的 Missouri 活动。

6	elementary schools		题目中问到哪个活动得到了小学的后续支持？这两个活动的对象都是 3 岁以前的儿童，并且，在 C、D、E 三段扫描也并没有出现 elementary schools，所以选 D
7	did not succeed	C 段 第 2 小段	该题与第 3 题类似，答案位置也相同，只要知道 Headstart 失败了就能选对。
8	support and training to parents	D 段	该题也不难，因为我们知道 Missouri 活动正是重视家长的作用才取得成效，这也是它与 Headstart 的区别之处。
9	insufficient funding	C 段 第 4 句	C 段第 4 句 A lot of money was poured into it. 告诉我们，Headstart 活动不缺钱，故排除 A 和 C 项；同时对 D、E 两段的扫描也没有发现对 insufficient funding 的描述。故选 D。
10	improve pre-schooler's educational development	C、D 段	两项活动不管方法、成效如何不同，初衷都是利用儿童早期时间，抓紧早期教育，力争能够提高学前儿童以后的教育发展。故选 C。

Questions 11 – 13

● 题型归类：TRUE/FALSE/NOT GIVEN

T/F/NG 类题考查考生对文章细节的把握与辨别能力，考查题目中细节信息和逻辑关系是否与文章中完全对应。因此在解题时，先要确保读懂题目，准确理解题目意思，然后根据题目定位词回到原文定位相关内容后与题目进行对照判断。

● 题目解析：

题目编号	题目定位词	答案位置	题解
11	"Missouri" programme, scored highly	E 段 第 1 小段	题目：大多数参加"密苏里"活动的 3 岁儿童在听力、口头表达、推理和与人交往能力方面表现很好。 根据题目中的定位词"Missouri" programme 可以首先将答案的搜索范围缩小到 D、E 两段。然后根据题目意思，将答案定位在描述该活动成效显著的 E 段。E 段多次提到通过对 3 岁儿童的测试，他们的 language abilities, other intellectual skills 等得分很高，题目符合原文意思，因此答案确定为 TRUE。
12	"Missouri" programme, parents, scored less highly	E 段 第 2 小段 第 1 句	题目：那些年轻、未受教育的单身家长的孩子在"密苏里"活动里测试结果相对较差。 该题同样是在对谈论"Missouri" programme 的成效，因此同样把答案定位在 E 段。在该段第 2 小段中，我们发现第一句话说：更为重要的是，传统意义上的"风险"因素，如家长的年龄，以及他们是否是单亲父母，都与这次孩子们的成就和语言发展关系不大。所以，题目不符合原文意思，孩子家长的背景与孩子的成绩并没有直接联系。故选 FALSE。

13	"Missouri" programme, richer families, stress levels	E 段第 2 小段	题目:家境富裕的家庭在"Missouri" programme 压力会更大。 该题与上题一样,都是在谈论"Missouri" programme 的成效,答案同样定位在 E 段。作者在该段的第 4、5 句中确实提到了 family stress:一个被认为是影响儿童发展的因素是家庭压力,它恶化了家长和孩子之间的互动和配合。在更为贫困的家庭中,这种互动和配合不见得会必然糟糕。作者承认了家庭压力的存在,但只是说在贫困家庭里因压力导致的互动与配合不见得就会必然糟糕,我们并不能反推出富裕家庭的压力会更大,原文中没有给出这样的逻辑关系,故选 NOT GIVEN。

参考译文

儿童早期教育

新西兰国家党教育部门新闻发言人洛克伍德·史密斯博士近来出访了美国和英国。下面是他关于这次访问的收获所做的报告,报告还指出了这些收获对于新西兰教育政策的影响。

《教育:影响未来》于去年八月出版。它是"新西兰政府儿童早期教育工作组"提交的报告。报告呼吁,儿童应该获得更加公平的受看护机会,并且儿童早期教育机构应该得到更好的资助。毫无疑问,我们确实需要这样做;但是既然家长们通常在孩子三岁之后才会把他们送到学前班,那我们是不是错过了他们人生中最宝贵的几年?

哈佛大学的一项长达 13 年之久的关于儿童早期成长的研究项目显示,大多数儿童在 3 岁的时候就已经具有理解大约 1,000 个单词的潜力。而这 1,000 来个单词将是他们日后日常交谈中所需要的大部分语言。

另外,研究还发现,虽然每位儿童都有天生的好奇心,但在他们 2 - 3 岁的时候,这种好奇心会受到极大的压制。研究人员声称,人的性格形成于人生的头两年,在头三年中,儿童将学到一些基本技能,而日后不论在家或是在学校的学习生活中,他们都将用到这些基本技能。一旦过了 3 岁,孩子们将继续扩展他们现有的关于这个世界的知识。

众所周知,家境贫寒的年轻人通常会在我们的教育体系中表现不佳。这一现象不仅存在于新西兰,也存在于澳大利亚、英国和美国。1965 年,美国为了解决家境贫寒的年轻人受教育效果不理想的问题,开展了一项名为"领先"的全国性活动。这项活动收到大量资金。它把 3 岁的儿童带进学前教育机构,希望能帮助来自贫困家庭的儿童在将来的学习中取得优秀成绩。

尽管资金来源充足,但是结果还是令人失望。人们认为有两点可以解释这次活动失败的原因。第一,这次活动开始得太晚。大多数年满 3 岁的儿童参加这次活动时就已经在语言方面及其他可衡量的智力方面落后于他们的同龄人。其次,孩子的家长并没有参与进来。每一天的活动结束时,孩子们又回到了卑贱依旧的家庭环境中。

越来越多的研究结果证实儿童前三年在其一生中的重要性,"领先"活动的结果也不尽如人意,这些都促使美国密苏里市开始启动一项实验性活动,专注于使家长担当孩子最初教师的角色。"密苏里"活动依托的研究表明:与家长们合作,而不是忽视他们,才能最有效地帮助孩子们找到最好的人生起点。这次为期 4 年的研究项目包括 380 个家庭,这些家庭不仅即将拥有他们的第一个孩子,而且具有广泛代表性,代表了来自社会中不同社会经济地位、年龄及家庭构成的群体。他们中不光有单亲家庭、双亲家庭，有两位家长都有工作的家庭，也有父亲、母亲中有一位无业在家的家庭。

此次活动内容包括让训练有素的家长教育专家前往每个家庭，与家长们——或是单亲家长——和孩子一起工作。活动提供孩子成长发展的信息，当孩子成长时指导家长如何照顾他们以及如何对他们有所期待，如何促进孩子的智力、语言、社会及运动技能的发展。活动定期全面检查孩子的教育进展及感觉官能（听觉和视觉）的发展，以期能查出可能存在的生理上和智力上的残缺，这种残缺将会干扰孩子的生长发育。活动还会就医学问题请教专家。

家长教育专家经常以个人身份拜访各个家庭，每月召开群体会议和其他新参加的家长们分享经验，一起讨论感兴趣的话题。位于学校建筑内的家长资源中心为各个家庭以及儿童看护人员提供学习材料。

等到参加此次“密苏里”活动的儿童年满 3 岁的时候，活动随机挑选出一些同样具有广泛代表性的，来自同样背景、社会经济条件的家庭的和他们同岁的儿童，与参加活动的儿童一道进行评估测试。评估结果令人振奋。这些参加活动的 3 岁儿童与他们的同龄人相比，在语言方面取得显著领先地位，在问题解决能力方面及其他智力技能和社会发展方面进步更快。事实上，在他们这个年龄段的孩子中，活动中的儿童在听力理解、文字表达及语言能力方面，平均排在前 15% - 20% 之间。

更为重要的是，传统意义上的“风险”因素，如家长的年龄，以及他们是否是单亲父母，都与这次孩子们的成就和语言发展关系不大。不管家庭社会、经济条件都多么不利，孩子们的表现同样喜人。虐待儿童现象几乎杜绝了。一个被认为是影响儿童发展的因素是家庭压力，它恶化了家长和孩子之间的互动和配合。在更为贫困的家庭中，这种互动和配合不见得会必然糟糕。

这些研究发现激动人心。在新西兰，越来越多的证据显示，来自贫困家庭的儿童进入学校时，自身发展差强人意，并且我们的教育体制有使这种劣势永久化的倾向。上述措施可以打破这种劣势的循环。这种与家长们在家里或者工作单位里一起配合的理念与儿童早期教育工作组所做的报告有明显的出入。工作组的注意力都放在了使儿童和母亲们都有机会得到儿童看护，从而使儿童早期教育制度化。毫无疑问，对 3 岁至 5 岁之间孩子的教育至关重要，但是有证据显示，如果不把同样的注意力放在对家长的教育上，对儿童前三年的重要性认识不够的话，这还不足以改变儿童受教育不平等的现状。

READING PASSAGE 2

文章结构

体　　裁	说明文
主要内容	本文主要论述了尼罗河三角洲地区由于得不到随尼罗河河水顺流而下的沉积物的补充，面临被侵蚀殆尽的危险。而阿斯旺大坝的建立被视为是造成这种情况的主要原因。
结　　构	A 段：Introduction 点出主题：尼罗河三角洲肥沃的土地不能像过去那样得到沉积物的补充。
	B 段：人们归咎于阿斯旺大坝的建立。大坝建立之前，尼罗河水带来的沉积物造福三角洲地区。大坝的建立改变了这一切。
	C 段：进一步说明大坝对尼罗河三角洲地区土壤补给的不利影响。
	D 段：尼罗河水分流至灌溉渠和淡水湖，进一步加剧尼罗河三角洲地区土壤补给问题。
	E 段：受污染的沉积物严重影响三角洲的农业和渔业，进而破坏该地区的生态平衡。
	F 段：世人开始关注这一问题，并试图提出办法解决。但难度较大。

词汇注释

文 章

A 段

fertile *adj.*（指土地）肥沃的，富饶的
delta *n.*（河口的）三角洲
erode *v.*（esp. passive 尤用于被动语态）侵蚀，腐蚀（某物）
Mediterranean *adj.*（似）地中海的
astounding *adj.* 使人震惊的
estimate *v.* 估计；估算
scour *v.*（指河流等）冲刷成（水道等）
current *n.*（水、气的）流，流动
replace *v.* 代替；取代
sediment *n.* 沉积物（如沙、砾等）

B 段

blame *v.* ~ sth. on sb. 责备；责怪；归咎于
dam *n.* 水坝；水堤
quantity *n.* 数目、数量（尤指巨大的）
interior *n.* 内地；内陆
deposit *v.*（尤指液体、河流）使（淤泥等）沉积
eventual *adj.* 最终；最后
region *n.* 地区
layer *n.* 层（尤指数层中之一）
silt *n.*（由流水带到河口、港口等的）淤沙、淤泥等
annual *adj.* 每年的；年度的；一年一次的
nutrient-rich 富含营养物质的
dispense with sb./sth. 用不着某人/某事物
fertilizer *n.* 肥料；化肥
electricity *n.* 电
irrigation *n.* 灌溉
drought *n.* 干旱（时期）
accumulate *v.* 积累，聚积（某物）
upstream *adj. adv.* 向上游（的）；逆流（的）

C 段

turn out to be sb./sth. 证明是某人/某事物
emerge *v.* 出来；现出；露出
sample *n.* 货样；样品；样本
gram *n.* 克（重量单位）
cubic *n.*（常作定语）立方的
ashamed *adj.* 感到羞耻；感到惭愧
significance *n.* 意义；意思；重要性
replenish *v.* 再将某物充满；补充某物
trap *v.* 使（某物）留在某处

D 段

divert *v.* 使某事物转向
canal *n.* 运河
freshwater *adj.*（常作定语）来自淡水的；淡水的
lagoon *n.*（大湖或江河附近的）小而浅的淡水湖
coastline *n.* 海岸线

E 段

plain *n.* 平原
aquaculture *n.* 水产养殖
account for 作某事物的解释；解释某事物的原因
laden *adj.*（常作表语）装满的；满载的
municipal *adj.*（常作定语）市的；市政的
pollutant *n.* 污染物质
investigation *n.* 调查研究
concur *v.* 同意；表示意见一致
mercury *n.* [化]汞；水银
lead *n.* [化]铅
copper *n.* [化]铜；紫铜
zinc [化]锌
coincide *v.*（指事情）同时发生
availability *n.*（指物）可用或可得到的
concentration *n.* 集中（于某事物）
poison *n.* 毒药；毒物
food chain 食物链
productivity *n.* 生产力；生产能力
stimulate *v.* 使某人/某事物奋发起来；激励；刺激
upset *v.* 扰乱；打乱
ecology *n.* 生态；生态学

F 段

erosion *n.* 腐蚀；侵蚀
principally *adv.* 多半；主要地

impact *n.* 影响	**waterway** *n.* 水路；航道
ecosystem *n.* 生态系统	**desalination** *n.* （从海水中）去除盐分；脱盐
artificial *adj.* 人造的；人工的	**devise** *v.* 设计；想出（计划、制度、工具等）

考题解析

Questions 14–17

● 题型归类：List of Headings

此类题型属于结构题，考查考生对文章整体结构的把握和概括能力。解答此类题型首先要分析题目中给出的选项，确定各选项的主要内容和相似选项之间的区别，接着要了解段落基本构成方式，准确寻找段落的主题句（通常集中在段落的首句和末句），如果主题句较难寻找，则需要迅速浏览全段后总结段落中心思想。

● 题目解析：

题目编号	段落主题句	题解
14	Up to now, people have blamed this loss of delta land on the two large dams at Aswan in the south of Egypt, which hold back virtually all of the sediment that used to flow down the river.	B 段首句告诉我们，人们认为阿斯旺大坝的建立阻碍了沉积物的天然流动，因此它背负起造成三角洲土地流失的罪名。为了证明这一说法，作者在这一段中使用正反对比手法：阿斯旺大坝建成之前沉积物随河水天然的流动以至最终形成尼罗河三角洲肥沃的土地；而大坝的建成阻碍了这一天然进程，沉积物转而在上游堆积。在各个选项中，我们发现只有第 4 个选项是在总结概括 B 段的内容，其他的都没有在该段体现。
15	Once north of Cairo, most of the Nile water is diverted into more than 10,000 kilometers of irrigation canals and only a small proportion reaches the sea directly through the rivers in the delta.	D 段首句开始就谈到大量的尼罗河水都被引导灌溉渠里去了，只有少部分直接入海。而从上文可以看出，沉积物是随着河水一起“旅行”，最终到达三角洲的。所以河水引入灌溉渠，沉积物自然随之进入渠内，沉入渠底。而随着入海的河水水量减少，沉积物自然也随之减少。灌溉渠对沉积物去留的影响正在于此。
16	These poisons can easily enter the food chain, affecting the productivity of fishing and farming.	E 段开头指出三角洲平原的农田、渔业和水产养殖为埃及提供了食物供给，但接下来却说随着大坝的建立、工业的发展，尼罗河水里的沉积物受到各种污染，而这些沉积物很多被用来为农田等提供天然肥料，所以污染物很自然就会进入食物链，威胁该地区的食物生产。该段的主题句也正说明了这一点，所以正确选项为第五个选项。 而第三个选项也可能成为干扰项，因为这个选项里含有“污染”这个字眼，很多考生看到它就会立即选择第三个选项。这一地区的食物虽然受到污染，但并没有谈到是否整个地中海都受到沉积物的污染，出题人在这里是偷换了概念。 另外，从文中可以得知，由于种种原因，进入地中海的沉积物不多，所以更不可能污染整个地中海。

17	According to Siegel, international environmental organizations are beginning to pay closer attention to the region, partly because of the problems of erosion and pollution of the Nile delta, but principally because they fear the impact this situation could have on the whole Mediterranean coastal ecosystem.	F段作为全文的总结段,从长远来看尼罗河三角洲水土流失问题的影响,勾画出解决这一问题的前景。首句指出国际组织之所以关注这一问题,不仅是因为三角洲的水土流失和污染加剧,更是从长远考虑,对整个地中海海岸线生态系统的失衡表示忧虑。选项中只有最后一项概括了这一问题,并且其关键词 impact 也出现在了本段的首句中。

Questions 18–23

● 题型归类:YES/NO/NOT GIVEN

Y/N/NG 类题考查考生对文章细节的把握与辨别能力,考查题目中细节信息和逻辑关系是否与文章中完全对应。因此在解题时,先要确保读懂题目,准确理解题目意思,然后根据题目定位词回到原文定位相关内容后与题目进行对照判断。

● 题目解析:

题目编号	题目定位词	答案位置	题解
18	coastal erosion, before the building of the Aswan dams	A段第二句	题目:在阿斯旺大坝建成之前埃及地中海沿岸就有海岸被侵蚀现象。 在A段第二句话我们就了解到海岸线上的土地以前就常被海水冲走(scoured away),只是又得到了新的沉积物的补充,而现在(大坝建成之后)没有新的土壤的补充。可见,海水冲刷海岸线一直都存在,与大坝的建立并没有直接关系。故选 YES。
19	predicted, the Aswan dams, cause land loss	B段首句	题目:有人在阿斯旺大坝建成之前就预言大坝会造成水土流失。明显出现人们对大坝态度的语句是出现在B段的第一句:时至今日,人们仍然把水土流失归咎于大坝的建立。但是至于是否有人在大坝建立之前就有这样的先见之明,我们不得而知,因为文中并没有谈到这一点。所以选择 NOT GIVEN。
20	the Aswan dams, increase the fertility of the Nile delta	B段第五句	题目:阿斯旺大坝的建立是为了使尼罗河三角洲更加肥沃。文章中明确谈到大坝建立宗旨的语句是B段第五句,作者用了两个带 to 的不定式说明大坝建立的目的:1)提供电量和灌溉;2)保护开罗及周边地区免受洪灾和旱灾之苦。我们并没有看到为三角洲增肥的目的。 再者,给三角洲提供肥料的一直都是作为天然肥料的沉积物。而现在,大坝的建立挡住了沉积物的流动,这明显与增肥的目标背道而驰。所以选 NO。

21	levels of sediment, Cairo	C 段第三句、末句	题目：史丹利发现在流至开罗的河水里沉积物含量相比而言较高。 此题较难，因为文中并没有出现史丹利对沉积物含量的具体表态，我们只能通过上下文及他说话的语气来推测他的真实态度。史丹利的调查发现流至开罗的河水里沉积物含量是大坝建成之前的一半，但是根据末句的说法，与进入地中海的河水相比，这里的含量还算是较高的，因为很少有沉积物会进入地中海。故选 YES。 这道题不仅涉及对文章细节的掌握，而且还牵扯到对说话人语气和文章整体的把握。
22	sediment, irrigation canals, causes flood	D 段	题目：尼罗河三角洲上灌溉渠里面的沉积物导致洪灾。 涉及到灌溉渠与沉积物的段落只有 D 段，二者有联系的地方只是灌溉渠里的沉积物被农民捞出来做肥料，并没有说沉积物与洪灾的联系。文章中倒是提到了尼罗河三角洲的annual flooding，但也没有说明它的成因。故选 NOT GIVEN。
23	water, pumped from the irrigation canals	D 段第三句	题目：水被从灌溉渠中抽出注入淡水湖里。 该题设计思路较为隐晦，D 段第三句中主要说沉积物沉入渠底，又被农民捞出，或是注入四大淡水湖中，主语都是sediment，只是在一个 with 引导的伴随结构中才见到 water 的出现，原来是沉积物是随着水的泵出才进入到淡水湖里的。故选 Yes。

Questions 24-26

● 题型归类：Summary

在做这类题时有一个诀窍：依据 summary 题型在试题中的位置确定答案在文章中的位置。如果 summary 位置靠前，那么答案一般会在文章的前面；如果 summary 位置靠后，则答案要么是对整篇文章的总结，要么是对文章后面某一部分的内容的体现。具体到这三道题，因为它们是这篇阅读理解的最后面的习题，所以这个 summary 是对最后一段的总结。这个诀窍可以使考生尽快定位答案，提高做题速度。

● 题目解析：

题目编号	题目定位词	答案位置	题解
24	increase, contained, silt	F 段首句	根据上文的说法，我们尽快回到 F 段寻找答案。首句告诉我们，现在三角洲地区面临两大威胁（partly... but principally...）。在第一个也是比较明显的威胁里，我们发现erosion是和 pollution 是并列的，而试题中只出现了 erosion，而不见后者，所以结合文章的意思，该空白应该选 F项。考生要注意，出题人把原文中的 pollution 换了说法，但都是在说同一件事。

25	in the short term	F 段 第 3 句	该题的答案不是很明显，因为原文中并没有出现 in the short term 这个词组，只有 in the immediate future。但是通过与下文的对比，我们知道 Stanley 实际上针对短期和长期提出了两个解决方法，短期的就是用 artificial floods 冲刷水道，这正是 A 项。
26	in the long term	F 段 第 4 句	该题应该与上题结合起来，上题提出了短期的解决方案，该题就是长期的方案。根据 Stanley 的想法，像脱盐这样的过程才是解决问题之道，故选 B。

参考译文

正在消失的三角洲

沿埃及地中海海岸线的尼罗河三角洲肥沃的土地正在以惊人的速度被侵蚀，在一些地区这个速度达到了每年 100 米。过去，海岸线上被地中海海水冲刷掉的土地总是被尼罗河带到三角洲的沉积物所取代，但是现在这种情况一去不复返了。

直到现在，人们还把三角洲的水土流失归咎于在埃及南部阿斯旺修建的两个大型水坝，这两个大坝拦截了几乎全部的沉积物，而在过去，这些沉积物总要顺流而下。大坝建成之前，尼罗河自由流动，从非洲北部内陆地区沿途携带大量沉积物，带到尼罗河三角洲沉积下来。这种情况持续了7,000年，最终形成了一块超过 22,000 平方公里的富含肥沃淤泥的土地。年复一年的洪水给三角洲地区带来了新的营养丰富的土壤，以取代那些被海水冲刷走的土壤，并且使埃及富饶的产粮区无需任何别的肥料。为了提供电力和灌溉，同时也为了使开罗这个人口稠密中心及其周边地区免受洪灾和干旱之苦，在 20 世纪建成阿斯旺大坝。但是随着大坝的建成，大量蕴含天然肥料的沉积物在位于纳赛尔人工湖上游南部的大坝里往上聚积，不再顺流而下，流至三角洲。

然而，这里发生的一切比上述所说的更多。现在看来，从阿斯旺大坝里流出的不含沉积物的河水在其流向开罗的 800 公里的"旅程"中，一路侵蚀河床和两岸，掘起淤泥和沙石。Smithsonian 研究所的丹尼尔·简·史丹利注意到，从在开罗采集到的河流到达三角洲之前的河水样本来看，有时一立方米的河水中含有 850 克的沉积物——几乎是大坝建成以前河水沉积物含量的一半。史丹利在《海洋地质学》里指出："我感到很羞愧，我看了 50、60 份研究报告之后才意识到这种情况的重要性。现在仍然有大量的沉积物进入到三角洲地区，但是基本上没有任何沉积物流入地中海来补充海岸线。所以这些沉积物肯定是滞留在三角洲地区了。"

以前在开罗北部，大多数的尼罗河水被分流到超过 10,000 公里的灌溉渠里，只有一小部分通过三角洲里的支流直接入海。史丹利解释说，灌溉渠里的河水要么静止不动，要么流动缓慢，所以不可能携带沉积物。沉积物沉入灌溉渠的底部，然后被农民捞起盖在田地里，或者跟河水一道被泵入位于三角洲外沿的四个大淡水湖里。所以实际上，只有极少量的沉积物会到达海岸线，取代那些被地中海海流冲走的土壤。

埃及的食物供应很大程度上依赖于三角洲平原的农田以及淡水湖里的渔业和水产养殖。但是当这些沉积物到达这些田地或淡水湖里时，它却充斥着来自开罗地区——在这一地区生活着四千万人口——的城市生活垃圾以及工业、农业垃圾。史丹利指出："污染物越积越快。"来自乔治华盛顿大学的弗莱德里克·希雅戈在对来自三角洲里的淡水湖的沉积物多次研究之后，对史丹利的说法表示赞同："举例来说，在我们建立阿斯旺大坝、得到价格低廉的电、发展一些大型的以电力为基础的工业的同时，Manzalah 淡水湖里的汞、铅、铜、锌元素也在增加。"从那时候起，汞元素的集中度显著增加。从使用含铅燃料的发动机里和以及从其他工业来源里渗出的铅元素同样增加很快。这些毒素很容易就能进入食物链，影响渔业和农业的生产。另外一个问题是：农业垃圾里会包含用来刺激淡水湖里作物增长的肥料，进而扰乱整个地区的生态平衡，这将严重影响渔业发展。

据希雅戈说，一些国际环境组织已经开始给与这个地区更多的关注，部分是因为尼罗河三角洲的侵蚀和污染问题，但主要是因为他们担心这种情形会影响整个地中海沿海生态系统。但是现在还没有解决问题的好办法。史丹利相信，在不久的将来，将使用人工产生的洪水冲刷三角洲里的水道，就像大坝建成之前的那些天然洪水的作用一样。但是他还指出，从长远来看，还会使用另外一种诸如脱盐的作法来增加河水的流量。史丹利说："在我看来，埃及必须设计出一个办法增加水量流经尼罗河和三角洲。"在这样一个人口急剧增长的沙漠地区，这样的方法说起来容易做起来难。

READING PASSAGE 3

文章结构

体　　裁	说明文
主要内容	本文阐述了"人工智能"这个概念在沉寂多年之后，又重新开始活跃。文章讲述了其从兴盛到淡出人们视野之外的经过，并对其未来的发展抱有信心。
结　　构	A 段：Introduction 点出主题："人工智能"这个名词重新活跃在人们的视野当中。
	B 段：从 1956 年的一次会议说起，讲述"人工智能"的由来。
	C 段：在对"人工智能"的幻想达到顶峰之后，人们开始反思，"人工智能"这个名词逐渐淡出。
	D 段：分析"人工智能"没落的原因，指出在一定程度上是受自己盛名之累。
	E 段："人工智能"又开始得到实际运用。
	F 段：分析"人工智能"重新得到重视的原因。
	G 段："人工智能"的理论虽然依旧不可捉摸，但人们对它还是抱有信心。

词汇注释

文　章

A 段

in the wilderness（习语）不再处于重要的或有影响的地位

artificial intelligence（**AI**）人工智能

poised *adj.*（指人、动物等）身体处于紧张状态，准备行动

vanish *v.* 消失

consciousness *n.* 明了；觉悟

release *n.* 影片、唱片、书籍的发行

ignite *v.* 使某物燃烧，着火

debate *n.* & *v.* 辩论；争论

executive *n.*（在企业、工会等中的）行政领导；经理；董事

irony *n.* 反语；反话

inverted comma 引号

hype *n.*（俚）天花乱坠的宣传报道

justification *n.*（做某事的）正当理由

admittedly *adv.*（尤用于句首）无可否认地，诚然

rehabilitation *n.* 恢复；复原

under-achieving *adj.* 成绩未如理想的

B 段

coin *v.* 创造（新词语）

attractive *adj.* 吸引人的，有魅力的

informative *adj.* 提供大量资料或信息的

encompass *v.* 包围，环绕，包含或包括某事物

previous *adj.* 在前的，早先的	**capture** *v.* 俘获，捕获，夺取
disparate *adj.* 全异的；不同的	**mimic** *v.* 模仿，摹拟
cybernetics *n.* 控制论（对信息传递和控制的研究，尤涉及人及动物大脑与机器及电子装置的差异）	**recognition** *n.* 识别
logic *n.* 逻辑，逻辑学，逻辑性	**unify** *v.* 统一，使成一体
	imagination *n.* 想象，空想，想象的事物，想象力
C 段	
peak *v.* 到达最高点；达到最高值	**backlash** *n.* 对某些事物的激烈的、通常诉诸暴力的反应
public *n.*（有共同爱好的）一群人	**ensue** *v.* 跟着发生，继起
rear *v.* 培养，饲养	**undue** *adj.* 不当的；过度的；过分的
science-fiction 科幻小说	**optimism** *n.* 乐观主义；乐观
expectation *n.* 期待，预料，指望，展望	**retrenchment** *n.* 节省，删除
imply *v.* 暗示；意味	**opt** *v.* 决定做某事；选择
breakthrough *n.* 突破	**align** *v.* 使结盟，使成一行
substantially *adv.* 实质上；大体上；基本上	**specific** *adj.* 专门的；特殊的
prototype *n.* 事物之原始形态；原型	**sub-discipline** *n.* 准学科
diagnosis *n.* 诊断	**neural network** 神经网络
materialize *v.* 成为现实；实现；发生	**agent technology** 代理技术
D 段	
ironically *adv.* 说反话地，讽刺地	**deem** *v.* 认为，相信
victim *n.* 受害人；牺牲品	**in the first place** 第一；首先
apparently *adv.* 显然地	**characterize** *v.* 表现…的特色，刻画的…性格
mundane *adj.*（常做贬义）平凡的；平淡的	**commercialization** *n.* 商业化，商品化
unattended *adj.* 没人照顾的；无人看管的	**implement** *v.* 贯彻，实现；执行
E 段	
tide *n.* 潮流，趋势	**camouflage** *v.*（军事上的）伪装，掩饰
reckon *v.* 认为（某事物）是…	**vehicle** *n.* 交通工具；车辆
approach *n.* 方法，步骤，途径，通路	**battlefield** *n.* 战场；沙场
promising *adj.* 有希望的；有前途的	**extract** *v.* 提出；取出
cluster *n.* 串，丛	**signal** *n.* 信号
processor *n.* 处理器	**emphasis** *n.* 强调；重点
F 段	
boost *v.* 推进	**explosion** *n.* 爆炸；激增
prospect *n.* 前景；前途	**web page** 网页
differentiate *v.* 区别；区分	**filter** *v.* 过滤
overload *v.* 超载；负荷过多	**categorize** *v.* 加以类别，分类
exacerbate *v.* 激怒，使加剧，使烦恼	**classic** *adj.* 经典的；第一流的
G 段	
feature *v.* 由（某人/某物）主演	**elusive** *adj.* 难懂的，难捉摸的
lip-read *v.* 唇读，观唇辨意	**comparison** *n.* 比较；对照
encapsulate *v.* 简述某事；总结某事	**match up to** 与某人/某事物同样好或相当
widespread *adj.* 分布广泛的；范围广的	**impressive** *adj.* 给人深刻印象的；感人的
transcribe *v.* 抄写或用打字机打印某物	
题目	
acceptable *adj.* 可接受的；合意的	**pattern-recognition** 模式识别
perform *v.* 履行；执行；完成任务	

考题解析

Questions 27－31

● 题型归类：Short-answer Questions

● 题目解析：

题目编号	题目定位词	答案位置	题解
27	military impact	E 段第 2 句	题目：AI 如何在军事方面发挥作用？ 该题考查考生对细节的把握能力。在 E 段出现了两个关键词组：battlefield 和 camouflaged vehicles，E 段第 2 句的意思是 AI 能侦察到战场上的伪装车辆，这就充分说明 AI 能在军事领域发挥作用，故选 E。 有的考生可能不熟悉 camouflaged（伪装）这个词，但是只要知道 battlefield 就能猜对该题。
28	brings together，a range of separate research areas	B 段	题目：AI 把一系列不同的研究领域整合到一起的事实。 在 B 段中，我们注意到出现了许多各不相同的学科，这些学科都有一个目标，就是利用机器模拟人类的能力，这实际上就是"人工智能"。而在该段的最后，作者说 AI 只是在名称上把这些学科统一起来。故选 B。
29	reason，topic of conversation，again	A 段第 2、3 句	题目：AI 之所以又成为人们的热门话题的原因。 文章的开头，作者就告诉我们 AI 这个名词又准备重新回到人们的视野了。而第 2、3 句告诉我们《人工智能》这部电影的上映更加激起人们热烈的讨论，同时 AI 又应用于电脑工业。这些都是在告诉我们为什么 AI 能够又火一把的原因。 在解题时，考生可能会选择 F 项，因为那也是在讲原因。不过 F 段是在说推动 AI 在将来美好前景的因素。
30	deal with，difficulties，information，electronically	F 段第 2 句	题目：AI 如何应付过量的电子信息？ 文章中只有一处谈到电子信息带来的困扰，这也是题目中所说的"difficulties"，并且指出 AI 最擅长这方面的事情：classic AI problems。故选 F。
31	expression，first used	B 段首句	题目：AI 这个名词在哪里首先被使用？ 该题不难，考生只要抓住 B 段首句的关键词 coined 就能选出答案，但是有些考生不知道 coin 除了"硬币"之外是否还有别的意思。其实，coin 作为动词，是"制造、创造"的意思，正是从"硬币"的意思中引申出来的：硬币——制造硬币——制造、创造。

Questions 32－37

● 题型归类：TRUE/FALSE/NOT GIVEN

● 题目解析：

题目编号	题目定位词	答案位置	题解
32	researchers, launched the field, other projects	B 段第 4 句	题目：那些开始 AI 领域的研究人员们曾经在别的项目一起工作过。 根据题目中的定位词，可以首先将答案的搜索范围缩小到 B 段，该段说研究人员虽然在 AI 项目上目标相同，但各有专攻。可是我们并不了解他们以前的工作关系，文章也没有交代。因此答案确定为 NOT GIVEN。
33	lowest point, 1985	C 段首句	题目：AI 在 1985 年到达最低潮。 涉及到 1985 年的只有 C 段首句，但题目的意思明显与原文背道而驰。Peak 是“达到顶点”的意思，故选 FALSE。
34	agent technology, neural networks	C 段末句	题目：研究代理技术要比研究神经网络花费多。 文章中出现这两个专有名词的地方只有 C 段末句，在这一句中，我们发现这几个研究领域是并列关系，同属于 specific sub-discipline 这个范畴，但文章中并没有说明谁的花费多，这也不是本文讨论的重点。故选 NOT GIVEN。
35	application of AI, success	E 段	题目：AI 的应用已经取得一定进展。 AI 的利好消息集中在 E、F 段里，这两段是对 AI 技术的支持。但是 F 段更多地是在讨论前景，只有 E 段里的 HNC 公司做出了实例，取得了成绩，比如侦查伪装车辆等，说明 AI 的应用确实取得了一定进展。故选 TRUE。
36	1967	C 段第 4 句	题目：在 1967 年以后，那些等着 AI 来解决的问题依然如旧。 涉及到 1967 年的只有 C 段第 4 句里马文·闵斯科的关于“人工智能”的断言。在那一年里，他说用不了多久，创造 AI 的问题就会得到实质性解决。而题目上说的是等着 AI 来解决的问题，两个“问题”不一样。故选 FALSE。
37	the film 2001: A Space Odyssey, contemporary ideas	G 段	题目：电影《2001 太空漫游》反映了当时人们对人工智能电脑潜力的理解。 在文章的最后，作者提到这部著名的电影，以电影的机器人主人公为例，说明它是当时乐观主义的体现：encapsulated the optimism of the 1960s that intelligent computers could be widespread by 2001。题目中的 AI computer 实际上就是原文中的 intelligent computers，而当时的 contemporary ideas 实际上就是 the optimism of the 1960s。故选 TRUE。

Questions 38-40

● 题型归类：Multiple Choices

● 题目解析：

题目编号	题目定位词	答案位置	题解
38	in the late 1980s	C 段末句	根据题目中出现的年代，我们将答案定位在 C 段。该段谈论的正是 AI 从顶点走向没落的过程，到了二十世纪八十年代后期，人们已经认识到了以前的盲目乐观，开始反思，并转而投向别的研究领域。B 项说，以前对 AI 的期望不现实，这正是人们当时的反思。A 项说 a general theory of AI would never be developed，但文中只是提到 elusive；C 项反映的正是当时的盲目乐观；而 D 项在文中找不到根据。
39	the reputation of AI	D 段第 4 句	该题较难，因为文中并没有具体谈到 AI 的名声（reputation），要做对这道题，考生必须了解两个知识点：1）move the goal-posts 意思是"不断变化原已认可的条件"，也就是 change perceptions；2）考生要明白 researchers joked that AI stood for "almost implemented" 的修辞手法。作者说，研究人员开玩笑说，AI 是"马上就要付诸实施"的缩写，这是对 AI 名声的一种损害。文章指出，正是不断变化认识，才导致 AI 得到这样一个"别名"。故选 A。
40	prospects, benefit from	F 段首句	该题目实际上是对 F 段首句变换了说法。原文说，factor that boost the prospects 其实是题目中的 benefit from。所以我们可以看到，该题不仅考查对细节的把握能力，也考查对语言的应用能力。投资商现在需要使用新技术而不是商业模式的公司，这正是他们的 priority。故选 D。

参考译文

人工智能的回归

人们又开始谈论电脑可以执行诸如解决问题和模式识别这样只有人类才能担当的任务了。

在淡出人们视线多年之后，"人工智能"（AI）这个名词好像又出现准备回归的态势了。在八十年代，"人工智能"火爆一时，但是到了九十年代就消失得无影无踪了。伴随着一部讲述机器人男孩的电影《人工智能》的公开上映，"人工智能"又准备重新回到人们的视野当中。这种情形激起了人们对于 AI 的广泛讨论，并且现在这个名词在电脑工业中又重新得到使用。如今，研究员、经理以及市场营销人员在用到这个名词时不带任何讽刺的意味，也不再使用引号了。同时，这个词也不再被天花乱坠地宣传。人们现在有理由把这个名词应用到一些依靠最早是 AI 研究人员开发出来的技术的产品上。诚然，这个名词要想完全恢复以前的风光，还要有很长的一段路要走，并且一些公司仍然拒绝使用它。但是，别的公司开始再次使用这个名词的事实证明，AI 已经不再是那个曾被视为雄心勃勃而又见效甚微的研究领域了。

在 1956 年的一次会议上，一群研究人员开始进入对这个领域的研究，并且创造出"人工智能"这个词。这群研究员包括马文·闵斯科，约翰·麦克卡斯，赫伯特·西蒙以及阿伦·纽威尔，他们日后成为该领域的领军人物。这个词给一个研究课题起了个引人入胜而又令人大开眼界的名字，这个研究课题涵盖诸如运算学、控制论、逻辑学和电脑科学这样的以前各不相同、互不相干的领域。这些学科领域的一个共同目标就是试图运用机器捕捉或者是模仿人类的能力。尽管如此，不同的研究人员以不同的方式专攻类似从语音识别到下象棋这样的不同问题；AI 只是从名字上把这些学科领域统一起来。但是这个名字确实迎合了当时公众的遐想。

大多数的研究人员都赞同，AI 在 1985 年前后曾达到一个顶峰。一群爱好科幻小说的人们被不断发展的电脑力量所激励，对 AI 抱有太高的期望。多年以来，AI 研究人员一直在暗示一次科学突破就近在咫尺。1967 年，马文·闵斯科指出，创造"人工智能"这个问题将在一代人的时间内得到实质性解决。医学诊断程序的雏形以及语音识别软件看起来正在不断取得进展。但是这只是一个虚假的前景。会思考的电脑和家用机器人最终没有能变成现实，随之而来的是反思思潮的高涨。印第安那大学的研究员大卫·里克指出："二十世纪八十年代早期人们过分乐观，所以当人们意识到问题的严峻时，就出现大量的削减现象。到了八十年代后期，'人工智能'这个名词已被许多研究人员抛弃，他们转而研究一些专门的准学科，例如神经系统、代理技术等，不一而足。"

具有讽刺意味的是，AI 在某种程度上受自己盛名之累。每当一个实实在在的问题被解决时，例如开发出一套可以实现在无人照看情况下降落飞机的系统，这个问题首先被理解成没有人工智能在里面起作用。正如里克博士总结道："只要是它起作用，它就肯定不是 AI。"这样不断变化原已认可的条件的后果是 AI 被认为是远不能实现商业化的"蓝天"研究。研究人员开玩笑说，AI 是"马上就要付诸实施"的缩写。同时，一些诸如语音识别、语言翻译和决策支持软件这样的把 AI 推向市场的技术并不被理解为 AI。其实，上述所说的这三项技术都是属于 AI 研究的范畴。

但是根据里克博士的说法，这种趋势已经开始发生逆转。受到政府部门支持的圣地亚哥 HNC 软件公司认为他们新的"人工智能"解决方法是至今被发现的最为有利、前途最为光明的方法。HNC 声称他们的系统建立在一串数量为 30 个的处理器的基础之上，可以用来在战场上侦查经过伪装的车辆，或者在嘈杂的背景中挑捡出一个声音信号，这样的任务人类可以完成的很好，但计算机却无能为力。里克博士说："不管他们的技术是否能够达到像他们所说的那样好，HNC 这样强调 AI 的应用这个事实本身就是一个有趣的进展。"

另外一个因素也在推动 AI 在不久的将来的美好前景，那就是投资者现在正在寻找那些使用智能技术，而不仅仅是使用聪明商业模式的公司，从而使自己脱颖而出。尤其值得一提的是，关于信息超载、人们饱受电子邮件和网页数量激增的困扰等问题意味着那些能够过滤和对信息进行分类的新技术有着更多的应用空间，而这正是 AI 所擅长的领域。这或许也意味着将有更多的人工智能公司崛起迎接这个挑战。

拍摄于 1969 年的电影《2001 太空漫游》由一个名叫 HAL 9000 的智能电脑主演。HAL 不仅能理解和讲英语，它还能下象棋，甚至还会唇读术。HAL 正是二十世纪六十年代乐观主义的映像，那时的人们相信智能电脑必定会在 2001 年实现普遍化。但是 2001 年已经过去，我们始终未见像 HAL 这样的电脑的踪影。虽然个人电脑系统能够下象棋或者是转录语音，但是机器智能这个广泛的理论仍然不可捉摸。但是，AI 和 HAL 的比较可能不再是那么重要，人们现在审视 AI 是看它能够做到什么，而不是看它在多大程度上能够比得上一部三十多年前的科幻电影。里克博士满怀希望地说："人们现在已经开始意识到这些系统也能做很多给人印象深刻的事情了。"

WRITING

WRITING TASK 1

a）*Question analysis, including discussion of main features, comparisons that need to be made, and possible misinterpretations of the question.*（审题）

"The map below is of the town of Garlsdon. A new supermarket（S）is planned for the town. The map shows two possible sites for the supermarket. Summarise the information by selecting and reporting the main features, and make comparisons where relevant."

Points to note.（审题要点）

1. Locations of S1 and S2.（选址 1 和选址 2 所在的位置。）
2. Zones—countryside, town center, housing, industry.（地区——农村、镇中心、住宅房屋、工业。）
3. Transport links—main roads and railways. Town center is a no-traffic zone.（交通连接——主干道路和铁路。镇中心是交通禁行区。）
4. Distance to other towns.（与其他市镇之间的距离。）
5. Population of Garlsdon and other towns.（加尔斯登以及其他市镇的人口。）

Main features and comparisons.（主要特征和比较）

1. S1 is in the countryside NW of Garlsdon.（选址 1 位于加尔斯登镇西北的乡村地区。）
2. S2 is in the town center.（选址 2 位于加尔斯登镇中心。）
3. The town center is surrounded by a housing zone.（镇中心被一片住宅区环绕。）
4. The two industrial zones are in the north and south of Garlsdon.（加尔斯登的两片工业区分别位于镇北部和南部。）
5. Transport links run near both S1 and S2.（选址 1 和选址 2 都邻近交通连接。）

Possible misinterpretations and problems.（审题误区）

1. Be sure to compare the locations S1 and S2.（务必对选址 1 和选址 2 所在的地点进行比较。）
2. Be sure not to mix the different zones.（确保不要把不同的地区混为一谈。）
3. Be sure to mention transport links, as these are a key factor in deciding where to locate any business.（务必提到交通连接，因为它是决定任何产业设施选址的重要因素。）
4. The map contains a lot of information. This is good because it means that it should be easy to write at least 150 words about it. However, it also means that you should not include every piece of information. The examiner knows that you only have 20 minutes to write the report and will not expect all the details.（地图包含了非常丰富的信息。这意味着要写出至少 150 词的短文难度应该不会太大。但是这也意味着不能试图在文中包含全部的信息。测试人知道你只有 20 分钟来写出这份报告，他们不会要求在文中看到所有的细节。）

b）*Suggested answer format, including contrast with possible unsuitable formats.*（写作思路）

The introduction should consist of rewriting "The map below is of the town of Garlsdon. A new supermarket（S）is planned for the town. The map shows two possible sites for the supermarket." The obvious changes are:（引言部分应该包含对题干说明"以下是加尔斯登镇的地图，这里计划要建起一家

新的超市,地图上显示了两处可能的选址"的改写。改写时明显可以采用的变化有:)

i) change ‘site’ to ‘location’.(将"选址"改成"地点"。)

ii) add that the map shows land use zones, transport links, and information about nearby towns.

Most candidates will examine each site in turn. This is completely correct. However, it would be a good idea to give an overview of Garlsdon (particularly zones and transport links) before doing this. (大部分考生会依次对两处选址进行描述和分析。这样做是完全正确的。不过如果在这样做之前先对整个加尔斯登镇的总体情况进行一个综述<尤其是地区划分和交通连接方面>,效果会更好。)

Most candidates will add an opinion about whether S1 or S2 is better. This is not required by the Question and should not be added. Hence, the report will not have a ‘conclusion’. (大部分考生会附上自己的观点——S1 与 S2,哪个会更好。这是题目没有作要求的,因此不应该加入。也就是说,这个报告应该是没有结论的。)

c) *Model answer.*(参考范文)

The map shows the town of Garlsdon (population 65,000), four types of land use (countryside, town center, housing, and industry), main road and rail connections to three nearby towns, and the two possible locations of a new supermarket for the town. (这是加尔斯登镇的地图<人口:6 万5 千>。地图体现了四种土地使用形式<农村、镇中心、住宅、以及工业区>,与附近市镇之间的主干道路和铁路连接,以及在镇里修建一家新的超级市场可能选择的两处位置。)

The town center is surrounded by a housing zone and there are two industrial zones—one in the north of the town and the other in the south. The area surrounding these three zones is countryside. A rail link runs through the town center, following a north-west to south-east direction. Three main roads run from the town center. One runs north-west to Hindon (population 10,000). Another goes south-east to Cransdon (population 29,000). A third goes south-west to Bransdon (population 15,000). (加尔斯登镇中心被一片住宅区环绕,此外镇里还有两片工业区——一片在镇北,另一片在镇南,这三片区域的周围是农村。镇中心有一条西北——东南走向的铁路线穿过,此外还有 3 条主干路从镇中心起始。其中一条往西北延伸,连接辛登镇<人口:1 万>。另一条往东南延伸,连接克兰斯登镇<人口:2 万9 千>。第三条往西南方向延伸,连接布兰斯登镇<人口:1 万 5 千>。)

The first possible site for the new supermarket (S1) is located in the countryside north-west of Garlsdon, between the main road to Hindon and the railway. Hence, it is accessible by both road and rail. The second possible site (S2) is located in the town center. As the town center is a no-traffic zone, it is inaccessible to road traffic. Although the town center is a no-traffic zone, there are the three roads to Hindon, Cransdon, and Bransdon leading from it. The railway line also runs through the town center, very close to S2. (新超市的可能选址 1 位于加尔斯登镇西北部的农村区,在连接辛登镇的主干路和铁路之间,因此通过铁路和公路都可以到这个位置。可能选址 2 位于镇中心。由于镇中心是交通禁行区,这里无法连接公路交通。但是尽管这里是交通禁行区,分别连接辛登镇、克兰斯登镇和布兰斯登镇的三条公路发自这里,此外铁路线也穿过镇中心,并且非常靠近选址 2。)

d) *Analysis of vocabulary and structures used in model answer, including possible mistakes made by candidates.*(语言分析)

This kind of task requires the use of different verbs to describe how things are linked. "A rail link runs through", "Another goes", "There are three roads . . . leading from it." These verbs will sometimes be used in the passive tense. "The town center is surrounded", "it is accessible", "is located in the countryside". Typical problems for candidates are that i) they have spent their time preparing for tasks that involve charts, not maps and ii) they do not use appropriate verbs correctly.(这种文章考查考生用不同的动词来描述事物连接方式的能力。范文中运用了"镇中心有一条铁路穿过","另一条往东南延伸","三条公路发自这里";还有一些以被动语态形式出现的动词:"镇中心被一片住宅区环绕","通过铁路和公路可以到达","位于农村区"。考生会出现的典型问题包括:1. 花了大量的时间来准备应对涉及图表的测试,而对地图没有准备;2. 用词不当。)

Remember to refer to S1 and S2 as possible sites for supermarkets, not actual ones.(记住,S1 和 S2 只是超市可能的选址,而非实际的选址。)

WRITING TASK 2

a) *Question analysis, including discussion of the points that need to be made in the essay, possible misinterpretations of the question, and brainstorming diagrams.*(审题)

"Some people think that a sense of competition in children should be encouraged. Others believe that children who are taught to co-operate rather than compete become more useful adults. Discuss both these views and give your own opinion."("有些人认为在儿童当中应该倡导一种竞争意识,然而也有人认为如果教导儿童如何共同协作,而不是相互竞争,那么他们会成长为更优秀的成年人。就这两种看法进行讨论,并且给出你自己的观点。")

Possible misinterpretations and problems.(审题误区)

1. The Question prompt clearly asks candidates to examine both points of view. Answers that do not do this will lose marks. However, it is not necessary to give equal weight to each point of view. In the model answers, each writer gives more weight to the view corresponding to his own.(题目很明确的要求考生考查两种观点。因此如果考生的文章中没有体现这一点就会丢分。不过考生倒是不必对两种观点给予同等程度的关注,在下面的范文中,作者分别侧重讨论了对应自己个人观点的看法。)
2. The Question prompt clearly asks candidates to give their own viewpoint. This can be stated at the beginning or at the end, or both. Candidates can take an extreme position or one, somewhere between. It is likely that most candidates will take a position in between, rather than extreme ones as in the model answers.(题目很明确的要求考生给出自己的观点。可以在文章开头提出,也可以在结尾提出,甚至于两处都提。考生的观点可以是在某一个极端,也可以是一个介于两端之间的位置。比较可能出现的情况是考生会选择一个介于两端之间的位置,而不是范文中体现的极端的观点。)
3. The Question prompt asks the candidates to assess how children being taught to compete and/or co-operate will affect them as adults, so make sure that your answers include reference to this.(题目要求考生分析儿童被教导来竞争和<或者>协作对他们成年之后的行为有怎样的影响。因此考生务必在文中涉及这方面的内容。)

b) *Suggested answer format, including contrast with possible unsuitable formats.*(写作思路)

For this question, the essay format should involve an introduction, two or three main paragraphs, and a conclusion. The introduction should be short and may or may not include the writer's opinion. Each of the main paragraphs should focus on a particular argument. However, these main paragraphs can either focus on one side of the argument or take into account the opposite point of view. The conclusion should be short and state the writer's opinion.(在答这个题目的时候,文章中间应该包括一个引入部分,两到三个主体段,以及一个结论段落。引入段应该很简短,可以包含考生的观点,也可以不包含。各主

体段应该分别着重讨论一个讨论的点。不过各主体段可以选择只是着重分析讨论点一方的观点，也可以选择同时考虑对立一方的观点。结论段应该很简短，并且包含作者的观点。）

The most important thing is to make sure that each of the main paragraphs focuses clearly on one argument. If several arguments are included in the same paragraph they could confuse the reader. It is also important that each argument be well developed, and having a separate paragraph for each will help the writer achieve this.（最重要的问题是要保证每个主体段清晰地集中关注一个讨论点。如果在同一个段落中出现了多个讨论点，那么读者会困惑不解。此外关于每个讨论点的分析应该很有组织地展开，如果采用一个独立的段落来讨论每个点对此会很有帮助。）

c）*Two model answers of around 300 words, each essay taking a different view.*（参考范文）

Model answer 1—agreeing with the first statement.（范文1，同意第一种观点）

The modern world is full of competition. Amongst adults, there is competition for jobs and amongst children there is competition at school. I believe that it is important to get children used to competition from an early age, so that they are better prepared for life.

Many of the things that people do early in life effect what they will be capable of later. For example, if a child does well at school, he or she will have a much greater chance of studying a subject he or she likes at university, and then going on to get a job in a field of his or her choice. This will not only have an effect on his or her working life, but also on his or her personal happiness. It will also have a direct effect on his or her capacity to earn money to satisfy his or her material needs.

There are, of course, situations where co-operation is necessary. However, usually, people co-operate with friends or colleagues in order to compete with others. For example, a sales team may be composed of several individuals, but their aim is to sell more than the sales teams from competing companies. Hence, learning to co-operate is useful, but learning to compete is far more important.

To conclude, it is vital that children are fully prepared for the modern world, a world in which competition is a key, inescapable feature of life. If they are not prepared for it, they cannot be expected to perform at their best.

译文：

当今世界充满了竞争。在成年人当中，我们有职场竞争；而对儿童来说，则有学校里的竞争。我认为应该让儿童从很小的时候就习惯竞争，让他们为将来的生活作好准备，这一点非常重要。

人们小时候所做的很多事情会决定他们成长之后能够应对怎样的情况。比如说，如果一个小孩在学校里表现良好，他就会更有机会在将来进入大学后学到自己喜欢的科目，并且随后根据自己的喜好找到一份职业。这不光是关系到一个人的工作生活，也关系到他的个人幸福。这也会直接影响到这个人是否有能力挣到足够的收入来满足自己的物质需要。

当然，在有些情形下，协作是有必要的。但是通常人们是在和自己的朋友或同事进行合作，从而与其他人竞争。比如说，一个销售团队可能是由好几个人组成的，但是他们的目标是要比其他公司的销售团队卖出更多的产品。因此，尽管学会协作有一定的作用，但是学会竞争却更重要。

因此，儿童为现代社会作好全面准备是至关重要的。在这个世界里，竞争是关键，是生活一个不可或缺的特质。如果儿童没有为此做好准备，他们就不可能达到最好的生活状态。

Model answer 2—agreeing with the second statement.（范文2，同意第二种观点）

Although competition is a part of life, I think that encouraging our children to co-operate will make them better people and more able to contribute to the society they live and work in.

Competition can be a good thing. It tells us who is the best at a particular activity and can even be entertaining, such as watching the Olympic Games or a talent show on TV. However, we often ignore the stress that competition puts on people. Top athletes are under great pressure to win. If they do not, they might lose sponsorship or access to the best facilities. The effects of this can lead to the use of performance enhancing drugs and/or injuries. If we encourage our children to compete, they might become people for whom the only important thing is victory.

If we encourage our children to co-operate, they will learn that winning isn't everything and that there are other pleasures in life. People generally feel great satisfaction from achieving things as part of a group. Group activities can help to create friendship between members of the group. Many children today are growing up in isolation, encouraged by their parents to view other children as competitors rather than as friends. Working together, people can achieve great things, such as sending a man into space or constructing an Olympic stadium.

In conclusion, although the modern world is competitive, we should try to encourage our children to co-operate, so that they do not suffer from too much pressure and learn the value of working with others to achieve more.

译文：

尽管竞争是生活的一部分，我还是认为鼓励我们的孩子们多参与协作才能够帮助他们成为更好的人，并且更有能力为他们生存和工作所在的这个社会做出贡献。

竞争是有它的积极作用的。它可以告诉我们在某一个特定的活动当中谁是最好的。它甚至是有娱乐价值的，比如奥运会或是电视上的才艺比赛节目。但是我们常常忽略了竞争对人们施加的压力。顶级的运动员需要承受巨大的追求获胜的压力。如果他们失败的话，他们可能或失去赞助或是使用最好的器材设施的机会。而这种压力可能会导致运动员使用能提高表现的药物和（或是）引起伤病。如果我们鼓励孩子们去竞争，他们可能会成为一群只看重胜利的人。

如果我们鼓励孩子们去协作，他们就会知道胜利并不能代表一切，生活中还有很多其他的快乐。在作为团队的一部分得到某种成就的时候，人们普遍会感受到极大的满足感。团队活动能够促进团队成员之间的友谊。现在很多小孩都是在孤立和隔离中成长，他们的父母会促使他们把周围的同龄人视为竞争对手而不是朋友。而在齐心协力工作时，人们可以实现更伟大的目标，例如把人类送到太空中或是修建起庞大的奥林匹克体育馆。

总的来说，尽管当今世界充满了竞争，我们仍然应该鼓励孩子们参与协作。这样他们就不需要去承受过大的压力，并且学会与他人合作，实现更加伟大的目标。

d) *Analysis of vocabulary and structures used in model answer, including possible mistakes made by candidates.*（语言分析）

"For example, if a child does well at school, he or she will have a much greater chance of studying a subject he or she likes at university, and then going on to get a job in a field of his or her choice." Notice that the writer doesn't just use 'will'. The writer expresses his/her exact meaning.（"比如说，如果一个小孩在学校里表现良好，他或她就会更有机会在将来进入大学以后学到自己喜欢的科目，并且随后根据自己的选择找到一份职业"。注意作者不只是用了"会"，作者表达了自己确切的意思。）

"There are, of course, situations where co-operation is necessary. However, usually, people co-operate with friends or colleagues in order to compete with others. For example, a sales team may be composed of several individuals, but their aim is to sell more than the sales teams from competing companies.

Hence, learning to co-operate is useful, but learning to compete is far more important." Notice how the writer structures the argument in this paragraph. The first sentence admits that co-operation is needed. The second sentence points out why people co-operate. The third sentence gives an example and the fourth gives the writer's conclusion. ("当然,在有些情形下,协作是有必要的。但是通常人们是在和自己的朋友或同事进行合作,从而与其他人竞争。比如说,一个销售团队可能是由好几个人组成的,但是他们的目标是要比其他公司的销售团队卖出更多的产品。因此,尽管学会协作有一定的作用,但是学会竞争却更重要。"注意作者是怎样在这个段落表达了看法。第一个句子承认了协作是有必要的。第二个句子指出了人们为什么要协作。第三句举出了协作的例子,第四句则表明了作者的结论。)

The writer of the second model answer does the same thing. "Competition can be a good thing. It tells us who is the best at a particular activity and can even be entertaining, such as watching the Olympic Games or a talent show on TV. However, we often ignore the stress that competition puts on people. Top athletes are under great pressure to win. If they do not, they might lose sponsorship or access to the best facilities. The effects of this can lead to the use of performance enhancing drugs and/or injuries. If we encourage our children to compete, they might become people for whom the only important thing is victory." (第二篇范文的作者也采用了同样的策略。"竞争是有它的积极作用的。它可以告诉我们在某一个特定的活动当中谁是最好的。它甚至是有娱乐价值的,比如奥运会或是电视上的才艺比赛节目。但是我们常常忽略了竞争对人们施加的压力。顶级的运动员需要承受巨大的追求获胜的压力。如果他们失败的话,他们可能或失去赞助或是使用最好的器材设施的机会。而这种压力可能会导致运动员使用能提高表现的药物和<或是>引起伤病。如果我们鼓励孩子们去竞争,他们可能会成为一群只看重胜利的人"。)

SPEAKING

a) *Question analysis, including possible misinterpretations of the questions.*

Do you prefer relaxing at home or going out in the evening? Why?

Many candidates will answer 'yes' or 'no' to this question, which is obviously incorrect.

When you go out for an evening, what do you like to do?

Remember to use the structure 'to do something' in your answer. You may also need to mention places and people in your answer.

How popular is this with other people in your country?

This Question continues from the previous one ('this'). Be sure not to switch the topic of conversation. The Question also refers to people in your country, not your friends or family.

Is there any kind of entertainment you do not like? Why? Why not?

Be careful to use the negative correctly—I don't like ...

Describe one of your friends.

This is a very straightforward Question and shouldn't present any major problems. Remember to describe just **one** friend! Also remember not to mix up 'he' and 'she'!

What do you think are the most important qualities for friends to have?

Almost all candidates will say 'honesty' in answer to this question, so it might pay to be original by choosing a different answer or by developing your 'honesty' answer in an interesting way.

Which are more important to people, their family or their friends? Why?

When you answer this question, be very careful with absolutes. Many candidates will say that family members or friends 'will' or 'cannot' do something. Take care not to do this.

What do you think causes friendships to break up?

There could be numerous reasons for this and you might find it useful to refer back to your answer about important qualities of friends.

What other types of relationship, apart from friends or family, are important in people's lives today?

Note that the Question says 'apart from friends or family'. Most candidates will talk about friends and/or family, meaning that they are not answering the question.

Have relationships with neighbours where you live changed in recent years? How?

The most important thing here is to talk about any **changes** there have been. Be careful to use the past tense and present perfect tense as appropriate.

How important do you think it is for a person to spend some time alone? Why? Why not?

Again, use words and phrases like 'very/quite important' to express your opinion.

b*) *Shortlist of useful vocabulary that candidates could use in their answers to each Question and brainstorming diagram for Part 2 questions.

Do you prefer relaxing at home or going out in the evening? Why?

Extrovert, outgoing, alone, shy, quiet, make/spend time with friends, stay out late, get up early, spend money/time.

When you go out for an evening, what do you like to do?

Café, bar, club, chat, relax, give advice, discuss problems, have a drink, eat some food/snacks, meet new people.

How popular is this with other people in your country?

Quite/very popular, prefer, rather, waste of time/money, stay at home.

Is there any kind of entertainment you do not like? Why? Why not?

Going to bars/clubs, watching sports/TV/films, playing sports/computer games, reading.

Describe one of your friends.

The process for answering this Question is similar to describing any person, such as a person you admire (see previous test).

Job—student, accountant, manager, teacher, secretary, taxi driver.

Where he/she works/lives—Beijing, university, office, CBD(中央商务区), factory.

Appearance—quite tall, slim, average build, long hair, pony tail, fashionable, dresses smartly.

Character—very quiet, generous, honest, kind, strange, polite.

Interests—going to cafés, reading, watching TV, playing computer games, surfing the Internet.

What do you think are the most important qualities for friends to have?

Honesty, trust, friendship, patience, understanding, kindness, fun, humorous.

Which are more important to people, their family or their friends? Why?

Basis of society, family members, support, look to someone, guidance, problems, advice.

What do you think causes friendships to break up?

Argument, disagreement, scream at each other, call each other names, listen to each other carefully.

What other types of relationship, apart from friends or family, are important in people's lives today?

People you work with, colleagues, boss, problems at work, appreciation, feel good, good feeling, do a favour for someone.

Have relationships with neighbours where you live changed in recent years? How?

Change a lot/little, (close) neighbourhood, help each other out, private people, mix with the other neighbours.

How important do you think it is for a person to spend some time alone? Why? Why not?

Quite/very important, study, think about problems, hobbies, reading, collecting stamps, isolated, share ideas/views.

c) Two model answers for each question.

Do you prefer relaxing at home or going out in the evening? Why?

I prefer staying at home. I'm a shy person and don't make friends easily. Of course, I do go out sometimes, but usually only to a quiet place with a few friends—you know, like a café.

I prefer going out, but I can't go out every evening because I have to get up early in the mornings. Besides, I don't have enough money to spend on going out too often. If I go out, I usually go to a bar with friends, or I go alone and try to make new friends.

When you go out for an evening, what do you like to do?

As I said, I go to a café. My friends and I chat, normally about our studies or what's been in the news. We also give each other advice about any problems we have.

As I mentioned, I enjoy going to bars. I like ones which are lively—you know, plenty of people and some good music. I love meeting new people and getting to know them. Of course, I normally have two or three beers too!

How popular is this with other people in your country?

I don't think it's very popular. A lot of people seem to prefer staying at home rather than going out. I think that they feel going out in the evening is a waste of money. Or maybe they're even shyer than I am!

I think going to bars and clubs is quite popular, but most people think they are bad places. I know many young people whose parents tell them that only bad people go to bars. I have to disagree. When you go to a bar, there's no rule that says you have to drink alcohol or find a boyfriend or girlfriend. I just go to relax and meet people.

Is there any kind of entertainment you do not like? Why? Why not?

I don't like watching sports. I know that most people do, but I think it's really boring. I don't mind playing sports. Playing sports is good for keeping fit, but just sitting and watching is something I find pointless.

I don't like playing computer games. I don't find them educational and people often play them for hours and hours on their own. I would much rather spend my free time with people than trying to kill aliens or whatever.

Describe one of your friends.

Actually, I don't have many friends, so choosing one isn't too difficult! Her name is Cindy and she lives here in Beijing. She is a student, like me, but we study at different universities. She studies literature, probably because she loves books. Her room is full of them! She is quite tall for a Chinese girl and average build. She has long hair which she ties in a pony tail. She is very quiet. Sometimes, when we go to a café, we just sit across the table from one another reading—not talking at all. You won't be surprised to hear that she doesn't have a boyfriend. She doesn't dress very fashionably—just the usual jeans and T-shirt. She looks so average and is so quiet that many people don't notice her when we go to a party.

I'd like to describe my best friend, Keith. He is a strange young man, but very popular with my classmates. He spends a lot of time on the Internet, finding strange facts to tell us. That's why he's so popular—he always has something interesting to say. He's slim, but not very tall. He almost always dresses smartly—even wearing a tie to class! He's polite to everyone and I don't think I've ever seen him get angry. Generally, he's quite a good student, but he doesn't get the best marks in class. I think that's because he spends so much time looking for information that we are tested on in class.

What do you think are the most important qualities for friends to have?

I think that friends need to be honest with each other. If you can't trust your friends, who can you trust? If your friendship is good, you can tell friends things that are true but that they may not like to hear. For example, you may need to tell a friend that her clothes are unsuitable or something.

I think that friends need to be patient with each other. Nobody is perfect and your friends are sure to occasionally say or do things that you don't like or disagree with. I think that understanding that people make mistakes and that people are different is very important.

Which are more important to people, their family or their friends? Why?

I think that their family is more important. Families are the basis of society and family members are usually in the best position to support each other. I think this is particularly true for young people, who often look to their parents for guidance and support when they have problems.

I think friends are more important. Very often, parents just tell their children what to do without understanding that the world young people grow up in today is different to that of 20 or 30 years ago. Friends understand the situation better and can offer more realistic advice.

What do you think causes friendships to break up?

I said before that honesty is the most important thing in a friendship. If people find that they cannot be honest with each other, the friendship is almost sure to end. If you are honest, I think people will respect that, even if they disagree with you.

I think that silly arguments are the biggest cause of friendships breaking up. By 'silly', I mean arguments over things that are unimportant. I've seen a lot of friends start arguing over something like that and, before they know it, they are screaming at each other, calling each other names. I think that this wouldn't happen so often if people listened to each other more carefully.

What other types of relationship, apart from friends or family, are important in people's lives today?

Well, there are relationships with people that you work with. I mean, you should be careful to get on well with your colleagues and your boss, to make sure that there are no problems at work.

I know that this sounds a little idealistic, but I think that people should try to make every relationship a pleasant experience. For example, be nice to the waitress who brings your food. A little appreciation will make her feel good. Maybe then she will pass on that good feeling to others, and so on. Besides, you never know when you might need that waitress to do a favour for you. Every little relationship is important.

Have relationships with neighbours where you live changed in recent years? How?

No, I don't think so. My neighbourhood is a very close one—everyone knows everyone else. People try to help each other out when they can. I'm not saying that there aren't problems, but relationships have always been very good.

Yes, they have. A lot of new people have moved into the neighbourhood and some of them are very private people who don't mix with the other neighbours. Relationships used to be very close, but now most people don't even know what jobs their neighbours do or what their hobbies are.

How important do you think it is for a person to spend some time alone? Why? Why not?

I think it's very important. I need to spend time alone to study and to think about any problems I might have. Most of my hobbies are things that a person usually does alone, like reading or collecting stamps.

I think it's important to have some time alone, but I think it's much more important to spend time with friends and other people. If you spend too much time alone, you become isolated and don't share ideas and views with others.

d) Text boxes showing how sentences can be completed. For example:

I don't have enough ...	money to spend on going out.
	time to go out often.
	energy to go out after work.

A lot of people seem to prefer ...	staying at home	in the evening.
	going to bars and clubs	
	watching TV	

He ... She ...	almost always	dresses smartly.
	usually	reads in a café.
	occasionally	spends time surfing the Internet.

I think that friends need to ...	be honest with each other.
	be patient with each other.
	have similar hobbies and interests.

I think that family is ...	more important than friends.
	as important as friends.
	not as important as friends.

Test 4

LISTENING

SECTION 1

谈话场景:学生租房咨询中心。
人物关系:咨询人员与欲租房的学生。
谈话话题:填写租房申请表。

词汇注释

fix up sb. with 为某人安排某事物
present *adj.* 现在的,当前的
definite *adj.* 明确的;一定的
extension *n.* 增加的一段时间;延长期
permit *n.* 许可证;通行证
occupation *n.* 职业
advanced *adj.* 高阶的;高级的
intermediate *adj.* 中级的
requirement *n.* 需求,要求,必要条件,需要的东西,要求必备的条件
diet *n.* 通常吃的食物;日常食物
vegetarian *n.* 素食者
facility *n.* [常作 facilities] 能够或易于做某事的环境,设备
en suite *n.* (法)(指房间等)构成独立单元
yard *n.* 院子
peaceful *adj.* 和平的,平静的,安宁的
serious *adj.* 认真的
obvious *adj.* 明显的;显而易见的
dependent *adj.* 依靠的,依赖的,由…决定的,随…而定的
approximate *adj.* 近似的,大约的
intended *adj.* 计划的;打算的;意欲的
maximum *n.* 最大量,最大限度

交际与语言表达

1. 本段对话是围绕一名想在英国租房的外国留学生展开的,重点在于如何填写相关租房表格,这些问题可能都是准备雅思考试的学生将来在英国将要面对的问题。
2. I **understand** you help fix up students with host families. 我听说你们帮助学生们安排住宿。这句话里的 understand 不能理解为"理解、了解"等意思,而是为了在交谈中展开对话而使用的交际常用语。说话人在使用这个词时,通常是已经了解到了一定信息,希望得到对方肯定的答复。
3. . . . are you interested in. . . ? Yes. . . "您是否想了解……?""是的……"在这段简短的对话中,双方都是只说了一半。这也是口语中经常见到的情形,说话双方对对方要说的意思心领神会。考生在听到这样的对话时,要有意识地自动根据已知信息补全对话的空白。
4. So when would be the best time to **catch** you? 那么最好是什么时候跟你联系呢? catch 这个词在这里不是"抓住、赶上"的意思,而是电话用语中的常用词汇,表示"与某人联系"。如 well, I catch you at last. 哎呀,我终于跟你联系上了。
5. I think I'd like to say "advanced" but my written work is **below** the level of my spoken, so I suppose it's intermediate. 我原想说是"高级的",但是我的笔头功夫不如我的口语,所以我想应该是"中等"吧。黑体标示的 below 在这里的意思是 not as good as,含有比较的意味。
6. Shall I say you are? It's probably easier that way. 我能写你就是(素食者)吗? 那样可能会更方便一些。申请者提到自己算是一个素食者(nearly a vegetarian),但咨询人员觉得有些为难,就劝他

不如就填是一个素食者,这样更方便一些。这句话有一些成分被省略,考生要通过上下文把握。咨询者听口音像是中国人,东方人的思维总是笼统含糊,总喜欢说“基本上”、“差不多”这样的话;而西方人思维偏重于精确具体。这段对话也是中西方思维方式的体现。

7. We usually have lots of families **up** there. 我们通常在那边有很多房源。考生应该掌握 up 这个小词的用法:up 在被用作是方向性副词时,通常表示“朝着重要地方或在重要地方”,比如说“去(在)伦敦”;或是“在一个国家或地方的北部”,比如本句中 up 的用法。同样的道理,“去小地方”或是“去南部”应该用 down。
8. I would prefer my own facilities—“**en suite**”, is that right? 我希望不跟别人混用,“单间”,是这样说的吗? 可能考生对 en suite 这个词不熟悉,它其实最早是一个法语词。英语中的单词有很多是法语词转化而来,但在口语中不是很常见。
9. Anyway, obviously all this is partly **dependent on** how much you're **willing to** pay. 总之,很显然,这一切一定程度上取决于你愿意付多少钱? 这句话中有三处值得我们注意:1) anyway 在这里是一个语气词,没有什么实质意义;2) be dependent on 的意思是“取决于,由……决定”,相当于 depend on;3) be willing to do sth 的意思是“心甘情愿、愿意做某事”。
10. Well I don't think we'd **have any problem finding** something for you. 那我肯定能够帮你安排。have problem/difficulty (in) doing sth.,做某事有困难。这里的 in 可以省略。咨询人员在听到这位学生报出的价格之后,觉得为他安排房子肯定没问题。

考题解析

Question 1

这类填表题难度一般不大,因为表格里面的问题基本上是顺着说话人的思路和对话设置的,并且对于大多数出题点说话人都会加以强调或解释,考生只要跟上说话人的节奏和逻辑就能填对答案。该题不难,题目中的问题在材料中都是原文重现。只是涉及到地名时,考生可能听不出来这个专有名词的拼写,可能写出一个音同字不同的单词来。其实,需要考生填写的地名一般都很常见,比如本题中的“14 Hill Road”,就是门牌号加街道名称。

Question 2

该题稍有难度,很多考生可能不知道问话人说的 catch 就是题目中的 contact 的意思,同时题目中的 NB 也难住了很多考生,它是书面语中一个常见的缩写,意思是“注意,留心”,用来提醒别人。另外,那位学生回答时也是含糊不清,首先是加了一个插入语 let me see,然后又给出一个省略的回答:half-past。考生在填写答案时,“between 9 and 9:30”或是直接“9 - 9:30”都是可以接受的。相比之下,后者更节省时间。

Question 3

首先,考生可能不知道题干上的 intended 的意思,它其实等同于原文中的 planning on。其次,说话人在同一句中给出两个不同的时间,再加上句子中的转折词 but,这可能也会使部分考生迷惑,认为考点肯定是在 but 之后的内容。但说话人紧接着说要申请延长期,延长至原先计划的一年,所以答案依旧是 1year,注意不要写成原文中的 a year。

Question 4

这道题说话人同样给出两个相互关联的说法来迷惑考生,实际上,这句话关键点在于最后一句,由 so 引导出总结性观点:说话人虽然口语不错(advanced),但笔头功夫比不上口语,所以自认为是“中等”(intermediate)。

这两道题告诉我们,当听到两个或两个以上备选答案时,不要着急,细心抓住关键词,综合考虑说话人给出的所有条件。

Question 5

这道题不难,虽然也有一个干扰项 in the center,但很容易排除,因为说话人说得很清楚:那是他学习的地方,而不是住的地方。填空时要注意 North-West 的大写形式,因为它们都是方位词。

Question 6

很多考生可能知道 vegetarian 这个词的意思,但不知道如何拼写。其实素食运动在西方也算是时尚之一,多留意西方报刊读物就会经常见到这个词。

Question 7

在提到其他要求时,说话人特地提到 a real garden,并补充说明他可以在那里安静地坐着,同时他还强调了 garden 与 yard 的区别,所以考生应该不难答对。在填空时,考生可以省去定冠词 a 和前置形容词 real,只留下 garden,这样难度也降低了。

Question 8

解题时考生如果能抓住 prefer 一般会跟介词 to 的话,就能迅速与题目挂钩,剩下的都是照搬原文了。另外,对方用了相近意思的表达:no other guest 来重复这一信息。no other 不正是 only 吗?

Question 9

该题与上面的 3、4 题一样,原文中含有多个干扰项。其实该题不难,既然题目要求是 maximum(最多的),那不就是 a hundred 吗?但是有的考生可能不认识 maximum 这个单词,它的反义词是 minimum(最小的)。

Question 10

该题不难,学生说要两个星期之后搬家,咨询人员就依当天(10th)算出了日子:23rd March。

SECTION 2

谈话场景:足球俱乐部会议。

人物关系:说话人为会议主持人。

谈话话题:通知下个赛季的活动内容及介绍新的委员会成员。

词汇注释

season *n.* (一年中有某事物或有某活动的)时期,时候	**fee** *n.* 会费
competition *n.* 竞赛;比赛	**equipment** *n.* 装备,设备,器材
clubhouse *n.* 俱乐部会所	**volunteer** *v.* 自愿做某事
picnic *n.* 野餐	**newsletter** *n.* (定期发给俱乐部、社团等成员的)简讯
presentation *n.* (尤指在仪式上)授予	**former** *adj.* 从前的;以前的
prize *n.* 奖励;奖项	**supervise** *v.* 监督;管理;引导
treasurer *n.* 财务员;出纳员	**refreshment** *n.* 小吃;点心

交际与语言表达

1. 雅思听力第二篇一般都是独白,本篇独白虽然是足球俱乐部会议主持人的会议发言,但并没有涉及太多的足球术语,用词较为简单,直白流畅,逻辑清楚。
2. Now I'd like to **take a few minutes** to tell you about some changes to the Soccer Club for the coming season. 现在,我利用一点时间给大家说说下个赛季俱乐部的一些变化。西方人发言时一般直奔

主题,并且通常说话时都有一定的套路,除了句子中的说法之外,还有:I would like to **use/avail myself of** this opportunity to say... 我想利用这个机会说一说……。

3. In the senior competition, there'll be four teams, **the same as** last year, and their games will be played on **Saturday afternoons** starting at 2:30, **no sorry**, it will be a 2 o'clock start,... 在高级别比赛中,与去年一样,将有四支队伍参加,他们的比赛定于每个周六下午的2:30,呃,对不起,应该是2点开始。这句话中有三点值得我们注意:1)如果两件事物完全相同,可以用the same as,其前还可用exactly, virtually, nearly等修饰,如:She's doing **the same** course **as** me. 她和我修同样的课;2)如果星期几和上/下午后面加复数,则表示这个时间已经固定下来,成为规律了;3)当说话人有口误(slip of tongue)时,说话人一般会说:I'm sorry/I beg your pardon/excuse me 等加以纠正。
4. **many thanks** to Robert for taking on the job of President. 非常感谢罗伯特承担主席这个职务。在表达"感谢,欣赏"的时候,除了用I am grateful to..., I extend my gratitude to..., thank you for...等之外,我们还可以使用句中的表达,把thanks当作名词使用。同样地,当我们表达歉意的时候,也可以说my apologies to sb for...。
5. If you have any information that may be useful, please **let David know** so that it can be included in these newsletters. 如果你有能派上用场的信息的话,请告诉大卫,这样他可以加到简报里去。在要求别人告诉某人信息、消息时,用let sb know要比please tell sb有礼貌,更地道。比如:If you have any problem here, please let us know so that we can make another arrangement. 如果您在这里有任何问题的话,请告诉我们,我们好另做安排。
6. 请注意主持人在介绍四位委员会成员时所使用的不同说法:1)let me **welcome** Robert Young, the new President... 2)next we **have** Gina Costello, she's the treasurer,... 3)Then **there's** David West who has volunteered to be the club secretary,... 4)also I'd like to **introduce** you to Jason Dokic who is the Head Coach. 从上面的不同的说法来看,与汉语不同,英语语言讲究变换多样(variety),不喜重复。
7. and we are very lucky to have such **an experienced coach and former player** at our club. 并且在俱乐部里能拥有这样一位经验丰富的教练和前运动员,我们感到很幸运。请注意:这里的教练员和前运动员都是指同一人,因为前面只有一个冠词。考生不要误以为出现两个不同的人物。

考题解析

Question 11

该题几乎就是原文的重现,结构与原文相同,并且clubhouse这个词说话人重复了两遍,相信大多数考生都能做对。

Questions 12–13

这两道题有些难度。在考试中,题目短小的反而会难一些,因为它里面包含的信息量少,不容易在原文中捕捉到出处。第12题问道"第一次活动是什么",许多考生见到这道题都有些摸不着头脑。其实说话人在发言的前半部分正好介绍了下个赛季一头一尾的活动:1)We hope to **begin** the season **with** a picnic,我们将以一次野餐来开始我们这个赛季;2)the last week of the season we usually have a dinner and presentation of prizes to the players,赛季的最后的一个星期我们将聚餐,给队员颁奖。这样一来,我们就知道了这两道题的答案。

另外,有些考生可能没听懂presentation of prizes是什么意思,只听到了dinner和to the players,所以虽然半信半疑,但还是硬着头皮把第13题的答案写成了dinner。

Questions 14–17

对于这类分门别类对照填表题,考生一定要事先看题目,知道说话人要谈论几类情况,这样才不至于把不同情况的细节混成一团。14 题的答案稍有干扰，说话人说 ten teams，**instead of** five，in the junior competition，考生只要弄清这两个数字的逻辑关系就能答对。这几道题都不是很难，只要抓住细节就能填对。

Questions 18–20

这三道题是根据主持人对委员会成员的介绍而设的，主持人介绍每一位成员都会简单交待一下他们的工作职责，只是在各段落中的位置不同，Gina 的工作职责在开始就交待了，David 的职责是在中间位置，而 Jason 的工作职责则放在最后才说，考生要注意听关键动词，因为动词之后的不定式就是答案所在，如：to send out newsletters，to supervise the teams 等。

SECTION 3

谈话场景：商学院课堂讨论。
人物关系：导师与两个学生。
谈话话题：讨论某公司面临的困境以及提出解决办法。

词汇注释

case study 案例研究	**assume** *v.* 假定；设想；以为
assessment *n.* 评价；评估	**dramatic** *adj.* 激动人心的；给人深刻印象的
track *v.* 追踪	**ambitious** *adj.* 有雄心的
summarize *v.* 概述，总结，摘要而言	**analysis** *n.* 分析
despite *prep.* 尽管；不论	**option** *n.* 选择；选项
campaign *n.*（政治或商业性）活动	**telecommunication** *n.* 电讯
expansion *n.* 扩充；扩张	**overcome** *v.* 战胜，克服，胜过，征服
competition *n.* 竞争；竞赛	**outline** *v.* 概述(某事物)
stall *v.*（使）停转，（使）停止，迟延	**intrinsic** *adj.*（指价值、性质）固有的，内在的，本质的
strike *n.* 罢工	**innovative** *adj.* 创新的；革新的
colossal *adj.* 巨大的；庞大的	**foregone conclusion** 可预料的必然结果
machinery *n.*（总称）机械；机器	**boost** *n.* 推进；促进
define *v.* 定义；详细说明	**outdated** *adj.* 过时的；不流行的
eventual *adj.* 最终；最后	**inevitable** *adj.* 不可避免的；必然的
be credited to 归因于	**realistic** *adj.* 现实的；实事求是的
favorable *adj.* 令人高兴的；有利的	**expectation** *n.* 期待，预料，指望，展望
cautious *adj.* 谨慎的；小心的	**innovation** *n.* 改革；创新

交际与语言表达

1. 本段对话是商学院导师与学生之间的课堂讨论，中间有许多商业术语，并且句子较为复杂，带有正式文体的色彩，充满思想的交锋，但这正是课堂讨论的特点。
2. It's interesting because they are **in the middle of** problems at the moment and I want you to **track** how they deal with them. 这个案例很有趣，因为他们现在正忙于解决这些问题，我想让你们查查他们是怎样应付的。本句中的 in the middle of 原意是“在……中间”，用在这里是把它的意思引申开来，表示他们现在正困在这些问题当中；而 track 原意是“追踪”，用到这里等于“investigate，

look into, scrutinize"。

3. **Having read through** the case study, can you just summarize what the problems were **that** Box Telecom had to **take on board**? 你已经通读了这个案例,现在能总结出那些伯克斯电讯公司应该承担责任的问题吗? 这句话有三点需要我们掌握:1) Having read through... 是动名词作状语。因为 read 这个动作已经先于谓语动词 summarize 之前完成,所以这里使用动名词的完成体;2) 黑体标示的 that 引导一个限制性定语从句,修饰 the problems,但是这个从句被后置,没有紧挨着先行词。这是因为这个定语从句太长,而主句,即 what 引导的作宾语的名词性从句太短。为了不造成歧义,就把定语从句后置;3) take on board 的意思是"承担(责任);承认(问题)",如:I'm too busy to take this new job on board at the moment. 我太忙,目前不能接受这项新工作。
4. **On top of** that immediate problem, **what** had also happened over the last two years was that, although they had invested in an expansion plan, they had to **face up to** increased competition. 除了这个直接的问题,过去两年尽管他们也在一个扩张计划上投资,但面临的竞争还是不断加剧。这句话虽然不长,但包含了四个重要的语法点:1) on top of 原意为"在……之上",但在这里的意思是"加在某事物之上;除了某事物之外";2) 黑体标示的 what 引导一个作主语的名词性从句;3) although 引导一个让步状语从句,却被当作一个插入语,夹在名词性从句与它的宾语之间;4) face up to 的意思是"诚实而勇敢地承认和处理令人不快的或困难的事物",如:He must face up to the fact that he is no longer young. 他应该勇于正视自己不再年轻这一事实。
5. At the same time, their longer-term problems, **which** were affecting their market share, where eventually **credited to** poor training—and **having looked at** the details in their last report I think that's right. 同时,他们的那些影响市场份额的长期问题,最终归因于糟糕的培训。我仔细看了他们最后一份报告,认为我这个观点是正确的。有些考生可能在听的时候,不知道这句话在说些什么,它包含了多个插入语及非谓语动词成分。其中,1) 黑体标示的 which 引导一个非限制性定语从句修饰 problems,把主句分隔开来,这可能是为了强调这些问题的严重后果;2) 黑体标示的动词短语 be credited to 许多考生可能也是第一次见到,其实它是 credit sth. to sb./sth.(把某事物归功于某人/某事物)的被动形式,而且意思也发生了变化;3) 最后用黑体标注的动名词结构作原因状语,修饰主句 I think that's right。说话人在说最后一句话时,稍稍停顿了一下,虽然没有连词引导,但是我们通过他的语气判断出这一句话是对前面观点的补充说明,是对自已观点可信度的补充说明。
6. well, you **mustn't** always assume that **dramatic** problems require **dramatic** solutions. 你可不能认为重病还得下猛药。mustn't 表示"禁止、不许",与其他情态动词相比语气更为强烈;英语语言虽然不喜重复,鼓励使用同义词,但是在同一句子中可以出现重复,并且两个相同的形容词用在这里,修辞意味更加强烈。
7. but a more ambitious approach, and **one which** I think would have more chance of success, would be to alter how they're running things—the management layers and the processes. 但是还有一个更加有雄心的办法,我也认为这个办法胜算更大,那就是变更他们现在的管理方法,即管理层和管理流程。在口语中,说话人因为不像书面语那样严谨,经常会对上一句话补充说明,所以会经常使用如黑体标示的同位语等手段。值得注意的是,这里的同位语 one 后面还接了一个定语从句来修饰。除了同位语来补充说明以外,还会用到如:I mean, in other words, let me put it in another way 等这样的短语插入补充说明;或者,干脆像本句中这样,直接加一个破折号说明。在考试中,那些被补充说明、着重强调的内容通常是试题的出题点。
8. I think it can but it's not a **foregone conclusion unless** they manage to attract the right level of investment. 我认为它能(重新振兴),但是如果他们不能吸引到足够的投资,那么能否这样还不好说。在这个句子里,我们首先注意黑体标示的习语 foregone conclusion 意为"可预料的必然结果",如:

The outcome of the election is a foregone conclusion. 选举结果已在预料之中。另外,黑体标注的 unless 引导一个条件状语从句,表示"除非……",主句为否定句的居多;最后,句子开头的 I think it can 后面实际上是省略了谓语动词,这也是对上文 Karin 的话的对应,如果补充完整,应该是 I think it can (recover)。

9. Personally I think the stock market is to **blame.** 我个人认为股票市场应该有责任。不定式的语态分为主动和被动两种。一般来说,当不定式的逻辑主语表示动作的执行者时,不定式应用主动语态;逻辑主语表示动作的承受者时,应该用被动语态。但有时不定时主动式表示被动意义,本句中黑体标示的就是这样的例子,这主要是因为在有些不定式作补语的句型中,不定式的主动式表示被动意义,如:The reason is not far to seek. 原因不难找。

10. And I **disagree with** you **about** the advertising campaign. 还有,在那个广告宣传方面我不敢苟同。这句话里含有一个重要词组,disagree/agree with sb. about sth. 在某事物上与某人持不同/相同意见。类似的表达还有:talk to sb. about sth. 等等。

考题解析

Questions 21–22

这里的图表填空题是针对 Karin 和 Jason 的回答设置的,其中 Karin 回应了导师关于 Box Telecom 公司出现的问题的提问,而 Jason 则解答了导师关于该公司出现这些问题的原因的提问,各有分工。考生必须先听清楚导师的提问,才能有的放矢,更有针对性。

导师要求 Karin 来 summarize the problems,有的考生可能没有听懂 take on board 在这里的意思,但这并不影响做题,只要听清 problems 即可。Karin 的回答包括三个方面,并且每一个方面都有并列或递进连词来引导,考生要注意抓住这些连词,按图索骥寻找答案。在解答 21 题时,考生要抓住 first 这个信息词,然后听到动词词组 suffer from,就知道距离答案不远了。但是有些考生可能没听懂 falling (下落、下降),与题干上的 drop 对不上号。

在解答 22 题时,词组 on top of 也会影响考生定位答案,考生没反应过来这就该说第二个原因了。但大多数的考生都知道原文中的 increasing 等于题干上的 growing,所以这也提醒了考生答案的位置。

Questions 23–24

这两道题是根据 Jason 的回答设置的。考生可能不知道导师问话中的 define 是什么意思,但还是听到了 reason 这个题眼。第 23 题较难,因为答案前面并没有我们所熟悉的表次序的词语或连词出现,而且关键性动词词组 set back 也不是我们所熟知的用法,幸亏我们抓住了题干上的形容词 high,能与原文衔接上。

第 24 题较为容易,不仅出现了关联性词组 at the same time,而且关键词 problems 也同样出现。只是出题人又设了一道关卡:把原文中的 poor training 换成了名词词组 lack of good training,不明白 lack 用法的考生又要吃亏了。

Questions 28–30

这三道题较难,需要考生对整篇对话有了整体把握后才能找齐三个人分散在对话中的观点,不光考查听力,还考查考生的归纳总结能力。另外,考生还要分清这三个人的身份,从话语中判断谁是 Karin,谁是 Jason,谁又是 tutor,然后才能正确判断他们的观点和态度。

三道题中第 28 题相对容易,因为他明确地表明了 Box Telecom 公司一定会重振旗鼓:Personally I' ve got great hopes for it. I think it will recover. 题干中显示这一积极的信息的只有 C 项:克服所有难题。Jason 的回答较为隐晦,但我们从他的第一句话 I' m not sure 得知,他对 Karin 的看法并不赞同。然后,他用了一个 unless 引导的条件状语从句表明自己的观点,中间还夹杂了一个不常见的习语 foregone conclusion,这些都给考生造成了很大麻烦。好在选项 B 里含有 investment 这个单词,许多考生猜对了这道题。

回答导师的态度之前，我们必须要了解 Karin 的想法，因为导师已经明确提出 I disagree with you about the advertising campaign Karin。Karin 认为该公司的 advertising campaign 很成功，所以导师的想法肯定会跟他相反。但是选项中并没有 advertising campaign 这个词组，只有 marketing campaign。有商业常识的人都知道，在商业中，市场营销在很大程度上靠广告，事实上，marketing 的意思就是指“（公司的）市场推广”。因此，导师的态度就是 D 项。

SECTION 4

谈话场景：面向大学新生的讲座。

人物关系：讲话者为新生培训督导员。

谈话话题：介绍图书馆资源使用方法。

词汇注释

settled *adj.* 稳定的；固定的
guidance *n.* 指导；领导
effectively *adv.* 有效地；有力地
guided *adj.* 有指导的；有向导的
muddle *v.* 使某人糊涂
series *n.* 连续；系列
talk *n.* 非正式的演讲或讲话
aspect *n.*（问题的）方面
resource *n.* 资源
literate *adj.* 有文化的
access *v.* 接近
available *adj.* 可用的或可得到的
permanently *adv.* 永久地；不变地
debatable *adj.* 可争议的
critical *adj.* 找出毛病的；指出缺点的；批评的；非难的
specialist *n.* 专业工作者；专家
reference *n.* 参考，参考书目
MLA（Modern Language Association）美国现代语言协会
updated *adj.* 最新的；更新的
journal *n.* 定期刊物；杂志
version *n.* 版本
accessible *adj.* 易接近的，可到达的
shelf *n.* 书架
intention *n.* 目的；意图
phase out 逐步或分阶段撤出或中止某事物
photocopy *v.* 影印
additional *adj.* 另外的，附加的
restricted *adj.* 受限制的；有限的
relevant *adj.* 有关的；相应的
supervisor *n.* 监督人，管理人，检查员，督学
oversee *v.* 检查；视察
induction *n.* 入门课
initial *adj.* 最初的
specialized *adj.* 专门的
dissertation *n.*（学术）论文
undergraduate *n.* 本科生
postgraduate *n.* 研究生
at the outset 开始；开端
chapter *n.* 章节
bibliography *n.* 参考书目
draft *n.* 草稿；草案
register *v.* 注册；登记

交际与语言表达

1. Ok, are you all settled? 都坐好了吗？这句话一般是讲话或讲座的开场白，意思是“我马上准备开始讲了，请做好准备”。
2. Some of you have asked about a guided tour but we find this **rather** muddles people. 你们有人想让人带着在图书馆里走一遍，但是我们发现这反而会使你们摸不着头脑。rather 用在动词前表示

"或多或少；相当地"，如：I rather suspect we're making a big mistake. 我有些怀疑我们可能犯了个大错。

3. You'll also find that to **get the most out of** this library you really do need to be computer **literate...** 你也会发现，为了能最大限度地利用图书馆，你必须会使用电脑。在这个句子里有一个作状语成分的不定式短语 to get the most out of，这个短语的意思是"最大限度地从某事物/某人处得到或获得"；黑体标示的 literate 本来是"有知识的；博学的"，如果前面加了一个作定语的名词修饰的话，就是指"具备某方面的知识"。
4. Clearly some of you will **find** the printed version more accessible as it sits on the shelves but I'm afraid the intention is to phase these out eventually. 很显然你们有人会觉得印刷版本更容易取得，因为它就在书架上，但是恐怕将来这些都会被逐渐取代。
5. The CD-ROMS contain exactly the same information **as** the reference books **as** the two are updated together. 光盘里包含了与参考书一样多的信息，因为二者是同步更新的。这句话中出现两个 as，第一个是属于短语 the same as，表示"与……一样"，第二个 as 是连词，引导一个原因状语从句。
6. This is because some of you may **prefer to** borrow a book **rather than** sit in the library. 这可能是因为你们有人宁愿把书借出去也不愿呆在图书馆。该句包含着一个典型的"prefer to... rather than"句型，表示"宁愿……也不……"。值得注意的是，prefer 与 rather than 二者是对应关系，后面跟的句子成分保持一致；prefer 后面的 to 不能理解为不定式的标志，而是一个介词。例如：I prefer to tea rather than coffee. 我宁愿要茶也不愿要咖啡。
7. ... if you do **get stuck** looking for thing, you should ask the relevant Cataloguing Assistant. 如果你在找资料的时候一筹莫展时，你可以找相关的管目录的助手帮忙。本句黑体标注的 get stuck 意为"不能动；不能继续做某事"，stuck 这是做表语；后面紧跟的动名词结构 looking for 作伴随状语。
8. Your department will discuss the planning stage of the dissertation—i. e. what you're going to do—with you and we will focus on the structure of it. 你所在的院系将和你探讨你论文的筹划阶段，也就是说你将要做的事情，而我们将专注于论文的结构。在口语中，人们经常会对上一句话做进一步的解释说明，这就需要短暂的插入语来引出下面的解释说明性文字。这样的插入语有文中i. e. 的，还有 in other words, to put it more (simply), that is (to say)等等。考生一般听到这些插入语时，就应该知道下面的文字是对上文的进一步阐释，这也说明，上文提到的内容比较重要，也是出题的重点。
9. Your tutors will tell you **at the outset how** to set out the chapters they require but you will need to ask them how they would like you to organize the bibliography because it varies **depending on** your subject area. 你的导师一开始就要告诉你如何按照他们的要求安排章节，但是你还需要问他们如何让你组织参考书目，因为这要视你的专业而定。这句话句子较长，句子成分较为复杂，包含多个语法现象：1) tell 和 ask 后面都跟了一个 how 引导的宾语从句；2) 习语 at the outset 等于 at/from the beginning，意为"开端；开始"；3) chapters 后面跟了一个不带关系代词 that 的定语从句，修饰前面的整个句子；4) depending on 构成一个作伴随状语的动名词结构。

考题解析

Question 31

在解答这道选择题时，考生要抓住一个关键词 talks，明白它在这里是"讲座、讲话"的意思，说话人说他们将要安排一系列讲座，讲解图书馆及图书馆资源的各个方面。其实，没有听懂这个词的考生也可以使用排除法做这道题，A 选项正是说话人所不赞同的，他觉得会 muddles people；而 C 选项在文章中根本找不到，我们并没有听见过 computer center 的说法。故选 B。

Question 32

作者虽然在讲话中推崇在网上寻找资料,认为这样做节省电脑空间,但也警告学生要小心网上的信息准确与否。考生这时要注意说话人的语气,他在发出警告时,语气放慢,以期能引起学生的注意,特别是说 useless 和 highly debatable 的时候。同时,他还告诫学生要 critical(批判性的)。综合以上考虑,A 选项的 unreliable 应该是说话人的态度,而其他两项并没有提及。

Question 33

说话人具体谈到 CD 的时候不多,这样也使考生容易定位答案。说话人在提到 CD 的好处时,用了一个习语:at very little extra cost,大多数考生都知道 cost 的意思。并且,说话人又补充说明了这一点,指出这样一来可以省下钱了去购置更多的书了。B 项的说法在他的讲话中找不到根据;而 C 项正好是对原文的曲解,说话人明明说到这两者是同步升级的:updated together。

Question 34

说话人在鼓励学生在线阅读期刊之前,先指出还是有学生觉得在图书馆的书架上借书要方便得多,但紧跟着就告诉学生这些书架上的书马上就要被分批撤走了。在他的这句话中,他用了一个抽象名词 intention 和一个习语 phase out,可能有的考生没有听懂他在说什么,而且他也没有再进行任何的补充说明,这就更增加了理解难度。

A 项说这些文章可以不用还到书架上,这个说法在讲话中找不到根据;B 项对比了在线阅读和影印文章的开支不同,而文章并没有提到这二者的对比,唯一提到的是学生在打印文本与影印文本之间作选择。排除了这两项之后,圈定答案为 C。

Question 35

这道题的答案不是那么直接,需要考生从说话人字里行间揣摩。说话人指出,虽然有很多 CD 存储,但还是准备了 the full range of classic reference books,因为有人宁愿把书借出去也不愿呆在图书馆。符合这一说法的只有 A 选项。

B 和 C 选项都是与说话人的意思不符,B 项中说参考书里的内容别的地方找不到,而说话人明明说 CD 光盘里的内容与参考书保持一致,因为两者是同步升级的:updated together;C 项说参考书借出的时间可以延长(extended),可说话人明确提出对于借书的时间有 a restricted loan time,这里的 loan 不是借贷的意思,而是“借书”这件事。

Question 36

这道题的答案比较明显,说话人特别强调了自己的职责是 oversee your induction,但是这个词组难住了不少考生。我们可以从他下面的话得出一点线索,他说他过了这个星期就不会再出现了,所以他能提供的帮助只能是方向性的、暂时的,不可能整天守在这里做支持(support)。而图书馆里的 Section Manager 是需要学生自己去找的,并且也不常见到,所以圈定答案为 B。

Questions 37–40

这四道题难度相对较大。凡是出现在最后的 Matching 题型,一般都是要考生对对话内容整体把握,寻找散落在对话中的答案,所以考生必须事先快速浏览题目,心中有数,听到相关信息时及时做记号,不要听完整篇文章再来回忆。

说话人提出图书馆将会提供专门的培训(offering specialized training),但是这种专门的培训包不包括电脑培训呢?说话人先卖了一个关子,转而提及研究生做论文,说到学生所在的院系和图书馆在学生论文指导方面的分工不同,这才提到培训中包括对电脑的培训,因为学生们要知道如何使用数据系统。所以,图书馆将会负责专门的电脑培训。

第 38 题相对容易一些,因为说话人指出像组织参考书目这样的事只能征询导师的意见,所以该题选 A 项。

在解答第 39 题时，考生要抓住说话人所说的 trainer 到底指谁，可能因为他说 here 的时候语速太快，有的考生没能跟上，但是应该猜到提供 training 的只有图书馆，应该选 B。

第 40 题较为明显，因为它的答案包含在最后一句话中，许多考生也听到了 international center 的位置，知道该去那里寻求语言帮助。

READING

READING PASSAGE 1

文章结构

体　裁	说明文。
主要内容	本文论述了"荒原旅游业"对当地生态环境和文化的影响。在客观指出其带来的不利影响之后，作者也提出只要措施得当，"荒原旅游业"可以促使当地经济和文化的发展。
结　构	A 段：Introduction 指出国际社会对"荒原"的定义以及荒原脆弱的特点。旅游业成为一些偏远地区的主要收入来源。
	B 段：旅游业对当地影响深远，不仅在经济和生存方式上，也在生态环境方面有着不利影响。
	C 段：只要当地措施得当，旅游业完全可以与当地的经济和文化发展结合起来，成为当地发展振兴的推动力。

词汇注释

文　章

A 段

tourism *n.* 旅游业
remote *adj.* 遥远的；偏僻的
boom *v.* 繁荣；兴盛
promote *v.* 促进，发扬，提升
wilderness *n.* 荒野，荒地
Arctic *n.* 北极；北极圈
wetland *n.* 沼泽地
attraction *n.* 吸引；吸引力
definition *n.* 定义
recognize *v.* 认可；承认
fragile *adj.* 易碎的；脆弱的
vulnerable *adj.* 易受攻击的；暴露于危险面前的
abnormal *adj.* 反常的；非常态的
ecology *n.* 生态
inhabitant *n.* 居民；居住者
significant *adj.* 有意义的；重大的；重要的
proportion *n.* 比例；一物与他物在数量、大小等方面的关系
characteristic *n.* 特性，特征
seasonality *n.* 季节性
harsh *adj.* 粗糙的，荒芜的
prevail *v.* 流行；盛行
consequently *adv.* 从而；因此
landscape *n.* 地形；地貌
indigenous *adj.* 本地的；土产的；土生土长的
isolated *adj.* 隔离的；孤立的
breed *n.* 品种；种类
adventure *n.* 冒险；冒险经历
hard currency 硬通货
prime *adj.* 主要的；最重要的
foreign exchange 外汇

B 段	
location *n.* 位置;场所;特定区域	**relatively** *adv.* 相关地
destination *n.* 目的地	**dependence** *n.* 依靠，依赖，信任，信赖
profound *adj.* 深刻的,意义深远的	**culprit** *n.* 犯过者;犯罪者
trekker *n.* 徒步旅行者	**undermine** *v.* 逐渐削弱或暗中破坏
output *n.* 产量;输出	**dilemma** *n.* 进退两难的局面，困难的选择
insufficient *adj.* 不足的;缺乏的	**erosion** *n.* 腐蚀;侵蚀
terrace *n.* 梯田的一层，梯田;台地	**deforestation** *n.* 采伐森林，森林开伐
irrigation *n.* 灌溉	**fuel** *n.* 燃料
traditionally *adv.* 传统上	**degradation** *n.* 降级;降格;退化
C 段	
legion *adj.* 极多;大批	**tundra** *n.* 苔原;冻土地带
inevitably *adv.* 不可避免地	**strategy** *n.* 策略
minimize *v.* 将…减到最少;最小化	**pueblo** *n.* 印第安人村庄
reinvigorate *v.* 使再振作;使复兴	**reservation** *n.*(美国印第安人)居留地
ensure *v.* 保证，担保，使安全	**handicraft** *n.* 手工艺;手工艺品
integrate *v.* 使成为整体;使一体化	**artwork** *n.* 艺术品;美术品
impose *v.* 将(不愉快的、不受欢迎的事物)强加于某人	**pottery** *n.* 陶器
renaissance *n.* 复兴;复活;新生	**penetrate** *v.* 穿透，渗透;进入或穿过某物
communal *adj.* 全体共用;分享的	**venture** *n.* 工程项目或事业
reliable *adj.* 可靠的;可信赖的	**aspiration** *n.* 热望;渴望
exploit *v.* 开拓，开发，开采，剥削，用以自肥	**demonstrate** *v.* 示范;证明;显示
transient *adj.* 短暂的;片刻的	**norm** *n.* 标准;规范
repatriate *v.* 遣返	**exception** *n.* 除外;例外
accrue *v.* 自然增长或利益增加;积累	

考题解析

Questions 1–3

● 题型归类:List of Headings

这类题型考查考生对文章整体结构的把握能力,以及总结归纳段落中心思想的能力,是雅思阅读中较难的题型之一。

● 题目解析:

题目编号	段落主题句	题解
1	As the 1992 United Nations Conference on Environment and Development recognized, these regions are fragile (i. e. highly vulnerable to abnormal pressure) not just in terms of their ecology, but also in terms of the culture of their inhabitants.	Section A 包含两部分内容,第一部分具体讲述荒原地区的定义,指出国际上公认的对“荒原”的认识,包括的地区以及显著的特点。第二部分照应开头,着重从经济角度分析了为什么偏远地区的旅游业如此兴盛。这一部分引出全文,首先对“荒原地区”下定义,然后初步解释“荒原旅游业”火爆的原因,为下文定好调子。选项中只有第三个选项符合整体段落大意,从两个方面总结段落。

	Tourists are drawn to these regions by their natural landscape beauty and the unique cultures of their indigenous people.	第一个和最后一个选项可能会具有一定的迷惑性，因为第一个选项看起来像是照应了文章第一句话。其实本段的主题句并不像其他主题句那样一般都是开头第一句话。本篇的开头只是描述现状，引出主题。而最后一个选项也只是对本段的第二自然段的总结，不够全面。
2	Once a location is established as a main tourist destination, the effects on the local community are profound.	Section B 的开头就说一些地区被确立为旅游区，这会对当地产生深远影响。而文中举出的例子都是带有负面色彩：农民放弃田地，产量下降，饮食习惯变化等；而最明显的莫过于第二自然段，阐述旅游者对当地环境及水资源的破坏，所以本段主题应该是第五个选项。可能有的考生不认识选项中的 disruptive，其实它与 disrupt，disruption 等都是同根词。 第四个选项可能会有迷惑性。该段确实提到了一些地区的传统食物供应手段，但是这只是为了说明旅游业给当地饮食带来的影响，不够全面。
3	Although tourism inevitably affects the region in which it takes place, the costs to these fragile environments and their local cultures can be minimized.	Section C 开头承认旅游业带来的不利影响，但注意转折词 yet 的使用，它标志着作者思路的转变。果然，作者从振兴当地文化和发展当地经济两个方面阐述旅游业可以帮助当地生活的改善，并就一些少数民族的具体做法展开讨论，探究具体平衡方法。 本文思路清晰，语言平实，方便考生迅速找到文章主题。

Questions 4–9

● 题型归类：YES/NO/NOT GIVEN

Y/N/NG 类题考查考生对文章细节的把握与辨别能力，考查题目中细节信息和逻辑关系是否与文章中完全对应。因此在解题时，先要确保读懂题目，准确理解题目意思，然后根据题目定位词回到原文定位到相关内容后与题目进行对照判断。

● 题目解析：

题目编号	题目定位词	答案位置	题解
4	low financial cost, attractive	Section A 第 1 段 第 3 句	题目：发展荒原旅游业不需要很多财政投入，这对很多国家来说很有吸引力。 第 1 自然段开头讲荒原旅游业近来十分火爆，很多国家都趋之若鹜，然后作者就初步分析其原因，指出这是因为不需要太多投资。题目把原文的名词 attraction 化为形容词 attractive，这对考生来说难度不大。故选 YES。
5	deserts, mountains, Arctic regions, examples, fragile	Section A 第 1 段 第 6 句	题目：沙漠、高山和北极地区是那些生态和文化上都很脆弱的环境的典型。 文章中集中谈到沙漠、高山和北极地区的地方只有 Section A，作者在解释完“荒原”的定义后，跟着就举

			出实例，说明哪些地区符合定义和特征。题目上的三者符合作者举出的例子和前提条件。故选 YES。
6	Wilderness tourism, throughout the year	Section A 第 1 段 第 7、8 句	题目：在脆弱的环境里，全年都可以实现荒原旅游。作者在说到荒原的特点时明显提出荒原的季节性，即一年中只有特定的时间段才适合人类的活动。所以题目明显是对原文的曲解，故选 NO。
7	fall, amount of food produced, hill-regions	Section B 第 1 段 第 3 句	题目：旅游业在一些高山地区的扩散已经导致了当地食物产量的下降。 在谈到旅游业对当地生态和文化的不利影响时，作者特地谈到了高山地区农民为了更好的报酬放弃田地，导致农业产量下降。故选 YES。
8	Traditional food-gathering, Distributed evenly	Section B 第 2 段 第 1、2 句	题目：多年以来，沙漠社会里的传统食物收集都是平均分配。 作者在谈到旅游业对沙漠地区饮食的影响时，指出当地人已经放弃了传统的食物采集习惯，转而依赖购买的外来食物，所以题目中传统的食物收集已经在有些地区不复存在了。故选 NO。
9	Government hand-outs, damage, tourism	Section B 第 2 段 第 3、4 句	题目：政府的福利发放对传统的食物收集方式造成的伤害比旅游业更大。 作者为了替旅游业辩解：Tourism is not always the culprit behind such changes，搬出有偿劳动、政府福利发放等来跟旅游业相提并论，指出还有别的因素也可能导致传统食物收集方式的改变，不能只怪罪旅游业。但我们并没有见到政府行为与旅游业之间具体的对比，不知道二者谁的危害更大，故选 NOT GIVEN。

Questions 10–13

● 题型归类：Table Completion

该类题考查考生对文章细节的辨别和掌握能力。在解题时，考生要迅速回归原文分门别类地寻找 Table 中出现的各项内容，根据关键词准确定位，而且需要特别注意空格处的语法成分以及题目中的字数限制。

● 题目解析：

题目编号	题目定位词	答案位置	题解
10	Swiss Pays d' Enhaut, revived production	Section C 第 2 段 第 2、3 句	根据题目的要求，该图表填空题应该是要在 Section C 里面寻找，因为它涉及当地如何正确对待旅游业的发展。 Section C 里面谈到 Swiss Pays d' Enhaut 的只有第 2 段，指出这个族群现在已经开始限制旅游人数的增长；同时，最后一句话指出他们又重新振兴了当地的

			集体奶酪生产。题目中的 revived 的意思相当于原文中的 renaissance(复兴;复活)。当 renaissance 大写的时候,意为"文艺复兴"。
11	Arctic communities	Section C 第 3 段 第 2 句	Section C 里面的第 3 段谈到 Arctic communities,这段是说北极地区的人们开始自己组织旅游项目了,并举例证明。该题不难,几乎完全是原文的重现,只要定位准确就能很快找到答案。
12	Acoma and San Ildefonso	Section C 第 4 段 最后一句	该题与下面的一道题同来源于一句话,但是原文中的说法并不直接,必须结合上下文理解。原句中的 establish 一词并不能直接理解为 produce and sell,同样 successful with 也不能直接理解为 produce and sell。该自然段开头谈到当地人改变策略,让旅游者购买(purchase)他们的工艺品,题目中提到的这两个族群的做法正是这一句的举例说明。
13	Navajo and Hopi	Section C 第 4 段 最后一句	参照上题的解答,答案应该是 jewellery 或是 jewelry,两种拼法都可以接受。

参考译文

荒原旅游业的影响

偏远地区旅游业的市场从来没有像今天这么火爆过。每个国家都在向出手阔绰的旅游者大力推广宣传他们的"荒原"地区,如高山、北极地带、沙漠、小岛和沼泽地。这些地区的吸引力显而易见:单从定义上讲,荒原旅游业不需要、或者很少需要原始投资。但是这并不意味着没有代价。召开于 1992 年的联合国环境和发展大会承认这些地区很脆弱(在反常压力下容易被破坏),这不仅就它们的生态平衡而言,更是就当地居民的文化而言。在这些方面,或者是就它们在地球表面所占的面积而言,脆弱环境有下列三种最为重要的类型:沙漠、高山和北极地区。它们的一个重要特征就是显著的季节性,一年好几个月都持续着恶劣的环境。所以,大多数的人类活动,包括旅游业,都限定在每年特定的时间里。

吸引旅游者来到这些地区的是它们美丽的天然景色和当地土著居民独特的文化。同时,这些偏远地区贫穷的政府一直都是欢迎这种新的"探险旅游",对它们带来的硬通货心存感激。多年以来,旅游业一直是尼泊尔和不丹最重要的外汇来源,它也是诸如拉普兰和阿拉斯加等北极地带地区和像澳大利亚艾尔斯巨石和亚利桑那纪念谷这样的沙漠地区的重要经济收入。

一旦某个地区被确定为主要的旅游胜地,就会给当地生活带来深远的影响。比如说,一个山上的农夫为外国徒步旅行者当几个星期挑夫,赚的钱就比他在田地里干一年活赚的还要多,所以就不难理解他为什么放弃了农田,把它留给家里的其他成员照料。在一些高山地区,这样的情况已经导致了农田产量的下降和当地饮食的变化,因为已经没有足够的劳动力维持田地和灌溉系统种庄稼了。所以结果是,这些地区的许多人已经转而依赖外来大米或其他食物了。

在北极和沙漠地区,传统上,一年的生计都依赖于在一个相对来说短暂的季节里的打猎、捕鱼、采摘水果等活动。但是,当一些居民投身于旅游业,他们就没有时间去采集野生食物;这样一来他们越来越依赖于买来的食物及店铺了。这些变化不应该都归咎于旅游业。所有类型的计酬工作,或者政府的福利发放,都容易损害传统意义上的生存系统。不管原因如何,面临的两难困境都是一样的:当没有这些新的外来收入时,我们该怎么办?

探险旅游的发展带来了另外一个新的问题,那就是旅游者对环境的影响。主要道路上的侵蚀吸引了很多关注,但是或许更应引起重视的是为了满足旅游者生火做饭和洗热水澡的需要而带来的森林砍伐和对水资源的影响。在高山地区和沙漠地带,生长缓慢的树木常常成为燃料的主要来源,由于过度利用,水资源很容易枯竭。

最近几年来,旅游者造成的问题数不胜数。但是这完全可以不成为一个问题。尽管旅游业不可避免地会影响到所在的地区,这些脆弱环境和当地文化付出的代价可以最小化。确实,它甚至可以成为重振当地文化的工具,尼泊尔珠峰区的舍尔巴人和一些阿尔卑斯村庄发生的事情证实了这一点。同时,越来越多的冒险旅游业开发商现在都在保证他们的活动从长远来看会造福于当地居民和环境。

在瑞士的阿尔卑斯山区,当地人已经决定他们的未来将依赖于使旅游业和当地经济更有效地结合在一起。在瑞士贝伊东地区,当地人担心他们会越来越依赖旅游业的发展,所以开始限制它们的增长。并且,当地的集体奶酪生产活动重新兴起,这样使当地人有了稳定的收入而不再依赖外来的旅游者。

许多北极地带的旅游区已经被外来的公司开发,它们雇佣临时工,把大多数的收入都回流至他们的家乡。但是一些北极地区的当地团体现在正自己组织旅游业,这样确保了当地人收益的增长。例如,阿拉斯加当地的一家公司雇佣本地人,经营一条从安克雷奇到柯泽堡的空中旅游线路,一路上,旅游者品尝北极食物,漫步在苔原上,欣赏当地的民间音乐和舞蹈。

居住在美国西南部沙漠地区的土著居民也采用相似的策略,鼓励旅游者参观他们的印第安人村庄和居留地,购买精美的手工艺品。Acoma 和 San Ildefonso 的印第安人村庄已经确立了高利润的陶器业,而 Navajo 和 Hopi 部落在珠宝业也取得了相似的成功。

面对旅游业的无孔不入,许多生活在脆弱环境里的居民已经失去了对当地经济、文化和环境的控制力。单单限制旅游业不是解决这种不均衡状态的办法,因为人们想去参观新地方的欲望是不会消失的。相反,在脆弱环境里生活的团体应当掌控当地的旅游业,来取得满足他们的生活之需与旅游业的要求的平衡。越来越多的当地团体已经证明,只要有坚定的集体决策能力,完全有可能做到这一点。当前最为关键的问题是这样的做法能否成为制度,而不只是临时之举。

READING PASSAGE 2

文章结构

体　裁	说明文。
主要内容	本文主要论述了钢化玻璃存在因为内含镍硫化物晶体而容易破碎这一问题。从钢化玻璃的制作过程详细谈起,深入分析问题症结所在,指出它的普遍性和不可预知性。
结　构	第 1 段:Introduction 点出主题:从发生在一个英国小镇的钢化玻璃破碎事件说起,引出文章主题。
	第 2 段:一权威人士承认问题的存在,但否认它的普遍性。
	第 3 段:另有专家驳斥上文观点,认为这一问题相当普遍。
	第 4 段:指出钢化玻璃到处受欢迎的原因。
	第 5 段:说明钢化玻璃的制作原理。
	第 6 段:从制作过程中分析问题产生的根源。
	第 7 段:继续上文的分析,指出两种晶体形式之间的转化不畅为问题产生埋下隐患。

	第 8 段:指出钢化玻璃破碎时间的不可预知性。
	第 9 段:指出除了不可预知,钢化玻璃破碎情况还可能成批出现。
	第 10 段:以具体实例证实钢化玻璃破碎的不可预知性以及容易成批出现。

词汇注释

文 章

第 1 段

pane *n.* 窗户上的单块玻璃
toughened glass 钢化玻璃
shatter *v.* 粉碎;破碎
frame *n.* 窗框
fragment *n.* 碎片;断片
analyze *v.* 分析;研究
giant *adj.* 庞大的;巨大的
manufacturer *n.* 生产厂商
minute *adj.* 极小的;微小的
crystal *n.* 晶体
nickel *n.* [化]镍
sulphide *n.* 硫化物
trap *v.* 使(某物)留在某处
failure *n.* 失灵;故障

第 2 段

be aware of 意识到;察觉到
committee *n.* 委员会
glazing *n.* 玻璃装配业
federation *n.* (社团、工会等)联合会
association *n.* 社团;协会
rare *adj.* 希罕的;稀有的
phenomenon *n.* 现象

第 3 段

on average 按平均数计算
related *adj.* 有关系的;相关的
consultant *n.* 顾问, 商议者, 咨询者
investigation *n.* 调查;研究
similar *adj.* 相似的;类似的
tip *n.* 顶;尖端;梢
iceberg *n.* 冰山

第 4 段

shelter *n.* 遮蔽物;庇护物
strength *n.* 强度
cube *n.* 立方体
razor-sharp *adj.* 像剃刀一样锋利的
shard *n.* [瓷]碎片
architect *n.* 建筑师
bolt *v.* 用螺栓将物体固定
transparent *adj.* 透明的

第 5 段

ordinary *adj.* 普通的;平凡的
soften *v.* (使)软化;(使)柔软
cool *v.* (使)冷却
jet *n.* 喷射流
contract *v.* (使)缩小;缩约
solidify *v.* (使)凝固;巩固
interior *n.* 内部
shrink *v.* 收缩;缩小
permanent *adj.* 永久的;持久的
compression *n.* 浓缩, 压缩, 压榨
tensile *adj.* 拉力的;张力的;紧张的
crack *n.* 裂缝
propagate *v.* 传播;繁殖
tension *n.* 紧张(状态);压力
compressive *adj.* 有压缩力的
resistant *adj.* 抵抗的;有阻力的

第 6 段

contain *v.* 包含;容纳
impurity *n.* 不纯;杂质
trace *n.* 极微的量
raw *adj.* 未加工的;处于自然状态的
alloy *n.* 合金
molten *adj.* 溶化的;熔融的
atom *n.* 原子
furnace *n.* 炉子;熔炉

第 7 段	
form *n.* 形式；形态	**compact** *adj.* 紧凑的；紧密的
dense *adj.* 密集的；浓厚的	**subsequent** *adj.* 后来的；接下来的
phase *n.* 阶段	**prime** *v.* 将某物准备好（以便投入使用或启动）
stable *adj.* 稳定的	**coil** *v.* 盘绕；卷曲
temperature *n.* 温度	**spring** *n.* 弹簧
convert *v.*（使）转化；转变	**revert** *v.* 恢复原状
第 8 段	
unleash *v.* 使某物不受控制；释放	**ironically** *adv.* 说反话地，讽刺地
elapse *v.*（时间）过去，消逝	**due to** 由（某人/某事物）引起的；由于（某人/某事物）
unpredictable *adj.* 不可预知的	**inclusion** *n.* 包含；内含物
decade *n.* 十年	
第 9 段	
data *n.* **datum** 的复数，［计］资料，数据	**batch** *n.* 一批
complicated *adj.* 复杂的；难解的	
第 10 段	
rash *n.* 令人不快的事情突然大量出现	**microfiche** *n.*［摄］单片缩影胶片
contamination *n.* 玷污，污染，污染物	**reader** *n.* 阅读器
studio camera 摄影棚用摄像机	**potential** *adj.* 潜在的；可能的
photographer *n.* 摄影师	**replace** *v.* 取代；更换；代替
cradle *n.*（依靠绳索及滑轮可沿外墙上下移动的）吊架；吊篮	**time-consuming** *adj.* 耗时间的
scan *v.* 扫描；细看	**alternative** *n.* 可能性中的选择
modified *adj.* 改良的；改进的	**re-clad** *v.* 重新覆盖
题目	
flawed *adj.* 有缺陷的；有瑕疵的	

考题解析

Questions 14–17

- 题型归类：Matching
- 题目解析：

题目编号	题目定位词	答案位置	题解
14	Brian Waldron	第 2 段	这类寻找说话人观点的题型相对容易，只需回到原文说话人名字出现的段落，揣摩说话人的观点或蕴藏的言外之意即可。Brian Waldron 这段话的大意是虽然承认钢化玻璃破碎这种事情的存在，但坚持认为这类事情并不多见。在 A – H 中，只有 G 符合原意。G 项中的 unusual 等于原文中的 rare。
15	Trevor Ford	第 3 段	这段话中出现人物较多，考生需辨清各人的观点。Ford 的话中包含着一个习语：the tip of the iceberg，考生应该根据他的话揣摩他的言外之意，即：还有很多类似的事件不为人知，被掩盖了。选项中，A 项符合原意。该项的 publicity 与 public 同词根，意为“为公众所知”。

16	Graham Dodd	第 8 段	第 8 段主要表明这类玻璃破碎的事件发生时间不可预知。从 Graham Dodd 的话中，我们看到了一例迄今为止发生破碎时间最晚的事件，一块时隔 27 年之后才因为内含镍硫化物晶体而破碎的玻璃。选项 H 适合题意，delay 意为"推迟"。
17	John Barry	第 10 段	John Barry 为了检查这栋玻璃破碎事件频发的大楼，运用先进仪器，仔细审看了每块玻璃：analyzed every glass pane in the building。因此选项 B 应该符合题意。值得注意的是，选项 E 具有一定的迷惑性，因为根据 John Barry 的调查，既然大楼里还有许多潜在的玻璃破碎事件，何不全部更换？但是根据 John Barry 的做法，他显然不愿采取这种全盘更换的做法，因为那样会耗资巨大：would have cost ten times as much。

Questions 18–23

● 题型归类：Summary

根据上个单元所说到的 Summary 做题技巧，这组题目应该是对全文的总结和概括，这样相对难度就会大一些。但是这篇 Summary 依旧是按照文章的逻辑顺序设置的，先讲钢化玻璃的优缺点，再从制作工艺上找到问题症结所在，分析难以预测破碎何时会发生。把逻辑顺序弄清楚后，解题时思路会更清晰。另外，正确猜测空白的词性也会对解题有所帮助。

● 题目解析：

题目编号	题目定位词	答案位置	题解
18	architects, ordinary glass, fragments	第 4 段	根据上面的分析，我们借助定位词回到第 4 段，看作者是如何表现钢化玻璃的优缺点的。优点是：这种玻璃硬度高，并且碎片不会像普通玻璃的那样 razor-sharp，所以选 F。
19	disadvantage	第 8 段	该题较难，因为它的答案与上题位置相差太远，考生必须统盘把握文章意思才能选对。从题目上看，因为 shatter 是不及物动词，第 19 题的空白所缺的词应该是副词。选项中是副词的只有 C、H、I 三项，根据文章原意，钢化玻璃破碎情况发生时间无法预知，所以选择 I 项。
20	heated, cooled	第 5 段	从这道题开始涉及钢化玻璃的制作过程。先加热，后用冷蒸汽迅速冷却是制作中的最开始步骤。原文中的 rapidly 只能与选项中的 C 项对等。
21	outer layer, inner layer	第 5 段	顺着上题的思路，快速冷却的结果是外层先于内层收缩以产生张力。原文中的 contract 在选项中可以找到原词。
22	unstable, expand, weather	第 8 段	文中涉及到天气的只有两处：第一处是在最开始，从 8 月的一天，一个小镇的玻璃破碎事件谈起；第二处便是第 8 段，作者举 sunlight 为例，说明天气炎热就会使扩张进程加快。实际上，这两处是紧密相连，前后呼应的。温度的上升（if the glass is heated）直接加快（speed up）玻璃破碎。所以此处应该选 E 项。

23	frequency, glass experts	第2、3段	根据题意，问题发生的频率也就是问题发生的数量的多少，考生应当记得玻璃专家们是怎样争论钢化玻璃破碎事件的数量多少的，专家们的意见分为两类，一类说这类事情rare，一类说是the tip of the iceberg。这说明尚有争议，所以选L。 P项也有迷惑性，文章确实给出了一项数据：one inclusion in 7 tonnes(7吨玻璃中有一例内含镍硫化物)，但是作者说的很明确，相关数据不可能拿到，所以怎么可能正确calculate呢？并且，上面的数据只是推算、假设(even if)，不能当真。

Questions 24–26

● 题型归类：TRUE/FALSE/NOT GIVEN

T/F/NG类题考查考生对文章细节的把握与辨别能力，考查题目中细节信息和逻辑关系是否与文章中完全对应。因此在解题时，先要确保读懂题目，准确理解题目意思，然后根据题目定位词回到原文，定位到相关内容后与题目进行对照判断。

● 题目解析：

题目编号	题目定位词	答案位置	题解
24	little doubt, reason, Bishops Walk accident	第1段	题目：主教路事件的原因已经少有争议了。 当主教路的一块钢化玻璃掉落下来后，专家们聚集在制造商那里，经过分析，一致同意内含的镍硫化物晶体是事件原因。大家对于原因并没有争议，有争议的是类似事件数量的多少，因此答案确定为TRUE。
25	same appearance, ordinary glass	第4段	题目：钢化玻璃和普通玻璃看起来一模一样。 在对比这两种玻璃的时候，二者的优缺点是对比的对象，至于二者的长相文中倒是没有提到。因此答案是NOT GIVEN。
26	documented evidence, available	第9段	题目：很多有案可稽的证据可以证明因内含镍硫化物晶体而导致玻璃破碎。 该题难度稍大，因为与之相对应的原句与题目相差较大，且作者一笔带过，很多考生印象不深，不知道这道题出自何处。 在第9段的开头，作者用了一个较为复杂的句型来表达题目相关内容：Data showing the scale of the nickel sulphide problem is almost impossible to find。作者先用一个动名词修饰Data，又用了一个不定式作主语补足语，且不定式主动形式表示被动意思。这都给考生带来麻烦。 理解了原句之后，不难发现题目的意思是与原句有出入的。故选FALSE。

参考译文

有瑕疵的美:钢化玻璃的问题

1999年8月2日,天气酷热,英国赛伦塞斯特小镇主教路上的一个购物中心里,一大块天花板上的钢化玻璃突然破碎,从窗框里掉落下来。专家们聚集在玻璃生产巨头皮尔金顿公司分析玻璃碎片(这块玻璃正是该公司的产品),他们基本上肯定正是隐藏在玻璃里面的细小镍硫化物晶体导致玻璃的破裂。

玻璃和玻璃安装联合会的标准委员会主席布里安·沃顿指出:"玻璃制造业已经意识到这个问题。"该联合会同时还是一个英国贸易协会,布里安·沃顿同时兼任皮尔金顿公司的标准开发官员。但是他坚称这类事件并不多见,指出:"这是一个非常罕见的现象。"

但是别人并不这样认为。"我每个月平均能见到一两栋建筑发生这种镍硫化物导致的破裂情况。"巴里·乔赛说。他是参加主教路事件调查的咨询工程师。还有别的专家也讲述了相似的经历。来自总部设在伦敦的咨询工程师托尼·威尔莫特,还有来自汉普郡克莱德技术协会的西蒙·阿姆斯特朗都宣称共了解到数百件类似的事件。"你所听到的只是冰山一角,"来自昆士兰瑞则沃工程设计公司的玻璃专家特沃·福特说。他说原因很简单:"没有人喜欢不利的报道。"

从汽车和巴士的挡风玻璃到全世界成千上万建筑物的窗户、墙壁和屋顶,到处可见钢化玻璃的踪影。原因很简单。这种玻璃的强度是普通标准玻璃的五倍,并且破裂时,它会碎成细小的立方体,而不是那种大块的如剃刀一样锋利的碎片。建筑师们喜欢使用它是因为大块的钢化玻璃可以用螺丝固定在一起,制成透明的玻璃墙,然后很容易地就可以把它变成天花板或地板。

钢化玻璃的制作方法如下:将一块普通玻璃加热至620°C使其逐渐软化,任由内部结构膨胀,然后用冷气快速喷射使其冷却。这会导致玻璃板外层先于内层收缩并固化。当内层最终固化并收缩时,就会对外层产生一个推力,使其处于一种永恒的压缩状态,于是就在玻璃内部产生了一种抗拉力。由于裂缝最容易在处于强压下的材质中蔓延,所以在玻璃板破碎之前,表面的压缩力必须得到抑制,这样就使得玻璃更经得住破裂。

玻璃内部包含镍硫化物杂质,这就是问题开始的源头。细微的镍和硫通常存在于用来制玻璃的原材料中,并且镍会经由镍合金碎片进入溶化的玻璃当中。当玻璃被加热时,这些原子反应形成细小的镍硫化物晶体。在熔炉中,十分之一克的镍可以产生50,000个晶体。

这些晶体可以以两种形式存在:一种密集的形式被称作阿尔法状态,在高温下还能保持稳定;另外一种不是很密集的形式被称作贝塔状态,在室温下保持稳定。固化过程中使用的高温将所有的晶体转化为密集结实的阿尔法状态。但是接下来的冷却速度太快,晶体来不及变回贝塔状态。这样一来,不稳定的阿尔法晶体就留在了玻璃中,像一个被上紧发条的弹簧,随时准备突然发力还原成贝塔状态。

当晶体还原时,它们可膨胀至4%。但是如果它们处在玻璃板紧张的中间区域时,膨胀时释放的压力可以粉碎整块玻璃。玻璃破碎何时发生无法预料,可能是制成后的几个月,或是数十年之后,尽管当玻璃受热时(比如说日照),这个过程可以加快。来自伦敦工程咨询集团的格拉姆·实德说,具有讽刺意味的是,目前所知的最早的因为包含镍硫化物而引起破裂的钢化玻璃板来自位于兰卡郡拉托姆的皮尔金顿公司的玻璃研究大厦。这块玻璃板已经有27年历史了。

现在几乎无法得到显示有镍硫化物问题的玻璃所占多少比重的数据。这些晶体通常成批出现,这使得这一问题更为复杂。所以,即使平均7吨的玻璃中只有一例这样的物质,或者你所在的建筑里只出现过一次因为包含镍硫化物而引起的玻璃破裂,这就可能意味着你会遇到多个类似的玻璃板。乔赛说过去十年里,在他工作过的15个建筑物中,玻璃破裂的事件已经达到两位数了。

最糟糕的一次事故是发生在完工于1990年的Waterfront Place。在接下来的十年中,一连串的类似事故发生在这座40层高的Brisbane大楼里。在专家最终被请来之前，已经有80块钢化玻璃因为包含镍硫化物而引起破裂。昆士兰大学的镍硫化物污染方面的专家约翰·巴瑞分析了大楼里的全部玻璃板。一名摄影师坐上吊篮，使用摄影棚用摄像机拍下所有的玻璃板。照片被放在一种改进过的单片缩影胶片阅读器下面仔细审看，寻找镍硫化物晶体的迹象。巴瑞指出："我们发现至少还有120块玻璃板内存在潜在的危险内含物，它们随后被替换了。这是一个耗时耗资的过程，还得需要六个月才能完成。"尽管这个项目耗费160万美元（将近70万英镑），但是另外一种方法——重新覆盖整幢大楼——的花费将会10倍于此。

READING PASSAGE 3

文章结构

体　裁	说明文。
主要内容	本文阐述了光在动植物生育繁殖方面的作用和影响，指出动植物根据光照时间的长短进化出不同的特性。
结　构	第1段：Introduction 开门见山，点出主题：光之所以对生物体意义重大，有两个原因可以解释。
	第2段：光照时间长度对于生物体生育繁殖来说是一个很好的提示。
	第3段：光照时间长度对于动物来说是生育季节的提示。
	第4段：在植物身上体现出来的对日照长度的适应性意义也同样清楚。
	第5段：一些植物的生育季节可以被拖得很长。
	第6段：光对于生物体很重要还有第二个原因，那就是它在光合作用中是最重要的因素。
	第7段：总体上，根据对光的适应性不同，植物可以分为两大类：耐阴型和非耐阴型。

词汇注释

文　章	
第1段	
organism *n.* 生物体；有机体	**seasonal** *adj.* 季节的；季节性的
cue *n.* 暗示；提示	**rhythm** *n.* 节奏；（事件或过程）有规律地反复出现
timing *n.* 适时，时间选择；时间的掌握	**assist** *v.* 援助；协助
第2段	
breeding *n.*（动物的）生育；繁殖；生殖	**physiological** *adj.* 生理上的；生理学的
reliable *adj.* 可靠的；可信赖的	**photoperiodism** *n.* 光周期现象
trigger *v.* 引起；引发；触发	**experimental** *adj.* 实验的；根据实验的
behavior *n.* 行为	**phenomenon** *n.* 现象
predictable *adj.* 可预知的；可预言的	**considerable** *adj.* 相当大（或多）的，相当可观的
pattern *n.* 模式；样式	**species** *n.* 物种；种
temperate *adj.*（指气候或有某种气候的地区）温和的	**induce** *v.* 劝诱，促使，导致，引起
temperature *n.* 温度	**artificial** *adj.* 人工的；人造的
fluctuate *v.* 变动，波动	**critical** *adj.* 关键的；决定性的
steadily *adv.* 稳定地；有规则地	**vegetative** *adj.* 有关植物生长的；植物的

regardless of 不理会(某人/某事物);不顾
neutral *adj.* 中立的;不偏不倚的
day length 日长
critical day length 临界日长
short-day plant 短日照植物
long-day plant 长日照植物
day-neutral 日中性植物
vegetative growth 营养生长

第 3 段

evolve *v.* (使)发展、进化、进展
offspring *n.* 子孙后代
survival *n.* 生存;幸存
reserve *n.* 储备(物),储藏量
reproduction *n.* 繁殖
fledging *n.* (刚会飞的)幼鸟
adequate *adj.* 适当的;足够的
assure *v.* 确保;保证

第 4 段

adaptive *adj.* 适应的
significance *n.* 意义;重要性
flower *v.* 开花
maximize *v.* 使(某事物)增至最大值;最大限度地利用某事物
be adapted for 为…做出调整
seedling *n.* 幼苗
fertilization *n.* 授精;受胎
insect *n.* 昆虫
ripen *v.* (使)某事物成熟
evolutionary *adj.* 进化的
advantage *n.* 优势
connection *n.* 关系;连接
favorable *adj.* 令人高兴的;有利的
annual *n.* 一年生植物;一季生植物
germinate *v.* 发芽;发育
suitable *adj.* 合适的;相配的
rainfall *n.* 降雨;降雨量

第 5 段

delay *v.* 耽搁;延迟
extraordinary *adj.* 非常的,特别的,非凡的
perennial *adj.* 四季不断的,(植物)多年生的
state *n.* 状态
fruit *v.* 结果实
climatic *adj.* 气候上的
simultaneous *adj.* 同时的;同时发生的
mass *n.* 大量;大批
centimeter *n.* 厘米
cope with 对付;应付
escape *v.* 逃脱;避开

第 6 段

essential *adj.* 本质的;最重要的
photosynthesis *n.* 光合作用
convert *v.* (使)转变;转化
carbon *n.* [化]碳(元素符号 C)
organic *adj.* 有机的
measure *v.* 衡量;测量
calculate *v.* 计算
uptake *n.* 摄取
photosynthetic *adj.* [生化]光合的
response *n.* 反应;响应
variation *n.* 变更,变化,变异,变种
intensity *n.* 强度;亮度
maximal *adj.* 最大的;最高的
sugarcane *n.* [植]甘蔗,糖蔗

第 7 段

tolerant *adj.* 容忍的;宽容的
classification *n.* 分类;分级
forestry *n.* 林学;森林学
horticulture *n.* 园艺
habitat *n.* (动植物的)生活环境,产地、栖息地,居留地,自生地,聚集处
a series of 一系列的
characteristic *n.* 特性,特征
occupy *v.* 占据;占领
component *n.* 组成成分
adaptation *n.* 适应;适应性

考题解析

Questions 27–33

● 题型归类:TRUE/FALSE/NOT GIVEN

● 题目解析：

题目编号	题目定位词	答案位置	题解
27	evidence, support, photoperiodism	第2段 第4句	题目：很多科学证据支持“光周期现象”。 Photoperiodism 这个名词的第一次出现是在第2段的第4句，考生应该很容易定位。这一句的前半句提出这个新名词，而后半句就紧接着指出，能证明这个现象的实验证据相当可观，并且下文紧跟了一个实例来证明。因此答案确定为 TRUE。 题目中把原文的 experimental 换成了 scientific，这应该不会影响考生的判断。
28	bird, breed out of season	第2段 第5句	题目：一些种类的鸟受到鼓励，错季生育。 这道题的出处紧连着上题，这有利于考生迅速定位题目。原文说，一些鸟类只是在人工增加日照长度的条件下，就能在隆冬季节生殖繁育。根据常识判断，隆冬季节肯定不是鸟类繁育的时间；句中的 be induced 意为“引诱、诱使”，等同于题目中的 be encouraged to do sth.。因此答案确定为 TRUE。
29	photoperiodism, geographic areas		题目：“光周期现象”只是在某些地理区域才会发生。 在解题时，考生会觉得拿不准。在 TRUE/FALSE/NOT GIVEN 这类题型中，凡是考生第一感觉拿不准的题目，一般都是 NG。这也是一个做题技巧。 本文说，根据对日照长度的反应不同，可以将植物分为三种：short-day plants, long-day plants, day-neutral plants。前两种都是需要光来提示的，而只有后者才不需要这种提示：regardless of photoperiod/the day length。所以 Photoperiodism 受物种的限制，至于会不会受地域的限制，文中没有提到。故选 NOT GIVEN。
30	desert annuals, long-day plants	第4段 最后一句	题目：沙漠一年生植物是长日照植物的典型。 考生很容易就会在原文中定位 desert annuals，这种植物的最大特点是 regardless of the day length，这是 day-neutral 植物的典型特点；再者，关键词出现的句子是一个例证（for example），证明上句提到的 day-neutral 植物具有进化优势。所以答案确定为 FALSE。
31	bamboos, flower	第5段	题目：竹子一生中开花数次。 作者在第5段提到竹子是那种生育季节推迟的多年生植物，开一次花需要多年的等待，一次轮回需要31年，怎么可能开花数次呢？故答案确定为 FALSE。
32	yet, Chusquea abietifolia's seasonal rhythm	第5段 第5句	题目：科学家尚未确定何为 Chusquea abietifolia's 竹子季节性生育规律的诱因。 该题的答案相对来说容易确定，文章中只有第5段提到

			过这种竹子,但至今对它的生育规律的成因了解不多:The climatic trigger for this flowering cycle is not yet known。因此答案确定为 TRUE。
33	Eastern hemlock, fast-growing plant	文章最后两句	题目:(加拿大)铁杉是一种快速生长的植物。 从文中考生了解到,(加拿大)铁杉是一种耐阴型植物,所以我们必须要知道耐阴型植物的生长特点。根据文章最后一段对植物的分类标准可得知,耐阴性植物光合作用速度低,因此生长缓慢:shade-tolerant plants have lower photosynthetic rates and hence have lower growth rates than those of shade-intolerant species。在解答此题时,考生只需做一个简单的归类即可。

Questions 34–40

● 题型归类:Sentence Completion

该类题型考查考生对文章细节的辨别和掌握能力。在解题时,考生先要准确理解题意,根据关键词准确定位,而且需要特别注意空格处的语法成分以及题目中的字数限制。

● 题目解析:

题目编号	题目定位词	答案位置	题解
34	day length, cue, breeding, unpredictable	第 2 段 第 2、3 句	读题后首先判断空格处应该填写名词或名词性短语。文章中第一次提到日照长度是生育的一个有效提示是在第 2 段。在进一步解释这一点时,作者以温带地区的春天这一特定时间段为例论证,因为这一地区到了春天,气温起伏不定:temperatures fluctuate greatly from day to day,但是日照时间却稳步增长。这说明,在这一地区,气温难以预料,不能用来作提示,只有日照时间是可靠的(reliable)。所以答案是 temperatures。
35	plants, do not respond to light levels	第 2 段 最后一句	从题目上看,空格中所需词语是一类植物的总称,在第 2 段作者根据对日照长度的反应不同,将植物分为三种:short-day plants, long-day plants, day-neutral plants。前两种都是需要光来提示的,而只有后者才不需要这种提示:regardless of photoperiod,所以后者是答案。
36	birds, temperate climates, longer days, nesting	第 3 段 最后一句	光不仅对于植物重要,对于动物也是一个重要的提示。第 3 段就是说明光对于动物生育规律的重要性。动物生育前必先准备好充足的食物支撑繁殖带来的能量消耗,为幼鸟们提供给养。随着日照时间增长,鸟类就知道春天到了,食物来源能得到保证:adequate food resources will be assured。日照时间对于鸟类来说,是开始储备粮食准备生育的提示。

37	plants, depend on, reproduce	第4段 第3句	题目中的 plants that flower when days are long 指的就是 long-day plants,第四段告诉考生这种植物的授精(fertilization)要靠昆虫。根据常识,授精是生育(reproduce)的第一步。所以解答这道题的时候,考生要能理解题目中涉及的基本生物知识。
38	desert annuals, signal, reproduction	第4段 最后一句	关于沙漠一年生植物前面已经出现过多次类似的题,所以考生应该很容易定位答案。这种植物是日中性植物,不依靠日照时间来作为生育的提示,它所依赖的是 suitable rainfall,只要下雨,它们就会发芽开花结籽。
39	no limit, photosynthetic rate	第6段 最后一句	首先我们在文中定位 photosynthetic rate,在第6段中我们发现植物的 photosynthetic rate 可以根据光强度的不同而不同,作者用了 some... others... 这个句型来进一步阐述。有些植物可以达到最大值(maximum),而有的则永远也达不到(never reach a maximum),像甘蔗。考生需要知道 no limit 在题目中的意思等于 never reach a maximum。
40	tolerance to shade, forestry, horticulture	第6段 第1、2句	题目中的定位词不难在文中发现,但是有的考生可能不知道 criterion 就是 criteria 的单数形式。第6段开头说明耐阴性和非耐阴性是植物的两大分类(classification),这种分类也常用于林学和园艺学。可以说,耐阴性和非耐阴性都是植物分类的标准(criterion)之一。

参考译文

光对植物和动物的影响

光之所以对于生物很重要,有两大原因:首先,它可以作为一天不同时刻和动植物体内的季节性节奏变化的提示;其次,它可以用来促进植物生长。

对于大多数生物来说,生殖和繁育只能在一年的某一时间段进行,所以就需要一个可靠的提示来引发生育行为。日照长度是一个很好的提示,因为它能提供一年内一个可预知的变化模式。春天的温带地区,气温每天变化不定,但是日照长度以一个可预知的数量稳步增加。日照长度给生理反应带来的季节性影响被称为"光周期现象",并且能证明这种现象的实验证据的数量也相当可观。例如,一些鸟类只是在人工增加日照长度的条件下,就能在隆冬季节生殖繁育(沃夫森 1964 年)。"光周期现象"的例子同样也在植物身上发生。当日照长度低于某一临界日长时,一株短日照植物就会开花。而某一临界日长被超出时,一株长日照植物就会开花。在这两种情况中,临界日长依物种不同而不同。那些不管日照时间经过一段时间营养生长后开花的植物,被称为日中性植物。

对于像鸟类这样的动物来说,生育季节已经进化成可以在一年中的某一特定时间段里进行,在这一段时间里它们的后代有最大的生存机会。在生育季节开始之前,它们必须储备充足的食物,不仅要支撑繁殖带来的能量消耗,还要为在巢中和即将成熟的幼鸟们提供给养。所以许多生活在温带地区的鸟类把春天里逐渐变长的日照长度当作提示,准备开始筑巢,因为这是能保证充足食物来源的时候。

在植物身上体现出来的对光周期现象的适应性意义也同样清楚。生活在温带地区的短日照植物是把春暖花开的时候作为最佳的种子生长时间。长日照植物需要通过昆虫代为授精或需要较长的种子成熟期。温带地区在秋天开花的短日照植物能够为生长季节和冬天的种子储存食物。当繁殖的最佳时间与日照长度的结合不是那么肯定的时候,日中性植物在进化上的优势就表现出来了。例如,只要下雨,不管日照时间多长,沙漠中的一年生植物就开始发芽、开花、结籽。

一些植物的生育季节可以被拖得很长。竹子是多年生草本植物,可以多年保持营养生长状态,然后突然开花、结果,然后死去(伊万斯1976年)。在1884年的时候,牙买加岛屿上的所有竹子都开花结籽,然后死去。下一代竹子是在1916至1918年之间开花结籽,然后死去。这表明一个轮回大约是31年。这种轮回的气候诱因现在尚不得知,但是它的适应性意义却很清楚。大批竹子的种子同时产生(有些种子埋在地下12-15厘米深处),使所有的以种子为生的动物一下子吃不光,所以有些种子就逃脱了被吃掉的命运,成长为下一代竹子(伊万斯1976年)。

光对于生物很重要还有第二个原因,那就是它在光合作用中是最重要的因素。在光合作用的过程中,植物利用来自太阳的能量将来自土壤或水的碳元素转化为生长所需的有机物质。光合作用的速度可以通过计算它摄取碳的速度来计算。随着光的强度的不同,植物的光合作用反应也不同。有些植物在充分光照的四分之一强时达到最大的光合作用;而像甘蔗这样的植物从来也达不到最大值,但是会随着光线强度的增加而持续光合作用的速度。

总体上,植物可以分为两大类:耐阴型和非耐阴型。这种分类办法在林业和园艺业也是广泛应用的。耐阴型植物光合作用速度低,因此生长速度低于那些非耐阴型植物。植物会适应某一特定的生活环境,并且在这一过程中,进化出一系列特性阻止它们占据别的生活环境。格雷姆(1966年)指出光可能是指引这些适应变化的几种重要的生长元素之一。比如,(加拿大)铁杉的种子就属于耐阴型的。它们可以在森林的底层靠着微弱的光线存活,因为它们的光合作用速度低。

WRITING

WRITING TASK 1

a) Question analysis, including discussion of main features, comparisons that need to be made, and possible misinterpretations of the question. (审题)

"The table below gives information about the underground railway systems in six cities. Summarise the information by selecting and reporting the main features, and make comparisons where relevant."

Points to note. (审题要点)

1. The table lists six cities and three pieces of information.(表中列举了六座城市和三种信息。)
2. The number of passengers each system carries is given in "millions per year".(各个地铁系统负载的旅客量以"百万每年"为单位。)
3. The geographical location of the cities (e.g. in Japan/America/Europe) is irrelevant.(各个城市所在的地理位置<例如:日本/美国/欧洲>与我们的讨论无关。)
4. Candidates should include as much of the information as possible.(考生需要在文中包含尽可能多的信息。)

Main features and comparisons. (主要特征和比较)

1. Three of the systems are old and three are new.(六个系统当中有三个是新的,另外三个历史较长。)

2. London's system is significantly longer and older than any other.（伦敦的系统远长于其他系统，历史也更久远。）
3. Kyoto and Los Angeles have very small systems and Los Angeles has a very new one.（京都和洛杉矶的系统规模较小，并且洛杉矶的系统非常新。）
4. Tokyo's system carries by far the most people.（东京的系统负载的旅客量要远大于其他系统。）
5. The systems in Paris and London carry very large numbers of people.（巴黎和伦敦的系统负载了相当大的旅客量。）
6. The systems in Kyoto and Los Angeles carry relatively few people.（京都和洛杉矶的系统负载相对较小的旅客量。）

Possible misinterpretations and problems.（审题误区）

1. The chart is very clearly laid out and there should be no problems misinterpreting the data.（本图表非常清晰地展示了相关信息，因此在对数据的解读上应该不会存在太大问题。）
2. The chart contains a lot of information. This is good because it means that it should be easy to write at least 150 words about it. You should try to include every piece of information, but it is not absolutely necessary for a good band score. The examiner knows that you only have 20 minutes to write the report.（图表中包含了相当多的信息。这意味着要写出至少 150 词的短文难度应该不会太大。你应该试图包含全部的信息，但是这不是取得高分的必要条件，因为测试人知道你只有 20 分钟的时间来完成这个报告。）

b）*Suggested answer format, including contrast with possible unsuitable formats.*（写作思路）

The introduction should consist of rewriting the sentence "The table below gives information about the underground railway systems in six cities." The obvious changes are:（引言部分应该包含对题干说明"下表给出了关于六座城市地下铁路系统的信息"的改写。改写时明显可以采用的变化有：）

i）add "three pieces of [information]".（加入"三种 <信息>"。）

ii）change "underground railway systems" to "subway networks".（把"地下铁路系统"改成"地铁网络"。）

iii）add on what the three pieces of information are.（补充说明这三种信息是什么。）

Candidates are faced with a choice of looking at each city in turn or examining each of the three pieces of information in turn. Either method is acceptable. However, the important thing to remember is that you should not simply list the information (e.g. "The subway networks in London, Paris, and Tokyo are 394, 199, and 155 kilometers long respectively.") This will certainly lose you points!（考生们面临着一个选择：到底是先依次考查各个城市还是依次考查各个方面的信息。两种方式都是可行的。但是很重要的一点是不能只是简单地列举所有的信息 <比如"伦敦、巴黎、东京的地铁网络的长度分别是 394、199、155 千米">。这肯定会让你丢掉分数！）

Writing a paragraph on each city is not a good idea. Each paragraph will be very short and it will appear that you are listing information rather than examining it. In the model answer, we have divided the six cities into two groups of three. This reflects the fact that three of the systems are old and three are new. Each of these groups shares certain characteristics—the three older systems carry the most passengers and are the longest. A short conclusion stating this is a good idea.（分别就每座城市各写一个段落，这样写不好。这样每个段落会很短，而且会显得你只是在列举信息，而没有进行分析。在范文当中，我们把六座城市分成了两个组，每组三座城市。这体现了其中三个系统历史相对较长，另外三个则历史较短。各组城市中的成员具备某些特定的共同点——三个历史较长的系统负载了最多的旅客，里程也最长。用一个简短的结论对此进行说明和总结是不错的选择。）

c) *Model answer.*（参考范文）

The table gives us three pieces of information about subway networks in six cities—the date that the system first opened, the total number of kilometers each system has, and the number of passengers each system carries per year.

London has the oldest system, opened in 1863, and the most extensive network, at 394 kilometers, almost double that of the next largest network (Paris). London's network carries 775 million passengers per year, less than Paris and Tokyo. Paris' system was opened in 1900 and is the second largest, at 199 kilometers. It also carries the second largest number of passengers—1191 million per year. Tokyo's network opened in 1927 and is 155 kilometers long. It carries more passengers than the others—1927 million per year. That is over 50% more than Paris and 2.5 times the number of passengers using London's system.

Washington DC has had a subway system since 1976. It is 126 kilometers long—close to Tokyo in length, but carrying far fewer passengers—144 million per year. Kyoto has had a network since 1981. It's the shortest of the six, at 11 kilometers, and carries the least number of people—45 million per year. The network in Los Angeles was opened in 2001, is 28 kilometers long, and carries 50 million people a year. This makes it the second shortest and second lowest in terms of number of passengers.

Overall, it can be seen that the three oldest networks are the most extensive and carry the most passengers, whilst the systems in Kyoto and Los Angeles are particularly small.

译文：

表格为我们给出了关于六座城市地铁网络的三种信息——系统最早开放的日期、各个系统总长度的千米数、以及各系统每年负载的旅客数量。

伦敦的系统历史最长，建成启动于 1863 年。它同时也是最长的网络，达到了 394 公里，几乎是第二大网络（巴黎地铁网络）的两倍之多。伦敦的网络每年要负载 7 亿 7 千 5 百万旅客，比巴黎和东京网络要少。巴黎的系统启动于 1900 年，也是第二长的系统，达到了 199 公里。它负载的旅客量排在第二——每年 11 亿 9 千 1 百万人。东京的网络启动于 1927 年，长度达到了 155 公里。它负载的旅客量比其他所有系统都要更大——每年 19 亿 2 千 7 百万人。这个数字比巴黎的要大百分之五十，而且是伦敦数字的二点五倍。

华盛顿特区的地铁系统启动于 1976 年。它的长度达到 126 公里——在长度上与东京很接近，但是在旅客负载量上却远远少于东京，仅有每年 1 亿 4 千 4 百万人。京都地铁系统启动于 1981 年。它的长度是六个系统中最短的，仅有 11 公里，负载的旅客量也是最小的——每年 4 千 5 百万人。洛杉矶地铁系统启动于 2001 年，长度达到 28 公里，每年负载了 5 千万乘客。它是六个系统中长度第二短的，旅客负载量也是第二少的。

总的来说，可以看出历史最长的三个网络是规模最大的，同时也负载了最多的旅客量，而另一方面京都和洛杉矶的系统规模则相当小。

d) *Analysis of vocabulary and structures used in model answer, including possible mistakes made by candidates.*（语言分析）

This can be a tricky Question for some candidates because they memorise vocabulary associated with trends over time—and none are shown in this table. Using words and phrases like 'climb', 'fall', and 'remain steady' is impossible in this task.（这个问题可能对有些考生来说有点难，因为他们识记的是体现数字随时间变化而变化的趋势的词汇——但是这些在这个表中没有体现。因此写这篇文章的时候，几乎无法用上例如"上升"、"下滑"、或是"保持稳定"等来表达。）

The writer uses the comparative and superlative forms of adjectives to compare cities—e. g. "London has the oldest system... and the most extensive network".（范文作者使用了形容词的比较级和最高级来比较各个城市——例如"伦敦的系统历史最长……它同时也是最长的网络"。）

The writer also uses numerical comparisons—e. g. "That is over 50% more than Paris and 2.5 times the number of passengers using London's system."（作者还使用了数字方面的比较——例如"这个数字比巴黎的要大 50%，而且是伦敦数字的 2.5 倍"。）

When talking about when the underground railway systems opened, the past tense will be used most often. However, it is possible to use the present perfect tense—e. g. "Washington DC has had a subway system since 1976."（在说明各个地下铁路系统启动时间的时候，过去时应该是使用频率最高的。但是还是有可能用到现在完成时——例如"华盛顿特区的地铁系统启动于 1976 年"。）

WRITING TASK 2

a) *Question analysis, including discussion of the points that need to be made in the essay, possible misinterpretations of the question, and brainstorming diagrams.*（审题）

"Research indicates that the characteristics we are born with have much more influence on our personality and development than any experiences we may have in our life. Which do you consider to be the major influence?"

Possible misinterpretations and problems.（审题误区）

1. The Question prompt clearly refers to the nature or nurture debate. Most Chinese candidates are familiar with it, so this Question shouldn't produce any major difficulties.（这个题目很明显涉及到了天生特质和后天培养之间的争议。大多数中国考生对这个问题都有所了解，因此它应该不会带来太大的麻烦。）
2. The Question asks, "Which do you consider to be the major influence?" This suggests that neither nature nor nurture is completely responsible for a person's character. However, you can take the view that one is completely responsible if you wish. Bear in mind that taking a position somewhere between might be wise, since there is plenty of evidence on both sides.（问题问道："你认为最主要的影响应该是哪一种？"这暗示了先天特质和后天培养都不能完全决定一个人的个性。但是如果你愿意的话，也可以选择这样的观点：其中一种完全决定了人的个性。牢记一点：选择一个介于两极之间的位置可能是比较睿智的选择，因为在两个方面都会有很丰富的证据。）
3. You should discuss both sides, but you can give more weight to one side than the other.（你应该讨论到两个方面，但是你可以更侧重讨论其中的某一个方面。）

b) *Suggested answer format, including contrast with possible unsuitable formats.*（写作思路）

For this question, the essay format should involve an introduction, two or three main paragraphs, and a conclusion. The introduction should be short and may or may not include the writer's opinion. Each of the main paragraphs should focus on a particular argument. However, these main paragraphs can either focus on one side of the argument or take into account the opposite point of view. The conclusion should be short and state the writer's opinion.（回答这个问题的时候，文章中应该包括一个引入部分，两到三个主体段，以及一个结论段落。引入段应该很简短，可以包含考生的观点，也可以不包含。各主体段应该分别着重讨论一个讨论的点。不过各主体段可以选择只是着重分析讨论点一方的观点，也可

以选择同时考虑对立一方的观点。结论段应该很简短，并且包含作者的观点。）

The most important thing is to make sure that each of the main paragraphs focuses clearly on one argument. If several arguments are included in the same paragraph they could confuse the reader. It is also important that each argument be well developed, and having a separate paragraph for each will help the writer achieve this.（最重要的问题是要保证每个主体段清晰地集中关注一个讨论点。如果在同一个段落中出现了多个讨论点，那么读者会困惑不解。此外关于每个讨论点的分析应该很有组织地展开，如果采用一个独立的段落来讨论每个点对此会很有帮助。）

c) Two model answers of around 300 words, each essay taking a different view. **（参考范文）**

Model answer 1—Nature.（范文 1，支持 Nature）

The debate about whether each individual person is born the way they are or is created by their environment is one that has been going on for centuries. In my opinion, the major influence is nature—a person is born as they are and that decides, in general, how they will be throughout their lives.

It is well known that a person's appearance depends largely on how their parents look. Genes from parents combine to create the genes of their children. It should be no surprise that scientists are now finding genes that influence things other than how a person looks. For example, scientists have discovered a gene that influences whether a person can run quickly over a short distance or less quickly, but for a longer distance. Scientists have also discovered genes that influence how quickly a person becomes violent. These and other discoveries may eventually help us to select athletes based on their natural talents and identify people who are more likely to commit violent crime.

I believe that nature influences people in another way. It is well known that people react to others partly, and often largely, on the basis of how they look—whether they are attractive, fat, have a particular skin colour, etc. Given that these characteristics have a natural basis, it is clear that how a person is when they are born has a great influence.

Clearly, a person's environment can have an influence on them. Everyone has good and bad experiences that help shape how they react the next time they are in a similar situation. However, I do not think that these experiences usually have a greater influence than natural, genetic factors.

In conclusion, neither nature nor nurture is 100% responsible for the way a person is, but I think that nature's influence is greater and that, as scientists uncover the meaning of more genes, this will become clearer.

译文：

关于人的个性是天生的还是后天生存环境所决定的争议已经持续了千百年。在我看来，天生特质是主要的影响因素——一个人的个性如何在出生时就已经确定了，也大体决定了在此后的生命过程中他们会是怎样的人。

正如大家所熟知的，人们的外表取决于他们父母亲的样子。父母亲的基因合在一起产生了子女的基因。现在我们已经毫不意外科学家们在逐渐发现影响人类外观以外的基因。举例来说，科学家已经发现了这样一种基因，它可以影响到人们到底是可以在短距离上跑得很快还是可以以慢一些的速度跑得更远。科学家们还发现了可以影响人们变得狂暴的过程快慢的基因。这些发现，以及其他同类发现，最终可以帮助我们根据人们的天赋来挑选运动员，或是确定哪些人会更有可能犯罪。

我认为天生特质还会以另一种方式影响人们。众所周知，人们对其他人的反应在一定程度上，常常是很大程度上，取决于这些人的外表——取决于他们到底是引人注目，是体型肥胖，还是肤色特别，诸如此类。考虑到这些特征都是基于人们天生的特质，很显然一个人在出生时是怎样的人有非常重大的影响。

很显然，人们所在的环境可以对他们产生影响。每个人都会有好的或是不好的体验来帮助他们在下次碰到类似情形时作出反应。但是我不认为这些经验通常会比天然的基因的因素产生的影响还大。

总的来说，天生特质和后天培养都不能完全决定一个人的个性，但是我认为天生特质的影响要更大一些，并且随着科学家们发现更多基因的意义，这一点会越来越明显。

Model answer 2—Nurture.（范文2，支持 **Nature**）

There has been an ongoing discussion as to whether a person is more influenced by nature (by their genes, inherited from their parents) or by nurture (the way that they are brought up and their experiences in life). In this essay, I would like to look at both points of view.

Each person, from the time that they are born, is influenced by the people, things, tastes, sounds, sights, and smells that surround them. These influence what people like to eat, listen to, the kind of people they enjoy spending time with, even the job that they decide to do. These things are the result of a person's experience. Whilst it is possible that genes have some influence, I find it hard to believe that they would count for more than all the thousands of experiences each person has.

Scientists have, in recent years, claimed to have discovered genes that influence people in ways that many people never thought possible. I recently read that a scientist claimed to have discovered a gene that made people more likely to commit crimes. Even if this discovery turns out to be true, it still doesn't mean that all people with this gene will become criminals. Therefore, a person's environment and upbringing must have a great influence. Like many people, I find it too simple to say that a person whose parents are criminals will become one too.

To conclude, I agree that genes do influence people and we will probably make more discoveries about their influence in the future. However, I firmly believe that a person's uncountable experiences have more bearing on the kind of person they are.

译文：

一直以来就有这样一个争议：到底人们是受天生特质（来自他们父母的基因）的影响更大，还是受后天培养（他们成长的方式以及在生活中的体验）的影响更大。在本文当中，我将对这两个观点都进行讨论。

每个人从出生的时候开始，就要受到身边的人、事物、味道、声响、情景和气味的影响。这些会影响到人们喜欢吃什么，听什么，喜欢和怎样的人共处，甚至于是他们决定要做的工作。这些都是一个人的体验导致的结果。尽管一方面人们的天生特质会有一定的作用，但是我觉得很难相信它所带来的影响会大于每个人成千上万的各种经历带来的影响。

近年来，科学家声称已经发现了某些基因会在人们从未想到过的方面对我们产生影响。我最近通过阅读了解到有一位科学家声称发现了一种基因，它会让人们更有可能犯罪。即使这个发现最终被证实是对的，它还是不能说明只要有这个基因的人就会成为罪犯。因此，一个人的环境和成长过程肯定会有重大的影响。和很多人一样，我觉得，断言父母都是罪犯的人其子女也会成为罪犯的观点太过武断。

总的来说，我同意基因会对人类产生影响，而且我们将来或许会对它们所能产生的影响有更多的发现。然而我坚定地相信一个人不可计数的各种体验，会更多地影响到这个人的成长。

d) *Analysis of vocabulary and structures used in model answer, including possible mistakes made by candidates.* (语言分析)

"In my opinion, the major influence is nature—a person is born as they are and that decides, in general, how they will be throughout their lives." The candidate has clearly expressed an opinion and the use of 'in general' indicates that it is not an extreme one. ("在我看来,天生特质是主要的影响因素———个人的个性如何在出生时就已经确定了,也大体决定了在此后的生命过程中他们会是怎样的人。"这位考生清楚地表达了个人的看法,而且使用"大体"表明了他的观点不极端。)

"It is well known that a person's appearance depends largely on how their parents look." The candidate begins by using the argument that our genes influence how we look, and then continues to point out recent scientific discoveries supporting his/her argument. "It should be no surprise that scientists are now finding genes that influence things other than how a person looks." ("正如大家所熟知的,人们的外表取决于他们父母亲的样子。"这位考生从我们的基因影响我们的外表这一点开始讨论,进而指出近来的科学发现支持他/她的观点。"现在我们已经毫不意外科学家们在逐渐发现影响人类外观以外的基因。")

"These and other discoveries may eventually help us to select athletes based on their natural talents and identify people who are more likely to commit violent crime." The candidate develops his/her answer by pointing out how these discoveries could prove useful. ("这些发现,以及其他同类发现,最终可以帮助我们根据人们的天赋来挑选运动员,或是确定哪些人会更有可能犯罪。"这位考生通过指出这些发现会怎样被证明有实用意义来进一步展开他/她的论述。)

"It is well known that people react to others partly, and often largely, on the basis of how they look-whether they are attractive, fat, have a particular skin colour, etc." The writer points out that our genetic (nature) characteristics influence our experiences (nurture). ("众所周知,人们对其他人的反应在一定程度上,常常是很大程度上,取决于这些人的外表——取决于他们到底是引人注目,是体型肥胖,还是肤色特别,诸如此类。"作者指出了我们的基因特点<天生特质>影响我们的体验<后天培养>。)

"There has been an ongoing discussion as to whether a person is more influenced by nature (by their genes, inherited from their parents) or by nurture (the way that they are brought up and their experiences in life)." The writer makes it clear that he/she understands that the Question is about the 'nature or nurture' debate. ("一直以来就有这样一个争议:到底人们是受天生特质<来自他们父母的基因>的影响更大,还是受后天培养<他们成长的方式以及在生活中的体验>的影响更大。"这里作者表明了他/她明白这里讨论的问题是关于"天生特质还是后天培养"的争议。)

"Each person, from the time that they are born, is influenced by the people, things, tastes, sounds, sights, and smells that surround them." The writer points out specific things that people experience every day. ("每个人从出生的时候开始,就要受到身边的人、事物、味道、声响、情景和气味的影响。"作者指出了人们每天会经历的一些具体的事情。)

"I recently read that a scientist claimed to have discovered a gene that made people more likely to commit crimes. Even if this discovery turns out to be true, it still doesn't mean that all people with this gene will become criminals." The candidate looks at the opposing argument and then rebuts it effectively. ("我最近通过阅读了解到有一位科学家声称发现了一种基因,它会让人们更有可能犯罪。即使这个发现最终被证实是对的,它还是不能说明只要有这个基因的人就会成为罪犯。"作者分析了对立的观点,同时有力地对它进行了反驳。)

"I find it too simple to say that a person whose parents are criminals will become one too." Notice that the candidate doesn't deny the possibility that children with parents who are criminals could themselves become criminals, jut that it is not something that is automatically true. ("我觉得,断言父母都是罪犯

的人其子女也会成为罪犯的观点太过武断。"注意这里作者没有否认父母都是罪犯的孩子同样也有成为罪犯的可能性，只不过这并不是一个必然要发生的情况。）

SPEAKING

a*) *Question analysis, including possible misinterpretations of the questions.

How important are clothes and fashion to you? Why? Why not?

Use words like 'quite' and 'very' to express the level of importance. Remember that for this series of Questions 'fashion' only refers to clothing.

What kind of clothes do you dislike? Why?

Don't say what you **like**!

How different are the clothes you wear now from those you wore 10 years ago?

Remember to use the past tense and the present perfect tense as appropriate. The Question asks 'How different...?', but if the clothes you wear are the same style, say so.

What do you think the clothes we wear say about us?

If you think that clothes say something about a person, you should give an example to illustrate your point. Be careful about making statements of certainty, for example using 'will'.

Describe a festival that is important in your country.

Candidates in China have prepared for this Question for years and so it shouldn't present any problems. Indeed, many examiners will regard this as a 'gift question'. Some candidates make the mistake of referring to more than one festival or of talking about a festival that is not important in China, e.g. a Western festival or a festival that is important only in their particular city or area. Make the examiner happy by not talking about the Spring Festival!

Why do you think festivals are important events in the working year?

Note that the Question talks about the importance of festivals in relation to work, so this should be the focus of your response, not culture or other aspects.

Would you agree that the original significance of festivals is often lost today? Is it good or bad, do you think?

If you give an example, make sure that you know the original significance of the festival. Many Chinese candidates choose examples of Western festivals and make mistakes because they do not know this.

Do you think new festivals will be introduced in the future? What kind?

Many Chinese candidates refer to Christmas or Valentine's Day in their answers to this question. These festivals have already been introduced into China—the Question asks if any "new festivals will be introduced".

b) Shortlist of useful vocabulary that candidates could use in their answers to each Question and brainstorming diagram for Part 2 questions.

How important are clothes and fashion to you? Why? Why not?

Wear, look fashionable/trendy, look/feel good, pay attention to fashion, appropriate, situation, celebrate, dress up, don't care, unfashionable, expensive, cheap, stylish, formal, informal, dark, brightly coloured, accessories.

What kind of clothes do you dislike? Why?

Horrible, awful, terrible, unfashionable, dirty, unclean, untidy.

How different are the clothes you wear now from those you wore 10 years ago?

Use words from the previous two questions.

What do you think the clothes we wear say about us?

Colours, style, optimistic, pessimistic, personality, follow fashion, sexy, can't tell much, rich, poor, judge a person by their clothes.

Describe a festival that is important in your country.

Chinese festivals—Spring Festival/Chinese New Year, Moon Festival, National Day, Dragon Boat Festival.
Significance—start of a new year, celebrate the founding of the PRC.
What people do—get a few days off work, give and receive presents, spend time with family and friends, keep traditions, eat and drink a lot, go shopping, visit places of interest, relax at home, dress up.

Why do you think festivals are important events in the working year?

Spend time with families and friends, go on a day trip, cultural meaning, treat them as days off work, have breaks from work.

Would you agree that the original significance of festivals is often lost today? Is it good or bad, do you think?

Doesn't (really) matter, different, (in)significant, remember, forget, meaning.

Do you think new festivals will be introduced in the future? What kind?

Celebrate, Western festivals, commercial, business, introduce.

c) Two model answers for each question.

How important are clothes and fashion to you? Why? Why not?

I love wearing fashionable clothes. I want to look trendy when I go out with my friends or boyfriend. When I look good, I feel good.

I don't pay much attention to fashion, but I do wear clothes that are appropriate to the situation I'm in. For example, if I'm celebrating something, I'll dress up a bit, but if I'm just relaxing with friends, even dirty jeans are OK.

What kind of clothes do you dislike? Why?

I dislike unfashionable clothes, but most of all I hate dirty clothes! Unfashionable clothes just don't look good, but dirty clothes are just horrible!

I can't think of any clothes I dislike. However, I think that some clothes are impractical. Actually, when I think about it, I don't like brightly coloured ties—you know, bright yellow or bright green. They look terrible!

How different are the clothes you wear now from those you wore 10 years ago?

Oh, ten years ago, I was just a little girl. I wore pretty dresses, and a uniform to school, whereas now I wear more fashionable clothes, like jeans, skirts, and all the accessories that go with them.

When I was younger, I wore smarter clothes. Now, I wear jeans and a T-shirt when I go out with friends, but before I wore smart trousers and a shirt. My dress style is far more casual now.

What do you think the clothes we wear say about us?

I think that the colours can tell us if the person is an optimistic or pessimistic person. The style tells us whether the person follows fashion or doesn't care about it. Some boys say that if a girl wears sexy clothes that means she is looking for a boyfriend, but I don't think that's true.

I don't think you can tell much about a person from the clothes they wear. For example, a friend of mine is really rich. He has a great job and he's a really nice guy. Girls don't like him because he just wears old jeans and a T-shirt when he goes out. They think he must be a poor guy with a bad personality, whereas the opposite is true. I think it's very dangerous to judge a person by their clothes rather than their personality.

Describe a festival that is important in your country.

I'd like to talk about Christmas. It's on 25th December, as you know, and the original meaning of the festival is that it celebrates the birth of Christ. However, I think that for many people it has lost its original significance and is simply a time when people get a few days off work and give and receive presents. I don't think that's really a bad thing. Giving presents to people you love and like, and spending time with them, is important. Most families keep Christmas traditions such as having a Christmas tree and putting presents under it. On Christmas Eve, children put stockings at the end of their beds for Santa Claus to fill with small presents. Sometimes I wonder how many of the children really believe that the presents come from Santa, rather than from their parents. Most people like to eat and drink a lot over the Christmas holiday. They buy turkey, Christmas pudding, chocolates, and all kinds of drinks.

The festival that I would like to talk about is Halloween—I'm sure you've heard of it. On this day, people in my country believe that ghosts walk the earth. To symbolise this, children dress up in scary costumes and go from house to house. At each house, they say "Trick or treat" and the person living there gives them candy or will have to suffer a trick. Almost everyone gives the children candy, which the children put into big bags. Adults don't generally celebrate this day, but they spend time helping their children make costumes and some parents go with younger children from house to house to make sure they are safe.

Why do you think festivals are important events in the working year?

They give people a chance to spend time with their families and friends. They can go on a day trip or have a picnic in a local park. I know that festivals originally had a greater cultural meaning, but I think that most people don't think about that much nowadays.

Festivals are an important part of a country's culture, but I think that most people treat them as days off work. It's certainly important to have breaks from work so that you can do the things that interest you.

Would you agree that the original significance of festivals is often lost today? Is it good or bad, do you think?

As I said before, yes, I agree. I don't think it really matters very much. Some people think that culture is something that stands still. It isn't. Our culture today is quite different from what it was 100 or 1000 years ago.

I would agree, but I think it is a bad thing. Culture is what holds a country together. If we lose it, for example by forgetting the original meanings of festivals, we will be no different from any other country in the world.

Do you think new festivals will be introduced in the future? What kind?

Yes, I do. We already celebrate Christmas and Valentine's Day and I believe that we will start celebrating other Western festivals. I think this will happen because businesses will see a chance to sell more during festivals, not because the people really have any interest in them.

I think we will start celebrating new festivals, particularly Western ones. I'm not sure what kind, as I'm not very familiar with foreign festivals. It would be nice to introduce some new festivals that aren't from abroad.

d) Text boxes showing how sentences can be completed. For example:

When I was younger, I ...	wore pretty dresses.
	wore smarter clothes.
	dressed differently.

I think it's ...	very dangerous	to judge a person by their clothes.
	very easy	
	OK	

Most people ...	eat and drink a lot	over the Christmas holiday.
Some people ...	visit their family and friends	during the Spring Festival.
Many people ...	celebrate	on National Day.

Festivals are ...	just days off work for most people.
	important breaks from work.
	an important part of our culture.

I think we will (not) ...	introduce new festivals	in the future.
	celebrate Western festivals	over the next few years.
	start celebrating new festivals	

General Training: Reading and Writing Test A

READING

SECTION 1

文章结构

体　裁	应用文
主要内容	新衣邮购宣传册

词汇注释

文　章

brochure *n.* 小册子
special *n.* (通过广告宣传的)大减价;优惠活动
cotton *n.* 棉花
woolen *adj.* 毛纺的
casual *adj.* 随意的;休闲的
patterned *adj.* 有图案装饰的;带花样的
belt *n.* 腰带
shirt *n.* 衬衫;衬衣
occasion *n.* 场合
variety *n.* 多样性;品种
motif *n.* 装饰的图案或式样
polyester *n.* 聚酯
blend *n.* 混合
plain *adj.* 简单的;朴素的
ironing *n.* 熨平衣服
colorfast *adj.* 不褪色的
hooded jacket 带帽夹克
waterproof *adj.* 防水的
zipper *n.* 拉链
gift voucher 礼券
purchase *n.* 购买
backpack *n.* 背包
postage *n.* 邮资
packing *n.* 包装
charge *n.* 费用
overnight *adj.* 晚上的;夜里的
surface mail *n.* 平信
minimum *n.* 最小值
airmail *n.* 航空邮件
delivery *n.* 递送(货物等)
destination *n.* 目的地

考题解析

Questions 1–7

● 题型归类:TRUE/FALSE/NOT GIVEN

雅思 G 类阅读的 TRUE/FALSE/NOT GIVEN 题型一般都比较直白,文章篇幅较短,结构明显,考生只需根据文中的信息做出简单比较和推测即可。

● 题目解析:

题目编号	题目定位词	答案位置	题解
1	women's cotton socks	For under $10 部分	题目:女袜要比男袜便宜。 在解答这类细节判断题时,要首先抓住文章给出的规律性信息。在本文中,厂家分别用三个黑体的代号 M,W,C 分别代表男性、女性、和儿童,这极大地加快了我们做题时的检索速度,尽快定位答案。 文中出现袜子的只有 For under $10 部分,但是考生发现那里只有儿童穿的袜子(C),没有题目中的男袜和女袜,所以二者的比较没有依据。因此答案是 NOT GIVEN。
2	men's silk shirt, five colors	For under $25 和 For under $50 部分	题目:男士丝质衬衫有五种颜色可选择。 文中出现男士丝质衬衫的有两个地方:For under $25 和 For under $50 部分,扫描结果发现,这种衬衫有五个尺寸,并且给出了颜色分别是 designer color 和 plain。考生可不要看花眼。因此答案是 NOT GIVEN。
3	children's T-shirts	For under $25 部分	题目:儿童短袖汗衫颜色多样。 出现儿童短袖汗衫的地方只有 For under $25 部分,原文是:a variety of animal motifs(多种动物图案可选择),出题人偷换了概念;而且原文中清楚地表示,T-shirts 的颜色是 white。故选 FALSE。
4	child's jacket, four pockets	For under $50 部分	题目:儿童夹克有四个口袋。 原文中的 jacket 前面还有一个定语 hooded,去掉它不影响做题。在产品描述中,这种夹克是带有口袋:large strong pockets,但没有说有多少口袋。出现 4 这个数字的是 4 sizes(4 个尺寸),出题人又想迷惑考生。这提醒考生做题时一定要谨慎,不要头脑发热。
5	$80, August	Additional monthly special 部分	题目:如果您在八月购衣超过 80 美元,可免费获赠一个闹钟。 在解题时,我们需要把题目中出现的所有有用信息回归到原文,看是否缺少限定条件。本题中的限定条件:$80, August 都与原文相符,闹钟也是条件的结果,因此答案确定为 TRUE。
6	special next-day delivery, in Australia	Note: Postage and packing charges 部分	题目:澳大利亚境内隔夜到达的快递收费金额为7.95 美元。 该题很好判断,收费金额为 7.95 美元的邮递方式是 regular post(普通邮件),故选 FALSE。

7	all clothing, within two months	Note: Postage and packing charges 部分	题目:所有的衣服都能保证在两个月内送达。该题实际上考查一个关键词:minimum(最小值)。原文说,国际邮递最少需要两个月(allow a minimum of two months for delivery)。这就自然驳斥了题目中的说法,故选 FALSE。

参考译文

邮购目录单

想带给全家更棒的穿衣点子吗?

七月衣服优惠标识:

M 代表男人　　W 代表女人　　C 代表儿童

10 美元以下的有:

棉袜 C ——纯棉制成,适合长时间穿着

毛袜 C ——在冬天为小孩子的脚保暖

运动袜 M ——可搭配牛仔和其他休闲衣着

带图案的腰带 W ——可搭配牛仔和其他休闲衣着

25 美元以下的有:

棉质衬衫 W ——适合白天与晚上穿着

丝绸衬衫 M ——5 个尺寸,颜色出自设计师之手,适合特别社交场合

短袖汗衫 C ——耐穿,白色,多种动物图案可选择

彩色短袖汗衫 M W ——棉、聚酯合成,素色,免熨

50 美元以下的有:

蓝色牛仔服 M W ——不缩水,不褪色,只有小号

丝绸衬衫 M W ——素色或带图案,所有尺寸都有

带帽夹克 C ——防风,4 个尺寸,带宽大结实口袋

夹克 W ——防水,拉链在前,所有尺寸都有

●也可购买礼券,别人也可选购。礼券有 10 美元,20 美元和 50 美元面额。

七月至九月还有更多每月优惠:

七月 ——凡购物超过 60 美元以上均可获赠价值 10 美元的礼券

八月 ——凡购物超过 80 美元以上(含 80 美元)可免费获得价值 19.95 美元的旅行闹钟

九月 ——凡使用信用卡消费满 75 美元以上可免费获赠儿童背包

注:邮资和包装费用说明

适用于下列各项:

澳大利亚境内
普通邮寄每件收费 7.95 美元
快递服务(夕发朝至)收费 17.95 美元

国际邮递
平信(最少需要两个月)
航空邮递(大约两周能到达大多数目的地)

文章结构

体　　裁	应用文
主要内容	介绍新发行的书籍

词汇注释

文　章

release *n.* 出版;发行
describe *v.* 描述
creativity *n.* 创造力
aboriginal *n.* 土著居民
stunning *adj.* 令人吃惊的;令人震惊的
reproduction *n.* 再现;复制
photography *n.* 摄影
informative *adj.* 提供大量资料或信息的
illustration *n.* 插图
nesting *n.* 筑巢
migration *n.* 迁徙
pattern *n.* 模式
classic *adj.* 经典的;第一流的
booklet *n.* 小册子
suitable *adj.* 适当的;相配的
packed *adj.* 充满了;挤满了
avid *adj.* 渴望的
hiker *n.* 徒步旅行者
practical *adj.* 实用的;应用的
continent *n.* 大陆
atlas *n.* 地图册
abundance *n.* 丰富;富饶
premier *adj.* 第一位的;首要的
guidebook *n.* 旅行指南
in-depth *adj.* 深入的;细致的
characteristic *n.* 特性;特征
fantastic *adj.* 了不起的;很好的
informative *adj.* 提供大量资料或信息的
graphic *adj.* 图表的;书写的
illustrate *v.* 阐明;举例说明
prehistoric *adj.* 史前的
definitive *adj.* 权威性的;确定的
handbook *n.* 手册
nutrition *n.* 营养
first aid *n.* 急救
scenic *adj.* 景色优美的
fascinating *adj.* 迷人的;引人入胜的
wilderness *n.* 荒野
otherwise *adv.* 否则

题　目

wheel *n.* 车轮;轮子
aborigines *n.* (尤指澳大利亚的)土著居民
pictorial *adj.* 图示的;图画的
dinosaur *n.* 恐龙
adventure *n.* 冒险;冒险活动
survival *n.* 生存
encyclopedia *n.* 百科全书

考题解析

Questions 8–14

● 题型归类：List of Headings

雅思 G 类阅读的 List of Headings 题型不像 Academic Reading 那样，需要通盘考虑整段话的意思。由于文章各段较短，它只是对于一句话的概括，对话语中的有效信息提炼加工，找准段落的中心词即可顺利解答题目，相对来说较为容易。

● 题目解析：

题目编号	题解
8	Book A 描述了居住在澳大利亚最干旱地区的土著居民的创造力，中心词是创造力：creativity。因为第三个选型“澳大利亚土著居民的丛林食物”里面包含 Aborigines 这个词，所以导致很多考生选择它。但是我们在原文中找不到 foods，只好排除。回到原文，我们发现了另外两处关键点：the driest parts 和 paintings，前者不正是沙漠吗？后者不正是艺术的一种吗？所以选择倒数第二个选项。人类的创造力这里是指艺术的创作。
9	Book B 的主题与上题一样比较隐晦，但是当看到 nesting（筑巢）时，考生应该联想起只有鸟类才会筑巢；另外，migration 是“迁徙”的意思，这也是鸟类的特点之一。所以，选择第一个答案。
10	Book C 的目标群体是 hiker（徒步旅行者），本书为他们提供徒步穿越南大陆丛林的各种有用信息和建议，所以答案只能是第五个选项。注意本题的关键点 hiker 这个词。
11	Book E 的中心词是 mountain biking（山地自行车运动），书中为参与这项运动的人提供了 guidebook（指南手册），介绍各种路线。选项中只有第二个选项符合题意：Two Wheels 不正是自行车吗？下面第七个选项中出现 4-wheel-drive，这是指汽车。
12	Book F 的中心词是 Australian native animals，并且内容详尽，将所有的动物按英文字母顺序全部排列出来，我们知道只有百科全书才这样做，所以答案选第九个选项。考生要注意 wild-life 就是野生动物的意思，还有 encyclopedia 的拼法，它有两种拼写法，都是可以接受的。
13	Book G 的主题相对隐蔽，中心词是 prehistoric animal（史前动物），究竟哪些才算是史前动物呢？第四个选项中出现 Dinosaur 这个词，许多考生不知道它就是“恐龙”的意思。恐龙是属于“史前动物”这个范畴的。其实，题目中的 graphic artists（画家）也可以帮助解题，画家参与的结果肯定是 pictorial 的。
14	Book H 的中心词是 outdoor safety（户外安全），书中包括许多有用的户外生存技能（survival techniques），所以选择第八个选项。

参考译文

新书一览

A. 该书描述了居住在澳大利亚最干旱地区的土著居民的创造力。令人惊异的绘画复制，美丽的照片和翔实的文字。

B. 口袋书式的地图册和画册，详尽说明了在澳大利亚的筑巢地点和迁徙模式。是一本经典的小册子，适宜于初学者和专家。

C. 本书为志存高远的徒步旅行者准备了大量资料，案头必备。照片、地图以及实用的建议将为您徒步穿越南大陆的森林提供向导。

D. 不仅仅是一本地图册——这本书包括地图、照片和全世界各国详细的地貌和气候介绍。

E. 澳大利亚最棒的山地自行车旅行指南——带您穿越众多国家级公园和森林。

F. 这里有澳大利亚本地动物的介绍：按英文字母顺序排列——通过精美的照片和内容翔实的文字，深度介绍它们的生活和习性。

G. 书画艺术家携手研究人员和科学家展现史前动物如何在澳大利亚大陆生老病死。

H. 户外安全的权威手册——深入聚焦装备、营养、急救、特别衣着和丛林技能。

I. 详尽介绍 15 条优美的驾车出游路线，沿着您可能会错过的引人入胜的荒原路径行进。

SECTION 2

文章结构

体　裁	应用文
主要内容	一家专业从事国际交换学生项目及相关服务的机构的广告宣传

词汇注释

文	章
escape *v.* 逃离；逃避	**directory** *n.* 姓名地址录，目录
unique *adj.* 唯一的；独有的	**emergency** *n.* 紧急情况；非常时刻
unbeatable *adj.* 无敌的；无与伦比的	**toll** *n.* 电话费用
fee *n.* 费用	**opportunity** *n.* 机会；时机
return flight *n.* 往返机票	**organization** *n.* 组织；机构；团体
onward *adj.* 向前的；前进的	**professional** *adj.* 专业的；职业的
insurance *n.* 保险费	**resort** *n.* 度假胜地
accommodation *n.* 住处；膳宿	**doughnut** *n.* 油炸圈饼
airport transfer *n.* 机场转机	**buzzing** *adj.* 嘈杂的；喧闹的
orientation *n.* 熟悉情况；认识环境	**duration** *n.* 持续时间
staff *n.* 职员；员工	**enroll** *v.* 入学
application *n.* 申请	**defer** *v.* 使推迟；使延期
assess *n.* （接近或进入某地的）方法；通路	**enthusiastic** *adj.* 热心的；热情的
extensive *adj.* 广阔的；广泛的	**sign up** 注册参加某一课程等
题	**目**
internal *adj.* 内在的；国内的	**restriction** *n.* 限制；约束
legal *adj.* 法律的	**upper** *adj.* 上面的；上部的

考题解析

Questions 15–20

● 题型归类：TRUE/FALSE/NOT GIVEN

● 题目解析：

题目编号	题目定位词	答案位置	题解
15	internal flights, within the USA	第一段	题目：活动费用包括在美国境内的机票。 该题较为简单，只需留意机票费用说明旁边的括号内容即可。有些考生可能不知道 onward 在这句话中的意思，它本意是“向前的”，为什么是向前的呢？因为飞机从澳大利亚飞来，停在洛杉矶，这是进入美国的最西边入口，再往前就是美国本土，所以括号的意思就是：不包括美国境内的旅行花费。因此答案是 FALSE。
16	emergency assistance, legal advice	第二段	题目：活动提供的紧急情况的协助包括法律咨询。 宣传单上说申请人还能得到全程的 24 小时紧急情况支持(24-hour emergency support throughout the length of the program)，但这是比较空泛的一句话，具体内容是什么我们不得而知，所以有没有含 legal advice(法律咨询)NOT GIVEN。
17	other countries	第三段	题目：InterExchange 在除美国之外的国家里也提供相同的活动。 第三段最后一句说：InterExchange can also offer you work opportunities in other countries. 这与题目说的一样，只是原文中具体的活动解释了题目中空泛的 similar program。因此答案确定为 TRUE。
18	government program	第四段	题目：InterExchange 是政府活动的一部分。 在 InterExchange 介绍自己时，它把自己定位于 a non-governmental organization(非政府组织)上面，所以它的活动自然不属于官方性质。故选 FALSE。
19	restrictions, type of job	第五段	题目：在你能做的工作选择上面没有限制。 第五段有一句话清楚地表示你在美国可以任意选择工作：you can choose any job that interests you anywhere in the USA，您可以挑选在美国任何一个地方您感兴趣的任何工作。接着，文章列举了美国各个地方的各种工作来证明这个说法。因此答案确定为 TRUE。
20	upper age limit	最后一段	题目：在申请时存在着年龄上限。 Upper limit 的意思是“上限”，文章中只是给出了申请人的最小年龄不能低于 18 岁：over 18 years old by November in the academic year（到这个学年的 11 月已经年满 18 周岁），至于有没有上限，我们不得而知，因此答案是 NOT GIVEN。

参考译文

去美国工作和旅游

想体验一下您从未有过的最好的暑假?

您是否刚刚毕业,想去海外寻找一份独一无二的经历?

1950 美元就能使这一切变为现实!

这个无与伦比的活动费用包括:

* 从悉尼至洛杉矶的往返机票(在美国境内的旅行费用不包括在内)
* 3 个月的保险费
* 到达后的 2 个晚上的食宿费,另加接机、欢迎和机场转机服务费
* 到达后由 InterExchange 经验丰富的员工提供指南咨询
* 签证申请费用

您还将拥有:

* 获得 JI 签证,可在美国工作
* 一份详细的雇主姓名地址录
* InterExchange 全程提供支持
* 活动全程的 24 小时应急支持

请拨打免费电话 1800 678 738

InterExchange 在国际交换学生项目上拥有 50 年的经验。每年全世界有 18,000 名学生通过该项目来到美国旅行。InterExchange 还能为您提供在别的国家的工作机会。

了解 InterExchange

InterExchange,国际交换学生项目及相关服务领域的领先者:

* 是一家非营利、非政府组织
* 在全世界 30 个国家拥有 700 名高素质员工
* 成立于 1947 年

InterExchange 面向全世界学生开放这些活动。它能为您提供来自训练有素、见多识广的职员的服务,在您的申请过程中提供全程服务。您可以挑选在美国任何一个地方您感兴趣的任何工作,不管是在波士顿的法律事务所或是在科罗拉多的著名滑雪胜地工作,或是在纽约喧闹的大街上售卖咖啡和炸圈饼。您可以选择您工作和旅行的时间;您可以选择工作 1 个月,然后旅行 3 个月,或者全程工作。选择权在您。

如果您符合下列条件,就可以抓住这个机会:

* 现是一所澳大利亚大学或 TAFE 学院的全日制学生
* 目前尚在学校注册,或完成这个学年,或推迟一年学习
* 到这个学年的 11 月已经年满 18 周岁,并且在该学年您已向 InterExchange 提出申请
* 对机会难得的体验充满热情……

现在就参加吧!

文章结构

体　　裁	应用文
主要内容	一所学校的网页介绍

词汇注释

文　章	
requirements *n.* 需求，要求，必要条件，需要的东西，要求必备的条件	**counsel** *v.* 劝告；忠告
orientation *n.* 指南	**credit** *n.* 学分
academic *adj.* 学术的	**commitment** *n.* 许诺；承诺
	assessment *n.* 评价；评估
题　目	
transcript *n.* 成绩报告单	**accredited** *adj.* 可信任的；可接受的
documentation *n.* 文件或证据的提供或备办	**seminar** *n.* 研讨会
automatic *adj.* 自动地	**tuition** *n.* 教学；讲授
membership *n.* 会员资格	**administrative** *adj.* 管理的；行政的
participate *v.* 参加；参与	**counselor** *n.* 顾问
achievement *n.* 成就；成绩	

考题解析

Questions 21–27

● 题型归类：Short-answer Questions

本篇文章的 Short-answer Questions 有些特殊，原文很简单，只是一所学院的网页，而题目很长，是网页中各项内容的解释或进一步链接，所以这些题目主要考查考生归纳推理以及提炼有效信息的能力。

● 题目解析：

题目编号	题目定位词	题解
21	results, award documentation	题目：当学生完成在学院的学习时，他们都会收到一份成绩报告单，记录成绩和相关奖项证明。 这道题的中心词是 results 和 award documentation，这强调了学生在校学习的结果，正是选项 J 所要表达的内容。
22	club, participate, activities	题目：一旦登记入学，所有学生自动成为社会俱乐部和公共演讲俱乐部的会员。学生可选择参加任一活动。学院鼓励并促进学生、老师和非教学人员之间的互动。 这道题看起来很长，但答案很容易确定，因为题目中的几个关键词与原文中的 K 选项不谋而合，题目的意思正是校园社团活动的具体内容。
23	achievement of A or B, course, university	题目：如果顺利完成一些课程，并取得 A 或 B 的成绩，可以使学生们在这些课程排名靠前，如果他们想进入大学深造的话。如果你想了解某一所大学是否认同一些课程，请给我们发邮件索取，邮件请附上那所大

		学的名字和你感兴趣的课程名称。 这段话同样很长,但是里面包含的中心意思很简单:学习好的同学可以继续进入大学深造。选项中只有 E 项含有这个意思,选项里的 credit 在这里不是"存款、贷方"的意思,而是指"学分",这不是一个十分常用的用法。
24	Arthur Philip College	题目:阿瑟·菲利普学院是澳大利亚悉尼顶尖商学院之一。该学院提供多种商业领域和其他相关领域的教育和培训项目。其备受信任的职业培训课程是专门为满足学生和行业需求而设置的。 该题较为简单,从题目中我们得知这是在介绍阿瑟·菲利普学院的教学情况,所以选择 A。
25	lectures, seminars, learning process	题目:在阿瑟·菲利普学院您将会从讲座、研讨会、案例学习、团队项目、个人作业和班级培训等受益匪浅。讲座和研讨班传授理念和想法,留有提问和回答时间。学生应该通过班级讨论、口头表达和其他项目积极参与学习过程。 这段话介绍了阿瑟·菲利普学院为学生提供了各种各样的学习方式(learning methods),学生应该积极参与。选项中只有 G 适合。
26	tuition time	题目:阿瑟·菲利普学院的课程一般安排为每周 25 学时,老师监督下的团队学习每周另有 5 学时。对于大多数课程而言,每周至少应该有 10 学时为个人学习时间。 这段话实际上是对学生在校的每周学习安排及相应时间指标,每项学习任务都包括一个规定的数字指标。所以这是学院对学生们的学习时间的承诺,应选 I。
27	from your first day	题目:在活动中,您将和教务长、老师和诸如学生住宿主管、学生咨询顾问等关键部门的行政人员见面,所以从入学第一天起,您就会知道在校期间他们将给与怎样的帮助。 该段话介绍了一大批校方领导,并且说以后他们会帮助你。这明显就是给新入学的学生介绍情况(orientation),所以答案是 C。

参考译文

网景浏览器

文件　　编辑　　视图　　转到　　交流　　帮助

内容:阿瑟·菲利普学院

A 关于阿瑟·菲利普学院
B 入学要求
C 新生指南
D 学业咨询服务
E 大学深造所需学分
F 留学生帮助
G 学习方法
H 课程费用
I 学习目标
J 评估与成绩
K 社会活动与社团
L 了解最新

SECTION 3

文章结构

体　　裁	说明文
主要内容	本文指出睡眠对人体的重要性，分析人类为什么会失眠，并提出相应治疗办法。
结　　构	Section A：指出每个人都需要足够的睡眠。
	Section B：指出睡眠的目的和作用。
	Section C：试验证明睡眠对人体健康的重要性。
	Section D：研究显示，睡眠分为五个不同的阶段。
	Section E：分类说明人为什么会失眠。
	Section F：介绍治疗失眠的方法。
	Section G：介绍一种利用荷尔蒙作用治疗失眠的新方法。

词汇注释

文　章

A 段

estimate *v.* 估计；估算
lecturer *n.* 演讲者；讲师
psychology *n.* 心理学
therapeutic *adj.* 治疗的；治疗学的
rare *adj.* 稀有的；罕见的
sizeable *adj.* 相当大的
minority *n.* 少数

B 段

purpose *n.* 目的
replenish *v.* 再将某物充满；补充某物
tissue *n.* [生]组织
regenerate *v.* 使新生，重建，革新
hormone *n.* 荷尔蒙；激素
somatotropin *n.* [生化]生长激素
compromise *v.* 危及…的安全；使某人/某事物陷入危险境地
immune system 免疫系统
muddle *v.* 使某人糊涂
depression *n.* (情绪)沮丧；低沉
anxiety *n.* 忧虑；焦急
irritability *n.* 易怒

C 段

deprive sb. of sth. *v.* 剥夺某人的某事物
viral *adj.* 病毒引起的
infection *n.* 传染
emotional *adj.* 精神上的；情绪上的
specialist *n.* 专门医师；专家
insomnia *n.* 失眠；失眠症
undermine *v.* 逐渐削弱或暗中破坏
vulnerable *adj.* 易受攻击的；暴露于危险面前的

D 段

despite *prep.* 尽管；不论
sequence *n.* 次序；顺序
blood pressure 血压
muscle *n.* [解]肌肉
progressive *adj.* 前进的；有进展的
slumber *n.* 睡眠、微睡
confused *adj.* 困惑的；迷惑的
disorientated *adj.* 失去方向的；迷惑的
episode *n.* 片断；一段情节
heartbeat *n.* 心跳
accelerate *v.* 加速；促进
paralyze *v.* 使瘫痪，麻痹

E 段	
consume *v.* 消费；消耗	**pregnancy** *n.* 怀孕
roughly *adv.* 大约地；概略地	**alcohol** *n.* 酒精；酒
disturbance *n.* 干扰；动乱；困扰	**handicap** *n.* 障碍；阻碍
F 段	
treatment *n.* 治疗	**benzodiazepine** *n.* ［化］苯异丙胺（用于制造各种镇静药）
relaxation *n.* 放松；缓和	
resort *n.* 可求助的人或事物；采取的应急手段或对策	**tranquilizer** *n.* 镇定剂
G 段	
advocate *v.* 提倡；鼓吹	**jet lag** 喷气飞行时差反应
melatonin *n.* ［生化］褪黑激素，N－乙酰－5－甲氧基色胺	**dramatically** *adv.* 戏剧性地；非常大地
	capsule *n.* 胶囊
pineal gland 松果腺；松果体	**tablet** *n.* 药片
biological clock 生物钟	**lozenge** *n.* 糖锭；（尤指口含的）锭剂
secrete *v.* ［生理］分泌	**herb** *n.* 草药
bloodstream *n.* 血流	**wean sb. off sth.** 使（婴儿或有小动物）断奶；使某人不再做某事（尤指逐渐地）
synthetic *adj.* 合成的；人造的	
version *n.* 版本	

考题解析

Questions 28－35

- 题型归类：Short-answer Questions
- 题目解析：

题目编号	题目定位词	答案位置	题解
28	amounts of sleep	A 段	题目：人们需要不同的睡眠时间。 A 段作者指出人们每天需要 7 个半小时至 8 个小时的睡眠，但也有人睡得很少，并且以撒切尔夫人为例证明。故选 A。
29	sleep deprivation	C 段	题目：一项关于睡眠被剥夺后的结果的调查。 该题的关键词 deprivation 是从 C 段首句的动词 deprive 变化过来的。在 C 段中，研究人员不让一群人在凌晨 3 点至 7 点之间睡觉：deprived a group of men of sleep between 3am and 7am on just one night，来观察结果。这正是本题的意思。有的考生选择 B 段，因为该段后半部分也是在说明睡眠不足的后果，但那只是作者的论点，C 段才是调查阶段。
30	reason， sleep disorder	E 段	题目：一些解释为什么人们可能受到睡眠问题困扰的原因。 题目中的 sleep disorders 实际上就是 insomnia（失眠），文章中讲到失眠原因的只有 E 段。作者给出了几个原因：年龄原因，吸烟，怀孕，饮酒等，这些都是造成 sleep disturbance 的原因。

31	lifestyle changes	F 段	题目:能改善睡眠问题的生活方式的改变。 生活方式的改变具体在文中何处体现呢?作者提到生活方式的改变是为了论述不用药物治疗也能克服睡眠问题,所以这样就很容易定位到F段,因为它主要说明了几个不用药物而注重人自身改变的方法,比如经常锻炼,严格规定起床和就寝时间等,这都属于生活方式的改变。
32	process	B 段	题目:一个睡眠有助于我们保持身心健康的过程。 题目的中心词是 process,睡眠如何保证我们身心健康呢?这也需要一个过程,而且这个过程是借助于睡眠完成。B 段开头具体解说了睡眠是如何有助于产生荷尔蒙,荷尔蒙又是如何促进组织修复的。这是一个复杂的过程,充足的睡眠保证了这个过程的完成。 该题出题思路较为隐蔽,需要考生细致归纳文章思路。
33	claims, commercialized, product	G 段	题目:声称一项治疗失眠的人造产品的商业成功。 文中提到的众多治疗手段中,只有 Regelson 教授的松果体激素药品取得了商业成功,因为一个商人声称:that sales of the pill have increased dramatically(这种药片的销量猛增)。所以选 G。
34	physical changes, sleeping habits	E 段	题目:身体上的改变在睡眠习惯中的作用。 这道题又给了两个从未直接出现过的短语:physical changes 和 sleeping habits。所谓 physical changes 在文中就是指人逐渐变老,而这会带来了荷尔蒙分泌模式的变化,进而影响到睡眠的习惯:老人容易患上失眠症。这种关系在 E 段体现得很明白。
35	processes	D 段	题目:睡眠中发生的活动。 睡眠中会发生什么活动?D 段给出了答案,即五个阶段和四个循环(five stages and four cycles)。

Questions 36-40

● 题型归类:TRUE/FALSE/NOT GIVEN

● 题目解析:

题目编号	题目定位词	答案位置	题解
36	cure illness	B 段	题目:睡眠可以治病。 在论述睡眠的作用的 B 段,我们发现睡眠对人体的重要性,但是没有提到它的治病功效,故选 NOT GIVEN。
37	stages of sleep	D 段	题目:睡眠的各个阶段一晚上可以重复多次。 回到论述睡眠阶段的 D 段,作者明确提出:in an average night... the sequence of stages is repeated。答案确定为 TRUE。

38	dreaming, sleeping-walk	D 段	题目:做梦和梦游发生在同样的睡眠阶段。 在解答此题时,考生需要仔细检查每个睡眠阶段都有哪些具体特征。我们发现,梦游和做梦不在同一阶段,前者在第四阶段,而后者属于最后一个阶段,故选 FALSE。
39	REM stage	D 段	题目:梦游多发生在"眼球快速运动"阶段。 此题属于偷换概念,在 REM 阶段多发生的是做梦,而不是梦游,故选 FALSE。 出题人把"梦游"解释成了 sleepers move around,这种变动应该对考生影响不大。
40	body temperature, elderly people	E 段	题目:老年人体温升高较早。 涉及到老年人的段落只有 E 段,这一段主要论述了随着年龄的增长,荷尔蒙分泌模式也有变化。老人在早上三四点钟时体温升高,而年轻人则在天亮时,所以老年人要早一些。答案确定为 TRUE。

参考译文

缺乏睡眠

据统计,正常男性或女性平均每天需要 7 个半小时至 8 个小时的睡眠。有些人完全可以睡得很少。比如说,据报道撒切尔女男爵担任英国首相时,一天只睡四个小时也可以照常工作。Jill Wikinson 博士是萨里大学的心理学高级讲师,同时也是《咨询与治疗实践中的心理学》一书的合著者之一。他说,很少有健康的人能做到 24 小时内睡眠不足 5 个小时或少至两个小时,但这也是一个相当可观的少数群体。

最近,人们相信,睡眠的主要目的是使身体得到休息和补充,能有时间修复,并让组织复原。有证据支持这个"休息和修复"理论,那就是能促进组织复原的生长激素的产生在我们睡眠时达到顶点。但是,缺乏睡眠会危及免疫系统,干扰思考能力,产生沮丧情绪,助长忧虑的增加,使人易怒。

圣地亚哥的研究人员有一天晚上曾不让一群人在凌晨 3 点至 7 点之间睡觉,发现他们体内的天然防御病毒感染的水平与第二天早上相比显著下降。"睡眠对于我们的身心健康来说十分重要,如果缺乏睡眠,我们白天的很多活动都要受其影响,"维吉尼亚大学的 William Regelson 教授指出。他也是研究失眠的专家。他说:"因为它可以极大地损害免疫系统功能,所以病人极易受到感染。"

对于很多人来说,缺乏睡眠很少是个人自愿的事情。有些人难以入睡,还有些人能一觉睡到天亮。尽管人们普遍认为睡眠是一个漫长的事情,但是研究表明,一个晚上的睡眠可以分为五个阶段和四次循环,其中,这些阶段不断依次更迭。在第一个浅阶段,心率和血压下降,肌肉放松。在接下来的两个阶段中,渐渐进入深层睡眠。通常一个小时之后,进入第四个阶段,睡眠层次更深。这时候如果把人叫醒,他会显得迷迷糊糊,失去方向感。梦游正是发生在这个阶段,一般时间不超过 15 分钟。在第五个阶段,也就是"眼球快速运动"阶段,心跳快速回到正常水平,大脑活动加快至日间水平或者更高,这时眼球不停地在紧闭的眼睑后面运动,好像在看什么东西。在这个阶段,身体几乎没有任何动作。这个"眼球快速运动"阶段也是我们做梦的阶段。

睡眠模式随着年龄的增长而改变,这也是为什么很多年过六旬的老人患有失眠症的原因。在美国,这个年龄段的人对催眠药物的消耗几乎占据了这个市场的半壁江山。关于这种年龄引起的改变的原因,有一个理论指出这是与荷尔蒙的改变有关。年轻人的体温在天亮的时候上升,而对于老年人来说，早上三四点钟是体温上升的时期。抛弃年龄因素不说，据统计，大约三个人中间有一个人会有睡眠困难的问题。怀孕、饮酒产生的精神压力以及心脏病等因素都可能是诱因。众所周知，吸烟是一个影响睡眠的因素，有调查显示，戒烟者可以在18分钟之内进入睡眠，而戒烟以前，这个数字是平均52分钟。

除了诸如经常锻炼这样的自助疗法，也有精神疗法，其中包括放松训练和针对摆脱睡前焦虑的疗法。还有减少睡眠疗法，目的是通过严格控制人们睡觉和起床的时间来提高睡眠质量。药物治疗通常被很多人视为是最后不得已的手段，通常采取药片的形式，大多数情况下是一种轻微的镇静剂：苯异丙胺。

Regelson 教授提倡引入褪黑激素来治疗睡眠问题。褪黑激素是一种人体自然分泌的荷尔蒙，位于大脑深处的松果腺内。这种荷尔蒙的主要功用是控制人体的生物钟，这样我们就知道何时入睡及何时起床。这种腺体能察觉射入眼睛的光线；当没有光线时，它就会分泌褪黑激素进入血流，降低体温，促进睡眠。褪黑激素药片含有一种人工合成的褪黑激素，通常治疗喷气飞行时差反应及其他睡眠问题。John Nicholls 是一家美国最大的健康食品商店的销售经理，他宣称这种药片的销量猛增。他解释说，这种混合草药的药物以胶囊、药片、糖锭的形式出售。尽管它并不是在所有的失眠症状治疗中都效果显著，但是很多服用者还是因为使用它而逐渐摆脱安眠药。

WRITING

WRITING TASK 1

***a*) *Question analysis, including discussion of main features, comparisons that need to be made, and possible misinterpretations of the question.*（审题）**

"Your neighbours have recently written to you to complain about the noise from your house/flat. Write a letter to your neighbours. In your letter

· explain the reasons for the noise

· apologise

· describe what action you will take"

Points to note.（审题要点）

1. The points do not have to be written in the same order as they are listed in the Question prompt.（虽然题目中有序地提出了几点对考生的写作内容要求，但是实际行文中却并不需要死板地按照题目中所给出的顺序写。）
2. You can choose the level of formality. You may be very friendly with your neighbours or you may hardly know them. Remember to keep the same level of formality (tone) throughout your letter for example by using an appropriate salutation and closure.（对于此篇书信的正式程度可由考生自行选择。在书信中，你与邻居的关系既可以显得关系密切、和善友好，也可以是初次相识、一无所知，但无论是哪一样，考生需切记要通过恰当的"语气"<例如相匹配的抬头和结束语>使行文的正式程度通篇一致。）
3. Think of a good reason for the noise. It should be something that has been going on for a while, not a party one evening.（要为家中所产生的噪音考虑一个恰当的理由。应当选择一个会使噪音持续相当一段时间，以至邻居开始抱怨的理由，而不能是例如像聚会这样一晚就会销声匿迹的不合理的借口。）

4. "Describe what action you will take". This can include action that you have already taken since receiving the letter from your neighbours.（关于"你将针对此问题所采取的方案"，可以包括一些自从你收到邻居的抱怨信后就已经开始采取的方案。）
5. Your letter should be polite at all times!（注意，无论何时你的回信都必须彬彬有礼！）

Possible problems.（审题误区）

1. Be careful to use correct tenses. You will probably need the past, present perfect, present, and future.（小心使用正确的时态。在信中，你将会用到过去时，现在完成时，现在时和将来时。）
2. Include all three points. If you do not, you will get a lower band score.（书信的内容必须包括题目中提出的三点，否则考生的分数将会得不到保证。）

***b) Suggested answer format, including contrast with possible unsuitable formats.*（写作思路）**

The easiest way to open the letter is to apologise for the noise. This serves two purposes. First, it sets a polite, friendly tone for the letter. Second, it covers one of the three points immediately—the rest of your letter can focus on the other two. Logically, the problem should be mentioned before any proposals you make for dealing with the situation. These two points should be in separate paragraphs. The final sentence can be a repetition of the apology.（首先，最简练的开头方式就是直接对噪音的干扰进行道歉，这样做有两个好处：第一，它使整篇书信的语气礼貌、友好；第二，简单的一两句话就已经完成了题目中的一个要求，可以拿出剩下的部分来完成题目提出的另两个要求。从逻辑严谨度上来说，在提出任何针对的解决方案前，就应先提及问题本身。也就是说，对除道歉以外的两点要求的完成，应形成分别的两个段落。同时，最后一句话可以就对开头道歉的话进行重复。）

In short, the letter will look like this:（简而言之，这封书信可以按照以下格式进行书写：）

Salutation.（抬头 <问候语>。）

Apology.（道歉。）

Reason for noise.（解释原因。）

Dealing with the problem.（解决方案。）

Apology.（再次道歉。）

Closure.（结束语。）

***c) Model answer.*（参考范文）**

Dear Jim and Mary,

I truly apologise for the noise that has annoyed you so much over the past week. I should have dropped by to explain that there would be a lot of it since we are replacing the lead piping in some parts of the house. I honestly cannot understand why the previous occupants used lead piping. It has been known for years that it can contaminate the water supply. I'm sure you understand why we feel we have to deal with it.

Unfortunately, as you have pointed out, there is a lot of noisy work involved. Since receiving your letter, I have discussed it with the workmen and they say that some of the noisy work can be avoided, though it will take longer to do. I have asked them to do this. However, there is still some unavoidable noisy work, so I have asked the workmen to do this during the weekday, when you are both out at work.

I apologise again and hope that you can be patient with us for a little while longer.

Best wishes,

David

译文：

亲爱的吉姆和玛丽：

首先我要对这一周来噪音对你们的干扰郑重道歉。其实自从我们决定更换房子中的部分铅制水管时，就应该拜访府上，对于将会由此造成的噪音问题进行解释的。说实话，我真是不知道这间房子的前任主人为什么要安装这些会污染房子供水的铅制水管。我相信您一定会对我们这次迫不得已的改装表示谅解的。

但是现在，正如您在信中所指出的，这项改装工程已经造成了很严重的噪音影响。在收到您的来信那天，我已经和施工的工人们就此问题进行了协商，他们说，可以尽量避免造成噪音污染的工作。虽然这样会延长工期，但我已经让他们就此标准进行施工了。当然，仍有一些噪音是在所难免的，因此，我已经知会工人们在你们二人出去上班时进行这类工作，不会在周末打扰你们的休息。

最后，再一次对于噪音对你们造成的不便进行道歉，并且衷心的希望你们再耐心的等候一段时间，以便我们完成改装工程。

祝好！

大卫

d) *Analysis of vocabulary and structures used in model answer, including possible mistakes made by candidates.*（语言分析）

It is important to be polite throughout the letter—e. g. "I truly apologise for..." , "I'm sure you understand why..."（首先，在信中，通篇语气显得彬彬有礼十分重要。例如，"I truly apologise for..." <我对……郑重道歉>；"I am sure you understand why..." <我相信您一定会对……表示谅解的>。）

It can be a good idea to say that you should have done something or admit a mistake—e. g. "I should have dropped by to explain that ..."（在信中直接承认错误或说明"you should have done something" <早就应该……而没做>是一种很好的思路。例如，"I should have dropped by to explain that..." <其实自从我们决定更换房子中的部分铅制水管时，就应该拜访府上，对于将会由此造成的噪音问题进行解释>。）

In this model answer, the writer points out that the noise was necessary. This depends, of course, on the reason you give for the noise.（在这篇范文中，作者指出制造噪音是在所难免的，当然，这一说法也要由考生所给出的形成噪音的原因而定。）

Note the use of the present perfect to describe what has been done since the letter of complaint was received—e. g. "I have discussed/asked ..."（注意，当在信中谈及在收到信后所采取的行动时，要使用"现在完成时态"。例如，"I HAVE DISCUSSED/ASKED" <我已经就……讨论过/我已经知会过……>。）

Note the use of appropriate idiomatic English (e. g. dropped by) and uncommon words (e. g. lead piping, contaminate).（注意在行文中使用适当的惯用语体 <例如，DROPPED BY> 和非惯用语体 <例如，LEAD PIPING，CONTAMINATE>。）

It is very important to keep the same tone (level of formality) throughout the letter. This is problem with many letters written by candidates. Remember that you can choose the level of formality, but you can't change it midway!（最后，在信件行文中，全篇通过语气的合理运用来保持正式度的一致是非常重要的，同时，这一问题也是考生们经常会犯的错误。请牢记，考生可以自由选择书信的正式程度，但决不能在行文中途进行语气改变！）

WRITING TASK 2

a) Question analysis, including discussion of the points that need to be made in the essay, possible misinterpretations of the question, and brainstorming diagrams. **(审题)**

"Some people believe that children are given too much free time. They feel that this time should be used to do more school work. How do you think children should spend their free time?"("有些人认为孩子们的课后闲娱时间太多了，他们认为这些时间应该用来让孩子们做更多的学校任务。那么，你认为孩子们应该如何利用这些课后闲娱时间呢？")

Possible misinterpretations and problems. (审题误区)

1. The Question prompt is easy to understand and the topic is one that Chinese candidates should be familiar with. Note that the Question prompt refers to children, not university students or adults. Answers that don't refer to children can expect to be penalised as irrelevant. (本题题目清晰易懂，而且是中国考生比较熟悉的一个话题。但需要注意，本题题目中所涉及到的讨论对象是儿童，并非大学生或成人，由此可以肯定，没有涉及儿童课余时间的作文将被视为跑题。)
2. The Question prompt doesn't specifically say it, but candidates are expected to agree of disagree with the statement. It is not necessary to look at both sides of the argument, but it is certainly a good idea, if only to demonstrate that you know there two sides to the debate. (虽然本题题目中并没有明确要求，但考生在行文中提出自己对于所讨论话题的主观态度却是非常有必要的<即同意与否>。对于本题，没有必要一定要谈及论证的两个方面，但是在掌握问题的两方面论据充足的前提下，双面论证亦不失为一个好方法。)

b) Suggested answer format, including contrast with possible unsuitable formats. **(写作思路)**

For this question, the essay format should involve an introduction, two or three main paragraphs, and a conclusion. The introduction should be short and may or may not include the writer's opinion. Each of the main paragraphs should focus on a particular argument. However, these main paragraphs can either focus on one side of the argument or take into account the opposite point of view. The conclusion should be short and state the writer's opinion. (对于这道题目，行文格式应包括以下三部分：一段开头，两到三段主体论证段落和一段结尾。首先，开头部分应该简短，同时是否点明作者的论点都可以；其次，在主题部分，每一段论证段落都应该围绕一个论证分论点，同时支持或反对论据都可以出现在主体论证部分中；最后，结尾部分不仅应该简短，也要点明作者的主论点。)

The most important thing is to make sure that each of the main paragraphs focuses clearly on one argument. If several arguments are included in the same paragraph they could confuse the reader. It is also important that each argument be well developed, and having a separate paragraph for each will help the writer achieve this. (在主体论证段落中，确保每一段都只有一个分论点进行论证是非常有必要的。如果在一段中出现多个分论点就会让读者<考官>感到非常疑惑，同时，对每一个分论点的充分论证也是非常重要的。所以，进行分段论证是一种必要的手段。)

c) Two model answers of around 300 words, each essay taking a different view. **(参考范文)**

Model answer 1—More school work. (范文 1，支持 more school work)

Some people think that children have too much free time and do not spend enough time on their school work. In this essay, I will explain why I agree with those people.

First, the world is a very competitive place and we need to be able to compete with businesses from other countries. Our children can help us achieve this aim in the future by becoming well educated, since becoming a leading economy requires a talented and intelligent work force. They need to study foreign languages in order to be able to communicate with people from other countries. They need to study science and technology so that they can use modern technological advances. They need to study business techniques in order to run companies more efficiently than their competitors.

Second, study gives children direction and something useful to focus their energy on. If children do not have something positive to put their energy into, they might find less productive, or even destructive, outlets, such as crime, playing computer games all day, watching endless TV programs, etc.

When we talk about school work, I would like to include useful non-academic subjects, such as music, art, and sports. These are taught at most schools and give students who are not so talented academically a chance to show that they can also contribute. Even though developing a strong economy should be our first aim, there are other important areas of life.

In conclusion, I believe that children should be given more school work and encouraged to take up suitable non-academic subjects at school to allow them to become useful members of society.

译文：

有些人认为孩子们的课后闲娱时间太多了，而且花在学习如学校作业上的时间并不充足。那么，在这篇文章中，我将说明一下我支持这些人观点的原因。

首先，现在的世界是一个充满竞争的地方，所以，我们必须具备与其他很多国家进行商业竞争的能力。而通过接受良好的教育，孩子们在未来可以帮我们实现这一目标，因为成为主体经济需要有才干的劳动力。例如说，他们需要学习好外语以便于更好地与外国人进行交流、沟通；需要学习科学、技术来操控现代科技产品；需要学习商业技巧，更有效的运营公司企业，超越竞争对手。

其次，学习也为孩子们提供了有益的精力消耗对象。如果孩子们不能将精力放在有积极意义的对象上，那么，消极甚至有毁灭性影响的东西也许会成为孩子们发泄精力的渠道，例如犯罪、整天打电脑游戏或沉浸在无尽的电视节目中等等。

同时，当我们谈及孩子们的作业时，我希望它可以包含一些如音乐，艺术或运动等有用的非学术性科目。这些科目在很多学校教授而且让那些在学术领域天赋不足的孩子们有了一展才华的机会。要知道，即使发展经济是我们的第一要务，但生活中其他领域的发展也是不可或缺的。

最后，我坚信，多给孩子们一些学校作业并鼓励他们在学校多参加一些适宜的非学术性科目，会将他们培养成一名有用的社会成员。

Model answer 2—More free time.（范文 2，支持 more free time）

There has been a lot of discussion about whether children have too much free time and whether this time would be better spent on school work. Personally, I believe that children already have too much school work and should be given more free time. In this essay, I will give my reasons for holding this opinion.

Here in China, parents often push their children very hard to do well at school and get high grades. I can understand their point of view. Very often, they have only one child and they expect this child to be able to provide for them in their old age. However, this leads to a vicious circle. Parents see other parents pushing their kids, which leads them to pressure their own children more, and so on. The parents lose sight of the effect that this has on their children. Their children become isolated from other children.

They can even become physically unhealthy through sitting and studying all day. They certainly won't know anything of the world beyond the school work that they are given by teachers. When they leave school, will they make useful employees?

Another reason why I believe that children should be given more free time is that each child is different and so all children should be given the opportunity to explore their talents in as many areas as possible. Children should try as many different sports as they can, to discover which ones they enjoy and are good at. Who knows where the next Ronaldo or Agassi will be found. Children should be given the chance to explore their artistic and creative sides. A good carpenter or artist can support a family as well as a manager or accountant.

To sum up, children should be given more free time so that they can become people who are not only good at studying and so that they can discover for themselves what they want to do and what they are best at, rather than having so much pressure placed on them from an early age.

译文：

现在，关于是否应该给孩子们更多的课余时间，亦或是让孩子们将更多的时间放在学校的课业上这一话题，已引起了无数讨论。就我个人而言，我认为孩子们已经在课业上花的时间够多了，应该给孩子们多一些课余时间好好喘口气了。在这篇文章中，我将说明一下我支持这一观点的原因。

首先，在中国，很多家长逼迫他们的孩子在学校努力学习，取得好成绩。我可以理解家长们的想法，因为他们通常只有一个孩子，而且有着“养儿防老”的思想。但是，这却形成了一个“恶性循环”。当其他家长看到这种实际上给孩子们带来很大压力的培养方式时，便也纷纷效仿。然而，他们却忽视了这样做带给孩子们的负面影响。他们的孩子被迫和其他的孩子“与世隔绝”，甚至在长时间的保持坐姿进行学习的同时，毁坏了身体健康。当然，除了学校老师所布置的作业外，孩子们更不会知道外面的世界有多精彩了。那么，当他们离开学校后，他们会成为有用的工作人员吗？

其次，我支持孩子们得到更多课余时间的理由还有一个。那就是，每一个孩子都是不一样的。所以，应该给孩子们尽可能多的机会去发掘他们在其他领域的才能。例如说，可以让孩子们尽量参加不同的体育项目，以便于发现哪一种项目他们更擅长或给他们带来更多的快乐。谁知道他们中会不会有下一个莱昂那多或阿加西呢？同时，孩子们也应该有机会去发掘他们在艺术及创造领域的才能。因为一个好的木匠或艺术家也同经理或顾问一样养家糊口。

最后，我坚信，应该给孩子们更多的课余时间。只有这样，才能避免使他们成为只知道学习的书呆子；同时，通过发现其所愿与所长，使他们避免陷入一个过早充满压力的童年。

d) *Analysis of vocabulary and structures used in model answer, including possible mistakes made by candidates.*（语言分析）

“Our children can help us achieve this aim in the future by becoming well educated, **since** becom**ing** a leading economy requires a talented and intelligent work force.” Note the use of ‘since’ to join the aim and the reason. Also note that a verb following a preposition will have ‘-ing’.（“而通过接受良好的教育，孩子们在未来可以帮我们实现这一目标，因为成为主体经济需要有才干的劳动力。”注意“SINCE”作为因果连接介词的使用方法，同时注意介词后的动词要加“ING”的语法规则。）

“They need to study foreign languages **in order to** be able to communicate with people from other countries.” Note the use of ‘in order to’ to join an action with a reason. This is also done in the following sentence. “They need to study science and technology **so that** they can use modern technological advances.”（“他们需要学习好外语以便于更好地与外国人进行交流、沟通。”注意“IN ORDER TO”作为连接原因与结果的词组的作用。这一用法与下文中的“SO THAT”相同。“需要学习科学、技术来

操控现代科技产品。”）

“If children do not have something positive to put their energy into, they might find less productive, or even destructive, outlets”. Notice that the writer makes a suggestion using ‘might’ rather than an assertion using ‘will’.（“如果孩子们不能将精力放在有积极意义的对象上，那么，消极甚至有毁灭性影响的东西也许会成为孩子们发泄精力的不二对象。”注意作者使用的是猜测性词汇“MIGHT”而非肯定性词汇“WILL”。）

“When we talk about school work, I would like to include useful non-academic subjects, such as music, art, and sports.” The writer realizes that non-academic subjects are important and includes them as school work because they are taught as subjects at most schools.（“当我们谈及孩子们的作业时，我希望它可以包含一些如音乐，艺术或运动等有用的非学术性科目。”作者意识到了非学术性科目的重要性而且将他们列入了学校作业的范畴之内，因为这些科目在很多学校都在进行教授。）

Personally, I believe that children already have **too much** school work”. Many candidates will look at this issue in a black and white way, and conclude that both school work and free time are necessary, which doesn’t really answer the question. The aim should be to assess whether children have ‘too much’ or ‘not enough’ school work.（“就我个人而言，我认为孩子们已经在课业上花的时间够多了。”很多的考生针对这一观点时，所秉持的态度往往是中立的，并且在最后总结出，学校作业与课余时间同样重要，但这却并没有真正的回答题目中所提出的问题。切记，本道题目的行文切入点应该是讨论孩子们的课余时间是否过多或者孩子们的学校作业是否不够。）

“However, this leads to a vicious circle.” The candidate has shown that he/she understands the opposing view and then goes on to point out why he/she disagrees.（“但是，这却形成了一个恶性循环。”首先，这位考生已经告诉了读者他/她是能够理解很多家长持有不同意作者的反面意见，但是接下来，他/她继续就自己的主要观点，进行下一步论证。）

“The parents **lose sight of** the effect that this has on their children.” Appropriate use of idiomatic language leads to higher band scores.（“但是，家长们却忽视了这样做带给孩子们的负面影响。”适当的惯用语体对于作文分数的提高非常有好处。）

“They can even become physically unhealthy through sitting and studying all day.” The use of ‘can even’ indicates that this is only true in extreme circumstances, not all. Change ‘can even’ to ‘will’ and see the difference in meaning.（“甚至在长时间的保持坐姿进行学习的同时，毁坏了身体健康。”使用“CAN EVEN”暗示了读者，这种极端环境对孩子们的负面影响只是一种可能，而不是必然的。一旦将“CAN EVEN”换成“WILL”，那么整句话的意思也将发生改变。）

“Children should try as many different sports as they can, to discover which ones they enjoy and are good at.” In contrast to the first writer, this candidate does not include sport as a school subject. Both views are possible—it depends on how you view sport.（“应该给孩子们尽可能多的机会去发掘他们在其他领域的才能。例如说，可以让孩子们尽量参加不同的体育项目，以便于发现哪一种项目他们更擅长或给他们带来更多的快乐。”与范文一的作者不同，这篇范文的作者并没有将体育运动归入到学校作业中去。这两种论证方法在论证过程合理的条件下，都是可行的。）

General Training: Reading and Writing Test B

READING

SECTION 1

文章结构

体　裁	应用文
主要内容	倡议行走募捐,并告知注意事项

词汇注释

文　章

annual *adj.* 每年的;一年一次的
charity *n.* 慈善活动
delightful *adj.* 令人愉快的;可喜的
sponsor *n.* 赞助人
instruction *n.* 指示;指导
transport *n.* 交通;运输
co-ordinator *n.* 协调员
refuse *v.* 拒绝
forecast *v.* 预报;预测
eventuality *n.* 可能发生的事;不测之事
registration *n.* 注册;报到
marshal *v.* 集结
n. (负责某些公共活动的)司仪、指挥
in single file 成单行
oncoming traffic 迎面驶来的车辆
checkpoint *n.* 检查站

题　目

footwear *n.* 鞋类
participant *n.* 参与者
frequency *n.* 频率

考题解析

Questions 1–7

● 题型归类:Short-answer Questions
● 题目解析:

题目编号	题目定位词	答案位置	题解
1	starting point, 30 km walk	倡议书的第一段图示	题目:30 公里行走路线的出发点是哪里? 倡议书的第一段就交待出三条线路的出发点都是 Weldown(Starting in Weldown),而且通过图示我们也证实了这一点。

2	latest start time, 20 km walk	活动说明的第一段	题目:20 公里行走路线最晚开始时间是多少? 该题答案较为明显,在 start times 一栏中,我们发现 20 公里行走路线的开始时间是 8 - 10:30 am,所以最晚开始时间为 10:30 am。请注意,这里的时间段不是行走所需时间,考生不要误会。
3	footwear	活动说明的第二段(穿衣)	题目:在鞋子的要求方面,你应该避免穿什么鞋? 在穿衣提示中,组织方特地强调要穿那种已经穿惯上脚的鞋(worn in),而不要穿新鞋。请注意,原文中的出现省略成分,new 后面省去了 shoes,但在填空时要加上。
4	officials, help participants	活动说明的第三段(地图)	题目:在队伍中帮助参与者的官员被称为什么? 该题出题思路正好与原文相反。原文中说参与者需要帮助的话,请告知他们的 marshals,所以本题的答案就是参与者寻求帮助的对象。
5	20 km walk, finish	活动说明的第四段(巴士)图示	题目:20 公里行走路线在哪里结束? 文章中并没有直接说明 20 公里行走路线的结束点,但说有一辆巴士等在 Fenton 接参与者回程:to take walkers back to Weldown,这说明终点就是在那里。通过图示我们也发现了这一点,虚线的终点到 Fenton 结束。
6	Bus, Fenton to Weldown	活动说明的第四段(巴士)	题目:Fenton 与 Weldown 之间的巴士发车频率是多少? 该题较为简单,考生只需注意到细节时间表述即可。请注意,"every + 时间段"表示"每隔;每逢"的意思。
7	Lower Brene	图示	题目:哪条线路不经过 Lower Brene? 这道题的答案只能从图示中去寻找了,我们看到虚线和粗线都经过 Lower Brene,只有细线没有到达这个地方,所以答案是细线所代表的 10 公里行走路线。 请考生注意:原文中出现的是公里的缩写形式,但答案中要求全称:kilometer/kilometre。

参考译文

为慈善而行走

亲爱的朋友:

请参加我们一年一度的"为慈善而行走"活动。活动出发点为 Weldown,您和您的朋友们可以选择一条怡人的 10 公里、20 公里或 30 公里的线路。

活动所筹得款项将为世界各地的人们提供帮助。现在开始寻找您的资助者吧,到那一天我们一起行走。请仔细阅读下面的说明,特别是您要乘坐交通工具来到或离开 Weldown 的话。

让我们相聚于 5 月 14 日,星期天。

V Jessop

行走活动协调员

又及：去年的行走活动收获颇丰，我们成功募得 21,000 英镑。这笔钱已经用于修建一座儿童操场。

开始时间：

30 公里线路：8 – 10 am

20 公里线路：8 – 10:30 am

10 公里线路：8 – 11:30 am

组织者有权拒绝迟到者。

穿衣应适合当天天气。如果预报有雨，请带上雨具，以备不时之需。最好穿上已经穿惯的鞋子，不要穿新鞋。

地图可在注册点领取。路线将用路标标示出，参加者将被编成纵队。在路线与车道重合的地方，行走队伍要靠一边成单行行走，并且会不停面对迎面开来的车辆。如果您在行走中需要帮助，请告诉其中的一位司仪。

可以在停车场和 Weldown 的街道边免费停车。

公共汽车

在 10 公里线路和 20 公里线路上，将有一辆公共汽车等候在 Fenton，将行走者带回 Weldown。巴士从中午开始运营，每半小时一班。巴士服务免费提供，没有必要预定。

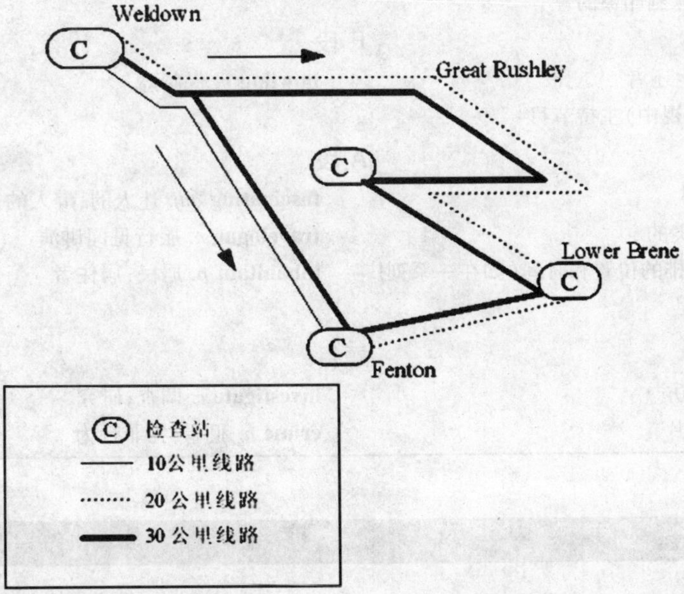

文章结构

体　裁	应用文
主要内容	介绍本周电视节目

词汇注释

文　章

A 段

private *adj.* 私人的
detective *n.* 侦探
a series of 一系列
robbery *n.* 抢掠；抢夺
authority *n.* 当局；有权利发号施令的人或团体

B 段

astronaut *n.* 宇航员
crashland *v.* (使)强行着陆
entire *adj.* 全部的；完整的
suspense *n.* 悬念
adventure *n.* 冒险；冒险经历
condition *n.* 条件；情形

C 段

encounter *n.* 突然或意外的相遇
supernatural *adj.* 超自然的；神奇的
deserted *adj.* 荒芜的；荒废的
mystical *adj.* 神秘的，奥秘的
previous *adj.* 在前的，早先的
ancestor *n.* 祖先；祖宗

D 段

tent *n.* 帐篷
set off 出发

E 段

launch *v.* 发行；投放市场
science fiction 科幻小说
impressive *adj.* 给人深刻印象的
special effect 特技
underground *adj.* 地下的；地面下的

F 段

survivor *n.* 幸存者；生还者
present *v.* (在广播电视中)主持节目
bowling *n.* 保龄球

A 段

account *n.* 讲述；说明
ideal *adj.* 理想的；完美的
slot *n.* 为某人某事安排的位置和时间(如在一系列广播、讲座中)
fascinating *adj.* 迷人的；醉人的
travelogue *n.* 旅行见闻讲演
inhabitant *n.* 居民；居住者

题目

interview *n.* 面谈；采访
documentary *n.* 纪录片
investigate *v.* 调查；研究
crime *n.* 犯罪；犯罪行为

考题解析

Questions 8–14

- 题型归类：Short-answer Questions
- 题目解析：

题目编号	题目定位词	答案位置	题解
8	personal interview	D 段	题目:这个节目以个人访谈的形式出现。 既然是个人访谈,就排除了以电影或电视剧为主的 A、B、C、E、F 段。G 段实际上是一个旅游节目,讲述人带我们走遍欧亚大陆的铁路线。这只是一个旅游见闻演讲节目(travelogue)。所以只剩下 D 段。该段说女主人公将喝着咖啡,讲着她自己的经历,这不正是 Personal interview 的场景吗?
9	documentary, technological development	F 段	题目:这个节目是关于技术发展的纪录片。 技术发展肯定是与科学有关,所以先锁定 F 段。该段讲到关于电脑驱动的汽车:computer-driven cars,这正是技术发展的例证。其余各段都是人文方面的节目,所以排除。
10	time travel	C E 段	题目:这两个节目是关于时间旅行的。 时间旅行肯定是属于科幻片范畴,所以锁定 B、C、E 三段,B 段讲的是一个宇航员闯入动物星球的事情,没有涉及时间旅行。C 段中的超自然能力使人能见到自己的祖先(meet their ancestors),而 E 段的主人公跑到了 23 世纪,所以这两段都是答案。
11	book	G 段	题目:这个节目源自一本书。 我们记得 G 段有这样一句话:Based on his own novel(根据他自己的小说),说明这个节目是作者改编自己的书而成。
12	introduction, a set of	E 段	题目:该电影是为一系列节目的介绍。 该题出题思路较为隐蔽。文中出现 a set of(系列)的意思只有 E 段开头:This is a TV film being used to launch a new science fiction series(这部电影将引出一套新的科幻系列电影)。有的考生不知道 launch 在本句中的含义,它是指“发行;投放市场”的意思,所以说,这部 TV film 的目的是为了迎接一套新的电影的出现。
13	present-day travelers	D G 段	题目:这两个节目都是关于当今旅行。 该题较为简单,除了到 23 世纪进行科幻旅行,只有 D、G 两段是关于旅行的:一个 walking around the world;一个 journey on the railways of Europe and Asia。
14	investigating, crime	A 段	题目:这个节目是关于调查一项可能存在的犯罪。 文章中涉及到 crime 的只有 A 段中看起来并不存在的 robbery 了,一个 detective 的任务不正是去 investigating 吗?

参考译文

本周最佳节目

A 狂野玫瑰（星期二 19:00）

该电视剧讲述一位被一伙纽约商人雇佣的年轻私家侦探的故事，她被商人们派到巴西去调查一系列发生在宾馆的抢劫案。当她到达那里之后，她发现过去的两年里被这些商人控制的宾馆空空如也，当地政府也没有任何抢劫案的纪录。

B 动物星球（星期三 23:00）

该片是一部拍摄于上世纪四十年代的经典黑白电影，讲述了宇航员查理·豪斯顿强行降落在一个完全被动物控制的星球上。这是一部一流的悬念冒险片，同时也不忘关注人类的情形，尽管这一部分在电影中并不是体现得很成功。

C 奇怪的相遇（星期六 21:00）

在这部构思巧妙、小规模的体现超自然能力的电影中，悬念被巧妙地编织进去。一对年轻的夫妇去看一座他们中意的废弃老屋，在那里遇到了一个奇怪的老太太，告诉他们这座房子的神奇力量，以及以前的房主是怎样穿越时空回到现在，来与他们的祖先见面的。

D 最长的行走（星期二 21:30）

Flyona Campbell 就要到达了。她现在所做的就是走过法国和英国，她已经成功走完全世界。今晚，她会在一个帐篷里喝着咖啡，讲述在她启程前往比利牛斯山脉之前她去 Janet Street-Porter 的故事。

E 卢比孔河 5（星期四 20:30）

这部电影将引出一套新的科幻系列电影。它有让人印象深刻的特技和强大的、令人信服的演员阵容，他们前往 23 世纪。故事发生在地下的城市，周围的一切都已被电脑所控制。

F 新科学（星期五 19:30）

这部广受欢迎的半小时科学杂志栏目连续第 29 年播出，这证明它是这个电视世界里的硬朗的幸存者。今晚将有 Carol Vorderman 主持，介绍五个报道，其中包括电脑控制驾驶的汽车和保龄球。

G 旅途归来（星期日 22:00）

Paul Theroux 讲述最近往返于伦敦和东京的旅行，这为今晚的旅游节目提供完美的素材。根据他自己的小说，他沿着亚欧大陆铁路（维多利亚火车站、巴黎、伊斯坦布尔）前行，他对这次旅行的讲述成为令人着迷的旅行见闻演讲，那里的居民逐渐从西方迁至东方。

SECTION 2

文章结构

体　裁	应用文
主要内容	一所地方学院的活动宣传

词汇注释

文	章
orientation *n.* 熟悉情况；认识环境	**residence** *n.* 居住；住所
inclusive *adj.* 包括的；包含的	**approximate** *adj.* 近似的，大约的
facilities *n.* 能够或易于做某事的环境，设备	**alternative** *adj.* 选择性的；其他的
European Union 欧盟	**welfare** *n.* 社会福利
custom *n.* 风俗习惯	**immigration** *n.* 移民
exclusive *adj.* 不包括某人/某事物	**essential** *adj.* 本质上；最重要
tuition fee 学费	**buffet** *n.* 自助餐
refundable *adj.* 可退还的；可偿还的	**excursion** *n.* 远足，游览，短程旅行

考题解析

Questions 15–20

● 题型归类：TRUE/FALSE/NOT GIVEN

雅思 G 类阅读的 TRUE/FALSE/NOT GIVEN 题型一般都比较直白，文章篇幅较短，结构明显，考生只需根据文中的信息做出简单比较和推测即可。

● 题目解析：

题目编号	题目定位词	答案位置	题解
15	arrive two days early	第一部分	题目：参与者应该提前一两天到达。 什么时候到达活动地点应该是首要通知的事情，所以锁定前面几段。涉及具体日期的是第一段，校方建议学生们应该 22 – 23 日到达伯明翰，算起来正是活动开始前的一两天。因此答案确定为 TRUE。
16	cost, European Union	第三部分	题目：来自欧盟的学生应缴费 195 英镑，里面不含住宿费。 该题容易定位，因为第三段专门谈 cost，考生只需分清欧盟和非欧盟学生的收费不同就行了。注意 exclusive 和 inclusive 的用法。
17	places, limited		题目：住宿地点数量非常有限。 在谈到住宿时，校方只是分了提前预订和未提前预订两种情况，并没有解释原因，我们也无从了解数量是否 limited。因此答案是 NOT GIVEN。
18	not charged extra, accommodation	第三部分	题目：一些学生在活动中，并不额外支付住宿费。 上题说到，住宿费的收取分为提前预订和未提前预订两种情况，其中提前预订的可以不用付住宿费：You do not have to pay extra for accommodation during the Orientation program. 因此答案确定为 TRUE。

19	accommodation, local families	第三部分	题目：校方会安排学生住进当地居民家。 除了上文提到的校方住宿安排，其实还有一种情况，那就是学生自行解决：you can arrange your own accommodation for that week in a flat, with friends or a local family（您也可以自己安排食宿，与您的朋友住在公寓里，或住在当地居民家里）。可见，不是校方，而是学生自己的安排。故选 FALSE。
20	breakfast	第四部分	题目：您可以额外付钱给校方购买早餐。 在第四部分的活动安排里面，专门有 Meals 这一项，特别提到：please note that breakfast is not available（请注意，不提供早饭）。可见不管你出多少钱，都在学校买不到早餐。故选 FALSE。 阅读中出现的特别提示，一般都是出题点。

参考译文

伯明翰地方性学院

外国留学生入学指南活动

活动简介：

这项活动将带您前往学院和伯明翰。在学期前一周举行，具体日期为9月24日至28日，但是您应该于9月22日或23日抵达伯明翰。

为什么这个活动很重要？

我们希望您的学习有一个良好的开始，您需要事先了解学院能提供给您的所有机会。这次活动的目标正是帮助您做到这一点。它会使您更了解学院、它的设施以及相关服务。您也可以有机会与我们的老师和同学们见面。

活动花费是多少？

<u>留学生（非欧盟学生）</u>

对于那些不是来自欧盟国家的学生来说，你们还没适应欧洲的文化和风土人情，这项活动非常重要，我们强烈建议您参加。基于此，这项活动的花费（不包括食宿）将计入学费中。

<u>欧盟学生</u>

欢迎欧盟学生参加此项活动，费用为195英镑，不包括食宿。费用不予退还。

<u>住宿费用（留学生和欧盟学生）</u>

如果您提前一年（41周）通过学院预定了学院宿舍（Cambourne House, Hanley House，学生公寓村或者学院合租屋），您不需再额外支付您在留学生指南活动期间的住宿费。如果您没有预定学院宿舍，您可以要求我们提前一周（活动开始的一周）为您提前预定宾馆房间，与其他留学生一起住宿。住宿费一周大约是165英镑。或者，您也可以自己安排食宿，与您的朋友住在公寓里，或住在当地居民家里。

这项活动都包含什么内容？

<u>膳食：</u>午餐和一顿晚餐将会作为活动的一部分提供，第一顿晚饭安排在9月23日星期天作为开始，以9月28日星期五中午的一顿午饭结束。请注意，不提供早饭。

<u>情况介绍：</u>包括下列专题：食宿、健康、宗教问题、社会福利、移民问题、学习技巧、职业以及其他

重要事宜。

社会活动：包括一次欢迎自助餐和一次半天的绕伯明翰的短途旅行。

交通：提供您的住宿地与学院主校区——也就是活动地点——之间的交通。

词汇注释

文章	
option *n.* 选择	**permit** *n.* 许可证
cater *v.* 提供饮食及服务	**allocate** *v.* 分配
en-suit(法)(指房间等)构成独立单元	**respectively** *adv.* 分别地
broadband *n.* 宽带(上网)	**initiative** *n.* 为解决困难而采取的行动
communal *adj.* 公共的;集体的	**payable** *adj.* 应付;可付
lounge *n.* 休息室	**radius** *n.* 半径(距离)

考题解析

Questions 21–27

● 题型归类：Short-answer Questions

● 题目解析：

题目编号	题目定位词	答案位置	题解
21	car owners	C 段	题目：这可能将给驾车者带来不便。 根据文章意思，能给驾车者带来不便的只有停车位的问题，不可能是汽车坏了等别的问题。文章中 C 段明确提出附近没有停车位(there is no space for parking nearby)。故选择 C 项。
22	the Web	A 段	题目：如果您喜欢上网，这是您最好的选择。 文章中提到能上网的住处只有 A 处，因为那里配有 broadband Internet connections(宽带接入)。
23	fewest students	D 段	题目：在所有的学生宿舍中，这里的人最少。 该题较为简单，只需查查数字即可，D 住处只有 120 人，明显最少。
24	new option	E 段	题目：这是学院提出的新选择。 如果考生认识 initiative 这个词的话就很容易判断，recent 的意思是“进来，新近”，根据这个形容词就能猜到答案。
25	parking a year at a time	B 段	题目：你不得不一次就得筹备一年的停车问题。 这道题问得比较含糊，但是它考查考生对细节的辨别和把握能力。文中明确提出停车办法的事 A 和 B，前者 60 英镑停一学期，后者 90 英镑停一学年，粗心的考生没看清后面的单位是一学期还是一年，就容易选错。

26	Does not belong to the college	D 段	题目:这个宿舍不属于学院。 在这五个宿舍中,只有 D 的性质是 privately-owned(私人拥有),故选 D 项。
27	bathroom	C 段	题目:在这里你肯定不会有自己的浴室。 在住宿中,有没有单独浴室也是很多人考虑的条件之一。五处宿舍中,A、D 明确提出有单独的浴室,B、E 没有明确提出有没有,而只有 C 明确提出没有单独浴室,只有 communal bathrooms(公共浴室)。故选 C。

参考译文

学生住宿

学院提供五种基本的住宿选择。您可根据以下信息决定:

A Cambourne House:饮食自理,学生住房,位于市中心,距离学院主校区 2 英里。最多容纳 499 名学生,公寓一套房间含 6、7 或 8 间卧室,每个都有单独的淋浴间。房租为一星期 64 英镑,含水电费(电话费不包括)。宽带上网及电话,公用厨房和休息室。有停车位,租金为一学期 60 英镑。

B 学生村:一套房间含 3、4、5 或 7 间卧室,饮食自理,250 名学生合租,靠近主校区。房租为一星期 60 英镑,含水电费(电话费不包括)。有停车位,租金为一学年 90 英镑。

C Hanley House:位于市中心的第二家现代的住所,饮食自理,152 名学生合租,每楼层 18 个房间,公用厨房、休息室、浴室和厕所。房租为一星期 53 英镑,含水电费(电话费不包括)。附近没有停车位。

D Clencarrick House:私人拥有并经营的学生宿舍,位于市中心,紧挨一座多层停车场,靠近一家主要夜总会,能容纳 120 名学生。学院住宿服务中心负责分配这里的房间。一间小单间房租为 58.50英镑,一间大单间为 68.50 英镑。用电需付费。

E House Shares:这是近年来的新办法,为 140 名学生开发一系列合租的房子,使之符合我们定下的标准,满足所有法律意义上的安全要求。房间为合租,租金为每周 45 英镑和 55 英镑,不含其他费用,与两个主校区都只有 4 英里距离。这里的房租与大学学生宿舍一样,都是按学期收费。

SECTION 3

文章结构

体　　裁	说明文
主要内容	本文主要介绍萤火虫这一种类繁多、历史悠久、分布很广的昆虫。

结　构	
	Section A：萤火虫种类繁多，其发出的光随着种类的不同而不同。
	Section B：萤火虫用途广泛，在地球上存在时间很早，遍布世界各地。
	Section C：萤火虫的生命分为四个阶段，每个阶段都有自己的特点。
	Section D：分析在一些国家萤火虫的数量下降的原因。
	Section E：新西兰的一个洞穴里聚集了大量萤火虫，这成了一道景观。

词汇注释

文　章

A 段

glow-worm *n.* 萤火虫
Lampyridae *n.* 萤科
species *n.*（动植物）种类
appealing *adj.* 吸引人的
dazzling *adj.* 眼花缭乱的，耀眼的
avoid *v.* 避免；消除
pulse *n.*（声波、光波、电流等）一次脉动
interval *n.* 时间间隔

B 段

magical *adj.* 神奇的；不可思议的
ancient *adj.* 古老的；远古的
encyclopedia *n.* 百科全书
pupil *n.* 学生
Confucius *n.* 孔子（公元前 551 – 479 年，中国春秋末期思想家、政治家、教育家，儒家的创始者）
folk *adj.* 民间的
inspiration *n.* 灵感
countless *adj.* 数不清的
anecdote *n.* 轶事；奇闻
emergency *n.* 紧急情况；非常时刻
battery *n.* 电池
thread *v.* 将线、细绳、带子等穿过某物
illuminate *v.* 照亮；照明
fossilize *v.*（使）成化石
concentration *n.* 聚集；集合
tropic *adj.* 热带的
Antarctic *adj.* 南极的

C 段

distinct *adj.* 清楚的，明显的，截然不同的，独特的
larva *n.* 幼虫
equivalent *adj.* 相等的，相当的，同意义的
caterpillar *n.* 毛虫
pupa *n.* [昆]蛹
chrysalis *n.* 蛹，茧
fragile *adj.* 脆弱的；易碎的
harden *v.* 使变硬，使坚强，使冷酷
shell *n.*（卵、种子等）外壳
hatch *n.* & *v.* 孵化
organ *n.* 器官
millimeter *n.* 毫米
matchstick *n.* 火柴杆
encase *v.* 装入；包住
complex *adj.* 复杂的；综合的

D 段

steady *adj.* 稳固的；稳定的
habitat *n.*（动植物的）生活环境，产地、栖息地，居留地，自生地，聚集处
destruction *n.* 破坏；毁灭
acre *n.* 英亩
pesticide *n.* 杀虫剂
fertilizer *n.* 肥料
pollutant *n.* 污染物质

E 段

damp *adj.* 潮湿的
spectacular *adj.* 引人入胜的；壮观的
surveyor *n.* 测量员；检察员
raft *n.* 筏；救生艇
myriad *n.* 无数；无数的人或物

题　目

variation *n.* 变化；变异
distribution *n.* 分布；分配

考题解析

Questions 28–33

- 题型归类：Short-answer Questions
- 题目解析：

题目编号	题目定位词	答案位置	题解
28	threats	D 段	题目：萤火虫面临的威胁。 该题容易判断。D 段谈到萤火虫数量下降，其中有很多原因，这都是对萤火虫的威胁。
29	ways, used	B 段 第 1 自然段	题目：萤火虫的用途。 在 B 段第 1 自然段，作者举出大量实例证明萤火虫用途广泛，全世界都在利用。
30	type	A 段	题目：萤火虫多种多样的种类。 文章一开始作者就说萤火虫是个大家庭，种类众多，为了互相区别，萤火虫的发光模式随种类的不同而各不相同。A 段具体说明这种 Variation 的表现。
31	distribution	B 段 第 2、3 自然段	题目：萤火虫的分布。 B 段主要谈了萤火虫的历史久远和分布广泛。作者说，除了南极和北极圈以内，全世界任何地方都可见到萤火虫踪影（today members of the firefly family can be found almost anywhere outside the Arctic and Antarctic circles）。
32	attraction	E 段	题目：萤火虫成为了一道景观。 萤火虫是常见之物，怎么可能成为景观呢？原来，文章最后把我们带到了新西兰的一个洞穴里，看到无数萤火虫聚在一起，成为一道景观。最后洞穴向旅游者开放，吸引无数游人（have attracted millions of people from all over the world）。
33	life-cycle	C 段	题目：萤火虫的生命周期 C 段把萤火虫的一生分为四个不同的阶段，我们对它的生命周期一目了然。

Questions 34–40

- 题型归类：TRUE/FALSE/NOT GIVEN
- 题目解析：

题目编号	题目定位词	答案位置	题解
34	exact number	A 段	题目：科学家只是到了最近才把萤火虫的种类具体数目列举出来。 文章开头说萤火虫种类繁多，每天还有新增的，但是科学

			家到底有没有全部列举出来呢？文中并没有提到，因此答案是 NOT GIVEN。 有考生说应该是 FALSE，因为数量每天都在增加，所以推理出科学家数不到头，这是把自己的推理强加在文章上了。
35	30 million years ago	B 段 第 2 自然段	题目：最早的萤火虫出现在三千万年以前。 文中出现这个数字是在 B 段第 2 自然段，那是化石形成的年代，但是不是萤火虫最早出现的年代，因为 and their ancestors were probably glowing long before then（它们的祖先可能早在它们之前就会发光了）。故选 FALSE。
36	decrease	D 段	题目：萤火虫数量在一些国家的下降速度快于其他国家。 D 段开头是提到在一些国家萤火虫数量的下降，但没有用别的国家来对比。因此答案是 NOT GIVEN。
37	larvae	C 段 第 1 自然段	题目：温度影响萤火虫幼虫的出现。 题目中的 production 可能会使有些考生感到疑惑，其实，这里它不是指"产量；生产"，而是说"出现，产生"。Heat 可以理解成 temperature。温度的变化使幼虫破壳的时间不定，因此答案确定为 TRUE。
38	adulthood, stage	C 段 第 3 自然段	题目：成虫期是萤火虫一生中最长的时期。 成虫身上没有嘴的部分，不能进食，所以支撑不了几天，这可能是它生命里最短的时期。故选 FALSE。
39	reason, decreasing	D 段	题目：萤火虫数量下降的确切原因尚不清楚。 D 段虽然给出了大量原因，但这都是各方的猜测，该段最后一句话说：a lot more research will be needed, however, before the causes of the glow-worm's gradual decline are clear（但是，在萤火虫数量递减的原因尚不明了之前，还有很多东西有待研究。）。因此答案确定为 TRUE。
40	wet areas	E 段第一句	题目：萤火虫通常在潮湿的地方被发现。 E 段第一句告诉我们：Although glow-worms are found wherever conditions are damp...（尽管潮湿的地方就有萤火虫），如果考生不知道 damp 的意思的话，这道题就不好做了。雅思出题时经常会使用原文中关键词的同义词，请考生平时复习时注意灵活掌握词汇，特别是注意词汇的同义词。

参考译文

萤火虫

萤火虫属于一个被称为"萤科"的昆虫大家族。萤火虫是一个有着两千多个种类的大群体，并且一直都有新的种类被发现。萤火虫之所以很吸引人是因为它们能够发出耀眼的光芒。成年萤火虫用这种光作为求偶的信号，并且每个种类必须发展出自己的"呼叫信号"，避免与也在附近发光的其他种类的萤火虫混淆。所以，在每一块地方，每个种类的萤火虫都在某种程度上与它的邻居区分开来，比如说，在光的颜色和模式上，每一次发光持续时间，光的脉动之间的间隔时间，还有它是在飞行中发光还是从地面上发光。

萤火虫神奇的发光吸引了世世代代的人们的注意。早在两千年前，孔夫子的一个学生就在一本古代的百科全书中描绘过萤火虫的发光。萤火虫经常出现在日本和阿拉伯人的民间药物中。它们还是全世界诗人、画家和小说家的灵感。比如在英国，有很多轶事奇闻记述了萤火虫是如何被用作读书的灯光，或是当自行车电池突然失灵时被用作自行车备用车灯。新大陆早期的旅行者都会带着类似的故事回来，讲述中美洲的人们是如何收集到一种萤火虫，然后把它们带到室内释放，点亮他们的小屋。女孩们用线把萤火虫穿在一圈，围在脚上点亮夜间的丛林小径。

一些成为岩石化石的萤火虫与我们今天所见到的萤火虫很类似，这些化石形成于三千万年以前，它们的祖先可能早在它们之前就会发光了。现在不可能完全肯定第一个萤火虫在什么时候什么地点出现的。今天我们发现的聚集程度最高的萤火虫集体生活在南美洲的热带地区，这可能意味着它们要么是从这里首先进化的，要么只是因为它们喜欢这里的环境而已。

不管它们最早从何而来，从那时起，萤火虫开始扩散到世界上的每一个角落。今天，除了北极和南极圈以内，任何地方都可以见到萤火虫大家庭的成员。

正如许多昆虫一样，萤火虫的一生可以被分为四个完全不同的阶段：卵，幼虫（相当于蝴蝶的毛虫），蛹（或者是茧）和成虫。萤火虫在秋天以一个浅黄色卵的形式开始它的生命。刚产出的卵非常脆弱，但是只需一天它的表层就硬化成坚硬的外壳。卵大约要花上35天孵化，但是确切的日期根据气温的不同而不同，天热时是27天，天冷时要超过45天了。当快要孵化时，萤火虫的发光器官已经完全发育，它的发光预示着这个卵马上就要孵化了。

幼虫离开卵之后，躯体慢慢从只有几毫米长到一个火柴棒那么大小。幼虫阶段是唯一一个能够进食的阶段。幼虫大部分时间都在进食和构建自己的食物储备，这样当它长成成虫时，它就可以专心致志地投入到寻找配偶和繁殖的任务中了。在为期15个月的幼虫阶段中，萤火虫发出明亮的光芒。幼虫的光芒要比成年雌性萤火虫暗淡得多，但是五米之外还是可以看得到的。

在萤火虫生命中的最后一个阶段，当一只简单的幼虫要变成更为复杂的成年飞虫时，幼虫换上一种蛹状皮肤。成年飞虫从蛹中破壳而出，雄性开始追求它可以交配的雌性。交配之后，雌性昆虫产下大约120只卵。成虫身体上没有嘴的部分，不能进食，因此只能存活几天。但人们说起看到一只萤火虫时，他们通常都是指发出耀眼光芒的成年雌性萤火虫。

在一些国家，萤火虫的数量开始下降。有证据显示，从20世纪50年代（或者更早）开始，英国萤火虫数量稳步下降。这种趋势的原因可能包括栖息地受到破坏，污染和天气变化。成千上万英亩的草地被覆盖，萤火虫的栖息地逐渐被隔开。杀虫剂和肥料的广泛使用可能也会危及萤火虫。萤火虫处于食物链的顶端，当它吃掉蜗牛时，它很可能吸收掉蜗牛吃进的所有污染物。全球变暖对于降雨和其他天气的影响也可能是萤火虫消失的因素之一。但是，在萤火虫数量递减的原因尚不明了之前，还有很多东西有待研究。

尽管潮湿的地方就有萤火虫，因为那里食物充足还有一面垂直的墙壁，但是在洞穴里它们才是最壮观的。一百年来，新西兰的萤火虫洞穴吸引了来自世界各地成千上万的游客。这些洞穴最早是由一个当地毛利族族长 Tane Tinorau 和一名英国测量员 Fred Mace 于1887年发现的。他们做了一只小筏划进一个水流入地下的洞穴，蜡烛是他们的唯一光源。当眼睛逐渐适应那里的黑暗之后，他们看见数不清的光芒反射在水面上。抬头一看，发现洞穴顶部被成千上万只萤火虫的光芒所点缀。后来他们多次回到洞穴进一步探究，一次 Tane 一个人回去时，他发现了洞穴的上层和一条捷径。有人建议当地政府由官方测量员绘出洞穴地图。1888年，Tane Tinorau 向旅游者开放了这个洞穴。

WRITING

WRITING TASK 1

a) *Question analysis, including discussion of main features, comparisons that need to be made, and possible misinterpretations of the question.* (审题)

"You have a full-time job and are also doing a part-time evening course. You now find that you cannot continue the course. Write a letter to the course tutor. In your letter describe the situation explain why you cannot continue at this time say what action you would like to take"

Points to note. (审题要点)

1. The points do not have to be written in the same order as they are listed in the Question prompt, but they are listed in the most logical order. (虽然题目中有序地提出了几点对考生的写作内容要求，但是实际行文中却并不需要死板地按照题目中所给出的顺序写。)
2. You can choose the level of formality. You may be very friendly with your tutor or you may not know him/her outside class. Remember to keep the same level of formality (tone) throughout your letter for example by using an appropriate salutation and closure. (对于此篇书信的正式程度可由考生自行选择。在书信中，你与邻居的关系既可以显得关系密切，和善友好，也可以是初次相识，一无所知，但无论是哪一样，考生需切记要通过恰当的"语气" <例如相匹配的抬头和结束语> 使行文的正式程度通篇一致。)
3. Think of a good reason for finishing the course. It should be something that prevents you from missing the whole of the rest of the course, not just one lesson. (考虑一个好借口以便于最终完成你的这次学习。你的理由应该是那种会使你无法继续剩下的所有课程的，而并非这么一次课。)

Possible problems. (审题误区)

1. Be careful to use correct tenses. You will probably need the past, present perfect, present, and future. (小心使用正确的时态。在信中，你将会用到过去时，现在完成时，现在时和将来时。)
2. Include all three points. If you do not, you will get a lower band score. (书信的内容必须包括题目中提出的三点，否则考生的分数将会得不到保证。)

b) *Suggested answer format, including contrast with possible unsuitable formats.* (写作思路)

The easiest way to open the letter is to point out that your job means you will not be able to complete the course. However, if you are not well known to your tutor, you may need to introduce yourself first, so that your tutor knows exactly who you are. This will take one paragraph. The second paragraph should say what you want to do about the situation and you could add a 'thank you' to the tutor to be polite. (首先，最简练的开头方式就是直接向你的老师说明你的工作将使你无法完成剩下的课程。但是如果你与你的老师并不熟悉的话，那么你首先就需要向你的老师进行自我介绍，以便于让你的老师确切地知道你是谁。这些需要用一段的行文量。在第二段中你要说明你针对这一境况将要采取的解决方案，而且为了以示礼貌，你可以在本段中加入一些感谢老师教导的话。)

In short, the letter will look like this: (简而言之，这封书信可以按照以下格式进行书写：)

Salutation. (抬头 <问候语>。)

Introduce yourself (optional). (介绍你自己 <可自行选择>。)

Say you cannot complete the course and why.（点明你无法完成剩下的课程并解释原因。）
Say what you would like to do.（说明你将采取的解决方法。）
Thank the tutor for his/her work (optional).（感谢老师对你的教导<可自行选择>。）
Closure.（结束语。）

c) *Model answer.*（参考范文）

Dear Mr. Jones,

I am one of the evening class students taking your Computer Studies course on Tuesdays and Thursdays from 7 to 9. Like many of the students in the group, I have a full-time job. Unfortunately, I have been asked to head a new project at work and will not be able to continue the course, as the project means I will have to work overtime in the evenings.

The course has been very useful and I really appreciate the patience you have had with those of us who find computing a little difficult. I will not be asking for a refund, since there are only a few classes remaining. Besides, I can use the materials you have given us in advance of the classes to do some self-study when I have less work to do.

Thank you once again for your excellent work. If possible, I will try to take another of your courses in the future.

Yours sincerely,

David Watts

译文：

亲爱的琼斯先生：

我是从7月到9月每周周二、四听您计算机课程的一名夜大学生。正如班上的其他同学一样，我也是一名专职工作者。但是这次上面通知我，任命我来带领一个新的工作项目，这也就意味着我每天都要加班工作，所以无法继续参加剩下的课程了。

说实话，我认为这门课程对我来说是非常有用的，同时，虽然实机操作对我们来说并不是一件简单的事，但是您对我们的耐心教导却让我非常感激。因为所剩课程已不太多，所以我不打算再退费了。另外，我也会在工作之余，利用您提前发给我们的教材进行自学。

最后，再一次感谢您对我们的悉心教导，如果有可能的话，我希望将来能够再参加您的其他课程学习。

大卫·瓦茨敬上

d) *Analysis of vocabulary and structures used in model answer, including possible mistakes made by candidates.*（语言分析）

"I am one of the evening class students taking your Computer Studies course on Tuesdays and Thursdays from 7 to 9." The writer introduces himself. Combined with the salutation "Dear Mr. Jones," we know that the two people do not have a close relationship. Therefore we can expect a more formal letter. ("我是从7月到9月每周周二、四听您计算机课程的一名夜大学生。"作者首先进行了自我介绍。再通过他的抬头—"亲爱的琼斯先生"，我们可以认定这位学生与老师之间并不熟悉，所以，本文的行文应当非常正式。）

"Like many of the students in the group, I have a full-time job. Unfortunately, I have been asked to head a new project at work and will not be able to continue the course, as the project means I will have to work overtime in the evenings." The writer has described and explained the situation. ("正如班上的

其他同学一样，我也是一名专职工作者。但是这次上面通知我，任命我来带领一个新的工作项目，这也就意味着我每天都要加班工作，所以无法继续参加剩下的课程了。"作者已然点明了无法完成剩下的课程并解释了原因。）

"The course has been very useful and I really appreciate the patience you have had with those of us who find computing a little difficult. I will not be asking for a refund, since there are only a few classes remaining. Besides, I can use the materials you have given us in advance of the classes to do some self-study when I have less work to do." The writer has explained what he will do.（"说实话，我认为这门课程对我来说是非常有用的，同时，虽然实机操作对我们来说并不是一件简单的事，但是您对我们的耐心教导却让我非常感激。因为所剩课程已不太多，所以我不打算再退费了。另外，我也会在工作之余，利用您提前发给我们的教材进行自学。"作者已经说明了他将采取的解决方法。）

"Thank you once again for your excellent work." The writer politely thanks the tutor.（"再一次感谢您对我们的悉心教导"，作者礼貌地对老师表示了感谢。）

"Yours sincerely". The closure matches the salutation.（"你诚挚的"，这一结束语与本文的抬头相匹配。）

WRITING TASK 2

a) *Question analysis, including discussion of the points that need to be made in the essay, possible misinterpretations of the question, and brainstorming diagrams.*（审题）

"Nowadays we are producing more and more rubbish. Why do you think this is happening? What can governments do to help reduce the amount of rubbish produced?"

Possible misinterpretations and problems.（可能产生的曲解和问题。）

1. The Question prompt clearly refers to governments. Answers that refer mainly to what companies, individuals, etc., can do will be penalised as irrelevant.（需要注意，本题题目中所涉及到的讨论对象是政府，由此可以肯定，没有涉及政府而是谈到公司、个人等等的作文将被视为跑题。）
2. The Question prompt clearly gives candidates two Questions to answer—why is there so much rubbish and what can governments do about it. The first Question will almost certainly take less time to answer than the second.（本题题目明显提出了两大要求——是什么造成了这一现象以及政府应做出什么样的努力来减少垃圾的数量。很明显，相较第一个要求，解决第二个要求应当占据较大的行文比例。）

b) *Suggested answer format, including contrast with possible unsuitable formats.*（写作思路）

For this question, the essay format should involve an introduction, two or three main paragraphs, and a conclusion. The introduction should be short and may or may not include the writer's opinion. Each of the main paragraphs should focus on a particular point. The first main paragraph should focus on the first question, with one or two main paragraphs focusing on solutions. The conclusion should be short and state the writer's opinion.（对于这道题目，行文格式应包括以下三部分：一段开头，两到三段主体论证段落和一段结尾。首先，开头部分应该简短，同时是否点明作者的论点都可以；其次，在主题部分，每一段论证段落都应该围绕一个论证分论点，第一个主要论证段落应当主要集中解决题目中的第一个要求。然后再用两到三段提出解决方案；最后，结尾部分不仅应该简短，也要点明作者的主论点。）

The most important thing is to make sure that each of the main paragraphs focuses clearly on one question. It is also important that each point be well developed, and having a separate paragraph for each will help the writer achieve this.（在主体论证段落中，确保每一段都解决题目中的一个问题是非常有必要的。同时，对每一个分论点的充分论证也是非常重要的。所以，进行分段论证是一种必要的手段。）

c) *Two model answers of around 300 words, each essay taking a different view.* (参考范文)

Model answer 1 (范文1)

There is no doubt that our world has to deal with more rubbish than ever before. In this essay, I would like to suggest why this problem has arisen and how governments could bring the problem under control.

Every society has produced waste. Archaeologists find waste when they examine ancient sites all over the world. The amount of waste produced by a society is generally in proportion to the amount that a society consumes. Nowadays, as people are becoming wealthier, not just in countries that are already rich, but also those that were once poor, more rubbish than ever is being produced as more people become big consumers. This is actually not the real problem, in my opinion. The real problem is, as we consume more and produce more waste, we have not implemented ways of dealing with all the extra rubbish that is created.

Although individuals and businesses can do a lot to reduce the problems created by so much waste, it is the government that needs to take the lead through legislation. One thing that governments can do is require individuals, households, and businesses to separate their waste into different categories, such as paper, metal, plastics, etc. The government (or private businesses) can then recycle as much of the waste as possible. Another thing that governments can do is make laws limiting the amount of packaging that products use. A lot of the waste we produce consists of packaging which is often unnecessary to keep the product clean, fresh, and protected.

In conclusion, the main reason that we have so much waste in the world is that we are producing and consuming more to satisfy our material needs and we have not yet implemented ways to deal with this rubbish. However, there is much we can do, if our governments choose to take the lead.

译文:

毫无疑问,相较以前而言,现在的世界不得不把更多的精力放在垃圾处理问题上。在这篇文章中,我将说明垃圾问题日趋严重的原因及急待政府实施的解决办法。

每一个社会都在制造产生垃圾。考古学家甚至在全世界每一个考古遗迹进行发掘时,都发现过垃圾。一个社会的垃圾量基本上是和其消耗量持平的。现如今,不管是在已然富有还是那些曾经贫穷的国家中,人们正在变得越来越富有。在成为大型消耗者的同时,我们也正在制造着越来越多的垃圾。然而,在我眼中,这却并不是最大的麻烦。真正的麻烦是,在我们现在大量消费、产生大量垃圾的同时,我们却拿不出解决垃圾增多问题的有效办法。

虽然个人及商家正在为解决垃圾问题做着不懈的努力,但是政府通过立法理应成为这场斗争的主力军。其中,政府可以做到的一项措施,就是可以要求个人、家庭及企业对他们所制造的纸张、金属和塑料等垃圾进行分类,然后政府(或部分企业)再尽量对这些垃圾进行循环利用。同时,政府还可以通过立法来限制商品包装袋的使用量,因为垃圾品中有很多是这种东西。原本人们认为这样做可以保护商品或使商品洁净、新鲜,但实际上它们却是可有可无的。

最后,我认为,世界上大量垃圾量形成的原因是因为我们在大量制造和消耗产品以满足人们物质需求的同时,却又没有制定出针对垃圾增长行之有效的解决方案。但是,我坚信,只要我们的政府愿意担当主力军,我们就可以做出更大的努力。

Model answer 2（范文 2）

Many people believe that the world is facing a crisis over the amount of waste that people produce. We need to be more attentive to the environment that we are creating and we need to think of better ways of dealing with rubbish than just dumping it or exporting it to other countries.

The reason that we have so much rubbish to begin with is that we have become a consumer society, where having material things is viewed as our aim in life. Even children hold this view, asking their parents for (often expensive) things, such as toys and electronics. Generally, people in the world are becoming richer and that means that they can buy more material things. As we consume more, more rubbish is being produced.

Governments can do many things to lessen the problem of waste. Individuals and businesses respond to financial incentives. Therefore, the government could introduce a system whereby individuals and companies that produce more waste must pay more money, to cover the cost of dealing with it. This should encourage people to produce less waste. The government can also finance research into developing new ways of dealing with rubbish. For example, at the moment, not all plastic can be recycled. The government could fund a team of scientists to develop a way of recycling all plastic waste.

In conclusion, more waste is being produced as a result of higher consumption by more people. However, there are measures that governments can take to reduce the problem.

译文：

很多人都相信，世界正面对着一场由人们所制造的垃圾而引起的危机。我们应该更多地参与到解决由我们造成的环境问题中来，并且积极地找出更好的针对垃圾问题的解决办法，而不是一味向国外出口或倾倒。

我们现在不得不去面对大量垃圾的原因，是因为我们已然进入了消耗型社会。在这样的社会中，追求物质繁荣成为了我们的生活目标。即使孩子们也同样受其影响，很多孩子在央求他们的父母为他们购买诸如玩具或电子商品等较为昂贵的东西。总体说来，人们正在变得越来越富有，同时也意味着我们可以去购买越来越多的物质商品。但是，我们消耗的越多，所制造的垃圾也就会随之水涨船高。

针对垃圾处理这一问题，通过个人及企业的资金投入，政府可以进行很多工作。当然，政府也可以引进新的行政体系来解决垃圾处理的资金问题，那就是让个人及企业为他们所制造的垃圾成比例地付费。这样也许会鼓励人们少制造垃圾。还有，政府可以投入资金支持新的垃圾处理技术的研发工作。例如，现在的技术并不能循环利用所有的塑料制品，那么，政府就可以注入资金组成一支专家队伍，针对所有塑料制品的再回收利用进行科研。

最后，垃圾的大量形成是越来越多的人大量进行消费的结果。但是，政府可以通过有效的手段缓解这一问题。

d) Analysis of vocabulary and structures used in model answer, including possible mistakes made by candidates. **（语言分析）**

"There is **no doubt** that our world has to deal with more rubbish than ever before." Use words and phrases like 'no doubt', 'undoubtedly', 'it is certain that' and 'certainly' only when a situation is absolutely clear—with no debate possible.（"毫无疑问，相较以前而言，现在的世界不得不把更多的精力放在垃圾处理问题上。"当考生要论证的背景清晰且毫无疑问时，可以使用"NO DOUBT"，"UNDOUBTEDLY"，IT IS CERTAIN THAT"和"CERTAINLY"等词汇，短语等。）

"The amount of waste produced by a society is generally in proportion to the amount that a society consumes." The writer concisely expresses his/her opinion.（"一个社会的垃圾量基本上是和其消耗量持平的。"通过这句话，作者准确地表达出了他/她的观点。）

"The real problem is, as we consume more and produce more waste, we have not implemented ways of dealing with all the extra rubbish that is created." The writer has developed his/her opinion in an appropriate way.（"真正的麻烦是，在我们现在高消耗量，高垃圾量的同时，我们却拿不出解决垃圾增多问题的有效解决方案。"通过这句话，作者完美地阐述论证了他/她的观点。）

"Although individuals and businesses can do a lot to reduce the problems created by so much waste, it is the government that needs to take the lead through legislation." The candidate focuses on the Question of what governments can do. Note the verbs that follow in the paragraph—'require', 'make laws'. These are things that governments can do.（"虽然个人及商家正在为解决垃圾问题做着不懈的努力，但是政府通过立法理应成为这场斗争的主力军。"在这一段中，考生明显地在围绕着"政府能做出什么样的努力"这一问题要求进行论证。注意到这一段中后面使用的动词"要求"，"立法"等，这些都是政府可以实施的举动。）

"However, there is much we can do, if our governments choose to take the lead." The writer makes it clear that it is not only governments that can do something, but they are a major influence.（"只要我们的政府愿意担当主力军，我们就可以做出更大的努力。"作者通过这句话，清晰地说明解决垃圾问题不仅是政府的问题，我们也可以起到很大的作用。）

"Individuals and businesses respond to financial incentives." This is good use of idiomatic languages and tells us in which direction the writer is taking us. We know that money is going to be mentioned soon.（"通过个人及企业的资金投入。"作者利用这一漂亮的惯用语体成功地告诉了我们他/她的论证方向，由此得知，资金问题马上就会被提到。）

"This should encourage people to produce less waste." The writer is admitting that it is not a certainty (some people might just pay the extra money), but it is a probability.（"这样也许会鼓励人们少制造垃圾。"作者承认这一结果只是预期结果 <因为有的人只会多付钱而不会去主动减少垃圾的制造量>，而并不是必然结果。）

"The government can also finance research into developing new ways of dealing with rubbish. For example, at the moment, not all plastic can be recycled." Governments already finance research into finding ways of dealing with rubbish, so the writer adds the word 'new' and gives an example.（"政府可以投入资金支持新的垃圾处理技术的研发工作。例如，现在的技术并不能循环利用所有的塑料制品。"因为政府已经开始为垃圾处理办法投入资金进行研究，所以作者使用"新的"一词并举例论证来说明这一点。）